HANDBOOKS

# NEW MEXICO

ZORA O'NEILL

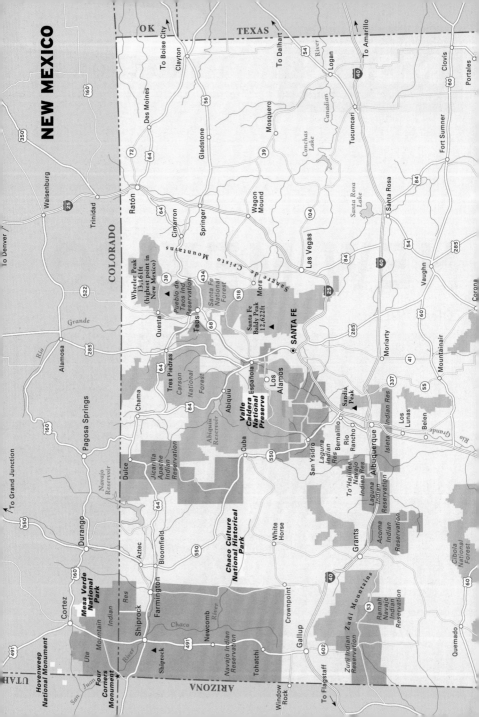

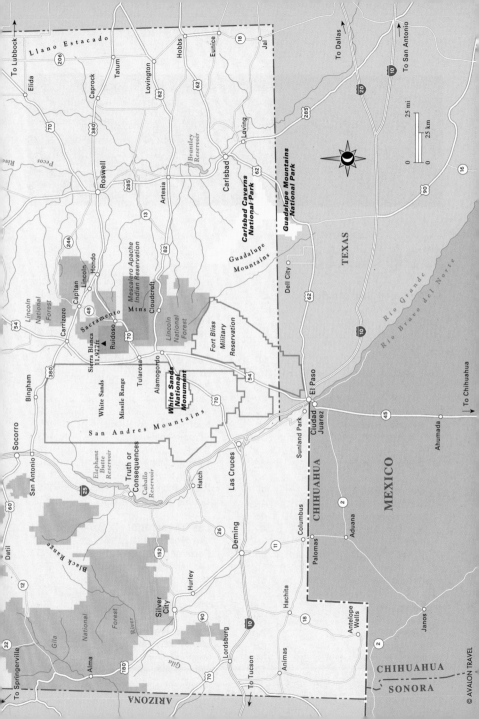

# Contents

# Discover New Mexico

There's a reason it's called the Land of Enchantment. The smells alone would be entrancing enough: lilacs in spring, ozone after summer thunderstorms, green chiles roasting in supermarket parking lots in fall, and fragrant piñon crackling in woodstoves and corner fireplaces. Listen, too, and you'll hear what makes the state special: Western tanagers warble in the trees, coyotes yelp in the night, and the deep boom of drums and jingle of bells resound at pueblo ceremonies. And that green chile adds a distinct taste to everything – it finds its way onto hamburgers and pizzas and even into ice cream and beer.

But none of that matches the majesty of the view: across austere mesas, down narrow sandstone canyons, or off snow-capped mountain peaks. Straight up is a cloudless dome the precise hue of the turquoise in the locally crafted jewelry. At night, stars clot the velvety sky, so close you can almost touch them. Many visitors to New Mexico feel disoriented by all this new sensory input – and perhaps by the dizzying altitude, which soars over 13,000 feet at its highest point. And on top of everything, they feel like Alice, shrunk away to nothing when compared with the vast landscape.

Indeed, New Mexico may as well be Wonderland. Sixteenth-century Spanish is spoken in tiny mountain towns in the northern part of the state, while Santa Fe is an adobe-looking utopia where the economy

magically thrives on nothing but art and politics. Los Alamos is a hidden city on a hill with a secret that changed the world, and half of Roswell, it seems, is still obsessed with an alleged UFO crash there in 1947. There are settlements named Truth or Consequences and Pie Town.

Visitors might need time to adjust – first to the altitude, and then to the laid-back attitude. But there's a point of entry for everyone. Outdoor adventurers can hike for an hour or a week, along mountainsides thick with yellow-leafed aspens, and camp on the surreal dunes of White Sands National Monument. Culture mavens thrive in Santa Fe, with its world-class contemporary art scene and an eclectic calendar of international film and music. History buffs can explore the ruined civilization at Chaco Canyon, spy ruts dug by thousands of passing wagon wheels on the Santa Fe Trail, or bunk down under a buzzing neon motel sign along Route 66.

At the end of the day, you can always pull yourself back into the present with a cold margarita and cuisine with a hot-chile kick – but that's no guarantee you'll shake off New Mexico's spell.

# Planning Your Trip

## ▶ WHERE TO GO

### Albuquerque

A modern Western city, Albuquerque sprawls over more than 100 square miles at the base of the Sandia Mountains. It's proud of its Route 66 style, and it's also preserving farmland along the Rio Grande and redesigning itself as a green burg. Head north to Santa Fe via the ghost towns of the Turquoise Trail, the hot springs in the Jemez Mountains, or the solitary trails of the Valles Caldera.

### Santa Fe

New Mexico's picturesque capital has a human scale and a golden glow (partly from the loads of money spent here). Museums are a major draw—for state history, folk art, and more—as are the scores of galleries. Outside of town are the cliff dwellings at Bandelier National Monument; the scenery of Abiquiu, which inspired painter Georgia O'Keeffe; and Los Alamos, birthplace of the A-bomb.

Yellow aspens line the Paseo del Bosque in Albuquerque.

### IF YOU HAVE . . .

- **FIVE DAYS:** Visit Santa Fe, with an overnight trip to Taos.
- **ONE WEEK:** Cruise the Navajo Nation in the northwest, or concentrate on Albuquerque and Santa Fe.
- **TWO WEEKS:** Follow the Grand Tour itinerary shown on page 12, or cover most of the southwest and southeast.
- **THREE WEEKS:** Go crazy: You have time for backpacking, rafting trips, or other wilderness excursions.

### Taos and North Central New Mexico

Taos melds artists, spiritual seekers, and ski bums—plus centuries-old Spanish and American Indian families. Make time to enjoy the atmosphere, cultivated in coffee shops and creative restaurants. A good day drive is the Enchanted Circle, a loop of two-lane roads with Wheeler Peak, the highest in New Mexico, at the center. Or head over the mountains to Chama, home to a historic steam train that forges the pass to Colorado.

### Las Vegas and the Northeast

Past the Pecos Mountains, Las Vegas, a.k.a. Meadow City, is a well-preserved historic town, often used as a Western film set. From there, the terrain, where the Santa Fe Trail once ran, is all short-grass prairie—once

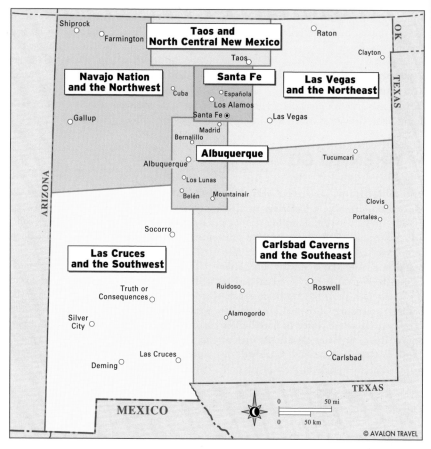

the western edge of the Dust Bowl. To get a view, drive the spiral road up Capulin Volcano, then soar across gorgeous Johnson Mesa to the mountain burgs of Raton and Cimarron.

## Navajo Nation and the Northwest

Stark volcanic landscape, lonesome roads, and tall mesas—this is some of the most dramatic desert terrain in the state, along with its oldest cultures. This quadrant (often called Four Corners, as it abuts three other states) is where the Ancestral Puebloans lived in Chaco Canyon, and where Gallup is the self-proclaimed American Indian capital. The city is surrounded by under-the-radar hiking and mountain biking trails.

## Las Cruces and the Southwest

This corner of the state has both the mountainous Gila Wilderness Area and the mesmerizing Chihuahuan Desert. It's a long drive between the river-fed farmland around Las Cruces and colorful, artsy Silver City, tucked in the mountains, but worth it—especially for birders, who can spot sandhill cranes and rare hummingbirds. Truth or Consequences reels in the curious, delivering hot springs and quirkiness.

## Carlsbad Caverns and the Southeast

Parts of this area feel more like neighboring Texas: Many flatland towns are dominated by the oil industry, and ski spots like Ruidoso are beloved by Texans. Most visitors make a beeline to the amazing natural wonders of White Sands National Monument and Carlsbad Caverns National Park. On the way, you can track outlaw Billy the Kid, who dueled in the mountain town of Lincoln, now an excellent outdoor museum.

## ► WHEN TO GO

With 300 days of sunshine a year, New Mexico doesn't have a bad time to visit. Summer high season is mid-May through mid-September. Summer is the only time to hike at higher elevations; for river rafting, plan on late May and early June, after snowmelt. Winter is busy (and pricier) in ski towns like Taos, but traditional celebrations preceding Christmas are wonderful. Many sights are closed or have limited hours. Towns at lower elevations, such as Truth or Consequences and Carlsbad, remain balmy, and prices in these places hold steady year-round. Book a hotel at least six months in advance for the week between Christmas and New Year's, Santa Fe's summer art markets, or the Albuquerque balloon fest in October.

The cheaper shoulder seasons are March and April, when ski season has wound down, and October and November, before it starts. Spring weather can be extreme, varying from snowfall (occasionally in May) to ceaseless, hot winds. But fall is beautiful: crisp temperatures, clear skies, and brilliant yellow aspen leaves in the mountains.

winter in the Sandia Mountains

# ▶ BEFORE YOU GO

## Getting Around

Most people fly into Albuquerque; Santa Fe receives only a few flights. You can get around the two cities on public transport—with planning in Albuquerque, and easily in Santa Fe, where parking is also difficult. Commuter rail links the two cities, with handy downtown stops. Amtrak serves a couple of destinations, but it's largely a novelty. In general, a car is essential.

## The Climate and What to Take

Be prepared for a wide range of temperatures whenever you visit. Even in the relatively low elevations of central Albuquerque, winter temperatures can dip well below freezing. If you think you'll attend winter pueblo dances, pack mittens, long underwear, double-thick wool socks, and a hat with earflaps—there's a lot of standing around outside.

Spring is mud season—if you hike or head to rural areas during this time, save a clean pair of shoes for around town. Summers are hot by day (July's average temperature is 92°F), but as soon as the sun sets, the temperature can drop 20°F or more, especially outside of city centers; always keep layers at the ready. In July and August, brief afternoon "monsoons" sometimes warrant an umbrella. In the sun, you'll be more comfortable in long-sleeve, light-colored shirts and pants rather than skimpy tops and shorts—covering up deflects the glare. Year-round, you should never be without sunglasses, heavy-duty sunscreen, and a brimmed hat.

As for style, New Mexicans are casual. Only if you'll be hobnobbing with Santa Fe's upper echelon need you pack something dressy—local formalwear for men is clean jeans, shined cowboy boots, and a bolo tie. When visiting churches and pueblos, women should cover shoulders and avoid short skirts.

the Cumbres & Toltec steam train on its descent into Chama

# Explore New Mexico

## ► 14-DAY GRAND TOUR

The multilevel adobe buildings of Taos Pueblo are framed by the surrounding mountains.

You could conceivably explore New Mexico for a month or so, seeking out ever more obscure towns, but two weeks gives just enough time to appreciate the distinct character of the major cities and enjoy bumpy back roads. This itinerary involves a lot of driving to cover all of the state's most scenic routes, but you'll still have opportunities for leisurely lunches and other out-of-car activities. If you want to cut down on some of the driving, you could fly out of El Paso, Texas, about one hour south of Las Cruces and substantially closer to White Sands—in this case, stay in Albuquerque for the first few days, then head out to explore.

### Day 1
Arrive at Albuquerque's Sunport airport; transfer to a hotel in the city or one of the excellent, rural-feeling bed-and-breakfasts in the North Valley. Have drinks and dinner in Nob Hill.

### Day 2
Visit the Indian Pueblo Cultural Center, then head west to Acoma Pueblo. Lunch in Grants and stay the night at the Zuni Mountain Lodge.

### Day 3
Get an early start for the long, bumpy ride along the back road to Chaco Culture National Historical Park. When you're done exploring, grab a late lunch at El Bruno's in Cuba, then take Highway 96 over the mountains to Abiquiu, where you'll spend the night.

### Day 4
If you like hiking, explore Abiquiu's red rocks at Ghost Ranch or drive down the road to Bandelier National Monument. If you prefer the city, head in to Santa Fe and the excellent museums around the plaza. In either

case, stay the night there, at classic La Fonda or more modern Hacienda Nicholas.

## Day 5

Take in Santa Fe's contemporary culture, with shopping, gallery-hopping, or a visit to the Museum of International Folk Art. End up on Canyon Road, with drinks and tapas, and maybe even dancing at El Farol.

## Day 6

Head to Taos via the high road, with stops at the chapel in Chimayó, where you can also pick up some delicious tamales, and in the villages of Truchas and Las Trampas. Settle into your hotel in Taos after a de rigueur margarita at The Adobe Bar.

## Day 7

Start with an early visit to San Francisco de Asis Church, followed by breakfast at Loka (for light eaters) or Michael's Kitchen

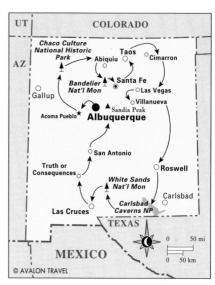

Santuario de Chimayó

(for heartier appetites). Then head to the Taos Art Museum at Fechin House for background on the town's art scene. Spend the afternoon at Taos Pueblo, then get green chile at Orlando's.

## Day 8

Drive the first leg of the Enchanted Circle, turning east at Eagle Nest to reach Cimarron. Lunch at the St. James Hotel, then head down to Las Vegas via I-25. Check in at the Plaza Hotel, then tour the surrounding historic buildings.

## Day 9

Today is a long day of driving, but you'll pass through pretty old villages like Villanueva and the flat plains around Vaughn. Have a late lunch in Roswell, where you might have time to visit either the International UFO Museum or the Anderson Museum of Contemporary Art. You're bunking down at Carlsbad's Trinity Hotel.

# WEIRD AND WONDERFUL NEW MEXICO

New Mexicans have a chip on their shoulder because other Americans often confuse the place with a foreign country. But sometimes it feels like an entirely different planet. Locals have a fine appreciation for the quirky, the offbeat, and the utterly strange. Here's where to see the state at its most eccentric.

## TRUTH OR CONSEQUENCES

From its attention-grabbing name (product of a 1950 publicity stunt) to its downtown full of galleries and odd shops (as remarkable for their wares as for their garrulous proprietors) and the labyrinthine **Geronimo Springs Museum,** this is a small town with more than its share of character.

## MADRID

First of all, it's MAD-rid, which gives you an idea about this ghost-town-turned-galleryville's wacky residents, who have brought the place back from the dead since the 1970s. Second of all, you should try to visit before Christmas, when the twinkly lights are strung so densely, they're probably visible from space. If you're lucky enough to arrive when it happens to be open, you can lunch at the **Ghost Town Kitchen.** South of here is **Tinkertown,** a miniature world whittled from wood, cobbled together from bottle caps and bits of string. You'll be inspired never to waste a scrap of wire or a minute of leisure time.

## SANTA FE AND TAOS

Poll your fellow hot-tubbers at **Ten Thousand Waves** about their past lives, or ask your neighbor at the **World Cup** coffee shop if he can hear the "Taos hum." While you're up in the northern reaches, check out the **Greater World Earthship Development,** a completely off-the-grid suburb of Taos where the buildings crafted from beer cans and tires look straight off a *Star Wars* set; you can even stay the night in one.

## LOS ALAMOS

This mesa-top town is where the atomic bomb was devised and scientists now toil in secrecy. One museum here touts the joys of nuclear science, while across town, the salvage yard **The Black Hole** stocks used lab equipment and office supplies, as well as a heavy dose of Cold War paranoia. Round out your visit to "the Hill" with a jaunt south to **Trinity Site,** where the bomb was first tested in July 1945; it's open to visitors only two days a year.

## ROSWELL

Ever have cryptic dreams about green creatures with big heads and long, skinny arms? You'll feel right at home at the **International UFO Museum & Research Center,** where alien visitations are treated as a matter of course. The work at the outstanding **Anderson Museum of Contemporary Art** depicts all manner of alternate realities.

## PLAINS OF SAN AGUSTIN

If Roswell gets you in the mood to peer into the solar system, cruise out to this installation of radio telescopes that make up the **The Very Large Array.** You might recognize the giant white dishes, all connected to a Y-shaped track that stretches more than 20 miles, from the film *Contact.* They don't actually receive messages from across the galaxy, but the images they take of deep space are nearly as illuminating.

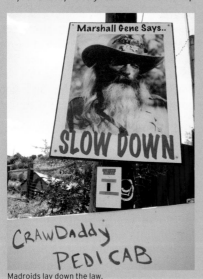
Madroids lay down the law.

## Day 10

Head out early to Carlsbad Caverns National Park. Back in town, have dinner at Danny's BBQ in Carlsbad and take in a movie at the Fiesta Drive-In, then head back to the Trinity for bed.

## Day 11

Head west to Alamogordo and White Sands National Monument, winding up in Las Cruces that evening. Have dinner in historic Old Mesilla.

## Day 12

Drive up I-25 to return to Albuquerque, stopping in Truth or Consequences for coffee and a snack and a dip in the hot springs. Plan on lunch at the Owl Café in San Antonio. You should be in Albuquerque by nightfall—check out the scene downtown.

inside The Big Room at Carlsbad Caverns

## Day 13

Take it easy today, but wind up at Sandia Peak around sunset, to take one last look at the Southwestern scenery.

## Day 14

Fuel up for your flight with breakfast at The Frontier, where you can also grab some house-made tortillas to take home.

The Sandia Peak Tramway ascends more than 3,000 feet.

# ▶ BLACK STONE, WHITE SANDS

Temperate climates, plain old "pretty" land-scapes—who needs 'em? New Mexico's extreme terrain, from stark lava beds to gleam-ing fields of gypsum, is much more exciting. Snow-capped peaks are just a short drive from arid deserts, and you can spot hardy animals, odd birds, and stunning rock formations ev-erywhere in between. Whether remote wilder-ness areas or lesser-known routes in popular parks, the otherworldly spots suggested here are almost always empty.

Which ones you visit depends a lot on what time of year it is and, equally important, what altitude you can handle. When you arrive in New Mexico and see the scenery, it's tempt-ing to put on your boots and head straight out, but unless you're coming from a compa-rable elevation, stick to clambering in foothills and scenic drives for the first couple of days. Drink plenty of liquids, and head to bed early. Every corner of the state holds some entic-ing natural adventure, but due to long driv-ing distances, you're better off limiting your exploration to one quadrant at a time. This way, you'll spend less time in the car and more time on the land.

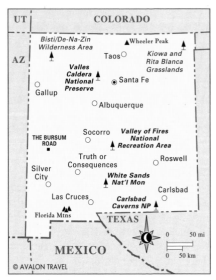

## Wheeler Peak

A hike up the state's highest mountain—which typically requires a few days, with a bivouac along the way—is not for the faint of heart, and shouldn't be attempted any time other than June, July, or August. If you're in

a beautiful vista at White Sands National Monument

# NOT JUST HOT TAMALES

Given the region's distinctive cuisine – from only-in-New-Mexico hot chile to gourmet creativity – it would be easy to plan a vacation entirely around eating.

## BEST TRADITIONAL NEW MEXICAN

"Red or green?" is the official state question, referring to the dilemma diners face when they order enchiladas, huevos rancheros, or anything else that can be drowned in an earthy red chile sauce or a chunky, vegetal green one.

- **Mary & Tito's:** An Albuquerque institution, this family restaurant was named a James Beard American Classic in 2009. Red chile is the star here (page 55).

- **San Felipe Restaurant:** In the category of restaurants in a gas station, this one's a winner: big enchilada platters, as well as pueblo favorites like blue-corn mush (page 65).

- **Horseman's Haven:** This place used to be in a gas station, but even in its slicker location, it still cooks up what's probably the hottest green chile in the state (page 99).

- **Orlando's:** The Taos favorite is known for its green-chile sauce – deceptively smooth and velvety, considering it's often the hottest thing in town (page 147).

## BEST GREEN-CHILE CHEESEBURGERS

This greasy treat is so genius, it has been immortalized in an official New Mexico Green Chile Cheeseburger Trail (www.newmexico.org). Here are just a few options:

- **Bobcat Bite:** Just outside Santa Fe is this restaurant that grinds its own meat and shapes the enormous patties by hand. There are other items on the menu, but they're just window dressing (page 99).

- **The Frontier:** With the all-you-can-ladle pot of green-chile stew at the condiment counter, you can add as much heat as you want to your burger at this colossal diner in Albuquerque (page 54).

- **Owl Café:** Often cited as the best GCCB in the state, the Owl's version requires a drive way down south of Albuquerque to the village of San Antonio. Once you're there, though, you can also sample the Owl's main rival, from Manny's Buckhorn, across the street (page 243).

- **Blake's Lotaburger:** A New Mexico chain, this place is more accessible than the Owl and (heresy) almost as delicious. No single Blake's is reviewed in this book – just keep an eye out for the icon of the man in the red-white-and-blue top hat.

## BEST LOCAL AND ORGANIC

New Mexico's extreme climate makes farming difficult – perhaps why locally grown produce is so treasured by the foodie set.

- **Jennifer James 101:** Minimalist chef James composes a short daily menu from local produce, and weekly "community tables" show off seasonal treats (page 55).

- **Los Poblanos:** Guests at this historic farm inn in Los Ranchos de Albuquerque enjoy fresh eggs for breakfast, among other treats (page 50).

- **Vinaigrette:** This "salad bistro" in Santa Fe grows its own greens on a nearby farm and can vouch for every other ingredient on its menu (page 98).

- **The Love Apple:** A chalkboard displays the sources of all the ingredients at this candlelit New Mexican bistro: Tucumcari cheese, Pecos beef, and more (page 148).

- **Gallup flea market:** As local as it gets: grilled lamb from sheep raised here, with a roasted green chile, on frybread made with flour from Colorado (page 209).

- **The Curious Kumquat:** Chef Rob applies global spices to local goodies, and the occasional line-caught salmon flown in by friends from Alaska (page 273).

moonrise at the Bisti/De-Na-Zin Wilderness Area

the Taos area outside this period, you can hike at lower elevations instead.

## Bisti/De-Na-Zin Wilderness Area

Top-heavy hoodoos—precarious, windswept sandstone towers—are the hallmark of this barren landscape south of Farmington. There are no trails and no services, and virtually no other hikers, so come prepared with plenty of water, a compass, and an appreciation for solitude.

## Valles Caldera National Preserve

The lush alpine meadows that line this ancient volcanic basin are some of the state's most pristine. Every season here is beautiful, whether the trout streams are high with spring runoff or the knee-deep snow is prime for snowshoeing. But if you plan just to hike on your own, without a larger group tour, plan for sometime between June and September, before the cold snap.

## Kiowa and Rita Blanca Grasslands

Once the edge of the brutal Dust Bowl, this protected prairie now looks a bit more hospitable, dotted with pronghorns and cattle. The real surprise comes when you drive down to Mills Canyon, a red-striped chasm with a lush bottom. Camping in this hidden spot, with hawks wheeling overhead, is like being hidden away from the world.

## The Bursum Road

For those who prefer to drive rather than hike, Highway 159, which runs into the east side of Gila National Forest, is one of the state's most thrilling routes. It's best taken in the fall, when the aspens that crowd in on this rugged track turn a brilliant gold—but don't wait too long, as the gate east of Mogollon is locked at the first hint of snow. You can also get out and stretch your legs, or even camp, at a number of spots along the road.

## Florida Mountains

A respite from the flat, hot Chihuahuan Desert around Deming, these little-visited crags foster vivid wildflowers, brightly colored birds, and even a few exotic mountain goats. Head for Spring Canyon Recreational Area in the spring or late summer, and be sure you're there at sunset.

## Valley of Fires National Recreation Area

The volcano that produced these badlands exploded just yesterday, relatively speaking— the blackened landscape hardened about 1,500 years ago, setting in wedges, whorls, and fantastically odd lumps. You'll bake if you hike the shadeless terrain in high summer; for surprising greenery, just after spring rains is best.

## White Sands National Monument

After you've slid down the gypsum dunes, really get to know this amazing place on a ranger-led car tour to the sands' source, Lake Lucero, or a hike on Alkali Flats Trail. Better still, camp here overnight after taking a hike or mountain biking tour under the full moon. Try to avoid the boiling peak of summer and midwinter, when periods of heavy rain can close off parts of the park.

## Carlsbad Caverns National Park

Go deeper—literally—than the average daytripper by signing up for the hardcore Spider Cave tour, on which you'll wiggle through tiny tunnels into lofty halls. The park supplies helmets and headlamps, but it's BYOB: bring your own batteries. Handily, the temperature underground holds steady year-round; just book ahead during peak summer months.

White Sands National Monument

## ► A WEEK IN THE WILD WEST

Gunslingers, cattle rustlers, and Apache warriors made New Mexico a colorful, if violent, place in the 19th century, and relics of that frontier lifestyle are still visible everywhere. History buffs can visit old forts, count bullet holes in saloon ceilings, and trace the fortunes of prospectors in ghost-town graveyards. Though the major cities have their share of history, this route takes you away from the modern centers and into

emptier quarters on the east side of the state. It can be expanded with a stop in Santa Fe or a more leisurely pace up to Las Vegas (Highway 3, which connects I-40 to I-25, for instance, is exceptionally pretty, if a bit out of the way).

### Day 1

Arrive in Albuquerque. Take in the western sunset at the base of the Sandia Peak Tram,

## RETRO NEW MEXICO

"Get your kicks," advises Nat King Cole's classic anthem of the Mother Road. Though officially decommissioned, Route 66 (now traced by I-40) is still alive in New Mexico in the form of neon signs and cruising culture. Far beyond the highway, many parts of the state foster a certain nostalgia for the mid-20th century.

Hit the road, preferably in a convertible, to enjoy good old-fashioned fun like **drive-in movie theaters** in Las Vegas (summers only) and Carlsbad. The car is still king in Clovis, where you'll find original **drive-ins,** such as Foxy, complete with car-hops – this is the way burgers and fries were meant to be eaten.

Clovis is also where 1950s crooner Buddy Holly recorded his early hits – check out the **Norman & Vi Petty Rock & Roll Museum** for the story, and come for the **Clovis Music Festival** every September. Real car fans can check out the **Route 66 Auto Museum** in Santa Rosa, or see one of Elvis's Caddies at **B-Square Ranch** in Farmington (the taxidermy museum here also seems like a relic of another age). And capture the real spirit of a road trip by heading out U.S. 60 to remote **Pie Town,** so named because it served intrepid motorists sweets in the

Historic Route 66 cuts straight through the state.

1930s. Two cafés keep this slice (pun intended) of Americana alive with mixed berry, chocolate cream, and more at the ready. For more sweets, head to **Carrizozo,** where Roy's mixes up chocolate ice cream sodas at an old fountain. Don't

in the foothills, then come back to the center of the city for dinner at the appropriately named and Western-themed The Frontier restaurant. Bed down at historic Mauger Estate or Los Poblanos Inn, amid horse farms in the North Valley.

### Day 2

Head southeast to Mountainair and the rustic-bizarre Shaffer Hotel; you'll also pass the Salinas Pueblo Missions. By mid-afternoon, you should be in Lincoln, where Billy the Kid earned his greatest notoriety. Tour the

buildings here, then settle in for the evening at the Wortley Hotel (book dinner ahead with a local restaurant).

### Day 3

After breakfast, you're headed north to Fort Sumner to see Billy the Kid's grave and a memorial to Navajo internment in the 1860s. Take an afternoon dip in the Blue Hole in Santa Rosa to fortify yourself for the last leg of the drive, to Las Vegas, where you'll stay and dine at the wonderfully restored Plaza Hotel.

miss the very groovy early-1960s signage on the short main street.

The best legacy of the Route 66 era is the motels. Tuck yourself in at the **Blue Swallow Motel** in Tucumcari, one of scores of motels here, and at **El Rancho** in Gallup, which hosted Ronald Reagan and other Western movie stars. Farther afield, in Raton, the **Budget Host Melody Lane** has vintage saunas in the rooms. And in Truth or Consequences (a town named for a 1950s radio show), the owners of **Blackstone Hotsprings** motel have decorated rooms as homages to *The Twilight Zone* and Lucille Ball. Sleep tight, and dream of the charm of yesteryear.

an all-American breakfast in Pie Town

## Day 4

Tour the Meadow City's historic buildings in the morning, with lunch at Estella's or Charlie's Spic & Span, then head for sprawling Fort Union in the afternoon—the slanting sun should highlight the ruts of the Santa Fe Trail off to one side. Return to Las Vegas for the evening.

## Day 5

I-25 north takes you to Raton, where you turn east to Capulin Volcano National Monument, which affords a grand view over the plains. Loop back via Folsom (site of numerous train robberies) and the awesome, empty expanse of Johnson Mesa. Have a late lunch in Raton at The Sands, then cruise down the road to Cimarron, where you'll spend the night in the spooky St. James Hotel.

## Day 6

Depending on your interests, hang out in Cimarron in the morning until the Old Mill Museum opens, or make a beeline through dramatic Cimarron Canyon to Eagle Nest and on to Taos. The long way around the

Enchanted Circle yields the best views and takes you past abandoned Elizabethtown, site of the state's first gold rush. In Taos, the Wild West is alive and well at the Sagebrush Inn—a must for drinks, after you've had a decadent dinner at Antonio's or Lambert's. The Historic Taos Inn or La Fonda de Taos both wear their years well.

### Day 7

Drive south back to Albuquerque via the low road and, if you have the time, the Turquoise Trail—you can have lunch at San Marcos Café or just a soda in tiny Cerrillos, where Mary's Bar feels like a Western film set. If you don't have to meet a flight out, plan on stopping in Madrid too, for burger or a beer at the Mineshaft Tavern.

the ruins at Abó, one of the Salinas Pueblo Missions

## ► NATIVE NEW MEXICO, ANCIENT AND MODERN

The culture that developed before the arrival of the Spanish in the 16th century is visible in both ruined and inhabited pueblos and in excellent museums that hold some of the state's finest treasures. Even if you're visiting only a small area on your trip, there's a lot of American Indian history to see in and around each place—but definitely try to schedule a visit around a dance ceremony at a pueblo, as this will give you the most memorable impression of the living culture. If you're serious about purchasing art and jewelry, you may want to time your visit with the Santa Fe Indian Market, which takes place every August and showcases more than 1,200 artisans. But you'll also have a chance to buy directly from craftspeople in Zuni, Acoma, Crownpoint, and Santa Fe. If you have plenty of time to explore, you could also

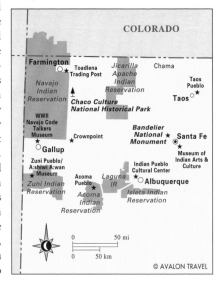

head south of Albuquerque to the Salinas Pueblo Missions, the Gila Cliff Dwellings, and the Bosque Redondo Memorial at Fort Sumner.

## Albuquerque

The Indian Pueblo Cultural Center should be your first stop, for its good museum and information on all the American Indian settlements. Also pay a quick visit to Petroglyph National Monument on the west side, to see ancient rock carvings and get a great view across the city. The Hyatt Tamaya resort, on the north side of town, is owned by Santa Ana Pueblo.

## Acoma Pueblo

West of Albuquerque, this weathered fortress village atop a monolithic mesa is accessible only by guided tour. At the base is an excellent cultural museum, which displays the pueblo's specialty, delicate white pottery painted with fine black lines. You can grab lunch here, or down the road in Grants.

## Zuni Pueblo

This is the only pueblo where you can stay overnight, at the Inn at Halona. It's also the source of beautiful jewelry. Take a walking tour of the mission church, with its resplendent kachina murals, and check out the A:shíwi A:wan Museum. The dance ritual Shalako, in late November or early December, is amazing, but you must book at the inn many months ahead.

## Gallup

Hosting a huge annual powwow, Gallup has the largest native population in the state, as well as the WWII Navajo Code Talkers Museum. Visit on a Saturday, for the funky and diverse flea market. About an hour's drive

Zuni drummer dressed in his finest moccasins

Zuni's *olla* maidens dressed for a dance

ruins on the valley floor at Bandelier National Monument

away is Crownpoint, which hosts a monthly rug auction—a must-visit even if you don't buy anything.

## Shiprock and Farmington

Head into the Navajo Nation via U.S. 491, passing the Toadlena Trading Post, which displays beautiful rugs. Shiprock offers another chance at a Saturday flea market, or traditional mutton stew at the fast-food joints—or hold out till Farmington and Ashkii's Navajo Grill. Farmington is usually the base for visiting Chaco Culture National Historical Park, a little over two hours south—though you can also camp at the site, under starry skies.

## Taos

Taos Pueblo is as much a relic as Acoma but still regularly used. If your visit doesn't coincide with a ceremonial dance there, stop by the Best Western Kachina Lodge in the early evening to see a demonstration performance (summer only)—but you should stay at Little Tree B&B, where the owner can give you a history lesson on the area.

## Santa Fe

Check out the modern arts scene at the Museum of Indian Arts & Culture and the Museum of Contemporary Native Arts, as well as several galleries representing pueblo artists. And don't miss the jewelry vendors under the portal at the Palace of the Governors. A short drive away are the ruins at Bandelier National Monument and the Puyé Cliff Dwellings, where Santa Clara residents lead the tours.

raw turquoise and shell for sale at the Gallup flea market

# ALBUQUERQUE

As a tourist destination, Albuquerque may labor in the shadow of the jet-set arts colonies to the north, but as a city, it's a thriving haven for those who pride themselves on being down-to-earth and sensible. If Santa Fe is the "City Different" (a moniker any Albuquerquean will razz for its pretentiousness), then New Mexico's largest city, with a population of nearly 900,000 in the greater metro area, is proudly the "City Indifferent"—unconcerned with fads, cultivated quirkiness, and flawless facades.

Which is not to say the city doesn't have its pockets of historic charm, well away from the traffic-clogged arteries of I-40 and I-25, which intersect in the center in a graceful tangle of looping, turquoise-trimmed bridges. The Duke City was founded three centuries ago, its

cumbersome name that of a Spanish nobleman, but its character the product of later eras: the post-1880 downtown district; the University of New Mexico campus, built in the early 20th century by John Gaw Meem, the architect who defined pueblo revival style; and Route 66, the highway that joined Albuquerque to Chicago and Los Angeles in 1926.

Spread out on either side of the Rio Grande, from volcanic mesas on the west to the foothills of the Sandia Mountains along the east, Albuquerque enjoys a striking natural setting. Accessible hiking and biking trails run through diverse environments: In the morning, you can stroll under centuries-old cottonwood trees near the wide, muddy river; in the afternoon, you can hike along the edge of a windswept mountain range with views across

© RON BEHRMANN

# HIGHLIGHTS

**◖ Rio Grande Nature Center State Park:** Savor a bit of country in the city in this bird-filled sanctuary along the river. Hiking and biking trails head north and south along the cottonwood-shaded irrigation channels (page 32).

**◖ San Felipe de Neri Church:** Built in 1793, this adobe church is the most striking building in Albuquerque's historic Old Town. It's still in regular use by local parishioners (page 33).

**◖ KiMo Theater:** A fantasia of Southwestern decorative styles, this former cinema is one of the few examples of Pueblo Deco style. Restored and run with city money, it's the showpiece of downtown (page 35).

**◖ Nob Hill:** Hobnob and boutique-hop in Albuquerque's quirkiest shopping district, developed in sleek modern style in the 1940s. Sidewalk cafés and bars provide a place to rest up afterward (page 36).

**◖ National Hispanic Cultural Center:** This grand institution, built in a historic barrio south of downtown, contains a great museum displaying art by Spanish-speakers from all over the United States and the globe. Try to catch a flamenco performance in the beautiful auditorium (page 36).

**◖ Sandia Peak Tramway:** Zip up the world's longest single-cable tram to the crest of the mountain that looms over the east side of Albuquerque. At the top, you'll get a vertigo-inducing view across the whole metro area and out to the hazy western horizon (page 37).

**◖ Petroglyph National Monument:** The city's west mesa is covered with fine rock carvings made centuries ago by the ancestors of the local Pueblo people. Don't miss the views across the city from the dormant volcanoes that stud the top of the ridge (page 39).

© AVALON TRAVEL

LOOK FOR ◖ TO FIND RECOMMENDED SIGHTS, ACTIVITIES, DINING, AND LODGING.

**◖ Tinkertown Museum:** An enthralling collection of one man's lifetime of whittling projects, this folk-art exhibit is inspiring for adults and a delight for kids. The more you look, the more you see (page 59).

**◖ Valles Caldera National Preserve:** In the crater formed by a collapsed volcano, some 89,000 acres of grassy valleys are set aside for very controlled public access. You must make reservations to hike here, but it's worth planning ahead (page 64).

the vast empty land beyond the city grid. And at the end of the day, you'll see Albuquerque's most remarkable feature, the dramatic light show as the setting sun reflects bright pink off the Sandia (Watermelon) Mountains.

The city is also an excellent (and reasonably priced) base for exploring the many interesting pueblos and natural attractions nearby, and it's just an hour's drive to Santa Fe, with easy day trips or long scenic drives through the mountains in between. In the Manzano Mountains southeast of town, for instance, lie a series of ruined pueblos, last inhabited during the early years of Conquest; the road that links them also winds past a canyon known for its fall colors and a historic hotel in a distinctly New Mexican style.

Whether you're en route to Santa Fe or just making a day loop, you have several ways to head north. The most direct is I-25, which cuts through dramatic rolling hills; take a short detour to Kasha-Katuwe Tent Rocks National Monument, where pointed white rocks tower above a narrow canyon. Beginning east of Albuquerque, the historic Turquoise Trail winds along the back side of the Sandias, then through the former mining town of Madrid, resettled as an arts colony, with galleries occupying the cabins built against the black, coal-rich hills.

The most roundabout route north is along the Jemez Mountain Trail, a scenic byway northwest of Albuquerque through the brick-red rocks surrounding Jemez Pueblo, then past a number of natural hot springs. The road runs along the edge of Valles Caldera National Preserve, a pristine valley where the daily number of visitors is carefully limited, so you can enjoy the vistas in solitude.

## PLANNING YOUR TIME

Because it's not so full of must-see historic attractions, Albuquerque really fares best as the primary focus of a trip, when you have time to enjoy the natural setting and the people. Ideally, you would spend a leisurely week here soaking up a little Route 66 neon, enjoying the downtown entertainment, hiking in the

Sandias, taking scenic drives, and bicycling along the Rio Grande.

But if you're also planning to visit other parts of the state, it is difficult to recommend more than a couple of days in Albuquerque. In this case, you'll probably want to allocate only two or three days on your way in or out—preferably the latter because Albuquerque's modern, get-real attitude is best appreciated after you've been in the adobe dreamland of Santa Fe for a bit. Spend a day visiting the Salinas pueblos, then the next relaxing and knocking around Old Town and the shops in Nob Hill. Or if you prefer a last dose of open sky, take the tramway up to Sandia Peak and hike along the crest trail—at the end of your trip, you'll be able to handle the elevation with no problem.

Any time of year is enjoyable in the city proper—even the winters are mild in the low basin around the river, though the Sandias often get heavy snow. As elsewhere, summer heat is broken by heavy afternoon rainstorms. And because Albuquerque is seldom top on tourists' lists, there's never a time when it's unpleasantly mobbed. Hotel prices are highest in summer, but not a dramatic hike from low-season rates.

## HISTORY

Even before tourists beat a path to points north, Albuquerque was a way station. It was established in 1706 as a small farming outpost on the banks of the Rio Grande, where Pueblo Indians had been cultivating crops since 1100, and named after a Spanish duke. When the Camino Real, the main trade route north from Mexico, developed decades later, the Villa de San Felipe de Alburquerque (the first "r" was lost over the years) was ideally situated, and the town prospered and soon outgrew its original adobe fortress, the central plaza ringed with one-story haciendas and a church.

Life continued relatively quietly through the transition to U.S. rule in 1848. But in 1880 the railroad came through town—or near enough. The depot was two miles from the original plaza, but investors were quick to construct "New Town," which became the

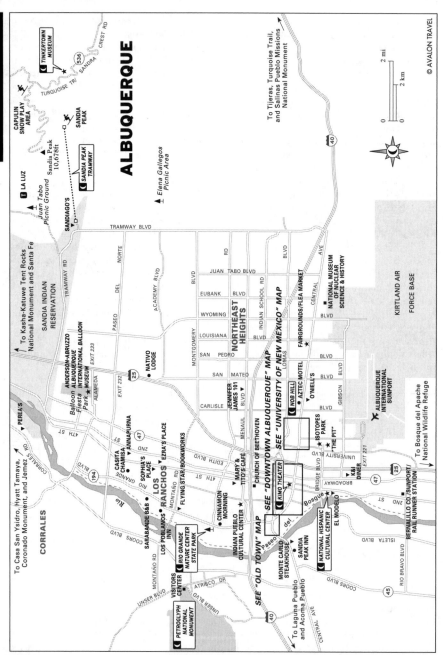

# ALBUQUERQUE

TINKERTOWN MUSEUM

536

CREST RD

SANDRA

TURQUOISE TR/

CAPULIN
SNOW PLAY
AREA

LA LUZ

Juan Tabo
Picnic Ground

SANDIAGO'S

SANDIA
PEAK

Sandia Peak
10,678ft

SANDIA PEAK
TRAMWAY

To Tijeras, Turquoise Trail,
and Salinas Pueblo Missions
National Monument

40

© AVALON TRAVEL

2 mi

2 km

Elena Gallegos
Picnic Area

TRAMWAY BLVD

KIRTLAND AIR
FORCE BASE

To Kasha-Katuwe Tent Rocks
National Monument and Santa Fe

SANDIA INDIAN
RESERVATION

TRAMWAY RD

NORTE

RD

BLVD

ACADEMY BLVD

DEL

JUAN TABO BLVD

BLVD

EUBANK BLVD

PASEO

WYOMING

INDIAN SCHOOL RD

CENTRAL AVE

NATIONAL MUSEUM
OF NUCLEAR
SCIENCE & HISTORY

NORTHEAST
HEIGHTS

FAIRGROUNDS/FLEA MARKET

LOUISIANA

BLVD

ANDERSON-ABRUZZO
ALBUQUERQUE
INTERNATIONAL BALLOON
MUSEUM

MONTGOMERY

EXIT 233

ALAMEDA

25

EXIT 232

NATIVO
LODGE

SAN PEDRO

SAN MATEO

LOMAS

BLVD

AZTEC MOTEL

O'NEILL'S

BLVD

GIBSON

BLVD

ALBUQUERQUE
INTERNATIONAL
SUNPORT

Balloon
Fiesta
Park

To Casa San Ysidro, Hyatt Tamaya,
Coronado Monument, and Jemez

CORRALES

PEREA'S

4TH ST

CORRALES BLVD

COORS BLVD

Rio

BLVD

194

RIO GRANDE

MONTAÑO RD

SARABANDE B&B

LOS POBLANOS
INN

47

2ND ST

ANNAPURNA

ST

CASITA
CHAMISA

SOPHIA'S
PLACE

LOS
RANCHOS

EZRA'S PLACE

FLYING STAR/BOOKWORKS

CINNAMON
MORNING

INDIAN PUEBLO
CULTURAL CENTER

RIO GRANDE
NATURE CENTER
STATE PARK

CARLISLE

MENAUL

JENNIFER
JAMES 101

EDITH BLVD

4TH ST

MARY &
TITO'S CAFE

CHURCH OF BEETHOVEN

SEE "DOWNTOWN ALBUQUERQUE" MAP

KIMO THEATER

SEE "OLD TOWN" MAP

Paseo

del

Bosque

NOB HILL

SEE "UNIVERSITY OF NEW MEXICO" MAP

ISOTOPES
PARK

"THE PIT"

UNIVERSITY BLVD

KAI
DINER

BROADWAY

2ND ST

BRIDGE BLVD

EL MODELO

MONTE CARLO
STEAKHOUSE

SANDIA
PEAK INN

NATIONAL HISPANIC
CULTURAL CENTER

EXIT 221

25

47

BERNALILLO CO./SUNPORT/
RAIL RUNNER STATION

To Bosque del Apache
National Wildlife Refuge

ISLETA BLVD

RIO BRAVO BLVD

COORS BLVD

45

VISITORS
CENTER

PETROGLYPH
NATIONAL
MONUMENT

UNSER BLVD

ATRISCO DR

UNSER BLVD

40

ATRISCO AVE

CENTRAL AVE

To Laguna Pueblo
and Acoma Pueblo

downtown business district. Railroad Avenue (now Central) connected the two communities, though increasingly "Old Town" fell by the wayside, its adobe buildings occupied primarily by the Mexican and Spanish population maintaining their rural lifestyle, while Anglos dominated commerce and the construction of the new city. In the early 20th century, Albuquerque's crisp air was lauded for its beneficial effect on tuberculosis patients, and sanatoriums flourished. Then Route 66 was laid down Central Avenue in the 1930s. By the next decade car traffic and business were booming, and by the 1950s, the characteristic neon signage on the numerous motor-court hotels and diners was in place.

Albuquerque's character changed again following World War II, when recruits trained at Kirtland Air Force Base returned to settle down. At the same time, the escalating Cold War fueled Sandia National Labs, established in 1949. Streets were carved into the northeast heights in anticipation of the tract houses these new workers would inhabit, and over the course of the 1940s, the population exploded from 35,000 to 100,000.

Growth has been steady ever since, and small outlying communities such as Bernalillo and Placitas have been incorporated into the larger metro area. Now they're primarily wealthy suburbs, though portions, such as Corrales and Los Ranchos de Albuquerque, both north of central Albuquerque along the river, retain a village feel that's not far from the city's roots three centuries back.

## ORIENTATION

Albuquerque's greater metro area covers more than 100 square miles, but visitors will likely see only a handful of neighborhoods, all of which are linked by Central Avenue (historic Route 66), the main east–west thoroughfare across town. Visitors typically start in Old Town: The city's best museums are clustered here, a few blocks from the Rio Grande, which runs north–south through the city. East from Old Town lies downtown, where most of the city's bars and clubs are located, along with the bus and train depots. Central Avenue then continues under I-25 and past the University of New Mexico campus. Just east of the school, the Nob Hill shopping district occupies about 10 blocks of Central. After this, the rest of Albuquerque blurs into the broad area known as the Northeast Heights, where there are only a few attractions of note—visitors will want to come up this way, to the farthest edge of the heights, to hike in the foothills and ride the Sandia Peak Tramway to the top of the mountain. The other notable parts of town—technically, separate villages—are Los Ranchos de Albuquerque and Corrales. These are two districts in the North Valley—the stretch of the river north of Central—that contain a few of the city's better lodging options; from Old Town, head north on Rio Grande Boulevard to reach Los Ranchos, then jog west over the river and north again to Corrales.

When you're trying to get your bearings, do as the locals do and keep your eyes on the mountain, along the east side of the city. Street addresses are followed by the city quadrant (NE, NW, SE, SW); Central Avenue forms the dividing line between north and south, while the east–west border is roughly along 1st Street and the train tracks. When locals talk about "the Big I," they mean the relatively central point where I-40 (east–west) and I-25 (north–south) intersect. You won't need to use the freeways for much until you head east to the foothills or west to Petroglyph National Monument.

# Sights

To cruise the major attractions in town, you could get on board with the **Albuquerque Trolley Co.** (303 Romero St. NW, 505/240-8000, www.abqtrolley.com, Apr.–Oct., $25). Departing from Old Town, its 75-minute tour loops through downtown and up to the university and Nob Hill, with informed commentary along the way. The company also offers an entertaining "Trolleywood" tour of the numerous film locations around the city.

## OLD TOWN AND THE RIO GRANDE

Until the railroad arrived in 1880, Old Town wasn't old—it was the *only* town. The labyrinthine old adobes have been repurposed as souvenir emporiums and galleries; the city's major museums are nearby on Mountain Road. Despite all the chile pepper magnets and cheap cowboy hats, the residential areas surrounding the shady plaza retain a strong

Hispano flavor, and the historic Old Town buildings have a certain endearing scruffiness—they're lived-in, not polished. A few blocks west of Old Town runs the Rio Grande, a ribbon of green space through the city and a quiet reminder of the city's agricultural history.

## Albuquerque BioPark

This kid-friendly park (2601 Central Ave. NW, 505/764-6200, www.cabq.gov/biopark, 9 A.M.–5 P.M. Mon.–Fri., 9 A.M.–6 P.M. Sat. and Sun. June–Aug., 9 A.M.–5 P.M. daily Sept.–May, $7) on the riverbank just west of Old Town contains two components. On one side is an aquarium, with a giant shark tank, a creepy tunnel full of eels, and displays on underwater life from the Gulf of Mexico and up the Rio Grande. The other half is botanical gardens, including a desert hothouse and a butterfly habitat. The most New

one of many courtyards in Old Town

in the children's garden at the BioPark

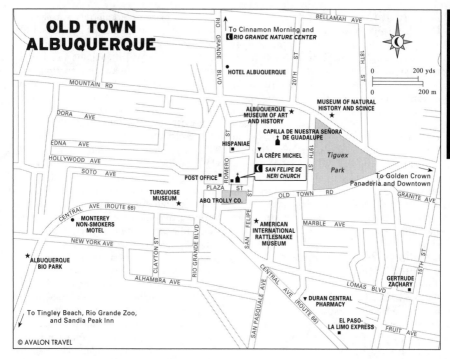

# OLD TOWN ALBUQUERQUE

BELLAMAH AVE

RIO GRANDE BLVD

To Cinnamon Morning and
RIO GRANDE NATURE CENTER

HOTEL ALBUQUERQUE

0        200 yds
0        200 m

MOUNTAIN RD

DORA AVE

EDNA AVE

HOLLYWOOD AVE

SOTO AVE

MUSEUM OF NATURAL
HISTORY AND SCINCE

ALBUQUERQUE
MUSEUM OF ART
AND HISTORY

CAPILLA DE NUESTRA SEÑORA
DE GUADALUPE

HISPANIAE

LA CRÊPE MICHEL

Tiguex

POST OFFICE

SAN FELIPE DE
NERI CHURCH

Park

To Golden Crown
Panaderia and Downtown

PLAZA ST

GRANITE AVE

TURQUOISE
MUSEUM

ABQ TROLLY CO.

OLD TOWN RD

CENTRAL AVE (ROUTE 66)

MONTEREY
NON-SMOKERS
MOTEL

AMERICAN
INTERNATIONAL
RATTLESNAKE
MUSEUM

MARBLE AVE

NEW YORK AVE

ALBUQUERQUE
BIO PARK

ALHAMBRA AVE

CLAYTON ST

RIO GRANDE BLVD

SAN FELIPE

CENTRAL AVE (ROUTE 66)

LOMAS BLVD

GERTRUDE
ZACHARY

DURAN CENTRAL
PHARMACY

To Tingley Beach, Rio Grande Zoo,
and Sandia Peak Inn

SAN PASQUALE AVE

EL PASO-
LA LIMO EXPRESS

FRUIT AVE

© AVALON TRAVEL

Mexico–specific installation, and the most interesting, is the 10-acre Rio Grande Heritage Farm, a re-creation of a 1930s operation with heirloom apple orchards and rare types of livestock, such as Percheron horses and Churro sheep. It's an idyllic setting near the river and fun for kids (especially if you're there for the apple harvest).

Pay an extra $5, and you also get admission to the **Rio Grande Zoo** (903 10th St. SW), as well as a ride on the miniature train that links the two areas. It's not particularly groundbreaking, but kids can run around among trumpeting elephants and screeching peacocks. The window into the gorilla nursery is probably the most fascinating exhibit. Between the zoo and aquarium, on the east bank of the river, south of Central, so-called **Tingley Beach** (505/764-6200, sunrise–sunset, free) is 18 acres of paths and ponds

for fishing; you can also rent pedal boats and bicycles here.

## Albuquerque Museum of Art and History

The museum (2000 Mountain Rd. NW, 505/243-7255, www.cabq.gov/museum, 9 A.M.–5 P.M. Tues.–Sun., $4) has a permanent collection ranging from a few choice Taos Society of Artists members to contemporary work by the likes of Nick Abdalla, whose sensual imagery makes Georgia O'Keeffe's flower paintings look positively literal. The history wing covers four centuries, with emphasis on Spanish military trappings, Mexican cowboys, and Albuquerque's early railroad years. Free guided tours run daily around the sculpture garden, or you can join the informative Old Town walking tour (11 A.M. Tues.–Sun. mid-Mar.–mid-Dec.).

## American International Rattlesnake Museum

You'd never guess this small storefront just off the plaza (202 San Felipe St. NW, 505/242-6569, www.rattlesnakes.com, 10 A.M.–6 P.M. Mon.–Sat., 1–5 P.M. Sun. June–Aug., $5) houses the largest collection of live snakes in the world, as you have to wade through an enormous gift shop full of plush snakes, wood snakes, little magnet snakes, and snakes on T-shirts to see the real critters. You'll also see some fuzzy tarantulas and big desert lizards, and the reptile-mad staff are usually showing off some animals outside to help educate the phobic. In the off-season, September–May, weekday hours are 11:30 A.M.–5:30 P.M. (weekends are the same).

## Capilla de Nuestra Señora de Guadalupe

Tucked away in a side alley off the main street, this tiny adobe chapel (404 San Felipe St. NW) is dedicated to the first saint of Mexico; her image dominates the wall facing the entrance. The dimly lit room, furnished only with heavy carved seats against the walls, is still in regular use, and the air is sweet with the smell of votive candles. Despite the building's small scale, it follows the scheme of many traditional New Mexican churches, with a clerestory that allows sunlight to shine down on the altar.

## Indian Pueblo Cultural Center

Just north of I-40 from Old Town, the Indian Pueblo Cultural Center (2401 12th St. NW, 505/843-7270, www.indianpueblo.org, 9 A.M.–5 P.M. daily, $6) is a must-visit before heading to any of the nearby Indian communities. A large museum traces the history of the first settlers along the Rio Grande, depicting the Spanish Conquest as a bizarre, faintly absurd enterprise. It's illustrated with some beautiful artifacts and showcases the best craftwork from each pueblo. The central plaza hosts dance performances (11 A.M. and 2 P.M. Apr.–Oct., noon Nov.–Mar.), one of the only places to see them outside of the pueblos themselves. The extensively stocked gift shop is a

very good place to buy pottery and jewelry; you can also have a lunch of posole and fry-bread at the Pueblo Harvest Café. Don't miss the south wing, which contains a gallery for contemporary art. At the information desk, check on ceremony schedules and get directions to the various pueblos.

## Museum of Natural History and Science

This large exhibit space (1801 Mountain Rd. NW, 505/841-2800, www.nmnaturalhistory.org, 9 A.M.–5 P.M. daily) contains three major attractions: a planetarium and observatory; a wide-format theater screening the latest vertigo-inducing nature documentaries; and a presentation of Earth's geological history. This latter section devotes plenty of space to the crowd-pleasers: dinosaurs. New Mexico has been particularly rich soil for paleontologists, and several of the most interesting finds are on display, such as *Coelophysis* and *Pentaceratops*. In addition, the *Startup* exhibit details the early history of the personal computer in Albuquerque; it was funded by former Duke City resident Paul Allen, who founded Microsoft here with Bill Gates, *then* moved to Seattle. Admission is $7 to the main exhibit space and $7 for the theater or the planetarium, though there are discounts if you buy tickets to more than one.

## ◖ Rio Grande Nature Center State Park

Familiarize yourself with river ecology at this green haven in the center of town (2901 Candelaria St. NW, 505/344-7240, www.rgnc.org, 8 A.M.–5 P.M. daily, $3/car). You enter the sleek, concrete visitors center (10 A.M.–5 P.M. daily) through a drainage culvert. Beyond an exhibit on water conservation and river ecology, a comfortable glassed-in "living room" lets you watch birds on the pond outside, from the comfort of a lounge chair and with the outdoor sounds piped in through speakers. Outside, you can walk several paved trails across the old irrigation channels and along the river, all shaded by towering cottonwood trees. In the spring

© ZORA O'NEILL

The Rio Grande Nature Center is an entry point to the Paseo del Bosque path along the river.

and fall, the area draws all manner of migrating birdlife; borrow binoculars from the staff if you want to scout on your own, or join one of the frequent nature walks (including full-moon tours) that take place year-round.

### San Felipe de Neri Church

Established in 1706 along with the city itself, San Felipe de Neri Church (2005 N. Plaza St. NW) was originally built on what would become the west side of the plaza—but it dissolved in a puddle of mud after a strong rainy season in 1792. The replacement structure, on the north side of the plaza, has fared much better, perhaps because its walls, made of adobe-like *terrones* (sun-dried bricks cut out of sod) are more than five feet thick. As they have for two centuries, local parishioners attend Mass here, conducted three times a day, once in Spanish.

Like many religious structures in the area, San Felipe de Neri received a makeover from Eurocentric Bishop Jean Baptiste Lamy of Santa Fe in the second half of the 19th century. Under his direction, the place got its wooden folk Gothic spires, as well as new Jesuit priests from Naples, who later added such non-Spanish details as the gabled entrance and the widow's walk. The small yet grand interior has brick floors, a baroque gilt altar, and an elaborate pressed-tin ceiling with Moorish geometric patterns. A tiny museum (9 A.M.–5 P.M. Mon.–Fri., 10 A.M.–3 P.M. Mon.–Sat., free) on the east side contains some historic church furnishings.

### Turquoise Museum

This place (2107 Central Ave. NW, 505/247-8650, 9:30 A.M.–5 P.M. Mon.–Fri., 9:30 A.M.–4 P.M. Sat., $4) is more of a consumer's resource than a museum per se. Sure, the less imaginative may see only exhibits on the geology and history of turquoise, along with specimens from all over the world, but most folks can't help but think of all the jewelry they plan to buy. So come here to learn the distinction between "natural" and "real" turquoise and otherwise arm yourself for the shopping ahead.

## DOWNTOWN

Once known as bustling New Town, the downtown area of Albuquerque, stretching along Central Avenue between the train tracks and Marquette Avenue, was the city's commercial center, crowded with mule-drawn streetcars, bargain hunters, and wheeler-dealers from the East Coast. Then, in the 1950s and 1960s, shopping plazas in Nob Hill and the Northeast Heights began drawing business away. By the 1970s, downtown was a wasteland of government office buildings that was utterly desolate after 5 P.M. But thanks to an aggressive urban-renewal scheme initiated in 2000, the neighborhood has regained some of its old vigor, and Central is now a thoroughfare best known for its bars and lounges. By day, you won't see too many specific attractions, but a stroll around reveals an interesting hodgepodge of architectural styles from Albuquerque's most optimistic era.

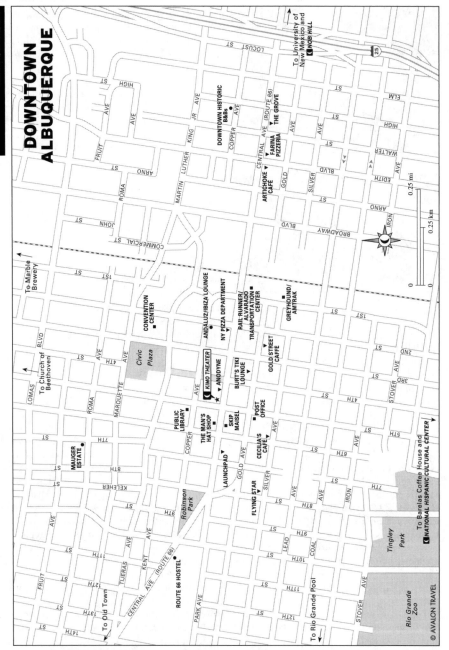

**DOWNTOWN ALBUQUERQUE**

## ◖ KiMo Theater

At the corner of Central Avenue and 5th Street is Albuquerque's most distinctive building, the KiMo Theater (505/768-3522 or 505/768-3544 event info, www.cabq.gov/kimo). In 1927, local businessman and Italian immigrant Carlo Bachechi hired Carl Boller, an architect specializing in movie palaces, to design this marvelously ornate building. Boller was inspired by the local adobe and native culture to create a unique style dubbed "Pueblo Deco"—a flamboyant treatment of Southwestern motifs, in the same vein as Moorish- and Chinese-look cinemas of the same era. The tripartite stucco facade is encrusted with ceramic tiles and Native American iconography (including a traditional Navajo symbol that had not yet been completely appropriated by the Nazi party when the KiMo was built). To get the full effect, you must tour the interior to see the cow-skull sconces and murals of pueblo life; enter through the business office just west of the ticket booth (8:30 A.M.–4:30 P.M., 11 A.M.–5 P.M. Sat.).

© ZORA O'NEILL

The splendid KiMo Theater is preserved and managed by the city.

## THE UNIVERSITY AND NOB HILL

The state's largest university was established in 1889, a tiny outpost on the far side of the railroad tracks. By 1909, under the guidance of president William George Tight, it had acquired the outline of its distinctive pueblo-inspired architecture (though Tight was then fired in part for his non–Ivy League aesthetics). Pueblo revival pioneer John Gaw Meem carried on the vision through the 1940s, and even with contemporary structures now interspersed among the original halls, it's still a remarkably harmonious vision, uniting the pastoral sanctuary feel of the great Eastern campuses with a soothing, minimalist interpretation of native New Mexican forms. Surrounding the campus is the typical scrum of cheap pizza places, bohemian coffeehouses, and dilapidated bungalow rentals. The next neighborhood east along Central is the city's best shopping district, Nob Hill, developed around a shopping plaza in the late 1940s and still showing that decade's distinctive style in marquees and shop facades.

### The University of New Mexico

Nearly 25,000 students use this campus, which sprawls for blocks beyond the old core bounded by Central Avenue and University Boulevard. Visitors can park in a complex just inside the UNM campus across from Cornell Street. The info center, where you can pick up a detailed map, is in the southwest corner of the structure. Just across the way, the **University Art Museum** (505/277-4001, 10 A.M.–4 P.M. Tues.–Fri., 1–4 P.M. Sat. and Sun., $5 donation) displays treasures from the permanent fine art collection of more than 30,000 pieces from all over the globe.

Wandering around the grounds, you'll see such classic Meem buildings as **Mesa Vista Hall** (now the Student Services Building) and **Zimmerman Library.** Rest up at the bucolic duck pond, then head for the **Maxwell Museum of Anthropology** (off University Blvd., north of M. L. K. Jr. Blvd., 505/277-4405, 10 A.M.–4 P.M. Tues.–Fri., free), a Meem building designed as the student union. The

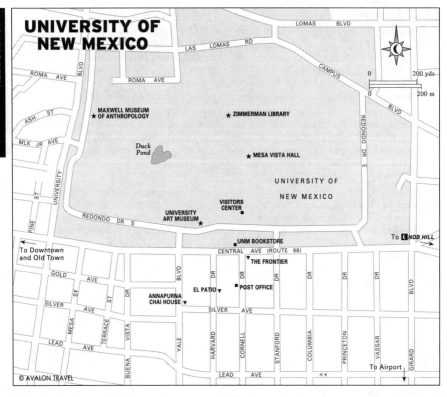

museum has a particularly good overview of Southwestern Indian culture.

## ( Nob Hill

Square frames trimmed in neon mark the Nob Hill district on Central Avenue at Girard Street and at Washington Boulevard. The area began to grow after 1937, when Route 66 was rejiggered to run along Central; the Nob Hill Shopping Plaza, at Central and Carlisle, signaled the neighborhood's success when it opened as the glitziest shopping area in town a decade later. The area went through a slump from the 1960s through the mid-1980s, but it's again lined with brightly painted facades and neon signs. The eastern half of the strip hasn't enjoyed quite the same renaissance, but wander down this way to see the **Aztec Motel** (3821 Central Ave. NE), a bizarre art project/ flophouse that a onetime resident decorated with a weird array of tiles, mannequin parts, plastic Christmas decorations, and rain-worn plush animals.

## ALBUQUERQUE METRO AREA

Beyond the neighborhoods described in the previous pages, Albuquerque is a haze of modern tract houses and shopping centers built during the 1960s and later—decades dubbed Albuquerque's "Asphalt Period" by an unkind local journalist. A few sights, particularly along the edges of the city, are well worth seeking out, however.

## ( National Hispanic Cultural Center

Just south of downtown (but not within walking distance) on 4th Street in the historic, and historically neglected, neighborhood of Barelas, the National Hispanic Cultural Center (1701 4th St. SW, 505/246-2261, www.nhccnm. org, 10 A.M.–5 P.M. Tues.–Sun., $3) is an impressive modern complex that lauds the cultural contributions of Spanish-speakers the world over. It has had a huge positive influence in this down-at-the-heels district: Even the McDonald's across the street mimics its architecture. The central attraction is the museum, which shows work ranging from the traditional santos and *retablos* by New Mexican craftspeople to contemporary painting, photography, and even furniture by artists from Chile, Cuba, Argentina, and more. Adjacent to the museum is the largest Hispanic genealogy library in existence, as well as the giant Roy E. Disney Center for Performing Arts.

## National Museum of Nuclear Science & History

Opened in 2009, this spiffy museum (601 Eubank Blvd. SE, 505/245-2137, www.nuclearmuseum.org, 9 A.M.–5 P.M. daily, $8) covers everything you wanted to know about the atomic era, from the development of the bomb on through current energy issues. Exhibits cover the ghastly elements of the atomic bomb, but also wonky tech details (check out the display of atomic-bomb decoders, set in suitcases for emergency deployment) and pop-culture artifacts, such as "duck and cover" films from the Cold War. Don't miss the beautiful posters by Swiss-American artist Erik Nitsche.

## ◖ Sandia Peak Tramway

The longest tramway of its type in the world, the tram (505/856-7325, www.sandiapeak. com, $1 parking, $20 round-trip, $12 one-way) whisks passengers 2.7 miles along a continuous line of Swiss-made cables, from Albuquerque's northeast foothills 4,000 feet up to the crest in about 15 minutes. If the wind is blowing, the ride can be a bit alarming—or thrilling, depending on your outlook. The service runs frequently all year-round (9 A.M.–9 P.M. daily June–Aug., 9 A.M.–8 P.M. Wed.–Mon., 5–8 P.M. Tues. Sept.–May), making it a convenient way

© ZORA O'NEILL

Zip up to Sandia Peak on the world's longest tramway.

# ALBUQUERQUE METRO AREA

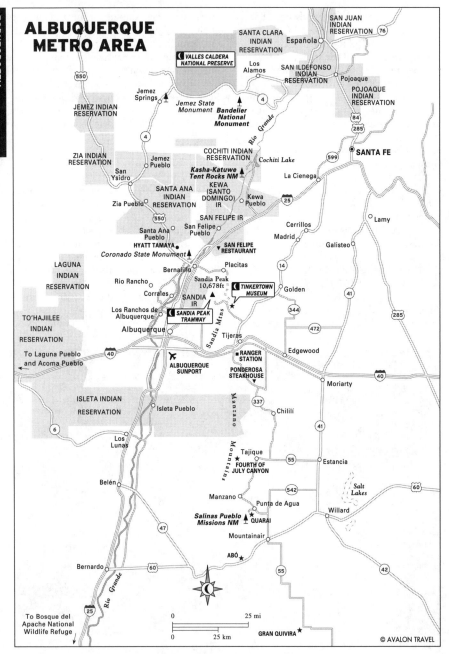

© AVALON TRAVEL

to get to the ski area; in the summer, you can ride up to the peak, then hike along the crest a few miles to the visitors center. At the base of the tram, there's a small free museum about skiing in New Mexico, and even from this point, the view across the city is very good—you may want to come to the casual Mexican restaurant here, **Sandiago's** (38 Tramway Rd., 505/856-6692, 11 A.M.–8:30 P.M. daily, $10), for a sunset margarita.

## ◖ Petroglyph National Monument

Albuquerque's west side is bordered by this national reserve area, 7,500 acres of black boulders that crawl with some 20,000 carved lizards, birds, and assorted odd beasts. Most of the images, which were created by chipping away the blackish surface "varnish" of the volcanic rock to reach the paler stone beneath, are between 400 and 700 years old, while others may date back three millennia. A few more recent examples of rock art include Maltese crosses made by Spanish settlers and initials

left by explorers (not to mention a few by idle 21st-century teenagers).

Stop in first at the **visitors center** (Unser Blvd. at Western Trail, 505/899-0205, www. nps.gov/petr, 8 A.M.–5 P.M. daily) for park maps, flyers on flora and fauna, and general orientation. You can see some of the largest groupings on two major trails: **Boca Negra Canyon,** a short paved loop, and in **Rinconada Canyon,** a 1.25-mile one-way hike. Boca Negra Canyon is the only fee area ($1/car on weekdays, $2 on weekends), and there are restrooms and water in the parking area. The Rinconada trailhead is less developed; the walk can be tedious going in some spots because the ground is sandy, but it's relatively flat. The clearest, most impressive images are in the canyon at the end of the trail. Keep an eye out for millipedes, which thrive in this stark environment; dead, their curled-up empty shells resemble the spirals carved on the rocks—coincidence?

The back (west) side of the parkland, the **Volcanoes Day Use Area** (9 A.M.–5 P.M. daily) is also a great place to survey the city.

© PETROGLYPH NATIONAL MONUMENT

Critters adorn the rocks at Petroglyph National Monument.

Access is via Paseo Volcan (exit 149) off I-40; turn right (east) 4.3 miles north of the highway at an unmarked dirt road to the parking area. From the base of three cinder cones, you can look down on the city and see how the lava flowed between sandstone bluffs that later crumbled away—hence the lava "fingers" that stretch east and the crumbled edges of the escarpment where the petroglyphs are found. If you go in the winter, you'll see that the volcanoes, which were last reported emitting steam in 1881, are still not entirely dead: Patches of green plants flourish around the steam vents that stud the hillocks, particularly visible on the middle of the three volcanoes.

## Anderson-Abruzzo Albuquerque International Balloon Museum

Boosters of Albuquerque's hot air balloon scene—which has been flourishing since the first rally in 1972—include locals Ben Abruzzo, Larry Newman, and Maxie Anderson, who in 1978 made the first Atlantic crossing by balloon in the *Double Eagle II* helium craft. Abruzzo and Anderson also crossed the Pacific and set a long-distance record (5,678 miles) in the *Double Eagle V*. These pioneers are honored at The Anderson-Abruzzo Albuquerque International Balloon Museum (9201 Balloon Museum Dr. NE, 505/880-0500, www.balloonmuseum.com, 9 A.M.–5 P.M. Tues.–Sun., $4), in Balloon Fiesta Park.

## Los Ranchos and Corrales Scenic Byway

For a pretty drive through these villages that have been all but consumed by greater Albuquerque, head north from Old Town on Rio Grande Boulevard; you first reach Los Ranchos, then cross the river at Alameda to Corrales Road and continue up the west bank. These districts remain pockets of pastoral calm where horses gambol and 18th-century acequias water organic herb gardens—a practical melding of old agricultural heritage with modern suburban bliss. The only real sights are in central Corrales, two blocks west of the

Albuquerque's balloon museum: the next best thing to going up, up, and away yourself

main road. The folk Gothic **Old San Ysidro Church** (505/897-1513, 1–4 P.M. Sat. and Sun. June–Oct.) stands where the center of the village was in 1868, when its bulging adobe piers were first constructed.

Across the road, **Casa San Ysidro** (505/898-3915, www.cabq.gov/museum, $4) was owned by obsessive collectors Alan and Shirley Minge, who lived in the place for nearly 40 years, heating with firewood and squirreling away New Mexican antiques and craftwork. The Albuquerque Museum gives tours regularly June–August (9:30 A.M. and 1:30 P.M. Wed.–Fri., 9:30 A.M., 10:30 A.M. and 1:30 P.M. Sat., 2 P.M. Sun.) and a little less frequently the rest of the year (9:30 A.M. and 1:30 P.M. Wed.–Sat., 2 P.M. Sun.). You can just turn up, but it's a good idea to call to confirm the times.

## Coronado State Monument

Though named for Spanish explorer Francisco Vásquez de Coronado, who camped on this lush spot by the river during his 1540 search for gold, the monument (485 Kuaua Rd., Bernalillo, 505/867-5351, 8:30 A.M.–5 P.M. Wed.–Mon., $3) is actually a Native American relic, the partially restored pueblo of Kuaua (Tiwa for "evergreen"), which was inhabited between 1300 and the early 1600s. The centerpiece is the partially sunken square kiva, its interior walls covered with murals of life-size human figures and animals in ritual poses. What you see are only reproductions—the originals have been removed for preservation,

and a few are on display in the visitors center. The setting is good for a picnic: Seated on a bench facing the river and the mountains, with the city hidden from view behind a dense screen of cottonwoods, you get a sense of the lush, calm life along the Rio Grande in the centuries before the Spanish arrived. To reach the monument, exit I-25 in Bernalillo and head west on Highway 550; Kuaua Road is on your right, before the Santa Ana Star casino. The monument is closed Tuesdays during the winter.

# Entertainment

## BARS AND CLUBS

When the city government promoted downtown as the nightlife district, it may have created too much of a good thing. Now it's the city's main bar and club scene, all packed in a few square blocks, which makes for handy hopping (or staggering) from place to place. A lot of the bars cater to students, with plentiful beer and other happy-hour specials, but a somewhat generic, slightly dressed-up atmosphere. It ends in a rowdy scene after the bars close on Fridays and Saturdays, and crowds spill out onto several blocks of Central that are closed to car traffic.

The more distinctive places are pure Albuquerque: unpretentious, with a remarkably varied clientele. Because there aren't enough members of any one particular subculture to pack a whole bar, even the most chic-appearing places will see an absent-minded professor and a veteran Earth First–er propping up the bar next to well-groomed yuppies.

### Downtown

The **Hotel Andaluz lobby** (125 2nd St. NW, 505/242-9090) touts itself as "Albuquerque's living room"—Conrad Hilton's original vision for the place—and it's a comfy spot to sip delectable cocktails (the watermelon-lime cooler is dangerously drinkable) and nibble Spanish-inspired snacks, especially if you reserve one

of the private "casbahs" on the weekend, when there's also live tango or salsa and a big crowd of dancers. Up on the second floor, the indoor-outdoor **Ibiza Lounge** (5 P.M.–1 A.M. Thurs.–Sat., $10 cover after 9 P.M. Fri. and Sat.) is a chic scene on weekends, a cooler alternative to the mayhem just over on Central.

The best all-purpose casual bar downtown is the second-floor **Anodyne** (409 Central Ave. NW, 505/244-1820), a long, wood-floor room filled with pool tables and a younger crowd sprawled on the thrift-store sofas. Choose from more than a hundred beers, and get some quarters to plug into the good collection of pinball machines.

To catch the latest touring indie-rock sensation or the local crew about to hit it big, head to the very professional **Launchpad** (618 Central Ave. SW, 505/764-8887, www.launchpadrocks.com). With free live music and a pool table, **Burt's Tiki Lounge** (313 Gold Ave. SW, 505/247-2878, www.burtstikilounge.com, 8 P.M.–2 A.M. Mon.–Sat.) has a funky feel and an eclectic bill, from British psychedelia to reggae.

Further out of the downtown fray, the **Marble Brewery** (111 Marble Ave. NW, 505/243-2739, 3 P.M.–midnight Mon.–Thurs., 2 P.M.–midnight Fri., noon–midnight Sat., noon–10 P.M. Sun.) is a cool space with a big patio out back, where you might catch a band.

# TRADITIONAL NEW MEXICAN MUSIC

Blaring mariachi ensembles, scratchy fiddles accompanying the Matachines dancers, booming tribal drums: The musical traditions of New Mexico are diverse. The best place to hear the mix is on KANW (89.1 FM) in Albuquerque, a public radio station that devotes most of its day and evening programming to homegrown music, with a heavy emphasis on mariachi, and such stars as Los Reyes de Albuquerque. There's also a vintage country show on Saturday nights, as a nod to Anglo listeners. On Sunday afternoons, KUNM (89.9 FM) turns the airwaves over to *Singing Wire,* where you'll hear traditional Native American music as well as pop anthems like Keith Secola's oft-requested "NDN Kars."

If you're out of range of these stations, look for the excellent Smithsonian Folkways CDs *Music of New Mexico: Hispanic Traditions* (which has the Matachines and Comanches dance songs alongside more widespread Mexican songs like "Las Mañanitas") and *New Mexico: Native American Traditions,* which is all traditional drumming.

And its beers are much better than other brew-pubs' in town.

## The University and Nob Hill

In the Nob Hill shopping plaza, **Gecko's** (3500 Central Ave. SE, 505/262-1848, 11:30 A.M.– late Mon.–Fri., noon–late Sat. and Sun.) is a good place for a snack (anything from Thai curry shrimp to chipotle hot wings) and a drink on the patio. Sporting its own breezy patio, **O'Niell's** (4310 Central Ave. SE, 505/255-6782, 11 A.M.–2 A.M. Mon.–Sat., 11 A.M.– midnight Sun.) is a great Irish pub that draws a varied crowd; the kitchen is open until midnight. If you want to watch more street life, **Kelly's** (3222 Central Ave. SE, 505/262-2739, 8 A.M.–11 P.M. daily, $9) has ample outdoor seating along the sidewalk in central Nob Hill. The rich Kelly Porter washes down beer-friendly food like so-so bison burgers and curly fries—but you're really here for the scene, the sun, and the suds. If you're more in the mood for a cozy indoor vibe, head to the cellar wine bar at **Zinc** (3009 Central Ave. NE, 505/254-9462, 5 P.M.–1 A.M. Mon.–Sat.), where you can try tasting flights while listening to a jazz trio or watching old movies.

## CREATIVE CULTURE

A young but beloved institution, Albuquerque's **Church of Beethoven** (505/234-4611, www.churchofbeethoven.

org, $15) is a Sunday-morning gathering for classical-music lovers and anyone who wants "church minus the religion," as the organizers envision it. It takes place at the funky coffee house The Kosmos (1715 5th St. NW), part of a larger warehouse-turned-art-studios complex. The "service" starts at 10:30 A.M. and lasts about an hour, with two musical performances, interspersed with a poem and a few minutes of silent contemplation. It's all fueled by free espresso.

## FESTIVALS AND EVENTS

The city's biggest annual event is the **Albuquerque International Balloon Fiesta** (505/821-1000, www.balloonfiesta.com), 10 days in October dedicated to New Mexico's official state aircraft, with more than 700 hot air balloons of all colors, shapes, and sizes gathering at a dedicated park on the north edge of town, west of I-25. During the fiesta, the city is packed with fanatical "airheads," who claim this is the best gathering of its kind in the world. If you go, don't miss an early-morning mass ascension, when the balloons glow against the dark sky, then lift silently into the air in a great wave.

You'll catch an equally colorful show at the **Gathering of Nations Powwow** (www.gatheringofnations.com), the largest tribal get-together in the United States, with more than 3,000 dancers and singers in full regalia

# CEREMONIAL DANCES

This is only an approximate schedule for ceremonial dances at Albuquerque-area pueblos – dates can vary from year to year. Annual feast days typically involve carnivals and markets in addition to dances. Confirm details and start times – usually afternoon, but sometimes following an evening or midnight Mass – with the **Indian Pueblo Cultural Center** (505/843-7270, www.indianpueblo.org) before setting out.

## JANUARY 1

- Jemez: Matachines

- Kewa (Santo Domingo): corn dance

## JANUARY 6

- Most pueblos: various dances

## FEBRUARY 2

- San Felipe: various dances for Candlemas (Día de la Candelaria)

## EASTER

- Most pueblos: various dances

## MAY 1

- San Felipe: Feast of San Felipe

## JUNE 13

- Sandia: Feast of San Antonio

## JUNE 29

- Santa Ana: Feast of San Pedro

## JULY 14

- Cochiti: Feast of San Bonaventura

## JULY 26

- Santa Ana: Feast of Santa Ana

## AUGUST 2

- Jemez: Feast of Santa Persingula

## AUGUST 4

- Kewa (Santo Domingo): Feast of Santo Domingo

## AUGUST 15

- Zia: Feast of the Assumption of Our Blessed Mother

## LABOR DAY

- Santo Domingo: arts and crafts market

## SEPTEMBER 8

- San Ildefonso: corn dance

## NOVEMBER 12

- Jemez: Feast of San Diego

## DECEMBER 12

- Jemez: Matachines

## DECEMBER 24

- Santa Ana: dances after midnight Mass

from over 500 tribes crowding the floor of the University Arena. Miss Indian World earns her crown by showing off traditional talents such as spearfishing or storytelling. The event takes place the last weekend in April.

The state's agricultural roots get their due at the **New Mexico State Fair** (www.exponm.com), a 17-day festival of fried foods and prizewinning livestock that begins just after Labor Day. It's your usual mix of midway craziness and exhibition barns, along with really excellent rodeos, which often end with shows by country music legends like Willie Nelson.

# Shopping

Old Town and the environs are where you can pick up traditional jewelry and pottery for very reasonable prices, while Nob Hill is the commercial center of Albuquerque's counterculture, with body-piercing studios adjacent to comic book shops next to herbal apothecaries.

## OLD TOWN AND THE RIO GRANDE

The slew of galleries and gift shops packed around the plaza can blur together after just a little bit of browsing, but a couple of places stand out: **Hispaniae** (410 Romero St. NW, 505/244-1533, 10 A.M.–5:30 P.M. Mon.–Sat., noon–5 P.M. Sun.) is three rooms crammed with Mexican craftwork, and the **street vendors** set up on the east side of the plaza are all artisans selling their own work, at fair prices.

Just outside of Old Town's historic zone, the

**Gertrude Zachary** showroom (1501 Lomas Blvd. NW, 505/247-4442, 10 A.M.–6 P.M. Mon.–Sat., 10 A.M.–5 P.M. Sun.) is the place to go for turquoise-and-silver jewelry, whether you want a traditional squash-blossom necklace or a contemporary reimagining of that design studded with other semiprecious stones.

For more traditional work, head to the shop at the **Indian Pueblo Cultural Center** (2401 12th St. NW, 505/843-7270, www.indian-pueblo.org, 9 A.M.–5 P.M. daily); not only are its prices reasonable, but the staff is happy to explain the work that goes into various pieces.

## DOWNTOWN

An emporium of American Indian goods, **Skip Maisel** (510 Central Ave. SW, 505/242-6526, 9 A.M.–5:30 P.M. Mon.–Sat.) feels like a relic from downtown's heyday—whether you want a war bonnet, a turquoise-studded watch, or

Skip Maisel, a classic Western-wear emporium

© ZORA O'NEILL

deerskin moccasins, it's all here in a vast, over-stocked shop with kindly salespeople. Don't miss the beautiful murals above the display windows in the foyer; they were painted in the 1930s by local Indian artists. Another throw-back is **The Man's Hat Shop** (511 Central Ave. NW, 505/247-9605, 9:30 A.M.–5:30 P.M. Tues.–Fri., 9:30 A.M.–5 P.M. Sat.), which stocks just what it promises, from homburgs to ten-gallons.

## THE UNIVERSITY AND NOB HILL

Start your stroll on the west end of the Nob Hill district, near Girard. **Masks y Más** (3106 Central Ave. SE, 505/256-4183, 11 A.M.–6 P.M. daily) deals in all things bi-zarre, most with a south-of-the-border fla-vor; here's where to get the outfit for your Mexican-wrestler alter ego. Tasteful (and ex-pensive) **Hey Jhonny** (3418 Central Ave. SE, 505/256-9244, 10 A.M.–6:30 P.M. Mon.–Sat., 11 A.M.–6 P.M. Sun.) stocks gorgeous sushi sets, hip handbags, and travel guides only to the coolest destinations.

On the next corner, **Mariposa Gallery** (3500 Central Ave. SE, 505/268-6828, 11 A.M.–6 P.M. Mon.–Sat., noon–5 P.M. Sun.) is one of the city's longest-established art vendors, dealing since 1974 in jewelry, fiber art, and other crafts. If you're looking for unusual postcards, head down the block to **Papers!** (114 Amherst Dr. SE, 505/254-1434, 10:30 A.M.–6:30 P.M. Mon.–Sat., 11 A.M.–5 P.M. Sun.), where the greeting cards are great, but the array of blank sheets may inspire you to make your own. **A, the Albuquerque Store** (3500 Central Ave. SE, 505/266-2222, 10 A.M.–6 P.M. Mon.–Sat., noon–5 P.M. Sun.) specializes in home fur-nishings for the Southwestern hipster, such as colorful flower-print Mexican tablecloth fabric and handmade candles. The jewelry

loose turquoise for sale at the Albuquerque flea market

© ZORA O'NEILL

here, much of it by local designers, is very good, too.

## ALBUQUERQUE METRO AREA

Every Saturday and Sunday, Albuquerque's **flea market** (505/222-9766, $2 parking) takes place at the fairgrounds (enter at Gate 9, on Louisiana just north of Central). It's an interesting outlet where you can pick up anything from new cowboy boots to loose nuggets of turquoise; socks and beef jerky are also well represented. Stop off at one of the myriad food stands for a snack—re-freshing *aguas frescas* (fresh fruit juices, in flavors such as watermelon and tamarind) and Indian frybread are the most popular. It allegedly starts at 7 A.M., but most vendors get rolling around 9 A.M. and go till a little after 4 P.M.

# Sports and Recreation

Albuquerque is a perfect city for outdoorsy types, with several distinct ecosystems and plenty of trails running through them. Late spring and summer are the best times to head to the higher elevations on the Sandia Mountains; once the cool fall weather sets in, the scrub-covered foothills and the bare, rocky West Mesa are more hospitable. The valley along the Rio Grande, running through the center of the city, is remarkably pleasant year-round: mild in winter and cool and shady in summer. As everywhere in the desert, always pack extra layers of clothing and plenty of water before you set out, and don't go charging up to Sandia Peak (10,678 feet above sea level) your first day off the plane.

## SKIING

**Sandia Peak Ski Area** (505/242-9052, www.sandiapeak.com, $45 full-day lift ticket) is open from mid-December through mid-March, though it often takes till about February for a good base to build up. The 30 trails, serviced by four lifts, are not dramatic, but they are good and long. The area is open daily in the holiday season, then Wednesday through Sunday for the rest of the winter.

Sandia Peak also has plenty of opportunities for cross-country skiing. The most popular place is the **Capulin Snow Play Area** ($3 parking), nine miles up Highway 536 to the crest, where there are also big hills for tubing and sledding. You can check the status of the trails at the Sandia ranger station (505/281-3304) on Highway 337 in Tijeras.

## HIKING

Between the West Mesa and the east mountains, Albuquerque offers a huge range of day hikes. The easiest option is the *bosque* (the wooded area along the Rio Grande), where level paths lead through groves of cottonwoods, willows, and olive trees; the **Rio Grande Nature Center** (8 A.M.–8 P.M. daily,

$3 parking) at the end of Candelaria, is the best starting point for any walk around the area. Anyone looking for some elevation gain will want to head to the Sandias. On the city side, the foothills are ideal in the winter but a little hot in the summertime—the best access is at **Elena Gallegos Picnic Area** (7 A.M.–9 P.M. Apr.–Oct., 7 A.M.–7 P.M. Nov.–Mar., $1 weekdays, $2 weekends), east of Tramway Boulevard and north of Academy, at the end of Simms Park Road.

The foothills are also the starting point for a much more challenging hike: the popular **La Luz Trail,** a 7.5-mile ascent to the Sandia Crest Visitor Center. The trail has a 12 percent grade at certain points, but the views are worth the effort, as is the experience of hiking through four climate zones (pack lots of layers) as you climb 3,200 vertical feet. Near the

© JEFF GREENBERG

The Sandia foothills are criss-crossed with biking and hiking paths.

# BIRDING ON THE PEAK

Sandia Peak in the dead of winter does not seem hospitable to life in any form, much less flocks of delicate-looking birds the size of your fist, fluffing around cheerfully in the frigid air. But that's precisely what you'll see if you visit in the iciest months, particularly right after a big snowfall. The feathered critters in question are rosy finches, a contrary, cold-loving variety (sometimes called "refrigerator birds") that migrate from as far north as the Arctic tundra between November and March to the higher elevations of New Mexico, which must seem relatively tropical by comparison.

What's particularly special about Sandia is that it draws all three species of rosy finch, which in turn draws dedicated birders looking to add the finches to their life lists. *Birder's*

*World* magazine praises Sandia Peak as "the world's most accessible location to see all three species of rosy finches." This is a boon for people who are more accustomed to kayaking through swamps and slogging through tropical forests to spot rare species. So if you see the finches – they're midsize brown or black birds with pink bellies, rumps, and wings – you'll probably also spy some human finch fans. But they might not have time to talk, as it's not unheard-of for the most obsessive birders – those on their "big year," out to spot as many species as possible in precisely 365 days – to fly into Albuquerque, drive to the crest, eyeball the finches, and drive right back down and fly out in search of even more obscure varieties.

top, you can take a spur that leads north to the Sandia Crest observation point or continue on the main trail south to the ski area and the Sandia Peak Tramway, which you can take you back down the mountain. Ideally you'd have someone pick you up at the bottom end of the tram because the 2.5-mile trail along the foothills from the tram back to the trailhead is dusty and lacking in shade. (You might be tempted to take the tram up and hike down, but the steep descent can be deadly to toes and knees.) La Luz trailhead ($3 parking) is at the far north end of Tramway Boulevard just before the road turns west.

If you want to enjoy the views without quite so much effort, you can drive up the east face of the mountain (I-40 to Highway 14) via scenic byway Highway 536, a.k.a. the Crest Road, and park at the Sandia Crest Visitor Center at the top ($3 day-use fee). From there, an easy loop of a little more than two miles runs south along the **Crest Spur Trail,** which dips below the ridgeline to connect to **La Luz,** which in turn goes on to the tram terminal. Then you can hike back to your car via the **Crest Trail.**

## BIKING

Albuquerque maintains a great network of paved trails for cycling in the city, and the mountains and foothills are lined with challenging dirt tracks. Recreational cyclists need head no farther than the river, where the **Paseo del Bosque,** a 16-mile-long, completely flat biking and jogging path runs through the Rio Grande Valley State Park. The natural starting point is at **Alameda/ Rio Grande Open Space** (7 A.M.–9 P.M. Apr.–Oct., 7 A.M.–7 P.M. daily Nov.–Mar.) on Alameda Boulevard. You can also reach the trail through the **Rio Grande Nature Center** (8 A.M.–8 P.M. daily, $3 parking), at the end of Candelaria, and at several other major intersections along the way. For details on this and other bike trails in Albuquerque, download a map from the city's bike info page (www.cabq.gov/bike). In the summer, you can **rent bikes** at Tingley Beach (part of the Albuquerque BioPark, in the *Sights* section; 10 A.M.–5 P.M. Mon.–Thurs., 10 A.M.–7 P.M. Sat. and Sun., $8/hour) and start biking along the river from there.

Mountain bikers can take the Sandia Peak

Tramway to the ski area, then rent a bike to explore the 30 miles of wooded trails. Bikes aren't allowed on the tram, though, so if you have your own wheels, you can drive around the east side of the mountain. Or you can stay in the city and explore the **foothills trails,** a web of dirt tracks all along the edge of the Northeast Heights. **Trail no. 365,** which runs for about 15 miles north–south from near the tramway down to near I-40, is the best run. You can start at either end, or go to the midpoint, at Elena Gallegos Open Space, off the north end of Tramway Boulevard at the end of Simms Park Road. Aside from the occasional sandy or rocky patch, none of the route is technical, nor steep. More complex trails run off to the east; pick up a map at the entrance booth at Elena Gallegos.

For hard-core road bikers, a popular tour is up to **Sandia Peak** via the Crest Road on the east side—you can park and ride from any point, but cyclists typically start somewhere along Highway 14 (the Turquoise Trail) north of I-40, then ride up Highway 536, which winds 13.5 miles along increasingly steep switchbacks to the crest. The New Mexico Touring Society (www.nmts.org) lists descriptions of the myriad of other ride options and organizes group rides.

## BASEBALL

Minor-league baseball thrives in Albuquerque, apparently all because of some clever name: The so-so Dukes petered out a while back, but a fresh franchise, under the name of the **Albuquerque Isotopes,** has been drawing crowds since 2003. It's hard to judge whether the appeal is the cool Isotopes Park (1601 Avenida Cesar Chavez NE, 505/924-2255,

Root for the home team at Isotopes Park.

www.albuquerquebaseball.com), the whoopee-cushion theme nights, or just the name, drawn from an episode of *The Simpsons*. Regardless, a summer night under the ballpark lights is undeniably pleasant; it helps that the best seats are just $12.

## SWIMMING

Beat the heat at the **Rio Grande Pool** (1410 Iron Ave. SW, 505/848-1397, noon–5 P.M. daily late May–mid-Aug., $2.25), one of Albuquerque's nicest places to take a dip; the outdoor 25-meter pool is shaded by giant cottonwoods.

# Accommodations

Because Albuquerque isn't quite a tourist mecca, its hotel offerings have languished a bit. Chain-operated towers are the norm, and some of the bed-and-breakfasts have a haphazard air. But a few places, particularly a downtown historic hotel and the inns in the pastoral areas of Los Ranchos and Corrales, on the north edge of the city, are quite nice, and you'll pay substantially less here than you would in Santa Fe for similar amenities.

## UNDER $100

Funky and affordable, the **Route 66 Hostel** (1012 Central Ave. SW, 505/247-1813, www. rt66hostel.com) is in a century-old house midway between downtown and Old Town and has been offering bargain accommodations since 1978; it's clean despite years of budget travelers traipsing through. Upstairs, along creaky wood hallways, are private rooms ($25–35) with various configurations. Downstairs and in the cool basement area are single-sex dorms ($20 pp). Guests have run of the kitchen, and there's a laundry and room to lounge. The most useful city bus lines run right out front. There have been complaints of staff not being on hand for early or late check-ins—be sure to call and confirm before you arrive.

Central Avenue is strewn with motels, many built in Route 66's heyday. Almost all of them are unsavory, except for ( **Monterey Non-Smokers Motel** (2402 Central Ave. SW, 505/243-3554, www.nonsmokersmotel.com, $68 s, $74 d), which is as practical as its name implies. Except for a jazzy neon sign, the place doesn't really capitalize on 1950s kitsch—it just offers clean, good-value rooms with no extra frills or flair. The location near Old Town is very convenient.

The only criticism to muster against the ( **Sandia Peak Inn** (4614 Central Ave. SW, 505/831-5036, $60 d) is that it's nowhere near the mountain; in fact, it's on the west side of the city, just over the river from Old Town. In all other respects, it's more than you could want in a bargain hotel: large, spotless rooms, all with bathtubs, fridges, microwaves, and huge TVs. Breakfast is included in the rate. There's a small indoor pool and free wireless Internet available throughout.

## $100–150

On the west edge of downtown you'll find the Queen Anne–style **Mauger Estate** (701 Roma Ave., 505/242-8755, www.maugerbb. com, $109 s). It gleams with polished dark wood paneling and floors. Luxe touches like triple-sheeted beds and fresh flowers contribute to an overall feeling of elegance.

The exceptionally tasteful **Downtown Historic Bed & Breakfasts of Albuquerque** (207 High St. NE, 505/842-0223, www.albuquerquebedandbreakfasts.com, $129 d) occupies two neighboring old houses on the east side of Downtown (walking distance to some very good food). Heritage House has more of a Victorian feel, while Spy House has a sparer, 1940s look—but both are refreshingly uncluttered.

The heart of ( **Cinnamon Morning** (2700 Rio Grande Blvd. NW, 505/345-3541, www.cinnamonmorning.com, $129 s), about a mile north of Old Town, is its lavish outdoor kitchen, with a huge round dining table and a fireplace to encourage lounging on nippier nights. Rooms are simply furnished, with minimalist Southwestern detail—choose from three smaller rooms in the main house, each with a private bath, or, across the garden, a two-bedroom guest house and a casita with a private patio and a kitchenette.

A strong option in the rural-feeling Los Ranchos district, **Sarabande B&B** (5637 Rio Grande Blvd. NW, 505/345-4923, www.sarabandebnb.com, $139 d) has six rooms in three configurations. Choose from a skylight, brick floors, and a potbellied wood stove; a private garden and a gas fireplace; or a wood-burning kiva fireplace and a soaking tub. They're all done in subdued Southwestern style. A small lap pool takes up the backyard, and a flower-filled patio with a fountain is the breakfast venue.

Los Poblanos Historic Inn was built by noted architect John Gaw Meem.

Hidden on a narrow road in Los Ranchos, the wonderfully private **Casita Chamisa** (850 Chamisal Rd. NW, 505/897-4644, www.casitachamisa.com, $105 d) is the sort of place that could exist only in New Mexico: The 150-year-old adobe house sits on an old acequia, amid the remnants of a Pueblo community established seven centuries ago. The site was partially excavated by the owner's late wife, an archaeologist.

**Nativo Lodge** (6000 Pan American Fwy., 505/798-4300, www.hhandr.com, $189 d) is comparable to sister property Hotel Albuquerque in style and comfort, with plush pillow-top beds and a cool "Pueblo Modern" style. But because it's on the north side of town—convenient only for the Balloon Fiesta or an early start to Santa Fe—it's substantially cheaper. Definitely request a room in the back, so you're not overlooking I-25, and try to book online, where the rates can drop substantially.

## $150-250

At Albuquerque's nicest place to stay, you don't actually feel like you're anywhere near the city. **( Los Poblanos Historic Inn** (4803 Rio Grande Blvd. NW, 505/344-9297, www. lospoblanos.com, $155 d) sits on 25 acres, the largest remaining plot of land in the city, and the rooms are tucked in various corners of a sprawling *rancho* built in the 1930s by John Gaw Meem for city bigwig Albert Simms and his wife, Ruth McCormick, former U.S. legislators who contributed enormously to the city's social and economic life. Main-house guest rooms, accented with Spanish colonial antiques and arrayed around a central patio, retain their old wood floors and heavy viga ceilings. A big sunny guesthouse is filled with colorful folk art, and even a new wing, opened in late 2010, fits right in, with fireplaces, wood floors, and beautiful views. There's also a saltwater pool and a gym, but the most special feature is access to the extensive gardens and organic lavender farm that take up much of the acreage.

If you prefer to be in the middle of the city, go for **( Andaluz** (125 2nd St. NW, 505/242-9090, www.hotelandaluz.com, $189 d), a beautiful relic of early 20th-century travel. Opened

© ZORA O'NEILL

COURTESY HOTEL ANDALUZ

a private "casbah" in the Andaluz lobby

are soothing and well designed, with a little Moorish flair in the curvy door outlines. The place is worth a visit for the lobby alone; check out the exhibits from local museums on the second-floor mezzanine.

**Hotel Albuquerque at Old Town** (800 Rio Grande Blvd. NW, 505/843-6300, www. hhandr.com, $219 d) is a good backup in this category—on the surface a little pricey, though rates are much lower when booked online. Sporting a chic Spanish-colonial style, the brick-red-and-beige rooms are relatively spacious. Opt for the north side (generally, even-numbered rooms) for a view of the mountains.

## OVER $250

The smell of piñon smoke and the sound of flute music set the tone at the **Hyatt Regency Tamaya** (1300 Tuyuna Tr., Santa Ana Pueblo, 505/867-1234, www.tamaya.hyatt.com, $265 d), an impeccably designed resort that's a cooperative project between Santa Ana Pueblo and the Hyatt chain. Even the standard rooms are quite large, with either terraces or balconies, though the mountain view is worth the premium. Three swimming pools and a full spa offer relaxation; the more active can play golf or tennis, take an archery class, or attend an evening storytelling program with a pueblo member.

in 1939 by New Mexico–raised hotelier Conrad Hilton, it received a massive renovation in 2009, keeping all the old wood and murals but updating the core to be fully environmentally friendly, from solar hot water heaters to a composting program. The neutral-palette rooms

# Food

Although Albuquerque has a few dress-up establishments that merit a little bit of credit-card debt, the real spirit of the city's cuisine is in its low-rent spots where dedicated owners follow their individual visions—whether that means funky lunch creations or the hottest chile in the state. Prices given are those of the average entrée.

## OLD TOWN AND THE RIO GRANDE

Aside from the couple recommended here, the restaurants in the blocks immediately adjacent

to the Old Town plaza are expensive and only so-so; better to walk another block or two for real New Mexican flavor, which can be found in a number of local hangouts around Old Town and up Rio Grande Boulevard in the North Valley.

### Cafés

Of the few places in Old Town proper, **La Crêpe Michel,** tucked in a courtyard on the back side of the art museum (400 San Felipe St. NW, 505/242-1251, 11:30 A.M.–2 P.M. and 6–9 P.M. Tues.–Sat., 11:30 A.M.–2 P.M.

Sun., $9), is one of the better. It serves French standards—not just crepes, but also quiches and *croque monsieurs*—in a snug front room and a covered back patio.

A 10-minute walk from Old Town, **Golden Crown Panaderia** (1103 Mountain Rd. NW, 505/243-2424, 7 A.M.–8 P.M. Tues.–Sat., $4–9) is a real neighborhood hangout. Famous for its green-chile bread and its biscochitos (the anise-laced state cookie), it also does dainty fried empanadas and other flaky, sweet treats. You can also order sandwiches and pizza (green-chile crust is an option), to take away or to eat at the picnic tables out back.

Stuck on a barren stretch of North 4th Street, where neighboring businesses are feed stores and car-repair shops, two exceptional restaurants are run by the same family. For breakfast and lunch, **( Sophia's Place** (6313 4th St. NW, 505/345-3935, 7 A.M.–3 P.M. daily, $8) is the sort of bohemian café that serves fresh farm eggs but doesn't brag about it. Get those eggs on a breakfast sandwich, which you're really ordering for the side of highly addictive red-chile-dusted home fries. At lunch, you can opt for a big bowl of noodles or a fat sandwich stuffed with your choice of grilled meats. For dinner, head to **( Ezra's Place** (6132 4th St. NW, 505/344-1917, 11 A.M.–3 P.M. and 5–9 P.M. Tues.–Sat., 9 A.M.–2 P.M. Sun., $12), which has a similarly eclectic menu with tons of specials every day, inspired by whatever's in season. A major selling point, on top of dishes like duck enchiladas with serrano-tomatillo salsa, is the funky location in a bowling alley (look for the sign for Lucky 66 Bowl).

### New Mexican

Not far from the plaza, **Duran Central Pharmacy** (1815 Central Ave. NW, 505/247-4141, 9 A.M.–6:30 P.M. Mon.–Fri., 9 A.M.–2 P.M. Sat., $6) is an old-fashioned lunch counter hidden behind the magazine rack in this big fluorescent-lit drugstore. Regulars pack this place at lunch for all the New Mexican staples: huevos rancheros, green-chile stew, and big enchilada plates. Cash only.

For New Mexican food with a heavier American Indian influence, hit the **Pueblo Harvest Café** (2401 12th St. NW, 505/724-3510, 8 A.M.–8:30 P.M. Mon.–Thurs., 8 A.M.–9 P.M. Fri. and Sat., 8 A.M.–4 P.M. Sun., $8), at the Indian Pueblo Cultural Center. The menu covers generic territory, but specialties such as mutton stew and a green-chile-and-lamb sandwich are rich and earthy and rarely found elsewhere. Breakfast is also good, with blue-corn pancakes and apple-raisin "Indian toast." (The "Rez Breakfast," with Spam on the side, is an interesting, if not delicious, cultural artifact.) There's live music Friday and Saturday evenings, as well as Sunday around noon.

## DOWNTOWN

With so many bars in this area, there's little room left for food, beyond a couple of solid cafés.

### Cafés

For coffee and pastry or for a full dinner with a glass of wine, head to **Gold Street Caffè** (218 Gold Ave. SW, 505/765-1633, 7 A.M.–2 P.M. Mon., 7 A.M.–10 P.M. Tues.–Fri., 8 A.M.–10 P.M. Sat., 8 A.M.–2 P.M. Sun., $11), where you can monopolize a sidewalk table while you sample tuna niçoise salad or mussels in a red-chile broth. It also serves breakfasts—the de rigueur huevos rancheros alongside innovations like poached eggs on green-chile brioche, plus the dangerously addictive honey-chile glazed bacon.

A branch of **Flying Star** (723 Silver Ave. SE, 505/244-8099, 6 A.M.–10 P.M. Sun.–Thurs., 6 A.M.–11 P.M. Fri. and Sat., $9) occupies a hiply restored 1950 John Gaw Meem bank building. See *The University and Nob Hill* listings for more.

If you're on the go—or just prefer to soak up the sun on the 4th Street pedestrian walk—you can grab a slice at **JC's New York Pizza Department** (215 Central Ave. NW, 505/766-6973, 11 A.M.–midnight Sun.–Thurs., 11 A.M.–2:30 A.M. Fri. and Sat., $6), which specializes in thin-crust pies named after the five boroughs (Da Bronx: cured pepperoni and mozzarella).

Past the railroad tracks in EDo (East Downtown), **(C The Grove** (600 Central Ave. SE, 505/248-9800, 7 A.M.–4 P.M. Tues.–Sat., 8 A.M.–3 P.M. Sun., $10) complements its local-organic menu with an indoor-outdoor feel, with big front windows facing Central and a screened-in patio. The chalkboard menu features big, creative salads (spinach, orange slices, and dates is one combo) as well as sandwiches and cupcakes; breakfast, with farm-fresh local eggs and homemade English muffins, is served all day. It's a notch above Flying Star in price, but you're paying for the very high-quality ingredients.

### New Mexican

Even though it's in the middle of Albuquerque's main business district, **Cecilia's Café** (230 6th St. SW, 505/243-7070, 7 A.M.–2:30 P.M. daily, $8) feels more like a living room than an office. Maybe it's the woodstove in the corner—as well as the personal attention from Cecilia and her daughters and the food that's clearly made with care. The rich, dark red chile really shines here.

### Fine Dining

Since it opened in 1989, the **Artichoke Café** (424 Central Ave. SE, 505/243-0200, 11 A.M.–2:30 P.M. and 5:30–10 P.M. Mon.–Fri., 5:30–10 P.M. Sat., 5:30–9 P.M. Sun., $24) has been top on locals' lists for a dinner treat, largely because the husband-and-wife owners have varied the menu with the times without seeming desperately trendy—influences are largely Mediterranean (asparagus-mushroom ravioli) and use local meats and cheeses to excellent effect. The blue-tinged dining room is simple without being austere, and the crowd is varied. Reservations are recommended. The neighboring **Farina Pizzeria** (510 Central Ave. SE, 505/243-0130, 11 A.M.–9 P.M. Mon., 11 A.M.–10 P.M. Tues.–Fri., 4–10 P.M. Sat., 5–9 P.M. Sun., $13), under the same ownership, shows the

same care for ingredients, in a cool, semi-industrial setting.

## THE UNIVERSITY AND NOB HILL

Thanks to the large student population, this area has some great and varied spots to grab a cheap bite, but Nob Hill has some upscale options too.

### Cafés

When you walk into **(C Flying Star** (3416 Central Ave. SE, 505/255-6633, 6 A.M.–11:30 P.M. Mon.–Thurs., 6 A.M.–midnight Fri. and Sat., $9), you'll be mesmerized by the pastry case, packed with triple-ginger cookies, lemon-blueberry cheesecake, and fat éclairs. But try to look up to appreciate the range on the menu boards: Asian noodles, hot and cold sandwiches, mac-and-cheese, and enchiladas. With speedy service and a huge magazine selection, it's a great place to zip in or to lounge around (wireless Internet access is free). This is the original location of what's now a mini-chain—you'll find one in nearly every neighborhood, including the North Valley (4026 Rio Grande Blvd. NW, 505/344-6714) and downtown.

Just a few blocks from the university, **Annapurna World Vegetarian Café** (2201 Silver Ave. SE, 505/262-2424, 7 A.M.–9 P.M. Mon.–Sat., 10 A.M.–8 P.M. Sun., $8) is a vegetarian's delight, serving a menu that's compatible with Ayurvedic dietary recommendations, with giant *masala dosas* (rice-flour crepes) as well as less strictly Indian dishes such as cardamom pancakes with maple syrup. It has a second branch in the North Valley (7520 4th St. NW, 505/254-2424, 7 A.M.–8 P.M. Mon.–Sat.).

Pick up goods for a picnic at **La Montañita Co-op** (3500 Central Ave. SE, 505/265-4631, 7 A.M.–10 P.M. Mon.–Sat., 8 A.M.–10 P.M. Sun.), where quinoa salads and stuffed grape leaves are all the rage; look in the dairy section for "sampler" pieces of locally made cheese. There's a bigger branch in the **North Valley**

(2400 Rio Grande Blvd. NW, 505/242-8800, 8 A.M.–10 P.M. daily).

## Mexican

A branch of the popular Santa Fe purveyor of fresh and fast Mexican, **Bumble Bee's Baja Grill** (3423 Central Ave. NE, 505/262-2862, 11 A.M.–8 P.M. daily, $4.50–11) specializes in grilled fish tacos, but the meatier ones, including a stewed lamb filling, are delicious too. They also do roast chicken, grilled trout, and a couple other full entrées. There's a great fresh salsa selection as well.

## Pizza

**Il Vicino** (3403 Central Ave. NE, 505/266-7855, 11 A.M.–11 P.M. Sun.–Thurs., 11 A.M.– midnight Fri. and Sat., $9) is a slick brewpub and pizza parlor. Order at the front counter from the list of high-grade pizza toppings, and the dough promptly gets slid into the wood-fired oven at the back—or opt for a grilled *panino* sandwich or a big fresh salad. Then squeeze into your seat and enjoy your pint of Wet Mountain IPA. In keeping with the upscale pizza-joint feel, there's also wine and Italian sodas.

## New Mexican

You haven't been to Albuquerque unless you've been to **❰ The Frontier** (2400 Central Ave. SE, 505/266-0550, 5 A.M.–1 A.M. daily, $6), a mammoth diner across from UNM. Everyone in the city passes through its doors at some point in their lives, so all you have to do is pick a seat in one of the five Western-theme rooms (Hmm, under the big portrait of John Wayne? Or maybe one of the smaller ones?) and watch the characters file in. You'll want some food, of course: a green-chile–smothered breakfast burrito filled with crispy hash browns, or a grilled hamburger, or one of the signature cinnamon rolls, a deadly amalgam of flour, sugar, and some addictive drug that compels you to eat them despite the hydrogenated goo they're swimming in. If you feel a little unhealthy, you can always get some fresh orange juice and restore your balance

© ZORA O'NEILL

The Frontier is the city's best spot for green-chile stew and people-watching.

by vegging out in front of the mesmerizing tortilla machine.

Near the university, **El Patio** (142 Harvard Dr. SE, 505/268-4245, 11 A.M.–9 P.M. Mon.–Thurs., 11 A.M.–9:30 P.M. Fri. and Sat., noon–9 P.M. Sun., $8) is the kind of old-reliable place that ex-locals get misty-eyed about after they've moved away. The green-chile-and-chicken enchiladas are high on many citywide favorite lists. It doesn't hurt that the setting, in an old bungalow with a shady outdoor space, feels like an extension of someone's home kitchen. The menu is more vegetarian-friendly than most New Mexican joints.

All sleek black and silver inside, stylish **Nob Hill Bar & Grill** (3128 Central Ave. SE, 505/266-4455, 11 A.M.–10 P.M. Tues.–Thurs., 11 A.M.–11 P.M. Fri. and Sat., noon–9 P.M. Sun.) is the domain of Sam Etheridge, renowned for his previous restaurant, Ambrozia. His newer effort is more casual, with hardly anything over $20 (or "20 bucks," in the folksy menu's parlance), and familiar dishes get a little twist of fancy: a crab BLT, for instance, or steak *frites* with a trio of homemade ketchups; salads are only "7 bucks." All-you-can-eat Sunday brunch ($20) is a gourmand's undoing: chocolate croissants alongside mole enchiladas and crab-cake Benedict.

## ALBUQUERQUE METRO AREA

Great places to eat are scattered all over the city, often in unlikely looking strip malls. These places are worth making a trip for, or will provide a pick-me-up when you're far afield.

### New Mexican

Experts agree: **Mary & Tito's Café** (2711 4th St. NW, 505/344-6266, 9 A.M.–6 P.M. Mon.–Thurs., 9 A.M.–8 P.M. Fri. and Sat., $7) is the place to go for *carne adovada,* the dish of tender pork braised in red chile. The only thing better is the "Mexican turnover," an uncooked flour tortilla filled with *carne adovada,* then deep-fried. But in fact, everything with red chile is delicious at this simple, home-style place north of downtown. You'll see locals cashing in their frequent-diner cards—even if you're in town for a short stay, you might want to get one.

Cruise down by the rail yards south of downtown to find **El Modelo** (1715 2nd St. SW, 505/242-1843, 7 A.M.–7 P.M. daily, $6), a local go-to for a hangover-curing *chicharrón* burrito, chile-smothered spare ribs, or tamales for the whole family. Because it's really a front for a tortilla factory, the flour tortillas are particularly tender, and you can order either a taco or a whole platter of food. If the weather's nice, grab a seat at a picnic table outside and watch the freight trains go by.

Just two blocks from the National Hispanic Cultural Center, popular **((** **Barelas Coffee House** (1502 4th St. SW, 505/843-7577, 7:30 A.M.–3 P.M. Mon.–Fri., 7:30 A.M.–2:30 P.M. Sat., $6) is confusing to the first-timer: The attraction is chile, not coffee—especially the red, which infuses hearty, timeless New Mexican standards like posole, *chicharrones,* and *menudo.* The restaurant occupies several storefronts, and even then there's often a line out the door at lunch. But it's worth the wait—this is timeless food.

Out in Corrales, **Perea's Restaurant & Tijuana Bar** (4590 Corrales Rd., 505/898-2442, 11 A.M.–2 P.M. Mon.–Sat., $7) is open only for lunch, but it's worth scheduling around if you know you'll be out this way. Everything's home-cooked, from Frito pie to *carne adovada.*

### Fine Dining

File under Best High-End Meal in a Strip Mall: Chef Jennifer James has been a fixture on Albuquerque's dining scene for years, but it wasn't until she opened **((** **Jennifer James 101** (4615 Menaul Blvd. NE, 505/884-3860, www.jenniferjames101.com, 5–10 P.M. Tues.–Sat., $24) that she finally got a nod from the James Beard Foundation, in a nomination for Best Chef Southwest in 2009. It hasn't gone to her head. Once inside, away from the traffic, the place is supremely calm, and your dinner is a confident mix of seasonal ingredients that sound plain on paper, but deliver intense flavor: lamb with rhubarb chutney, for instance, or a pasta with fiddlehead ferns and mushrooms. Check the website for special events: occasional prix-fixe "dinner parties" on Sundays, and the Tuesday and Wednesday "community table"—eight seats with a set seasonal menu and matched wines. For $50, it's a bargain, and a social treat for solo travelers. You must reserve ahead at all times.

# Drives from Albuquerque

Within 45 minutes of the city, you'll find some great natural attractions. A winding road through the mountains southeast of town brings you past the ruined Salinas Pueblo Missions—an intriguing bit of early Conquest history, and little visited. To the east is the start of one of three routes to Santa Fe, the Turquoise Trail, which leads through some vestiges of New Mexico's mining past. An equally scenic route north is the more circuitous Jemez Mountain Trail, past red rocks and hot springs. Or you can zip directly up the interstate, where you'll pass the windswept region known as Tent Rocks.

## SALINAS PUEBLO MISSIONS NATIONAL MONUMENT

Set on the plains behind the Manzano Mountains, the scenically decaying mud-brick buildings at Quarai, Gran Quivira, and Abó represent one of the Franciscans' bigger challenges during the early years of the Conquest. The national monument designation actually applies to three separate sites. Visiting them all will take a full day, and the route (Highway 337, beginning in Tijeras, just east of the city) also passes by the little town of Mountainair, as well as one of the area's most beautiful fall hiking spots.

### Tijeras

To reach Highway 337, take I-40 east to exit 179. Settled in the 1850s, the village of Tijeras (Scissors, for the way the canyons meet here) is still a stronghold of old Hispano traditions, though it doesn't look too distinctive on the surface. Beginning the ascent along the mountains, you leave it behind in a matter of minutes. Very soon you pass the **Ponderosa Steakhouse** (10676 Hwy. 337, 505/281-8278, 4–9 P.M. daily, $8), which is really more of a bar, populated by mountain men far more grizzled than you'd expect this close to the big city. The place represents the East Mountains of old, before the area was considered a suburb.

But the steak (and especially the steak fajitas) is good and inexpensive—you could drive the route backward if you want to end with dinner here.

### Fourth of July Canyon

Past the Spanish land grant of Chililí (its terms have been contested ever since the Treaty of Guadalupe Hidalgo), Highway 337 runs into Highway 55—make a right and head to Tajique, then turn onto Forest Road 55 to reach Fourth of July Canyon. The area in the foothills of the Manzanos, seven miles down the dirt road, is a destination in late September and early October, when the red maples and oak trees turn every shade of pink, crimson, and orange imaginable. (Amazingly, the place got its name not for this fireworks-like show of colors, but for the date an Anglo explorer happened across it in 1906.) It's also pretty in late summer, when the rains bring wildflowers. You can explore on the short **Spring Loop Trail** or **Crimson Maple Trail,** or really get into the woods on **Fourth of July Trail** (no. 173), which wanders into the canyon 1.8 miles and connects with **Albuquerque Trail** (no. 78) to form a loop.

Forest Road 55 loops back to meet Highway 55, but the second half, after the campground, can be very rough going. It's usually maintained in the fall, but at other times of the year, you might want to backtrack rather than carry on, especially if you're in a rental car.

### Quarai

The first ruins you reach are those at Quarai (505/847-2290, 9 A.M.–6 P.M. daily June–Aug., 9 A.M.–5 P.M. Sept.–May, free), a pueblo inhabited from the 14th to the 17th century. Like the other two Salinas pueblos, Quarai was a hardscrabble place with no natural source of water and very little food, though it did act as a trading outpost for salt, brought from small salt lakes farther east (hence the name). When the Franciscans arrived, then,

© ZORA O'NEILL

**Folk artist "Pop" Shaffer was highly creative with rocks.**

they put more than the usual strain on this community of 400 or so Tiwa-speakers; they nonetheless managed to build a grand sandstone-and-adobe mission, the most impressive of the ones at these three pueblos. In addition to a struggle with the local population, the priests found themselves at odds with the Spanish governors, who helped protect them but also undermined their conversion work by encouraging ceremonial dances. At the same time, raids by Apaches increased because any crop surplus no longer went to them in trade, but to the Spanish. Oh, and there were terrible famines between 1663 and 1670. No wonder, then, that the place was abandoned even before the Pueblo Revolt of 1680. Only the mission has been excavated; the surrounding hillocks are all pueblo structures.

## Mountainair

Highway 55 meets U.S. 60 in the village of Mountainair, which hosts the **Salinas Pueblo Missions Visitors Center** (505/847-2585, 8 A.M.–5 P.M. daily), on U.S. 60 west of the intersection—though it offers not much more information than what's available at the

small but detailed museums at each site. The **Mountainair ranger station** (505/847-2990, 8 A.M.–noon and 12:30–4:30 P.M. Mon.–Fri.) is also here, for those who want trail maps for the Manzanos and the like. Coming from the north, follow signs west off Highway 55, before you reach the U.S. 60 intersection.

Mountainair is also home to the weird architectural treasure that is the **Shaffer Hotel** (103 Main St., 505/847-2888, www.shafferhotel.com), a 1923 Pueblo Deco confection with a folk-art twist, built by one Clem "Pop" Shaffer, who had a way with cast concrete—look for his name in the wall enclosing the little garden. Redone in late 2005, the hotel has unfortunately not been kept up well, and its rooms (from just $28 for one with a shared bath) are recommended only if you have a chance to inspect them first—don't reserve ahead. Better to stop in just for a snack or a drink at the adjacent **Shaffer Café** (10:30 A.M.–3:30 P.M. Mon., Wed., and Thurs., 8:30 A.M.–6:30 P.M. Fri. and Sat., 8 A.M.–3 P.M. Sun.), where the wood ceiling is Shaffer's masterpiece: intricately carved and painted, it crawls with turtles, snakes, and other critters.

For real sustenance, hit **Alpine Alley** (210 N. Summit Ave., 505/847-2478, 6 A.M.–2 P.M. Mon.–Fri., 8 A.M.–2 P.M. Sat.), just north of the main intersection on Highway 55. This small-scale café makes everything from scratch, including great baked goods, creative sandwiches, and soups. It's a treat, and a real social center for the village.

## Gran Quivira

South from Mountainair 26 miles lies Gran Quivira—a bit of a drive, and you'll have to backtrack, but on the way you'll pass **Rancho Bonito,** another Pop Shaffer creation—his actual home. As it's private property, you can't go poking around, but from the road you can see a bit of the little log cabin painted in black, red, white, and blue. (If you happen to be in Mountainair in May for its art tour, the house is open for tours then.)

Right where Highway 55 makes a sharp turn east, Gran Quivira (505/847-2770, 9 A.M.–6 P.M. daily June–Aug., 9 A.M.–5 P.M. Sept.–May, free) looks different from the other two Salinas pueblos because it is built of gray San Andres limestone slabs, not sandstone, and finished with plaster that was painted with symbols. It's the largest of three, with an estimated population between 1,500 and 2,000, likely devoted to trade, as the large array of feathers and pottery styles found here indicate. Like the people of Abó, the residents spoke Tompiro, and the Spanish dubbed them Los Rayados, for the striped decorations they wore on their faces. It appears they outwardly accepted the Franciscan mission after the first sermon was preached here in 1627. But they took their own religion literally underground, building hidden kivas underneath the residential structures even as they toiled on two successive missions ordered by the Catholics. Nonetheless, the place was deserted by 1671, after more than a third of the people had starved to death.

## Abó

From Gran Quivira, drive back the way you came and turn west on U.S. 60 in Mountainair to reach Abó (505/847-2400, free), nine miles

a warren of interconnected rooms at Gran Quivira

© ZORA O'NEILL

on. The visitors center here has the same hours as the other sites (9 A.M.–6 P.M. daily June–Aug., 9 A.M.–5 P.M. Sept.–May, free), but the ruins themselves are open all the time—it's nice to drop by here just as the setting sun is enhancing the red glow of the rocks. Abó was the first pueblo the Franciscans visited, in 1622; the mission here, constructed over more than 60 years, shows details such as old wood stairs leading to the choir loft. (The Franciscans were so dedicated to re-creating the Catholic church experience here in the desert that they brought in portable pipe organs and trained their converts to sing.) Unlike Gran Quivira, though, Abó seems to have had some agreement regarding kivas, as there is one built right in the center of the convento (the compound adjoining the mission), dating from the same period—something that no archaeologist or historian has yet explained. The excellent condition of all of these ruins is due in part to a family that owned the land from the mid-19th century on—one member, Federico Sisneros, is buried near the mission, at his request.

From Abó, you can continue west through the mountain pass, then down into the long, flat Rio Grande valley on U.S. 60, which runs straight into I-25 at Bernardo. If you're heading back to Albuquerque, you can take Highway 47 northwest to Belén, about 25 miles closer to the city.

## THE TURQUOISE TRAIL

This scenic back route to Santa Fe, which runs along the east side of the Sandias and up across high plateaus, revisits New Mexico's mining history as it passes through a series of ghost towns. Take I-40 east from Albuquerque to exit 175. If you want to pick up hiking maps of the area, bear right to go into the village of Tijeras and the **Sandia ranger station** (11776 Hwy. 337, 505/281-3304). Go left to continue directly to the junction with Highway 14, the beginning of the Turquoise Trail.

### ◖ Tinkertown Museum

The four-lane road heads north through alternating communities of old Spanish land grants and modern subdivisions collectively

referred to as the East Mountains. Six miles on, you come to a large triangle intersection—to the left is Highway 536, the Crest Road up to Sandia Peak, a beautiful winding drive through steadily thinning forests until you reach the exposed top of the mountain, more than 10,000 feet above sea level and more than 5,500 feet above the center of Albuquerque. Even if you don't drive to the crest, do head 1.5 miles up the Crest Road to Tinkertown Museum (505/281-5233, 9 A.M.–6 P.M. daily Apr.–Oct., $3), a temple to efficient use of downtime.

Ross Ward, an artist and sign painter who learned his trade doing banners for carnivals, was also a master whittler and creative engineer who built, over 40 years, thousands of elaborate miniature figures and dioramas out of wood, some of which he even animated with tiny pulleys and levers: a man with a cleaver chases chickens in a circle, circus performers soar, the blacksmith's bellows huff and puff. Many of the buildings themselves are Ward's creations as well—undulating walls made of bottles and studded with odd collectibles, for

© TINKERTOWN

wise words from Ross Ward, who built Tinkertown

instance; the museum, like an amoeba, even seems to have taken over a friend and neighbor's 35-foot wooden boat. Ward died in 2002; his family keeps up the museum, and even though it's no longer growing as it used to, it remains a remarkable piece of pure folk art.

## Golden

Back on Highway 14, continue north through rolling hills and ever-broader sky. After 15 miles, you reach the all-but-gone town of Golden—so named because it was the site of the first gold strike west of the Mississippi, in 1825. But all that's left now is a handful of homes, an attractive adobe church, and **Henderson Store** (10 A.M.–3:30 P.M. Tues.–Sat.), a general store open since 1918. It's largely given over to Indian jewelry and pottery, but prices are reasonable and quality is generally quite high. Antique trinkets line the upper shelves, remnants of Golden's moment of glory.

## Madrid

Thirteen miles beyond Golden, and about midway along the drive, Madrid (pronounced MAD-rid by locals) is a ghost town back from the dead. Built by the Albuquerque & Cerrillos Coal Co. in 1906, it once housed 4,000 people, but it was deserted by the end of World War II, when natural gas became more widespread. By the late 1970s, though, a few of the sway-backed wood houses had been reoccupied by hippies who were willing to live where indoor plumbing was barely available. Over the decades, Madrid slowly revived. Portable toilets are still more common than flush models, but the arts scene has flourished, and a real sense of community pervades the main street, which is lined with galleries and pretty painted bungalows. In 2006, the village was the setting for the John Travolta film *Wild Hogs,* and the set-piece café built for the production has become a minor pilgrimage site for bikers.

You can learn more about Madrid's history at the **Old Coal Mine Museum** (Hwy. 14, 505/438-3780, www.themineshafttavern.com, 11 A.M.–5 P.M. Fri.–Mon., $5), where you can wander among sinister-looking machine parts, and even walk partway down an abandoned mineshaft—a great disciplinary tool for kids

It's not really a diner – it's a set from *Wild Hogs,* now housing a souvenir shop.

© ZORA O'NEILL

who've been acting up in the car. You'll feel the "ghost" in "ghost town" here. There's an Old West costume photo studio in the lobby, and, if it gets revamped to meet fire codes, the melodrama-ready **Engine House Theatre**— check the website for updates.

A more vibrant remnant of Madrid's company-town days is the **Mine Shaft Tavern** (2846 Hwy. 14, 505/473-0743, 11:30 A.M.– 10 P.M. daily), where you can belly up to a 40-foot-long pine-pole bar, over which hang murals by local artist Ross Ward, who built the Tinkertown Museum in Sandia Park. "It is better to drink than to work," reads the Latin inscription interwoven among the mural panels, and certainly everyone in the bar, from long-distance bikers to gallery-hoppers, is living by those encouraging words.

For coffee and local gossip, hit **Java Junction** (2855 Hwy. 14, 505/438-2772, www.javajunction.com, from 7:30 A.M. daily), which also rents a **guestroom** ($109 d). For more substance, head straight to **Mama Lisa's Ghost Town Kitchen.** When it's open (seemingly not on a regular basis, but chances are better in the summer), it's a true treat, a cozy place with an all-over-the-map menu: buffalo chalupas, Austrian-style pork chops, rhubarb pie, and hibiscus mint tea, which you can enjoy out on the tree-shaded front patio. When it's closed, all you can do is press your face against the window and dream—or go down the street to **The Hollar** (Hwy. 14, 575/471-4821, 11 A.M.–3 P.M. Mon.–Wed., 11 A.M.–9 P.M. Thurs.–Sat., 11 A.M.–3 P.M. and 5–8 P.M. Sun., $9), which dishes up Southern standards like po' boys, fried green tomatoes, and ooey-gooey cheese grits—it's casual by day and more refined in the evening, making it the kind of place Santa Feans drive to for a treat.

## Cerrillos

By contrast with Madrid, Cerrillos, once the source of turquoise that has been traced to Chaco Canyon, Spain, and Chichén Itzá in Mexico's Yucatán Peninsula, hasn't been gallerified like its neighbor down the road. A trading post sells cow skulls, antique bottles, taxidermied jackalopes, and turquoise nuggets; an adjacent petting zoo has a llama and a sheep. And there's one bar, **Mary's,** whose proprietress is into her 10th decade of life and has been running the place since 1977. The bar doesn't look particularly open from the outside, but do stop in and have a beer and a chat with Mary Trujillo, who can tell some fine tales of putting unruly drunks in their place (including the cast of *Young Guns,* which was filmed here). You can go **horseback riding** through the canyon (Broken Saddle Riding Co., 505/424-7774, www.brokensaddle.com, $80 for two hours) and in **Cerrillos Hills Historic Park** (head north across the railroad tracks, www.cerrilloshills.org), more than 1,000 acres of rolling hills and narrow canyons that are also good for mountain biking.

After ascending from the canyons around Cerrillos onto a high plateau (look out for antelope), you're on the home stretch to Santa Fe—but you'll pass one more dining option, the 🅒 **San Marcos Café** (3877 Hwy. 14, 505/471-9298, 8 A.M.–2 P.M. daily, $9), which shares space with a working feed store where chickens scratch in the yard. Breakfast in the country-style dining room (a potbellied stove lurks in one corner) is especially delicious, with great cinnamon buns, homemade chicken sausage, and a variety of fresh-tasting egg dishes.

From here, Highway 14 continues on to become Cerrillos Road, the very slow and unscenic way into Santa Fe; the more direct route is via I-25 to Old Santa Fe Trail. Keep an eye out for the highway on-ramp—signs point to Las Vegas.

## THE JEMEZ MOUNTAIN TRAIL

Beginning just northwest of Albuquerque, the Jemez (HAY-mez) Mountain Trail is an exceptionally beautiful drive, as it passes through Jemez Indian Reservation, the Santa Fe National Forest, and the Valles Caldera National Preserve. It's the least direct way of getting to Santa Fe—you actually wind up near Los Alamos and must backtrack a bit south to reach town—but nature lovers will want to set aside a full day for the trip, which is especially beautiful in the fall, when the aspen leaves turn vivid yellow against the rich red stones. Unlike the Turquoise Trail, it's not based on any particular historical route but rather on the sheer beauty of the scenery. The drive begins on U.S. 550, which goes northwest out of the satellite town of Bernalillo, just west of I-25. At the village of San Ysidro, bear right onto Highway 4, which forms the major part of the route north.

## Jemez Pueblo

This community of some 3,000 tribal members settled in the area in the late 13th century, and Highway 4 runs through the middle of the 89,000 acres it still maintains. Before the Spanish arrived, the Hemish people (which the Spanish spelled Jemez) had established more than 10 large villages in the area. One of the few pueblos in the area that has not opened a casino (though it was under consideration in 2010), it's quite conservative and closed to outsiders except for ceremonial dances. Because Jemez absorbed members of Pecos Pueblo in 1838, it celebrates two feast days, San Diego's (November 12) and San Persingula's (August 2). It's also the only remaining pueblo where residents speak the Towa language, the rarest of the related New Mexico languages (Tewa and Tiwa are the other two). The pueblo operates the **Walatowa Visitors Center** (575/834-7235, www.jemezpueblo.org, 8 A.M.–5 P.M. daily Apr.–Dec., 10 A.M.–4 P.M. Jan.–Mar.), about five miles north of San Ysidro. The center is easy to miss because you'll be gawking off the east side of the road at the lurid red sandstone cliffs at the mouth of the **San Diego Canyon.** From April till October, vendors selling traditional Indian frybread and enchiladas are another tasty distraction. The visitors center has exhibits about the local geology and the people of Jemez and doubles as a ranger station, dispensing maps and advice on outdoor recreation farther up the road, such as hiking trails, campgrounds, fishing access points, and the various hot springs that well up out of crevices

all through the Jemez Mountains. You can take a one-mile guided hike ($5) up into the red rocks; it's a good idea to call ahead and arrange a time.

## Jemez Springs

This charming small resort town—really just a handful of little clapboard buildings tucked in the narrow valley along the road—is the most convenient place to indulge in some of the area's springs, which are a stew of minerals and trace elements like lithium that have inspired tales of miraculous healing since people began visiting in the 1870s. **Giggling Springs** (Hwy. 4, 575/829-9175, www.gigglingsprings. com, 11 A.M.–sunset Tues.–Sun., $17/hour or $48/day), built in the 1880s, has a luxe-meets-rough feel, with a spring-fed pool enclosed in an attractively landscaped flagstone area right near the Jemez River. In winter, it's open only Wednesday–Sunday. The **Jemez Springs Bath House** (Hwy. 4, 575/829-3303, www. jemezsprings.org, 10 A.M.–8 P.M. daily, $157 per hour) is operated by the village. Here, the springs have been diverted into eight soaking tubs; they're private, but have a somewhat clinical feel. Call ahead to reserve; massages and other spa treatments are available as well.

For a bite to eat and a place to stay, **Laughing Lizard Inn & Café** (Hwy. 4, 575/829-3108, www.laughinglizard.com, $70 d) offers four pretty little rooms opening onto a long porch. The café occupies an old tin-ceiling general store and serves an eclectic menu of Moroccan chicken, pizzas, and fresh salads (about $10). If all that seems too healthy and modern, head to **Los Ojos Restaurant & Saloon** (17596 Hwy. 4, 575/829-3547, 11 A.M.–midnight Mon.–Fri., 8 A.M.–midnight Sat. and Sun., $8), where horseshoes double as window grills and the atmosphere hasn't changed in decades. Its odd, but the satisfying Jémez Burger sports black olives and Swiss cheese, but you can get green chile as well, of course. Closing time can come earlier if business is slow, so call ahead in the evenings.

If you're planning to explore the wilderness

© ZORA O'NEILL

Battleship Rock is a landmark north of Jemez Springs.

and missed the Walatowa Visitors Center at Jemez Pueblo, you can stop at the **Jemez Ranger District Office** (Hwy. 4, 575/829-3535, 8 A.M.–5 P.M. Mon.–Fri.) for info. There's also a **visitors center for Valles Caldera National Preserve** (Hwy. 4, 575/661-3333, 8 A.M.–4:30 P.M. Mon.–Fri.) here too—stop in to arrange reservations for the park, or to see if there are last-minute openings. Both are on the north edge of town.

## Jemez State Monument

Just north of Jemez Springs, you pass this set of ruins (Hwy. 4, 575/829-3530, 8:30 A.M.–5 P.M. Wed.–Mon., $3), where the ancestors of the present Jemez people settled more than 700 years ago and lived until the Pueblo Revolt of 1680. More striking than the old pueblo, which was named Giusewa, is the crumbling Franciscan mission that rises up in the middle of it. The convent and church of San José de los Jémez were built around 1620, using forced labor from the pueblo; the result was remarkably lavish, but the friars had abandoned their work by 1640, probably because they'd thoroughly antagonized their would-be parishioners. Today the remnants of the two different cultures have nearly dissolved back into the earth from which they were both built, but the church's unique octagonal bell tower has been reconstructed to good effect. The place is closed Tuesdays in the winter; pay $5 admission, and you can also visit Coronado State Monument, on the north edge of Albuquerque, on the same day.

A couple of curves in the highway past the monument, you reach the rocks of **Soda Dam** off the right side of the road. The pale, bulbous mineral accretions that have developed around this spring resemble nothing so much as the top of a root beer float, with a waterfall crashing through the middle. You can't really dip in the water here, but it's a good photo op.

## Hot Springs

Outside of the town of Jemez Springs, you pass several other opportunities to take a hot bath. Five miles north, where the red rocks of the canyon have given way to steely-gray stone and Battleship Rock looms above the road, is the trail to **McCauley Springs.** These require a two-mile hike along East Fork Trail (the parking area for the trailhead is just past Battleship Rock Picnic Area) but are an excellent motivator for a not-too-strenuous climb. Follow the trail until it meets a small stream flowing down from your left (north), then walk up the creek about a quarter mile to the spring, which has been diverted so it flows into a series of pools of ever-cooler temperatures (only 85°F at most points). Because the trail runs along the streambed, though, it's usually impassable in the high-flow winter and spring.

The most accessible pools are **Spence Springs,** about half a mile north of Battleship Rock. A sign marks a parking area on the east side of the road, and the trail to the springs starts immediately south of the dirt pullout. A short hike (0.4 mile) leads down to the river then up the steep hillside to two sets of 100°F pools. The place is well known, and although there are signs insisting on clothing, don't be surprised if you encounter some people bathing nude.

## Hiking

Several trails run through the Jemez, but one of the best for a day hike is **East Fork Trail** (no. 137), which runs from Battleship Rock Picnic Area to Las Conchas. At 10 miles one-way, the whole route is a bit ambitious, so it's preferable to start the trail where it crosses Highway 4, about 3 miles after the highway makes its hairpin turn southeast, when you descend a bit and enter a small valley. From this point, the eastern half of the trail, about 4.5 miles one-way, is the most scenic, following a stream up through a pine forest, where wild berries grow in the summer; or you can head west one mile to Jemez Falls, where water cascades through a narrow canyon.

## ◖ Valles Caldera National Preserve

Spreading out for 89,000 acres to the north of Highway 4, this protected parkland (866/382-5537, www.vallescaldera.gov) is a series of vast green valleys, rimmed by the edges of a volcano that collapsed into a huge bowl millennia ago. At the center is rounded Redondo Peak (11,254 feet). The park was a private ranch, which the U.S. government purchased in 2000 and then created an experimental structure to manage the new preserve, with the goal of making the area self-sustaining, independent of government funds. To this end, use fees are high (starting at $10 per person), and for all but two trails, you must make reservations at least 24 hours ahead online, as there are restrictions on how many people may enter the park each day. The reward is a hike through land that feels utterly untouched, where you will see herds of elk grazing and eagles winging across the huge dome of the sky. Hiking is best June–September, and in winter months, the park is open for cross-country skiing. There are also limited elk-hunting and fishing seasons. A full roster of guided activities is available too: group day hikes, full-moon snowshoeing and sleigh rides, overnight winter yurt camping, tracking classes, horseback riding, and more.

If you haven't planned ahead, you can still use the **Coyote Call Trail,** a three-mile loop off the south side of Highway 4, and the **Valle Grande Trail** (two miles round-trip), off the north, without prior reservations.

Past Valles Caldera, Highway 4 goes into Bandelier National Monument. If you're carrying on to Santa Fe, go through White Rock and join Highway 502, which leads through Pojoaque to U.S. 285, which then goes south to the capital.

## THE INTERSTATE TO SANTA FE

The most direct route north to Santa Fe is along I-25, a drive of about 60 miles. The road, which passes through the broad valley between the Sandia and Jemez mountain ranges, is not as scenic as the more meandering routes, but it does cross wide swaths of undeveloped pueblo lands (Sandia, San Felipe, and Kewa, formerly Santo Domingo) with impressive vistas.

© ZORA O'NEILL

Kasha-Katuwe Tent Rocks National Monument

At exit 252, hop off for a meal at the ◖ **San Felipe Restaurant** (26 Hagan Rd., 505/867-4706, 6:30 A.M.–9 P.M. daily, $8), alongside a gas station and past a short hall of dinging slot machines. Its broad diner-ish menu of spaghetti and meatballs as well as New Mexican favorites is superlative, especially pueblo dishes like posole with extra-thick tortillas. The crowd is just as diverse: pueblo residents, day-trippers, long-haul truckers.

You also have the opportunity to detour to one of the region's most striking natural phenomena, **Kasha-Katuwe Tent Rocks National Monument** (Forest Rd. 266, 7 A.M.–7 P.M. daily mid-Mar.–Oct., 8 A.M.–5 P.M. daily Nov.–mid-Mar., $5/car), where the wind-whittled clusters of volcanic pumice and tuff do indeed resemble enormous tepees, some up to 90 feet tall. To reach the parklands, leave I-25 at exit 259 and head west toward Cochiti Pueblo on Highway 22, then turn south in front of Cochiti Dam,

which blots out the horizon around mile 15; before you reach the pueblo, turn right on Indian Route 92. From the monument parking area, you have the choice of two short trails: an easy, relatively flat loop runs up to the base of the rocks, passing a small cave, while a longer option runs 1.5 miles into a narrow canyon where the rock towers loom up dramatically on either side. The latter trail is level at first, but the last stretch is steep and requires a little clambering.

On your way out from the hike, you can drive through **Cochiti Pueblo,** the northernmost Keresan-speaking pueblo, which claims its ancestors inhabited some of the ruins at Bandelier National Monument. The core of the community is still two ancient adobe kivas; the people who live in the surrounding houses sell craftwork. Nearby **Cochiti Lake** (reached by continuing along Highway 22 past the dam) is a popular summer destination for boaters, though it's not particularly scenic.

ALBUQUERQUE

# Information and Services

## TOURIST INFORMATION

The **Albuquerque Convention and Visitors Bureau** (800/284-2282, www.itsatrip.org) offers the most detailed information on the city, maintaining a kiosk on the Old Town plaza in the summer and a desk at the airport near the baggage claim (9:30 A.M.–8 P.M. daily). You can also get excellent information on events at the **Hotel Andaluz**, at the computer terminals on the second floor mezzanine. The **City of Albuquerque** website (www.cabq.gov) is very well organized, with all the essential details about city-run attractions and services.

### Books and Maps

The **University of New Mexico bookstore** (2301 Central Ave. NE, 505/277-5451, 8 A.M.–6 P.M. Mon.–Fri., 10 A.M.–5 P.M. Sat.) maintains a good stock of travel titles and maps, along with state history tomes and the like. On the west side, **Bookworks** (4022 Rio Grande Blvd. NW, 505/344-8139, 9 A.M.–9 P.M. Mon.–Sat., 9 A.M.–7 P.M. Sun.) is a great resource, with a large stock of New Mexico–related work as well as plenty of other titles, all recommended with the personal care of the staff.

### Local Media

The *Albuquerque Journal* publishes cultural events listings in the Friday entertainment supplement. On Wednesdays, pick up the new issue of the free weekly *Alibi* (www.alibi.com), which will give you a hipper, more critical outlook on city goings-on, from art openings to city council debates. The glossy monthly *ABQ The Magazine* (www.abqthemag.com) explores cultural topics, while the free *Local Flavor* (www.localflavormagazine.com) covers food topics.

### Radio

KUNM (89.9 FM) is the university's radio station, delivering eclectic music, news from NPR and PRI, and local-interest shows such as *Native America Calling*. KANW (89.1 FM) is a project of Albuquerque Public Schools, with an emphasis on New Mexican music of all stripes, but particularly mariachi and other traditional forms; it also carries a lot of the most popular NPR programs.

## SERVICES

### Banks

Banks are plentiful, and grocery stores and pharmacies increasingly have ATMs inside. Downtown, look for **New Mexico Bank & Trust** (320 Gold Ave. SW, 505/830-8100, 9 A.M.–4 P.M. Mon.–Thurs., 9 A.M.–5 P.M. Fri.). In Nob Hill, **Wells Fargo** is on Central at Dartmouth (3022 Central Ave. SE, 505/255-4372, 9 A.M.–5 P.M. Mon.–Thurs., 9 A.M.–6 P.M. Fri., 9 A.M.–1 P.M. Sat.). Both have 24-hour ATMs.

### Post Offices

Most convenient for visitors are the **Old Town Plaza Station** (303 Romero St. NW, 505/242-5927, 10 A.M.–4 P.M. Mon.–Fri., noon–3 P.M. Sat.), **Downtown Station** (201 5th St. SW, 505/346-1256, 9 A.M.–4:30 P.M. Mon.–Fri.), and an office near UNM (115 Cornell Dr. SE, 505/346-0923, 8 A.M.–5 P.M. Mon.–Fri.).

### Internet

The main branch of the **Albuquerque Public Library** (501 Copper Ave. NW, 505/768-5141, www.cabq.gov/library, 10 A.M.–6 P.M. Mon. and Thurs.–Sat., 10 A.M.–7 P.M. Tues. and Wed.) offers Internet access with the one-time purchase of a $3 card that's good for three months for out-of-towners; wireless access is free. City-maintained wireless hotspots are listed at www.cabq.gov/wifi; many businesses around town also provide the service.

# Getting There and Around

## BY AIR

**Albuquerque International Sunport** (ABQ, 505/244-7700, www.cabq.gov/airport) is a pleasant single-terminal airport served by all of the major U.S. airlines. It's on the south side of the city, just east of I-25, about four miles from downtown. There's free wireless Internet access throughout the complex and a nice collection of art on the walls. Near baggage claim, you'll find a desk maintained by the convention and visitors bureau.

From the airport, there are several bus services: The city ABQ Ride bus Route 50 runs from the airport to the main bus hub, the Alvarado Transportation Center at Central and 2nd Street downtown. Buses depart the airport weekdays every half hour 7 A.M.–8 P.M., and on Saturdays every hour and 10 minutes 9:45 A.M.–7:05 P.M.; there is no Sunday service. The ride takes 25 minutes. On weekdays, there's also an express shuttle (Route 350) to the same stop downtown, with six departures (5:48 A.M.–6:09 P.M.) timed to meet the commuter train to Santa Fe; the ride takes 15 minutes and costs $1. One other weekday-only bus (Route 222) runs to the nearest commuter train stop, just 20 minutes away; departures are eight times a day. Verify the latter two schedules online at www.nmrailrunner.com, as the train schedule often changes.

## BY CAR

All of the major car-rental companies have offices in a single convenient complex adjacent to the airport, connected by shuttle buses. **Hertz** and **Enterprise** offer service at the Amtrak depot (really just a refund for the cab ride to the airport offices), and Hertz has two other locations around town—substantially less expensive because you bypass the airport service fee. (If you're up for a public-transit adventure right off the plane, you could potentially get from the airport to the San Mateo Hertz office on the city bus, Route 222 eastbound, then Route 140/141.)

## BY BUS

**Greyhound** (800/231-2222, www.greyhound.com) runs buses from all major points east, west, north, and south, though departures are not frequent. The bus station (320 1st Street NW, 505/243-4435) is just south of the Alvarado Transportation Center. Cheaper *and* nicer are the bus services that cater to Mexicans traveling across the Southwest and into Mexico, though they offer service only to Santa Fe and Las Cruces; **El Paso-Los Angeles Limousine Express** (1611 Central Ave. SW, 505/247-8036, www.elpalimo.com) is the biggest operator.

With **ABQ Ride** (505/243-7433, www.cabq.gov/transit) public buses, it's possible to reach all of the major sights along Central Avenue, but you can't get to the Sandia Peak Tramway or anywhere in the east mountains.

The most tourist-friendly bus is Route 66, the one that runs along Central Avenue, linking Old Town, downtown, and Nob Hill. The double-length red **Rapid Ride** buses (Route 766) follow the same route, but stop at only the most popular stops; service runs until 3 A.M. on summer weekends. The fare for all buses, regardless of trip length, is $1; **passes** are available for one ($2), two ($4), and three ($6) days, and can be purchased on the bus.

## BY TRAIN

**Amtrak** (800/USA-RAIL, www.amtrak.com) runs the Southwest Chief through Albuquerque, arriving daily in the afternoon from Chicago and Los Angeles. The depot, just south of the larger bus travel center, is downtown on 2nd Street, south of Central Avenue. The **Rail Runner** (866/795-RAIL, www.nmrailrunner.com) runs from downtown Santa Fe through Albuquerque and as far south as Belén. The main stop in Albuquerque is the downtown Alvarado Transportation Center, at Central and 1st Street. It's fantastic service to or from Santa Fe, but within Albuquerque, the system doesn't go anywhere visitors typically go. If you ride, keep your ticket—you do get a free transfer from the train to any city bus.

# SANTA FE

One of Santa Fe's several nicknames is "Fanta Se," a play on the name that suggests the city's disconnection from reality. This small cluster of mud-colored buildings in the mountains of northern New Mexico does indeed seem to subsist on dreams alone, as of the 67,000 people who live here, there's a larger proportion of writers, artists, and performers than in any other city in the United States. In the local Yellow Pages, "Art galleries" take up five pages, and "Artists" have their own heading, while billboards advertise work space: "Your art might suck. Your studio shouldn't have to." In all, nearly half of the city is employed in the larger arts industry. (Cynics would lump the state legislature, which convenes in the capitol here, into this category as well.)

The city fabric itself is a byproduct of this creativity—many of the "adobe" buildings that make up the distinctive downtown area are in fact plaster and stucco, built in the early 20th century to satisfy a collective vision of what Santa Fe ought to look like to appeal to tourists. And the mix of old-guard Spanish, Pueblo Indians, groovy Anglos, and international jetsetters of all stripes has even developed a soft but noticeable accent—a vaguely Continental intonation, with a vocabulary drawn from the 1960s counterculture and alternative healing.

What keeps Santa Fe grounded, to use the local lingo, is its location, tucked in the foothills of the Sangre de Cristos. The outside is never far, even if you're just admiring the mountain view from your massage table at a Japanese-style spa or dining on locally raised lamb at an elegant restaurant. You can be out

© ZORA O'NEILL

# HIGHLIGHTS

**◖ Santa Fe Plaza:** On the city's lively main square, teenage hippies play hacky-sack, while local Pueblo vendors sell their wares under the eaves at the Palace of the Governors (page 73).

**◖ La Fonda:** The Santa Fe Trail came to an end on the doorstep of this hotel, which has witnessed the city's fluctuating fortunes – and harbored its assorted colorful characters – for centuries (page 78).

**◖ Canyon Road:** More than 200 galleries line this winding street that's the heart of Santa Fe's art scene. It's also the main artery of its social life when it's packed with potential collectors and party-hoppers on summer Friday nights (page 79).

**◖ Museum of International Folk Art:** In the main exhibition hall, all the world's crafts, from Appalachian quilts to Zulu masks, are jumbled together in an inspiring, if slightly overwhelming, display of human creativity (page 81).

**◖ Los Alamos:** Driving up to "the City on the Hill," you can't help but imagine what the Manhattan Project scientists must have thought when they arrived in this remote outpost where they would soon develop the atomic bomb (page 101).

**◖ Bandelier National Monument:** The hidden valley of Frijoles Canyon was once home to the ancestors of today's Puebloans, in an elaborate urban complex and cliff-side cave apartments (page 105).

**◖ Ghost Ranch:** The spread where Georgia O'Keeffe kept a studio occupies a patch of dramatic red-rock cliffs and windblown pinnacles. Learn about the dinosaurs unearthed there, and hike up to Chimney Rock for the best view across Abiquiu (page 110).

LOOK FOR **◖** TO FIND RECOMMENDED SIGHTS, ACTIVITIES, DINING, AND LODGING.

**◖ Chimayó:** The faith is palpable in this village, where an adobe chapel has become known as "the Lourdes of America," thanks to the healing powers attributed to the holy dirt found in a small "well" in a side room (page 111).

**◖ Las Trampas:** In this remote mountain village on the high road to Taos, the San José de Gracia Church is a flawless example of colonial Spanish adobe design. Visit in the summer for a better chance of seeing the beautiful carvings inside (page 113).

SANTA FE

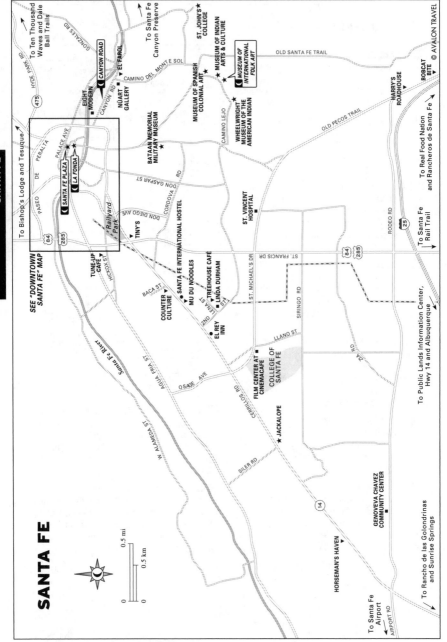

SANTA FE

of town at a trailhead in 15 minutes, skiing down a precipitous slope in 30, or wandering among the hills you've seen in Georgia O'Keeffe's paintings of Abiquiu in 60.

Santa Fe's history, too, gives the community strong roots—officially established around 1609, it's the second oldest city in the United States. (St. Augustine, Florida, beats it by 44 years.) The city is surrounded by pueblos that have been inhabited since well before the Spanish arrived, alongside remnants of older settlements, such as Tyuonyi in Bandelier National Monument. As the former capital of the Spanish territory of Nuevo México, Santa Fe was the gateway to the wilder, emptier lands to the north—and it still is, with two scenic routes running north to Taos: The high road winds along mountain ridges, while the low road follows the Rio Grande through apple orchards and canyons.

If you need a break from Santa Fe and all its history, head for the town of Española, a modern and unlikely mix of lowrider-proud cruisers and convert Sikhs, and a great place for New Mexican food. Or seek out isolated Los Alamos, home of the atomic bomb—the biggest reality check of all.

## PLANNING YOUR TIME

If you're considering a short trip, a three-day weekend in the city is a perfectly good getaway. Add a few days more to take a hike outside of town or make the drive to Taos, Los Alamos, or Abiquiu. Mobs arrive in July and August, especially for Spanish Market and Indian Market (the latter coincides with closing night at the Santa Fe Opera), so you'll find the city a bit calmer—and the heat less overpowering—in spring and fall. Choose spring if you'll be primarily in the city—lilacs bloom in May, tumbling over adobe walls and filling the air with scent—but opt for the fall if you plan to do a lot of hiking because October is when the dense groves of aspen trees on the Sangre de Cristo Mountains turn bright yellow, a gorgeous sight enhanced by the crisp, spicy air at that time of year. If you do come in the summer, however, you'll find the gallery scene in full swing—plan to be in the city on a Friday night, when Canyon Road galleries have their convivial openings.

## HISTORY

Founded in 1609, La Villa Real de la Santa Fé (The Royal City of the Holy Faith) was built to be the capital of Spain's northernmost territory in the New World. The Camino Real, the route that connected the outpost with Mexico, ended in the newly built plaza. The 1680 Pueblo Revolt set back the Spanish settlers' plans, but not for long: Don Diego de Vargas returned with troops in 1693, bent on reconquering the city. After a pitched battle, the Spanish moved back in (ousting the Indians from the state house, which they'd turned into storerooms and apartments) and established a shaky truce with the local population, after which more Spaniards began to settle in small villages north of Santa Fe.

Mexico's independence from Spain in 1821 marked a major shift in the city's fortunes, as the new government opened up its northernmost territory to outside trade—something the Spanish had refused to do. Soon enough, the Santa Fe Trail, a route from Missouri to New Mexico first blazed in 1792, was booming with trade, and the city was a cosmopolitan commercial hub where Mexicans and Americans swapped goods and hard currency. The Americans earned an easy victory in New Mexico during the Mexican-American War, when General Stephen Kearny peaceably brought the territory under U.S. control in 1846. But Santa Feans still had to contend with the more domineering figure of Bishop Jean Baptiste Lamy, appointed in 1850. For more than three decades, the Frenchman struggled with both Spanish Catholics and Indians. His attempts to "elevate" the city to European standards can be seen in the grandiose stone St. Francis Cathedral.

The Americans had a little more luck taming the frontier capital when the railroad came through, in 1880. Although it effectively killed the Santa Fe Trail (and the trade economy with it), it opened up the city to what's still its

# IT'S NOT *ALL* ADOBE

Santa Fe maintains its distinctive historic core through the stringent Historic Styles Ordinance, which dictates even the shade of brown stucco finish required for buildings around the plaza. But look closely, and you'll see several different styles. **Colonial** is the term applied to adobe (or adobe-look) buildings, usually one story, with their typical rounded edges and flat roofs supported by vigas – long crossbeams, made of single tree trunks. The style was developed by the Spanish colonists in the 16th, 17th, and 18th centuries, based on their previous experience with adobe architecture and forms they saw in the pueblos.

In the 19th century, when New Mexico became a territory of the United States, American influence came in the form of timber-frame houses, often two stories with balconies, and ornamented with brick cornices or coping and Greek revival details, such as carved wood fluted columns and pediments above windows. This **territorial** style, as it's called, can still be seen on the plaza at the two-story Catron Building on the northeast side, but a lot of the best examples were lost during the **pueblo revival** period in the early part of the 20th century. Architects such as John Gaw Meem and Isaac Rapp (the latter designed the Museum of Fine Arts on the northwest corner of the plaza) took their inspiration from both the Spanish colonial-era mission churches and the traditional pueblo buildings, where they saw a clean-lined minimalism that was in keeping with the developing modernist sensibilities. Because they used contemporary frame construction, pueblo revival buildings could be much bigger: Meem's additions to La Fonda make it five stories tall. The architectural trend coincided with the city's aggressive move to court tourism and the idea of developing a comprehensive "look" for the city, so many of the wood-frame territorial houses were simply covered over in a thick layer of plaster. The result is not precisely "historic," but the city planners achieved their goal: Santa Fe looks like no other city in the United States.

lifeblood today: tourism. As locals moved south to do business in the now-booming city of New Albuquerque, where the train tracks went right by their front doors, loads of curious Easterners, undeterred by the 18-mile trip up from the depot at Lamy, took their places. Along with them came freight cars full of odd materials such as bricks and timber, used to build new houses that were the most visible evidence that New Mexico was no longer a Spanish colony.

Some of these early visitors were artists who helped popularize Santa Fe as a retreat well before the territory was granted official statehood in 1912. By 1917, the Museum of Fine Arts (now the New Mexico Museum of Art) had opened, and the first Indian Market was held in 1922. A new element was added to Santa Fe's mix in 1943, when the building at 109 East Palace Avenue became the "front office" and only known address for Los Alamos, where the country's greatest scientists were developing the atomic bomb under a cloud of confidentiality.

But the rational scientists left little mark on Santa Fe. Right-brain thinking has continued to flourish, and the city is a modern, creative version of its old self, a meeting place where international art dealers swap goods and ideas.

## ORIENTATION

For all the things to see and do in Santa Fe, it's easy to forget you're in a small town. Not only are most of the major sights within walking distance from the central plaza, but visitors will have little reason to see large swaths of town. Generally, you'll find yourself within the oval formed by Paseo de Peralta, a main road that almost completely circles the central district. On its southwest side it connects with Cerrillos Road, a main avenue lined with motel courts, shopping plazas, and chain restaurants. Compared with the central historic district, it's unsightly, but there are some great local places to eat along this way, as well as the few inexpensive hotels in town.

# Sights

One of the city's best tourist deals, a $20 **museum pass,** good for four days, grants access to five institutions—the Museum of Fine Arts, the New Mexico History Museum, the Museum of Indian Arts & Culture, the Museum of International Folk Art, and the Museum of Spanish Colonial Art. You can purchase it at any of the five participating museums. A one-day pass ($15) admits you to any two museums (except the Spanish colonial one).

## DOWNTOWN

The city's most visited sights are within a few blocks of the central plaza.

### ◖ Santa Fe Plaza

When Santa Fe was established in 1610, its layout was based on strict Spanish laws governing town planning in the colonies—hence the central plaza fronted by the Casas Reales (Palace of the Governors) on its north side. The plaza is still the city's social hub, and the blocks surrounding it are rich with history. In the center of the plaza is the **Soldiers' Monument,** dedicated in 1867 to those who died in "battles with…Indians in the territory of New Mexico"—the word "savage" has been neatly excised, a policy applied to historic markers throughout the state.

### New Mexico History Museum and Palace of the Governors

Opened in 2009, the new state history museum (113 Lincoln Ave., 505/476-5200, www.nmhistorymuseum.org, 10 A.M.–5 P.M. Sat.–Thurs., 10 A.M.–8 P.M. Fri., $9, free 5–8 P.M. Fri.) finally gave a little breathing room for a collection that had been in storage for decades. Oddly, though, it feels like very few actual objects are on display—or they may be simply overshadowed by all the other display elements. If you're already familiar with the state's storied past, you won't find much new here—the exhibits give a fairly basic overview.

Which is not to say you shouldn't go. The admission ticket also covers the Palace of the Governors, the former seat of Santa Fe's government (120 Washington Ave., 505/476-5090, www.palaceofthegovernors.org). Built 1610–1612, it's one of the oldest government buildings in the United States, giving it plenty of time to accumulate stories: De Vargas fought the Indian rebels here room by room when he retook the city in 1693, ill-fated Mexican governor Albino Pérez was beheaded in his office in 1837, and Governor Lew Wallace penned *Ben Hur* here in the late 1870s.

The exhibits here are far more detailed and showcase some of the most beautiful items in the state's collection: trinkets and photos from the 19th century, as well as the beautiful 18th-century Segesser hide paintings, two wall-size panels of buffalo skin depicting, on one, a meeting between two Indian tribes, and

The plaza is the city's main gathering spot.

SANTA FE

© ZORA O'NEILL

SANTA FE

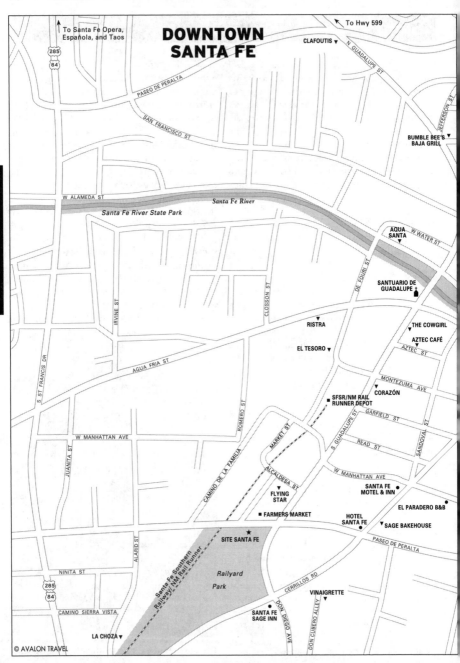

**DOWNTOWN SANTA FE**

To Santa Fe Opera, Española, and Taos

To Hwy 599

285 84

PASEO DE PERALTA

SAN FRANCISCO ST

N GUADALUPE ST

JEFFERSON ST

CLAFOUTIS ▼

BUMBLE BEE'S BAJA GRILL ▼

W ALAMEDA ST

Santa Fe River

Santa Fe River State Park

AQUA SANTA ▼    W WATER ST

DE FOURI ST

CLOSSON ST

SANTUARIO DE GUADALUPE ✝

IRVINE ST

RISTRA ▼

THE COWGIRL ▼

AZTEC CAFÉ ▼

EL TESORO ▼

AZTEC ST

S ST FRANCIS DR

AGUA FRIA ST

MONTEZUMA AVE

CORAZÓN ▼

SFSR/NM RAIL RUNNER DEPOT ■

ROMERO ST

GARFIELD ST

SANDOVAL ST

W MANHATTAN AVE

JUANITA ST

READ ST

S GUADALUPE ST

MARKET ST

CAMINO DE LA FAMILIA

ALCALDESA ST

W MANHATTAN AVE

FLYING STAR ▼

SANTA FE MOTEL & INN ●

EL PARADERO B&B ●

FARMERS MARKET ■

HOTEL SANTA FE ●

SAGE BAKEHOUSE ▼

ALARID ST

SITE SANTA FE ★

PASEO DE PERALTA

NINITA ST

Railyard Park

285 84

Santa Fe Southern Railway/NM Rail Runner

CERRILLOS RD

VINAIGRETTE ▼

DON DIEGO AVE

CAMINO SIERRA VISTA

SANTA FE SAGE INN ●

DON CUBERO ALLEY

LA CHOZA ▼

© AVALON TRAVEL

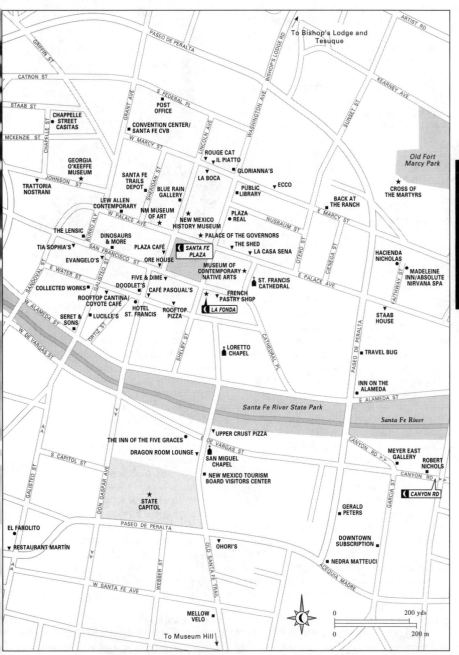

on the other, a battle between the French and a Spanish expedition in Nebraska. These works, along with the room they're in (trimmed with 1909 murals of the Puyé cliffs) are worth the price of admission. In a couple of the restored furnished rooms, you can compare the living conditions of the Mexican leadership circa 1845 to the relative comfort the U.S. governor enjoyed in 1893.

**Walking tours** depart from the Lincoln Avenue side of the museum at 10:15 A.M. (Mon.–Sat. mid-April–mid-Oct., $10), covering all the plaza-area highlights in about two hours.

## St. Francis Cathedral

Santa Fe's showpiece cathedral (131 Cathedral Pl., 505/982-5619, 7 A.M.–6 P.M. daily, free), visible from the plaza at the end of East San Francisco Street, was built over some 15 years in the late 19th century. It was Jean Baptiste Lamy's folly. The French priest had been assigned by the church to a newly created post that would formally separate New Mexico's Catholics from those in Mexico, but when he arrived in 1851 full of fire and zeal to uplift the barbarous population, he promptly alienated much of his would-be flock.

Lamy was not only shocked by the locals' ways of worship (the cult of the Virgin of Guadalupe was already well established, and the Penitente brotherhood was performing public self-flagellation), but he was also horrified by their aesthetics. How could a person possibly reach heaven while praying on a dirt floor inside a building made of mud? Lamy took one look at the tiny adobe church dedicated to St. Francis of Assisi and decided he could do better. Construction on the Romanesque revival St. Francis Cathedral began in 1869, under the direction of architects and craftsmen from Europe—they used the old church as a frame for the new stone structure, then demolished all of the adobe, save for a small side chapel. Lamy eventually ran short of cash, however—hence the stumpy aspect of the cathedral's corners, which should be topped with spires.

Inside is all Gothic-inspired light and space and glowing stained glass windows, but the

a procession in front of St. Francis Cathedral
© ZORA O'NEILL

salvaged adobe chapel remains off to the left of the altar. It is dedicated to the figure of La Conquistadora, a statue brought to Santa Fe from Mexico in 1625, carried away by the retreating Spanish during the Pueblo Revolt, then proudly reinstated in 1693 and honored ever since. She glows in her purple robes, under a heavy viga ceiling—all of which probably makes Lamy shudder in his crypt in front of the main altar (he died in 1888).

On your way out, peek at the great cast-bronze doors—they're usually propped open, so you'll have to peer behind to see the images depicting the history of Catholicism in New Mexico. One plaque shows the Italian stoneworkers constructing the cathedral, and another shows families fleeing from attack in 1680—perhaps the only depiction of the Pueblo Revolt in the state that's sympathetic to the Spanish.

## Loretto Chapel

Step inside this small chapel (207 Old Santa Fe Tr., 505/982-0092, 9 A.M.–6 P.M. Mon.–Sat.,

10:30 A.M.–5 P.M. Sun., $2.50), and you leave the Southwest behind. Initiated by Bishop Lamy in 1873, the building was the first Gothic structure built west of the Mississippi. The decorative elements reflect his fondness for all things European: the stations of the cross rendered by Italian masons, the harmonium and stained glass windows imported from France. Even the stone from which it was built was hauled at great expense from quarries 200 miles south.

But what really draws the eye is the marvelously elegant spiral staircase leading to the choir loft. Made entirely of wood, it makes two complete turns without a central support pole. It was built in 1878 by a mysterious carpenter who appeared seemingly at the spiritual behest of the resident Sisters of Loretto. These nuns—who had in 1853 trooped to New Mexico from Missouri to found a school at Lamy's request—had resorted to prayer because the funding from Lamy hadn't been quite enough. The carpenter toiled in silence for six months, the story goes, then disappeared, without taking any payment. He was never heard from again—though some historians claim to have tracked him down to Las Cruces, where he met his end in a bar fight. The Sisters of Loretto finally went broke in 1968; the chapel was desanctified when it sold in 1971, but it's still a popular wedding spot. The chapel closes at 5 P.M. every day in winter.

## New Mexico Museum of Art

Famed as much for its building as for the art it contains, the New Mexico Museum of Art (107 W. Palace Ave., 505/476-5041, www.nmartmuseum.org, 10 A.M.–5 P.M. Tues.–Sun., also Mon. June–Aug., $9, free 5–8 P.M. Fri.) is dedicated to work by New Mexican artists. Built in 1917, it is a beautiful example of pueblo revival architecture, originally designed as the New Mexico pavilion for a world expo in San Diego two years prior. The curvaceous stucco-clad building is an amalgam of iconic pueblo mission churches—the bell towers, for instance, mimic those found at San Felipe. Inside, the collection ranges from Gerald Cassidy's *Cui*

© CHRIS CORRIE

The staircase in Loretto Chapel is allegedly miraculous.

SANTA FE

*Bono?,* a perpetually relevant oil painting that questions the benefits of pueblo tourism (it has been on display since the museum opened in 1917), to contemporary video installations. Look out for an excellent collection of Awa Tsireh's meticulous watercolors of ceremonial dances at San Ildefonso pueblo, alongside other local American Indian artists.

On your way out, don't miss the adjacent St. Francis Auditorium, where three artists adorned the walls with art nouveau murals depicting the life of Santa Fe's patron saint. It's rare to see a secular style usually reserved for languorous ladies in flowing togas used to render such scenes as the apotheosis of Saint Francis and Santa Clara's renunciation, and the effect is beautiful.

### Georgia O'Keeffe Museum

Opened in 1997, this museum (217 Johnson St., 505/946-1000, www.okeeffemuseum.org, 10 A.M.–5 P.M. Sun.–Wed., 10 A.M.–8 P.M. Thurs.–Sat. May–Sept., 10 A.M.–5 P.M. Sat.–Thurs., 10 A.M.–8 P.M. Fri. Oct.–Apr., $8, free 5–8 P.M. Fri.) honors the artist whose name is inextricably bound with New Mexico. The contrary member of the New York avant-garde first visited the state in the 1920s, then moved to Abiquiu permanently in 1949 after the death of her lover, photographer Alfred Stieglitz.

Initially, the museum was a bit of a hollow monument, as O'Keeffe's finest works—her signature sensuous, near-abstract flower blossoms, for instance—have already been ensconced in other famous museums. But in mid-2005, the museum received the collection of the Georgia O'Keeffe Foundation, the trust that managed the artist's assets since her death in 1986. The transaction brought some exciting new treasures—although much of the space is still given over to exhibitions on her contemporaries, or those whose work she influenced or admired.

### Museum of Contemporary Native Arts

Set in the city's former post office building, this museum (108 Cathedral Pl., 505/983-8900, www.iaiamuseum.org, 10 A.M.–5 P.M. Mon.–Sat., noon–5 P.M. Sun., $5) is the showcase for students, professors, and alumni of the prestigious Institute of American Indian Arts. Come here if you're burned out on old pots in glass cases—instead you'll see the contemporary American Indian experience rendered in oil, charcoal, glass, bronze, and conceptual installations. The collection of works by confident colorist and the institute's most famous professor, Fritz Scholder, is particularly strong. And while the work on the walls is often very experimental, the gift shop stocks a good blend of modern and traditional styles and is quite well priced.

### ◖ La Fonda

"The Inn at the End of the Trail," (100 E. San Francisco St., 505/982-5511) on the corner of San Francisco Street and Old Santa Fe Trail, has been offering respite to travelers in some form or another since 1607. This hotel boomed in the early years of the Santa Fe Trail and the gold-digging era, with a casino and saloon. It hosted the victory ball following General Kearny's takeover of New Mexico in the Mexican-American War. And during the Civil War it housed Confederate general H. H. Sibley. Lynchings and shootings took place in the lobby. In the 1920s, it got a bit safer for the average tourist, as it became part of the chain of Harvey Houses along the country's railways. Since the 1960s, it has been a family-owned hotel.

The stacked pueblo revival place you see today dates from 1920, and its interior still hums with history—something about the tile floors, painted glass, and heavy furniture conveys the pleasant clamor of conversation and hotel busyness the way more modern lobbies do not. Guests still pick up their keys at an old wood reception desk, drop their letters in an Indian-drum-turned-mailbox, and chat with the concierge below a poster for Harvey's Indian Detours car trips. Also look around at the great art collection, including wall-size portraits of Kit Carson and Native American dancers, as well as a mural of a Santa Fe Trail

a funky counterpoint to the fancier galleries on Canyon Road

© ZORA O'NEILL

and in the fourth-floor Governor's Gallery, and don't forget to look up at the stained glass skylight over the rotunda, which has an Indian basket-weave pattern. When the legislature is in session—late January through February in even-numbered years, late January through March in odd—you're welcome to sit in the galleries and watch the proceedings.

## ◖ CANYON ROAD

Ground zero for Santa Fe's art market is the intersection of Paseo de Peralta and Canyon Road, the beginning of a half-mile strip that contains more than 80 galleries. In the summer, Canyon Road is a solid mass of strolling art lovers, aficionados and amateurs alike. It's especially thronged on Friday evenings, when most galleries have an open house or an exhibition opening. There's a city parking lot at the north end of the road, and public restrooms (9:30 A.M.–5:30 P.M. daily) are near the south end, in the complex at 225 Canyon Road, behind Expressions gallery.

Hard to believe, but this street wasn't always chockablock with thousand-dollar canvases. It used to be farmland (irrigated by the "Mother Ditch," Acequia Madre, which still runs parallel one block to the south), and only a few decades ago, it was still unpaved, a muddy gully when it rained. In addition to the galleries, you'll also pass the mid-19th-century house **El Zaguán,** which contains the offices of the **Historic Santa Fe Foundation** (545 Canyon Rd., 505/983-2567, www.historicsantafe.org, 9 A.M.–noon and 1:30–5 P.M. Mon.–Fri., free). Its garden, laid out in the late 19th century, is a lovely place to rest in the summer; it's open on Saturday as well. The **Quaker meeting house** (630 Canyon Rd.) is the former home of Olive Rush, who painted the Old Santa Fe Trail mural at La Fonda and willed her house to the Quakers after her death.

## GUADALUPE AND THE RAILYARD DISTRICT

Guadalupe Street runs south and north from just west of the plaza; its southern stretch developed around the depot for the rail spur

SANTA FE

wagon train. La Plazuela restaurant, in the sunny center courtyard, is a beautiful place to rest, and the bar is timeless.

### Cross of the Martyrs

This white cross at the top of a hill overlooking downtown Santa Fe is a memorial to the Spanish settlers who were killed in the Pueblo Revolt. This new cross is at the end of a zigzagging paved path uphill. It's not a strenuous walk, and the bird's-eye view from the hilltop is excellent. The path up to the cross begins on Paseo de Peralta just east of Otero Street.

## NEW MEXICO STATE CAPITOL

A round building (491 Old Santa Fe Tr., 505/986-4589) with an entrance at each of the cardinal points, the 1966 state capitol mimics the zia sun symbol used on the state flag. Inside, the Roundhouse, as it's better known, is a maze of concentric halls lined with an excellent collection of art by the state's best-known creative types—all accessible for free. Look in the halls on the senate side, the upstairs balcony area,

up from the main line at Lamy, but today it is lined with a clutch of cafés and shops that feel quite different from the plaza. The area along the tracks was recently renovated, with new parks around the Rail Runner station. **Santa Fe Southern Railway** (410 S. Guadalupe St., 505/989-8600, www.sfsr. com) runs vintage trains from the same depot out to Lamy, where there's a café in a groovy restored dining car.

## Santuario de Guadalupe

Built 1776–1796, this is the oldest shrine to the Virgin of Guadalupe in the United States (100 S. Guadalupe St., 505/988-2027, 9 A.M.–4 P.M. Mon.–Sat., free). The interior is spare, just folding chairs set up on the wood floor, in front of a Mexican baroque oil-on-canvas altar painting from 1783. Mass is still said regularly, and musical groups, particularly the Santa Fe Desert Chorale, use the space's excellent acoustics. A museum in the small anteroom displays relics from earlier

The Santuario de Guadalupe was the first church in New Mexico dedicated to the Virgin.

© ZORA O'NEILL

incarnations of the building, such as Greek-style columns carved in wood. The chapel is closed on Saturdays during the winter.

## SITE Santa Fe

In sharp contrast to the Guadalupe chapel, this boxy, modern exhibition space (1606 Paseo de Peralta, 505/989-1199, www.sitesantafe. org, 10 A.M.–5 P.M. Wed., Thurs., and Sat., 10 A.M.–7 P.M. Fri., noon–5 P.M. Sun., $10, free on Fri.) is dedicated to all things new in the art world. It puts on high-concept one-off shows that make use of its very flexible space. SITE hosts the Santa Fe Biennial in even-numbered years.

## OLD SANTA FE TRAIL

From its end at La Fonda, the historic trade route runs off to the east. Just past Paseo de Peralta and the small Santa Fe River, it passes through Barrio de Analco, one of Santa Fe's oldest residential neighborhoods, established by the Tlaxcala Indians who came from Mexico as servants of the first Spanish settlers. The road then runs past the state capitol and to a junction with Old Pecos Trail, the main route to I-25 (and historically the cattle-drivers' route to Mexico).

### San Miguel Chapel

This sturdy adobe building (401 Old Santa Fe Tr., 505/983-3974, 9 A.M.–5 P.M. Mon.–Sat., 10 A.M.–4 P.M. Sun., $1) is the oldest church structure in the United States, built around 1610, then partially rebuilt a century later after it was set aflame in the Pueblo Revolt. Its stone buttresses are the product of a desperate attempt to shore up the sagging walls in the late 19th century. The interior is snug and whitewashed, with painted buffalo hides on the walls and a splendid altar screen that was restored in 1955 after having been covered over in house paint for decades. The late-18th-century work is attributed to the anonymous Laguna Santero, a Mexican artist who earned his name from the intricately carved and painted screen at the Laguna Pueblo church, near Albuquerque.

## Bataan Memorial Military Museum and Library

The Bataan Death March, one of World War II's many atrocities, was a particular tragedy in New Mexico because most of its national guard, drafted as the 200th Coast Artillery, was among the more than 70,000 U.S. and Filipino soldiers subject to torture, malnourishment, random execution, and three years' imprisonment. Of the 1,800 who started in the regiment, fewer than 900 came home, and a full third of those men died in the first year back. The catastrophe is recalled with newspaper clippings, maps, and testimonials at this homegrown museum (1050 Old Pecos Tr., 505/474-1670, 9 A.M.–4 P.M. Tues.–Fri., 9 A.M.–1 P.M. Sat., free), which also contains Civil War memorabilia and exhibits on Native American contributions in U.S. wars, such as the Choctaw and Navajo code talkers. The museum opens one hour later and closes one hour earlier in winter.

## MUSEUM HILL

A cluster of major exhibitions on Camino Lejo, on Santa Fe's southeast side, are worth leaving the plaza area.

## Museum of Spanish Colonial Art

The Museum of Spanish Colonial Art (750 Camino Lejo, 505/982-2226, www.spanishcolonial.org, 10 A.M.–5 P.M. Tues.–Sun., $6) opened in 2002 with a strong collection of folk art and historical objects dating from the earliest Spanish contact, which had been growing since the Spanish Colonial Arts Society was established in Santa Fe in 1925. One-of-a-kind treasures—such as the only signed *retablo* by the 19th-century *santero* Rafael Aragón—are shown alongside more utilitarian items from the colonial past, such as silk mantas, wool rugs, and decorative tin. New work by contemporary artisans is also on display—don't miss Luis Tapia's meta-*bulto*, *The Folk-Art Collectors*.

## Museum of Indian Arts & Culture

This excellent museum (710 Camino Lejo, 505/827-6463, www.miaclab.org, 10 A.M.–5 P.M. daily July–Aug., 10 A.M.–5 P.M. Tues.–Sun. Sept.–May, $9) is devoted to Native American culture from across the country, with the cornerstone exhibit Here, Now & Always, which traces the New Mexican Indians from their ancestors on the mesas and plains up to their present-day efforts at preserving their culture. It displays inventive spaces (looking into a HUD-house kitchen on the rez, or sitting at desks in a public schoolroom), sound clips, and stories. Another wing is devoted to contemporary art, while the halls of craftwork display gorgeous beaded moccasins, elaborate headdresses, and more. The gift shop is particularly extensive, stocked with beautiful jewelry and other tidbits from local artisans.

## ◖ Museum of International Folk Art

This marvelous hodgepodge of a museum (708 Camino Lejo, 505/476-1200, www.moifa.org, 10 A.M.–5 P.M. daily June–mid-Sept., 10 A.M.–5 P.M. Tues.–Sun. mid-Sept.–May, $9) is one of Santa Fe's biggest treats—but the easily overwhelmed should steer clear of the main exhibition space, the collection of modernist designer Alexander Girard. About 10 percent of his collection—10,000 pieces from more than 100 countries—is on permanent display in one hall, hung on walls, set in cases, even dangling from the ceiling. Pieces are juxtaposed to show off similar themes, colors, and materials, an approach that initially seems jumbled but in fact underscores the universality of certain concepts and preoccupations around the world.

Elsewhere in the museum, a wing is dedicated to northern New Mexican Hispano crafts—a good complement to the Museum of Spanish Colonial Art—and a lab area where you can see how pieces are preserved. Temporary exhibits take up the rest of the space, usually with colorful, interactive shows on Carnival celebrations around the world, for instance. Don't skip the gift shop, which stocks some smaller versions of the items in the galleries, along with a great selection of world-music CDs.

## Wheelwright Museum of the American Indian

Mary Cabot Wheelwright, an adventurous East Coast heiress, made her way in the early 1920s to New Mexico, where she met a Navajo medicine man named Hastiin Klah. Together they devised this museum (704 Camino Lejo, 505/982-4636, www.wheelwright.org, 10 A.M.–5 P.M. Mon.–Sat., 1–5 P.M. Sun., free), which opened in 1937 as the House of Navajo Religion. The mission has since been broadened to incorporate all Native American cultures, with exhibits of new work by individual artists rotating every few months. The building—modeled after the Navajo hogan, with huge viga timbers supporting the eight-sided structure—has two levels: the ground-floor exhibition space and the basement gift shop, really a re-creation of a 19th-century trading post. The shop would feel like a tourist trap if it weren't for the authentically creaky wood floors and the beautiful antique jewelry on display in the overcrowded cases.

## SANTA FE METRO AREA
### Rancho de las Golondrinas

The "Ranch of the Swallows" (334 Los Pinos Rd., 505/471-2261, www.golondrinas.org, 10 A.M.–4 P.M. Wed.–Sun. June–Sept., $6), about 15 minutes' drive southeast of Santa Fe, is a 200-acre museum in the form of a restored Spanish colonial *paraje,* a way station on the Camino Real. Museum staff members in period costumes demonstrate crafts and other aspects of early New Mexican history in the blacksmith shop, the schoolhouse, and the mills. Kids who love the American Girl dolls will probably already know it as the home of Josefina Montoya—there's a special guided tour available a few days a week ($10 adults, $7 children) that talks about the buildings shown in the book. The ranch hosts big to-dos—a sheep-shearing fair in early June and a frontier-theme horse show in August—and outside the regular season, opens just for special theme weekends like a Civil War reenactment in late April and an October harvest festival.

# Entertainment

## BARS AND CLUBS

With balmy summer evenings and a populace that always seems to knock off work a little early, Santa Fe is a great place to savor happy hour. The patio at **The Cowgirl** (319 S. Guadalupe St., 505/982-2565, 11 A.M.–midnight Mon.–Fri., 11:30 A.M.–midnight Sat., 10 A.M.–11 P.M. Sun.) is packed 5–7 P.M. with neighbors swilling margaritas. Sunset is also a great time to hit **The Ore House** (50 Lincoln Ave., 505/983-8687, 2:30–11 P.M. daily), on the plaza, where the upstairs balcony bar serves more than 40 kinds of margaritas (happy hour is only 4–6 P.M., though, and you have to request fresh lime juice). The **Rooftop Cantina** at the otherwise skippable Coyote Café (132 W. Water St., 505/983-1615, 5:30–10 P.M. daily, $36) has a long table overlooking the street. But don't drink so much you get hungry—the food here is only serviceable. Over at La Fonda

hotel, the outdoor **Bell Tower Bar** (100 E. San Francisco St., 505/982-5511, Apr.–Oct.) provides a fine view from its fifth-floor rooftop haunt, but it shuts just after sunset. In wintertime, the regulars decamp to the lobby watering hole, **La Fiesta Lounge,** decorated with portraits of rodeo queens; live local country acts grace the small corner stage.

For any time of the night, **El Farol** (808 Canyon Rd., 505/983-9912, 11 A.M.–12:30 A.M. Mon.–Thurs., 11 A.M.–1:30 A.M. Fri. and Sat., 11 A.M.–midnight Sun.) is a perennial favorite. A bar since 1835, it's the gallery owners' clubhouse, and exuberant dancing occasionally breaks out on the tiny dance floor. The vintage glam **Staab House** (330 E. Palace Ave., 505/986-0000, 11:30 A.M.–11 P.M. daily) at La Posada de Santa Fe has history of another kind. The 1882 Victorian home of the prominent Jewish merchant Abraham Staab, it still

# CEREMONIAL DANCES

This is only an approximate schedule for ceremonial dances at pueblos in the Santa Fe area – dates can vary from year to year, as can the particular dances. Annual feast days typically involve carnivals and markets in addition to dances. Confirm details and start times – usually afternoon, but sometimes following an evening or midnight Mass – with the Indian Pueblo Cultural Center (505/843-7270, www.indianpueblo.org) before setting out.

## JANUARY 1
- Ohkay Owingeh (San Juan): cloud or basket dance

## JANUARY 6
- Picurís: various dances
- Nambé: buffalo, deer, and antelope dances

## JANUARY 22
- San Ildefonso: vespers and firelight procession at 6 P.M.

## JANUARY 23
- San Ildefonso: Feast of San Ildefonso, with buffalo, Comanche, and deer dances

## JANUARY 25
- Picurís: Feast of San Pablo

## FEBRUARY 2
- Picurís: various dances for Candlemas (Día de la Candelaria)

## MARCH/APRIL (EASTER)
- Nambé: bow dance
- San Ildefonso: various dances

## JUNE 13
- Ohkay Owingeh (San Juan), Santa Clara, and Picurís: Feast of San Antonio

## JUNE 24
- Ohkay Owingeh (San Juan): Feast of San Juan Bautista

## JULY 4
- Nambé: celebration at the waterfall

## AUGUST 9-10
- Picurís: Feast of San Lorenzo

## AUGUST 12
- Santa Clara: Feast of Santa Clara

## SEPTEMBER 8
- San Ildefonso: corn dance

## OCTOBER 4
- Nambé: Feast of San Francisco de Asís

## NOVEMBER 12
- Tesuque: Feast of San Diego

## DECEMBER 12
- Pojoaque: Feast of Nuestra Señora de Guadalupe

## DECEMBER 24
- Picurís and Ohkay Owingeh (San Juan): torchlight procession at sundown, followed by Los Matachines dances
- San Felipe, Tesuque, and Nambé: various dances, beginning after midnight Mass

## DECEMBER 25
- San Ildefonso, Ohkay Owingeh (San Juan), Picurís, and Tesuque: various dances

## DECEMBER 26
- Ohkay Owingeh (San Juan): turtle dance

## DECEMBER 28
- Picurís and Santa Clara: children's dances to celebrate Holy Innocents Day

SANTA FE

SANTA FE

# GOODBYE, OLD MAN GLOOM!

Every fall a raucous chant fills the air in Santa Fe's Fort Marcy Park: "Burn him! Burn him! Burn him!" It's not a witch hunt but the ritual torching of Zozobra, a 50-foot-tall marionette with long, grasping arms, glowering eyes, and a growly voice. It represents the accumulated worries, sorrows, and chronic problems of the populace; burning him to ashes purges these troubles and allows for a fresh start.

This Santa Fe tradition dates from the 1920s, when artist Will Shuster and a few friends wanted to liven up the annual Fiesta de Santa Fe. Shuster, who had moved to Santa Fe in 1920 to treat the tuberculosis he'd developed in World War I, was inspired by the Mummers Parade, a fixture in his native Philadelphia. He also drew on the traditions of the Yaqui Indians in Tucson, Arizona, who burn Judas in effigy during the week preceding Easter.

The first Zozobra, built in 1924, was just 18 feet high, with a disproportionately small head. By 1926, Shuster had perfected the scale and developed the spectacle. A *Santa Fe New Mexican* article from that year relates:

© CHRIS CORRIE

**Zozobra begins to burn.**

> Zozobra...stood in ghastly silence illuminated by weird green fires. While the band played a funeral march, a group of Kiwanians in black robes and hoods stole around the figure.... [Then] red fires blazed at the foot of the figure... and leaped into a column of many colored flames.... And throwing off their black robes the spectators emerged in gala costume, joining an invading army of bright-hued harlequins with torches in a dance around the fires as the band struck up "La Cucaracha."

Shuster oversaw Zozobra nearly every year until 1964, when he ceded responsibility to the Kiwanis Club. In the late 1930s, Errol Flynn, in town with Olivia de Havilland and Ronald Reagan to film *The Santa Fe Trail*, set Zozobra aflame. A few years later, during World War II, the puppet's face had the features of the era's baddies – and was called Hirohitlomus. In 1950, Zozobra appeared on the New Mexico state float in the Rose Bowl parade and won the national trophy.

Shuster, who died in 1969, is a local legend – he's also credited with inventing piñon-juniper incense and starting the tradition of citywide bonfires on Christmas Eve. And thanks in part to another of the artist's innovations – collecting and stuffing the figure with outdated police reports, pictures of ex-girlfriends, papers from paid-off mortgages, and other anxiety-inducing scraps of paper – the 30,000 people who gather to watch the conflagration are happy to see Zozobra go up in smoke.

bears mezuzahs on the doorframes, along with ornate woodwork and gas chandeliers. The far funkier **Dragon Room Lounge** (406 Old Santa Fe Tr., 505/983-7712, 11:30 A.M.–2 A.M. Mon.–Sat., 5 P.M.–midnight Sun.) is so dim you might not notice at first the huge tree growing up from the left side of the bar. Guys in cowboy hats chat with mountain bikers and dressed-up cocktail drinkers. There's live music Tuesday, Thursday, and Evangelo.

For more music, hit **Evangelo's** (200 W. San Francisco St., 505/982-9014, 11 A.M.–1 A.M. daily), where soul and blues bands take the small stage at the back; when there's no band, there's room at the pool tables. At **Corazón** (401 S. Guadalupe St., 505/983-4559, 8:30 P.M.–2 A.M. Mon., Tues, Thurs., and Sat., 7 P.M.–2 A.M. Wed. and Fri., 8 P.M.–midnight Sun.), if there's not a band, there's usually an eclectic DJ spinning reggae, Latin hits, or some other genre. And **Rouge Cat** (101 W. Marcy St., 505/983-6603, 4:30 P.M.–late Wed.–Sat.) is the closest Santa Fe comes to a full-blown

club, with a multilevel space where you can sip cocktails, nibble snacks, and, on the lower level ($10 cover), dance with a mixed crowd to "trash disco" or other themes; it also has happy hour 4:30–6:30 P.M.

## PERFORMING ARTS

The 2,128-seat **Santa Fe Opera** (U.S. 84/285, 505/986-5900, www.santafeopera.org) is the city's premier arts venue. The elegant open-air amphitheater seven miles north of Santa Fe acts as "summer camp" for the country's best singers to perform a mix of repertory and modern works during July and August. Even if you think opera is all about tuxes, plush seats, and too-long arias, you shouldn't miss the SFO, where half the fun is arriving early to "tailgate" in the parking lot, which involves gourmet goodies, lots of champagne, and time to mill around and check out other attendees' bolo ties. In addition to your picnic dinner, also pack blankets to ward off the chill after the sun sets. If you have kids to entertain, look into visiting on a designated "youth night," special dress rehearsals with extra info to introduce young ones to the art form.

Set in a 1931 Moorish curlicued palace, the **Lensic Performing Arts Center** (211 W. San Francisco St., 505/988-1234, www.lensic.com) is Santa Fe's best stage after the opera house, with everyone from Ladysmith Black Mambazo to the Santa Fe Chamber Orchestra playing to the 821-seat house. The two-month-long **Santa Fe Chamber Music Festival** (www.sfcmf.org) schedules events here, as well as at the St. Francis Cathedral, with performances nearly every day in July and August.

## FESTIVALS AND EVENTS

The city's biggest annual event is **Santa Fe Indian Market** (505/983-5220, www.swaia.org), when 1,200 Native American artisans present their jewelry, pottery, weaving, and other wares, ranging from the most traditional forms to wildly inventive ones. Tented booths fill the plaza and surrounding streets, and the city swells with some 100,000 visitors. It's a bit of a frenzy during the selling proper, for one

© ZORA O'NEILL

the Lensic Performing Arts Center, Santa Fe's most diverse stage

weekend near the end of August, but the atmosphere is festive, as the booths are augmented by free music and dance performances.

**Spanish Market** (505/982-2226, www. spanishmarket.org) has a similar feel the last weekend in July. Emphasis is on traditional crafts, with New Mexico's most respected *santeros* and *santeras* selling their work alongside weavers, tinworkers, and furniture-makers. Finally, the **International Folk Art Market** (505/476-1197, www.folkartmarket.org) showcases traditional crafts from all over the globe. Unlike the other two markets, this one takes place mostly on Museum Hill, so the center of the city is a bit less disrupted.

After all the frenzy of summer tourism, locals celebrate the arrival of the calmer fall season with the **Burning of Zozobra** (www. zozobra.com), a neo-pagan bonfire on the Thursday after Labor Day that's as much a part of Santa Fe's social calendar as the opera season. The ritual kicks off the weeklong **Fiesta de Santa Fe** (505/204/1598, www. santafefiesta.org), which has been celebrated in some form since 1712. It begins with a re-enactment of De Vargas's *entrada* into the city, then a whole slew of balls and parades, including the Historical/Hysterical Parade and a children's pet parade—eccentric Santa Fe at its finest.

# Shopping

Even people who hold their purse strings tight may be a little undone by the treasures for sale in Santa Fe. The most expensive shops are more like free museums; the cheapest are shameless places eternally on the brink of "going out of business" and should be avoided. Downtown around the plaza are souvenir shops and a few influential galleries; on Canyon Road, galleries of all stripes; and on South Guadalupe Street, more funky and fun shops.

One of the most familiar sights of Santa Fe is the north side of the plaza, where Native American vendors from all over New Mexico spread out their wares under the portal at the **Palace of the Governors,** as they've been doing for more than 80 years. Some 1,000 vendors are licensed to sell here; every morning the 63 spots, each 12 bricks wide, are doled out by lottery. Expect anything from silver bracelets to pottery to *heishi* (shell bead) necklaces to freshly harvested piñon nuts. It's a great opportunity to buy direct from a skilled artisan and learn about the work that went into a piece.

The popular **Santa Fe Farmers Market** (505/983-4098, www.santafefarmersmarket. com, 7 A.M.–noon Tues. and Sat. mid-Apr.– Oct., 9 A.M.–1 P.M. Sat. Nov.–mid-Apr.) is a great place to pick up fresh treats as well as souvenir chile *ristras*. It's in a market hall on the north end of the Railyard complex, off Paseo de Peralta near Guadalupe Street.

## GALLERIES

With every other storefront downtown occupied by a gallery, aimless wandering is a straight ticket to art burnout. Whether you're just browsing or actually looking to buy, decide first what you're most interested in—American Indian crafts, Taos Society of Artists' work, new abstract painting—and stick with that, at least to start with. Summer hours are given here; in the winter, most galleries are closed at least Mondays and Tuesdays.

### Contemporary

**Linda Durham Contemporary Art** (1807 2nd St., 505/466-6600, 10 A.M.–5 P.M. Tues.–Sat.) helped pull Santa Fe out of the mire of Western Americana with her first gallery in Galisteo, opened in the early 1980s. She has now relocated to a large space in an edgy part of town and deals in big names like Joel-Peter Witkin as well as up-and-comers—her taste runs to punchy, pop, and conceptual.

Similarly influential gallery **LewAllen**

**Contemporary** (129 W. Palace Ave., 505/988-8997, 9:30 A.M.–5:30 P.M. Mon.–Sat., 11 A.M.–5 P.M. Sun.) represents Judy Chicago in Santa Fe, as well as a range of other artists in every medium, though most are figurative to some degree.

On Canyon Road, real cutting-edge work is rare, but do check out **Nüart Gallery** (670 Canyon Rd., 505/988-3888, 10 A.M.–5 P.M. daily), which showcases lots of Latin American magical realism, and **Eight Modern** (231 Delgado St., 505/995-0231, 9:30 A.M.–5:30 P.M. Mon.–Sat., 11 A.M.–4 P.M. Sun.), for the colorful, abstract, and pop. A nice transition from some of the fustier Western galleries to the contemporary scene, long-established **Meyer East** (225 Canyon Rd., 505/983-1657, 9 A.M.–5 P.M. Mon.–Sat., 11 A.M.–4 P.M. Sun.) shows many landscapes, though this can range from hyperrealism to the spare geometry of Jesse Wood.

North of Santa Fe in the village of Tesuque, the bronze foundry **Shidoni** (Bishop's Lodge Rd., 505/988-8001, 10 A.M.–5 P.M. Mon.–Sat.) has two large gardens full of metalwork sculpture, open from sunrise to sunset every day. If you want to see the foundry in action ($1), show up at noon on a weekday or anytime between 9 A.M. and 5 P.M. on Saturday. Immediately adjacent, **Tesuque Glassworks** (Bishop's Lodge Rd., 505/988-2165, 9 A.M.–5 P.M. daily) functions as a co-op, with a whole range of glass artists using the furnace and displaying their work. To get to Tesuque, head north out of Santa Fe on Washington Avenue, which becomes Bishop's Lodge Road; Shidoni will be on the left side.

### Native American and Southwestern

Near Canyon Road, **Gerald Peters** (1011 Paseo de Peralta, 505/954-5700, 10 A.M.–5 P.M. Mon.–Sat.) and **Nedra Matteucci Galleries** (1075 Paseo de Peralta, 505/982-4631, 8:30 A.M.–5 P.M. Mon.–Sat.) are the biggies when it comes to Taos Society of Artists and other Western art, though Gerald Peters has other figurative contemporary artists too. Even if nothing inside hits the spot, the one-acre sculpture garden in back of Nedra Matteauci is a treat.

For more contemporary work, check out **Blue Rain Gallery** (130 Lincoln Ave., 505/954-9902, 10 A.M.–6 P.M. Mon.–Sat.), which showcases work from many pueblo residents, such as Tammy Garcia's modern takes on traditional Santa Clara pottery forms—she sometimes renders bowls in blown glass or applies the geometric decoration to jewelry. **Robert Nichols Gallery** (419 Canyon Rd., 505/982-2145, 10 A.M.–5 P.M. Mon.–Sat., 11 A.M.–5 P.M. Sun.), specializes in Native American pottery and has an excellent, and often funny, collection of boundary-pushing work.

### CLOTHING AND JEWELRY

Get the Santa Fe look at **Lucille's** (223 Galisteo St., 505/983-6331, 10 A.M.–6 P.M. Mon.–Sat., 11 A.M.–4 P.M. Sun.), which overflows with flowing cotton skirts, bohemian tunics, and chunky jewelry. There's always good stuff on the sale rack.

**Glorianna's** (55 W. Marcy St., 505/982-0353, 10 A.M.–4:30 P.M. Mon., Tues., and Thurs.–Sat., often closed for lunch 1–2 P.M.) is a treasure trove of beads, packed to bursting with veritable eggs of raw turquoise, trays of glittering Czech glass, and ropes of African trade beads, as well as boxes full of smaller treasures, like delicate iridescent seed beads and antique sequins. And you can pick up a pair of boots fit for the Opry at **Back at the Ranch** (209 E. Marcy St., 505/989-8110, 10 A.M.–5:30 P.M. Mon.–Sat., noon–5 P.M. Sun.), stocked floor-to-ceiling with ostrich-skin ropers and loads of belt buckles.

### GIFTS AND HOME DECOR

If it's an odd knickknack, it's at **Doodlet's** (120 Don Gaspar St., 505/983-3771, 9:30 A.M.–5 P.M. Mon.–Sat.), a corner shop and Santa Fe institution (open since 1955) filled to the brim with goodies high and low: toy accordions, oven mitts emblazoned with Mexican skeletons, and every sort of novelty light you can imagine. Endless browsing

© ZORA O'NEILL

rugs for sale in Santa Fe

potential—and kids can practice the xylophone while you shop.

Rockhounds and paleo-freaks will go wild in **Dinosaurs & More** (137 W. San Francisco St., 505/988-3299, 10 A.M.–5:30 P.M. daily). The owner is a feverish collector and has a story to tell about nearly every piece in the gallery-like space: meteorites, fossils, and geodes straddle the border between natural treasures and art.

The owner of **Seret & Sons** (224 Galisteo St., 505/988-9151, 9 A.M.–5:30 P.M. Mon.–Fri., 9 A.M.–6 P.M. Sat., 9:30 A.M.–5 P.M. Sun.) is a Santa Fe icon who deals in finely woven rugs, antique doors, and life-size wooden elephants from his cavernous warehouse just south of the plaza. For funky folk art that won't break the bank, head for the equally gigantic **Jackalope** (2820 Cerrillos Rd., 505/471-8539, 9 A.M.–6 P.M. daily), where seemingly acres are given over to mosaic-topped tables, wooden

chickens, Mexican pottery vases, and inexpensive souvenirs. Sharing the space is a community of prairie dogs—good distraction for children while adults cruise the breakables.

Some goods for foodies, **Todos Santos** (125 E. Palace Ave., 505/982-3855, 10 A.M.–6 P.M. Mon.–Sat.) adds the sweet smell of chocolate to the flower-filled air in Sena Plaza. The closet-size shop has the perfect (if short-lived) Santa Fe souvenir: *milagros,* the traditional Mexican Catholic prayer charms shaped like body parts, rendered in Valrhona chocolate and covered in a delicate layer of gold or silver leaf. If your preference is for nuts and chews, head to longtime candy vendor **Señor Murphy** (100 E. San Francisco St., 505/982-0461, 10 A.M.–5:30 P.M. daily) for some "caramales" (chewy balls of caramel and piñon nuts wrapped up in little corn husks) and other New Mexico–inspired sweet treats.

# Sports and Recreation

It's no accident *Outside* magazine has its offices here. On weekends, Santa Feans leave the town to the tourists and scatter into the surrounding mountains on foot or bike. You'll find something to do all four seasons, though high-altitude hikes shouldn't be attempted till mid-May at least. If you're in town in the fall, don't miss the leaves turning on the aspens, usually in mid-October (for a great view, ride the lift at the ski basin if you're not up for anything more strenuous). The main access route for most activities is Highway 475—it starts out from the north side of Santa Fe as Artists Road, then the name changes to Hyde Park Road, and farther north locals call it Ski Basin Road.

Just off Highway 14, immediately south of I-25, the **Public Lands Information Center** (301 Dinosaur Tr., 505/954-2002, www.publiclands.org, 8 A.M.–4:30 P.M. Mon.–Sat.) is the best starting point for any outdoor activity.

## SKIING AND SNOWSHOEING

Sixteen miles northeast of town in the Santa Fe National Forest, **Ski Santa Fe** (Hwy. 475, 505/982-4429, www.skisantafe.com, $60 full-day lift ticket) is a well-used data area with 73 fairly challenging trails. A major selling point: virtually no lift lines.

The only regularly groomed trails for cross-country skiers are the **Norski Trails,** about a quarter of a mile before the Ski Santa Fe parking lot, off the west side of the road. The standard route is about 2.5 miles, winding through the trees and along a ridgeline, and you can shorten or lengthen the tour by taking various loops and shortcuts, as long as you follow the directional arrows. To blaze your own trail, **Aspen Vista,** on Highway 475 just after mile marker 13, is a wide 10-mile-long road with a gradual climb and good views—great for either skiing or snowshoeing. It's closed to motorized vehicles, so it's relatively peaceful too.

Just seven miles out of town along the road to the ski area, **Hyde Memorial State Park** has a couple of nicely maintained **sledding**

runs, as well as some shorter cross-country ski routes. **Cottam's Ski Shop** (740 Hyde Park Memorial Rd., 505/982-0495, www.cottamsskishops.com) is the biggest rental operation in the area—it's handily located on the way up to Aspen Vista.

## HIKING

Some hikes start very near the center of town, while others call for a half-hour drive at the most. The most popular are the trails in the Sangre de Cristo foothills: the Atalaya, Dale Ball, and Winsor trails. The latter two are described in the *Mountain Biking* section.

### Atalaya Mountain

One of the most accessible trails in the Santa Fe area (you can take the "M" city bus to the trailhead on the campus of St. John's College) is also one of the more challenging. The hike heads up to a 9,121-foot peak, starting out as a gentle stroll along the city's edge, then becoming increasingly steep, for a round-trip of approximately seven miles.

### Santa Fe Canyon Preserve

For an easy saunter close to town, head for this 190-acre patch of the foothills managed by the Nature Conservancy (505/988-3867). The area is open only to people on foot—no mountain bikes, and no pets either. The preserve covers the canyon formed by the now-diverted Santa Fe River, which farmers once attempted to tame by building a two-mile-long rammed-earth dam (a herd of goats did the ramming). An easy interpretive loop trail leads around the area for 1.5 miles, passing the remnants of the dam and winding through dense stands of cottonwoods and willows. The trailhead is on Cerro Gordo Road just north of its intersection with Upper Canyon Road.

### Randall Davey Audubon Center

Birders of course will want to start a hike here, but even general visitors will also be intrigued by the house of artist Randall Davey (1800 Upper Canyon Rd., 505/983-4609, 8 A.M.–4 P.M. daily) and two very pretty trails that lead into the forest and canyons behind ($2). The beautifully painted back rooms of the house are open for a guided tour at 2 P.M. every Friday ($5), and a free guided bird walk departs from the parking lot at 8:30 A.M. every Saturday.

## Aspen Vista

Heading farther up the mountain, Aspen Vista is the most popular trail in the Sangre de Cristos. But don't be put off by the thought of crowds, as the promised views of golden aspen groves are indeed spectacular—in the densest spots, when the sun is shining through the leaves, the air itself feels yellow. Even though it's at a high elevation, it's an easy hike, on a wide path with a gradual slope across the 10 miles.

# BIKING

Mountain bikers have fantastic outlets very close to Santa Fe, while those who prefer the open road will love the challenges in the winding highways through the mountains north of the city. **Rob & Charlie's** (1632 St. Michael's Dr., 505/471-9119, 9:30 A.M.–6 P.M. Mon.–Sat., noon–5 P.M. Sun.) is a reliable shop for road bikers, and closer to the plaza, **Mellow Velo** (638 Old Santa Fe Tr., 505/995-8356, 9 A.M.–5:30 P.M. Mon.–Sat.) rents both mountain and road models (from $35 per day) and also runs shuttles and tours.

## Mountain Biking

The **Dale Ball Trails** are a 30-mile network of single-track routes used by both hikers and mountain bikers, winding through stands of piñon and juniper in the foothills. Two trailheads give access to the North, Central, and South Sections of the trail: From the northern trailhead, on Sierra del Norte (immediately off Highway 475 after mile marker 3), the North Section trails vary a bit in elevation, but the Central Section (south from the parking area) is more fun because it's a longer chunk of trails. The southern trailhead,

on Cerro Gordo just north of its intersection with Canyon Road, gives access to the Central Section and a newer South Section, which is very difficult, for advanced riders only. Note that the trail that starts at the southern trailhead lot, part of the Santa Fe Canyon Preserve, is for foot traffic only—ride your bike one-tenth of a mile down Cerro Gordo to the start of the Dale Ball system.

A popular run is **Winsor Trail** (no. 254), which provides a great range of scenery and terrain. It has become best known as an awesome downhill joyride, with a local shuttle service providing drop-offs at the top. But local riders strongly discourage this tactic—the Forest Service has considered closing the trail to bikes because of accidents and damage done by sloppy skidding. Instead, it's recommended you earn the great descent by pedaling up first—there are few deadly steep ascents, so it's tiring but not impossible, and you'll rarely have to hike-a-bike.

The main trail begins near Tesuque: Take Washington Avenue north out of the center of Santa Fe, continuing as it becomes Bishop's Lodge Road (Highway 590). After not quite four miles, turn right onto County Road 72-A, also signed as Big Tesuque Canyon. There are two small pullout areas for parallel parking, and the trail starts about one-tenth of a mile up the road from the second parking area—the first half mile is through private land. It's not cheating too badly to shorten the uphill leg by starting at Chamisa Trail, six miles up Highway 475 (Hyde Park Road), which connects with Winsor after 2.5 miles—but you'll need to arrange a pickup at the bottom.

If you just want an easy out-and-back cruise, the **Santa Fe Rail Trail** is perfect. The wide gravel path begins at Rabbit Road (take St. Francis Drive south and under I-25) and runs along the railroad tracks through town and on to Lamy, a trip of about 11 miles that's almost completely level. If you're feeling especially leisurely, you can bike down and then take a train back with the Santa Fe Southern Railway tours (see *Guadalupe and the Railyard District* in the *Sights* section).

© ZORA O'NEILL

Ten Thousand Waves is a Japanese bathhouse with New Mexican touches.

## Road Biking

Make sure you're acclimated to the altitude before you set out on any lengthy trip—the best tour, along the **high road to Taos,** will take you through some of the area's highest elevations. Find the full driving route in the *Outside Santa Fe* section in this chapter. Starting in Chimayó shaves some not-so-scenic miles off the ride and gives you a reasonable 45-mile jaunt all the way to Taos. The annual **Santa Fe Century** (www.santafecentury.com) ride takes place every May, running a 104-mile loop south down the Turquoise Trail and back north via the old farm towns in the Galisteo Basin, southeast of Santa Fe.

## SPAS

**Ten Thousand Waves** (3451 Hyde Park Rd., 505/992-5025, www.tenthousandwaves.com, 9 A.M.–10:30 P.M. Mon., Wed.–Sun., 3:45–10:30 P.M. Tues.) is such a Santa Fe institution that it could just as well be listed under the city's major attractions. This traditional Japanese-style bathhouse just outside of town has two big communal pools and seven smaller private ones tucked among the trees so as to optimize the views of the mountains all around; many have adjoining cold plunges and saunas. The place also offers full day-spa services, with an elaborate menu of intense massages and luxe facials and body scrubs. Prices are reasonable, starting at $20 for unlimited time in the public baths and $99 for one-hour massages. In the winter (Nov.–June), hours are shorter Monday–Wednesday.

In town, **Absolute Nirvana Spa** (106 Faithway St., 505/983-7942, www.absolutenirvana.com, 10 A.M.–6 P.M. daily) offers Balinese treatments and massages. Afterward, you can relax in the gardens with a cup of tea and some organic sweets from the adjacent tearoom.

## SPORTS FACILITIES

**Genoveva Chavez Community Center** (3221 Rodeo Rd., 505/955-4001, www.chavezcenter.org, 6 A.M.–10 P.M. Mon.–Thurs., 6 A.M.–8 P.M. Fri., 8 A.M.–8 P.M. Sat., 10 A.M.–6 P.M. Sun., $4) is the city's biggest recreational facility, with a large swimming pool with a slide and a separate lap pool (both are indoors); basketball and racquetball courts; a gym; and a year-round ice rink. In the winter, there's also a small ice rink at **Hyde Memorial State Park** (505/983-7175), seven miles northeast of town on the way to the ski area.

SANTA FE

# Accommodations

Santa Fe offers some great places to stay—historic hotels that conjure the old trading days as well as cozy, fantastically decorated bed-and-breakfasts—but none of them are very cheap. Prices quoted here for the bigger hotels are the standard rack rates. Chances are, you'll be able to find substantially lower ones just by calling or by booking online, at least at the higher-end properties. Prices spike in July and August, often up to holiday rates; if you're coming for Indian Market or Christmas, try to book at least eight months in advance.

## UNDER $100

As hostels go, **Santa Fe International Hostel** (1412 Cerrillos Rd., 505/988-1153, www.hostelsantafe.com) is not the worst, but neither is it one of the more inspiring. The dim dorms ($18 pp) and private rooms ($25 s, $35 d) can be recommended only for the financially desperate. Daily chores, including cleaning, are required of guests—which means the place isn't terribly clean.

For camping, the closest tent sites to the center are at **Hyde Memorial State Park** (Hwy. 475, 505/983-7175), about four miles northwest of the city, with both primitive ($8) and developed sites with electricity ($14). Or head to the commercial **Rancheros de Santa Fe** (736 Old Las Vegas Hwy., 505/466-3482, www.rancheros.com, Mar.–Oct.), east of town about seven miles (a 20-minute drive from the plaza) and pleasantly rural. Tent sites ($22) are private and shady and well away from the RVs, and there are small cabins ($47) as well, plus a nice pool. Reserve ahead in the summertime.

A fabulous deal for anyone willing to consider an unhosted place, **The Chapelle Street Casitas** (209 Chapelle St., 505/995-9689, www.casitas.net) offers by-the-night rentals just blocks from the plaza. Every house is a little different, ranging from cozy studios ($78) to a three-bedroom place with a private patio ($298). Considering that Santa Fe hotels can't change sheets more often than every four days

due to water restrictions, you're not missing too much by going it alone at a rental property—and you gain the feeling of being a Santa Fe native, waving at passersby from your front porch and mixing up margaritas in your fully outfitted kitchen. The online booking system can be a little flaky, so better to call directly to reserve.

## $100-150

◖ **Santa Fe Motel & Inn** (510 Cerrillos Rd., 505/982-1039, www.santafemotel.com, $139 d) is your best budget bet close to the center, with rooms done up in simple, bright decor that avoids motel sameness despite the generic motor-court layout. A few kitchenettes are available, along with some more private casitas with fireplaces. Lots of nice touches—such as bread from the Sage Bakehouse across the street along with the full breakfast—give the place a homey feel without the tight quarters of a typical bed-and-breakfast.

The bones of ◖ **Santa Fe Sage Inn** (725 Cerrillos Rd., 866/433-0335, www.santafesageinn.com, $125 d) are a standard highway motel, but the super-clean rooms are done in sharp, modern red and black, with Southwestern rugs hung on the walls. Little touches such as free Wi-Fi, plush beds, and an above-average breakfast (fresh bagels, fruit, yogurt, and more) make this an excellent deal—the place even has a swimming pool. It may be on Cerrillos Road, but it's still walking distance to the center, and it's right across the street from the new Railyard Park.

Leaving aside its location, ◖ **El Rey Inn** (1862 Cerrillos Rd., 505/982-1931, www.elreyinnsantafe.com, $99 s, $135 d), about two miles from the plaza, counts as one of the best hotels in Santa Fe based on charm alone. Built in 1935, it has been meticulously kept up and adjusted for modern standards of comfort, with beautiful gardens, a hot tub, a big swimming pool, and a fireside open-air Jacuzzi. The 86 rooms, spread over 4.5 acres, vary considerably in style (and in price), from the oldest section with snug adobe walls and heavy viga ceilings to airier rooms with balconies, so ask to see a few before you choose. Rooms at the back of the property are preferable, due to noise from busy Cerrillos Road.

With 12 rooms in an old adobe, plus an adjacent Victorian with two suites, **El Paradero B&B** (220 W. Manhattan St., 505/988-1177, www.elparadero.com, $145 d) is a flexible place: It has a variety of room configurations that can suit families, solo travelers, and friends traveling together. Upstairs rooms have balconies, and a few others have fireplaces. The look throughout is subdued Southwestern, with soothing whitewashed walls.

## $150-250

East of the plaza, twin bed-and-breakfasts under the same ownership offer two kinds of style: The rooms at **Hacienda Nicholas** (320 E. Marcy St., 505/992-8385, www.haciendanicholas.com, $160 d) have a tasteful Southwest flavor, decorated with a few cowboy trappings and Gustave Baumann prints; two of the rooms have fireplaces. Across the street, **Madeleine Inn** (106 Faithway St., 505/982-3465, www.madeleineinn.com, $150 d) is set in a wood Victorian, but the guest rooms aren't lacy—they're done in rich Balinese fabrics. In both places, breakfast is a continental spread, but that doesn't mean you'll go away hungry—the banana bread is fantastic.

In 2009 and 2010, one local hotel group renovated both **Hotel St. Francis** (210 Don Gaspar Ave., 505/983-5700, www.hhandr.com, $199 d) and **Hotel Plaza Real** (125 Washington Ave., 505/988-4900, hhandr.com, $229 d), and both offer good value very near the plaza. The St. Francis is a California mission–style building that dates from 1923, and the rooms have wood floors and lots of fresh, white linens, while the Plaza Real has earth-tone décor to match its territorial-style architecture; upstairs rooms have private balconies, and some suites have fireplaces. For both, rates are substantially lower when booked online.

A very nice bed-and-breakfast in this category is **El Farolito** (514 Galisteo St., 505/988-1631, www.farolito.com, $195 d), where the eight rooms have private entrances, small patios, and fireplaces. Decor ranges from Southwestern to international folk art (in Casita Peralta, which has two double beds), and the breakfast is very good.

Majority-owned by Picurís Pueblo, **Hotel Santa Fe** (1501 Paseo de Peralta, 800/825-9876, www.hotelsantafe.com, $229 d) is both a successful business experiment and a very nice hotel, with one of the few large outdoor pools in town, set against the neo-pueblo hotel walls. The standard rooms are a bit small—the real value is in the ultra-luxe Hacienda wing (officially $518 and up), where the huge rooms with fireplaces and butler service can be more than half-price online—making them a steal compared with other high-end places in town.

**Inn on the Alameda** (303 E. Alameda St., 505/984-2121, www.innonthealameda.com, $230 d) is a good option for people who want adobe style *and* space, and its location is handy for gallery-hoppers. The big rooms have triple-sheeted beds, wireless Internet access, and overstuffed armchairs that are only lightly dusted with Southwestern flair; most also have a patio or balcony. The premium charged for a fireplace ($75 in high season) is a bit steep. The continental breakfast spread is very generous, and there's a wine-and-cheese hour every afternoon.

A wonderfully restful spot is **Houses of the Moon** (3451 Hyde Park Rd., 505/992-5025, www.tenthousandwaves.com, $239 d), the guest cottages at Ten Thousand Waves spa. Some have more of a local feel, with viga ceilings and kiva fireplaces, while others are straight from Japan (both samurai era and contemporary anime). There's even a tiny Airstream trailer ($139), a riff on the Japanese "capsule" hotel, that's a great value considering access to the communal hot tubs is included in the rate.

**Bishop's Lodge** (1297 Bishop's Lodge Rd., 505/983-6377, www.bishopslodge.com, $179 s, $199 d) occupies 450 acres, the core of which is the former country estate of Bishop Lamy. Just a 10-minute drive from the plaza, the resort is still far enough into the foothills that you can go horseback riding, hiking, or mountain biking in solitude—or you can join group activities like the Friday "cowboy cookout." Of the fifteen buildings, South Lodge rooms are the oldest, with creaky porches and thick adobe walls, while Chamisa Lodge is all new, with huge bathrooms and gas fireplaces. The Ridge Lodge has a view across the valley.

## OVER $250

From the outside, **( The Inn of the Five Graces** (150 E. De Vargas St., 505/992-0957, www.fivegraces.com, $360 per suite) looks like a typical historic Southwestern lodge, a collection of interconnected adobe casitas. But inside, there's a certain air of opium dream—the 24 sumptuous suites are done in antique Turkish kilims, heavy wood doors, and mosaics. The result is not typical "Santa Fe style," but it perfectly captures the Santa Fe aesthetic:

decadent international bohemian. Rates include a full breakfast, delivered to your room if you like.

While other hotels have put a hip gloss on their history, **La Fonda** (100 E. San Francisco St., 505/982-5511, www.lafondasantafe.com, $319 d), just off the plaza, remains pleasantly unchanged and still family-owned, its lobby of waxed saltillo tile floors and heavy Spanish-style wood decorated as it has been for decades, its bar populated by a mix of cowboys, layabouts, and lunchtime schmoozers. The cozy rooms have been upgraded with plush beds and soft lighting, and some have their original kiva fireplaces and *latilla* ceilings, but many are still small. Basically, you're paying for the feel of Santa Fe before it was a trendy spa-and-shopping destination. If you do want some modern trappings, spring for the Terrace-level penthouse suites done in chic earth tones. Fortunately, rates on the hotel's website are occasionally marked down.

# Food

Dining is one of Santa Fe's great pleasures—considering the tiny population, it's remarkable what a range of flavors and what high quality you can choose from. You can get a cheese-smothered, crazy-hot plate of green-chile chicken enchiladas, but most locals eat more globally than that—"Santa Fean" cuisine cheerfully incorporates Asian, Southwestern, and Mediterranean flavors, with an emphasis on organic and holistic.

## DOWNTOWN

Food is a bit ho-hum on Santa Fe Plaza itself (except for the fajita cart, when it's set up), but the blocks surrounding it, within the ring formed by Alameda Street and Paseo de Peralta, contain some classic Santa Fe spots to which everyone makes a trek at some point, along with a few hidden treats.

## Coffee

Although Starbucks is near the plaza, disguised by an adobe facade, you might want to get your latte at a local joint such as **Ecco** (105 E. Marcy St., 505/986-9778, 7 A.M.–9 P.M. Mon.–Thurs., 7 A.M.–10 P.M. Fri., 8 A.M.–10 P.M. Sat., 8 A.M.–7 P.M. Sun.), which is packed with coffee junkies and Wi-Fi fanatics in the mornings; later, people come in for panini (at the counter next door) and exceptional gelato. The excellent bookstore **Collected Works** (202 Galisteo St., 505/988-4226, 8 A.M.–8 P.M. Mon.–Sat., 8 A.M.–6 P.M. Sun.) has a comfortable coffee bar inside—it's a mellow place to start the day, or to relax in the afternoon. It opens at 9 A.M. in the winter. If you don't mind a walk, head over to **Ohori's Coffee, Tea & Chocolate** (507 Old Santa Fe Tr., 505/988-7026, 8 A.M.–6 P.M. Mon.–Fri., 9 A.M.–6 P.M. Sat., $3), Santa Fe's small-batch coffee epicures. You can drink a cup of the black-as-night brew there and buy a pound or two to take home.

## Breakfast and Lunch

The **French Pastry Shop** (100 E. San Francisco St., 505/983-6697, 6:30 A.M.–5 P.M. daily, $7) doles out sweet crepes, buttery pastries, *croque monsieurs,* and chewy baguette sandwiches. Early mornings attract a fascinating crew of Santa Fe regulars. Another solid French option is **Clafoutis** (402 N. Guadalupe St., 505/988-1809, 7 A.M.–5 P.M. Mon.–Sat., $8), a cozy, farmhouse-like café where you'll be greeted with a cheery "Bonjour!" This place is great at lunch, for sandwiches, and *cagettes,* platters of charcuterie or smoked fish, along with cheese and salad—sort of the French equivalent of a bento box.

**Tia Sophia's** (210 W. San Francisco St., 505/983-9880, 7 A.M.–2 P.M. Mon.–Sat., $8) is one of the last places in the plaza area that feels untouched by time and tourists, serving old-time New Mexican plates without a touch of fusion—so authentic, in fact, the kitchen claims to have invented the breakfast burrito.

Show up early in the morning at █ **Plaza Café** (54 Lincoln Ave., 505/982-1664, 7 A.M.–9 P.M. daily, $8) to eavesdrop on local political gossip (the mayor's phone number is posted on the wall, along with the weather forecast), as regulars roll in to read the paper and load up on coffee and great renditions of New Mexican and American diner favorites. This is no greasy spoon, though—the "harvest oatmeal" and piñon blue-corn pancakes are a great change of pace from breakfast burritos. Lunch and dinner are equally good and fresh. If you're lucky, it'll be someone's birthday, which calls for a serenade with the Mexican tune "Las Mañanitas" (though locals fondly remember the old days, when the birthday anthem was "And Then There's Maude").

For a very casual lunch, stop in at the **Five & Dime General Store** (58 E. San Francisco St.,

505/992-1800, 8:30 A.M.–8 P.M. Mon.–Sat., 9 A.M.–6 P.M. Sun., $5), on the south side of the plaza. Formerly a Woolworth's where, allegedly, the Frito pie was invented (Frito-Lay historians beg to differ), the knickknack shop has maintained its lunch counter and still serves the deadly combo of corn chips, red chile, onions, and cheese, all in the Fritos bag. Eat in, or, better, lounge on the plaza grass—and don't forget the napkins.

## New Mexican

**The Shed** (113½ E. Palace Ave., 505/982-9030, 11 A.M.–2:30 P.M. and 5:30–9 P.M. Mon.–Sat., $14) has been serving up platters of enchiladas since 1953—bizarrely, with a side of garlic bread. But that's just part of the tradition at this colorful, comfortable, marginally fancy place that's as popular with tourists as it is with die-hard residents. There are perfectly decent distractions like lemon-garlic shrimp and fish tacos on the menu, but it's the red chile you really should focus on.

## Mexican

At █ **Bumble Bee's Baja Grill** (301 Jefferson St., 505/820-2862, 11 A.M.–9 P.M. daily, $5) fat bumblebee piñatas dangling from the ceiling set a cheerful tone. The specialty at this upscale taco joint is Baja shrimp tacos—but made healthy by grilling rather than frying. They're garnished with shredded cabbage and a creamy sauce, plus a spritz of lime and your choice of house-made salsas. Lamb tacos are also delicious, as are the fried-fresh tortilla chips and that Tijuana classic, Caesar salad. In the morning, fresh and tasty breakfast burritos are served, and you might catch a live jazz act on Saturday nights. The place closes an hour earlier in the winter.

## Santa Fe Eclectic

Open since the late 1970s, █ **Café Pasqual's** (121 Don Gaspar St., 505/983-9340, 8 A.M.–3 P.M. and 5:30–9:30 P.M. daily, $28) has defined its own culinary category, relying almost entirely on organic ingredients. Its breakfasts are legendary, but the food is delicious any time of day—just brace yourself for the inevitable line, as the brightly painted dining room seats only 50 people, and loyal fans number in the thousands. Expect nearly anything on the menu: smoked-trout hash or Yucatán-style *huevos motuleños* are what's for breakfast; at dinner, sure, the mole enchiladas are good, but don't miss the Vietnamese squid salad.

Cozy creative-tapas joint **La Boca** (72 W. Marcy St., 505/982-3433, 11:30 A.M.–10 P.M. Mon.–Sat.) is a great place to stop in for a late-afternoon snack of bruschetta with mushrooms and egg, though you might end up staying for a dinner of grilled salmon with parsnip-bacon hash. Ranging from $6 to $12, the little plates can add up fast, unless you're there 3–5 P.M. weekdays, when they're on special. There's also a three-course tasting menu for $45, and lunchtime specials for about $10.

## Italian

Of all of the opportunities in Santa Fe to blow your rent money on a decadent dinner, ◖ **Trattoria Nostrani** (304 Johnson St., 505/983-3800, 5:30–10 P.M. Tues.–Sat., $29) is one of the most worthy—even though it incorporates none of its Southwestern surroundings. The cuisine in this four-room house with glossy wood floors and white tablecloths is pure northern Italian, executed flawlessly: delicate fried squash blossoms to start, perhaps, then rich ravioli filled with salt cod and potato and topped with lump crab. An ethereal *panna cotta* or biscotti served with sweet *vin santo* makes the perfect finishing touch.

Locals head to amber-lit **Il Piatto** (95 W. Marcy St., 505/984-1091, 11:30 A.M.–2 P.M. and 5:30–9:30 P.M. Mon.–Fri., 5–9 P.M. Sat. and Sun., $18) for casual Italian and a neighborly welcome from the staff, who seem to be on a first-name basis with everyone in the place. Hearty pastas like *pappardelle* with duck are served in generous portions—a half order will more than satisfy lighter eaters. This is a

great place to take a breather from enchiladas and burritos without breaking the bank.

With the options of whole-wheat crust and green chile as a topping, the pies at **Upper Crust Pizza** (329 Old Santa Fe Tr., 505/982-0000, 11 A.M.–11 P.M. daily, $10), next to Mission San Miguel, are more Santa Fean than Italian. Hot deli sandwiches and big, super-fresh salads round out the menu. Delivery is free, but then you'd be missing the live music on the little front deck. Winter closing time is 10 P.M.

**Rooftop Pizzeria** (60 E. San Francisco St., 505/984-0008, 11 A.M.–10 P.M. Sun.–Thurs., 11 A.M.–11 P.M. Fri. and Sat., $13) is a good place to enjoy a view along with your meal, on a long balcony overlooking Water Street (enter on the plaza side of the shopping complex and head upstairs). This *is* Santa Fe, so you have the option of a crust with a hint of blue-corn meal, and toppings range from plain old onions to duck and crab, and they come in combinations like the BLT (the lettuce is added after the pie comes out of the oven, luckily). It also has a good selection of wines by the glass.

## Fine Dining

At **La Casa Sena** (125 E. Palace Ave., 505/988-9232, 11:30 A.M.–3 P.M. and 5:30–10 P.M. Mon.–Sat., 5:30–10 P.M. Sun., $31), the emphasis is on hearty meats: bacon-wrapped lamb, for instance, or antelope loin. Even the fish dishes need to be attacked with gusto: The trout baked in clay gets cracked open at the table, releasing a perfectly moist and tender fish. Sunday brunch (11 A.M.–3 P.M., $12) involves eggs Benedict with chipotle hollandaise. There are better-value restaurants of the same caliber in town, but the patio is a dreamy place to dine in the warm months.

## GUADALUPE AND THE RAILYARD DISTRICT

An easy walk from the plaza, these few square blocks hold some of the better, quirkier dining options in town.

## Cafés

In a funky wood house off Guadalupe Street, **Aztec Café** (317 Aztec St., 505/820-0025, 7 A.M.–8 P.M. Mon.–Thurs., 7 A.M.–11 P.M. Fri. and Sat., 8 A.M.–7 P.M. Sun., $8) pours java for Santa Fe's tattooed and guitar-strumming set. An impromptu acoustic serenade on the side porch shouldn't distract from the food, which is inexpensive and veggie-friendly and includes great ice cream in summer. Even coffee addicts should consider the Mexican hot chocolate. In winter, the place closes at 7 P.M. Monday–Saturday and 6 P.M. on Sunday.

Make room in your morning for an almond croissant from **[** **Sage Bakehouse** (535 Cerrillos Rd., 505/820-7243, 7 A.M.–5 P.M. Mon.–Fri., 7 A.M.–2 P.M. Sat., $4). Washed down with a mug of coffee, these butter-soaked pastries will have you set for hours. Before you leave, pick up some sandwiches for later—classic combos like smoked turkey and cheddar on the bakery's excellent crust. And maybe a pecan-raisin wreath. And a cookie too.

**El Tesoro** (500 Montezuma Ave., 505/988-3886, 8 A.M.–6 P.M. Mon.–Sat., 11 A.M.–5 P.M. Sun., $8), in the Sanbusco Center, is a great spot for breakfast, with chile and eggs in every possible combination.

And right by the Rail Runner station is a branch of Albuquerque's **Flying Star** (500 Market St., 505/216-3939, 7 A.M.–9 P.M. Sun.–Thurs., 7 A.M.–10 P.M. Fri. and Sat., $9), much to the dismay of Santa Feans, who see the cheerful chain as an invasion. But visitors can enjoy coffee, pastries, decent full meals, and plenty of space and free Wi-Fi without any inner conflict.

## New Mexican

The under-the-radar cousin of The Shed, **La Choza** (905 Alarid St., 505/982-0909, 11 A.M.–2:30 P.M. and 5–9 P.M. daily, $13) has a similar creative New Mexican menu but is more of a local hangout—though it has become better known now that the rail yard has been developed around it. This also makes it a handy destination if you're coming to Santa Fe

on the train—just walk back down the tracks a few minutes.

## American

All things Texan are the specialty at **The Cowgirl** (319 S. Guadalupe St., 505/982-2565, 11 A.M.–midnight Mon.–Fri., 11:30 A.M.–midnight Sat., 10 A.M.–11 P.M. Sun., $14)—but it's been a Santa Fe fixture for so long that it doesn't seem like "foreign" food. It's a kitsch-filled spot that's as friendly to kids as it is to margarita-guzzling, barbecue-rib-gnawing adults. Non-meat-eaters won't feel left out: An ooey-gooey butternut squash casserole comes with a salad on the side. Both carnivores and veggies can agree on the pineapple upside-down cake and the ice-cream "baked potato."

## Fine Dining

Where Santa Fe foodies eat on a casual night, **[** **Aqua Santa** (451 W. Alameda St., 505/982-6297, noon–2 P.M. and 5:30–9 P.M. Wed.–Fri., 5:30–9 P.M. Tues. and Sat., $18) feels like dining at a friend's house—the open kitchen occupies more than a third of the small building, leaving space for just a handful of tables in the whitewashed room with a fireplace. Dinner, served on old-fashioned flower-print plates, capitalizes on punchy combinations, such as hot baby artichokes with cool, creamy burratta cheese, and entrées are limited to five or so very strong choices—quail stuffed with chorizo, for instance. There's a solid wine list as well.

Elegant but not flashy, regulars' favorite **Ristra** (548 Agua Fria St., 505/982-8608, 11:30 A.M.–2:30 P.M. and 5:30–9:30 P.M. Tues.–Sat., 5:30–9 P.M. Sun. and Mon., $30) applies a French treatment to Southwestern cuisine: Squash blossoms are fried up like ethereal beignets, while duck is spiced with a hint of pasilla chile. It's in a white-walled bungalow with tables in the front yard in warm weather; the pretty bar area is a good place to sample appetizers and tapas.

As of 2010, **Restaurant Martín** (526 Galisteo St., 505/820-0919, 11:30 A.M.–2 P.M. and 5:30–10 P.M. Tues.–Sun., $29) was the

© ZORA O'NEILL

SANTA FE

Lunch at Restaurant Martín employs local farm produce.

new hot spot, as longtime local hero Chef Martín Rios finally set up his own shop. His "progressive American" food can be a little overwrought, but it's a good deal for a grown-up lunch—smooth service and a mix of full plates as well as sandwiches like a Southwest-ified reuben with spicy dressing and homemade sauerkraut ($13).

## CANYON ROAD

Gallery-hopping can make you hungry—but there are only a handful of places to eat on Canyon Road, and not many of them are all that satisfying. For a caffeine hit, jog off the strip to **Downtown Subscription** (376 Garcia St., 505/983-3085, 7 A.M.–6 P.M. daily), an airy coffee shop that stocks perhaps a million magazines and attracts potential readers for even the most obscure titles. Wednesday nights occasionally see poetry readings after normal hours.

At the north end of Canyon Road, stalwart **◖ El Farol** (808 Canyon Rd., 505/983-9912, 11 A.M.–12:30 A.M. Mon.–Thurs.,

11 A.M.–1:30 A.M. Fri. and Sat., 11 A.M.–midnight Sun., $8) is a very popular bar, but its selection of Spanish tapas is also worth noting—grilled octopus with olive pesto, for instance. You can also take in a bigger meal in a small side room that's quieter than the main bar; the *zarzuela* (fish soup) is recommended.

Santa Fe's two splurgiest restaurants are also on Canyon Road: **The Compound** (653 Canyon Rd., 505/982-4353, noon–2 P.M. Mon.–Sat. and 6–9 P.M. daily, $29) and **Geronimo** (724 Canyon Rd., 505/982-1500, 5:45–9 P.M. daily, $36). Honestly, there's far better dining value elsewhere in town, but of the two, the Compound has more inventive food (apricot-glazed duck) while glitzier Geronimo (with a weird "global French Asian" menu) puts on a better show, and the snug bar with a fireplace is a good place to rest your feet after a Canyon Road cruise.

## CERRILLOS ROAD

This commercial strip isn't Santa Fe's most scenic zone, but you'll find some great culinary gems out this way.

### Cafés

Don't feel guilty if you're on green-chile-and-cheese overload—just head to **◖ Vinaigrette** (709 Don Cubero Alley, 505/820-9205, 11 A.M.–9 P.M. Mon.–Sat., $14) and dig into a big green salad, along with half of Santa Fe. The so-called "salad bistro" uses largely organic ingredients from its farm in Nambé, and you can pick from their imaginative combos (baby lettuce with peas, bacon, and sautéed mushrooms, say) or create your own. It sounds like a cheesy chain-restaurant premise, but the setting is pure Santa Fe, with a pretty patio off a little side street just at the top of Cerrillos Road.

The decor—all light pine, metal, and chalkboard menus—at **Counter Culture** (930 Baca St., 505/995-1105, 8 A.M.–3 P.M. Sun. and Mon., 8 A.M.–3 P.M. and 5–9 P.M. Tues.–Sat.) is spartan, but the colorful crowd of, well, countercultural types fills the void. At lunch the eclectic menu runs from fat burgers to cold sesame noodles, with prices around $9; in general, Asian flavors are good, as are the soups. Dinner is a bit more formal, and a bargain, as prices max out at $15. Breakfast, served till 11 A.M., is great—then you can indulge in the gigantic muffins and coffee cakes as a main meal, rather than dessert; on Sunday, breakfast is served all day. Cash only.

The all-vegetarian **Treehouse Pastry Shop & Café** (1600 Lena St., 505/474-5543, 8 A.M.–3 P.M. Mon.–Sat., 9 A.M.–2 P.M. Sun., $9) has impeccable ecological credentials, from the ingredients to its compost system. Fortunately, the all-veggie food, from quinoa salad to cherry pie, is delicious too. Settle in for a wait, though—as one regular says, "It's like they're just having a nice day cooking, and they only occasionally realize the customers exist."

### New Mexican

The white-stucco dining room is too bright, and the beer-sign-filled lounge is too dim, but that's part of the charm at **Tiny's** (1015 Pen Rd., 505/983-1100, 11 A.M.–2 P.M. and 6–10 P.M. Mon.–Sat., $8), a haven of undiluted New Mexico style, right down to its name. All the old favorites are on the menu—the only concession to "modern" trends is that you might get butter with your sopaipillas. Dinner starts and ends an hour earlier in the winter.

New Mexican green chile has been getting milder over the years—but not at **Horseman's Haven** (4354 Cerrillos Rd., 505/471-5420, 8 A.M.–8 P.M. Mon.–Sat., 8:30 A.M.–2 P.M. Sun., $7), which claims to serve the hottest green chile in Santa Fe. Locals grumbled when it moved out of its gas-station digs into a shinier new building across the street, but the chile continues to knock your socks off.

### Asian

A little oasis of Asian-inflected organic food in a chain-restaurant part of town, ◖ **Mu Du Noodles** (1494 Cerrillos Rd., 505/983-1411, 5:30–9 P.M. Tues.–Sat., $18) cuts the strip-mall glare with warm-hued walls and bamboo screens. The menu ranges from Central Asia to Japan, offering lamb pot stickers, coconutty

and spicy Malaysian *laksa,* and Indian yellow curry along the way. Reviving citrus-ade with ginger is delicious hot or cold, or you can order beer or wine. On Sundays, it serves just small snacky plates.

## SANTA FE METRO AREA

Make the drive for some of these places—it's well worth it. Not far out of the Paseo de Peralta loop, the **Tune-Up Café** (1115 Hickox St., 505/983-7060, 7 A.M.–10 P.M. Mon.–Fri., 8 A.M.–10 P.M. Sat. and Sun., $7) is a homey one-room joint that locals love, whether for fish tacos or a suitably Santa Fe–ish brown-rice-and-nut burger. The Salvadoran pupusas are tasty.

Out on Old Las Vegas Highway—the frontage road for I-25—there's a string of excellent places to eat. First up is ◖ **Harry's Roadhouse** (96-B Old Las Vegas Hwy., 505/989-4629, 7 A.M.–10 P.M. daily, $8), where chocolate mousse, lemon meringue, and coconut cream pies could be crowding the pastry case at any given time. And if you're looking for a reason to spend more time on the front patio with a great view across the flatlands, the rest of the menu is solid, too: cold meatloaf sandwiches, catfish po' boys, lamb stew, and shrimp satay, plus tasty margaritas and an awe-inspiring breakfast burrito.

Farther on, hamburgers at **Bobcat Bite** (420 Old Las Vegas Hwy., 505/983-5319, 11 A.M.–7:50 P.M. Tues.–Sat., $8) are legendary: thick, freshly ground sirloin, piled high with chopped green chile and oozy cheese. Try to go near the end of typical lunch hours to avoid the crowds.

Finally, right at exit 290 off I-25, ◖ **Real Food Nation** (624 Old Las Vegas Hwy., 505/466-3886, 7:30 A.M.–7:30 P.M. Tues.–Fri., 8 A.M.–3 P.M. Sat. and Sun., $9) shows its all-organic, Slow Food cred starting with all-edible landscaping. Inside, pick from fresh salads, soups, and killer desserts. Dinner is usually a few entrées with a good vegetarian option—check online or call before you make the drive. Kids have room to play outdoors or in the beanbag corner.

And last of all, but certainly not least, **☾ Terra** (198 Hwy. 592, 505/946-5800, 11:30 A.M.–2 P.M. and 5:30–10 P.M. daily, $30), at the Encantado resort in Tesuque, is by far the best restaurant to really go all out in the Santa Fe area. Chef Charles Dale does confident, rustic food that trots all over the globe, with judicious use of local flavors: In his Chinese pork buns, chipotle adds a smoky kick to hoisin sauce, and Anasazi beans lend earthiness to a cassoulet with succulent locally raised lamb. Desserts are simple and satisfying, but perhaps the best offering is the cheese plate, with "additional enhancements," a too-modest name for the delectable fruit concoctions devised for each cheese. And if the assured waitstaff—easily the best in the area—has a wine recommendation, take it.

# Outside Santa Fe

Less than an hour's drive from Santa Fe lie all manner of fascinating destinations, whether you're interested in the six-century-old ruins of ancestral Puebloan culture at Bandelier or the 20th-century atomic developments in Los Alamos, home of the Manhattan Project. Abiquiu, best known as Georgia O'Keeffe country, is a landscape of rich red rocks along the tree-lined Rio Chama. The most popular day or overnight outing from Santa Fe is to Taos, but even that presents several possibilities. The main options are the low road along the Rio Grande or the high road that passes through tiny Hispano mountain villages. You can also take a more roundabout route through Ojo Caliente, a village built around hot springs.

## THE PUEBLOS

Between Santa Fe and Taos lie seven pueblos, each set on a separate patch of reservation land. Unlike scenic Taos Pueblo, which opens its centuries-old buildings to visitors, most of the others are not worth visiting for their ancient architecture—they're typically a mix of old and new, and some are closed to outsiders all or part of the year. Do visit on feast days or for other ceremonial dances if you can, though.

Directly north of Santa Fe, U.S. 84/285 runs right through the closest pueblos—the overpass bridges are decorated with the original Tewa names. **Tesuque** (Te Tesugeh Owingeh, "village of the cottonwood trees") is marked by **Camel Rock,** a piece of sandstone on the west side of the highway that has eroded to resemble a creature that looks right at home in this rocky desert. Though this stretch of casinos and tax-free cigarette shops isn't particularly scenic, don't be tempted to race through it—the area is a major speed trap. **Pojoaque** manages the **Poeh Museum** (U.S. 84/285, 505/455-3334, 8 A.M.–5 P.M. Mon.–Fri., 4–9 P.M. Sat., free), in a striking old-style adobe building. It functions as a community arts gallery, with rotating exhibits and some of the finest work for sale, as well as a permanent installation relating to the Pojoaque people's path *(poeh)* through history.

On the land of **Santa Clara** (Kha P'o, or Shining Water), on Highway 30 south of Española, are the beautiful **Puyé Cliff Dwellings** (888/320-5008, www.puyecliffs. com), which were occupied until the early 1600s. They're accessible only by guided tour, and a somewhat expensive one at that: $20 for one-hour walks along the cliff side or the mesa top, or $35 for both. But tour leaders come from the pueblo and connect the ancient ruins with current culture in an intimate and fascinating way. At the base of the cliffs is a stone building from the Harvey Tours days of the early 1900s, when carloads of intrepid visitors would trundle out to these exotic sights; it now houses a small museum. You must buy your tickets at the Puyé Cliffs Welcome Center—better recognized as a gas station on Highway

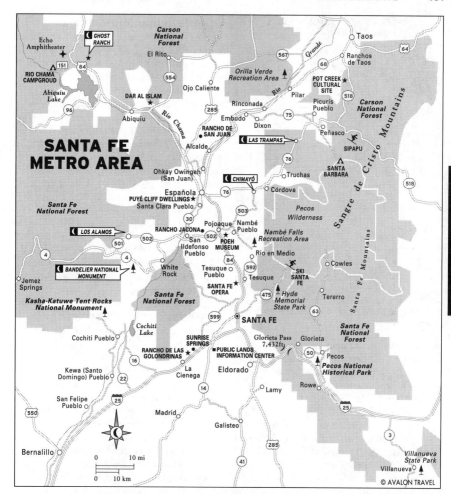

SANTA FE

30, at the turn to the cliffs. Tours run on the hour 9 A.M.–5 P.M. daily from the Monday after Easter through Labor Day; the rest of the year, tours run 10 A.M.–2 P.M.

**San Ildefonso,** best known for the black-on-black pottery of María Martinez and her husband, Julian, is off Highway 502, on the way to Los Alamos. A small **visitors center and museum** (Hwy. 502, 505/455-3549, 8 A.M.–4 P.M. Mon.–Fri., $5/car) shows the pottery-making process, and there are several crafts shops. Immediately north of Española,

at the junction of the Rio Chama and the Rio Grande, is **Ohkay Owingeh** (Strong Village, formerly San Juan), the birthplace of Popé, who led the Pueblo Revolt.

# ◖ LOS ALAMOS

Unlike so many other sights in New Mexico, which are cloaked in centuries of history, Los Alamos is an emblem of the modern age. During World War II, what had been only an elite, rugged boys' school was requisitioned by the army to become the top-secret base for

Sturdy pine poles hold up Fuller Lodge in Los Alamos.

## Orientation and Information

Los Alamos is spread out over three long mesas that jut like fingers from Pajarito Mountain. Highway 502 arrives in the middle mesa, depositing you on Central Avenue and the main downtown area; the north mesa is mostly residential, while the south mesa is occupied by the labs and two routes running back down the mountain and connecting with Highway 4. (Stray too far off the beaten track, and you start passing ominous Explosive Area signs.) Stop at the **tourist info center** (109 Central Park Square, 505/662-8105, http://visit.losalamos.com, 9 A.M.–5 P.M. Mon.–Sat., 10 A.M.–3 P.M. Sun.) for maps and the handy *50 Hikes in the Los Alamos Area* booklet. There's another helpful office in **White Rock** (35 Rover Blvd., 505/672-3183, 9 A.M.–4 P.M. daily mid–Mar.–Oct., 10 A.M.–2 P.M. Nov.–mid-Mar.), just off Highway 4.

## Los Alamos Historical Museum

Even a manufactured town like Los Alamos has a history. See what the area was like pre–Manhattan Project at this fascinating museum (1921 Juniper St., 505/662-6272, 9:30 A.M.–4:30 P.M. Mon.–Sat. and 1–4 P.M. Sun. in summer, 10 A.M.–4 P.M. Mon.–Sat. and 1–4 P.M. Sun. in winter, free) set in an old building of the Los Alamos Ranch School, the boys' camp that got the boot when the army moved in. The exhibits cover everything from relics of the early Tewa-speaking people up to juicy details on the social intrigue during the development of "the gadget," as the A-bomb was known.

In front of the museum is historic **Fuller Lodge,** originally the Ranch School's dining room and kitchen. It was built by John Gaw Meem, who handpicked the vertical logs that form the walls and designed the cowboy-silhouette light fixtures. It houses the **Los Alamos Art Center** (10 A.M.–4 P.M. Mon.–Sat.).

The museum is just west of the main street, Central Avenue—you'll see Fuller Lodge on Central, with the museum set back behind it.

development of the nuclear bomb, home for a time to J. Robert Oppenheimer, Richard Feynman, Neils Bohr, and other science luminaries. The Manhattan Project and its aftermath, the Cold War arms race, led to the establishment of Los Alamos National Labs (LANL) and the growth of the makeshift military base into a town of about 18,000 people (if you count the "suburb" of White Rock, just down the hill on Highway 4).

The highway up the mountainside is wider than it used to be, but the winding ascent to "Lost Almost"—as the first scientists dubbed their officially nonexistent camp—still carries an air of the clandestine. The town itself has a jarring newness about it, only emphasized by the dramatic, timeless landscape spreading out in all directions from the mesa edge on which it's perched. It's a beautiful starting point for hikes—after you've gone to the museums and cruised Bikini Atoll Road, Trinity Boulevard, and Oppenheimer Drive.

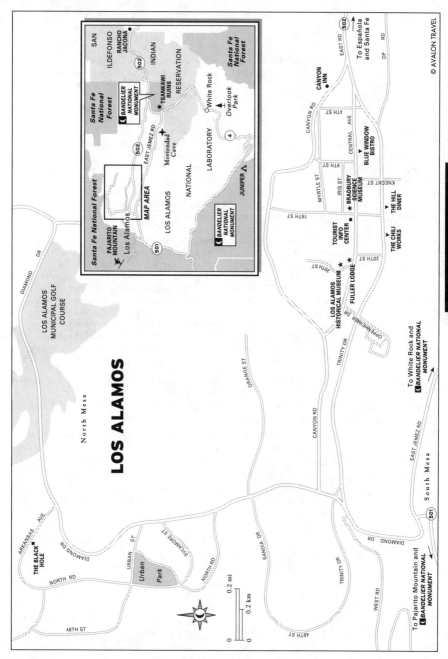

SANTA FE

# TRIBAL ECONOMIES IN THE GAMING AGE

North of Santa Fe on U.S. 84/285, Cities of Gold Casino looms beside the road, a sight that would've dazzled any conquistador in search of El Dorado. This, it seems, is the true fabled jackpot of the New World.

Pojoaque opened Cities of Gold in the 1990s after much deliberation in the small pueblo. The main argument for getting into the gaming business – effectively permitted by the federal Indian Gaming Regulatory Act in 1988 and then legalized in New Mexico in 1994 – was simply a need for cash and jobs in communities that had virtually no industry. At the time, up to 72 percent of pueblo residents were jobless, and the average income in many communities was less than $10,000 per year – almost inconceivably below national standards.

Pojoaque now boasts zero unemployment as well as attractive new apartment housing and a beautifully appointed museum funded by casino profits. And it has invested in developing the even more massive (but gambling-free) Buffalo Thunder Resort. But not all pueblos have followed that community's lead down the gaming path. For instance, Picurís's social conservatism as well as more practical concerns, such as its remote location, deterred the pueblo from opening its own gambling palace; the elders did eventually agree to co-owning the Hotel Santa Fe, a venture initiated by a few Anglo entrepreneurs who saw an opportunity to capitalize on a unique relationship with a pueblo. Jemez Pueblo remains staunchly reliant on its own agriculture and crafts and does not even take advantage of its status to sell tax-free cigarettes. The divisions between gaming and nongaming pueblos are not dramatic, but they are visible – especially as they're enhanced by a difference in economic status.

Puebloans and Anglos alike complain about the aesthetics of the gaudy, brightly lit casinos springing up on previously empty land, and others worry about the apparent loss of tradition that goes along with courting lowest-common-denominator tourism. But for many people who had previously been not much more than a scenic backdrop in New Mexico – a mute patch of "local color" – there's no incongruity at all. As George Rivera, the governor of Pojoaque, has put it, "You don't have to be poor to have your culture."

## Bradbury Science Museum

This LANL-sponsored exhibit (1350 Central Ave., 505/667-4444, www.lanl.gov/museum, 1–5 P.M. Sun. and Mon., 10 A.M.–5 P.M. Tues.–Sat., free) on the miracles of atomic energy has the feel of a very-high-grade science fair, with plenty of buttons to push and gadgets to play with. There's also an air of a convention sales booth—the museum's mission is definitely to sell the public on LANL's work and nuclear technology in general, though a public forum corner gives space to opposing views. More interesting are the relics of the early nuclear age: the Fat Man and Little Boy shell casings, gadgetry from the Nevada Test Site, and the like.

## Recreation

The mountains and canyons around Los Alamos are filled with some excellent hiking trails, in addition to those at Bandelier National Monument, farther west. In White Rock, the **White Rock Rim Trail** runs three miles along the cliff edge—you'll have suburban tract homes to your back and a dizzying canyon out in front of you. Even if you don't much feel like a hike, stop by where the walk starts in Overlook Park, just for the view; follow signs from Highway 4 at the first stoplight in town.

A bit of a locals' secret, **Pajarito Mountain** (505/662-5725, www.skipajarito.com, 9 A.M.–4 P.M. Fri.–Sun. and holidays) offers good skiing and snowboarding ($55 for a full day), with five lifts giving access to bunny slopes as well as double-black-diamond trails. The area is just a few miles northeast of Los Alamos, off Highway 501, and luckily escaped all damage from the Cerro Grande fire.

## Accommodations

The few hotels in Los Alamos cater primarily to visiting engineers, which is a shame considering the city's proximity to Valles Caldera National Preserve—it's a handy place to bunk if you want to get an early start on a hike. One decent place, the **Canyon Inn** (80 Canyon Rd., 505/662-9200, $85 s, $95 d), has four carpeted rooms with wireless Internet and private bathrooms; it's in a convenient location downtown. Guests have the run of a shared kitchen and can fix themselves breakfast when they like.

## Food

The Los Alamos old guard favors **The Hill Diner** (1315 Trinity Dr., 505/662-9745, 11 A.M.–8 P.M. daily, $8), where the vibe is Early Cold War: wood paneling, checked tablecloths, massive slices of coconut cream pie, and hot dinners like chicken-fried steak served with your choice of two sides. It's open an hour later in the summer.

For lunch, semi-elegant **Blue Window Bistro** (813 Central Ave., 505/662-6305, 11 A.M.–2:30 P.M. and 5–9 P.M. Mon.–Fri., 5–9 P.M. Sat., $15) is a treat, with a menu of sandwiches and pastas. For dinner, it's a bit spendy, but it's still your best bet in town.

## ◖ BANDELIER NATIONAL MONUMENT

One of New Mexico's most atmospheric ancient sites, Bandelier (www.nps.gov/band, $12/car) comprises 23,000 acres of wilderness, including the remarkable Frijoles Canyon, which is lined on either side with cave "apartments," while the remnants of a massive settlement from the 16th century occupy the valley floor. The Edenic canyon and the fun of clambering up ladders and around caves make for a grand day out—but everyone else thinks so too, and the place is packed from late April through the end of the summer. Come early on a weekday, if at all possible, or plan an overnight hike in the backcountry to avoid the crowds. Better still, join a torch-lit, silent **night walk** ($6) into Frijoles Canyon, a trip that sparks the imagination. They typically fall on Wednesday nights; check online for the schedule.

Start at the **visitors center** (505/672-3861, 8 A.M.–6 P.M. daily June–Aug., 9 A.M.–5:30 P.M. Apr., Sept., and Oct., 9 A.M.–4:30 P.M. daily Nov.–Mar.), which has a small museum and the usual array of maps and guides; pick up a Falls Trail guide even if you're not hiking that way, as it has good illustrations of the various plants and wildflowers that grow in the area. You can also get a free backcountry permit and thorough topo maps here.

## Main Loop Trail and Alcove House Trail

A paved walkway leads out the back of the visitors center into Frijoles Canyon, passing the ruins of the major settlements—or at least the ones that have been thoroughly excavated. You first reach **Tyuonyi** (chew-ON-yee), a circle of buildings that was settled for about 200 years, beginning in the 1300s. Built of bricks cut from tuff (the volcanic rock that makes up most of the area) and adobe plaster, some of the 250 rooms at one time stood several stories tall.

The trail then goes up next to the cliffs, dotted with small caves dug out of the soft stone, and to **Long House,** the remnants of a strip of condo-style buildings tucked into the rock wall. Paintings and carvings decorate the cliff face above. If you're here near sunset, keep an eye on the **bat cave** near the end of the strip, home to about 10,000 of the animals.

After Long House, the trail continues another half mile to the **Alcove House,** where you can climb up to a restored kiva high in the cliffs—well worth the extra mileage, unless you have trouble with heights (140 feet of ladders are involved). Rangers run free guided walks around the main loop a few times a day, or you can pick up the trail guide for $1 in the visitors center.

## Other Trails

**Falls Trail,** which leads southeast from the visitors center, is a showcase for the area's geology, rather than archaeology—the 2.5-mile route leads down through a canyon to two separate waterfalls and, eventually, the Rio Grande. Allow at least two hours for the full trip, as the trail is quite steep.

Well before you reach the main entrance to Bandelier, you pass **Tsankawi** on the east side of Highway 4. Unique pottery excavated in this separate section, disconnected from the main park, suggests that it was inhabited by a different people from those who settled in Frijoles Canyon, and some sort of natural border seems to have formed here, despite a shared cliff-dwelling culture: Today the pueblos immediately north of the Bandelier area speak Tewa, while those to the south speak Keresan. A 1.5-mile loop, with ladders to climb along the way, leads past unexcavated ruins, cave houses, and even a few petroglyphs.

## Camping

**Juniper Campground** ($12), just inside the park's northern border, is usually open year-round, with 94 sites. There are no hookups or showers—you're directed to the Los Alamos YMCA up the hill instead. No reservations are taken, but it's usually not full. The scenery up on the plateau isn't as striking as down in the canyon, but you will get an early start on the day if you stay overnight here.

## ESPAÑOLA

Although it's just a few miles from San Gabriel, the first town established by Don Juan de Oñate in 1598, Española itself is a relatively modern city of about 10,000 people, founded in the 1880s as a stop on the Chili Line, the railway between Denver and Santa Fe. It's still a crossroads: Take Highway 68 (called Riverside Drive in town) north from here to Taos, or continue on U.S. 84 to Abiquiu or U.S. 285 to Ojo Caliente. Highway 76 leads east to Chimayó, then to Truchas and the other high-road towns on the way to Taos. Highway 30 is the back road to Los Alamos.

Superficially, the place is not enticing, but really, Española is all about the food: Come here for authentic northern New Mexican cuisine, never watered down for interlopers'

tastes. Española is also the state's unofficial lowrider capital—keep your eyes out for cruisers in, say, the Wal-Mart parking lot, or at the Saints and Sinners package liquor store (its neon sign should also get landmark status) on U.S. 84/285 at the south end of town. Two incongruously nice hotels make it an even more tempting stopover.

## Chimayó Trading Post

No, you haven't made a wrong turn—you're still in Española. This adobe trading post (110 Sandia Dr., 505/753-9414, 10 A.M.–4 P.M. Wed.–Sat.) on the west side of the main highway relocated here in the 1930s, after several decades at its original location in Chimayó. Now it's a listed landmark, as one of the last remaining historic trading posts, and it has everything you'd expect: creaky wood floors, dim lighting, and a jumbled stock of treasures that includes not only Chimayó rugs but also ones from Iran; Nepalese silver jewelry; cut-tin candleholders, made locally; long skeins of handmade wool yarn; postcards; and even free coffee. The remaining elderly owner (one of a pair of airline employees, back in the real jet-set age) is no longer seriously replenishing

© ZORA O'NEILL

Chimayó Trading Post, a landmark at the crossroads in Española

his stock, but there are still some nifty finds. Hours can be a bit erratic.

## Accommodations

Española has a few hotels that are so nice, you might rethink your itinerary. A project of the local pueblo, the **Santa Claran** (460 N. Riverside Dr., 877/505-4949, www.santaclaran.com, $89 d), opened in 2010, has enormous rooms, tastefully done in subdued grays and browns with carved wood—the "modern Pueblo" look that distinguishes many new hotels in the area. Perks include fridges and laundry machines; Internet is wired only in rooms and wireless in the lobby (where there's a Starbucks outpost). You'd pay more than twice as much for similar quality in Santa Fe. The **Inn at the Delta** (234 Paseo de Oñate, 505/753-9466, www.innatthedelta.biz, $110 s, $140 d) is a beautiful rambling adobe complex with enormous rooms with fireplaces and fresh flowers in the rooms; rates include breakfast. Again, compared with Santa Fe, it's a bargain.

South of town, on the road to Los Alamos,

▌ **Rancho Jacona** (277 County Rd. 84, 505/455-7948, www.ranchojacona.com, $165 d) is a working farm dotted with 11 casitas, each with a kitchen and space for three to eight people. You'll likely get some fresh chicken eggs for breakfast, and kids can frolic in the pool. There's a three-day minimum.

## Food

If you're just driving through on your way north, stop off for a quick bite at **El Parasol** (603 Santa Cruz Rd., 505/753-8852, 7:30 A.M.–8 P.M. daily, $3), a takeout stand with picnic tables under cottonwood trees and a Spanglish menu ("pollo with guacamole taco"). If you've got more time, head indoors to neighbor **El Paragua** (505/753-3211, 11 A.M.–8:30 P.M. Mon.–Fri., 9 A.M.–8:30 P.M. Sat., 11 A.M.–8 P.M. Sun., $15) in a big two-story hacienda filled with wagon wheels, wrought-iron bric-a-brac, and vintage newspaper clippings. The place is constantly packed with locals stuffing themselves with big plates of carnitas, chiles rellenos, and the most delectable, perfectly fried sopaipillas in the region. Turn for both of these places at the sign for Highway 76, which is called Santa Cruz Road in town—the restaurants are immediately on the left.

For a quieter dining experience, look for **Matilda's** (424 Corlett Rd., 505/753-3200, 10:30 A.M.–8 P.M. Tues.–Thurs., 10:30 A.M.–9 P.M. Fri., 9 A.M.–9 P.M. Sat. and Sun., $7) to the southeast off the main road (if you're heading north and pass the Chimayó Trading Post, you've gone too far). The place strikes a homey tone from its front steps, filled with pots of geraniums; Matilda and her family cook up the very traditional (read: heavy on the chile, light on the cheese) northern New Mexican goods, often using ingredients they've grown themselves.

On the main drag (Highway 68/Riverside Drive), diner-style **JoAnn's Ranch O Casados** (938 N. Riverside Dr., 505/753-1334, 7 A.M.–8 P.M. Mon.–Sat., 7 A.M.–3 P.M. Sun., $10) serves breakfast all day, along with very good and inexpensive enchiladas, fajitas, and more. The red chile is rich and mellow, and you can get half-orders of many dishes.

## OJO CALIENTE

Twenty-six miles north of Española on U.S. 285, Ojo Caliente (Hot Spring) is, like Jemez Springs, an old resort village based around natural mineral water, now sporting a funky, post-hippie ambience. Set among red cliffs, the pools are attractive and worth a stop if you're driving through, but not necessarily deserving of a day trip from Santa Fe (unless you're tired of Ten Thousand Waves there). The main pools are managed by **Ojo Caliente Mineral Springs** (505/583-2233, www.ojocalientespa. com, 8 A.M.–10 P.M. daily) and built around a 1916 hotel building and several paved pools—one big public one ($16 Mon.–Thurs., $24 Fri.–Sun., $12/$20 after 6 P.M.) and several private options (an additional $40 for two for 50 minutes). You can also stay the night here, in cozy cottages ($199 d) or in the historic hotel building ($139 d), or in the campground ($20); room rates include access to the springs for the day of arrival and the day of departure. There's also a nice bed-and-breakfast in town, **The Inn**

**at Ojo** (505/583-9131, www.ojocaliente.com, $85 s, $115 d).

From here, you can continue on to Taos via a back route: Take U.S. 285 north, then turn east on Highway 567. This road ends at a T-junction—turn left on a new paved route, heading north, and you meet U.S. 64 about one mile west of the Rio Grande Gorge; Taos is to the right.

## ABIQUIU

Northwest of Española, along U.S. 84, the valley formed by the muddy Rio Chama is one of the most striking landscapes in northern New Mexico. Lush greenery on the river bottom clashes with bright red mud; roaming sheep and cattle graze by the roadside. The striated hills represent dramatic geological shifts, from 200-million-year-old purple stone from the dinosaur era to red clay formed by forests, then gypsum from sand dunes, then a layer of lava from only 8 million years back. More recently, Abiquiu has become inextricably linked with the artist Georgia O'Keeffe, who made the valley her home for more than 40 years, entranced all the while by the glowing light and the dramatic skyline.

Although Abiquiu often refers to the whole river valley, the unofficial town center is **Bode's** (Hwy. 84, 505/685-4422, 6:30 A.M.–7 P.M. Mon.–Fri., 7 A.M.–8 P.M. Sat., 7 A.M.–8 P.M. Sun.), an old-fashioned general store (the name's pronounced BO-deez) where you can get gas, pastries and sandwiches, fishing licenses and tackle, and local crafts; in winter, it closes earlier on weekends. The actual village of Abiquiu, established in 1754 by *genízaros* (Hispanicized Indians) through a land grant from the Spanish Crown, is up the hill on the opposite side of the road. O'Keeffe's house forms one side of the old plaza; on the other is the Santo Tomas de Abiquiu Church, built in the 1930s after the community opted for the legal status of village rather than pueblo. Continue uphill past O'Keeffe's house to see the village *morada*, dramatically set on a hilltop. You're not really encouraged to poke around, however—the

© ZORA O'NEILL

the view from Abiquiu

village maintains a privacy policy similar to those of the pueblos.

## Georgia O'Keeffe House

The artist's main residence, where she lived 1949–1984, fronts the small plaza in the village center of Abiquiu. The house is open to guided tours mid-March–November (505/685-4539, $40). The schedule depends on the month, but there are at least five tours each day Tuesday–Friday; extras are added from June on. The rambling adobe, parts of which were built in the 18th century, is interesting, especially to see how O'Keeffe juxtaposed her modernist design sense with the more organic feel of the adobe home. The tour price is shockingly high, though, and in many ways the surrounding landscape reflects O'Keeffe's work more than her home does. Tours depart from the Abiquiu Inn on U.S. 84; you must make reservations at least a month in advance.

## Dar al Islam

In another chapter of New Mexico's long utopian history, a few American converts established Dar al Islam (505/685-4515, www.daralislam.org), an intentional religious community, in 1979. A village for about 150 families on 8,300 acres just south of the village of Abiquiu proper, it was meant to be a place in which Muslims could practice their religion in every aspect of life, from education to food. The village concept never quite took off, though, and Dar al Islam has been reinvented as a retreat center that's open to visitors. Egyptian architect Hassan Fathy's adobe mosque, all organic sinuous lines, is beautiful and harmonizes flawlessly with the land surrounding it. The most direct route to the community is via Highway 554, which runs east from U.S. 84 south of Abiquiu (follow signs for El Rito); immediately after crossing the river, turn left on County Road 155, which leads to the main entrance.

If you leave the mosque by the far side, continuing on County Road 155 on its loop back to meet U.S. 84, you pass the towering gypsum formations of **Plaza Blanca** (White Place), an oft-photographed patch of land that looks like a pile of bleached bones. You can park your car anywhere and wander among the pinnacles.

## Abiquiu Lake

An Army Corps of Engineers dam project created this 4,000-acre lake with fingers running into the canyons all around. The view coming in is marred by the power station, but past that the water glimmers at the base of the flat-topped flint mountain Pedernal Peak, the distinctive silhouette that found its way into so many of O'Keeffe's paintings. ("It's my private mountain," she often said. "God told me if I painted it often enough, I could have it.") The overly paved campground at the lake is open year-round, but water and electric hookups are available only in the summer.

## ◖ Ghost Ranch

Ghost Ranch (U.S. 84, 505/685-4333, www.ghostranch.org), a 21,000-acre retreat now owned by the Presbyterian Church, is famous for several things: First, Georgia O'Keeffe owned a small parcel of the land and maintained a studio here. Then, in 1947, paleontologists combing the red hills discovered about a thousand skeletons of the dinosaur *Coelophysis* ("hollow form," for its hollow, birdlike bones), the largest group discovered in the world.

The grounds are open to visitors by day, to see the **Florence Hawley Ellis Museum of Anthropology** and the **Ruth Hall Museum of Paleontology** (9 A.M.–5 P.M. Tues.–Sat., $2), which have small but interesting collections displaying the local finds, including remnants of the prehistoric Gallina culture that lived on the ridge above the valley and an eight-ton chunk of *Coelophysis*-filled siltstone in the process of being excavated. Both museums are also open 1–5 P.M. on Sundays and Mondays in the summer. Guided tours of the ranch grounds, with an emphasis on O'Keeffe's legacy, run mid-March–mid-November (1:30 P.M. Tues. and Thurs.–Sat., $25); reserve ahead.

In spring and early summer, **horseback riding** is available, with one-hour rides for $40, on mellow horses. You can also **hike** on your own after registering at the reception desk. The best trek, which takes about 1.5 hours round-trip, is to **Chimney Rock,** a towering landmark with panoramic views of the entire area. Don't be daunted—the steepest part of the trail is at the start—but do slather on the sunscreen, as there's no shade on this route. **Box Canyon** is an easier, shadier, all-level walk that's about four miles round-trip. **Kitchen Mesa Trail,** which starts at the same point, is much more difficult, requiring some climbing to get up the cliffs at the end (though you could hike the easy first two-thirds, then turn around).

## Echo Amphitheater

This bandshell-shape rock formation, a natural wonder of acoustics, is a great place to let kids run around and yell to their hearts' content. It's four miles north of Ghost Ranch. There are pleasant picnic areas tucked among the brush and a couple of campsites ($2 day-use fee).

## Accommodations and Food

The **Abiquiu Inn** (505/685-4378, www.abiquiuinn.com) functions as the area's visitors center. Lodging ($140 d) consists of some pretty casitas at the back of the property, with great views of the river, and a cluster of motel rooms closer to the front (opt for rooms 2–6, which face away from the road); solo travelers should reserve well ahead for "El Vado Económico," a cozy one-bed room. Its restaurant, **Café Abiquiu** (7 A.M.–9 P.M. daily, $7–13) serves steak sandwiches, as well as bigger entrées like fried trout.

You can also stay at **Ghost Ranch** (U.S. 84, 505/685-4333, www.ghostranch.org) when it's not full for retreats—cabins start at $45, or you can camp for $16. Thirteen miles down a rocky dirt track, **Christ in the Desert Monastery** (Forest Rd. 151, 801/545-8567, www.christdesert.org, $60 s) delivers on solitude; day visitors are welcome, or you can stay overnight (two-night minimum) for a suggested donation. Out the same road (at the 11.5-mile mark), **Rio Chama Campground** is remote but beautiful—preferable to Abiquiu Lake if you really want to get away from it all.

# THE HIGH ROAD TO TAOS

Córdova, Truchas, Las Trampas, Peñasco—these are the tiny villages strung, like beads on a necklace, along the winding highway north through the mountains. This is probably the area of New Mexico where Spanish heritage has been least diluted—or at least relatively untouched by Anglo influence, for there has been a long history of exchange between the Spanish towns and the adjacent pueblos. The local dialect is distinctive, and residents can claim ancestors who settled the towns in the 18th century. The first families learned to survive in the harsh climate with a 90-day growing season, and much of the technology that worked then continues to work now; electricity was still scarce even in the 1970s, and adobe construction is common. These communities, closed off by geography, can seem a little insular to visitors, but pop in at the galleries that have sprung up in a couple of the towns, and you'll get a warm welcome. And during the **High Road Arts Tour** (www.highroadnewmexico.com), over two weekends in September, craftspeople famed particularly for their woodcarving skills open their home studios.

The drive straight through takes only about an hour and a half, but leave time to dawdle at churches and galleries, take a hike, or have lunch along the way. Start the driving route by leaving Santa Fe via North St. Francis Road, then continuing on U.S. 84/285 to the junction with Highway 503 (just past the turn for Los Alamos); turn right, following signs for Nambé Pueblo.

## Nambé Pueblo

To the right off Highway 503 just a few miles is **Nambé Falls Recreation Area** (505/455-2304, www.nambefalls.com, $10/car), open to the public for swimming and fishing; it also has beautiful camping spots ($25, including day pass). The highlight is the falls themselves, a double cascade through a narrow crevice, marking the break between the Sangre de Cristo Mountains and the Española Basin. Incidentally, the Nambé line of high-end housewares has nothing to do with this pueblo

of 1,700 people—weaving and micaceous pottery are some of the traditional crafts here. The biggest annual event is Fourth of July, celebrated with dances and a crafts market.

## ◖ Chimayó

Continue on Highway 503 to a T-junction, where you make a hard left to follow the main road and begin the descent into the valley of Chimayó, site of the largest mass pilgrimage in the United States. During Holy Week, some 50,000 people arrive in town on foot, starting days in advance to arrive on Good Friday and often bearing large crosses.

The inspiration for the group treks, a tradition begun in 1945 as a commemoration of the Bataan Death March, is the **Santuario de Chimayó** (www.holychimayo.us, 9 A.M.–6 P.M. daily May–Sept., 9 A.M.–5 P.M. daily Oct.–Apr.), a small chapel that has gained a reputation as a healing spot, as it was built in 1814 at the place where a local farmer, Bernardo Abeyta, is said to have dug up a miraculously glowing crucifix.

Unlike many of the older churches in this area, which are now open very seldom, Chimayó is an active place of prayer, always busy with tourists as well as visitors seeking solace. (Mass is said weekdays at 11 A.M. and on Sunday at 10:30 A.M. and noon year-round.) As you approach from the parking area, you will see that previous visitors have woven twigs into the chain-link fencing to form crosses, each set of sticks representing a prayer. Outdoor pews made of split tree trunks accommodate overflow crowds, and a wheelchair ramp gives easy access to the church.

But the little adobe chapel seems untouched by modernity. The front wall of the dim main chapel is filled with an elaborately painted altar screen from the first half of the 19th century, the work of Molleno (nicknamed "the Chile Painter" because forms, especially robes, in his paintings often resemble red and green chiles). The vibrant colors seem to shimmer in the gloom, forming a sort of stage set for Abeyta's crucifix, Nuestro Señor de las Esquípulas, as the centerpiece. Painted on the screen above

© ZORA O'NEILL

Santuario de Chimayó

the crucifix is the symbol of the Franciscans: a cross over which the arms of Christ and Saint Francis meet.

But most visitors make their way directly to the small, low-ceiling antechamber that holds *el pocito,* the little hole where the cross was allegedly first dug up. From this pit they scoop up a small portion of the exposed red earth, to later apply to withered limbs and arthritic joints, or to eat in hopes of curing internal ailments. (The parish refreshes the well each year with new dirt, after it has been blessed by the priests.) The adjacent sacristy, formerly filled with handwritten testimonials, prayers, and abandoned crutches, is now a bit tidier and devoted to a shrine for Santo Niño de Atocha, a figurine that is also said to have been dug out of the holy ground here. (Santo Niño de Atocha has a dedicated chapel just down the road—the artwork here is modern, bordering on cutesy, but the back room, filled with baby shoes, is poignant.)

If you want to spend the night in the area, or

use it as a base for exploring, **Casa Escondida** (Hwy. 76, 505/351-4805, www.casaescondida. com, $109 d) is a lovely place, with a big backyard, a hot tub, and a sunny garden.

For lunch head right across the parking lot from the Santuario de Chimayó to **Leona's** (505/351-4569, 11 A.M.–5 P.M. Thurs.–Mon., $2), where you can pick up bulk chile and pistachios as well as delicious tamales and crumbly *bizcochitos.* For a more leisurely sit-down lunch, **( Rancho de Chimayó** (County Rd. 98, 505/351-4444, www.ranchodechimayo. com, 11:30 A.M.–9 P.M. daily May–Oct., 11:30 A.M.–9 P.M. Tues.–Sun. Nov.–Apr., $11) offers great red chile on a beautiful terrace—or inside the old adobe home by the fireplace in wintertime. The place is also open for breakfast on weekends, 8:30–10:30 A.M., and it's a popular special-occasion spot for Santa Feans.

## Córdova

Turning right (east) on Highway 76 (west

© ZORA O'NEILL

### SANTO NIÑO DE ATOCHA

Santo Niño de Atocha, patron saint of the imprisoned

takes you back toward Española), you begin the climb back up the Sangre de Cristo Mountains. Near the crest of the hill, about three miles up, a small sign points right and down to Córdova, a village best known for its unpainted, austere santos and *bultos* done by masters such as George López and José Dolores López. Another family member, **Sabinita López Ortiz** (9 County Rd. 1317, 505/351-4572, variable hours), sells her work and that of five other generations of wood-carvers. **Castillo Gallery** (County Rd. 1317, 505/351-4067, variable hours) mixes traditional styles with more contemporary work.

### Truchas

Highway 76 continues to wind along the peaks, eventually reaching the little village of Truchas (Trout), founded in 1754 and still not much more than a long row of buildings set into the ridgeline and facing the expansive valley below. On the corner where the highway makes a hard left to Taos is the village *morada,*

the meeting place of the local Penitente brotherhood; head straight down the smaller road to reach **Nuestra Señora del Rosario de las Truchas Church,** tucked into a small plaza off to the right of the main street. It's open to visitors only June–August—if you do have a chance to look inside the dim, thick-walled mission, you'll see precious examples of local wood carving. Though many of the more delicate ones have been moved to a museum for preservation, those remaining display an essential New Mexican style—the sort of "primitive" thing that Bishop Lamy hated. They're preserved today only because Truchas residents hid them in their houses during the late 19th century. In this part of the village, you'll also find the most established gallery, **Hand Artes** (137 County Rd. 75, 505/689-2443, variable hours).

### Las Trampas

Back on Highway 76, the village of Las Trampas was settled in 1751, and its showpiece, **San José de Gracia Church** (10 A.M.–4 P.M. Sat. and Sun. June–Aug.), was built nine years later. It remains one of the finest examples of New Mexican village church architecture. Its thick adobe walls, which are covered with a fresh coat of mud every year or two, are balanced by vertical bell towers; inside, the clerestory at the front of the church—a very typical design—lets light in to shine down on the altar, which was carved and painted in the late 1700s. Other paradigmatic elements include the *atrio,* or small plaza between the low adobe boundary wall and the church itself, utilized as a cemetery, and the dark narthex where you enter, confined by the choir loft above, but only serving to emphasize the sense of light and space created in the rest of the church by the clerestory and the small windows near the viga ceiling.

### Picurís Pueblo

For all the signs that point to Picurís, from every possible surrounding highway, you would imagine it's a glittery tourist extravaganza. In fact, as one of the few Rio Grande pueblos that has not built a casino, Picurís Pueblo, the smallest in New Mexico, instead capitalizes on its beautiful natural setting, a lush valley where bison roam and aspen leaves rustle. You can picnic here and fish in small but well-stocked Tu-Tah Lake. After the **San Lorenzo de Picurís Church** collapsed due to water damage in 1989, pueblo members rebuilt it by hand, following exactly the form of the original 1776 design—a process that took eight years. As at Nambé, local traditions have melded with those of the surrounding villages; the Hispano-Indian Matachines dances are well attended on Christmas Eve. Start at the **visitors center** (575/587-1099 or 575/587-1071, 9 A.M.–5 P.M. Mon.–Sat.) to pick up maps. The pueblo is a short detour from the high road proper: At the junction with Highway 75, turn left, then follow signs off the main road.

### Peñasco

The next community along the road is Peñasco, best known to tourists as the home of **Sugar Nymphs Bistro** (15046 Hwy. 76, 575/587-0311, 10 A.M.–3 P.M. and 5:30–7:45 P.M. Thurs.–Sat., 10 A.M.–3 P.M. Sun., $10), where you can get all kinds of treats such as grilled lamb, fresh-pressed cider, piñon couscous, and pizzas. Hours can be more limited in the winter, so it's best to call ahead. This is also the northern gateway to the **Pecos Wilderness Area**—turn on Forest Road 116 to reach Santa Barbara Campground and the Santa Barbara Trail to Truchas Peak, a 23-mile round-trip that requires advance planning. Contact the **Española ranger district office** (1710 N. Riverside Dr., 505/753-7331, 8 A.M.–4:30 P.M. Mon.–Fri.) or the one in the town of Pecos for conditions before you hike.

### Sipapu

Detouring right (east) along Highway 518, you reach Sipapu (Hwy. 518, 800/587-2240, www.sipapunm.com), an unassuming, inexpensive **ski resort**—really, just a handful of cabins at the base of a 9,255-foot mountain. Cheap lift

tickets ($39 full-day) and utter quiet make this a bargain getaway.

Returning to the junction, continue on to Taos via Highway 518, which soon descends into a valley and passes **Pot Creek Cultural Site** (575/587-2255, 9 A.M.–4 P.M. Wed.–Sun. July–Aug.), a mildly interesting diversion for its one-mile loop trail through ancestral Puebloan ruins from around 1100.

You arrive in Taos at its very southern end—really, in Ranchos de Taos, just north of the San Francisco de Asis Church on Highway 68. Turn left to see the church, or turn right to head up to the town plaza and to Taos Pueblo.

## THE LOW ROAD TO TAOS

The lush farmland around the Rio Grande is the highlight of this drive north—the valley filled with apple orchards is as green as New Mexico gets. The road is at first a bit unpromising, as it passes through the modern town of Española, but it soon winds into an ever-narrower canyon and finally emerges at the dramatic point where the high plains meet the mountains. This route is more direct than the high road and has fewer scenic stopping points, so if you're pressed for time, this is the way to go.

### Embudo and Dixon

The village of Embudo is really just a bend in the river, but it offers a couple of good eating options. First up is beautiful **Embudo Station** (Hwy. 68, 505/852-4707, 11 A.M.–8 P.M. Thurs.–Mon. Apr.–Nov., $14), a little lodge right on the water where you can have a succulent local-beef burger under the shade of a big cottonwood, with a side of greens grown just up the road in Dixon. By the time you read this, the place should also be serving local craft beers and wines.

If you want something faster, or just messier, look out for **Sugar's** (Hwy. 68, 505/852-0604, 11 A.M.–6 P.M. Thurs.–Mon., $5), just past Embudo Station on the opposite side of the road. It's just a small trailer, but it doles out seriously big food: barbecue brisket burritos,

© ZORA O'NEILL

© CREDIT

random roadside attractions in Embudo

or a more traditional BBQ platter with beans and corn on the cob. It's takeout only, but there are a few plastic picnic tables where you can sit down.

Down Highway 75 a few miles is the pleasant little town of **Dixon,** known for its dense concentration of artists, organic farmers, and vintners—a worthwhile detour in itself, especially in early November for the long-running **Dixon Studio Tour** (www.dixonarts.org), or for the **farmers market** village on summer and fall Wednesdays (4:30–7 P.M.).

## Pilar

Beginning just south of the village of Pilar and stretching several miles north, **Orilla Verde Recreation Area** ($3/car) is public land along either side of the Rio Grande, used primarily as a put-in or haul-out for **rafting,** but you can **camp** on the riverbanks as well—Petaca

and Taos Junction have the best sites ($7 per night). The **Vista Verde Trail** runs about 1.2 miles one-way along the west rim, an easy walk with great views and a few petroglyphs to spot in a small arroyo about a third of the way out; the trailhead is on the other side of the river, half a mile up the hill from the Taos Junction Bridge, off the dirt road Highway 567 (turn left off the highway in Pilar, then follow signs into Orilla Verde). Stop first on the main highway at the **Rio Grande Gorge Visitors Center** (Hwy. 68, 575/751-4899, 8:30 A.M.–4:30 P.M. daily June–Aug., 10 A.M.–2 P.M. Fri.–Sun. Sept.–May) for maps and other information. Across the road, **Pilar Yacht Club** (Hwy. 68, 575/758-9072, 8 A.M.–5 P.M. daily Apr.–Nov., 9 A.M.–2 P.M. Thurs.–Sun. Dec.–Mar.) is the center of the action, serving food to hungry river rats and functioning as an office for a couple of outfitters.

# Information and Services

## TOURIST INFORMATION

The **Santa Fe Convention and Visitors Bureau** (201 W. Marcy St., 800/777-2489, www.santafe.org, 8 A.M.–5 P.M. Mon.–Fri.) hands out its visitors guide and other brochures from its offices at the convention center. The New Mexico Tourism Department runs a **visitors center** near San Miguel Chapel (491 Old Santa Fe Tr., 505/827-7336, 8 A.M.–5 P.M. Mon.–Fri.).

For info on the outdoors, head out to the comprehensive **Public Lands Information Center** (301 Dinosaur Tr., 505/954-2002, www.publiclands.org, 8 A.M.–4:30 P.M. Mon.–Fri.), just off Highway 14, south of I-25. You can pick up heaps of free flyers, including detailed route descriptions for the most popular area day hikes, as well as buy guidebooks, detailed topo maps for all the wilderness areas, and hunting and fishing licenses.

### Books and Maps

Santa Fe has two particularly good bookshops right in the center of town. **Travel Bug** (839 Paseo de Peralta, 505/992-0418, 7:30 A.M.–5:30 P.M. Mon.–Sat., 10 A.M.–3 P.M. Sun.) specializes in maps, travel guides, gear like luggage and GPS gadgets, and free advice. For more general stock, **Collected Works** (202 Galisteo St., 505/988-4226, 8 A.M.–8 P.M. Mon.–Sat., 8 A.M.–6 P.M. Sun.) is the place to go—excellent staff recommendations and a trove of local-interest titles. In winter, it opens at 9 A.M.

### Local Media

The *Santa Fe New Mexican* is Santa Fe's daily paper, which publishes events listings and gallery news in its *Pasatiempo* insert on Fridays. For left-of-center news and commentary, the *Santa Fe Reporter* is the free weekly rag, available in most coffee shops and cafés.

### Radio

Santa Fe supports a number of niche radio stations: KLBU (102.9 FM) brings Ibiza-style chill-out electronica to the mountains, while KBAC (98.1 FM) is better known as Radio Free Santa Fe, a dynamic community station with eclectic music and talk. Tune in Friday afternoons for news on the gallery scene.

## SERVICES

### Banks

**First National Bank of Santa Fe** (62 Lincoln Ave., 505/992-2000, 9 A.M.–5 P.M. Mon.–Fri.) is on the west side of the plaza. **First Community Bank** (100 N. Guadalupe St., 505/946-4100, 9 A.M.–5 P.M. Mon.–Thurs., 9 A.M.–6 P.M. Sat.) is walking distance from the plaza, but also easily accessible by car.

### Post Office

Santa Fe's **main post office** (120 S. Federal Place, 505/988-2239, 8 A.M.–5:30 P.M. Mon.–Fri., 9 A.M.–4 P.M. Sat.) is conveniently just north of the plaza, near the district courthouse.

### Internet

**Travel Bug** (839 Paseo de Peralta, 505/992-0418, 7:30 A.M.–5:30 P.M. Mon.–Sat., 10 A.M.–3 P.M. Sun.) bookstore offers free Internet access and also serves coffee. **Santa Fe Public Library** (145 Washington Ave., 505/955-6780, www.santafelibrary.org, 10 A.M.–9 P.M. Mon.–Thurs., 10 A.M.–6 P.M. Fri. and Sat., 1–5 P.M. Sun.) has several public Internet terminals with free access; call ahead to reserve a time slot if you can.

# Getting There and Around

## BY AIR

**Santa Fe Municipal Airport** (SAF, 505/955-2900), west of the city, receives direct flights from Dallas and Los Angeles with American Eagle. Typically, fares are better to Albuquerque (ABQ), less than an hour's drive away.

## BY CAR

Ideally, you would not have a car while in Santa Fe—the area around the plaza is a maze of one-way streets, and parking is difficult. There are only a couple of small municipal lots, and hotels usually charge a premium for parking. **Hertz, Budget, Avis,** and **Thrifty** all have branches on Cerrillos Road.

## BY BUS AND SHUTTLE

**Sandia Shuttle Express** (888/775-5696, www.sandiashuttle.com) does hourly pickups from the airport 8:45 A.M.–10:15 P.M. and will deliver to any hotel or B&B ($27 one-way).

The reasonably useful city bus system, **Santa Fe Trails** (505/955-2001, www.santafenm.gov), can take you to all of the major sights from the handy central depot on Sheridan Street just north of the plaza. The "M" route goes to Museum Hill; Route 2 runs along Cerrillos Road. Buses on all routes run only every 30 to 60 minutes. The Museum Hill and Cerrillos Road buses run on Sundays. Fare is $1, or you can buy a day pass for $2, payable on board with exact change.

## BY TRAIN

**Amtrak** (800/USA-RAIL, www.amtrak.com) runs the Southwest Chief through Lamy, 18 miles south of Santa Fe and a dramatic place to step off the train—you'll feel very Wild West, as there's no visible civilization for miles around. Trains arrive once daily from Chicago and Los Angeles. Amtrak provides a shuttle van for passengers coming and going to Santa Fe.

Closer to home, the **Rail Runner** (866/795-RAIL, www.nmrailrunner.com) runs from Albuquerque to downtown Santa Fe—the final stop is at the rail yard in the Guadalupe district. The 90-minute ride costs $7, or $8 for a day pass, and the trains are timed so that you could eat dinner in Santa Fe (but not stay for a later drink) and take a return train back.

# TAOS AND NORTH CENTRAL NEW MEXICO

Though adobe houses cluster around a plaza, and art galleries, organic bakeries, and yoga studios proliferate, the town of Taos is much more than a miniature Santa Fe. It's more isolated, reached by curving two-lane roads along either the winding mountain-ridge route or the fertile Rio Grande river valley, and it has a rougher, muddier feel. The glory of the landscape, from looming Taos Mountain to the staggered blue mesas dissolving into the flat western horizon, can be truly breathtaking. Add to that the intense mysticism surrounding Taos Pueblo and the often wild creativity of the artists who have lived here, and the lure is irresistible. People flock here on pilgrimages—to the ranch where D. H. Lawrence lived, to the hip-deep powder on the slopes at Taos Ski Valley, to the San Francisco de Asis Church

that Georgia O'Keeffe painted—then simply wind up staying. The person pouring your coffee at the café probably has a variation on this same story.

Celebrity residents like Julia Roberts and Donald Rumsfeld have lent the place a certain reputation of wealth and exclusivity, but this is hardly the case. Spanish farmers in Valle Valdez scrape by on their acequia-fed farm plots just as they have for centuries. The same goes for residents of old Taos Pueblo, the living World Heritage Site that still uses no electricity or running water. Add to that a strong subculture of ski bums, artists, off-the-grid eco-homesteaders, and spiritual seekers, and you have a community that, while not typically prosperous, is more loyal and dedicated to preserving its unique way of life than

# HIGHLIGHTS

**【 Taos Art Museum at Fechin House:** In the early 1930s, Russian artist Nicolai Fechin designed his home in a fantastical fusion of Tartar, Spanish, and American Indian styles. Today, his paintings hang next to the wood lintels and furniture he carved (page 127).

**【 Millicent Rogers Museum:** A 1950s' socialite amassed an astounding trove of American Indian and Spanish artwork in just a few short years in Taos. Her collection is on view in her former house, and it provides a thorough introduction to the region's oldest cultures (page 128).

**【 Mabel Dodge Luhan House:** See where America's counterculture thrived in the mid-20th century, as encouraged by the arts doyenne who made Taos her home. Countless writers, painters, and actors visited Mabel here in her idiosyncratic home (page 131).

**【 San Francisco de Asis Church:** With its massive adobe buttresses and rich earthy glow, this 350-year-old Franciscan mission is one of the most recognizable in the world, thanks to its frequent depiction in paintings and photographs (page 132).

**【 Taos Pueblo:** The stepped adobe buildings at New Mexico's most remarkable pueblo seem to rise organically from the earth. Don't miss the ceremonial dances here, about eight times a year (page 133).

**【 Rio Grande Gorge:** Think how dismayed the first homesteaders must have been when they reached "New Mexico's Grand Canyon," an 800-foot-deep channel cut through the rock to the west of Taos. Think how overjoyed today's white-water rafters are in the spring, when mountain runoff surges through the rift (page 134).

**【 Taos Ski Valley:** This is the purist's mountain: deep powder, impossibly steep slopes, and until very recently, no snowboards. Don't ski? Drive up here just to crane your neck up at the top, and consider taking lessons (page 136).

**【 Cumbres & Toltec Scenic Railroad:** Ascending the pass through the Rockies into Colorado on this rumbling old steam train, soot and wind in your hair, you'll feel like you've climbed to the very top of the world (page 152).

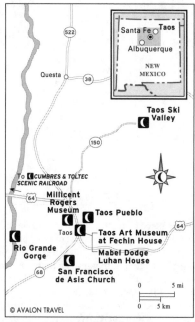

LOOK FOR **【** TO FIND RECOMMENDED SIGHTS, ACTIVITIES, DINING, AND LODGING.

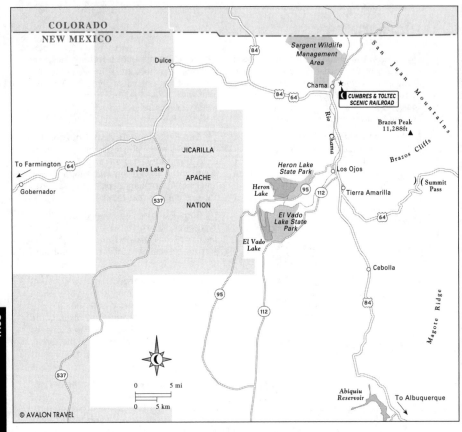

COLORADO
NEW MEXICO

Sargent Wildlife
Management
Area

Dulce

Chama ★

CUMBRES & TOLTEC
SCENIC RAILROAD

San Juan Mountains

JICARILLA

Brazos Peak
11,288ft ▲

Rio Chama

Brazos Cliffs

To Farmington 64

La Jara Lake

APACHE

Heron Lake
State Park

Los Ojos

Summit
Pass

Gobernador

NATION

Heron
Lake

95

112

Tierra Amarilla

537

El Vado
Lake State
Park

64

El Vado
Lake

Cebolla

95

112

Magote Ridge

84

0    5 mi

0    5 km

Abiquiu
Reservoir

To Albuquerque

© AVALON TRAVEL

TAOS

perhaps any other small town in the western United States.

Jump the Taos Gorge on U.S. 64 west out of town for a beautiful drive over the mountains to Tierra Amarilla, where centuries of shepherding continue to this day. North from here, you're nearly at the Colorado border when you reach Chama, best known as the depot for a scenic steam train up a narrow mountain pass.

North and east from Taos, the grandly named Enchanted Circle scenic byway loops around Wheeler Peak, the highest mountain in New Mexico at 13,161 feet. The area was settled primarily by miners and ranchers in the late 19th century, so it has a different atmosphere from the centuries-old Spanish-and-Indian legacy in the rest of northern New Mexico. Along the way, you can stop at a mining ghost town, a moving Vietnam veterans' memorial, or a rowdy Old West–style steakhouse. Likewise, the ski resorts of Angel Fire and Red River offer a somewhat less extreme, but no less fun, alternative to Taos Ski Valley.

## PLANNING YOUR TIME

Taos's busiest tourist season is the arid summer, when a day's entertainment can consist simply of gallery-hopping then settling in to watch the afternoon thunderheads gather and churn, then the sun set under lurid red streaks across the broad western mesas. Wintertime is of course

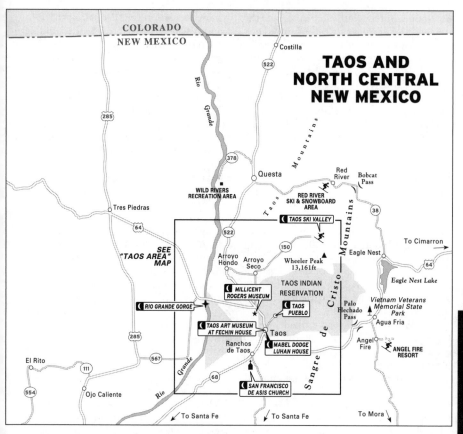

**TAOS AND NORTH CENTRAL NEW MEXICO**

busy with skiers between November and April, but as they're all up on the mountain during the day, museums scale back their hours, and residents reclaim the town center, curling up with books at one of the many coffee shops. The Taos Pueblo also closes to visitors for up to 10 weeks in February and March. By May, the peaks are relatively clear of snow, and you can hike to high meadows filled with wildflowers. Fall is dominated by the smell of wood smoke and the beat of drums, as the pueblo and the rest of the town turn out for the Feast of San Geronimo at the end of September.

If you're coming straight from Albuquerque, the trip takes about 2.5 hours along the most direct route, the "low road" through the river valley, or three hours along the high road. You'll want to stay over at least a couple of nights to make the drive worthwhile. From Santa Fe, it's possible to visit Taos as a day trip—as plenty of people do in the summertime—but you'll of course get a better sense of the place if you stay overnight. A three- or four-night visit will give you a chance to explore at a leisurely pace, with an afternoon at Taos Pueblo, a couple of mornings at galleries and museums, time for hiking or skiing, and a day tour of the Enchanted Circle. But you can also get a nice taste of Taos over a weekend, and a number of distinctive bed-and-breakfasts make it a perfect place for a short romantic getaway.

You can easily make the drive to Chama and

back in a day, though if you plan to ride the train, you'll have to get an early start or book a hotel there. As for the Enchanted Circle, the 84-mile loop is typically done as a day trip, but you may want to stay overnight in Eagle Nest or Red River, the better to take in the skiing, hiking, and rock climbing in the area. By no means attempt to visit Taos and do the Enchanted Circle loop in a single day—you'd be terribly rushed, and this is hardly the spirit of the place.

## HISTORY

The first full-time inhabitants of the area at the base of Taos Mountain were Tiwa-speaking descendants of the Ancestral Puebloans (also called Anasazi) who migrated from the Four Corners area around A.D. 1000. Taos, from Tiwa for "place of the red willows," was a thriving village when Spanish explorers, part of Francisco de Coronado's crew, arrived in 1540. By 1615, settlers had arrived and established their own small community.

The Spanish initially had difficulty establishing a toehold. The Pueblo Revolt of 1680 succeeded in driving Spanish settlers out of New Mexico for 12 years. Under the heavy hand of Governor Diego de Vargas, most of the area was reclaimed in 1692, but the Taos Pueblo Indians held out for four more violent years before they formally surrendered. The only thing that held the truce was that the Pueblo people and the Spanish both had to defend themselves against Comanche and Jicarilla Apache raiders.

By the middle of the 18th century, Taos had become moderately more secure and was an integral part of a crucial trade network, thanks in part to French fur trappers who had discovered wealth in beaver pelts from the lakes in the surrounding mountains. The little village became a place to gather and swap goods brought from Mexico and the surrounding wilderness.

Early in Taos's history, the population was so scarce and life so hard that it took only one energetic person to have a significant impact. Padre Antonio José Martinez, son of an established trader, was one of the area's most dynamic leaders in the first half of the 19th century. In 1835, he acquired the first printing press in the American west and began producing books and a newspaper. He also established a co-ed school, a seminary, and a law school. Jean Baptiste Lamy, the Frenchman appointed bishop of Santa Fe in 1853, earned the enmity of Taoseños by curtailing the popular Padre Martinez's work, even filing an order to excommunicate him. Although the papers don't appear to have been processed, Martinez claimed to have been cast out of the church, and he set up a private chapel at his house, from which he ministered until his death in 1867.

When Mexico declared independence from Spain in 1821, little changed for Taos. But in 1846, the transition to U.S. rule, following the Mexican-American war, caused much more upheaval. Wealthy Spanish landowners and Catholic priests (including Padre Martinez) foresaw their loss of influence under the Americans and plotted a rebellion. On January 19, 1847, the leaders incited a mob, many of them Indian, to kill New Mexico's first American governor, the veteran merchant Charles Bent. Elsewhere in town and the larger region, scores of other Anglo landowners were massacred before U.S. cavalry came from Santa Fe to squelch the uprising.

The last half of the 1800s saw the establishment of a mining industry in Twining (now Taos Ski Valley) and a gold rush in nearby Elizabethtown, but the 1879 arrival of the railroad in Raton to the north bumped Taos from its role as trading hub, and it slipped into backwater status. Nonetheless, the era brought colorful characters to town, some of whom would soon work their way into local legends. The six-foot-tall outlaw "Long" John Dunn, for instance, made a business in toll bridges across the Rio Grande; he also set up a gamblers' hotel and was the first car owner in Taos. He finally died in 1955.

Equally legendary were Bert Geer Phillips and Ernest Blumenschein, two painters on a jaunt from Denver in the summer of 1898 who "discovered" Taos when their wagon wheel snapped near town. After being happily

## TAOS: FACT AND FICTION

Just as San Francisco de Asis Church has inspired countless painters and photographers, the people of Taos have found their way into novels and short stories.

One of Taos's more revered figures is Padre Antonio Martinez, a popular priest and leader in the mid-1800s. So some Taos residents aren't fond of Willa Cather's *Death Comes for the Archbishop* (New York: Vintage, 1990), even if it is a literary classic. The 1927 novel is based on the mission of Jean Baptiste Lamy, who became archbishop of Santa Fe, with sympathy for his efforts to straighten out "rogue" Mexican priests like Martinez. The *padre* gets more balanced coverage in *Lamy of Santa Fe* (Middletown, Conn.: Wesleyan University Press, 2003), a biography by Paul Horgan that won a Pulitzer Prize after it was published in 1975.

Frank Waters, famous Western novelist and a Taos resident for almost 50 years, fictionalized Edith Warner, a woman who ran a small café frequented by the Los Alamos scientists while they developed the nuclear bomb. *The Woman at Otowi Crossing* (Athens, OH: Swallow Press, 1987) is his portrait of a woman who seeks isolation in the New Mexico wilderness but is drawn back into the world through

the largest event of her time. The novel is true to Warner's life, but it's rounded out by a biography, *The House at Otowi Bridge: The Story of Edith Warner & Los Alamos* (Albuquerque: University of New Mexico Press, 1979), by Peggy Pond Church, who lived at Los Alamos for 20 years before the area was taken over by the military.

Another Taos writer, John Nichols, earned acclaim for his comic novel *The Milagro Beanfield War* (New York: Owl Books, 2000), later made into a film by Robert Redford. The war of the title is an escalating squabble in a tiny village over the *acequia*, the traditional irrigation ditch that's still used in Valle Valdez and other agricultural communities in the area.

If that's all too highbrow, you can find pure pulp in Ruth Laughlin's *The Wind Leaves No Shadow* (Caldwell, ID: Caxton, 1978), a bodice-ripper based on the steamy life of Doña Barcelo Tules, who was born a pauper but grew up to be a powerful madam and gambling queen in 1830s Taos, then decamped to Santa Fe to run a high-end card house. She was the lover of Manuel Armijo, the last Mexican governor of New Mexico, then attended the U.S. Victory Ball in 1846 on the arm of American general Stephen Kearny. Allegedly.

waylaid in this inspirational place, Phillips stayed, marrying the town doctor's sister, Rose Martin. Blumenschein eventually returned with others and established the Taos Society of Artists (TSA) in 1915. In the 12 years of the TSA's existence, not only did these and other artists make names for themselves as painters of the American West, but they also put Taos on the map.

More important, the TSA piqued the curiosity of influential East Coasters. One was Mabel Dodge, a well-off, freethinking woman who had fostered art salons in New York City and Florence, then decamped to Taos in 1916. Her name—with "Luhan" appended, after she married Taos Pueblo member Tony Luhan—is now inextricably linked with Taos's

20th-century history because she had an eye for budding artists and writers and encouraged them to come live with and meet one another in Taos. D. H. Lawrence dubbed the place "Mabeltown," and figures as grand and varied as Greta Garbo, Willa Cather, Ansel Adams, Georgia O'Keeffe, Robinson Jeffers, and Carl Jung made the long trek to this dusty mountain town at her behest.

The next generation, in the 1960s, was even more dedicated to living together and sharing ideas. The New Buffalo commune in Arroyo Hondo was documented in *Easy Rider,* which in turn inspired another wave of countercultural immigrants. Longtime locals, living by very traditional mores, were horrified at the naked, hallucinogen-ingesting, free-loving, long-haired aliens who had appeared in their midst; more than a decade of antagonism followed. Eventually, however, the most extreme communes disbanded and everyone mellowed a bit with age; even members of old Spanish families now talk about maximizing the solar gain of their adobe houses.

## ORIENTATION

The area usually referred to as Taos encompasses not only the historic old town, which fans out from a main plaza, but a number of smaller surrounding communities. If you come via the low road, on Highway 68, you pass first through Ranchos de Taos. Once a distinct village, it's now connected to Taos Plaza by the least scenic part of town, a stretch of chain stores and cheap motels. Paseo del Pueblo Sur, as Highway 68 is called from Ranchos on, continues north to the central crossroads, the intersection with Kit Carson Road (U.S. 64).

After the light, the street name changes to

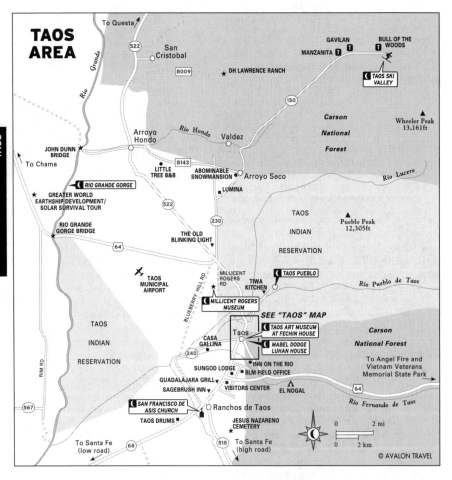

Paseo del Pueblo Norte. Where it curves west, at the northern end of the central business district, a smaller road continues north about two miles to Taos Pueblo. Paseo del Pueblo Norte carries on through the village of El Prado (now also overtaken by greater Taos) to a four-way intersection that will forever be called "the old blinking light," even though the flashing yellow signal was replaced with a newfangled three-color job in the 1990s. Here U.S. 64 regains its name, shooting west to the Rio Grande, and Highway 522 leads northwest to the outlying village of Arroyo Hondo, then to Questa and the Enchanted Circle. Highway 150, commonly called Taos Ski Valley Road, goes north to Arroyo Seco, another peripheral town that usually gets lumped in with Taos, and eventually to the base of the ski area.

# Sights

## TAOS PLAZA

Even more confusing than the patchwork of interlinked towns and highways is the fact that you can drive straight through Taos and completely miss its historic center if you're not alert. The central plaza, enclosed by adobe buildings with deep portals, is just west of the main intersection of Kit Carson Road and Paseo del Pueblo Sur. Once an informal area at the center of a cluster of settlers' homes, the plaza was established around 1615 but then destroyed in the Pueblo Revolt of 1680. New homes were built starting in 1710, but fires repeatedly gutted the block-style homes, so the buildings that currently edge the plaza all date from around 1930.

In the center is a monument to New Mexicans killed in the Bataan Death March of World War II. The U.S. flag flies day and night, a tradition carried on after an incident during the Civil War when Kit Carson and a

© ZORA O'NEILL

**Taos Plaza maintains its old adobe architecture.**

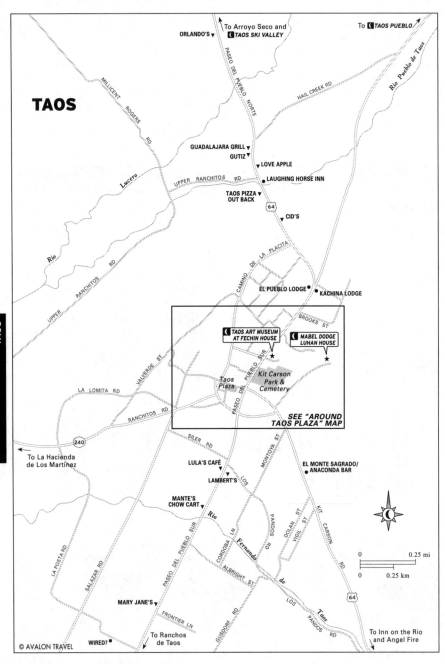

TAOS

# TAOS

To Arroyo Seco and
( TAOS SKI VALLEY
ORLANDO'S ▼

To ( TAOS PUEBLO

HAIL CREEK RD

MILLICENT ROGERS RD

Rio Pueblo de Taos

GUADALAJARA GRILL ▼
GUTIZ ▼
▼ LOVE APPLE
● LAUGHING HORSE INN

UPPER RANCHITOS RD

Lucero

TAOS PIZZA
OUT BACK ▼

64

▼ CID'S

Rio

UPPER RANCHITOS RD

CAMINO DE LA PLACITA

EL PUEBLO LODGE ●
● KACHINA LODGE

BROOKS ST

( TAOS ART MUSEUM
AT FECHIN HOUSE
★

( MABEL DODGE
LUHAN HOUSE
★

VALVERDE ST

PASEO DEL PUEBLO SUR

Taos
Plaza

Kit Carson
Park &
Cemetery

LA LOMITA RD

RANCHITOS RD

SEE "AROUND
TAOS PLAZA" MAP

240

SILER RD

To La Hacienda
de Los Martinez

LULA'S CAFÉ ▼

LAMBERT'S ▼

MONTOYA ST

EL MONTE SAGRADO/
● ANACONDA BAR

MANTE'S
CHOW CART ▼

Rio

LOS

PANDOS RD

DOLAN ST

VIGIL ST

KIT CARSON RD

LA POSTA RD

SALAZAR RD

PASEO DEL PUEBLO SUR

CORDOBA LN

Fernando

ALBRIGHT ST

de

Los

Taos

64

MARY JANE'S ▼

FRONTIER LN

GUSDORF RD

PANDOS RD

To Inn on the Rio
and Angel Fire

© AVALON TRAVEL

WIRED? ■

To Ranchos
de Taos

0          0.25 mi

0     0.25 km

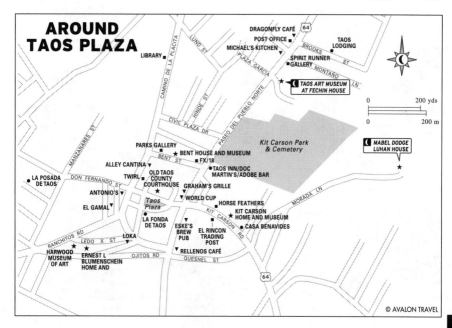

AROUND TAOS PLAZA

LUND ST
DRAGONFLY CAFÉ 64
POST OFFICE
MICHAEL'S KITCHEN
BROOKS ST
TAOS LODGING
LIBRARY
PLAZA GARCIA
SPIRIT RUNNER GALLERY
MONTANO
CAMINO DE LA PLACITA
HINDE ST
TAOS ART MUSEUM AT FECHIN HOUSE
PASEO DEL PUEBLO NORTE
CIVIC PLAZA DR

Kit Carson Park & Cemetery

0          200 yds
0          200 m

MABEL DODGE LUHAN HOUSE

MORADA LN

MANZANARES ST
PARKS GALLERY
BENT HOUSE AND MUSEUM
BENT ST
FX/18
ALLEY CANTINA
TAOS INN/DOC MARTIN'S/ADOBE BAR
DON FERNANDO ST
TWIRL    OLD TAOS COUNTY COURTHOUSE
LA POSADA DE TAOS
GRAHAM'S GRILLE
ANTONIO'S
WORLD CUP
EL GAMAL
Taos Plaza
HORSE FEATHERS
KIT CARSON HOME AND MUSEUM
KIT CARSON RD
LA FONDA DE TAOS
CASA BENAVIDES
RANCHITOS RD
LEDO X ST
LOKA
ESKE'S BREW PUB
EL RINCON TRADING POST
HARWOOD MUSEUM OF ART
ERNEST L BLUMENSCHEIN HOME AND
OJITOS RD
RELLENOS CAFÉ
QUESNEL ST
64

© AVALON TRAVEL

TAOS

crew of his men hoisted the flag and guarded it to keep Confederate sympathizers from taking it down. In front of the historic La Fonda hotel, a large bronze statue of local hero Padre Martinez gestures like a visionary—his enormous hands suggest his vast talent and influence. On the plaza's north side, the **old Taos County courthouse** contains a series of WPA-sponsored murals painted in 1934 and 1935 by Emil Bisttram and a team of other Taos artists. The door isn't always unlocked, but definitely try to get in: Enter on the ground floor through the North Plaza Art Center and go upstairs, toward the back of the building.

### Taos Inn

Distinguished by its large glowing thunderbird sign, the oldest neon sign in town, the inn was as central to previous generations of Taoseños' lives as it is now. Granted, today it's the hotel bar that everyone goes to, but starting in the 1890s, it was the home of Dr. T. P. Martin, Taos's first and only county doctor, who had a good reputation for accepting chickens or venison from his poorer patients in lieu of cash. His home looked out on a small plaza and a well—which has since been covered over and made into the hotel lobby.

## MUSEUMS

The Museum Association of Taos (www. taosmuseums.org) manages five museums in town—all of those listed below except for the Governor Bent House and the Kit Carson Home and Museum. At any of these museums, you can purchase a $25 pass, valid for a year, that grants you a single admission to all five. With individual admissions costing $7 to $10, it can be worth it if you visit three places.

## ◖ Taos Art Museum at Fechin House

This sunny space (227 Paseo del Pueblo Norte, 575/758-2690, 10 A.M.–5 P.M. Tues.–Sun., $8), former home of artist and wood-carver Nicolai Fechin, is a showcase not only for a great collection of paintings, but also for Fechin's lovely woodwork. When the Russia native moved to

The hand-built Fechin House is as beautiful as the art collection it contains.

Taos in 1927, hoping to cure his tuberculosis, he purchased seven acres of land, including the small two-story house, and, with the tools that are hidden in a small cabinet in the dining room, proceeded to hand-carve the lintels, staircases, bedsteads, and more, in a combination of Russian Tartar and local styles. His blending of traditions is flawless and natural— a small altar, also in the dining room, is set with Orthodox icons but could just as easily hold local santos.

The collection of paintings shown here is eclectic: Victor Higgins's 1936 *Indian Nude* recalls Gauguin, while Dorothy Brett's *Rainbow and Indians* from 1942 is more enamored of the powerful landscape. One room is dedicated to Fechin's own portrait work, characterized by broad, dynamic brushstrokes and a canny eye for distinctive facial features. One work is an etching of the same set of haggard, mustachioed twins rendered in oil by Ernest Hennings on a canvas hanging at the Harwood Museum. After all the work he did on the house, Fechin stayed in Taos only six years, when his wife divorced him. He moved on to Los Angeles with his daughter, Eya (her sunny study, on the ground floor, contains the child-scale furniture that her father made for her). After her father died in 1955, Eya, by then practicing psychodrama and dance therapy, returned to live in the studio (the back building that also houses the gift shop) and helped establish the main house as a museum.

### ◖ Millicent Rogers Museum

While today's style-makers jet to Dakar and Bhutan for inspiration, Millicent Rogers, a dashing, thrice-married New York City socialite and designer, moved to Taos in 1947 on a tip from a friend, Hollywood actress Janet Gaynor. Rogers brought her eye for style with her, adopting Navajo-style velvet broomstick skirts and *concho* belts and donning pounds of turquoise-and-silver jewelry for photo spreads in *Vogue* and *Harper's Bazaar*. Though she died just six years after she moved, in 1953 at the age of 51, she managed to accumulate a fantastic amount of stuff. Her namesake museum

(1504 Millicent Rogers Rd., 575/758-2462, 10 A.M.–5 P.M. daily, $10) was established by her son, Paul Peralta-Ramos, and is set in the warren of adobe rooms that make up her former home. It reflects her discerning taste, with flawless pieces of pottery, rugs, and jewelry—both local works and her own designs. Peralta-Ramos has also recently started contributing his own growing collection, including beautiful pieces of Hispano devotional art that were put on display in 2005. Aside from the individual beauty of the works, they also make up an excellent broad introduction to the artisanal work of the area, from ancient times to modern. But it's not all rooted in local culture: Rogers's goofy illustrations of a fairy tale for her children fill the last room. The gift shop here is particularly thorough and includes beautiful (though pricey) vintage jewelry and very old rugs.

## Harwood Museum of Art

This museum (238 Ledoux St., 575/758-9826, 10 A.M.–5 P.M. Tues.–Sat., noon–5 P.M. Sun., $7) set in the sprawling pueblo revival–style home of the Harwood patrons, tells the story of Taos's rise as an art colony, beginning with Ernest Blumenschein's fateful wagon accident of 1898. Modern Taos painters are represented as well in the temporary exhibit spaces upstairs, and it's interesting to see the same material— the mountain, the pueblo, the river, local residents—depicted in different styles over the decades. Also upstairs is a small but very good assortment of Hispano crafts, including a couple of santos by Patrocinio Barela, the Taos wood-carver who modernized the art in the 1930s, and some beautiful 19th-century tinwork. A separate back wing is dedicated to the ethereal abstractions of painter Agnes Martin.

## Blumenschein Home & Museum

Ernest Blumenschein, one of the founding fathers of the Taos Society of Artists, moved into this house (222 Ledoux St., 575/758-0505, 10 A.M.–5 P.M. Mon.–Sat., noon–5 P.M.

Sun., $8) in 1919 with his wife, Mary Shepard Greene Blumenschein, who was herself an accomplished artist. The house's decoration largely reflects her taste, from the sturdy wood furnishings in the dining room to the light-filled studio and the cozy wood-paneled library. Throughout, the walls are hung with sketches and paintings by their contemporaries; some of the finest are in the back "Green Room," including a beautiful monotype of Taos Mountain by Oscar E. Berninghaus. The main bedroom, entered through a steep arch, is decorated with Mary's lush illustrations for *The Arabian Nights*. Throughout, you can admire the variety of ceiling styles, from rough-hewn split cedar *(rajas)* to tidy golden aspen boughs *(latillas)*.

## La Hacienda de los Martinez

The word *hacienda* conjures a sprawling complex and rich surrounding lands, but the reality in 19th-century Taos was quite different, as this carefully restored adobe home (708 Hacienda Rd., off Ranchitos Rd., 575/758-1000, 10 A.M.–5 P.M. Mon.–Sat., noon–5 P.M. Sun., $8) from 1804 shows. Its builder and owner, Severino Martinez, was a prominent merchant who hosted the Taos trade fairs at the hacienda and eventually became the mayor of Taos in the 1820s. His oldest son was Padre Antonio Martinez, the valley leader who clashed with the French bishop Jean Baptiste Lamy. Despite the family's high social standing, life was fairly rugged, cramped, and cold: 21 simple rooms arranged around two courtyards allowed room for sleeping, cooking, and, in the single room with a wood floor, dancing. Some of the spaces have been furnished to reflect their original use; others are dedicated to exhibits, such as a very interesting display on slavery in the area, and an especially creepy wood carving of Doña Sebastiana, Lady Death, with her glittering mica eyes, in the collection of Penitente paraphernalia. During the summer months, local craftspeople are on hand to demonstrate weaving, blacksmithing, and the like in the

TAOS

© ZORA O'NEILL

**Get a glimpse of colonial life at La Hacienda de los Martinez.**

house's workshops; in the fall, the trade fair is reenacted.

## Kit Carson Home and Museum

Old photographs, memorabilia, and assorted trinkets from the frontier era conjure the spirit of the legendary scout at the Kit Carson Home and Museum (113 Kit Carson Rd., 575/758-4945, 11 A.M.–5 P.M. daily in summer, Wed.–Sun. only in winter, $5). The definitive mountain man, Carson was just one of many solitary scouts, trackers, and trappers who explored the American West. He was an intrepid adventurer who joined a wagon train headed down the Santa Fe Trail as a teenager; he arrived in Taos in 1826. His talent for tracking, hunting, and translating from Spanish and various Indian languages soon put him in high demand. Whether he was scouting for explorer John C. Frémont as Frémont mapped the trails west to Los Angeles or serving as an officer in the Civil War (or, less heroically, forcing the Navajos on the Long Walk to Fort Sumner), he used Taos as his base camp and called the

place home. He bought this house in 1843 with his third wife, Josefa Jaramillo, and they died there in 1868.

## Governor Bent House and Museum

Although it's not a member of the Museum Association of Taos, this dusty little backroom exhibit space (117 Bent St., 575/758-2376, 10 A.M.–5 P.M. daily Sept.–May, $2) is definitely worth a visit. It's the former residence of Charles Bent, who, following the Mexican-American War, was appointed the first governor of the territory of New Mexico in 1846, based on his extensive experience as a western trader (he and his brother had built Bent's Fort, an important trading center in Colorado). But Bent died in 1847, at the hands of an angry mob dissatisfied by the new American government. Amid the slightly creepy clutter (a malevolent-looking ceremonial buffalo head and more) is the very hole in the very wall that Bent's family quickly dug to escape, while Bent tried to reason with the murderous crowd. The back room only gets stranger, with surreal taxidermy, sinister doctor's instruments, and lots of old guns. The whole place may feel like an antiques store where nothing's for sale, but it still gives a surprisingly good overview of the period.

## OTHER ATTRACTIONS
### ◖ Mabel Dodge Luhan House

Now used as a conference center and B&B, arts patroness Mabel Dodge Luhan's home (240 Morada Ln., 575/751-9686, 9 A.M.–7 P.M. daily, free) is open to curious visitors as well as overnight guests. Knock at the main building first; the caretaker will give you information for a self-guided tour. Bordering the Taos Reservation, the house was built to her specifications starting in 1918, a year after she had moved to New Mexico to be with her third husband (she was Mabel Dodge Sterne at that point), then divorced him. Alongside a small original structure—a low row of adobe rooms that were already a century old at that point—she added a three-story main building, topped with a huge sunroom open on three sides. This, and the similarly glass-enclosed bathroom on the second floor, seemed a bit scandalous to her neighbors, the pueblo residents. One of them, however, didn't seem to mind—Tony Luhan, the foreman of the construction project, became her next husband. But Mabel's custom love-nest brought out some latent prurience even in D. H. Lawrence, who objected to the curtainless bathroom windows;

COURTESY TOWN OF TAOS

Mabel Dodge and her husband, Tony Luhan

### DENNIS HOPPER IN TAOS

In 1968, a Taos Pueblo elder told Dennis Hopper, "The mountain is smiling on you!" No wonder the *Easy Rider* actor and real-life renegade made the town into what he called his "heart home." His early years here were wild: He's notorious for his behavior at the Mabel Dodge Luhan House, which he bought in 1969. At one point, he rode his motorcycle across the roof. (Fortunately, it didn't cause permanent damage.) Over the decades, Taos locals came to think of him as one of their own. He mellowed just a bit, and in 2009, as part of a 40th anniversary celebration of the Summer of Love, the Harwood Museum mounted an exhibit of his photography and paintings, along with that of some of his compatriots from that era.

Hopper died not long after, in 2010, and it was no surprise he chose to be buried in Taos, after a funeral at the San Francisco de Asis Church. In attendance were fellow 1960s veterans Peter Fonda and Jack Nicholson. Following Pueblo tradition, he was buried in a pine box under a dirt mound, in Jesus Nazareno Cemetery. Fans can pay their respects there, north off Highway 518 via Espinoza Road. Or they can celebrate a new state holiday, established in 2010 by then-governor Bill Richardson: Dennis Hopper Day, decreed on May 17, the actor's birthday.

to soothe his sensibilities, if not Mabel's, he painted colorful swirls directly on the glass; you can still see them today.

## Kit Carson Cemetery

After seeing where Mabel Dodge Luhan lived, you can also visit her grave, in Taos's oldest cemetery. A shady sprawl of gravestones in a corner of Kit Carson Park, on Paseo del Pueblo Norte north of the Taos Inn, it was established in 1847 to bury the dead from the Taos Rebellion (the melée in which Governor Charles Bent was murdered). It earned its current name when the bodies of Carson and his wife were moved here in 1869, according to his will. Many of Taos's oldest families, particularly the merchants of the late 1800s, are buried here. Mabel had been a very close friend of the trader Ralph Meyers, and they often joked about being buried together. When Mabel died in 1962, a few years after Ralph, writer Frank Waters

recalled their wishes and suggested that Meyers's grave be scooted over to make room for Mabel. She was the last person to be buried in the cemetery, in 1962, and her grave is squeezed into the far southwest corner. Other local luminaries at rest here include Padre Antonio Martinez and Englishman Arthur Manby, whose grave actually stands outside of the cemetery proper, due to his lifetime of shady business deals, land grabs, and outright swindles perpetrated in town. Manby was found beheaded in his mansion in 1929, and the unsympathetic populace was happy to call it natural causes.

## ◖ San Francisco de Asis Church

Just as photographs of the Great Pyramid of Cheops seldom show the sprawl of modern Cairo crowding up to its base, San Francisco de Asis Church (east side of U.S. 68 in Ranchos de Taos, 575/758-2754, 9 A.M.–4 P.M. daily, Mass 7 A.M., 9:30 A.M., and 11:30 A.M. Sun.,

The hulking buttresses of San Francisco de Asis Church get remudded every year.

donation) as depicted in, say, Georgia O'Keeffe's paintings or Ansel Adams's photographs, is always a shadow-draped fortress isolated on a hilltop. So it's often a surprise to visitors to see the cluster of buildings that ring the small plaza in front of the church, which was built in the first half of the 18th century as a Franciscan mission for the farming community of Ranchos de Taos.

Today the adobe houses around the church hold more T-shirt shops than homes, but you can nonetheless see what has fascinated so many artists: the clean lines, the shadows created by the hulking buttresses, the rich glow of the adobe in the sun. At bottom, the church is a sort of living architecture, as much a part of the earth as something raised above it. As with every traditional adobe structure, it must be refinished every year with a mix of clay, sand, and straw; it is then coated with a fine layer of water and sand, and buffed with sheepskin. (This happens over two weeks in June, during which the church is open only at lunchtime and on Sunday.)

Inside, the whitewash walls are covered with santos and *retablos*. In the parish hall is the 1896 painting *The Shadow of the Cross* (9 A.M.–3:30 P.M. daily, $3), an eight-foot-high canvas in which the figure of Christ can be seen to luminesce—allegedly miraculously.

# ◖ TAOS PUEBLO

Even if you've been in New Mexico for a while and think you're inured to adobe, Taos Pueblo (575/758-1028, www.taospueblo.com, 8 A.M.–4:30 P.M. daily, closed for 10 weeks around Feb.–Mar., $10) is an amazing sight. Two clusters of multistory mud-brick buildings make up the core of this village, which claims, along with Acoma Pueblo, to be the oldest continually inhabited community in the United States. The current buildings, annually repaired and recoated with mud, are essentially from the 1200s, though perhaps all their components have been fully replaced several times since then. About 150 people (out of the 2,000 or so total Taos reservation members) live here year-round. The dedication of pueblo residents along with the town's designation as a UNESCO World Heritage Site have kept the place remarkably as it was in the pre-Columbian era, save for the use of adobe bricks (as opposed to clay and stone) as the main structural material, which was introduced by the Spanish. The apartment-like homes, stacked up in stages and connected by wood ladders, have no electricity or running water, though some use propane gas for heat and light.

As you explore, be careful not to intrude on spaces that are not clearly marked as shops, and stay clear of the ceremonial kiva areas on the east side of each complex. These kivas form the ritual heart of the pueblo, a secret space within a generally private culture.

## San Geronimo Church

The path past the admission gate leads directly to the central plaza, a broad expanse between **Red Willow Creek** and San Geronimo Church. The latter, built in 1850, is perhaps the newest structure in the village, a replacement for the first mission the Spanish built in 1619, using forced Indian labor. The Virgin Mary presides over the room roofed with heavy wood vigas; her clothes change with every season, a nod to her dual role as the Earth Mother. (Taking photos is strictly forbidden inside the church at all times and, as at all pueblos, at dances as well.)

The older church, to the north behind the main house, is now a cemetery—fitting, given the tragic form of its destruction. It was first torn down during the 1680 Pueblo Revolt; the Spanish rebuilt it about 20 years later. In 1847 it was again attacked, this time by American troops sent in to quell the rebellion against the new government—retaliation for the murder of Governor Charles Bent. The counterattack brutally outweighed what had sparked it: More than 100 pueblo residents, including women and children, had taken refuge inside the church when the Americans bombarded and set fire to it, killing everyone inside and gutting the building. Since then, the bell tower has been restored, but the graves have simply intermingled with the ruined walls and piles of dissolved adobe mud. All of the crosses—old carved wood to new finished stone—face sacred Taos Mountain.

## Pueblo Crafts

You are welcome to wander around and enter any of the handful of craft shops and galleries that are open—a good opportunity to see inside the mud structures and to buy some of the distinctive Taos pottery, which is only very lightly decorated but glimmers with mica from the clay particular to this area; these pots are also renowned for cooking, especially tender beans. On your way out of the pueblo, you may want to stop in at the **Oo-oonah Arts Center** (575/770-2110, 10 A.M.–4 P.M. daily Apr.–Oct.), where the gallery displays the work of pueblo children and adults enrolled in its craftwork classes. Just next door, stop for local herb tea at **Tiwa Kitchen** (575/751-

1020, 11 A.M.–5 P.M. Mon.–Sat., $8); there's a full menu of traditional food, though it's a bit uneven.

## ◖ RIO GRANDE GORGE

Heading west on U.S. 64 from the "old blinking light," you pass the Taos airstrip on the left, then, after a few more miles, the ground simply drops away. This is the Rio Grande Gorge, plunging at its most alarming point 800 feet deep into malevolent-looking black basalt. The river winds below, but it's not just millions of years of rushing water that have carved out the canyon—seismic activity also caused a rift in the earth's surface. The crack extends north to just beyond the Colorado state line and south almost to Española. The elegant, unnervingly delicate-looking bridge that spans it was built in 1965. At 650 feet above the river, the cantilever truss was a stunning engineering feat; it is still the fifth-highest of the bridge is the stretch of canyon called

© ZORA O'NEILL

View the inner workings of an eco-friendly home on the Solar Survival Tour.

## NEW MEXICO'S COMMUNES

Something about New Mexico's vast empty spaces inspires utopian thinking, as if the landscape were a blank slate, a way to start over from scratch and do things right. Spanish settlers felt it in the 16th century. Would-be gold miners banked on it in the 1800s. And in the 1960s, hippies, freethinkers, free-lovers, and back-to-the-landers fled crowded cities and boring suburbs to start life fresh in communities such as the Hog Farm and the New Buffalo Commune, both near Taos. For a while, New Mexico was the place to be: Dennis Hopper immortalized New Buffalo in his film *Easy Rider*, Janis Joplin chilled out in Truchas, and Ken Kesey drove his bus, *Further*, through the state.

To the rest of the United States, these experimental communities and their ideals seem to have been just a brief moment of zaniness –

their legacy appears to be Hog Farm leader Wavy Gravy's consecration on a Ben & Jerry's label. But in New Mexico, many of the ideals set down by naked organic gardeners and tripping visionaries have taken root and sprouted in unexpected ways. Yogi Bhajan, a Sikh who taught mass kundalini yoga sessions in New Mexico in 1969, later became a major contributor to the state economy through all the businesses he established. Buddhist stupas dot the Rio Grande Valley, the product of Anglo spiritual seekers working with Tibetan refugees brought to New Mexico by Project Tibet, co-founded by John Allen, who also ran the commune Synergia Ranch near Santa Fe. Allen was also instrumental in building Biosphere 2, the experimental glass dome in the Arizona desert – probably the most utopian vision yet to have sprouted in New Mexico.

the Taos Box, two words that will inspire wild tales in any seasoned river-runner. The Class III and IV rapids, which start around the John Dunn Bridge to the north, are held to be the best place for white-water rafting in New Mexico.

### Greater World Earthship Development

If you brave the slender bridge and continue on the west side of the gorge on U.S. 64, you soon see some odd apparitions along the right side of the road. These whimsically curved and creatively stuccoed houses are Earthships: modular, low-priced homes that function entirely separate from the public utility grid by using collected rainwater and wind and solar power. Whether it's due to the latent hippie culture or the awe-inspiring landscape, the homes have proved very popular, and you'll see them dotted around the area, as well as clustered together here at Greater World, the largest of three all-Earthship subdivisions in the area. Although they look like fanciful Hobbit homes or Mars

colony pods on the outside, Earthships are made of rather common stuff: The walls, usually built into hillsides, are stacks of used tires packed solid with rammed earth, while bottles stacked with cement and crushed aluminum cans form front walls and colorful peepholes.

The Greater World subdivision maintains a visitors center, 1.8 miles past the bridge, that's the most unconventional model home and sales office you'll ever visit. You can take the self-guided **Solar Survival Tour** (575/751-0462, www.earthship.com, 10 A.M.–4 P.M. daily, $5) of a basic Earthship and watch a video about the building process and the thinking behind the design. If you're hooked, you can of course get details on buying a lot in the development, or purchasing the plans to build your own place. Or try before you buy: You can stay the night or a week in an Earthship here, starting at $120.

### ARROYO SECO

Bemoaning the gallerification of downtown Taos? The sheer touristy mayhem? From the

TAOS

old blinking light, head north on Highway 150 to the village of Arroyo Seco, a cluster of buildings at a bend in the road to the ski area, and you'll slip back a couple of decades. Sure, there's some art up here too, but this smaller community, though only a half-hour drive from the Taos plaza, maintains an even more laid-back and funky attitude than Taos—if such a thing is possible.

"Downtown" Arroyo Seco has grown up around **La Santísima Trinidad Church,** set back from Highway 150 on the left. **Arroyo Seco Mercantile** (Hwy. 150, 575/776-8806) is the town's former general store, now a highly evolved junk shop that has maintained the beautiful old wood-and-glass display cases. Its stock ranges from the practical (books on passive-solar engineering and raising llamas) to the frivolous and the beautiful, like antique wool blankets. Across the street, **Abe's Cantina y Cocina** (489 Hwy. 150, 575/776-8643, 7 A.M.–5:30 P.M. daily) is a very old-style bar propped up by locals for countless decades; visit the adjacent lunch counter and peek in the side, if you don't fancy making a dramatic front-door entrance to a crowd of taciturn Spanish men in cowboy hats. **Taos Cow** (485 Hwy. 150, 575/776-5640, 7 A.M.–6 P.M. daily), the coffee shop next door and known as "The Cow," is the hangout for everyone who doesn't fit in at Abe's—many of them guests at The Abominable Snowmansion hostel down the block.

## TAOS SKI VALLEY

Heading out of Arroyo Seco, Highway 150 briefly edges fertile Valle Valdez, then begins to weave up through the Hondo Canyon, the steep mountain slopes crowded with tall, dense pines. In the wintertime, the mountaintops are often obscured by a wreath of clouds. The road dead-ends at Taos Ski Valley, a resort area that is technically an incorporated village, but only the mountain, along with the snow on top of it, matters to most people. When you finally get out of the car at the base of the ski runs and take in the vertiginous view toward Kachina Peak (elevation 12,481 feet and often white-capped even in July), you'll see why it inspires legions of reverential skiers every winter, when an average of 305 inches of snow falls on the mountain—almost 10 times the amount they get down in town.

And in fact, for decades, it was *only* skiers here. Snowboarders were banned, allegedly because of the seriously precipitous slopes—more than half the trails are rated expert level, and many of them are left ungroomed. But the slopes were finally opened to all in 2008, in the last days of the ski season. It's a sea of change for TSV's seriously loyal customers, and it leaves just three resorts in the country that don't allow snowboarding (Utah's Deer Valley and Alta, and Mad River Glen in Vermont).

In the summertime, Hondo Canyon's many trails make for very good hiking or picnicking. The road is dotted on either side with picnic areas and campgrounds—Cuchilla del Medio is a particularly nice area for a picnic.

# Entertainment

Taos is a small town. That means no glitzy dance clubs, no bars where you're expected to dress up. Nighttime fun is concentrated in a handful of places where, if you visit frequently enough, you'll get to know the regulars quickly. The various town-wide celebrations—including music and dancing on the plaza on summer Thursdays—draw a full cross-section of the population.

## BARS
### Taos Pub Crawl
Starting around 5 P.M., the **Adobe Bar** (125 Paseo del Pueblo Norte, 575/758-2233), in the lobby of the Taos Inn, is where you'll run into everyone you've seen over the course of the day, sipping a Cowboy Buddha ($10) or some other specialty margarita—the best in town. Mellow jazz or acoustic guitar sets the mood Wednesday–Sunday. To give the poor hotel residents a break, the bar closes at 10 P.M., which forces all the regulars to move on down the road to the next phase of the evening: the dance floor at the **Sagebrush Inn** (1508 Paseo del Pueblo Sur, 575/758-2254). It gets packed with cowboy-booted couples stepping lively to decent country cover bands whose members always seem to resemble Kenny Rogers. The scene encompasses all of Taos, from artists to pueblo residents to mountain men with grizzled beards. Booze is a bargain, and the fireplace is big. After the band wraps up around midnight, the most dedicated move on to **The Alley Cantina** (121 Teresina Ln., 575/758-2121) for another hour or so. This warren of interconnected rooms (one of which claims to be the oldest in Taos . . but don't they all say that?) can be baffling after a few drinks. There's shuffleboard for entertainment if you're not

TAOS

## PUEBLO DANCES: WHAT TO EXPECT

Visiting a pueblo for a ceremonial dance or feast-day celebration is one of the most memorable parts of a visit to northern New Mexico. The animal dances are particularly transporting – dressed in pelts and mimicking the movements of a deer, for instance, the dancers transform the plaza into a forest glade. While the state's American Indian culture can occasionally seem exploited for its tourism value, a pueblo dance is not at all for the benefit of tourists. It is a ceremony and a religious ritual, not a performance – you are a guest, not an audience.

Keep this in mind as a guide to your own behavior. Applause is not appropriate, nor is conversation during the dance. Queries about the meaning of the dances are generally not appreciated. Never walk in the dance area, and try not to block the view of pueblo residents. The kivas, as holy spaces, are always off-limits to outsiders. During feast days, though, some pueblo residents may open their doors to visitors, perhaps for a snack or drink – but be considerate of others who may also want to visit, and don't stay too long. Photography is strictly forbidden at dances, sometimes with the exception of Los Matachines, which is not a religious ritual. Don't even think about trying to sneak a shot with your camera phone, as tribal police will be more than happy to confiscate it.

On a practical level, be prepared for a lot of waiting around. Start times are always approximate, and everything depends on when the dancers are done with their kiva rituals. There will usually be a main, seasonal dance – such as the corn dance – followed by several others. If you go in the winter, dress very warmly, but in layers – a Christmas Eve Mass may start inside the close-packed, overheated church and then dances may continue outside in the near-freezing cold.

## CEREMONIAL DANCES AT TAOS PUEBLO

In addition to the Feast of San Geronimo, visitors are welcome to attend ceremonial dances. This is only an approximate schedule – dates can vary from year to year, as can the particular dances. Contact the pueblo (505/758-1028, www.taospueblo.com) for times, or check the listings in the *Tempo* section of the paper for that week. Every night May through October, there are dance performances as the Best Western Kachina Lodge (413 Paseo del Pueblo Norte) – sure, a little touristy, but nice if your trip doesn't coincide with a ceremonial dance at the pueblo itself.

**JANUARY 1**
- Turtle dance

**JANUARY 6**
- Deer or buffalo dance

**MAY 3**
- Feast of Santa Cruz: corn dance

**JUNE 13**
- Feast of San Antonio: corn dance

**JUNE 24**
- Feast of San Juan: corn dance

**JULY 25 AND 26**
- Feast of Santiago and Santa Ana: corn dances and footraces

**SEPTEMBER 29-30**
- Feast of San Geronimo

**DECEMBER 24**
- Sundown procession and children's dance

**DECEMBER 25**
- Various dances

into the ensemble onstage—its name usually ends in "Blues Band"; a $3 or $4 cover usually applies on weekends. The kitchen is open until 11 P.M., and it's not a bad place for a lunchtime burger ($6) either.

### Other Bars

In addition to the Big Three, a few other watering holes draw a crowd, usually for live music of some kind. Wood-paneled **Eske's Brew Pub** (106 Des Georges Ln., 575/758-1517) is across from the plaza, tucked back from the southeast corner of the intersection of Paseo del Pueblo Sur and Kit Carson Road. With live music on Fridays and Saturdays, it serves its house-made beer to a chummy après-ski crowd. You're in New Mexico—you should at least *try* the green-chile ale.

Named for its location one mile from the landmark traffic signal, **The Old Blinking Light** (100 Hwy. 150, 575/776-8787) is a casual, sprawling restaurant and bar where locals head for live bands. The food is only so-so (except for the deadly Mud Pie), but the atmosphere is very mellow and friendly, especially Monday nights for live music and on weekend afternoons, when people bring their kids to run around the back garden. If you're on the lookout for Julia Roberts, this is a good bet; so far, Donald Rumsfeld hasn't been spotted.

Taos's swankiest boîte—really, the only place in town that could be called a boîte—is the moodily lit **Anaconda Bar** in El Monte Sagrado resort (317 Kit Carson Rd., 575/758-3502), where deep semicircle leather booths curve around tables built of African drums. Skilled bartenders whip up pomegranate margaritas, and the list of wines by the glass is varied. Starting around 9:30 P.M. most nights, there's a not-too-intrusive live band.

### FESTIVALS AND EVENTS

Taos's biggest annual festivity (for which many local businesses close) is the **Feast of San**

**Geronimo,** the patron saint assigned to Taos Pueblo by the Spanish when they built their first mission there in 1619. The holiday starts the evening of September 29 with vespers in the pueblo church and continues the next day with footraces and a pole-climbing contest. La Hacienda de los Martinez usually reenacts a 19th-century Taos trade fair, with mountain men, music, and artisans' demonstrations.

Taos galleries put out their finest at the spring (Apr.–May) and fall (Sept.–Oct.) at **Taos Arts Festival** (www.taosfallarts.com), two-week-long exhibitions of the works of more than 150 Taos County artists. And if it's counterculture you're after, every June the **Taos Solar Music Festival** (www.solarmusicfest.com) takes place at an off-the-grid stage near the Earthship development west of the Rio Grande Gorge. The event draws a wild mix of dedicated campers and sun-worshippers, as well as diverse performers that have included Steve Earle, Harry Belafonte, and Los Lobos.

The glow of luminarias and torchlight on snow produces a magical effect—perhaps that's why Taos has so many winter events. On the first weekend in December, the **tree-lighting ceremony** on the plaza draws the whole town, and the rest of the season sees numerous celebrations, such as the reenactments of the Virgin's search for shelter, called Las Posadas, which take place at Our Lady of Guadalupe Church west of the plaza on the third weekend in December. At the pueblo, vespers is said at San Geronimo church on Christmas Eve, typically followed by a children's dance. On Christmas Day, the pueblo hosts either a deer dance or the Spanish Los Matachines dance.

# Shopping

Taos Plaza is ringed with less-than-inspiring souvenir stores. Two further clusters of boutiques and art dealers lie just north of the plaza—very pleasant places to browse, though you certainly won't find any bargains. The beginning stretch of Kit Carson Road has a more varied selection of shops with more affordable prices.

## GALLERIES

If you're hoping to discover Taos's next big art star, poke around smaller operations on back streets and in Arroyo Seco, or just keep your eyes open when you get your morning coffee—nearly every business doubles as a gallery in this town.

The town's best gallery for contemporary art is **Parks Gallery** (127 Bent St., 575/751-0343, 10 A.M.–5 P.M. Mon.–Sat.), where the selection of styles and media is extremely varied. Halfway to Arroyo Seco, turn off Highway 150 to reach **Lumina** gallery and sculpture gardens (11 Hwy. 230, 575/776-0123, 10:30 A.M.–5:30 P.M. Thurs.–Mon.), which has a very broad stable of artists, from a local from Santa Clara Pueblo who inlays pottery bowls with turquoise and shells to very contemporary photomontage artists. The elegant Japanese gardens are studded with monumental sculptures.

And visiting some of the town institutions can round out your experience at the museums. **Spirit Runner** (303 Paseo del Pueblo Norte, 575/758-1132, 10 A.M.–5 P.M. Tues.–Sun.), for instance, is operated by Ouray Meyers, son of Ralph Meyers, the first Anglo man to deal in Indian art in his trading post. His gallery is as much a social hub as an art dealership, and he has some tales to tell.

## GIFTS AND JEWELRY

Gussy yourself up in Western trappings from **Horse Feathers** (109-B Kit Carson Rd., 575/758-7457, 10:30 A.M.–5:30 P.M. daily), where you can pick up a full cowpoke getup, from ten-gallon hat to jingling spurs. The big money is in the room full of vintage cowboy boots, but you can find less expensive,

El Rincon was the first trading post in Taos to deal in crafts and jewelry from Taos Pueblo.

eclectic gift items, such as giant belt buckles or campfire cookbooks from 1900. **El Rincon Trading Post** (114 Kit Carson Rd., 575/758-9188, 9:30 A.M.–5:30 P.M. Tues.–Sun.) is crammed with stuff, some of it perhaps dating back to 1909, when Ralph Meyers established his Mission Shop trading post. Today the trove is managed by his daughter, who has put aside many of the best pieces in an informal "museum," but there are still plenty of one-of-a-kind *concho* belts and other jewelry, as well as beads and baubles from elsewhere in the world. And if you want more of this odd browsing, make sure you get out to **Arroyo Seco Mercantile,** described in more detail in the *Arroyo Seco* section in *Sights.*

**FX/18** (103-C Bent St., 575/758-8590, 10 A.M.–5 P.M. Thurs.–Tues., noon–5 P.M. Wed.) has a great selection, from groovy housewares to lively kids' stuff to nifty stationery. The selection of contemporary Southwest-style jewelry is particularly good.

Outside Taos are a number of sheep ranches, and **La Lana Wools** (136-C Paseo del Pueblo Norte, 575/758-9631, 10 A.M.–5:30 P.M. daily) shows off many of their products, from skeins of richly colored yarn (knitters will swoon) through to handwoven cloaks.

Not so soothing but a whole lot of fun, **Taos Drums** (3956 Hwy. 68, 800/424-3786, 8 A.M.–5 P.M. Mon.–Fri.) is a giant shop and factory dedicated to making Taos Pueblo–style percussion instruments, from thin hand drums to great booming ones made of hollow logs. Trying out the wares is encouraged—it's a good place to bring the kids. The shop is located on the west side of the highway five miles south of the plaza.

## TOYS

Taos is also home to an exceptionally magical toy store, **Twirl** (225 Camino de la Placita, 575/751-1402, www.twirlhouse.com, 10 A.M.–6 P.M. daily). Tucked in a series of low-ceiling adobe rooms, it's crammed with everything from science experiments to wooden trains to fairy costumes. Even the kiva fireplace gets a fantastical 1,001 Nights treatment, and there's a big roster of activities in the huge play space out back.

# Sports and Recreation

If you don't go hiking, mountain biking, or skiing in Taos, you're missing a lot of the town's appeal—the wild setting presses in all around, and Taos Mountain looms up behind every town view. Downhill skiing is the main draw in the winter, just a 45-minute drive from central Taos, but you can also try more solitary snowshoeing and Nordic skiing. In summer, peak-baggers will want to strike out for Wheeler Peak, the state's highest, while rafters, rock climbers, and mountain bikers can head the other direction, to the dramatic basalt cliffs of the Rio Grande Gorge where river-runners challenge the churning rapids of the legendary Taos Box (late May and early June is the best season for this).

Stop in at the **Carson National Forest Supervisor's Office** (208 Cruz Alta Rd., 575/758-6200, 8:30 A.M.–4:30 P.M. Mon.–Fri.) for advice, booklets on recommended trails, and maps. Just down the street, the **Bureau of Land Management Taos Field Office** (226 Cruz Alta Rd., 575/758-8851, 8 A.M.–4:30 P.M. Mon.–Fri.) can help you prepare for a rafting or longer camping trip, with plenty of maps and brochures.

Sudden thunderstorms are common in the summer months, as are flash floods and even freak blizzards. Well into May, snow can blanket some of the higher passes, so wherever you go, always carry more warm clothing than you think you'll need, and don't skimp on the sunscreen, even when it's below freezing.

## SKIING AND SNOWSHOEING

**Taos Ski Valley** (866/968-7386, www.skitaos. org, $71 full-day lift ticket) is the premier spot for downhill skiing. The resort is open from late November through the first weekend in April, with 110 trails served by 12 lifts and snowmaking capacity on all beginner and intermediate areas in dry spells. The dedicated can do the hike up to Kachina Peak, an additional 632 feet past where the lift service ends. Don't be too intimidated by the trails:

The highly regarded Ernie Blake Snowsports School is one of the best places to learn the basics or polish your skills. Novice "yellowbirds" can take one ($90) or two ($150) days of intensive instruction specially geared to new skiers.

For cross-country skiing and snowshoeing, **Enchanted Forest,** between Elizabethtown and Red River on the Enchanted Circle loop, offers miles of groomed trails, and there are also easy access points in the Carson National Forest—at Capulin Campground on U.S. 64, for instance, five miles east of Taos; along **Manzanita Trail** in the Hondo Canyon on the road to the ski valley; and, especially good for snowshoeing, the **Bull of the Woods Trail,** which starts off Twining Road, at the far end of the ski area parking lot, and leads in about 2.5 miles to a high pasture, then another 5.5 miles up to Wheeler Peak, if you're feeling extremely energetic.

Snowboarders were allowed at Taos Ski Valley only in 2008.

Don't have your own gear? **Cottam's Ski & Outdoor** (207-A Paseo del Pueblo Sur, 575/758-2822, 7 A.M.–7 P.M. Mon.–Fri., 7 A.M.–8 P.M. Sat. and Sun.) has the biggest stock of rental skis, snowboards, and snowshoes. The shop also sells everything else you'll need to get out and enjoy the snow; there's another location at the ski valley (575/776-8719) and one at Angel Fire (575/377-3700).

## HIKING

With Taos Mountain in the backyard, hiking around here ranges from rambles along winding rivers to intensive hauls that gain 2,000 feet in less than four miles. Be prepared for a cold snap or storm at any time, and don't plan on doing much before May. The most accessible and varied trails are along the road to Taos Ski Valley: Off Twining Road, in the base of the ski valley, the grueling trail to **Wheeler Peak** begins, a 16-mile roundtrip that only the very fit should attempt in one day. The **Gavilan Trail** is also recommended—it's plenty steep as well but leads to a high mountain meadow. The route is five miles roundtrip, or you can connect with other trails once you're up on the rim. If this sounds too strenuous, you can always take the chairlift up to the top of the mountain (10 A.M.–4:30 P.M. Thurs.–Mon. late June–Sept., $10), then wander down any of several wide, well-marked trails, all with stunning views. A variety of trails course through **Taos Canyon** east of town, with numerous campgrounds and trailheads off U.S. 64, including the **South Boundary Trail,** 22 miles up and over the pass, with views onto Moreno Valley.

## BIKING

A popular trail ride close to town is along the west rim of the Rio Grande Gorge, either from the gorge bridge up to John Dunn Bridge, about 15 miles round-trip, or from the gorge bridge south to the Taos Junction bridge near Pilar, about 18 miles out and back. Either way, you'll have great views and fairly level but rugged terrain. A more aggressive ride is the 22-mile South Boundary Trail (see *Angel Fire* in *The Enchanted Circle* section). **Native Sons**

**Adventures** (1033-A Paseo del Pueblo Sur, 575/758-9342, www.nativesonsadventures. com) can provide maps and shuttle service to and from trailheads. It also runs half- and full-day tours to these and several other trails, as well as hiker-biker combo trips. Angel Fire and Red River both open their slopes to mountain bikers in the summer, with access to the peaks on the chairlift.

If you prefer road touring, you can make a pleasant loop from Taos through Arroyo Hondo and Arroyo Seco. The 25-mile route has no steep grades and is a good way to get adjusted to the altitude. Head north up Paseo del Pueblo Norte, straight through the intersection with Highway 150, then turn right in Arroyo Hondo onto County Road B-143; this road winds up into Arroyo Seco, eventually dead-ending on Highway 230. Turn right, and you'll merge with Highway 150 in a couple of miles. The standard challenge is the 84-mile Enchanted Circle loop; every September sees the Enchanted Circle Century Bike Tour, sponsored by the Red River chamber of commerce (800/348-6444 for information). A mountain-biking race takes place the day after.

**Gearing Up** (129 Paseo del Pueblo Sur, 575/751-0365, 9:30 A.M.–6 P.M. Mon.–Sat., noon–6 P.M. Sun.) rents mountain and hybrid bicycles for $35 per day, with discounts for longer terms. If you're bringing your bicycle with you, consider having it shipped here, and they'll reassemble it and have it waiting when you arrive.

## RAFTING AND TUBING

The **Taos Box,** the 16-mile stretch of the Rio Grande south of the John Dunn Bridge down to near Pilar, provides perhaps the best rafting in New Mexico, with Class III rapids with ominous names like Boat Reamer and Screaming Left-Hand Turn. The river mellows out a bit south of the Taos Box, then leads into a shorter Class III section called the Racecourse—the most popular run, usually done as a half-day trip. Beyond this, in the Orilla Verde Recreation Area around Pilar, the water is wide and flat, a place for a relaxing float with kids or other water newbies; you can flop in an inner tube if you really want to chill out. North of the John Dunn Bridge, there's another intermediate run called La Junta that's a half-day trip. **Los Rios River Runners** (575/776-8854, www.losriosriverrunners.com) leads trips to all these spots, as half-day outings ($48), day trips (from $89), and overnight trips. The best season is late May and early June, when the water is high from mountain runoff. **Far-Flung Adventures** (575/758-2628, www.farflung.com) is another outfitter, and can add on rock climbing and horseback riding as well. With both organizations, you can choose whether you want a paddle boat—where you're actively (and sometimes strenuously) paddling—or an oar boat, where guides row, and you can sit back.

## SPORTS FACILITIES

The **Taos Youth and Family Center** (407 Paseo del Cañon, 575/758-4160, 9 A.M.–9 P.M. Mon.–Sat., 10 A.M.–7 P.M. Sun.) has a big indoor pool, as well as an ice-skating rink.

© ZORA O'NEILL

The whitewater surges on the Rio Grande from Taos to Pilar.

# Accommodations

Taos hotels can be a bit overpriced, especially on the lower end, where there are few reliable bargains. But because Taos is awash in centuries-old houses with impressive cultural and historic pedigrees, bed-and-breakfasts have thrived. For those skeptical of B&Bs, don't despair: The majority of them have private bathrooms, separate entrances, and not too much country-cute decor. Certainly, just as in Santa Fe, the Southwest trim can be applied with a heavy hand, but wood-burning fireplaces, well-stocked libraries, hot tubs, and big gardens can make up for that.

Also consider staying outside of Taos proper. Arroyo Seco is about a half-hour drive from the plaza, as is the Earthship subdivision, and rates here and in Ranchos de Taos are a little lower. In the summer, the lodges near the ski valley cut their prices by almost half—a great deal if you want to spend some time hiking in the canyon and don't mind driving into town for food and entertainment. If you're arriving in town without a car, a few good budget choices are served by Taos's Chile Line bus, which caters to skiers in the winter, from down on the southern end of town all the way up to the ski valley.

## UNDER $100

The best lodging bargain in the Taos area is **The Abominable Snowmansion** (Hwy. 150 in Arroyo Seco, 575/776-8298, www.abominablesnowmansion.com, $22 pp). Conveniently set midway to the Taos Ski Valley in bustling "downtown" Arroyo Seco, this is a cheerful HI hostel offering bunks in dorm rooms ($22 in winter, $19 in summer) and private rooms with shared or private bath ($44–55). In the summer, you can camp or sleep in a tepee, and nosh on veggies from the hostel garden. But as the name suggests, winter sports fanatics are the main clientele, and if you don't want to be woken by skiers racing for the Chile Line bus outside, opt for an individual cabin with shared bath ($32).

Of the various motels on the south side, **Sungod Lodge** (919 Paseo del Pueblo Sur, 575/758-3162, www.sungodlodge.com, $60 d) is one of the better options, with a grassy central courtyard and more personal feel than the chains. The room decor is dated (teal and dusty rose abound), but new owners are gradually sprucing things up. To avoid traffic noise, you might prefer the back building, where some rooms have fireplaces.

**The Laughing Horse Inn** (729 Paseo del Pueblo Norte, 800/776-0161, www.laughinghorseinn.com, $68 d), one of Taos's most popular budget B&Bs, cultivates an eccentric reputation, with a guest list of starving artists and Europeans on vision quests. Ten rooms in the main adobe house give new meaning to the word "snug" (some have loft beds; one has a sauna) and share three bathrooms. Solo travelers can get better value elsewhere, but for couples or families, the place isn't a bad deal. The penthouse A-frame suite, which conjures some of the bygone hippie charm, has a big deck and room for six to sleep ($160 for two). An honor-system kitchen, a clothing-optional hot tub, and continental breakfasts of organic, locally farmed foodstuffs add to the throwback feel.

Not a hotel at all, but simply a clutch of well-maintained one- and two-bedroom private casitas, **Taos Lodging** (109 Brooks St., 575/751-1771, www.taoslodging.com, $75 studio) is in a quiet, convenient block about a 10 minutes' walk north from the plaza. The eight cottages, arranged around a central courtyard, have assorted floor plans, but all have porches, full kitchens, and living rooms, as well as access to a shared outdoor hot tub. The smallest, a 350-square-foot studio, sleeps two comfortably; the largest ($130 for two), at 800 square feet, sleeps up to six.

**El Pueblo Lodge** (412 Paseo del Pueblo Norte, 575/758-8700, www.elpueblolodge.com, $74 s, $89 d) is a budget operation with

slightly spacey management but nice perks such as free laundry. Rooms vary wildly, from a tiny, very atmospheric nook in the oldest adobe section to new, slick motel rooms complete with gas fireplaces; those in the 1960s motel strip are a good combo of atmosphere and tidiness. The grounds are pleasant, with a heated pool, a hot tub, and hammocks slung between the big cottonwoods in the summertime.

In addition to being a tourist attraction, the ◖ **Mabel Dodge Luhan House** (240 Morada Ln., 575/751-9686, www.mabeldodgeluhan.com, $98 d) also functions as a homey bed-and-breakfast. Choose one of the snug little rooms in the oldest adobe section, all furnished with rickety antiques, floors worn down from years of treading, and tiny fireplaces; or one of the rooms in the main house: Mabel's original bedroom ($195) is the grandest (you can even sleep in her bed), but for those who don't mind waking at the crack of dawn, the upstairs solarium ($125) is gloriously sunny with gorgeous views of the mountain. Either way, you'll feel a little like you're bunking in a historical museum.

## $100-150

**Casa Benavides** (137 Kit Carson Rd., 575/758-1772, www.taos-casabenavides.com, $105 s) calls itself a B&B, but now it feels a bit more like a small hotel, as it sprawls down Kit Carson Road in a series of interconnected buildings, one of which is a wood Victorian built around 1900. The owners, a local family, have put a lot of care into the decoration of the 39 rooms with Taos-style furniture and Western artifacts. Each one is different, which makes the options a little overwhelming—but if you have an odd-size group, there's likely a room configuration for you. The two small (and cheap) upstairs rooms in the Benavides family home have balconies with mountain views.

A relatively generic chain hotel, **Best Western Kachina Lodge** (413 Paseo del Pueblo Norte, 575/758-2275, www.kachinalodge.com, $119 d) is notable because it can be a great deal when booked online, often less than $100. Rooms are large and reasonably

© ZORA O'NEILL

Mabel Dodge Luhan hosted arts salons and famous visitors in her sprawling home.

TAOS

well kept, a full breakfast is included in the rate, and there's a big pool.

For an only-in-Taos experience, stay the night in an **Earthship** (U.S. 64, 575/751-0462, www.earthship.com, $120 d). Three of the curvy, off-the-grid homes are available, with room for up to six people in the largest one. Not only does an Earthship feel like a Hobbit house with banana trees (in the south-facing greenhouse areas), but you're out in the larger, all-Earthship subdivision, with great views of the mountain. And yes, there's running water, refrigerators, and all the other comforts.

**( Inn on the Rio** (910 E. Kit Carson Rd., 575/758-7199, www.innontherio.com, $124 d) might be more accurately called Motel on the Creek. But what a motel: Each of the 12 thick-walled rooms is meticulously decorated with an artistic eye. Rich colors liven up the walls, and vintage Southwestern knickknacks add flair without being kitschy. The vintage wall heaters, still cranking from the old motor-court days, keep the rooms as toasty as a fireplace would. A hot tub between the two wings, plus luxe sheets and locally made bath gels, add

unexpected luxury. Pair this with longtime resident owners and a great morning meal, and you have all the benefits of a bed-and-breakfast without the feeling that you have to tiptoe in late at night.

Out near Arroyo Hondo, the house-proud owner of **( Little Tree B&B** (226 Hondo–Seco Rd., 575/776-8467, www.littletreebandb.com, $135 d) is a history buff—his expertise is a perk that comes with a stay at this snug inn with four rooms. The house and its small outbuilding are rare examples of old-school adobe (no stucco finish) *without* the stamp of history; a Taos Pueblo expert built them in 1990 using a range of mud finishes and decorative techniques. The feeling is rustic, authentic, but also very comfortable. One of the three rooms has a private hot tub, and all three have wood-burning fireplaces or stoves.

## $150-250

**( La Posada de Taos** (309 Juanita Ln., 575/758-8164, www.laposadadetaos.com, $150 d) hits the sweet spot between luxury comforts and casual charm—all the amenities are here, such as wood fireplaces (in five of the six rooms) and whirlpool tubs (in three), but the overall atmosphere is very homey and informal, and the decor is distinctly Taos without being heavy-handed, with sparing country touches. The price is right too, coming in on the lower end compared to other places with the same perks. El Solecito, in the older adobe section with its own back terrace, is recommended.

Of the two landmark hotels in town, **Hotel La Fonda de Taos** (108 S. Plaza, 575/758-2211, www.lafondataos.com, $160 d) has a few more modern perks. With gas fireplaces rather than wood, the rooms don't ooze atmosphere, but the beds are very nice, there's DSL, and you can feel quite grand opening your balcony doors over the plaza (request no. 301 or 302). Don't miss the small collection of D. H. Lawrence's erotic paintings (10 A.M., noon, 2 P.M., 4 P.M., and 6 P.M.; $3 admission); they're tucked in a small room behind the front desk. But the **Historic Taos Inn** (125 Paseo del Pueblo Norte, 575/758-2233, www.taosinn.com, $105 s, $165 d) has a cozier feeling. Rooms in the main building are subject to noise from the popular bar, but only until 10 P.M. (and can be a bargain for solo travelers). In the courtyard section or other outbuildings, you may get a kiva fireplace.

If you like eye candy, you'll love **Casa Gallina** (613 Callejon, 575/758-2306, www.

casagallina.net, $160 d), a collection of three guest cottages, each decorated with an artist's eye for color and texture to showcase beautiful handicrafts from Taos and around the globe. Two of three have full kitchens, and the other has a kitchenette—you can stock them with occasional goodies from the garden and eggs from the resident hens (they're also pressed into service for the fresh and delicious breakfasts). And it doesn't hurt that the meticulous owner also happens to be a massage therapist.

A successful experiment in sustainable development is also Taos's most luxurious lodging: **El Monte Sagrado** (317 Kit Carson Rd., 575/758-3502, www.elmontesagrado.com, $169 d), a soothing retreat that's still walking distance from the plaza. If they weren't pointed out to you, you'd probably never even notice the solar panels and the ingenious water-reuse system. Instead, eclectic style draws the eye, at least in the casitas ($199), some decorated with hand-painted trout, or in a deluxe global suite ($419) filled with Chinese antiques. The Taos Mountain rooms are a little less exciting, with their standard white-linens-and-dark-wood look, but a reasonable price for entry into the swank grounds, which include a lovely spa. The online booking system doesn't differentiate room styles well—if you have your eye on a particular room, it's better to call to reserve.

# Food

For a town of its size, Taos has a surprisingly broad selection of restaurants—though some of the most creative are open only for breakfast and lunch. If you're in town during a holiday or peak ski season, you might want to make reservations, but otherwise they're not necessary, and the whole Taos dining scene is exceptionally casual. The breakfast burrito—a combo of scrambled eggs, green chile, hash browns, and bacon or sausage wrapped in a flour tortilla—is commonly wrapped up in foil and served to

go, perfect if you want an early start hiking or skiing.

## COFFEE AND DESSERT

The location of **World Cup** on the corner of the plaza (102-A Paseo del Pueblo Norte, 575/737-5299, 7 A.M.–7 P.M. daily, $3) makes it a popular pit stop for both tourists and locals—the latter typically of the drumming, dreadlocked variety, lounging on the stoop. At the top of Ledoux Street, **Loka** (112-E Camino de la

Placita, 575/758-4204, 8 A.M.–3 P.M. Mon.–Sat., $3–8) is a sunny gallery/coffee bar where the baked goods are as gorgeous as the contemporary art on the walls. As a historical side note, it occupies the former offices of *El Crepúsculo de la Libertad,* the paper started by Padre Antonio Martinez.

In Arroyo Seco, most people start the day at **Taos Cow** (485 Hwy. 150, 575/776-5640, 7 A.M.–6 P.M. daily), a chilled-out coffee bar par excellence, with writers scribbling in one corner and flute players jamming in another. But it's the ice cream that has made the Taos Cow name: Cherry Ristra, for instance, is vanilla with piñon nuts, dark chocolate, and cherries. Sandwiches ($8) are an option too, if you want real sustenance.

## BREAKFAST AND LUNCH

**Michael's Kitchen** (304-C Paseo del Pueblo Norte, 575/758-4178, 7 A.M.–2:30 P.M. Mon.–Thurs., 7 A.M.–8 P.M. Fri.–Sun., $8) is famous for New Mexican breakfast items like huevos rancheros and blue corn pancakes with pine nuts, served all day, but everyone will find something they like on the extensive menu at this down-home wood-paneled family restaurant filled with chatter and the clatter of dishes. "Health Food," for instance, is a double order of chile cheese fries. The front room is devoted to gooey doughnuts, cinnamon rolls, and pie.

Euro-Latino might be the best catch-all term for the menu at ◖ **Gutiz** (812-B Paseo del Pueblo Norte, 575/758-1226, 8 A.M.–3 P.M. Tues.–Sun., $9), but of course you'll find green chile in some dishes—and then there's the unclassifiable French toast, which involves raspberry cream and peanut butter (honest, it's good!). Other inventive breakfast dishes include poached eggs and salsa on subtly spiced Spanish rice. Or you can opt for a more traditional *croque monsieur* for lunch.

At the homey **Dragonfly Café** (402 Paseo del Pueblo Norte, 575/737-5859, 11 A.M.–9 P.M. Mon. and Wed.–Sat., 9 A.M.–3 P.M. Sun. $15), you can choose your table according to which novelty set of salt-and-pepper shakers you prefer. The menu is eclectic and hearty (a tender lamb kebab, for instance, or a veggie-filled bowl of Korean *bibimbop*); Sunday brunch features delicious baked goods and innovations like gingerbread given a French-toast treatment.

Just west of the plaza, **El Gamal** (112 Doña Luz St., 575/613-0311, 7 A.M.–6 P.M. Sun.–Thurs., 7 A.M.–5:30 P.M. Fri., $7) brings the best of Israeli street snacks to Taos, with *shakshuka* (spicy scrambled eggs) for breakfast and falafel and *sabich* (eggplant and egg) sandwiches at lunch, washed down with a fizzy yogurt soda. There's also more standard hippie fare on the menu: homemade granola and the like.

In the Taos Inn, elegant **Doc Martin's** (125 Paseo del Pueblo Norte, 575/758-1977, 7:30 A.M.–2:30 P.M. and 5:30–9 P.M. daily, $10) serves all three meals, but breakfast is when the kitchen really shines—especially on dishes like the Kit Carson (poached eggs on yam biscuits topped with red chile) or blue corn pancakes with blueberries. The lunch menu is also tasty and doesn't reach the stratospheric prices of dinner. Despite the trendy flavor combos on the menu, the chile and beans are made by a Taos local, as they have been for decades.

Up in Arroyo Seco, ◖ **Abe's Cantina y Cocina** (489 Hwy. 150, 575/776-8643, 7 A.M.–5:30 P.M. daily, $4), a creaky old all-purpose general store/diner/saloon, has earned fans from all over for its satisfying and cheap breakfast burritos—and don't miss the sweet, flaky empanadas next to the register. (For coffee, though, you'll want to go next door to the Taos Cow.)

## NEW MEXICAN

A small, gaily painted place on the north side of town, the family-run **Orlando's** (1114 Don Juan Valdez Ln., 575/751-1450, 10:30 A.M.–3 P.M. and 5–9 P.M. daily, $10) is invariably the first restaurant named by anyone, local or visitor, when the question of best chile comes up. That said, there have been occasional whisperings about inconsistency (heresy!), but Orlando's still generally serves very satisfying, freshly made New Mexican standards, such as green-chile chicken enchiladas. The posole is quite good too—perfectly firm, earthy, and flecked with oregano. It's always busy, but a fire pit outdoors makes the wait more pleasant. Cash only.

For nourishment in Taos Ski Valley, fortify yourself with a green-chile cheeseburger or bowl of smoky-hot green-chile stew at **Tim's Stray Dog Cantina** (105 Sutton Pl., Taos Ski Valley, 575/776-2894, 11 A.M.–9 P.M. daily, $12), which gets busy after 3 P.M., when tired skiers come down from a day on the slopes. In the summer, it's a nice destination for a drive, as you can sit on the deck and listen to the river flow by.

## MEXICAN

*New* Mexican items may be front and center on the menu at **◖ Antonio's** (122 Doña Luz St., 575/751-4800, 11 A.M.–9 P.M. Mon.–Sat., 11 A.M.–3 P.M. Sun., $15), but the real good stuff here is from south of the border: rich *rellenos en nogada* (stuffed poblano peppers in walnut sauce), *carnitas* (crispy pork) with a tangy green salsa, and succulent *barbacoa de borrego* (pit-roasted lamb). Summer in the courtyard patio is lovely, with seats upstairs and down, and the interior is cozy in the winter. For a more casual bite and a somewhat more limited but no less satisfying menu, hit tiny **Rellenos Café** (135 Paseo del Pueblo Sur, 575/758-7001, 11 A.M.–9 P.M. Mon.–Sat., $6–10).

Or stop in at **Guadalajara Grill** (1384 Paseo del Pueblo Sur, 575/751-0063, 10:30 A.M.–8:30 P.M. Sun.–Thurs., 10:30 A.M.–9 P.M. Fri. and Sat., $10). It may be in a strip mall, but the food transports you straight to western Mexico, with enormous portions of gooey *queso fundido* (fondue-like cheese) and shrimp sautéed in garlic. There's a branch on the north side as well (822 Paseo del Pueblo Norte, 575/737-0816).

## TAOS ECLECTIC

Locals like **Graham's Grille** (106 Paseo del Pueblo Norte, 575/751-1350,

Tim's Stray Dog Cantina is cozy in winter and sunny in summer.

7:30 A.M.–2:30 P.M. and 5–9 P.M. Mon.–Fri., 8 A.M.–2:30 P.M. Sat. and Sun.) because its menu satisfies simple cravings—for mac-and-cheese with green chile, say—and some you didn't even know you had, such as one for fresh nacho chips drizzled with chocolate, a genius salty-sweet fusion. Creatively, falafel is the vegetarian option in dishes such as burritos. Spacious and airy, with lots of blond wood, the space is restful, and so are the prices—nothing's over $20. There are two entrances and two separate dining rooms—the smaller seating area at the back entrance (in the alley off the plaza) looks onto an open kitchen.

**◖ The Love Apple** (803 Paseo del Pueblo Norte, 575/751-0050, 5–9 P.M. Tues.–Sun., $16) wears its local, organic credentials on its sleeve, and the food delivers in simple but powerful flavor combinations, such as a quesadilla made sweet with apple and squash, and posole enriched with local lamb and caramelized onions. The setting is like a French bistro filtered through a northern New Mexican lens: a thick-walled adobe chapel, with candles glimmering against wine bottles along the walls. It can get hot inside in the summer, though, so go early to snag a table in the patio outside—where you'll also get a good view of the big chalkboard listing the sources of all the food you'll eat that night.

**Lula's Café** (316 Paseo del Pueblo Sur, 575/751-1280, 11 A.M.–9 P.M. Mon.–Sat., $9) looks like a standard sandwich shop, but the ingredients make the difference: house-roasted free-range chicken goes into the "Free Bird," and the meatloaf sandwich oozes with chipotle mayo and spicy slaw. Allot half your dining mission to sweets: peanut-butter thumbprint cookies topped with caramel, blueberry coffee cake, and more. You can sit in the sunny yellow room or on picnic tables out front.

## FINE DINING

Open since 1988, **Lambert's** (309 Paseo del Pueblo Sur, 575/758-1009, 5:30–9 P.M. daily, $32) is a Taos favorite, where everyone goes for prom, anniversaries, and other landmark events. Its New American menu is a bit staid, but everything is executed perfectly—trend-following foodies can't quibble that the chile-dusted rock shrimp with house-made cocktail sauce doesn't taste good. Get one of the game-meat specials if you can; otherwise, the signature pepper-crusted lamb is fantastic. A full liquor license means good classic cocktails, which you can also enjoy in the snug, couch-filled lounge.

## QUICK BITES

It looks temporary, but the truck that houses **Mary Jane's** (616 Paseo del Pueblo Sur, 575/751-4252, 7:30 A.M.–2 P.M. Mon.–Fri., $5) has been sitting in the parking lot for years. One of the off-menu specialties is *chicharrones* (fried pork skins) with "everything" (guacamole, salsa, etc.)—imagine a superdeadly version of nachos.

Hands down, **Taos Pizza Out Back** (712 Paseo del Pueblo Norte, 575/758-3112, 11 A.M.–9:30 P.M. daily, $7) serves up the best pie in town, using mostly local and organic ingredients. A glance at the menu—with items like green chile and beans, and the popular portobello-gorgonzola combo—often makes first-timers blanch, but after a bite or two they're converts, like everyone else in town. Soups and salads are also available, if you want to round out your meal.

A drive-through never offered something so good: **Mante's Chow Cart** (402 Paseo del Pueblo Sur, 575/758-3632, 6 A.M.–9 P.M. Mon.–Thurs. and Sat., 6 A.M.–10 P.M. Fri., $5) specializes in breakfast burritos, as well as genius inventions like the Susie, a whole chile relleno wrapped up in a flour tortilla with salsa and guacamole. Perfect road food.

## GROCERIES

Planning a picnic? Stop at **Cid's** grocery (623 Paseo del Pueblo Norte, 575/758-1148, 8 A.M.–8 P.M. Mon.–Sat.) for great takeout food, as well as freshly baked bread and a whole range of organic and local goodies, from New Mexican wines to fresh elk steaks.

**TAOS**

# West to Chama

U.S. 84 on its own is one of the more spectacular drives in northern New Mexico—you could also start this route in Española, close to Santa Fe, and drive up through Abiquiu. But coming through the mountains from the east gives you a dramatic descent into the Chama Valley.

## TIERRA AMARILLA AND LOS OJOS

U.S. 64 climbs up and over the Brazos Mountains, the view from the pass taking in the sheer limestone of 3,000-foot-high cliffs to the north. Descending into the golden valley along the Rio Chama, you soon reach the junction with U.S. 84 and the village of Tierra Amarilla, off the east side of the highway. There's little to see here now, but the courthouse was the site of a major struggle over land rights—still a contentious issue—in this largely Hispano region. Next door is the cool little **Three Ravens Coffeehouse** (15 Hwy. 531, 575/588-9086, 7 A.M.–4 P.M. Mon.–Fri.), a labor of love and active community center; ask the owner about how he renovated the ancient adobe building.

Just a few miles north of Tierra Amarilla and west of the highway, Los Ojos is a two-block-long main street of adobe and Victorian wood-frame buildings, most connected in some way with **Ganados del Valle,** a cooperative established in 1983 to preserve the economy in the region, which for hundreds of years had been based on raising sheep and selling their products. But young people could no longer earn a living from this, and many of the most traditional weaving and spinning techniques had already been lost. The cooperative was gradually able to provide employment for dozens of artists, administrators, and sheepherders, and in 1990, one of its founders, Maria Varela, who got her start as a Chicana activist in the Student Nonviolent Coordinating Committee in the 1960s, earned a MacArthur "genius grant" for her efforts.

Over the decades, Ganados del Valle has served as a model for rural development elsewhere in the state, and its offshoot retail store **Tierra Wools** (91 Main St., 575/588-7231, www.handweavers.com, 9 A.M.–6 P.M. Mon.–Sat., 11 A.M.–4 P.M. Sun. June–Oct., 10 A.M.–5 P.M. Mon.–Sat. Nov.–May) has become a sort of pilgrimage site for anyone engaged in traditional weaving arts. The shop showcases the work of many village women—rugs, pillows, ruanas—as well as brilliantly dyed skeins of hand-woven wool yarn from the hardy, four-horned Churro sheep, a heritage breed that the conquistadors introduced to New Mexico. If you're at all interested in the process, ask to see the dye vats out back. The last weekend in April, the **Spring Harvest Festival** involves demonstrations of sheep-shearing, hand-spinning, and more, along with music and other entertainment.

a roadside shrine near Los Ojos

© ZORA O'NEILL

## KING TIGER AND THE *MERCEDES*

The pastoral village of Tierra Amarilla gives little indication that it was once a battleground in the Chicano rights movement and the local Hispano fight for land-grant restitution. Established in the early 19th century, the Tierra Amarilla *merced* (land grant) was meant to be preserved, according to the Treaty of Guadalupe Hidalgo, when Nuevo México became a U.S. territory in 1848. But it was gradually appropriated by cattle ranchers and the national forest system. By the 1960s, many families in largely Hispano Rio Arriba County found themselves landless and subsisting on less than $1,500 per year.

Around this time, Reies López Tijerina, a charismatic activist in the growing Chicano consciousness movement, took up the land-grant cause. In 1967, he and more than 150 local men stormed the Tierra Amarilla courthouse, calling themselves the Political Confederation of Free City States and bearing a banner proclaiming "Give Us Our Land Back." Their plan was to make a citizen's arrest of the district attorney. But the D.A. was nowhere around, the activists wound up taking everyone in the courthouse hostage, and 300 National Guard troops were called in. The incident made headlines across the country

and made Tijerina an overnight legend. The press dubbed him King Tiger, and he was praised in the ballad "El Corrido de Rio Arriba," penned within weeks by the band Los Reyes de Albuquerque.

Trials the next year were equally gripping: Tijerina wept on the witness stand, a lawman present at the raid turned up murdered, and even New Mexico's governor gave heartfelt testimony. Tijerina came away with a minimal sentence for second-degree kidnapping. He went on to lead the Chicano faction as part of Martin Luther King Jr.'s Poor People's Campaign.

In Tierra Amarilla, meanwhile, the battle lines became hopelessly tangled. With seed money from a generous donor, the Sierra Club announced in 1970 that it would donate a new "land grant" to the area, but it failed to materialize – perhaps because environmentalists soon were battling the local sheepherders and their overgrazing animals. In 1995, a local shepherd successfully sued Sierra Club for the never-applied donation, and the economic situation in the valley has somewhat improved. But many people must lease land on which to graze their sheep, resentments run deep, and the heroism of King Tiger is still recalled with feeling.

## EL VADO LAKE AND HERON LAKE STATE PARKS

These two reservoirs west of Tierra Amarilla are nearly linked. Of the two, El Vado Lake State Park (575/588-7247, www.nmparks.com, $5/car) is smaller but busier, as motorboats are permitted here, and it's a popular recreation spot, with large campgrounds at its south end (accessible via Hwy. 112, 17 miles southwest of Tierra Amarilla).

A great 5.5-mile hiking trail leads from Shale Point, north of all of the campgrounds, up along the Rio Chama, across a bridge, up past Heron Dam, and into the south end of Heron Lake State Park (575/588-7470), which is also accessible via U.S. 64/84 and Highway 95. This lake is much quieter, as boat traffic is

more restricted. It's a favored spot for wintering bald eagles and hawks, and several pairs of rare and enormous ospreys (raptors with wingspans of nearly five feet) settle here as well. During the week, free ranger-led hikes are available on request—ideally, call ahead to the park office to let the staff know you're coming. There are scores of attractive campsites all along the banks here.

Both lakes offer excellent fishing—trout in summer, and kokanee salmon in winter—though you'll need to arrange for a boat at **Stone House Lodge** (Hwy. 95, 575/588-7714, www.stonehouselodge.com. $80 d), as there are no rentals at the lake itself. The stretch of the Chama River from El Vado Dam to Abiquiu Lake is an excellent rafting

© ZORA O'NEILL

**boat docks at "no-wake" Heron Lake**

run—if you're considering a multi-day trip, this is one of the best stretches in the state for it. **Kokopelli Rafting Adventures** in Santa Fe (505/983-3734, www.kokopelliraft.com) and **Los Rios River Runners** in Taos (575/776-8854, www.losriosriverrunners.com) both run trips through these remote canyons; expect to pay about $475 for a three-day outing.

## CHAMA

A tiny high-mountain town, Chama is a perfect getaway for people who find Durango or Silverton, Colorado, too crowded. With just 1,200 residents, the place was and still is focused on the railroad that begins here and threads its way between the mountains to Antonito, just over the state line. And Chama can't grow much more, as it's hemmed in on both sides by land belonging to the Jicarilla Apache. The tribe operates an elite hunting ranch, The Lodge at Chama, that's a favorite politico getaway. But the natural attractions here are accessible to all—with the Rio Chama running right through town, you

could theoretically walk out the front door of your (very affordable) rental cabin, snag a trout, and cook it up for dinner. On a day visit, the star of the show is the great steam train and its depot. If you stay a little longer, you'll have a chance to appreciate the remarkable vistas—particularly in the fall, when the mountains are blanketed with a thick patchwork of color.

## ◖ Cumbres & Toltec Scenic Railroad

The biggest attraction in Chama is this historic steam-driven rail line (575/756-2151, www.cumbrestoltec.com) that has been running 64 miles from Chama up to Antonito, Colorado, since 1880. It passes through stunning high-altitude scenery (and even if the train isn't your thing, you can drive north on Highway 17 for the views).

You can travel the route in several ways, depending on how much of a train ride you want. The standard outing is from Chama to the midpoint, the ghost town of Osier, just over the state border—you hop off there, have lunch, stroll around, and get back on the train for the ride back down the pass ($75 adults, $38 kids). The whole trip takes a little more than six hours. Hardcore rail fans can go the whole way to Antonito—stopping in Osier for lunch—and return to Chama by bus, which takes eight hours ($91 adults, $50 kids); this way, you'll get to see the dramatic Toltec Gorge, just north of Osier. Trains run most frequently in June, July, and early August, then again from mid-September to mid-October, for the autumn leaf season. Reservations are advised, and you can choose from three classes of service (windows open in tourist class, which is fun, but soot from the steam engine can make things a little gritty). The hot lunch included in the ticket price is pretty generous, with turkey and all the standard vegetables, plus buttermilk pie to finish.

You can also prowl around the depot and rail yards. Pick up a flyer at the station that identifies all the structures, as well as distinguishes between drop-bottom gondolas, flangers, and other specialized train cars.

## Recreation

Elk are prevalent throughout the mountains around Chama, and you can often see them at **Sargent Wildlife Management Area,** just off the north edge of town. In September and October, the elk's distinctive mating call, or bugle, can be heard—there's a viewing spot just inside the borders of the reserve, overlooking a big basin where the animals often graze. You can also hike into the center of the 20,000 acres, along the Rio Chama (for excellent fishing)—ask at the Chama visitors center for more information, and other area hiking spots.

## Accommodations

Chama has a reasonable selection of places to stay. The south side of town is largely devoted to rustic riverside cottage operations—**Little Creel** (2631 Hwy. 64, 575/756-2382, www.littlecreelresort.com, $65 and up) is certainly the nicest, with 16 individual cabins in various configurations (some have fireplaces), as well as a huge number of RV spots ($22 and up).

Up near the depot, the lodging is a bit less rustic. The pretty 🄲 **Chama Station Inn** (423 Terrace Ave., 575/756-2315, www.chamastationinn.com, $75 d) is just across from the train. Most of the nine rooms have wood floors, and all are decorated sparingly with country touches; the extra $10 for a deluxe room is well worth it, as it gets you a fireplace, a graceful high ceiling, and a little more space.

The least expensive bed can be found at funky **Foster's Hotel** (393 4th St., 575/756-2296, www.fosters1881.com, $53 d), an 1881 building that used to be a Harvey House operation. You'll definitely feel like you're sleeping upstairs at the old saloon (which is still a popular town watering hole—you might want earplugs). Rooms have low ceilings and simple furniture, but relatively new carpet.

Campers will do well at the **Rio Chama RV Park** (U.S. 64, 575/756-2303), on the north edge of town, where tent sites ($14) are nestled amid tall trees and the river flows right by. It's open May–mid-October.

## Food

A café across from the train station, **Carlatte's** (425 Terrace Ave., 575/756-1663, 7 A.M.–2 P.M. Mon.–Sat., $7) does basic breakfast and lunch—sweet rolls, omelets, and sandwiches—in a groovy atmosphere with big picture windows. There's Wi-Fi and a computer here, for Internet junkies.

For an honest steak and potato, plus not-so-carnivorous items like grilled trout and cold beer, head to the rough-and-tumble **High Country Restaurant & Saloon** (2299 S. Hwy. 17, 575/756-2384, 11 A.M.–9 P.M. Mon.–Thurs., 11 A.M.–10 P.M. Fri. & Sat., 8 A.M.–9 P.M. Sun., $10–20), a big wood-paneled operation that's popular with through-bikers as well as locals; it serves a massive breakfast buffet on Sundays 8 A.M.–noon.

## Information and Services

Chama's **visitors center** (575/756-2235, 8 A.M.–6 P.M. daily) is located right at the junction of U.S. 64/84 and Highway 17, on the southern edge of town. In addition to maps and other info (for the whole state, as it's maintained by the N.M. Tourism Board), it also provides free Internet access, coffee, and even apples from the tree outside, if you're there in the fall. In the winter, the office closes one hour earlier.

TAOS

# The Enchanted Circle

The loop formed by U.S. 64, Highway 38, and Highway 522, going past the ski resorts of Angel Fire and Red River as well as a handful of smaller towns, is perhaps too generously named, but the views of the Sangre de Cristo Mountains, including Wheeler Peak, the tallest in the state, are breathtaking. The area is also a cultural change of pace from Taos. Many of the towns along the north and east sides of the loop were settled by Anglo ranchers and prospectors in the late 1800s, and the Wild West atmosphere persisted well into the 20th century, today reinforced by the large population of transplanted flatlander Texans enamored of the massive peaks. You can drive the 84-mile route in a short day, with time out for a short hike around Red River or a detour along the Wild Rivers scenic byway.

Most guides and maps run the route clockwise, heading north out of Taos to Questa, but if you're doing the outing as a day trip, it makes more sense to head counterclockwise, going through Angel Fire and arriving in Red River or Questa, where there's better food, around lunchtime (or you could pack a lunch to enjoy at any of the picnic areas along the small river west of Red River). You'll also enjoy fantastic views at the end of the drive, descending into the Taos valley from Questa. If you're staying overnight, either direction will work, with the most lodging available in Red River. Because the ski areas value their customers, the roads are generally cleared quickly in the winter; the only patch that may be icy is Palo Flechado Pass west of Angel Fire.

To start, head east on Kit Carson Road, which eventually turns into U.S. 64, winding through the Taos River valley and past numerous campgrounds and hiking trails. At the pass, the road descends into the high Moreno Valley, a gorgeous expanse of green in the spring and a vast tundra in the winter.

## ANGEL FIRE

A right turn up Highway 434 leads to this tiny ski village. Although the mountain here looks like a molehill in comparison with Taos Ski Valley, **Angel Fire Resort** (800/633-7463, www.angelfireresort.com, $64 full-day lift ticket), with a summit elevation of 10,677 and a vertical drop of 2,077 feet, has one important thing going for it: A large portion of the runs are devoted to snowboarding, including four terrain parks and a half-pipe designed by Chris Gunnarson. For those with no snow skills at all, the three-lane, 1,000-foot-long tubing hill provides an easy adrenaline rush. Otherwise, there are few independent attractions in the cluster of timber condos at the base of the mountain. If you're around in the winter, book a sleigh ride with **Roadrunner Tours** (Hwy. 434 in town, 575/377-6416, www.rtours.com, $30 for 35 minutes); the experienced equestrian team can also arrange trail rides into the high mountains—a great summer trip.

In the summer, in addition to the small, trout-stocked Monte Verde Lake, managed by the ski resort, the main diversion here is mountain biking. On the mountain itself, the resort maintains about 30 miles of trails. But the real challenge is the storied **South Boundary Trail**, which runs from a trailhead off Forest Road 76 south of Angel Fire. The route to Taos is about 5 vertical-seeming miles up and over the pass, then another 22 or so back to El Nogal trailhead on U.S. 64, a couple of miles east of Taos. Maps are a must; contact **Native Sons Adventures** in Taos (1203 King Dr., 575/758-9342, www.nativesonsadventures.com).

For a lunch of burgers or brisket, stop off at **Zebadiah's** (Hwy. 434, 575/377-6358, 11 A.M.–9 P.M. daily), a big wood-paneled room that caters to hungry snowboarders in the winter and folks fishing at Eagle Nest in the summer. The bar, which is open till about 2 A.M., is the main hangout in the area. For dinner, you can have a slightly fancier meal

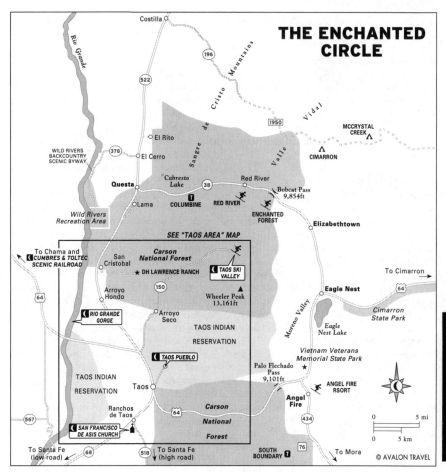

# THE ENCHANTED CIRCLE

at **The Roasted Clove** (48 N. Angel Fire Rd., 575/377-0636, 5–9 P.M. Wed.–Mon.). It has a somewhat formal dining room where you can have grilled elk tenderloin ($35), and the more casual (and better value) "upstairs bistro" is where you can get tasty gourmet mini-tacos and the like ($14).

The Angel Fire Chamber of Commerce maintains a **visitors center** (Centro Plaza, 3407 Hwy. 434, 575/377-6661, www.angel-firechamber.org, 9 A.M.–5 P.M. Mon.–Thurs., 9 A.M.–1 P.M. Fri.). The lobby is open 24 hours,

so you can load up on glossy brochures even when the office is closed.

## Vietnam Veterans Memorial State Park

Back on U.S. 64, a few miles past the turn for Angel Fire, a swooping white structure rises on the hill to your left. This is the Vietnam Veterans Memorial State Park (575/377-2293, www.nmparkscom.com, 9 A.M.–5 P.M. daily, chapel open 24 hours), built by Victor Westphall as a remembrance for his son David, who died in the war. When Westphall commissioned Santa Fe architect Ted Luna to design the graceful white chapel in 1968, it was the first such memorial for the casualties of Vietnam; an adjacent visitors center was built later and has expanded over the years. The complex is a site of pilgrimage for many, and the front grounds and bulletin boards testify to veterans' and families' devotion, as they are covered with additional informal monuments and messages.

## EAGLE NEST

Heading north on U.S. 64 from the Vietnam memorial, you soon see Eagle Nest Lake on the left. The lake was created in 1918 with the construction of a dam on the Cimarron River. In addition to agricultural and mining uses, the lake also supplied an ice-block industry in the winter. Today it's a state park, stocked with trout, and a popular summertime recreation spot (the huge Fourth of July fireworks display is legendary). In addition to all the activity at the lake, there are very good hiking trails in **Cimarron Canyon State Park** (575/377-6271, www.nmparks.com, $5/car), just east of Eagle Nest Lake on U.S. 64.

Vacation homes are clustered down by the water, but the town itself is farther north, at the junction with Highway 38. A small strip of wooden buildings along Therma Drive (U.S. 64) are all that's left of a jumping (illegal) gambling town in the 1920s and 1930s, when enterprising businessmen would roll slot machines out on the boardwalks to entice travelers on their way to Raton and the train, and bars like the Laguna Vista Saloon hosted roulette and blackjack. The **restaurant** ($8) at "The Guney" is passable, with a burgers-and-enchiladas menu in a rustic pine-paneled setting. Unfortunately, the adjoining **Laguna Vista Lodge** (575/377-6522, www.lagunavistalodge.com) doesn't rent rooms in the historic old building; instead, there are standard motel rooms connected by a screened porch ($70–105 d), as well as cabins and apartments with a view of the lake.

The **Eagle Nest Chamber of Commerce** (50 Therma Dr., 575/377-2420, www.

eaglenestchamber.org, 10 A.M.–4 P.M. Tues.–Sat.) has limited hours but an enthusiastic staff.

## ELIZABETHTOWN

Blink and you'll miss it: A small sign on the right side of the road 4.8 miles past Eagle Nest points the way to the former gold-rush site of Elizabethtown, the first incorporated village in New Mexico. After gold was discovered in 1866, it grew to more than 7,000 people, then faded to nothing when a dredge-mining project failed in 1903. It's now a ghost town overshadowed by the stone ruins of the Mutz Hotel, the former center of social activity. The only signs of life are, ironically, in the **cemetery,** which is still used by residents of Colfax County and contains graves dating as far back as 1880. The quirky **Elizabethtown Museum** (575/377-3420, 10 A.M.–5 P.M. daily June–Aug., $2 donation) details Elizabethtown's brief but lively history with items collected from local families' troves, from the gold-rush years and much later (vintage pinball machines!).

Continuing on Highway 38, you reach Bobcat Pass. Halfway down, the **Enchanted Forest** cross-country ski area (575/754-6112, www.enchantedforestxc.com, 9 A.M.–4:30 P.M. in season, $15 full-day pass) has more than 20 miles of groomed trails through the trees and up the mountainside. Nonskiers can rent snowshoes.

## RED RIVER

Descending into the valley, a somewhat bizarre apparition awaits: tidy rows of wooden buildings, all done up in Old West–look facades, complete with boardwalks and swinging saloon doors. No, it's not Elizabethtown of yore, it's the ski village of Red River. Although Taos loyalists dismiss **Red River Ski & Snowboard Area** (575/754-2223, www.redriverskiarea.com, $63 full-day lift ticket) as an amateur's playground, it's nothing if not convenient: The trails run right into town, so it's walking distance from anywhere to the chairlift.

Like Elizabethtown, Red River was once a community of wild prospectors, carving

© ZORA O'NEILL

**Old Western style in Red River**

copper, silver, and gold out of the hillsides. When that industry eventually went bust, the town salvaged itself by renting out abandoned houses to vacationers needing a respite from the summer heat at lower elevations. Just when air-conditioning started to become widespread in the 1950s, the ski area opened, saving the town from a major slump. Red River still thrives, with a year-round population of only about 450. The town hosts a rowdy Memorial Day Motorcycle Rally, as well as a surprisingly large Fourth of July parade and a Mardi Gras street party; contact the **Red River Chamber of Commerce** (575/754-2366, www.redrivernewmex.com) for more details.

### Hiking

This is the back side of Wheeler Peak, so the ascents are much more gradual, while still yielding dramatic views. Stop in at the **visitors center** (100 E. Main St., 575/754-3030, www.redriver.org, 8 A.M.–5 P.M. daily), in the town hall, for area maps and trail guides. The least strenuous hiking option is the **Red River Nature Trail**, which starts in town at

Brandenburg Park and runs two miles one-way, with signs identifying plants and geological formations.

West of town, the road leads past a number of trailheads that make for a good amble. **Columbine Trail,** on the left (south) seven miles out, starts out easy, crossing Deer Creek, but soon moves to a series of long switchbacks that lead through a large aspen grove, then above the tree line to the ridge, a total of about five miles. As an incentive, wild berry bushes flourish alongside the trail in the late summer. The right side of the road, however, is a little less scenic because a molybdenum mine has stripped a good chunk of the mountain.

### Food

Red River is a good place to stop for a late lunch if you're craving meat—but if you're hungrier for spicy New Mexican, hold out till Questa. Business turnover can be high here, but the town's most reliable eatery is the long-established **Texas Reds** (400 E. Main St., 575/754-2922, 5–9 P.M. daily, $18), which has relocated twice and still packs 'em in for big

TAOS

steaks in a wood-paneled Western-look hall. For something lighter, **Dairy Bar** (417 E. Main St., 575/754-2479, 11 A.M.–4 P.M. daily, $5) does burgers, chile, quesadillas, and of course soft-serve ice cream.

## QUESTA

Arriving in Questa, at the junction of Highway 38 and Highway 522, you're back in Spanish New Mexico. The town, which now has a population of about 1,700, was established in 1842 and is still primarily a Hispano farming village, though a few Anglo newcomers have set up art galleries here. The heart of town is the 1841 **San Antonio Church,** a handsome white stucco structure with a red metal roof and the distinctively New Mexican spiral pine columns on either side of the front door. Just south of the junction, look for signs to the **Northern New Mexico Historical Society & Museum** (noon–5 P.M. Thurs.–Sun. June–Aug., free), started by a Questa native who's enthusiastic about showing visitors through the restored adobe house that holds beautiful quilts and other local relics, WPA-era photos of the town, and a room dedicated to the history of the Molycorp mine.

### Food

Turning south on Highway 522, you're on the final leg of the Enchanted Circle loop. The **Questa Café** (575/586-9631, 6 A.M.–8 P.M. Mon.–Sat., 6 A.M.–3 P.M. Sun., $6), about half a mile south of the junction, is the best place in town for hearty New Mexican home cooking, including very good sopaipillas.

### Wild Rivers Recreation Area

Visitors usually breeze straight through Questa on their way to the Wild Rivers Recreation Area, a portion of Carson National Forest that encompasses the confluence of the Rio Grande and Red River, and the dramatic canyons forged by the two flows. Steep hiking trails lead down into the gorge and along the river, so you can make a full loop, and whitewater rafting is very popular here in the Class III rapids of the Red River Confluence run.

Five developed campgrounds (but no RV hookups) on the rim can be reached by car, or you can hike in to campsites by the river. The area feels very remote and wild, especially once you get down one of the trails—you will probably see red-tailed hawks circling over the gnarled, centuries-old piñon and juniper trees that line the rim of the gorge. The access road is three miles north on Highway 522 from the main Questa intersection, then west on Highway 378, which leads through the town of El Cerro and to the area's **visitors center** (575/586-1150, 9 A.M.–6 P.M. daily June–Aug., $3 day use, $7 camping).

### The D. H. Lawrence Ranch

After Questa, the view opens up as you descend into the valley, with mesas stretching far to the west. Just south of San Cristobal, a turn to the left (County Road B-009) leads five miles on a rutted road to the 160-acre ranch where English writer and provocateur D. H. Lawrence lived in 1924 and 1925 with his wife, Frieda, and the painter Dorothy

Pay your respects to D. H. Lawrence at his mountainside shrine.

TAOS

Brett—all as a gift from Mabel Dodge Luhan. Though there's not very much to see here, it is as good a reason as any to drive up a back road and into the fragrant pine forests (though not too early in the spring—the dirt road near the end is rutted and shady, leaving it iced over often through March).

Lawrence soon returned to Europe, and he died of tuberculosis in France in 1930; Frieda had the ashes returned to New Mexico. This plan sparked anger among Lawrence's other friends, including Mabel, who characterized Frieda's planned site for the ashes as "that outhouse of a shrine." Tales abound about how the ashes never made the trip, whether by accident or sabotage. Some of the earliest visitors to pay their respects at the ranch include Tennessee Williams and Georgia O'Keeffe, whose dramatic painting *The Lawrence Tree* is based on the view from the base of a gnarled pine in front of the Lawrences' cabin, farther down the hill. The aforementioned shrine is indeed small; aside from what may or may not be Lawrence's ashes mixed into a concrete slab, the modest building contains a guest book with wishes left by previous literary pilgrims, plus an official-looking certificate declaring the ashes to be genuinely Lawrence's.

To reach the ranch coming from the north, turn left at the second sign for County Road B-009 (the first is in the town of San Cristobal). Coming up from Taos, look for the historic marker on the right side of the road, immediately before the turn.

# Information and Services

## TOURIST INFORMATION

The **Taos Visitors Center** (1139 Paseo del Pueblo Sur, 575/758-3873, www.taosvacationguide.com, 9 A.M.–5 P.M. daily) is an expansive and helpful place a few miles south of the plaza. Stop here for flyers and maps galore, free coffee, and a copy of the very thorough weekly news and events bulletin (also posted online), which includes gallery listings, music, and more. The staff can also advise on the Enchanted Circle.

### Books and Maps

**Moby Dickens** (124-A Bent St., No. 6 Dunn House, 575/758-3050, 10 A.M.–6 P.M. daily) is Taos's best bookstore, exceedingly well informed on local history and culture and stocking plenty of maps, as well as rare books, a good CD collection, and assorted gift items.

At the intersection with Kit Carson Road, **Fernandez de Taos** (102 Paseo del Pueblo Norte, 575/758-4391, 8:30 A.M.–5 P.M. Mon.–Sat., 9 A.M.–5 P.M. Sun.) is a good enough bookstore, but it also has the town's best newsstand.

### Local Media

The *Taos News* comes out every Thursday, and it contains the *Tempo* entertainment section, with music, theater, and film listings. Many hotels offer free copies of *Tempo* to their guests. The *Albuquerque Journal* publishes a special northern edition daily, focused on local issues, but if you really want to dip in the muck of local politics, pick up a free copy of the *Horse Fly,* published monthly as the voice of cantankerous Taos.

### Radio

While you're in town, don't miss tuning in to KTAO (101.9 FM), a local radio station that's all solar-powered. The musical programming is broad, and you're sure to learn an interesting tidbit about the community in the process.

## SERVICES
### Banks

**First Community Bank** (120 W. Plaza, 575/758-6653, 9 A.M.–5 P.M. Mon.–Fri.), just off the southwest corner of the plaza, is the most convenient bank and ATM while on foot. The drive-through service at **Centinel Bank of Taos** (512 Paseo del Pueblo Sur,

TAOS

575/758-6700, 9 A.M.–5 P.M. Mon.–Fri.) is easily accessible from the main drag.

## Post Offices

The Taos **post office** (710 Paseo del Pueblo Sur, 575/751-1801, 9 A.M.–1 P.M. and 2–4:30 P.M. Mon.–Sat.) is on the south side; there's another on the north side (318 Paseo del Pueblo Norte, 8:30 A.M.–5 P.M. Mon.–Fri.), next to the Dragonfly Café.

## Internet

**Wired?** (705 Felicidad Ln., 575/751-9473, www.wiredcoffeeshop.com, 8 A.M.–6 P.M. Mon.–Fri., 8 A.M.–3 P.M. Sat. and Sun.), behind Raley's off La Posta Road, is a laid-back Internet café and business center with a big garden, good veggie and raw-food meals, and free wireless access for laptops; computer use is $2 for 15 minutes.

# Getting There and Around

## BY CAR

You'll likely need a car in Taos, but then feel bad for contributing to the daily traffic jam on Paseo del Pueblo. There are paid parking lots close to the plaza, and a free one down Kit Carson Road less than a quarter-mile. For rental cars, **Enterprise** (1354 Paseo del Pueblo Sur, 575/758-5333, www.enterprise. com, 8 A.M.–5 P.M. Mon.–Fri., 9 A.M.–noon Sat.) has a convenient office.

## BY BUS AND SHUTTLE

**Twin Hearts Express** (575/751-1201) runs a shuttle five times a day (every two hours 11:30 A.M.–5:30 P.M.) between the Albuquerque airport and Taos ($50 one-way). From Santa Fe, **Taos Express** (575/751-4459, www. taosexpress.com, $10) runs five times a day on Friday, Saturday, and Sunday. It coordinates its schedule with the Rail Runner's arrival in Santa Fe, making it a potentially seamless trip all the way from Albuquerque, and twice a day, it stops at the Santa Fe airport.

Within Taos, the **Chile Line bus** (575/751-4459) runs north–south from the Ranchos de Taos post office to the Taos Pueblo, approximately every 35 minutes 7:30 A.M.–5:30 P.M. Monday–Saturday. The fare (exact change only) is $0.50. December–April, one shuttle runs to Taos Ski Valley, leaving the Sagebrush Inn at 8 A.M. and stopping at a few other major spots along the way; the ride takes one hour. The return bus leaves at 4:30 P.M.

# LAS VEGAS AND THE NORTHEAST

Historically and geographically, the northeast section of the state acts as a bridge connecting central New Mexico to the great American plains. The alpine Pecos Wilderness Area forms a natural barrier east of Santa Fe, then the land levels out into a rolling, grassy vista stretching to the horizon. This was the northern frontier for the Spanish, and only after Mexico gained its independence in 1821 were these grasslands open to traders' wagon trains from Kansas. For the three decades when the Santa Fe Trail was at its peak of activity, followed by the prosperity brought in by the railroad, northeastern New Mexico was a lively place.

Now, though, it's a relatively sleepy swath of territory, traversed only by cattle and motorists, who usually stick to the interstate that runs north to Colorado. A few people stop to visit the town of Raton, at the base of a harrowing pass over the Rockies, or Cimarron, deeper in the mountains and that much more untouched by time. Just off I-25 in the lowlands, Las Vegas is the region's biggest center of activity. No bright lights and high rolling here: This Vegas is a college town with a population of about 15,000, a sedate place extending from a tree-shaded plaza edged with colonial and Victorian buildings that manage to be well preserved without feeling like a theme park—which can be a blessed change after Santa Fe's enforced historicism.

The other major landmark on the plains is Capulin Volcano, which was active 60,000 years ago. Its cinder cone rises a thousand feet above the surrounding land, and from its rim

© ZORA O'NEILL

# HIGHLIGHTS

**◖ Las Vegas Plaza:** The heart of "Meadow City" is this grassy spread surrounded by grand territorial and old adobe buildings. It's so well preserved, it has been used frequently as a movie set – but it's blessedly free of souvenir shops (page 169).

**◖ Montezuma Castle:** The glamour of the early railroad era is captured in this Queen Anne-style confection built as a resort hotel, now used as a college student center. Schedule a tour of the interior if possible, and don't miss the nearby hot springs (page 170).

**◖ Fort Union National Monument:** The largest fort in the Southwest is now an expanse of eroding adobe. Go early or late in the day to see the shadowy traces of the Santa Fe Trail stretching to the horizon (page 177).

**◖ Clayton Lake State Park:** Stop by this oasis in the prairie to stand in – or at least near – the footsteps of giants. Dinosaurs left their immense tracks in the prehistoric mud here 100 million years ago (page 180).

**◖ Capulin Volcano National Monument:** To get a great view across the plains, wind your way along the unnervingly narrow road that spirals up this perfectly round peak. You can also hike down into the crater (page 181).

**◖ Johnson Mesa:** Outside of Taos, this is probably the most striking scenery in northern New Mexico – the Rockies rise up to the north, and the plains slip away far below the edge of this empty pastoral expanse (page 183).

**◖ Shuler Theater:** The renovated gem of Raton's downtown is an almost poignant emblem of the town's past. Certainly nothing else on the main street can match the fantastical painted interior and beautiful embroidered curtains (page 185).

**◖ St. James Hotel:** The history – and present day – of Cimarron is intrinsically caught up with this old inn, the state's best 19th-century hotel (page 188).

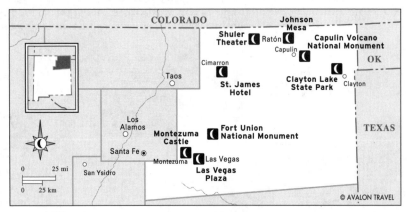

LOOK FOR ◖ TO FIND RECOMMENDED SIGHTS, ACTIVITIES, DINING, AND LODGING.

you can see the earth slope away to the edge of the Sangre de Cristo Mountains. This area may not exude the barren drama of New Mexico's western desert or the thrill of the rugged mountains, but these placid flatlands, interrupted by only a few roads and small towns, offer a sense of space and tranquility unmatched elsewhere in the state.

## PLANNING YOUR TIME

On the surface, Clayton, Las Vegas, Raton, and Cimarron are all one-night towns, as there are few formal sights and little to do in the evenings. But you could easily settle down somewhere for a few days (Cimarron or Las Vegas are the strongest candidates) while you investigate the spaces in between as well. You'll find plenty of ways to pass the time hiking, fishing, or just driving the pretty back roads that wend through the mountains and across the flatlands. In particular, the drive to Las Vegas on I-25 is a fairly dull one just for a day trip from Santa Fe, but if you're heading farther into the plains, the town is a lovely diversion. Few tourists make it all the way to Clayton, in the farthest corner. But if you think of it as a point of contrast with central, mountainous New Mexico, it can be a worthwhile journey. Be aware that tourist services in Raton and Cimarron are severely curtailed beginning in September and lasting through the end of April, and a cold snap in early fall is not uncommon.

## HISTORY

Dinosaurs traipsed through in the Early Cretaceous (most notably leaving footprints north of Clayton), and Comanche and other Plains Indians crisscrossed the area for hundreds of years before the Spanish arrived. But northeast New Mexico is even more indelibly marked by the Santa Fe Trail. The trade route proved to be the thin end of the wedge in opening up the West to American domination: First came goods from Missouri to the hungry market in Santa Fe (previously restricted to trading only with Spain), then came military supplies during the Mexican-American war, followed by homesteaders, prospectors, and entrepreneurs.

It was these prospectors who caused substantial trouble in the Rocky Mountains when, in 1866, gold was discovered not far from where the northern route of the Santa Fe Trail ran. In flooded scores of hopeful miners—never mind that the strike was on the Maxwell Land Grant, 1.7 million acres of privately owned land. By the 1870s, a battle was brewing between the land-grant owners and the squatters who'd moved in. The resulting Colfax County War was a struggle that involved assassinations, lynchings, and Republican conspiracies in Santa Fe. Finally, an 1887 Supreme Court ruling gave squatters the boot, along with Spanish families who had been settled for generations. But by then, the railroad was bringing surer money than gold anyway—as well as another point of conflict. Anglo businessmen piled off the train in Raton and East Las Vegas, buying up land and earning the wrath of the Hispano shepherds who had been living in a much simpler economy for centuries.

Meanwhile, homesteaders on the plains northeast of Las Vegas had set the stage for another drama. Beginning in 1862, when the Homestead Act doled out 160-acre parcels to any family with enough nerve to move to the frontier, the would-be farmers struggled to work the thin topsoil that lay over a hard limestone bedrock. They were able to displace the native Plains Indian tribes in many areas, but they had no defense against the drought that struck in the 1920s. Soon, this was the western edge of the Dust Bowl, where the sky would turn black for days and children would die from inhaling the grit. It was an unrivaled economic and environmental disaster that effectively emptied the region of all but the ranchers who had initially settled the area for the United States.

After many decades, the northern plains' fortunes finally turned, with the discovery of carbon-dioxide fields and the expansion of cattle ranching. But the area remains sparsely populated, just as much of the former Maxwell Land Grant is still relative wilderness.

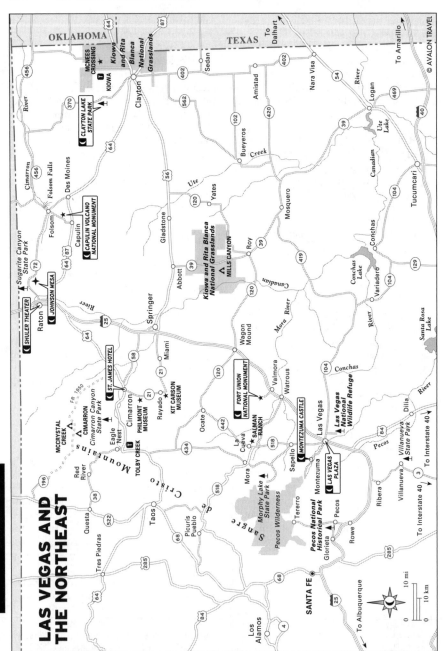

**LAS VEGAS AND THE NORTHEAST**

# Pecos and Villanueva

Santa Fe backs up against the vast **Pecos Wilderness Area,** the second-largest nature reserve in the state (after the Gila), 223,000 acres of high country where the mountain streams seethe with trout and elk ramble through emerald meadows. The former logging town of Pecos, where mountain men now live side by side with alternative healers and monks, is the jumping-off point for any trip into the woods. To reach the village, head east along I-25 to Glorieta (exit 299) and Highway 50; there's an alternate route via Highway 63 (exit 307), which passes the ruins of Pecos Pueblo, the regional power before the Spanish arrived. **Villanueva,** a small village near a gem of a state park, is 14 miles farther on I-25, then 10 miles south.

On the drive out, near exit 295, you pass the site of the westernmost Civil War battle in the United States. The **Battle of Glorieta Pass** raged March 26–28, 1862, part of a Confederate plan to invade the West with a force of Texans—a plan that was foiled in this decisive rout. Look for annual reenactments of the fight.

## PECOS NATIONAL HISTORICAL PARK

When the Spanish made first contact in 1540, Pecos was the largest pueblo in the region, home to some 2,000 people, living in four- and five-story complexes built of stone sealed with mud. The ruins of this grand community (Hwy. 63, 505/757-7200, www.nps.gov/peco, 8 A.M.–6 P.M. daily June–Aug., 8 A.M.–5 P.M. Sept.–May, $3) are accessible to visitors via Highway 63, then a 1.5-mile paved interpretive trail that winds through the remnants of the Pecos Pueblo walls, a couple of restored kivas, and, most striking, the remainder of a Franciscan mission. Free guided tours around various parts of the site run daily at 10 A.M. and at 2 P.M. during the summer and Friday–Sunday at 1:30 P.M. in winter. In winter, the visitors center closes at 4:30 P.M.

© ZORA O'NEILL

ruins of a Franciscan mission inside Pecos National Historical Park

On a ridge facing out to the plains to the northeast and to the mountains behind, the Pecos Pueblo setting provides a beautiful view today; around 1100, when the area was being settled with the first villages, it also provided a livelihood. The ridge was part of a natural trade path between the Rio Grande farmers and the buffalo hunters of the Great Plains—both groups met in Pecos, itself an agricultural community, to barter. What began as a series of villages consolidated in the 14th century into a city, with a layout so orderly it appears to have been centrally planned. By 1450, the fortress of Pecos was the major economic power in the area.

Perhaps it was the city's trading culture and relative worldliness that made the Pecos Indians welcome Francisco Vásquez de Coronado and his men in 1540 with music and dancing, rather than bows and arrows. Nearly 60 years later, Don Juan de Oñate visited the area and ordered that a mission church be built—a giant structure with six bell towers and buttresses 22 feet thick in some spots. The building was destroyed during the Pueblo Revolt, after which the Pecos people dug a kiva smack in the middle of the ruined convent area—symbolic architecture, to say the least.

But soon enough, the Spanish were back, and they were even welcomed and aided at Pecos. When they built a new church in the early 1700s, it was noticeably smaller, maybe as a form of compromise. But even as a hybrid Pueblo-Spanish culture was developing, the Indian population was gradually falling victim to disease and drought. When the Santa Fe Trail opened up in 1821, Pecos was all but empty, and in 1838, the last city-dwellers marched to live with fellow Towa-speakers at Jemez Pueblo, 80 miles west; their descendants still live there today.

## PECOS WILDERNESS AREA

Stop in at the **ranger station** (Hwy. 63, 505/757-6121, 8 A.M.–4:30 P.M. Mon.–Fri.) on the north end of Pecos town to buy topographical maps and inquire about conditions on the trails and at the eight developed campgrounds.

At this high elevation, summer temperatures are rarely above 75°F and can dip below freezing at night, so pack accordingly.

Highway 63 runs north out of town, following the Pecos River past the tiny settlement of Tererro and several fishing access points. At the general store in Tererro, you can inquire about **horseback-riding** trips (Hwy. 63, 505/757-6193, www.pecoswilderness.com, $50 per hour). The road then narrows and rises to reach what used to be the mining camp of Cowles—now just a wide spot in the road. Immediately north, Forest Road 223 leads 4.5 miles to Iron Gate Campground and **Hamilton Mesa Trail** (no. 249), a fairly level 3.8-mile hike to a wide-open meadow—look out for strawberries among the wildflowers.

At the end of Highway 63 (bear right where the dirt road forks), **Cave Creek Trail** (no. 288), which runs out of Panchuela Campground, is an easy 3.6-mile out-and-back that follows a small waterway up to some caves that have been carved out of the white limestone by the stream's flow. You can make this hike more ambitious by pressing on past the caves, up a steep hillside, and on to Horsethief Meadow; this adds an extra 3 (very strenuous) miles. You could make this into an overnight trip, as the meadow is a beautiful place to camp. More ambitious still is **Jack's Creek Trail** (no. 257), which goes out of Jack's Creek Campground. Pecos Baldy Lake is 7.5 miles in—doable as an out-and-back with a very early start, but better as an overnight hike. All trails in this area require a $2 trailhead parking fee; additional fees apply for camping or picnicking, depending on the spot.

## FOOD AND ACCOMMODATIONS

At the main crossroads in Pecos, where Highway 50 meets Highway 63, **Frankie's at the Casanova** (Hwy. 63, 505/757-3322, 7:30 A.M.–2:30 P.M. and 5:30–8:30 P.M. Tues.–Fri., 8 A.M.–2 P.M. and 5:30–8:30 P.M. Sat. and Sun., $9) is the best all-around restaurant in town, serving massive breakfasts (ham and eggs!), giant lunches (burgers stuffed with green chile and cheese!), and also rather large dinners, which range from plain old enchiladas to pasta Alfredo with shrimp. During the winter, the place is open only for breakfast and lunch.

If you want to get an early start hiking, consider staying the night in Pecos. The **Benedictine Monastery** (Hwy. 63, 505/757-6600, www.pecosmonastery.org, $75 s) maintains four austere hermitages with beautiful views; the rate is a suggested donation. Several mountain lodges, such as **Los Pinos Ranch** (505/757-6213, www.lospinosranch.com, $135 pp), offer multi-day packages with all meals and a variety of outdoor activities.

## VILLANUEVA

From exit 323 off I-25, Highway 3 is a beautiful drive south. The two-lane road runs through a narrow valley that's a change of scenery from the mountains, with rich red earth cut into small farm plots. The villages of Ribera and El Pueblo were founded in the late 18th century, after the establishment of the San Miguel del Vado land grant in this valley. Named for a ford (*vado*) on the Pecos River, this area later became the official customs point for caravans entering Mexican territory via the Santa Fe Trail.

You'll also pass ( **La Risa Café** (Hwy. 3, 575/421-3883, 11 A.M.–8 P.M. Thurs.–Sat., 8 A.M.–6 P.M. Sun., $8), where the shady screened patio is a popular stop for locals and day-trippers to enjoy spicy New Mexican food and astounding slices of pie. Farther along is the tiny, family-run **Madison Winery** (Hwy. 3, 575/421-8028, noon–6 P.M. Mon.–Fri., 10 A.M.–5 P.M. Sat., noon–5 P.M. Sun. in summer), between El Pueblo and Sena.

**Villanueva,** centered on its own historic church, is the largest settlement along the road; it has a small general store that stocks supplies for people using the nearby campground.

### Villanueva State Park

The small but beautiful Villanueva State Park (575/421-2957, 7 A.M.–9 P.M. daily in summer, 7 A.M.–7 P.M. in winter, $5/car) occupies a bend in the Pecos River against 400-foot-tall sandstone cliffs. Because the parkland is small, it doesn't draw big crowds—even in the summer, it's only busy on the weekends. During the week, you'll probably have the 2.5-mile Canyon Trail to yourself, and the choice of camping ($8) either on the cottonwood-shaded river bottom or up on the canyon rim amid juniper and piñon; the riverside sites are near flush toilets and a shower. The river is stocked with trout and can be deep enough for canoeing. Spring comes early in the valley, making for flower-filled paths by late April; fall is a burst of red scrub oak and yellow cottonwood leaves, in sharp contrast to the evergreens.

# Las Vegas

The city in New Mexico that suffers most from misplaced expectations, Las Vegas is in fact a quiet community about 50 miles northeast of Santa Fe. Its centerpiece is a pretty, shady plaza, and nearly a thousand registered historic buildings stand in the surrounding blocks.

Set near Starvation Peak—a landmark butte on the Santa Fe Trail—the city was a Spanish settlement well before it was a stop on the trade route. In the middle of town, the Gallinas River still marks the historic division between the 1835 settlement of Nuestra Señora de los Dolores de las Vegas (Our Lady of Sorrows of the Meadows) and the railroad boom town of East Las Vegas, begun in 1879. The old Hispano plaza-centered town and the new, largely Anglo community didn't merge into a single entity until 1970—probably because for decades East Las Vegas was huge, shockingly lawless, and populated with cattle rustlers, scam artists, and outlaws like Doc Holliday, who owned a saloon here for a year. Poor relations between the two towns were also exacerbated by fights over land use—a band of

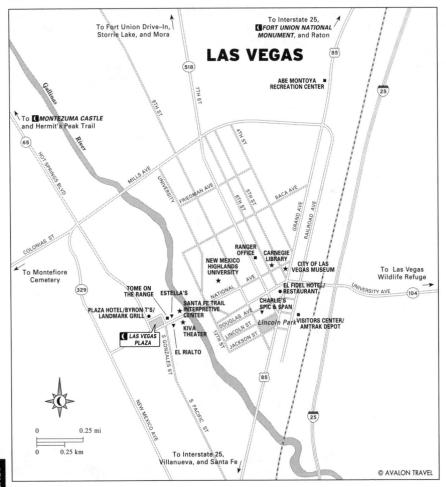

Hispano vigilantes called the Gorras Blancas (White Caps) went around snipping through Anglo fencing in the night, so that their sheep could continue to graze.

But the changes wrought by the railroad were irrevocable, and along with Anglo economic supremacy came telephones, an electric streetcar, an opera house, and other trappings of modern life. For a period in the late 19th century, "Meadow City" was the biggest metropolis between Missouri and San Francisco. Times have changed, but the New Mexico Normal School,

established during this early boom period to train teachers, is now Highlands University, and philanthropist Armand Hammer established a branch of the United World College system outside of town in the 1980s. Together, the two institutions cater to several thousand students, who give the town a lot of its life.

## SIGHTS

The best way to explore Las Vegas and appreciate its historic architecture is on foot—start on the old plaza and notice how the building styles and the street layouts change as you head east across Bridge Street, which leads toward the New Mexico Highlands University campus. Douglas Avenue, two blocks south, is the main shopping district on the east side; still farther east are the rail yards, now relatively derelict but at one time the liveliest part of town.

If Las Vegas looks vaguely familiar to you, maybe it's because you watched the Cold War scare flick *Red Dawn* too many times as a child, or you're a fan of Tom Mix westerns such as *The Tenderfoot's Triumph*. The city was the setting for scores of silent films shot in the early 20th century, as well as later productions such as *Easy Rider, All the Pretty Horses,* and *No Country for Old Men. Red Dawn* used the area most thoroughly; the "Calumet Says Howdy" mural just off Grand Avenue is a relic of the shoot.

You can pick up a thorough walking tour guide from the visitors center or from the **Citizens' Committee for Historic Preservation** (116 Bridge St. 10 A.M.–3 P.M. Mon.–Sat.). The pamphlet covers the plaza as well as outlying historic districts, each of which has its distinctive building styles; some structures date back as far as 1846. The group also occasionally organizes tours inside many of the private homes.

## Las Vegas Plaza

Looking around the large tree-edged plaza on the west side of town, you can see only remnants of the original Spanish settlement, which had originally been built entirely of adobe, in a defensive ring meant to be sealed off against Apache raids. Many of the buildings later got spruced up with territorial details when the railroad started to bring in bricks, tin cornices, and other modern details. **Desmarais House/ Our Lady of Sorrows Parish Hall** (1810 E. Plaza) is one of the few older adobe structures (built before 1883), though the curvy roofline is a later bit of 1930s whimsy. The old *acequia madre* (the mother ditch) runs along South Pacific Street, one block south of the plaza.

Also look out for **Tapetes de Lana Weaving Center** (1814 Plaza, 505/426-8638,

afternoon on the plaza in Las Vegas

© ZORA O'NEILL

7 A.M.–6:30 P.M. Mon.–Sat., 9 A.M.–3 P.M. Sun.), run by a nonprofit organization that helps preserve local textile traditions and provides employment in the small villages north of Las Vegas. You can pick up reasonably priced rugs here, as well as see antique looms in use. The rest of the plaza is ringed with a few very respectable antiques shops.

### Bridge Street

Bridge Street, which leads toward the Gallinas River, was built up in the mid-19th century and is now a great combination of old and new: A tattoo parlor and an herb store have filled in empty spaces next to the long-standing Popular Dry Goods, which deals in rodeo wear. The exhibits at the **Santa Fe Trail Interpretive Center** (116 Bridge St., 10 A.M.–3 P.M. Mon.–Sat.) aren't the most scintillating—they're heavy on yellowed documents in display cases. But entrance is free, and the place is run by the local historic preservation group, members of which are happy to answer questions of all kinds.

THE NORTHEAST

## East Las Vegas

New Mexico Highlands University occupies either side of the street once you cross the river. Up the hill and past the campus, you enter some of the finer residential districts, with many examples of beaux arts and Queen Anne architecture—the best of this is around **Carnegie Park** (4th St. and National Ave.). The park's green lawn surrounds the elegant domed **Carnegie Library** (500 National Ave., 505/426-3304, 8 A.M.–5 P.M. Mon.–Fri., 8 A.M.–noon Sat.), a mini-Monticello. It's one of more than 2,500 libraries around the world funded by steel magnate and philanthropist Andrew Carnegie beginning in 1883, and true to Carnegie's vision, it still houses the public library—the only one of three in the state to have survived.

About five blocks south of here is Douglas Avenue, where the commercial buildings all have a bit of historic flair—whether sleek 1940s storefronts or the enormous **Romanesque Masonic Temple** (514 Douglas Ave.) of 1895. Farther south still, **Lincoln Park** (Lincoln and 7th Sts.), is another square surrounded by gracious large homes.

## City of Las Vegas Museum and Rough Riders Memorial Collection

It takes almost more time to say the name of this museum (727 Grand Ave., 505/426-3205, www.lasvegasmuseum.com, 10 A.M.–4 P.M. Tues.–Sat., $2 donation) than it does to tour it, but the exhibits are informative and based on well-chosen artifacts. It starts with a glass case of pots and baskets from the pre-Columbian era, but quickly gets to Vegas's glam years in the late 19th century, when the town supported two opera houses and had all the trappings of high society and general civilization, including the first telephone line in the state, installed in 1879.

One room is dedicated to souvenirs from Teddy Roosevelt's Rough Riders, the spirited regiment he led in the Spanish-American war of 1898. The soldiers, chosen for their skills with horses and guns, were volunteers from all over the West, with the majority from New Mexico; they chose Las Vegas as the site of their first reunion and continued to gather over the years, until the last soldier died in 1975.

## Montefiore Cemetery

On the west edge of town at the end of Colonias Street (you'll probably want to drive here), this rambling cemetery is an interesting place to visit, especially the back corner, which is dedicated to the sizeable Jewish population that settled here in the mid-1800s and set up stores and other trade operations. After walking around downtown, you'll recognize many of the names: Charles Ilfeld, for instance, and Samuel Nahm of the Stern & Nahm building on Bridge Street. Although this community established the first synagogue in the state, Congregation Montefiore, in 1881, only about 40 Jews are left in Las Vegas today.

## ◖ Montezuma Castle

Head north off the plaza on Hot Springs Boulevard (Highway 65), then out of town 4.3 miles to reach Montezuma Castle, a 10,000-square-foot architectural confection perched on the mountainside. The turreted Queen Anne–style building stands as a reminder of more glamorous travel days, when the Atchison, Topeka & Santa Fe Railroad envisioned an elite resort here, connected to the main line with a spur track. The firm of Burnham & Root (one of whose principals went on to make his name with the Chicago world's fair complex of 1893) created the spectacular building, which opened to guests in 1885. But despite the patronage of Billy the Kid as well as American presidents, the place closed after less than 20 years. It later became the Montezuma Baptist College, then a Jesuit seminary for Mexican priests until 1972.

It was nearly in ruins when the **Armand Hammer United World College of the American West** (505/454-4221, www.uwc-usa.org) acquired it in 1981, with plans to renovate it as the center of its new campus. After more than $10 million invested, the building was restored to its former glory, but unfortunately it is closed to visitors except during free twice-monthly tours, on Saturday

© ZORA O'NEILL

Montezuma Castle was a resort in the early railroad era.

afternoons—call or check the website for the schedule. Beautifully restored, but with modern touches such as vivid Dale Chihuly chandeliers, the interior is as lavish as the exterior—it's well worth seeing if your schedule allows.

Also on the college grounds is **Dwan Light Sanctuary** (505/454-4200), which *is* open to the public, preferably between 8 A.M. and 5 P.M. (though it's open all the time); register first at the visitors booth. The serene meditation space dazzles with prism installations by Charles Ross, an artist who is building an earthwork sculpture nearby called *Star Axis* (www.staraxis.org).

While you're in the area, you might want to take a dip in **Montezuma Hot Springs** (5 A.M.–midnight, free), the waters that first inspired the construction of the castle resort. They're alongside Highway 65—just drive half a mile past the main entrance to the school and look for signs and breaks in the guardrail on the right side of the road. Those farthest along are the most appealing, a series of round concrete pools, screened from the road with a rustic fence.

In the winter, Montezuma Pond, just west of the campus, may be frozen solid enough for **ice skating** (call 505/454-4200 for info). The pond was originally built by the hotel for ice harvesting.

## ENTERTAINMENT AND EVENTS

Even though it's a college town, Las Vegas isn't particularly rambunctious, and it rolls up its sidewalks entirely on Sunday.

### Nightlife

In the summer, the plaza hosts live music on Fridays (4–6 P.M.) in the summer, after which you could check out the **Fort Union Drive-In** (3300 7th St., 505/425-9934, Fri.–Sun. May–Sept.), a great little relic of cinematic history, or the **Kiva Theater** (109 Bridge St., 505/454-0152, www.myspace.com/kivatheater), which has been open since 1912, making it the second-oldest cinema in the state, after the Fountain Theater in Mesilla. After the nightly movie, you could head to **Byron T's** (230 Plaza, noon–midnight daily) bar at the Plaza Hotel, with its dark wood paneling, big show windows overlooking the square, and a great mix of local drinkers. **El Rialto** (141 Bridge St., 505/454-0037) has a more modern-feeling bar.

## Events

If you're in town over Fourth of July weekend, you'll see the **Fiestas de las Vegas** (www.lasvegasnmfiestas.com), when vendors of traditional foods (as well as fair staples like caramel apples) set up all around the plaza and down Bridge Street and bands perform on the gazebo. Festivities last five days, beginning with Mass at Our Lady of Sorrows Church, one block west of the plaza, and ending with the crowning of the Reina de las Fiestas. On the second Saturday evening of each month, Bridge Street gets lively with the town **Artwalk,** when galleries and shops are open late.

## SPORTS AND RECREATION

It's easy to head up into the Pecos Mountains or out onto the flatlands. For maps and current conditions in the mountains, visit the **Pecos/Las Vegas Ranger District office** (1926 7th St., 505/425-3534, 8 A.M.–5 P.M. Mon.–Fri.).

### Santa Fe National Forest

Hikers will want to head north out of Las Vegas on Highway 65, which winds up an ever-narrowing valley to the borders of Santa Fe National Forest and **El Porvenir Campground,** in a pretty patch of pine forest, with campsites ($8) near a stream shaded by ponderosas. **Hermit's Peak Trail** (no. 223) leads 9.5 miles to the 10,160-foot summit. The peak's name refers to wandering mendicant Giovanni Maria Augostini, who walked from Kansas City to Las Vegas with a wagon train in the 1860s; he eventually wound up in the Organ Mountains near Las Cruces, where he was killed.

### Storrie Lake State Park

Just a few miles north of town, Storrie Lake State Park (Hwy. 518, 505/425-7278, www.

nmparks.com, $5/car) is heavily used for water-skiing and windsurfing. But as a place to camp, you can do much better, as it's rather barren, and campsites are so close to the highway that you hear the rush of traffic. As long as you're not hauling an RV, head instead to **Morphy Lake State Park** (575/387-2328, www.nmparks.com, $5/car), in the Mora Valley, which is much quieter.

### Las Vegas National Wildlife Refuge

Southeast of town via Highway 104, the remarkably lush Las Vegas National Wildlife Refuge is part of a chain of wetlands cultivated to accommodate migratory birds. A number of bald eagles winter here, and Swainson's hawks and more than 10 other species of raptors pass through every fall. A rectangular driving route cuts through the 8,672-acre area, passing **McAllister Lake,** where you can also camp. Be prepared: The second half of the circuit is unpaved and can get quite muddy.

Stop in first at the **visitors center** (Hwy. 281, 505/425-3581, 8 A.M.–2 P.M. Mon.–Fri.) to get an idea what birds are visiting; ask, too, if the secondary driving route is open, as it occasionally is in the late fall. If you want to stretch your legs, take the short **Prairie Trail,** which begins next to the gate at the center's driveway, or the half-mile **Gallinas Canyon Trail,** in the southwest corner of the refuge. The latter hike descends into a small canyon, where you can usually spot prairie falcons and swallows; register first (weekdays only) at the visitors center.

### Sports Facilities

Las Vegas's **Abe Montoya Recreation Center** (1751 N. Grand Ave., 505/426-1739, 5:30 A.M.–9 P.M. Mon.–Thurs., 5:30 A.M.–7 P.M. Fri., 9 A.M.–7 P.M. Sat.) has an indoor pool with a big slide ($1), plus ball courts ($3), a skateboard park, and a gym.

## ACCOMMODATIONS

Just about all of Las Vegas's hotels and motels, both chain and independent, are on North

Grand Avenue. The newest chains are on the far north end, at exit 347.

Las Vegas actually has two historic hotels. **El Fidel Hotel** (500 Douglas Ave., 575/425-6761, www.hotelelfidel.com, $45 s, $63 d) gets less press than its rival on the plaza, but you can't beat the price. Rooms are a bit small and basic, and the windows don't open, but the vast tile-floor lobby is relaxing (you can get Wi-Fi here, but not in the rooms). You're also right next to an excellent restaurant, and there's pretty much always a vacancy. And did we mention the low, low rates?

But if you want to do it right, the best place to stay is the beautiful **( Plaza Hotel** (230 Plaza, 505/425-3591, www.plazahotel-nm.com), the first building on the main square to get a solid rehab in the 1960s, and still the grandest. The standard rooms ($149) are perfectly nice, but the larger premium rooms and suites ($174 and $199), in the original building, have the most atmosphere, with towering ceilings, velvet drapes, and stately antiques. Rates include a basic hot breakfast in the hotel's sunny dining room. Prices are significantly lower if you book online.

## FOOD

Aside from the chains on Grand Avenue, dining choices are limited in Las Vegas, but there are a couple of gems.

### Cafés

Make room in your schedule (and your stomach) for a meal at **( Charlie's Spic & Span Bakery and Café** (715 Douglas Ave., 505/426-1921, 6:30 A.M.–5:30 P.M. Mon.–Fri., 7 A.M.–5 P.M. Sat., 7 A.M.–3 P.M. Sun., $8), where the glass cases burst with monster-size éclairs, jelly doughnuts, and gooey cinnamon buns. But the roomy restaurant's real specialty is the flour tortilla—be sure to get one with whatever you order, whether it's chile-smothered eggs (breakfast is served all day) or spicy green-chile stew, or just a green-chile cheeseburger. After tasting the delectably fluffy things, you'll be ruined for the

supermarket variety, so pick up a to-go bag of them at the door.

### New Mexican

Las Vegas's most beloved New Mexican restaurant is probably tiny **( Estella's** (148 Bridge St., 505/454-0048, 11 A.M.–3 P.M. Mon.–Wed., 11 A.M.–8 P.M. Thurs. and Fri., 7 A.M.–2 P.M. Sat., $7), which has been serving up bowls of chile and platters of *carne adovada* since 1950; there's also a chicken-fried steak sandwich on the menu for those who don't like heat.

If you miss Estella's somewhat limited operating hours, head to **El Rialto** (141 Bridge St., 505/454-0037, 10:30 A.M.–8:30 P.M. Mon.–Sat., $12) across the street, a bigger, slicker operation with a lively bar and great patio space.

### Steaks and More

For dinner, the Plaza Hotel's **Landmark Grill** (230 Plaza, 505/425-3591, $14) is popular with local politicians and the like for its steaks, pork chops, and chiles rellenos, served up in a wood-trimmed dining room off the hotel's lobby. The restaurant also does breakfast, lunch, and Sunday brunch, all quite good—a fine option if you're not staying at the hotel but want to enjoy its atmosphere.

A welcome addition to the generally down-home dining scene, **( El Fidel Restaurant** (510 Douglas Ave., 505/425-6659, 11 A.M.–2 P.M. and 5–10 P.M. Mon.–Fri., 5–10 P.M. Sat., 9 A.M.–2 P.M. and 5–10 P.M. Sun., $11–17) feels like it was beamed in from a much bigger city, with a crisp black-and-white interior and jazz playing softly. This could just seem pretentious, but the semi-organic menu is both creative and satisfying, with great flavor combos such as lamb meatballs with walnut-mint pesto. If you're coming from Santa Fe, you might not be stunned, but if you're coming in from the country, it's like an oasis of urbanity.

## INFORMATION AND SERVICES

The Las Vegas **visitors center** (800/832-5947, www.lasvegasnewmexico.com, 9 A.M.–6 P.M.

Mon.–Fri., 11 A.M.–7 P.M. Sat., noon–6 P.M. Sun.), run by the chamber of commerce, occupies a tiny office in the former rail depot where Lincoln Avenue dead-ends at the tracks. The town's on-demand bus service, **Meadow City Express** (505/454-8583), may run a tour of the historic districts at noon daily; confirm in the visitors center.

You can get online at the **Carnegie Public Library** (500 National Ave., 505/426-3304, 8 A.M.–5 P.M. Mon.–Fri., 8 A.M.–noon Sat.), a great excuse to go inside this beautiful building.

### Books and Maps
**Tome on the Range** (158 Bridge St., 505/454-9944, 10 A.M.–6 P.M. Mon.–Fri., 10 A.M.–5 P.M. Sat., noon–4 P.M. Sun.) is an excellent bookstore, with a fine selection of local history and other Western lore, along with all the best-sellers.

### GETTING THERE AND AROUND
**Amtrak** (800/USA-RAIL, www.amtrak. com) stops in the tiny but nicely remodeled old train depot, with service once daily each way from Chicago and Los Angeles. You could take the train up from Albuquerque—it takes about three hours and costs $29. There is no Greyhound service. Once you're there, **X-Press Rent-A-Car** (505/425-6770) has a small office in the depot, next to the tourist office.

# Mora Valley

Highway 518 heads north out of town, running along the edge of the Sangre de Cristo foothills. It eventually turns west to begin the ascent over the mountains—here you'll find the communities of La Cueva and Mora, which are culturally and historically linked with the Hispano towns on the other side of the range, such as Peñasco. A drive through here will take only a few hours (or the better part of a day, if you come during raspberry season), but several mountain retreats might entice you to stay a while.

## MORPHY LAKE STATE PARK
Gem-like Morphy Lake (575/387-2328, www. nmparks.com, $5/car) used to be one of the most difficult-to-reach parks in New Mexico. The narrow road up to the lake, off Highway 94 (turn in Sapello), has been paved, but the place still isn't accessible to RVs. Moreover, the lake is open only to rowboats or craft with electric engines, so the quiet isn't disturbed. The deep-blue water is stocked with trout and ringed with tall ponderosa pines, which provide shade for the primitive campsites ($8).

## LA CUEVA
At the junction of Highways 518 and 442, La Cueva was settled as part of the Mora Land Grant in the early 19th century; it's now a designated national historic site. The **old mill,** built in the 1870s, still creaks and clanks as the acequia streams over the water wheel, which generated electricity for nearby homes until 1949. To the northeast, the small adobe **San Rafael Mission Church** displays the French gothic windows in vogue in 1862, when it was built. **Salman Raspberry Ranch** (575/387-2900, www.salmanraspberryranch.com) now occupies some of the La Cueva outbuildings, as well as its more derelict ruins: It has built beautiful rambling gardens inside the mill complex's old adobe walls, which are a wonderful place to stretch or enjoy a picnic in the summertime. The you-pick berry farm is usually open from early August to mid-October, depending on the weather, with a basic **café** (11 A.M.–4 P.M. Tues.–Fri., 11 A.M.–5 P.M. Fri. and Sat.) alongside. Year-round, you can also get raspberry jam and vinegar, fresh berries (in season), and other local foodstuffs in the

The water wheel at La Cueva Mill has been running since the 1870s.

**farm store** (9 A.M.–5 P.M. daily July–Dec., 9 A.M.–4 P.M. Thurs.–Mon. Jan.–June).

## MORA AND CLEVELAND

The center of the 1835 land grant and of the lush valley, the town of Mora is also the county seat—though that doesn't mean this is a bustling metropolis in any way. Visitors often come for **Tapetes de Lana** (Main St., 575/387-2247, www.tapetesdelana.com, 10 A.M.–5 P.M. Mon.–Sat.), at the main intersection in Mora (the job-training group operates another store in Las Vegas). Inside, locally spun yarn (from the nearby mill) and hand-woven rugs are for sale. The group works with Churro sheep and locally raised alpaca wool.

Some of this wool comes from **Victory Ranch** (Hwy. 434, 575/387-2254, www.victoryranch.com, 10 A.M.–4 P.M. daily mid-Mar.–Dec., $3), up the road about a mile from the highway junction. With feedings of the fuzzy little camelids at 11 A.M., 1 P.M., and 3 P.M., it's a great place to take the kids.

About a mile down the road in the neighboring village, the **Cleveland Roller Mill Museum** (Hwy. 518, 575/387-2645, 10 A.M.–3 P.M. Sat. and Sun. June–Aug., $2) is a two-story adobe structure built around 1900 and kept in use until the mid-1950s. It doesn't look too impressive from the outside, but the building houses a complex system of heavy-duty machinery, from the massive steel rollers that crushed the wheat to the "sock dusters" that absorbed the potentially explosive flour dust. Everything's intact and put into use every Labor Day for the annual Millfest, when there's also live music and arts and crafts booths.

### Accommodations and Food

In the center of Mora, **Hatcha's Café** (Hwy. 518, 575/387-9299, 10 A.M.–7 P.M. Mon.–Fri., 8 A.M.–2 P.M. Sun.) does a mean green-chile stew. Across from the Cleveland Roller Mill Museum, **Mora Inn & RV Park** (575/387-5230, www.morainn.com, $55 d) is a quiet spot to bunk for the night, with motel rooms as well as campsites. It also has a café, open for breakfast and lunch.

© ZORA O'NEILL

THE NORTHEAST

# The Northern Plains

A subtly shifting blanket of gold, brown, or green, depending on the season, New Mexico's plains require a certain mindset to appreciate. The trick is to stop craving switchbacks, vertigo-inducing views, and all the other adrenaline-fueled drama of the mountains. Then you'll find this area incredibly relaxing, as the low-hanging, puffy clouds scud out to the horizon. After a bit of driving, you'll begin to discern the smallest changes: a shimmer of silver where a certain grass flourishes, or the brief contrast afforded by a dark rock outcropping.

Granted, there's very little to do. The major public lands, the Kiowa and Rita Blanca Grasslands, are virtually indistinguishable from the surrounding private ranches and offer very little in the way of recreation. The whole area is home to herds of pronghorn, some elk, and thousands and thousands of cows, the lifeblood of the economy in these parts. It's modern cowboy country, but it's also scarred by the traumatic Dust Bowl years, when dirt lay in drifts up to the fence posts. Many of the older locals still recall those hard times. You'll see few galleries or other signs of modern gentrification—these are unreconstructed small towns. If you're interested in prehistoric goings-on, though, the place is fascinating.

## ALONG THE SANTA FE TRAIL

Whether Bing Crosby was crooning about it, Ronald Reagan riding along it, or even a modern traveler retracing it, the Santa Fe Trail has earned a certain golden glow in American popular culture. The route, which cut across the frontier from Missouri to the middle of New Mexico, was used for less than 60 years, but it has become one of the great symbols of American westward expansion, all bundled up with the era when the cowboy and his horse were the masters of the new land.

The trail holds up well under the pressure of symbolism, especially when you consider the effort it took to traverse its 900 miles. A certain entrepreneur named William Becknell is credited with making the first trading trip, in 1821, without even knowing yet that the Mexican government, newly independent from Spain, had opened the borders of Nuevo México to outsiders. When Becknell was welcomed in Santa Fe, rather than imprisoned, and made a profit of 2,000 percent on his first load of calico cloth, it wasn't long before wagons, loaded with more than three tons of goods, were groaning across the plains.

Not that it was easy money. On this highway, wagons took up to three months for the full trip. At the far edge of Kansas, traders had to make a choice: Take the slow-going Mountain Route through frigid Colorado and the brutal Raton Pass, or risk Comanche and Apache attack on the Cimarron Cut-off, which was level and easy through the plains, but also short on water. The biggest wagon trains, bursting with everything from basic cotton cloth to fripperies like parasols and playing cards, had no choice but to take the latter. Despite the dangers, the traders forged on, driven by dreams of profit. In the process, they also carried the dreams of the expansionist United States – an abstract concept until the U.S. Army used the Santa Fe Trail for supply caravans when it went to war with Mexico in 1846.

So many tons of trade goods and, later, settlers to the new American territory were hauled along the plains that in places, the earth is still scored by wagon ruts. But even such an influential, profitable trail was not a permanent one. First the trail shortened as America's frontier border moved west; then the railroad displaced it entirely. But perhaps the very fact that the Santa Fe Trail was outmoded so quickly by more modern technology is what has fixed it so well in the American imagination.

Dinosaurs roamed through the mud, and then so-called Folsom Man hunted bison during the last ice age; you can see the lingering evidence in several places.

## ◖ FORT UNION NATIONAL MONUMENT

On a barren plain 80 miles from Santa Fe, Fort Union (Hwy. 161, 505/425-8025, www. nps.gov/foun, 8 A.M.–6 P.M. daily June–Aug., 8 A.M.–4 P.M. daily Sept.–May, $3) was the largest military depot in the southwest, located strategically where the two branches of the Santa Fe Trail joined. Built largely of adobe, the fort has melted away, leaving not much more than the outlines of the buildings; however, you can still get a good idea just how vast the complex was, and the experience is heightened by some informative audio clips that play in front of buildings like the jail and the latrine.

old adobe walls at Fort Union, the largest fort in the Southwest

But it took three tries to get the fort to this point. The first, built of logs, was built in 1851 as a base for campaigns against Apache raiders, but it soon rotted away. A second was a star-shaped earthen fortification built in a hurry to defend against a rumored Confederate attack in 1861; fortunately, the Union triumphed in the Battle of Glorieta Pass, just a year later, and the troops could abandon the muddy hovel.

The third structure, the stone and adobe outlines of which are preserved today, became the largest fort in New Mexico, with relatively luxurious officers' quarters and plenty of room for both a military post and a supply depot. The latter portion was actually busier, receiving and redirecting all kinds of goods that arrived via the Santa Fe Trail. But like so many settlements in New Mexico, Fort Union became obsolete when the railroad was laid through the state, and by 1891, this massive installation had been decommissioned.

Walk out northeast from the ruins to see the ghostly imprints of wagon ruts from the Santa Fe Trail—they're most visible early or late in the day.

## EAST FROM WAGON MOUND

Named for a rock outcropping that faintly resembles a Conestoga wagon, the small town at exit 387 is the turning point for Roy—if you're heading out to Clayton, this is a much prettier route than U.S. 56 from Springer. There's not much here but a couple of gas stations, though on Labor Day weekend, Wagon Mound hosts **Bean Day,** a century-old harvest celebration when there's rodeos, a free barbecue, and a big parade—bigger than the tiny downtown can hold, so it runs through twice.

### Highway 120 to Roy

You're really getting off here for Highway 120, which heads east across flatlands that are often surprisingly green. Another surprise: the dip down into Canadian River Canyon, striated with red and white. The road then heads to Roy—home to not quite 500 people, giving it the dubious title of the largest town in Harding County. Its last claim to fame was

© ZORA O'NEILL

that western-swing bandleader Bob Wills penned "San Antonio Rose" here in 1927, as he worked as a barber by day. At the time, Roy was much livelier, as a shipping point for coal to Tucumcari and a major dry-ice manufacturing site, given its location on top of the Bravo Dome carbon-dioxide field.

## La Frontera del Llano Scenic Byway

Although the highway from Wagon Mound is arguably more awe-inspiring, Highway 39, which runs north and south from Roy, is an *official* scenic route, a section of La Frontera del Llano Scenic Byway. To the south and east, the "Edge of the Plains" route goes to the cattle-ranching centers of **Mosquero** and **Bueyeros,** passing pink-striped buttes, a string of beautiful old churches, and dilapidated little bars. You can follow the route south to the end of the byway at Logan, near I-40, or head north at Bueyeros to make a roundabout route up to Clayton.

The northern stretch of Highway 39 from Roy runs through the **Kiowa and Rita Blanca National Grasslands,** part of 235,000 acres of short-grass prairie that are federally managed to maintain the natural flora, so as to avoid a repeat of the 1930s devastation. The land is home to quail, bobcats, and lots of pronghorn, but don't expect pristine wilderness—cattle are still allowed to graze here. You can camp at **Mills Canyon,** 10 miles north of Roy on Highway 39, then about 10 miles east, where a narrow, rocky road leads 800 feet down into the canyon. A former commercial farm, the sheltered river bottom still harbors a few fruit trees, as well as wildlife such as mule deer and Barbary sheep, introduced in 1950. During dry stretches of the summer, the campground can be closed due to fire danger—call the grasslands headquarters in Clayton (575/374-9652) to check the status before heading out here.

Highway 39, and the scenic byway, ends at the town of Abbott, at the junction with U.S. 56—from here, it's virtually a straight shot east to Clayton.

## SPRINGER

Springer is at the exit for U.S. 56, which runs directly to Clayton. Formerly named Maxwell, for Lucien B. Maxwell, whose land grant covered all of Colfax County, Springer was the county seat between 1882 and 1898 (Raton now holds the title). When political power moved away, so did most of the action. Now there's not much here except a vast antiques store, **Jespersen's Cache** (403 Maxwell Ave., 575/483-2349).

The other reason to visit is the very nice and unpretentious **Brown Hotel** (302 Maxwell Ave., 575/483-2269, $50 s, $60 d), which also serves as the town's main **café** (6 A.M.–7 P.M. Mon.–Sat., 7 A.M.–2 P.M. Sun. in summer, call for winter hours, $7). Its hearty, homemade American and New Mexican food is a treat in the middle of nowhere. The hotel has a rooming-house feel, with chenille bedspreads and furniture your grandmother might've owned; the view onto Springer's (almost always quiet) main street adds to the feel, as does the lack of TVs and phones. A group of the least expensive rooms share a bath, while others are arranged in pairs around a single bathroom with a tub— if the place isn't full, you'll probably get the facilities to yourself. When reserving, you might want to specify wood floors or carpeting; also, a few of the beds are a bit saggy, so feel free to check out the options. Rates include a full breakfast at the café.

## CLAYTON

Only 12 miles from Texas, Clayton is a place where most of the 2,500 people in town spend their days on horseback or otherwise engaged in the large cattle operations on the surrounding ranches and feedlots. (If the wind blows the wrong way, the smell is hard to ignore, though on a crisp autumn evening, there's a positive spin: You definitely get a sense of place.) By night, attention focuses on the gem of a vintage movie theater or the high school football stadium. The big annual event is the rodeo on Fourth of July weekend, and there are easily more churches than restaurants in town. In short, you're a long way from Santa Fe.

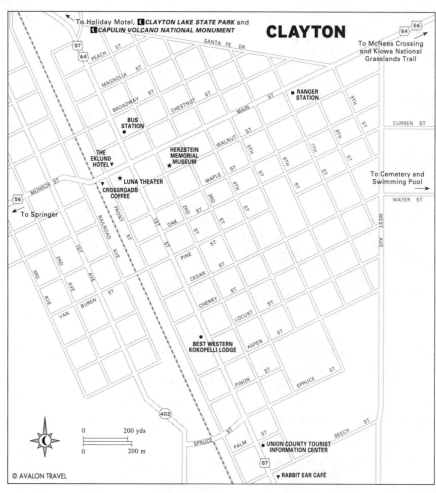

To Holiday Motel, ◖CLAYTON LAKE STATE PARK and ◖CAPULIN VOLCANO NATIONAL MONUMENT

# CLAYTON

To McNees Crossing and Kiowa National Grasslands Trail

SANTA FE DR

87
64
PEACH ST

MAGNOLIA ST

BROADWAY
CHESTNUT ST
MAIN ST
■ RANGER STATION
9TH ST

BUS STATION ■

WALNUT ST
8TH ST
CURREN ST

THE EKLUND HOTEL ▼
HERZSTEIN MEMORIAL MUSEUM ★
6TH ST
7TH ST

★ LUNA THEATER
MAPLE ST
4TH ST
To Cemetery and Swimming Pool

56
▼ CROSSROADS COFFEE
2ND ST
3RD ST
WATER ST

To Springer
RAILROAD AVE
FRONT ST
1ST ST
OAK ST
ST
WEST AVE

2ND AVE
1ST AVE
ST
PINE ST

3RD AVE
BUREN ST
CEDAR ST

VAN
CHERRY ST

LOCUST ST

● BEST WESTERN KOKOPELLI LODGE
ASPEN ST

PINON ST
SPRUCE ST

402
SPRUCE ST
BEECH ST

0      200 yds
0      200 m
PALM ST
■ UNION COUNTY TOURIST INFORMATION CENTER
87
▼ RABBIT EAR CAFÉ

© AVALON TRAVEL

THE NORTHEAST

Clayton was established relatively late by New Mexican standards—in 1888, well after the railroad. But it soon rocketed to notoriety as the place where outlaw Thomas "Black Jack" Ketchum met his end, two years after he was picked up for attempting to rob a train near Folsom.

## Sights

Bone up on local history at the interesting **Herzstein Memorial Museum** (S. 2nd St. at Walnut St., 575/374-2977, 10 A.M.–5 P.M. Tues.–Sun., free), a collection of local ephemera bequeathed to the town by a prominent shopkeeper. Spread over two floors of a stately 1919 Methodist church, the displays are surprisingly un-dusty, with period furniture, clothing, and medical equipment alongside vitrines dedicated to local luminaries such as Cowgirl Hall of Famer and single mom Bernice McLaughlin. There's also a small but fascinating display on the Dust Bowl. Tucked away in a small hall are photographs of Black Jack Ketchum being hanged

footsteps of giants at Clayton Lake State Park

© ZORA O'NEILL

THE NORTHEAST

on the courthouse square in 1901, a grisly event that ended in his accidental beheading. Ketchum (both parts) is buried in the **cemetery** (Princeton Ave.), at the southeast corner of town.

### ◖ Clayton Lake State Park

Fifteen miles north of Clayton, sunk down just below the level of the surrounding plain, Clayton Lake (Hwy. 370, 575/374-8808, www.nmparks.com, $5/car, $8 camping) is a lovely haven for day use or camping. But the real attraction is the **dinosaur footprints** in the sandstone at the east end of the lake. Made some 100 million years ago in what was then mud, they are part of a long series of tracks from Mosquero Creek in Harding County up to Fort Collins, Colorado, a route that ran along the edge of an ancient sea. They're accessible via a quarter-mile-long paved trail—look for signs to the right as you enter the park. Try to go early in the morning or in late afternoon, when the longer shadows make the prints stand out more clearly. The visitors center at the park

also has a small display about dinosaur life in this area.

### Sports and Recreation

**McNees Crossing** gets frequent mention in tourist literature, but even true Santa Fe trail enthusiasts will find little to see from the marker on Highway 406, east and north of Clayton. Better to head for the **Kiowa National Grasslands Hiking Trail,** which leads to some very well-preserved wagon ruts, as well as a ruined homestead. Getting there requires zigzagging along dirt ranch-access roads. Head east on U.S. 64/56, then 13 miles north on Highway 406; turn left (west) on Campbell Road and go 3 miles, then north 1 mile to a small pullout for parking. On your way out of Clayton, you might want to stop at the **ranger station** (714 Main St., 575/374-9652) for a map.

Should you need to cool off, the **municipal swimming pool** (Water St., 12:30–5:30 P.M. Tues.–Fri., noon–6 P.M. Sat., 1–6 P.M. Sun.) is a good-sized outdoor facility with a kiddie slide. It's on the east side of town—go through the gate to the armory and the airport.

### Entertainment

If you're a vintage cinema buff, don't miss the **Luna Theater** (4 Main St., 575/374-2712), built in 1916 as a vaudeville house. Pay the $5 admission at the Luna regardless of what's showing, just to see the glowing interior, set with art deco sconces and a beautiful embroidered velvet curtain from the 1930s. You can also try knocking during the day—if someone's there, they'll show you around. Showtime is 7:30 P.M. May–October and 7 P.M. November–April.

### Accommodations

Locally owned independent **Holiday Motel** (U.S. 87, 575/374-2558, $49 s, $59 d) is a gem—not much to look at on the outside, but scrupulously clean inside. The owners are so enthusiastic, they fold the towels into animal shapes. It's on the northwest edge of town, about a quarter-mile out from the big bridge.

Among the chain hotels, by far the best is the **Best Western Kokopelli Lodge** (702 S. 1st St., 575/374-2589, www.bestwestern.com, $120 d). It's a million times nicer than it has to be, considering the feeble competition from the neighbors, with an outdoor pool, wireless Internet, a free hot breakfast buffet, and plush, spacious rooms.

There's also a historic hotel, the Eklund, on Main Street. As of 2010, it was closed, but there were rumors it would be reopened. Check before you go—it's a trove of history, with a cool saloon.

### Food

The most popular restaurant in town is the **Rabbit Ear Café** (1201 S. 1st St., 575/374-3277, 7 A.M.–2 P.M. Mon., 7 A.M.–9 P.M. Tues.–Sat., 8 A.M.–2 P.M. Sun., $10)—which doesn't mean it's great. It's inconsistent, but when it's good, the chile is hot and the burritos are stuffed. Either way, it's a good slice of life in Clayton.

The other option is **Crossroads Coffee** (2 S. Front St., 575/374-5282, 6:30 A.M.–2 P.M. and 4–7 P.M. Mon.–Fri., 7–11 A.M. Sat., $7), a funky wood-paneled place in the old feed store that also happens to be an unlikely outpost of espresso with house-roasted beans. It has daily lunch specials (fajita wraps, turkey pesto sandwiches) and breakfast burritos in the morning, plus a bulging pastry case.

### Information and Services

The **Clayton-Union County Tourist Information Center** (1103 S. 1st St., 575/374-9253, www.claytonnewmexico.net, 8 A.M.–5 P.M. Mon.–Fri.) has a few brochures, plus souvenir postcards from the Dust Bowl. There's a free Internet station here, as well as wireless access all around the center of town. You can also get more detailed info online at the municipal website (www.claytonnewmexico.net).

### Getting There

**Greyhound** (800/231-2222, www.greyhound.com) runs through here, but only via Amarillo, Texas, dropping you off at the station (113 E. Chestnut St., 575/374-9924, 8 A.M.–5 P.M. Mon.–Fri.).

## WEST TO RATON

U.S. 64/87 heads roughly northwest out of Clayton, another hypnotizing drive through golden prairie. The terrain changes a bit halfway along, as defunct volcanoes punctuate the horizon. The most distinctive is the perfectly conical peak of Capulin; a drive up to the top (an adventure in itself) gives you a break from all the flatness, as well as a stunning view.

From Capulin, you can detour north to the ghost town of Folsom, a starting point for two smaller, more scenic roads. Backtrack east along a rough byway through the washes and ridges strung along the border with Colorado, or keep heading west on Highway 72, which takes you across a dramatic high mesa, the perfect way to meet the mountains at Raton.

### ◖ Capulin Volcano National Monument

An unmissable landmark, the domed top of Capulin Volcano (575/278-2201, www.nps.gov/cavo, 8 A.M.–5 P.M. daily June–Aug., 8 A.M.–4 P.M. daily Sept.–May, $5/car) reaches 8,182 feet above sea level and stands approximately as tall as the Empire State Building. About 60,000 years ago, Capulin spewed hot ash and rock into the air, which then settled into an almost perfect cone—its top edge looks like a carefully opened soft-boiled egg. At the summit, you can walk a short trail down into this crater, where steam vents are noticeable in the winter, as the surrounding patches are covered with greenery. Or hike up around the rim: From this vantage point you can see more clearly how this whole region was shaped by volcanic activity, from the lava-topped mesas to the hulking Sierra Grande. The latter formation is another dormant volcano, about a million years old, that's also the largest lone mountain in the United States, covering 50 square miles and rising 2,200 feet above the surrounding plain. Guided tours in summer at 10 A.M. and 2:30 P.M. can point out more details.

Dormant volcanoes dot the plains northwest of Clayton.

But to reach the top of Capulin, you first have to negotiate a two-mile road that spirals up the side of the volcano. It's narrow and doesn't have as many guardrails as you might expect; put your steeliest driver in charge, and take it slow. It's much easier coming down, as you're on the inside lane the whole time. Also watch out for mule deer in the road around the base. The area at the top has limited parking, so if you're visiting in the busy months of July and August, go very early or late in the day, or you'll have to wait to drive up.

## Folsom

Hard by the railroad tracks, late-19th-century Folsom drew cattle-traders and outlaws (most notably "Black Jack" Ketchum, whose gang held up trains three times here). Then in 1908, a flood demolished a good part of the town, and even claimed the life of the village telephone operator, who stayed at her post to warn residents of danger. Around the same time, floods also uncovered a collection of bison skeletons embedded with spear points in a wash west of town. When the site was finally

excavated in 1927, the spear points were determined to be at least 10,000 years old—a shock to archaeologists, who'd previously thought American Indians had arrived on the continent only around 2000 B.C.

At the intersection of Highways 325 and 456, **Folsom Museum** (575/278-3616, 10 A.M.–5 P.M. daily June–Aug., 10 A.M.–5 P.M. Sat. and Sun. May and Sept., $1.50) tells these stories in more detail, if not in a very illuminating way. It occupies a big old general store, and with all the dusty knickknacks in the old display cases, it's hard to remember that you're in a museum rather than a junk shop. Perhaps the best item is the odd diorama of the Ketchum hanging, but it's a perfectly decent place to stretch your legs, and perhaps avail yourself of the "colas and crackers" proffered for sale.

## Dry Cimarron Scenic Byway

A network of rural highways stretching into Colorado and Oklahoma, this route roughly follows the path of the Dry Cimarron River, with Highway 456 as the backbone; it eventually winds up back in Clayton.

© ZORA O'NEILL

Folsom Falls

About 3.5 miles northeast of Folsom on Highway 456, on the right (southeast) side of the road, look for a pullout and a sign warning against swimming. A small trail leads a short way to **Folsom Falls,** where water pours directly out of the rock face. It's visible from the edge of the shallow canyon, but you'll need to clamber down the rocks to get to the water's edge.

From here, Highway 456 zigzags across the river bottom as it heads east. At the junction with Highway 370, you can drive south to Clayton Lake State Park, but if you continue east, you'll pass towering buttes dubbed Battleship and Wedding Cake. You then loop back to Clayton via Highway 406.

## ◖ Johnson Mesa

U.S. 64/87 may go to Raton more directly, but if weather permits, don't skip the drive along Highway 72 out of Folsom, which is one of the most beautiful in New Mexico. Technically, this stretch of highway is also part of the Dry Cimarron Scenic Byway, but the terrain is so different as to seem like you're in an entirely different state. The narrow paved byway dips and rises, rollercoaster-like, as it gradually climbs the foothills, and then you're deposited on the top of Johnson Mesa, a bucolic expanse of grazing land studded with smaller hills, such as the perfectly round Red Mountain. At one point, the road passes close to the mesa edge, and you realize just how high up you are as you see the land plunge away. About the only evidence of human habitation up here is a small stone church, **St. John's Methodist,** built in 1896; now no one lives on the mesa regularly, though a few hardy souls come up for the summer along with the livestock. If you drive this way at dusk, watch out for deer on the road, even on the fringes of Raton.

**THE NORTHEAST**

# The Rockies

Where the laden caravans of traders struggled through Raton Pass on the Santa Fe Trail's mountain route, drivers now zip up with ease. Raton is still a watering hole, but it sates visitors with fast-food restaurants and travel centers; press past the off-ramp economy to see the town's century-old core, laid out along the now-silent railroad depot. South and west of Raton, smaller Cimarron was another stopping point on the mountain route, and one that wears its history well.

## RATON

The glowing red RATON sign on the hilltop on the northwest side of town suggests this mountain burg is a lot glitzier than it is. Traces of past glamour can be seen in the art deco fire station on North 2nd Street, for instance, and the quirky castle facade on the Raton Theater. But it owes everything to the mountain that juts up behind it: Travelers crossed precipitous Raton Pass (allegedly named by Spanish traders for the wood rats that lived in the forests

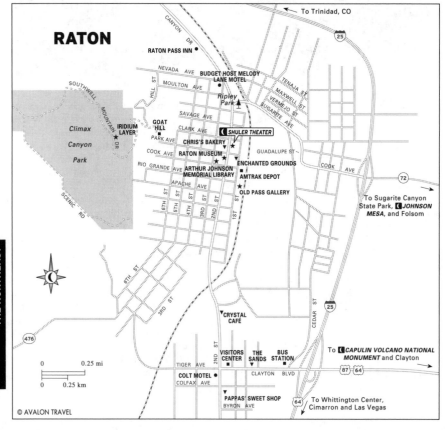

© AVALON TRAVEL

here), then rested after the strenuous trip. In 1866, an entrepreneur by the name of Richens Wootton took it upon himself to blast out a proper road through the mountains, wide enough to accommodate wagon trains—then he set up a toll gate and charged Santa Fe Trail traders to come through. "Uncle Dick," as he was known, sold his road to AT&SF Railroad for $1 and a lifetime grocery stipend. The railroad helped keep the town of Raton in money too, and some wealth came from coal mining in the surrounding mountains, though nothing like the giddy get-rich-quick silver and gold mines in the south. All of this was enough to bring big theaters and the first public school in the state—though, like everywhere in the late-19th-century West, it had its fair share of lynchings, mob violence, and more.

Now it's a more peaceful town, one that overlooks the plains to the east but still has its heart in the Rockies. If you are just passing through, note that nearly everything shuts down on Sundays—you'll be hard-pressed to find somewhere to eat outside of the usual chains.

## C Shuler Theater

The gem of 2nd Street is this rococo auditorium (131 N. 2nd St., 575/445-4746, www.shulertheater.com), beautifully restored by the town and used for live performances. Visitors can tour the theater weekdays 9 A.M. to 5 P.M.—definitely worth a stop to see the 1930s lobby murals and the beautiful cloud-studded "sky" above the proscenium. Three of the original drop curtains survive as well—they're painted with scenes depicting a Roman villa, the palisade cliffs near Cimarron, and Raton's Ripley Park. Building the theater was a bit of a battle, as the city council used money that had been earmarked for a new city hall. Later, the municipal auditorium was named in honor of the mayor who'd perpetrated the boondoggle, in a council resolution that was worded to effectively tell Raton residents, "See, we told you you'd love it."

## Other Sights

The main thoroughfare for cars is 2nd Street, where the **Raton Museum** (108 S. 2nd St., 575/445-8979, 10 A.M.–4 P.M. Tues.–Sat. in summer, 10 A.M.–4 P.M. Wed.–Sat. in winter, donation), occupies two huge tin-ceiling rooms. Displays on the coal camps and other facets of local life are nicely presented, along with vintage dolls, works by Taos painters and some good santero carvings in the front upstairs area. Pick up a walking-tour brochure here to guide you on a stroll along 1st Street, Raton's **historic downtown** where the handsome old storefronts are trimmed in cast-iron garlands, graceful figureheads, and jutting cornices. Business isn't exactly booming, but there are a few antiques shops and the **Old Pass Gallery** (145 S. 1st St., 575/445-2052, 10 A.M.–4:30 P.M. Tues.–Sat.), run by the local arts council. It occupies a renovated Wells Fargo office, and next door is the train depot, the only surviving building of a huge complex that used to manage the comings and goings of more than 60 trains a day.

You could also seek out the **Arthur Johnson Memorial Library** (244 Cook Ave., 575/445-9711, 1–6 P.M. Mon., 10 A.M.–6 P.M. Tue., Wed., Fri., and Sat., 10 A.M.–9 P.M. Thurs.), between 2nd and 3rd Streets, a neoclassical structure built as a post office in 1917, then converted to a library under the Carnegie program. It houses a good collection of Southwest-theme art, including some of the early Taos artists.

By car, you can drive up to **Goat Hill,** where the RATON sign is perched; take Moulton Avenue west to Hill Street. This hill is geologically famous, as it has a visible stripe of iridium running through it—the stripe of detritus that marks the meteorite crash that ended the dinosaurs. Just before the top of the hill, bear right rather than left at the fork—this dirt road will carry you around the ridgeline a few miles to a marked spot and a scenic overlook.

## Sports and Recreation

The closest outdoor getaway to Raton, **Sugarite Canyon State Park** (Hwy. 526,

575/445-5607, www.nmparks.com, $5/car) encompasses 3,600 acres along either side of Chicorica Creek and Lake Maloya, which is favored for trout fishing and casual boating. The area is also beautiful in spring, when the mountain slopes are dotted with wildflowers. From behind the visitors center, two miles up Highway 526, the Coal Camp Trail runs through the ruins of a mining settlement and up to two old mine shafts; a few longer trails lead up to the bluffs that line the road—ask at the visitors center for maps.

Hunting is a very big deal in the high mountains around Raton. Many outdoorsy types start at **Whittington Center** (Hwy. 64, 575/445-3615, www.nrawc.org), a 52-square-mile complex established in 1973 by the National Rifle Association. It's the largest gun club in the United States, offering classes for beginners and experts, target and skeet shooting, plus real-life hunting for deer, antelope, and even mountain lions. There's also space to camp or simple cabins.

## Accommodations

Most motels are located on Clayton Boulevard, which runs from exit 451 off I-25, but you don't need to rely on the big chains because you've got the ◀ **Budget Host Melody Lane Motel** (136 Canyon Dr., 575/445-3655, www.budgethost.com, $70 s, $75 d), on the quieter north side of town. It's a flawlessly maintained old motor court whose owner is a fanatic about cleanliness (she credits the nuns who raised her). Whatever the reason, you'll enjoy firm beds and new carpeting in the wood-paneled rooms with cozy-feeling slanted ceilings. Some bathrooms have a vintage built-in sauna—such a treat you could even check in here for the afternoon and call it a day spa. Though you can book online, the owner advises calling, as she often holds back rooms, and you can make special requests.

Just up the road, **Raton Pass Inn** (308 Canyon Dr., 575/445-3641, $52 d) is another excellent choice, though it's open only mid-April through October. It's run by a relative of the Budget Host owner, and the standards

© ZORA O'NEILL
vintage sleeping comfort in Raton

are equally scrupulous. The exterior looks like a standard 50-year-old motor court, but each of the 14 large rooms is decorated with a special touch and include Wi-Fi, mini fridges, and microwaves.

If you want unadulterated vintage-motel ambience, check out the **Colt Motel** (1160 S. 2nd St., 575/445-2305, www.coltmotel.com, $61 s, $67 d), where each room comes with its own little carport—very handy if you're coming through during the snowy season (when rates drop substantially). Modern amenities like fridges and wireless Internet complement the thick old walls, varied room layouts, and groovy bathroom tile (showers only, though); the owners are rightly proud of the way they've preserved the place.

## Food

Raton's restaurants have limited opening hours, and if you don't plan well, you'll be relegated to the fast-food joints on Clayton Boulevard. For morning coffee, **Enchanted Grounds Espresso Bar** (111 Park Ave., 575/445-2129, 7 A.M.–2 P.M. Mon., 7 A.M.–4:30 P.M.

Tues.–Fri., 7:30 A.M.–4:30 P.M. Sat.) is the place to go; it also serves French toast, egg sandwiches, and light lunches. If you like a doughnut with your coffee, detour to the bare-bones **Chris's Bakery** (134 N. 2nd St., 575/445-3781, 6:30 A.M.–2 P.M. Mon.–Fri., 7:20 A.M.–2 P.M. Sat.); they're so delectably crispy and light, you might need two.

**Pappas' Sweet Shop** (1201 S. 2nd St., 575/445-9811, 11:30 A.M.–1 P.M. and 5–8 P.M. Mon.–Fri.) bears mention just because it has been around so long. Originally an ice cream parlor, it has a menu that appeals to palates young and old, with pot roast, steaks—and cocktails.

The throwback **Crystal Café** (1021 S. 2nd St., 575/445-9461, 9 A.M.–1 P.M. and 5–8 P.M. Mon.–Fri., 5–8 P.M. Sat., $9) does diner breakfast and lunch. At night, it's all about good old Italian-American food like spaghetti and meatballs, served over paper placemats with a map of Italy.

After 8 P.M., your only non-chain choice is **The Sands** (350 Clayton Blvd., 575/445-4024, 6 A.M.–10 P.M. Mon.–Sat., 7 A.M.–9 P.M. Sun., $12), a Mexican-theme diner staffed by waitresses in frilly tops. The food isn't stupendous, but there's a range of stuff, from chimichangas to vegetarian specials.

### Information and Services

The **New Mexico visitor information center** (100 Clayton Blvd., 575/445-2761, www.raton.info, 8 A.M.–5 P.M. daily), maintained by both the Raton chamber of commerce and the state tourism board, can acquaint you with Raton, but it's more accustomed to dealing with through travelers looking for info on the rest of the state (which is presented in a particularly orderly fashion).

For Internet access, head to the **Arthur Johnson Memorial Library** (244 Cook Ave., 575/445-9711, 1–6 P.M. Mon., 10 A.M.–6 P.M. Tue., Wed., Fri., and Sat., 10 A.M.–9 P.M. Thurs.).

### Getting There

**Amtrak** (800/USA-RAIL, www.amtrak.com) trains pull in to the historic depot on 1st Street once each day on the eastbound and westbound routes. The trip from Albuquerque takes about 4.5 hours and costs $40. **Greyhound** (800/231-2222, www.greyhound.com) is impractical from Albuquerque. The only direct buses come in from Denver and Amarillo, Texas, and drop you off at the station (524 Clayton Blvd., 575/445-9071, 8–9 A.M. and 11 A.M.–1 P.M. Mon.–Fri., 11 A.M.–1 P.M. Sat.).

## VALLE VIDAL

South of Raton, U.S. 64 bears west away from I-25 and deeper into the mountains. About five miles outside of Cimarron is the turn for Forest Road 1950, the only access point to Valle Vidal, a 102,000-acre portion of the Carson National Forest that straddles some of the highest peaks in the Sangre de Cristo range. The border of the reserve is actually northwest of Cimarron—it's a good 25-mile drive up the forest road to the entrance. But if you're seeking pristine wilderness, it's worth the trek—Valle Vidal is perhaps the last, best place to get a sense of what New Mexico was like in the 19th century, when the Maxwell Land Grant was laid out. The place is home to the state's largest elk herd, and its watershed is essential for the rare Rio Grande cutthroat trout.

Though little visited, it is probably one of the best-known public lands in New Mexico, as it has been the topic of strenuous debate since 1982, when Pennzoil traded the land to the National Forest Service in exchange for tax breaks. Valle Vidal's status was always a bit vague, with no clear management plan for the natural-gas deposits beneath it. A strong grassroots campaign finally led to a law prohibiting mining and drilling, passed in late 2006.

There are no services in the wilderness, very few trails, and only two camping areas. Coming from the Cimarron side, the first one you reach is **McCrystal Campground,** set on a flat plain, with a few ponderosas providing shade; this is where people exploring on horseback often camp. If you want more privacy, head eight more miles to the 35 sites at the higher-elevation **Cimarron Campground,** which are tucked amid trees; many trout-fishing creeks are right nearby. For current conditions and advisories (parts of the valley are closed seasonally to protect the elk), contact the **Questa Ranger District office** (575/586-0520), on the west side, which manages the whole area.

## CIMARRON

There are few false-front buildings here, and no shoot-out reenactments at high noon, but Cimarron still feels like a 19th-century mountain town. A few times a year, the streets are filled with horses being driven to various pastures on the vast Philmont Ranch that adjoins the community, and the assorted rivalries of the Colfax County War are spoken of as though they happened yesterday—perhaps because so much of the town's social life takes place at the old St. James Hotel, where the ceiling is pocked with bullet holes.

But more than this violent history, the wilderness is what defines Cimarron. Established in 1861 by Lucien Maxwell, the town was the most substantial settlement on the giant land grant that Maxwell would later own outright. The surrounding mountains (and all the wildlife they harbor) still press in close, so that when the sun starts to set and the stars glimmer overhead, you're reminded just how small the town is. Amid so much empty land, you have to wonder what all the fighting was about…and was that a bear rustling over there in the trees?

By day, everything seems much more benign. A handful of galleries line 9th Street, one block north of U.S. 64 and the old acequia, and the fish jump in the Cimarron River. You can hike between granite cliffs or tour the mansion of the oilman who ran Philmont Ranch and dedicated it to the Boy Scouts of America. But at the end of the day, you'll likely be back at the St. James, drinking a beer and talking about the past.

### ◖ St. James Hotel

The center of Cimarron's social life, past and present, is the St. James Hotel (Hwy. 21, 575/376-2664), a beautifully maintained building that's as packed with legends, lore, and (perhaps) ghosts as it is with beautiful antiques and stuffed buffalo heads. Opened first as a saloon by a French chef named Henri Lambert (former employer: Abraham Lincoln) in 1872, the St. James rapidly became a Wild West playground bar none, with just about every famed outlaw passing through its swinging doors at some point. Buffalo Bill Cody met Annie Oakley in the saloon, Jesse James always requested the same room, and Billy the Kid, Black Jack Ketchum, and Wyatt Earp all signed the guest register. Cimarron was considered calm and quiet when three days passed without the sound of gunfire in the St. James; bullets are still embedded in walls and ceilings, particularly in the main dining room.

Specifically, one act of the **Colfax County War** played out here, when in 1875 the ranch hand and freelance shootist Clay Allison killed Francisco Griego in alleged self-defense, as Griego was seeking vengeance for the murder of his nephew, the constable Cruz Vega, whom Allison had lynched, in retaliation

© ZORA O'NEILL

THE NORTHEAST

REV. F. J. TOLBY
ASSASSINATED
SEPT. 14 1875
AGED 33 YRS

Casualties of the Colfax County War are buried in Cimarron's cemetery.

for his alleged participation in the murder of Franklin Tolby, a young minister who supported the rights of the local settlers. Sound complicated? It was, and it only got more so, as some 200 people were killed trying to settle the debate over who got to live on the Maxwell Land Grant.

All that history still feels very present in the chandelier-lit hallways lined with peeling wallpaper. Visitors are welcome to poke around on the ground floor, where some of the guestroom doors are left open.

### Other Sights

Round out the local history with a visit to the **Old Mill Museum** (Hwy. 21, 575/376-2913, 10 A.M.–5 P.M. Mon.–Wed., Fri. and Sat., 1–5 P.M. Sun. June–Aug., weekends only May and Sept., $3), just across the street from the hotel. Built by Lucien Maxwell in 1864, the structure now houses relics of the Colfax County War. You can also visit the **cemetery,** a short walk south on Highway 21, where the grave of Reverend Franklin Tolby sits alongside more recent (and longer-lived) Cimarron residents.

### Sports and Recreation

West of town about 12 miles, straddling U.S. 64 and stretching nearly to Eagle Nest, **Cimarron Canyon State Park** (575/377-6271, www.nmparks.com, $5/car) is known for its excellent trout fishing in the Cimarron River and its tributaries, as well as the dramatic granite palisades that form the canyon walls. Backcountry camping is not permitted, and the only established campgrounds are several spots fairly close to the road. Hiking, however, is excellent, especially on **Clear Creek Trail,** a 7 mile out-and-back you can do in about three hours. The route runs along a creek and passes several small waterfalls while gaining about a thousand feet; it's particularly nice in the fall, when the aspens turn yellow. Look for a signed pullout around mile marker 292. At about 6 miles one-way, **Tolby Creek Trail** makes a much longer outing—most of the trek is pleasantly shaded and damp, ending in beautiful

high meadows. This trail is not so clearly marked—you should double-check the route at the **park office,** across the highway from the trailhead at the western park boundary, just before you reach the town of Eagle Nest.

### Accommodations

Needless to say, the ◖ **St. James Hotel** (Hwy. 21, 575/376-2664) is the top pick here—but part of what makes the place so atmospheric is the artfully maintained level of antiquity in the 14 rooms in the main building, most with private baths with small tubs ($105–140), and a few sharing a more deluxe facility in the hall ($70–85). Your bed will certainly be comfortable, but prepare yourself for creaky floors, slightly awkward but original corner marble sinks, and other fusty details. If you can't bear impractical plumbing and no TV or phone, opt for one of the 10 modern rooms in the annex ($80–170).

Just up the road, **Cimarron Inn & RV Park** (U.S. 64, 575/376-2268, www.cimarron-inn.com) is a converted old motel with snug, thick-walled rooms, each one done in a different western theme. Four small rooms ($45) are a steal for solo travelers or couples, while the eight larger rooms ($60 d) are divvied up like tiny apartments, so there's a wall separating beds. Families or groups might like the Cowboy Cabin ($125), which sleeps up to six people, or the Casita ($180), with room for a dozen. If there's no vacancy here, **Canyon Inn** (31039 U.S. 64, 575/376-2336, www.cimmaroncanyoninn.com, $65 d) will do—it's a refurbished motor court with spacious rooms but not as much mountain charm as its neighbors.

### Food

Cimarron has few dining options, but fortunately a couple of places are very good. As with everything else, the main action is at the St. James Hotel: The menu at **Express** (Hwy. 21, 575/376-2664, 7–10:30 A.M. and 11 A.M.–9 P.M. daily, $8–20) covers the usual tacos-and-burritos territory, as well as standard burgers and steaks, and the more local grilled trout. The bar here is the only one in town; it's open from noon till midnight or "whenever the bartender gets tired of looking at people."

For breakfast or lunch, [( **The Porch Deli** (636 9th St., 575/376-2228, 7:30 A.M.–2 P.M. Mon.–Fri., $6) is also recommended, for strong coffee, pastries, and great chicken salad. The porch in question faces U.S. 64, but the entrance is on 9th Street, one block north.

### Information and Services

Cimarron's **visitors center** (575/376-2417, www.cimarronnm.com, 9 A.M.–5 P.M. daily May–Aug.,10 A.M.–3 P.M. Sept.–Apr.) occupies a small house just off U.S. 64 at Lincoln Avenue—look for a cowboy mural. You can pick up a walking-tour brochure here, along with other background info. To really get into the history of the place, you could take the **Legends by Lantern Light** tour (575/445-8373, 7:30 P.M. Wed. and Sat. in summer, $8) to hear the tales of local outlaws.

## PHILMONT RANCH

South out of Cimarron, Highway 21 takes the roundabout way back to Springer at I-25. The first leg roughly follows the old Santa Fe Trail route, passing the headquarters of Philmont Ranch (575/376-2281, www.scouting.org), the 127,000-acre spread that's now the property of Boy Scouts of America. More than 21,000 scouts come for backpacking trips every year. Practically an independent village, the place has its own post office, fire brigade, and hospital.

Visitors are welcome at **Philmont Museum & Seton Memorial Library** (8 A.M.–5 P.M. daily June–Aug., 8 A.M.–noon and 1–5 P.M. Mon.–Sat. Sept.–May, free), which displays a history of Philmont, photos of the Santa Fe Trail, and the art collection of Earnest Thompson Seton, a co-founder of the Boy Scouts. Fans of luxury manors will want to make reservations with the Philmont Museum to see **Villa Philmonte** (call for tour schedule, free), the vacation home of Oklahoma oilman Waite Phillips, the Boy Scouts' benefactor. His Spanish Mediterranean manse was built in 1926, and it's still chockablock with European antiques, as well as Waite's collection of Western paraphernalia.

Philmont Ranch also manages the **Kit Carson Living History Museum** (Hwy. 21, 8 A.M.–5 P.M. daily June–Aug., free), about seven miles farther down Highway 21. The adobe building is near where Lucien Maxwell and his friend Kit Carson set up a camp in the late 1840s, to deal with Santa Fe Trail traders (ruts are still visible where the trail crosses the Rayado River), and the museum re-creates life in that period, with costumed "mountain men" demonstrating how to fire a black-powder rifle, forge a horseshoe, and cook up a meal on a campfire.

# NAVAJO NATION AND THE NORTHWEST

Too often, American Indian culture is relegated to museums, its crafts and relics preserved behind glass or mounted on walls. But in northwestern New Mexico, native traditions are lived every day. The Navajo Nation, the largest reservation in the United States, occupies much of this region and stretches across 27,000 square miles into Arizona and Utah. The Jicarilla Apache have their own land near the Colorado border, while the Acoma, Laguna, and Zuni reservations are three outlying Puebloan communities. Visitors can appreciate a remarkable continuity of culture, from ancient ruins to contemporary powwows. The backdrop is slablike mesas, jagged canyons, spired red-rock buttes—the sort of classic Southwestern scenery that has photographers, mountain bikers, and hikers all reaching for their gear.

The most common route around the area begins heading west on I-40 from Albuquerque toward Acoma Pueblo. A thousand-year-old settlement atop a natural fortress of stone, "Sky City" is one of the most striking spots in New Mexico, rivaling Taos for the title of oldest inhabited town in the United States. Farther on, Gallup is the self-proclaimed Indian capital of the world, a major business hub for more than a hundred years. It has few tourist attractions aside from its old-fashioned trading posts, but it's emerging as a great outdoor destination, thanks to some excellent trails and rock-climbing sites nearby.

Heading north along a dead-straight and nearly empty highway brings you into the heart of Diné Bikéyah (Navajo land) and past Shiprock, a great plume of volcanic stone

© ZORA O'NEILL

# HIGHLIGHTS

**◖ Acoma Pueblo:** This windswept village on a mesa west of Albuquerque is one of the oldest communities in the United States. Visit for the views as well as for the delicate black-on-white pottery made only here (page 195).

**◖ Crownpoint Rug Auction:** Pick up a beautiful piece of handmade craftsmanship, and a good story while you're at it. This monthly auction in a Navajo village is a shopping event like no other (page 200).

**◖ El Malpais National Monument:** Explore "the Badlands" either down on the rugged black lava fields, full of rocky caves and dotted with hardy plants, or along the red rock cliffs that formed a natural barrier for the molten rock as it spread east (page 200).

**◖ El Morro National Monument:** *"Pasó por aquí,"* Don Juan de Oñate scratched in stone in 1605. He was just one of the many famous travelers who left his mark this cliff face, making it New Mexico's de facto guestbook over the centuries (page 202).

**◖ Nuestra Señora de Guadalupe Church:** Stunning murals decorate the whitewashed walls of Zuni Pueblo's oldest adobe church. Colorful and intricately detailed, the kachinas look vividly real (page 203).

**◖ B-Square Ranch:** Just outside of Farmington, Tom Bolack's mind-bogglingly huge collection of taxidermy and his son's museum of electrical relics make for one of the oddest, and most passionate, roadside attractions in the state. You'll come away debating the meaning of the word "environmentalist" (page 217).

**◖ Bisti/De-Na-Zin Wilderness:** Hiking this windswept landscape of dusty gray, red, and black stones is like taking a trip to another planet. There are no marked trails, but the weird mushroom-shaped rocks make good landmarks (page 219).

LOOK FOR ◖ TO FIND RECOMMENDED SIGHTS, ACTIVITIES, DINING, AND LODGING.

**◖ Aztec Museum & Pioneer Village:** In the vast field of small-town historical museums, this local endeavor stands out simply for being bigger than all the others – so big, in fact, that it even re-creates a frontier town in the backyard (page 223).

**◖ Pueblo Bonito:** The largest set of ruins at **Chaco Culture National Historical Park,** this 12th-century complex was also the largest building in North America in pre-Columbian times, marking the center of a vast, complex network of trade and culture (page 229).

sticking straight out of the plain that, like so many natural features in this area, is the subject of scores of legends and tales.

Just beyond the eastern border of the reservation, Farmington is a friendly small town with an outdoorsy bent. It makes a good base for exploring the last big site on the circuit: Chaco Canyon, where between A.D. 850 and 1250, the ancestral Puebloans (Anasazi) built a nine-mile-long city, a metropolis that served as the ceremonial and religious capital for this influential culture.

## PLANNING YOUR TIME

Because the driving distances are not so great here, you could cover this territory in as little as three days, staying one night in Zuni or Gallup and the next in Farmington, but this would leave you time to see only, say, Acoma Pueblo the first day, a long scenic drive including Four Corners the next, and the ruins at Chaco Canyon on the third. If you really want to appreciate how this part of New Mexico is culturally different from the other parts of the state, four days will give you a little more time to stop and catch your breath, and maybe take a hike or two, while a full week would of course be giving the place its proper due. For anyone with more than a passing interest in ancient archaeological sites, Chaco can take a whole day, or even three. Mountain bikers and hikers could easily just concentrate on the trails around Gallup—a great mix of mountains and rugged rock, and a couple of good places to hang out in town at night.

With few mountain ranges, a lot of the terrain in this region is devoid of shade—if you're planning any outdoor activities, try to avoid passing through at the peak of summer. The lower elevations relative to the rest of the state mean that most of this area does not get heavy snow in the winter, but the road to Chaco will be more difficult going.

## HISTORY

Northwestern New Mexico shows evidence of human occupation as early as 8000 B.C., but it was not until the middle of the 9th century

A.D. that people really began to flourish here: A.D. 850 marks the approximate point when the residents of Chaco Canyon moved from their sunken pit houses into larger, above-ground complexes that soon grew into multistory blocks, then into a network of communities as far north as Mesa Verde and as far south as Zuni, all displaying a similar architectural style and connected by skillfully engineered roads. For unknown reasons, though, they eventually left these towns behind and dispersed, some toward the Rio Grande, some to Zuni, and some onto the Hopi lands in what is now Arizona.

Meanwhile, bands of Navajo had migrated from northern climes into the desert a bit west of Chaco. No one has been able to pinpoint the date of their arrival here; the tribe's oral tradition says that Chaco was still inhabited, but archaeological evidence suggests the Navajo were not in their current territory until after Chaco was empty, around 1300, and perhaps not even until shortly before the Spanish made their first *entrada,* in 1540. In any case, the Navajo settled in quickly, and when the Spanish brought livestock, they added sheepherding—as well as raiding on horseback—to their already highly developed agricultural practices.

Simply because it was farther away from Santa Fe and the trade routes along the Rio Grande, the region avoided some of the worst suffering brought by Spanish rule. The real trouble began when the United States took control of the New Mexico territory in 1846, and optimistic homesteaders began flooding into the lands occupied by often hostile Navajo, Apache, and others; it didn't help that the American expansionists had already discovered rich mineral deposits in the Navajo homeland. The worst confrontations came in the 1860s, the era when federal Indian agent Kit Carson embarked on a scorched-earth campaign, burning crops, slaughtering sheep, and chopping down orchards. On the brink of starvation, the Navajo began to surrender in 1863, and Carson promptly marched them all, in the dead of winter, 400 miles southeast to Fort Sumner. Thousands died during "the Long Walk" and in the following years of

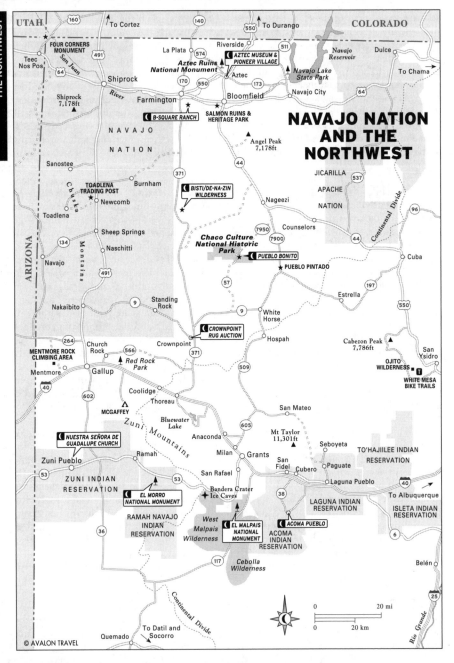

UTAH    160    To Cortez    140    550    To Durango    COLORADO

FOUR CORNERS MONUMENT

Teec Nos Pos    491

La Plata    574    Riverside    511    Navajo Reservoir    Dulce

Shiprock    64    **Aztec Ruins National Monument**    AZTEC MUSEUM & PIONEER VILLAGE    Navajo Lake State Park    To Chama

San Juan    170    Aztec

Shiprock 7,178ft    River    550    Bloomfield    173    Navajo City    64

Farmington

B-SQUARE RANCH    SALMON RUINS & HERITAGE PARK

N A V A J O    Angel Peak 7,178ft

N A T I O N    **NAVAJO NATION AND THE NORTHWEST**

Sanostee    371    44    JICARILLA    537

TOADLENA TRADING POST    Burnham    BISTI/DE-NA-ZIN WILDERNESS    APACHE

Newcomb    Nageezi    NATION    96

Toadlena    7950    Counselors

Sheep Springs    7900    44    Cuba

134    Naschitti    **Chaco Culture National Historic Park**

Navajo    491    PUEBLO BONITO

Chaska Montains    PUEBLO PINTADO    Estrella    197    550

Nakaibito    9    Standing Rock    57

9    White Horse    Cabezon Peak 7,786ft    San Ysidro

MENTMORE ROCK CLIMBING AREA    264    Church Rock    566    CROWNPOINT RUG AUCTION    Hospah    OJITO WILDERNESS

Mentmore    Red Rock Park    Crownpoint    371    WHITE MESA BIKE TRAILS

40    Gallup    509

Coolidge    602    Thoreau    San Mateo

MCGAFFEY    Bluewater Lake    605    Mt Taylor 11,301ft    Seboyeta    TO'HAJIILEE INDIAN RESERVATION

Zuni Mountains    Anaconda

NUESTRA SEÑORA DE GUADALUPE CHURCH    Milan    Grants    San Fidel    Cubero    Paguate

Zuni Pueblo    Ramah    San Rafael    Laguna Pueblo    40    To Albuquerque

53    ZUNI INDIAN RESERVATION    53    Bandera Crater Ice Caves    38    LAGUNA INDIAN RESERVATION    ISLETA INDIAN RESERVATION

EL MORRO NATIONAL MONUMENT    6

RAMAH NAVAJO INDIAN RESERVATION    West Malpais Wilderness    EL MALPAIS NATIONAL MONUMENT    ACOMA PUEBLO    ACOMA INDIAN RESERVATION    Belén

36    117    Cebolla Wilderness

Continental Divide

0    20 mi    25

0    20 km    Rio Grande

Quemado    To Datil and Socorro

© AVALON TRAVEL

ARIZONA

captivity. They finally returned to a federally granted reservation in 1868.

Much of modern Navajo history takes place in Arizona, where wrangling with the federal government, private energy interests, and the neighboring Hopi people over the use of coal deposits has been going on for more than a century—but these same factors (minus the Hopi) are constantly at play in New Mexico as well.

# West to Gallup

Heading out from Albuquerque, I-40 climbs the West Mesa and heads straight across a plateau lined with flat mesas—archetypal Southwest scenery that makes up for otherwise dull freeway driving. Ancient Acoma Pueblo is built on top of one of these mesas, an amazing place to visit and meet the people whose ancestors have lived here for nearly a thousand years. At the small town of Grants, you can turn south from the highway to enter the volcanic badlands of El Malpais; nearby is El Morro National Monument, a natural pool amid cliffs adorned with centuries-old graffiti. If you're on this loop on Highway 53, you'll next reach Zuni Pueblo, and Gallup (and I-40) is straight north from there.

## LAGUNA

About 18 miles west of Albuquerque, I-40 crosses the border onto the 45 square miles of Laguna Pueblo (505/552-6654, www.lagunapueblo.org), on which nearly 8,000 Keresan-speaking Ka-waikah (Lake People) live in six villages. From the highway, the only impression you get of Laguna is its Dancing Eagle Casino, but if you have time, it's worth getting off at exit 114 to visit the **San José Mission Church.** Established in 1699 when the Laguna people requested a priest (unlike any other pueblo), it stands out for its stark white stucco coating, but this is a relatively recent addition, following a 19th-century renovation. It was mudded and whitewashed every year until the 1950s, when the boom in uranium mining in the area left no time for this maintenance; it's now sealed with stucco.

Inside is the really key element of the church: Between a packed-earth floor and a finely wrought wood ceiling, the fine late-18th-century altar screen commands the full focus of the room. It's the work of the so-called "Laguna Santero," an innovative, anonymous painter who placed his icons inside a crowded field of decorative borders and carved and painted columns, creating a work of explosively colorful folk art that was copied elsewhere in the region in subsequent decades.

If you're lucky, **Alfred Pino** (505/274-5599), a local artist and informal guide, will be hanging around the church and offer you a personal tour and explanation of the symbols on the altar and the painted elk hides on the walls, in exchange for a tip and donation to the church. The church is officially open 8 A.M. to 4:30 P.M. weekdays (after a 7 A.M. morning Mass), but it's often open later and on weekends if Alfred's around.

Each of the six villages of Laguna celebrates its own feast day, then the whole pueblo turns out at the church September 17–19 for the **Feast of San José,** one of the bigger pueblo events in the Albuquerque area. Along with traditional dances and an arts-and-crafts market, Laguna hosts the All-Indian Baseball Tournament, in which the very sports-minded pueblo fields five semi-pro teams.

## ◖ ACOMA PUEBLO

At exit 102 off I-40, visitors to Acoma turn south. The road soon crosses up and over a ridge, and you may feel as though you've crossed through a pass into a Southwestern Shangri-La, for none of this great basin is visible from the highway. The route runs directly toward a flat-topped rock that juts out of the plain like a tooth.

# CEREMONIAL DANCES

This is only an approximate schedule for ceremonial dances – dates can vary from year to year. Annual feast days typically involve carnivals and markets in addition to dances. Confirm details and start times – usually afternoon, but sometimes following an evening or midnight Mass – with the Indian Pueblo Cultural Center (505/843-7270, www.indian-pueblo.org) before setting out. For the Navajo dances in Shiprock, check with the organizers of the Shiprock Navajo Fair (505/368-3727, www.shiprocknavajofair.org).

### JANUARY 6
- Laguna (Old Laguna): Feast of Los Tres Reyes

### MARCH 19
- Laguna (Old Laguna): Feast of San José

### EASTER
- Most pueblos: various dances

### JULY 26
- Laguna (Seama): Feast of Saint Anne

### AUGUST 10
- Acoma (Acomita): Feast of San Lorenzo

### AUGUST 15
- Laguna (Mesita): Feast of the Assumption

### SEPTEMBER 2
- Acoma (Sky City): Feast of San Esteban

### SEPTEMBER 8
- San Ildefonso: corn dances
- Laguna (Encinal): Feast of the Nativity of the Blessed Virgin Mary

### SEPTEMBER 19
- Laguna (Old Laguna): Feast of San José

### SEPTEMBER 25
- Laguna (Paguate): Feast of Saint Elizabeth

### EARLY OCTOBER
- Shiprock: Ye'iibichei dances

### OCTOBER 17
- Laguna (Paraje): Feast of Saint Margaret Mary

### OCTOBER 24-27
- Laguna (Old Laguna): harvest dance

### LATE NOVEMBER/EARLY DECEMBER:
- Zuni: Shalako

### DECEMBER 24
- Acoma (Sky City): luminaria display
- Laguna: dances after evening Mass

### DECEMBER 25-28
- Acoma (Sky City): Christmas dances
- Laguna: Christmas dances, all villages

Atop this rock is the original Acoma Pueblo, the village known as Sky City. The community covers about 70 acres and is built entirely of pale, sun-bleached adobe, as it has been since at least 1100. Only 50 or so people live on the mesa top year-round, given the hardships of no running water or electricity, but many families maintain homes here, and the place is thronged on September 2, when the pueblo members gather for the **Feast of San Esteban.** The rest of the 2,800 Acoma (People of the White Rock, in their native Keresan) live on the valley floor, which is used primarily as ranchland.

© LYNN BAKER

adobe houses at Acoma Pueblo

## Visiting Sky City

The fragile nature of the windswept village accounts in part for the particularly stringent tourism policies. All visitors must stop at the **Sky City Cultural Center and Haak'u Museum** (Indian Rte. 23, 800/747-0181, www.skycity.com, 8 A.M.–7 P.M. daily Apr.–Oct., 8 A.M.–4 P.M. daily Nov.–Mar.) on the main road, which houses a small café and shop stocked with local crafts, along with beautiful rotating exhibits on Acoma art and tradition. From here, you must join a guided tour ($20), which transports groups by bus to the village. The one concession to modernity has been the carving of this road to the top; previously, all goods had to be hauled up the near-vertical cliff faces. The tour lasts one hour, after which visitors may return by bus or hike down one of the old trails, using hand- and footholds dug into the rock centuries ago. Tours start at 9:30 A.M. and go every 45 minutes or so. In summer, the last one goes at 5 P.M., but it's shorter than the others; in winter, the last tour goes at 3 P.M.

The centerpiece of the village is the **Church of San Esteban del Rey,** one of the most iconic of the Spanish missions in New Mexico. Built between 1629 and 1640, the graceful, simple structure has been inspiring New Mexican architects ever since. (Visitors are not allowed inside, however, or into the adjoining cemetery.) As much as it represents the pinnacle of Hispano-Indian architecture in the 17th century, it's also a symbol of the brutality of Spanish colonialism, as it rose in the typical way: forced labor. The men of Acoma felled and carried the tree trunks for the ceiling beams from the forest on Mount Taylor, more than 25 miles across the valley, and up the cliff face to the village.

Acoma is well known for its pottery, easily distinguished by the fine black lines that sweep around the curves of the creamy-white vessel; on the best works, the lines are so fine and densely painted, they shimmer almost like a moiré. Additionally, the clay particular to this area can be worked extremely thin to create a pot that will hum or ring when you tap it. Throughout the village, you have opportunities to buy samples. Given the constraints of the tour, this can feel like a scam, but in many cases, you have the privilege of buying a piece directly from the artisan who created it.

## Accommodations and Food

The cultural center contains the **Yaak'a Café** (9 A.M.–6 P.M. mid-Apr.–mid-Oct., 9 A.M.–4:30 P.M. mid-Oct.–mid-Apr., $6), which serves earthy local dishes like mutton stew, posole, and bread made in traditional *horno* ovens—as well as Starbucks coffee. Acoma Pueblo operates the small-scale **Sky City Casino & Hotel** (877/552-6123, www.skycity.com, $89 s, $99 d), also at exit 102. Its rooms will do in a pinch.

## GRANTS

This town of 8,000 has gone through several career changes since its start in the 1880s. It began as a railroad camp, but it soon grew into a lumber town, based on the rich forests of the Zuni Mountains to the south. In the

## ACOMA VS. OÑATE: GRUDGE MATCH

In 1640, after more than a decade of construction using slave labor, the Church of San Esteban del Rey was complete at Acoma Pueblo. As if to add insult to injury, the Spanish friars then presented the church to the people as "restitution" for an earlier brutal incident that had started with a nasty attack on the pueblo in 1599 by conquistador Don Juan de Oñate, the first governor of Spain's newest province. The battle, which Oñate called justice for an earlier ambush on a handful of his men (which in turn was provoked by a previous disagreement), resulted in the deaths of hundreds of Acoma – the hilltop village was more than decimated.

But Oñate was not content. After the battle, he brought his enemies into a makeshift court and tried them for murder. The sentence for the inevitable guilty verdict was that every male in Acoma over the age of 25 would have one foot cut off; everyone between the ages of 12 and 25 was pressed into slavery; and the children were sent to convents in Mexico.

Oñate was eventually recalled from his post and chastised for his actions, but it was to this maimed populace that the Franciscans presented the "gift" of a Catholic church 30 years later. As a further gift of salvation, the friars publicly purged and hanged the village's spiritual leaders in the churchyard.

Variations on this treatment happened up and down the Rio Grande, eventually inspiring the Pueblo Revolt of 1680. But Oñate's particular brand of viciousness is probably the most remembered. Shortly after a monument to the conquistador was erected north of Española in 1998, the right foot of the bronze statue turned up missing – someone, or some group of people, had snuck in at night and sawed it clean off. An anonymous letter to newspapers stated that the act was "on behalf of our brothers and sisters at Acoma Pueblo." Rumor adds that the prankster vandals also left behind at the statue two miniature feet made of clay, attached to a shield inscribed with the words "The Agony of Defeat."

---

1940s, logging restrictions kicked in, and locals turned to farming, mustering the questionable boast of "carrot capital of the world."

But just a decade later, Grants reinvented itself as the much more *au courant* "uranium capital of the world," after a local sheepherder happened across some of that valuable ore just outside of town. It turned out to be one of the largest uranium fields in the world. With the best ore depleted in the 1980s and the last mine closed in 1999, Grants is now retired, so to speak. (Though recent interest in alternatives to fossil fuel might bring it back for one last job.) Meanwhile, Grants welcomes guests for a meal and a story or two about its past before they carry on to Gallup or Albuquerque. Mount Taylor just to the north is also a destination for hikers.

### New Mexico Mining Museum

If you're just driving through town, try to make time for this surprisingly good museum (100

N. Iron Ave., 505/287-4802, 9 a.m.–4 p.m. Mon.–Sat., $3), where you descend below the earth into a mock mine shaft. The narration from former miners gets pretty technical, but the narrow tunnels and clanking machinery give you a very real appreciation for the physical labor and risk involved in mining. The museum is on the west side of town, at the corner of Santa Fe Avenue, the main east–west drag.

### Mount Taylor

Heading north out of town, 1st Street (Hwy. 547) turns into Roosevelt Avenue then Lobo Canyon Road, headed toward Mount Taylor, a.k.a. Tsoodzil to the Navajo, who count it as one of their nation's four sacred mountains (although it is not technically on the reservation). About 10 miles up Highway 547, **Coal Mine Canyon Campground** (505/287-8833, open May–Sept.) is thick with pines and has some nice shady sites, with a stream running nearby.

Just as the pavement on Highway 547 ends, a right turn onto gravel Forest Road 193 takes you five miles to the head of **Gooseberry Springs Trail** (no. 77). From here, you can hike 3.5 miles to the mountain's summit, at 11,301 feet. Although the elevation gain is 2,400 feet, it's not a very strenuous climb, and it delivers an incredibly rewarding view—on a clear day, you can see as far as the Arizona border. Allow about three hours for the round-trip.

### Food

If you just want to nip off the highway for a quick bite, **Badlands Burgers** (1204 W. Santa Fe Ave., 505/287-9300, 10:30 A.M.–9 P.M. Mon.–Sat., $6), near exit 81, does a mean green-chile cheeseburger—it won a 2009 championship at the state fair, thanks to its double patties, bacon, and guacamole, along with the green stuff. Farther along, at exit 79 (really Milan, just west of Grants), **Wow Diner** (1300 Motel Dr., 505/287-3801, 6 A.M.–midnight Tues.–Sun., $8) is a true old-style diner, its stainless steel gleaming in the sun. The menu has something for everyone, from pork *carnitas* to spinach salad to old-fashioned ice-cream shakes.

In Grants proper, **La Ventana** (110 Geis St., 505/287-9393, 11 A.M.–11 P.M. Mon.–Sat., $12) is a respectable steakhouse that's open late; Geis Street is one block east of First Street, running north off the main drag.

### Information

Definitely stop in at the helpful and attractive **Northwest New Mexico Visitors Center** (1900 E. Santa Fe Ave., 505/876-2783, 9 A.M.–6 P.M. daily in summer, 8 A.M.–5 P.M. daily in winter), just south of I-40 at exit 85. Pick up maps, brochures, and suggested driving routes and hiking tours in this corner of the state.

## THOREAU

This curiously named town (pronounced thu-ROO) inspires no Walden-style reveries, what with its terrain of sagebrush, tumbleweeds, and asphalt. But it is the turn-off for one of

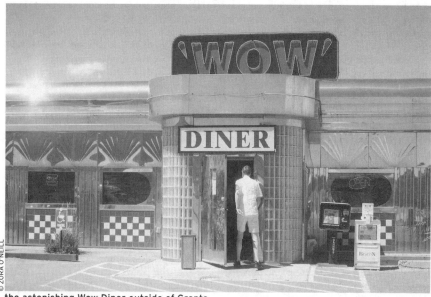

© ZORA O'NEILL

the astonishing Wow Diner outside of Grants

the best shopping experiences in northwestern New Mexico.

## Crownpoint Rug Auction

The small Navajo community of Crownpoint, 25 miles north of I-40 at the Thoreau exit (#53), is best known for its monthly rug auction, which has been drawing buyers and sellers from all around the region since 1968. It draws casual shoppers as well as bigwig gallery owners from Santa Fe. Jewelers and potters set up tables in the hall, and vendors sell food in the parking lot, giving the event a bit of a fair feel. It's easy to find in the tiny town—turn left from Highway 371 and look for lots of parked cars.

Rugs are on view from 4 P.M. to 6:30 P.M.; bidding starts at 7 P.M. and usually lasts till around 10 P.M. Often with more rugs on offer than customers, there's a good chance you'll find something you like for a reasonable price—a good 4-foot-by-6-foot rug can go for $300 or so, and small sampler rugs can go for $30. But even if you're not interested in shopping, it's worth a visit just for the cultural experience and a chance to see some beautiful work up close—the largest, finest-woven pieces are literally breathtaking when they're unfurled onstage.

For the schedule and other details, check the website of the **Crownpoint Rug Weavers Association** (505/786-7386, www.crownpointrugauction.com)—auctions are often on the second Friday of the month, but not always. Cash is the only payment accepted; there's an ATM in the gas station across from the school, but don't rely on it for any big purchase.

## Accommodations

There's nowhere to stay in Crownpoint, so you'll have to make a long drive at the end of the night. The closest option is **Zuni Mountain Lodge** (40 Perch Dr., 505/862-7616, www.zuniml.com, $85 s, $115 d), back down Highway 371 and 13 miles south of Thoreau and I-40. It's in a beautiful forested setting, and the seven rooms in the big old house have private baths. Rates include dinner and breakfast.

## EL MALPAIS NATIONAL MONUMENT

The product of three volcanic events, this lava-strewn landscape (505/783-4774, www.nps.gov/elma, free) is not exactly the barren terrain *el malpaís* (el-mal-pie-EES, literally, the badlands) suggests. A surprising amount of greenery has taken root in the millennia since the last eruption between 2,000 and 3,000 years ago, and in the spring, wildflowers stand out starkly against the jagged black rock. Out in the lava fields, you can explore deep, cave-like tubes that formed as the hot rock cooled. Some of the most scenic areas, however, are along the monument's eastern border, where the lava meets red sandstone cliffs, as well as New Mexico's largest natural arch.

If you want to make only a quick stop, the easiest access point is **Sandstone Bluffs Overlook,** where you can look down on the lava fields from one of the eastern cliffs, and north to Mount Taylor; you can walk a little way north along the cliff edge here too. It's about 11 miles south from I-40 on Highway 117. Drive another 7 miles to reach **La Ventana Arch,** a great sandstone arc; a short trail leads to a scenic viewing spot.

For details on longer hikes or drives into the park, go to the **Northwest New Mexico Visitors Center** (1900 E. Santa Fe Ave., 505/876-2783, 9 A.M.–6 P.M. daily in summer, 8 A.M.–5 P.M. daily in winter), near I-40 at exit 85—it's midway between the two highways that access different parts of the badlands. National Park Service employees can give you detailed maps and current conditions, and from there you can decide whether to take Highway 53 or Highway 117 south into the monument area. The monument **information center** (505/783-4774, 8 A.M.–4:30 P.M. daily) is less conveniently located on Highway 53, 23 miles south of I-40.

In addition to the hikes detailed below, there are more demanding but worthwhile places to explore outside the borders of the national park, in the BLM land designated **Cebolla Wilderness** (off the southeast border of the park) and **West Malpais Wilderness** (to the south and west)—ask at the visitors center for details on these areas as well.

If you're not carrying on to El Morro National Monument, farther west on Highway 53, you can loop back to I-40 via County Roads 50 and 49, a good gravel route that leads through ponderosa forests and some scenic canyons. And if you have a sturdy car, you can drive the **Chain of Craters Backcountry Byway** (County Rd. 42), a rugged track around the southern border of the lava flows that connects Highways 117 and 53. But don't think of it as a shortcut: The 32-mile drive can take up to two hours to traverse.

## Zuni-Acoma Trail

By far the most strenuous hike, this shadeless 7.5-mile route cuts across the lava beds roughly along the path used for centuries by the Puebloans in this region. It's rough going because the ground is so uneven, but if you're interested in the plants and animals that thrive in El Malpais, this can be a rewarding trek.

lava tubes at El Malpais National Monument

There's a trailhead on Highway 117 and one on Highway 53.

## Lava Falls Area

For the best up-close look at the lava, head farther south on Highway 117. Here the black rock is just 3,000 years old, and you can still make out the swirls and eddies of the molten stuff as if it had cooled yesterday; the variety of shapes and textures is fascinating, as are the odd pockets of stunted trees that manage to flourish here. The three-mile route (a mile-long loop with a one-mile spur) is marked only by rock cairns, so definitely bring a compass, as landmarks are sparse and it's easy to get disoriented.

## El Calderon Area

At this spot on Highway 53, a three-mile loop trail heads to **El Calderon Cinder Cone,** the area around the lava vent, and then back to the parking lot via a dirt road. It's also where lava tubes are closest to the road—a short walk from the car reveals the entrance to **Junction Cave,** a tube that has collapsed at one point, so you can walk through the first short section while seeing a sliver of daylight ahead the whole time (though you should still take flashlights, as it's hard to make out details once you get away from the openings). You can also head the other direction from the collapse, much deeper into the longer end of a pitch-black tunnel. Calderon Crater is the oldest of the three lava flows that make up the area, dating back some 115,000 years—as a result, the rock is more weathered, and not the stark black found around younger McCartys Crater. If you're in this area at sunset, head for **Bat Cave,** less than a mile from the parking area, where you can see a big circling cloud of the nocturnal critters as they head out for their evening insect feast.

## Big Tubes Area

For the weirdest terrain, you'll need a high-clearance truck to get to this network of 17 miles of lava caves on the west side of the monument. The main route is between the caves called Big Skylight and Four Windows;

© ZORA O'NEILL

it requires a lot of sliding, shimmying, and clambering. You should come prepared with headlamps (with extra batteries), sturdy boots, and heavy work gloves to protect your hands from the jagged rocks.

## Bandera Crater Ice Caves

A family-run tourist attraction that was grandfathered in when El Malpais was made a national monument, the ice caves (Hwy. 53, 888/ICE-CAVE, www.icecaves.com, $10) are an impressive natural sight, especially during the heat of summer, when you can descend from 90°F outside to 31°F underground, the chill emanating from a permanent layer of greenish ice at least 20 feet thick. Although the same phenomenon is visible elsewhere in El Malpais (for much less money), this is the most accessible spot, and generally more impressive. The other half of the attraction, Bandera Crater, 750 feet deep, is actually not much to look at—literally, just a big hole in the ground. Hours vary according to the season—daily from 8 A.M., and closing one hour before sunset.

## ◖ EL MORRO NATIONAL MONUMENT

This area may seem like relative wilderness today, but in fact, it has always been a fairly well-traveled route. The proof is at this national monument (Hwy. 53, 505/783-4226, www.nps.gov/elmo, 9 A.M.–7 P.M. daily in summer, 9 A.M.–6 P.M. in spring and fall, 9 A.M.–5 P.M. in winter, $3), where Don Juan de Oñate carved his name in the bluff (*morro*) and darkened the inscription with lamp soot, as a way of passing the time while his men rested and horses drank at the natural pool formed by snowmelt. It's also tangible proof of the early Spanish power in the Southwest—Oñate made his mark in 1605, seven years after his first official colonizing mission, and two years before the English even set foot in the New World. In the centuries since, seemingly every celebrity of the American West, major and minor, has left a graffiti autograph: Don Diego de Vargas was here in 1692, early

in his campaign to reclaim Nuevo México following the Pueblo Revolt of 1680. P. Gilmer Breckenridge, who led an experimental caravan of 25 camels from Texas to California, visited in 1857, and his compatriot, E. Pen Long, left a curlicue signature that gets the prize for best penmanship.

The half-mile **Inscription Loop Trail,** is paved and leads first to the year-round pool at the base of the rocks, then along the cliff face. The longer you stare at the rocks, the more names—as well as figures, carved by the Zuni centuries earlier—pop out. The natural ground level has sunk over the centuries too, so the graffiti crawls up the cliffs well above your head. For a view, continue on up the back side of the bluffs on the **Mesa Top Trail,** a two-mile trek that leads to Atsinna, the ruins of a small pueblo occupied by the Zuni in the 13th and 14th centuries. The last entrance to the trails is one hour before the visitors center closing time.

### Accommodations and Food

With just nine primitive sites, El Morro **public campground** ($5) is usually very quiet—though of course it's almost impossible to get a spot in the summer, when it's first-come, first-served. The water is shut off after the first freeze, usually in October; through the rest of the winter, there's no fee. If the public campground is full, or you just want a little more comfort, **El Morro RV Park & Cabins** (Hwy. 53, 505/783-4612, www.elmorro-nm. com), immediately east of the national monument, is a great place to stay out in the wilderness. Tent campsites are $10 per night, while tidy little cabins with queen and double beds start at $65; RV sites are $25. It's not too rustic, though—there's free wireless Internet throughout. The onsite **Ancient Way Café** does tasty brisket and beans.

### RAMAH

Ramah is a small Navajo community 12 miles west of El Morro. There's not much to see, but the local Ramah Navajo Weavers Association, like the collective in Tierra Amarilla in northern New Mexico, has helped revive an economy based on sheep, particularly the old Churro breed.

Before you reach Ramah, you pass the turn for **Wild Spirit Wolf Sanctuary** (505/775-3304, www.wildspiritwolfsanctuary.com, 11 A.M.–3:30 P.M. Tues.–Sun., $7), where you can hang out with some 50 captive-bred wolves and wolf-dogs that would otherwise go homeless. You can also camp here ($15 for tents or RVs)—then you're here in the morning to help feed the animals (another $25pp). Signs off Highway 53 point to Mountainview and Pine Hill; it's another 12 miles on Indian Route 125 and 120.

# Zuni Pueblo

Covering more than 600 square miles and with a population of more than 10,000, Zuni is the largest of the pueblos. For centuries, the Zuni people were spread over a wide area in several settlements. The current pueblo, Halona:wa (Anthill), around which the modern town of Zuni is based, was established long ago, but did not become the center of population until 1692, after the people made a peace agreement with Don Juan de Oñate and gathered here. With plenty of new, cinder-block construction, the town doesn't look all that special, but if you stay overnight (it's the only pueblo where you can do so), you'll have a better appreciation for the community. If you can't spend the night, certainly take the tour of the small historic core of the village—otherwise Zuni's appeal may be lost in the dust.

Isolation from the Rio Grande–area pueblos has helped keep Zuni culture more distinct—its *olla* maidens," for instance, perform a traditional dance with pots balanced on their heads. Zuni is also famous for its delicate inlay **jewelry,** called "needlepoint," in which the tiniest bits of turquoise, coral, and other stones are set in intricate patterns on a silver field; the texture almost resembles beadwork. Collectors also hold Zuni kachinas (figurines of spirit beings) and fetishes (tiny carved animals) in high esteem. If you're coming here to shop, though, you'll want to avoid late June and late December, when a period of fasting called Deshkwi bans buying or selling. Late July is the Zuni Arts & Cultural Expo.

## SIGHTS
Register first at the **visitors center** (Hwy. 53, 505/782-7238, www.zunitourism.com, 8:30 A.M.–5:30 P.M. Mon.–Fri., 10 A.M.–4 P.M. Sat., noon–4 P.M. Sun.), midway through town on the north side of the road. Here you can get information on artists' studios as well as arrange a highly recommended **walking tour** around Old Zuni—a somewhat spendy endeavor, but worth it. Resign yourself to asking plenty of directions: The hand-drawn map dispensed here is pretty but confusing.

## ◖ Nuestra Señora de Guadalupe Church
The core of the historic area called the Middle Village is the mission church, where the walls, first erected in 1629 and rebuilt in 1692, are painted with larger-than-life Shalako figures and other elements of the Zuni tradition as they function in the four seasons. The brilliantly colored paintings, created over more than 20 years beginning in 1970, are the work of one esteemed pueblo artist, Alex Seowtewa, and his sons. Together with the blankets and buffalo heads, this is one of the most syncretic churches in the state—a beautiful, fervent expression of faith over millennia.

The church is accessible only by guided tour (10 A.M., 1 P.M., and 3 P.M. Mon.–Sat., 1 P.M. and 3 P.M. Sun.), which departs from the Zuni visitors center. Theoretically, two separate tours are offered: one around the old town and one to the church, each for $10. But in practice, all visitors are usually lumped into a single tour of everything for $15. But don't fret—it's worth it just to see the inside of the church. The whole combined tour takes a little over an hour.

## A:shíwi A:wan Museum & Heritage Center

Zuni's only museum (2 E. Ojo Caliente Rd., 505/782-4403, www.ashiwi-museum.org, 9 A.M.–6 P.M. Mon.–Fri., free) is a fascinating one. It tells the story of the Zuni people, from creation myths through more contemporary issues with archaeologists and other researchers, such as Frank Cushing, who brought the pueblo to broader attention in the 19th century and became a local hero for a time. Cushing's endeavors are portrayed in a few hilarious cartoons by a Zuni artist. Also on display is a selection of artifacts from the ancestral settlement of Hawikku, excavated in 1916. They had been whisked away to a basement in a branch of the Smithsonian; Zuni leaders negotiated for these to be returned, leaving the remainder to be better preserved at the Smithsonian.

The museum is just south of Highway 53: Turn at the major stoplight and cross the small river to find yourself at the center of old Zuni—the museum is to your right, on the northwest corner of the intersection.

## EVENTS

The largest event of the year, the ritual of **Shalako** (also spelled Sha'la'ko) marks the end of the agricultural season and the beginning of winter in late November or early December. Although many of the prayers and dances take place in areas closed to visitors, it is still a remarkable time to visit the pueblo.

The Shalako, part of the extensive pantheon of kachinas, act as messengers between man and gods; when they depart the village, they are bearing the Zuni prayer for rain in the spring. For this ceremony, they are men who are elected each year to impersonate these god-like forces, and they spend the entire year preparing. The 24-hour ritual begins around noon, but the real excitement comes at dusk,

when the men descend from the sacred mesa south of town. With giant eagle-feather masks with goggle eyes and wooden beaks, they are transformed into frightening, noisy, 10-foot-tall creatures; they are an awesome sight as they swoop through the crowds and the bonfires, their beaks clacking and the drums pounding behind them. As they proceed around the village, lit only by bonfires, the effect is transporting.

Shortly after Shalako, the whole community gathers for the **Give-Away**, to thank the clans involved in the ritual—preparation is a massive expense. People bring specific gifts as well as all manner of unused items, from deer meat to refrigerators, which are redistributed according to need. Again, it's a ceremony that outsiders may not entirely get, but it's a festive time to be in town.

## SHOPPING

**Pueblo of Zuni Arts & Crafts** (1222 Hwy. 53, 505/782-5531, 9 A.M.–6 P.M. Mon.–Fri., 9 A.M.–5 P.M. Sat., 10 A.M.–3 P.M. Sun. in summer only) is the main outlet, a village-sponsored business with a wide selection of traditional and more modern jewelry, all at fair prices. Additionally, some 80 percent of the homes in Zuni are dedicated to some kind of craftwork, and many studios are open for tours—ask at the visitors center for more information.

## ACCOMMODATIONS AND FOOD

Unlike most pueblos, where visitors are welcome for the day or as customers at a glitzy casino, Zuni offers a unique opportunity to stay overnight and just soak up the atmosphere of the place: wood smoke, red dirt, and sparkling stars. The supremely comfortable **C Inn at Halona** (23-B Pia Mesa Rd., 505/782-4418, www.halona.com, $79) is run by an Anglo couple with roots on the reservation that go back a century. The older main house has five rooms (no. 4 upstairs is beautifully sunny, while the basement no. 5 is big yet cozy-feeling), but you might prefer the side house if you prefer to sleep late because the scene in the main house's breakfast room can get pretty animated. Guests dig in to what seems like an endless array of breads, eggs, meats, and other treats (definitely get the blue-corn pancakes).

At night, there's virtually nothing to do (alcohol is banned on the reservation), nor anywhere to go to eat. Luckily, the inn proprietors also own the adjacent general store, **( Halona Plaza,** where the deli counter serves up excellent fried chicken ($5) with smoky-hot red chile sauce on the side—New Mexican fusion at its finest. Book well ahead if you plan to be in town during any special events.

## Gallup

Initially just a wide spot along the railroad, Gallup took its name from the man who doled out cash in exchange for the coal that companies hauled in from the surrounding mines in the 1880s. By the 1920s, Gallup was known for its exceptionally pure coal, which meant higher wages for workers, who flooded in from Britain, China, Italy, Greece, and scores of other places, making the town a polyglot community from early on. The mining business has slowed, but at least a hundred trains still rumble through every day—it's a near-constant background noise, and as the freight loads cruise right through the center of town, you often have the disconcerting sensation of looking down a street and seeing the background in motion.

The other disconcerting effect of Gallup is the sense that you've stepped back in time, or at least onto a movie set. In fact, the place was a popular Hollywood location, and it's not hard to see why, what with the glowing neon on Route 66, the red sandstone cliffs, and the jagged Hogback Mountains, which inspire

© ZORA O'NEILL

the pueblo revival McKinley County Courthouse

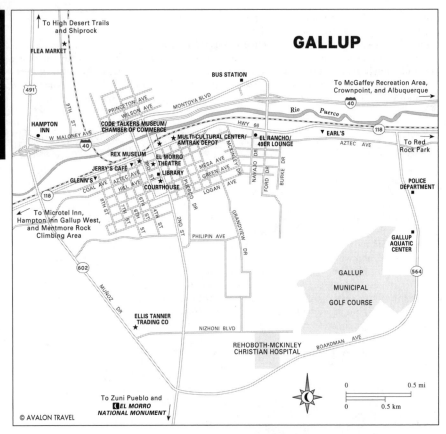

visions of Wild West adventure. Less glamorously, Gallup has struggled for decades with a grim image, due to high unemployment, stratospheric drunk-driving rates, and boarded-up businesses. But all that seems to be improving, and now downtown is clean and lively, and a sense of civic pride is palpable.

## SIGHTS

Gallup is divided by the railway and I-40. The historic downtown area is on the south side; Highway 66 and Coal Avenue are lined with the most notable buildings and shops. The far east and west ends of town cater to through travelers on the interstate, with all the chain hotels and restaurants.

### Downtown

You can cover most of Gallup's attractions on foot after parking downtown. There are a couple of museums, but some of the best art is outdoors—keep an eye open for the many murals around town, some painted by the WPA in the 1930s and others put up in the last few years. There's one dedicated to the Navajo code talkers on South 2nd Street just south of Highway 66, as well as a great modern one on the side of the city hall (Aztec Avenue at South 2nd Street) that depicts the more unglamorous, yet still evocative, modern life in Gallup: kids in pickup trucks, road construction, and rodeo events.

Downtown is anchored by the pueblo revival **McKinley County Courthouse** (207 W. Hill

# FROM THE REZ TO THE JUNGLE: THE NAVAJO IN WORLD WAR II

The ingeniousness and heroism of the Navajo code talkers of World War II has gotten a lot of press (and a big Hollywood budget, in 2002's *Windtalkers*) in recent years, but it wasn't always so. Though the code itself was declassified in 1945, the documents were not made public until the late 1960s, by which time Americans were caught up in a different war. As a result, this team of more than 300 men (and even one Anglo fighter fluent in the language) has become a novel footnote in the history of the war, rather than a crucial element in the U.S. military's victory. In fact, the Navajo code was an essential part of the Battle of Iwo Jima, and the code talkers were involved in every Marine battle in the Pacific.

Twenty-nine recruits formed the first team of code talkers, and these men were also responsible for developing the details of the code. At its core, the system used Navajo words to represent letters of the alphabet — these could be used to spell literally, or combined to form larger words and concepts. For instance, *w* was represented by the Navajo word for weasel, *gloe-ih*. To say "when," the code talker actually said "weasel" and "hen": *gloe-ih-na-ah-wo-hai;* "which" was "weasel" plus "hitch," or *gloe-ih-a-his-tlon;* "will" was *gloe-ih-dot-sahi,* or "sick weasel." Military terms required creative use of Navajo vocabulary: a *bish-lo,* or "iron fish," was a submarine, for instance.

The Japanese managed to break every other American code system but this one. The advantage of Navajo was that it was a highly complex yet completely oral language, with only a handful of nonnative speakers. Moreover, it was extremely fast to transmit, because unlike previous systems, it didn't require a machine at either end.

Even if the rest of the country has been slow to recognize the code talkers, they have long been a point of pride for the Navajo themselves, especially as symbols of the power of speaking the ancestral language. See if you can pick up a few of the words: A mural by Be Sargent on South 2nd Street in Gallup depicts the code in visual form, showing the original 29 code talkers along with the various animals and objects used as keys in the code.

St.), one block south of Coal Avenue, and **El Morro Theatre** (110 W. Aztec Ave., 505/726-0050, www.elmorrotheatre.com), built in 1926 in the Spanish colonial revival style. If you ask nicely and it's a slow day, you can walk around inside the courthouse and admire the tile work, the punched-tin light fixtures, and the 2,000-square-foot WPA mural in the main courtroom. Painted by Lloyd Moylan, it's the largest surviving work from that period in the state.

## WWII Navajo Code Talkers Museum

Adjoining the chamber of commerce, the WWII Navajo Code Talkers Museum (103 W. Hwy. 66, 505/722-2228, 8 A.M.–5 P.M. Mon.–Fri., free) is a large collection of memorabilia from World War II, arranged in fluorescent-lit glass cases—ask the chamber employees to turn the lights on. No frills here: The room is mostly used for business meetings, but the collected papers, photographs, and clippings trace the use of the Navajo language as code through the fight. Given the importance of the code to the success of the U.S. campaign, it's a little depressing to realize this is one of the largest exhibits on the subject (the next largest is inside the Burger King in Kayenta, Arizona). There are plans afoot to build a larger space in Window Rock, Arizona, but they were still at the fundraising stage in 2010.

## Multi-Cultural Center

The old Santa Fe Rail station has been converted into a well-used community arts center. Visitors will enjoy the **Storyteller Museum**

(201 E. Hwy. 66, 505/863-4131, 8 A.M.–5 P.M. Mon.–Fri., free) upstairs. The nifty collection of dioramas—scenes involving model trains, a replica trading post—are accompanied by headphones to listen to a local's explanation of the scene. You'll also find a café, the **Kiva Cinema,** and the **Ceremonial Gallery,** which exhibits local student art. In the summer, Navajo, Hopi, and other dance and music groups perform out front every night at 7 P.M.

### Rex Museum

Like many small-town collections, the Rex Museum (300 W. Hwy. 66, 505/863-1363, 8 A.M.–3:30 P.M. Mon.–Fri., $2 donation) is a hodgepodge, from roller skates to programs from the Inter-Tribal Ceremonial. But it's most interesting to see the traces of the various immigrant groups that have settled in Gallup, from Chinese to Greeks.

### Red Rock Park

East of town about six miles, Red Rock Park is Gallup's public party spot, with rodeo grounds and an outdoor amphitheatre. If you're just driving by (or finishing up a hike), stop by the surprisingly large **Red Rock Museum** (505/722-3839, 8 A.M.–noon and 1–5 P.M. Mon.–Fri., $2 donation). It feels as though it was set up in a fit of civic pride in the 1970s, then left to its own devices. The display cases, filled with information on the Zuni, Hopi, and Navajo, are a little dusty; you'll probably have to turn the lights on yourself. You'll see one of the most elaborate displays of Zuni kachinas anywhere—all the figurines labeled, and their roles explained. There's also a model hogan (the traditional Navajo home) and a representative selection of local jewelry styles. Access to the park is via the frontage road (E. Hwy. 66), from exit 33 or exit 26 off I-40, then turn north on Highway 566.

## ENTERTAINMENT

On an average day, the streets of Gallup are not exactly hopping. You will notice a significant rush on weekends, though, as people from surrounding communities come into town to shop and do business, nearly doubling the population. And expect crowds during the two big annual events, a powwow and a balloon rally.

### Nightlife

In part because Gallup chronically battles a high rate of alcoholism, liquor laws are extremely strict, and few places stay open very late. Even **Coal Street Pub** (303 W. Coal Ave., 505/722-0117, 11 A.M.–10 P.M. Mon.–Thurs., 11 A.M.–11 P.M. Fri. and Sat.), the main bar downtown, serves only beer and wine. It's a convivial place in the evening, often with some kind of live music on the weekends. It also serves a good menu of hearty stuff like steak and fried fish, with red chile on the side.

The **49er Lounge** (1000 E. Hwy. 66, 5 P.M.–1 A.M. daily) in the El Rancho Hotel does serve booze, but you might not need it because the setting is disorienting enough—like the rest of the hotel, this place exudes an overwhelming aura of decaying Western glamour. Go early, as it tends to close before the posted time if business is slow.

On weekends, you might also find mellow live music at **Angela's Café con Leche** (see the *Food* listings).

### Special Events

For four days in late July or early August, Gallup hosts the **Inter-Tribal Indian Ceremonial** (505/863-3896, www.theceremonial.com), which draws more than 20,000 participants from various tribes in Canada and Mexico, as well as all over the United States. General admission to exhibits is $6, but expect to pay about $15 for dances and $8 for the rodeo. Also on the schedule are a beauty pageant, a fashion show, and lots of music.

The other big annual event is the **Red Rock Balloon Rally** (505/979-1231, www.redrockballoonrally.com), on the first weekend in December. With about 200 participating hot air balloons, it has been going strong since 1981, probably because the setting, against the vibrant sandstone at Red Rock Park, is unbeatable. The balloonists often need extra volunteers, so it's a good chance to get a free ride or join a chase crew—show up early and ask around.

## SHOPPING

With a historic trading post or overstocked pawn shop seemingly every 10 feet, Gallup can be an exciting or overwhelming place to shop, depending on your point of view. But even if you don't feel up to sifting through treasure troves of antique Navajo turquoise, the **trading posts,** some in business for the better part of a century and still doing business primarily with the local Indian population, are worth a visit simply as another town attraction—they're stocked with everything from hand-spun skeins of wool to crisp new blue jeans, and of course, heaps and heaps of jewelry. One of the oldest, most respected trading posts downtown is **Richardson's Trading Co. & Cash Pawn** (222 W. Hwy. 66, 505/722-4762, 9 A.M.–6 P.M. Mon.–Sat.), where the warren of storefronts is permeated with the smell of old leather. The mammoth **Ellis Tanner Trading Co.** (1980 Hwy. 602, 505/863-4434, 8 A.M.–7 P.M. Mon.–Sat.) has deep roots in Gallup, though the building is relatively new; check inside for a huge mural by local artist Chester Kahn, honoring locals who have been good role models.

Another shopping hotspot is **City Electric Shoe Shop** (230 W. Coal Ave., 505/863-5252, 10 A.M.–6 P.M. Mon.–Sat.), where you can pick up a pair of street-ready moccasins in butter-soft suede or an embossed leather belt—both are made in a workshop in the basement.

But perhaps the best shopping experience in Gallup is at the 9th Street **flea market** (505/722-7328) every Saturday on the north side of town. Drawing hundreds of people from the Navajo reservation as well as from town, it's a great swap meet where you can pick up anything from a beaded necklace to a wolf-mix puppy to a bale of hay—not to mention all kinds of tasty prepared foods and fresh produce. Business gets rolling around 10 A.M. (sometimes earlier on the first Saturday of the month, when there are usually more vendors), and winds up in the mid-afternoon. To get

prime shopping on Historic Route 66

© ZORA O'NEILL

there, head up U.S. 491, then cut east to North 9th Street on West Jefferson Avenue.

## SPORTS AND RECREATION

Just since 2005, the city of Gallup has virtually reinvented itself as a destination for outdoor fun, capitalizing on its location between gorgeous sandstone bluffs and the ponderosa-covered Zuni Mountains. There's a lot to do in a relatively small area, and it's all still crowd-free.

### Biking

The main mountain biking network is the **High Desert Trails System,** built by a local group. The three interconnecting loops, each rated for a different skill level, run along the mesas just northwest of town. In addition to great views over cliff edges and some pretty tricky constructed switchbacks, the trails are marked by occasional public art—so just when you think the weird rock formations are sculpture enough, you might look up to see a black steel bobcat peering down from a cliff edge.

The main trailhead, called Gamerco, is two miles north on U.S. 491, then left on Chino Loop; the gravel parking lot is on the left (south) side of the road.

For shady forest biking, head to **McGaffey Recreation Area,** a patch of national forest in the Zuni Mountains southeast of Gallup. From exit 33 on I-40, Highway 400 runs south about six miles to the beginning of the popular **Quaking Aspen Trail,** at mile marker 3. These eight miles of single-track run up through ponderosa forests and aspens; at the top of the ridge, you can either backtrack or come down a rough road. For both areas, download maps from the City of Gallup website (www.gallupnm.org). For more suggestions pick up the handy guide *Gallup Waypoints,* available online at www.gallupwaypoints.com.

## Hiking

Hikers are also welcome on the High Desert and McGaffey trails, though two-wheelers have the right-of-way. In the latter area, **Strawberry Canyon Trail,** which begins in McGaffey Campground (follow Highway 400 to mile marker 0), is a shady, easy 1.5-mile hike up to a lookout tower, and it runs along a rough forest road, so there's room for both bikers and hikers.

But at two accessible trails close to town, you get the whole place to yourself. They both start in Red Rock Park: **Pyramid Rock Trail** is a three-mile round-trip that heads up to 7,487 feet to the top of this aptly named butte for a panoramic view. **Church Rock Trail** is just two miles round-trip but has you clambering up stairs cut into slick stone and takes you to the base of some dramatic rock formations. You can combine the two by hiking to Church Rock, then returning via Pyramid Rock—this takes between three and four hours. To reach the trailheads, drive past the rodeo grounds and horse barns, and a little way up the canyon—the trail starts on your left.

## Rock Climbing

A well-maintained public park east of town,

**Mentmore Rock Climbing Area** is frequented by only a handful of local regulars. With 31 sport routes and 50 bolted top-rope climbs spread over six different walls, along with quite a few bouldering options, there's more than enough fun to go around. At least some of the rocks get sun all the time, so it's climbable in the winter, but check the weather before heading out. The sandstone is fragile when wet, so local policy is to stay off the rocks for a couple of days after a heavy rain. To get there, take exit 16 from I-40 and head west on Highway 66 for half a mile; turn north on County Road 1, then bear west as it turns into Mentmore Road, leading directly to the parking area. If you'd like some climbing lessons or a general tour of other spots in the area, contact **Kokopelli Adventures** (1000 E. Hwy. 66, 505/863-9941, www.kokopelliadventures.org), based at El Rancho Hotel.

## Swimming

**Gallup Aquatic Center** (620 S. Boardman Ave.) is a kid's dream, with curvy slides galore, cactus-shaped sprinklers, and even a "lazy river" setup; adults get a separate competition-size pool for laps. It's all indoors, but still a lot of fun.

## ACCOMMODATIONS

Even if you don't plan to spend the night, do stop in at **《 El Rancho Hotel & Motel** (1000 E. Hwy. 66, 505/863-9311, www.elranchohotel.com, $82 s, $94 d). The lobby alone is a Western fantasia of rustic wood paneling, furniture made of bull horns, a giant stone fireplace, and glossy photos of all the Hollywood actors who passed through the doors back in Gallup's heyday as a movie backdrop (it helped that the man who built the place in 1937 was D. W. Griffith's brother). Rooms named after Kirk Douglas, Ronald Reagan, and others are kitted out with wagon-wheel headboards and vintage bathroom tile; some even have back porches. A separate motel wing has significantly less character but perfectly clean and functional rooms—rates here

Ronald Reagan slept here.

Jerry's Café dishes up the best chile in Gallup.

start at $56. Guests at both have access to a decent swimming pool, and there's Wi-Fi in the lobby. Practically speaking, rooms in the main hotel seem faintly overpriced. But for sheer atmosphere, this place ranks with La Fonda in Santa Fe by giving you a taste of what tourism must've been like back when New Mexico really was the wild frontier. Better to ignore the unreliable online booking engine (which doesn't show the motel rooms)—just call to reserve.

Aside from El Rancho, you have the usual chain-hotel choices, clustered on the east and west edges of town. Of these, the **Hampton Inn Gallup-West** (111 Twin Buttes Rd., 505/722-7224, www.hamptoninn.com, $89 d) is fairly spiffy and has a whirlpool; the other, more centrally located Hampton Inn (1460 W. Maloney Ave.) is also good. On the low end, the **Microtel Inn** (3270 W. Hwy. 66, 505/722-2600, www.microtelgallup.com, $50 d) will do in a pinch, though be sure to confirm your room rate.

## FOOD

As with the hotels, all the chain places (and a couple of vintage diners) are near the freeway exits. You definitely get more local flavor, in every sense, if you venture into the center of town.

### Cafés

The whitewashed **Coffee House** (203 W. Coal Ave., 505/726-0291, 7 a.m.–3 p.m. Mon.–Fri., 8 a.m.–3 p.m. Sat., $6) has an old tin ceiling, contemporary photography on the walls and a mellow atmosphere where Navajo artists and fleece-clad mountain bikers mingle; evenings often see some local singer-songwriter. The menu ranges from fresh salads and big sandwiches to a full breakfast.

With a nice small-town diner vibe, **Angela's Café con Leche** (201 E. Hwy. 66, 505/722-7526, 8:30 a.m.–4 p.m. Mon., 8:30 a.m.–5 p.m. Tues., 8:30 a.m.–9:30 p.m. Wed.–Fri., $7), in the cultural center in the former train station, pours bottomless cups of coffee to locals for breakfast and lunch. In the evenings, there's occasionally acoustic music.

**Glenn's Bakery** (900 W. Hwy. 66, 505/722-4104, 6 A.M.–8 P.M. Mon.–Sat., $3–10) is impressive first for its dazzling doughnut case, which includes wonderfully flaky cinnamon rolls. If you need more than a sugar fix, settle in alongside locals reading the morning papers for breakfast burritos, pizza, or one of the daily specials, such as lamb stew.

### New Mexican
Family-owned, with a battered neon sign, **Jerry's Café** (406 W. Coal Ave., 505/722-6775, 8 A.M.–9 P.M. Mon.–Sat., $8) has a crowd of dedicated followers (read: addicts) who drive miles for the stuffed sopaipilla, drenched in super-hot red chile sauce. The place is tiny and often packed with courthouse employees during lunchtime, so go late or early.

It may not have the absolute best food in town, but **Earl's** (1400 E. Hwy. 66, 505/863-4201, 6 A.M.–9 P.M. Mon.–Sat., 7:30 A.M.–3 P.M. Sun., $8), conveniently located close to the east-side freeway exit, has a timeless atmosphere that can't be beat. Since 1947, it has been serving biscuits and gravy, Navajo tacos, and enchiladas. It gets packed after the Saturday flea market, and you'll either love or hate the fact that local artisans go table to table selling their wares.

## INFORMATION AND SERVICES
Conveniently located right downtown, the staff at the **chamber of commerce** (103 W. Hwy. 66, 505/722-2228, www.gallupnm.org, 8 A.M.–5 P.M. Mon.–Fri.) can answer just about any question. From Memorial Day to Labor Day, it's also open Saturdays, from 8:30 A.M. to 5:30 P.M.

You can get **Internet access** at the public library (115 W. Hill Ave., 505/863-1291, 9 A.M.–8 P.M. Mon.–Thurs., 10 A.M.–6 P.M. Fri., 9 A.M.–6 P.M. Sat.).

## GETTING THERE
**Trains** stop at Gallup's station on Highway 66 once a day each for eastbound and westbound. Coming from Albuquerque, the trip takes about 2.5 hours and costs $33, making it a very pleasant alternative to the bus. Note that the station, which is used as the Multi-Cultural Center, is not staffed; you'll have to contact **Amtrak** (800/USA-RAIL, www.amtrak.com) for tickets and train status.

**Greyhound** (800/231-2222, www.greyhound.com) serves Gallup from Albuquerque, with departures from the station (827 E. Montoya Blvd., 505/863-3761, 6 A.M.–1:30 P.M. and 2:30–8:30 P.M. Mon.–Sat., 11:30 A.M.–1 P.M. Sun.) three times daily. There is no direct bus to Farmington, however (part of the reason you see so many hitchhikers outside of town here)—you must double back to Albuquerque.

# Navajo Nation

Covering some 27,000 square miles in New Mexico, Arizona, and Utah, the Navajo Nation is the largest reservation in the United States, and with nearly 300,000 people claiming Navajo ancestry (about 250,000 of whom live on the reservation), the Navajo are the largest tribe in the country. They call themselves Diné (The People); the name Navajo came from Tewa via the Spanish, translating as cultivated field, for which these settled people were already well known when the conquistadors met them.

Although the reservation was granted in 1868, the Navajo Nation didn't take on its current shape until decades later, when the eastern border was expanded through a series of complex land swaps with the U.S. government—the ruins at Chaco Canyon, for instance, are on federal land but surrounded by Navajo territory. This fringy edge is often referred to as the

## CLOUDS OVER SHIPROCK

Pink mesas, orange bluffs, red earth . . . brown sky? The only blemish on the desert landscape of northern New Mexico is the undeniable cloud of pollution hanging over the coal-fired Four Corners Power Plant in Fruitland, southeast of Shiprock – one of the largest coal plants in the country, and also one of the dirtiest. Since the plant opened in 1963 on Navajo land, it has been cause for heated debate. The money from leasing the land and selling the coal is a significant part of the reservation's economy, but its residents are also disproportionately affected by mercury contamination in streams and lakes as well as chronic respiratory problems.

As of late 2006, the Environmental Protection Agency was examining the plant in order to regulate emissions. In the meantime, though, a few people have discovered a surprising perk: The 1,200-acre man-made lake adjacent to the plant makes an excellent windsurfing and kite-surfing spot. The water, used for cooling, is usually bathtub-warm – perfect, considering the best wind comes during the winter. Now if only it could blow the smog away too . . . .

Checkerboard. Some portions of the reservation, such as Ramah, near Zuni, are completely separate from the rest of the "Big Rez."

The main thoroughfare through New Mexico's Navajo land is the route north from Gallup, U.S. 491. Until 2003, the highway was known as U.S. 666, but the Department of Transportation finally got sick of the chronic sign theft and changed the number. It still hasn't completely shaken its nickname, Devil's Highway, due to regular car crashes, hitchhikers being run down in the dark, and tales of people being attacked by "skinwalkers" (shapeshifters) along its most remote stretches.

The drive north to Shiprock is a beautiful but solitary one. You pass only a few chapter houses (reservation administrative centers), and the occasional hogan, the traditional Navajo ceremonial building. With their straight, faceted sides, hogans resemble the cliffs that often tower above them, and their doors always face the sunrise.

The terrain shifts to a sandy pink as you head north, punctuated only by the Chuska Mountains, off to the west on the border with Arizona, then the occasional mesa. Finally, there is Shiprock, a dramatic spike that does look like a prow gliding through the sandy sea—or, as the Navajo see it, a "rock with wings" (Tse' Bit'a'i).

## TOADLENA TRADING POST

Two Grey Hills is widely considered to be the source of some of the finest rugs in the Navajo tradition—delicately shaded neutral tones, often un-dyed wool carefully selected for its natural color, then woven into intricate geometric patterns rich with symbolic meaning. This trading post (505/789-3267, 9 A.M.–6 P.M. Mon.–Sat.) near Newcomb is one of the main places where Two Grey Hills rugs are sold, and it has a museum dedicated to skilled artisans like Clara Sherman, whose weavings are nearly as tight and thin as paper. About an hour north of Gallup, make a left at the Shell station and follow signs.

## SHIPROCK

Not to be confused with Window Rock (the Navajo Nation capital in Arizona), the town of Shiprock is the largest community in the Navajo Nation, home to 10,000 people, Diné College, a regional hospital, and a major Bureau of Indian Affairs office. Visitors won't find a whole lot going on, though, unless they're in town for the **flea market,** in the parking lot at the intersection of U.S. 491 and U.S. 64—it's appealing not just for the random assortment of merchandise (CDs from Navajo rock bands, as well as crafts and jewelry) but also for the seriously traditional

along the "Devil's Highway" north from Gallup

Navajo food, such as blue-corn mush and stewed sumac. If you're staying in Farmington, the flea market is definitely worth the short drive over. It allegedly now runs daily (8 A.M. to 5 P.M.), but it's biggest and most interesting on Saturdays.

The big annual event is **Shiprock Navajo Fair** (505/368-3727, www.shiprocknavajofair.org), which celebrates its centennial in 2011. It happens the first weekend in October, when there's a major powwow, the Miss Northern Navajo pageant, a free barbecue, and a frybread cook-off, as well as the nine-day Ye'iibichei dance ritual.

The rest of the time, it's as good a place as any to fill up on gas and admire the view across the San Juan River and desert plateau. In the strip mall at the intersection with U.S. 64, look out for **Navajo Fine Jewelry and Collectibles** (9 A.M.–8 P.M. Mon.–Sat., noon–6 P.M. Sun.). It may not have the charm of an old trading post, but as a project of the Navajo Nation government, it's very well priced and shows some excellent work. Look for Yei rugs, patterned with tall, skinny Yei deities—they're a specialty of the Shiprock region.

## Food

If you miss the flea market, you can get mutton stew and frybread tacos at **Mannings Thatsaburger** (U.S. 491, 505/368/4019, 10 A.M.–8 P.M. daily, $6) and at **KFC** (U.S. 491, 505/368-4805, 10 A.M.–9 P.M. Sun.–Wed., 10 A.M.–10 P.M. Thurs.–Sat., $4). The stuff is better at Mannings, but there's great novelty value in subverting the fast-food establishment by marching up to the plastic KFC counter and ordering the local goods.

## FOUR CORNERS MONUMENT

In 2009, the monument (U.S. 160, 928/871-6647, 8 A.M.–7 P.M. daily, $3) where the state boundaries of New Mexico, Arizona, Utah, and Colorado all meet came under scrutiny, as analysis of old surveying techniques suggested that the point might be a good 2.5 miles off. But rebuttal from the National Geodetic Service settled the matter, and the monument rests easy again. It's not much to see, though: even after a renovation, it's recommended only for aficionados of roadside Americana, fans of Twister, and land surveyors.

It's a long way to drive, but if you're looking for an excuse to tour around the barren, butte-spiked lands up here, then this destination is as good as any, and you'll be wanting to get out and stretch your legs just about the time you pass by the entrance on U.S. 160. And what a stretch you'll get, as you put one limb in each state and pose for your travel companion's camera. There's also a gift shop and some frybread vendors (but no public water source).

Nearby, farther north on U.S. 160, just past the San Juan River, be sure to stop at the scenic overlook for an awesome view across the flatlands to Shiprock (occasionally marred by smog from the power plant).

# Farmington

Even though (or perhaps in part because) it's set right against the border of the Navajo Nation, Farmington has an entirely different feel from Shiprock. The largely Anglo population of 40,000 prospers from coal, oil, and natural-gas deposits, and the nearby Four Corners Power Plant is a major employer. It's the most common base for visiting the ruins at Chaco Canyon to the south and is a pleasant enough city in its own right, tidy and filled with parks.

Farmington's first settlers, from England, were attracted by the fertile land around the confluence of the San Juan, La Plata, and Animas Rivers (the Navajo name for the area is Tótah, the place where the waters meet). The first well was drilled in the 1890s—but the investor was dismayed to hit gas rather than the water he'd been looking for. The Farmington Oil & Gas Co. was established in 1906, but it wasn't until 1922 that the industry really got any attention, with a wildcat well in Hogback producing crude so pure that cars could run on the stuff, no refining necessary. In the meantime, though, Farmington's growth was based on the prosperous farms and orchards in the surrounding river valley. The 1950s marked the first real oil boom, when many of the orchards were plowed under to make room for new houses; another came in the 1970s, thanks to the limited supply from overseas. And with current tensions in the world oil market, it's doing quite well once again.

## SIGHTS

The town proper has only a handful of typical attractions; pick up the *Footloose in Farmington* brochure for a walking tour of some of the nicer historic buildings downtown. The town of Aztec and the ruins there

© ZORA O'NEILL

downtown Farmington

THE NORTHWEST

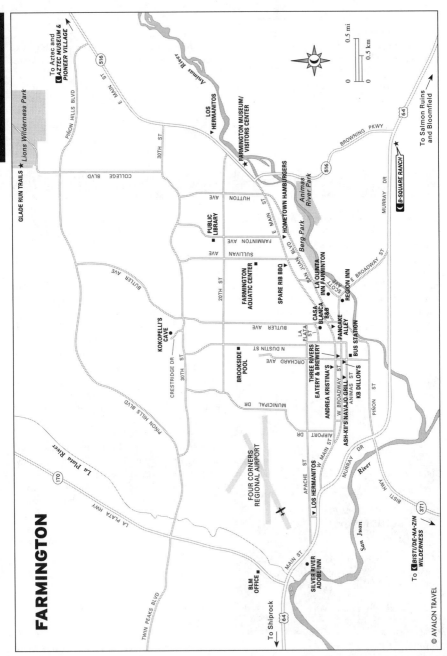

**FARMINGTON**

To Aztec and
AZTEC MUSEUM &
PIONEER VILLAGE

GLADE RUN TRAILS ★ Lions Wilderness Park

Animas River

To Salmon Ruins
and Bloomfield

0.5 mi

0.5 km

PIÑON HILLS BLVD

E MAIN ST

30TH ST

COLLEGE BLVD

LOS HERMANITOS

FARMINGTON MUSEUM/
VISITORS CENTER

BROWNING PKWY

B-SQUARE RANCH

MURRAY DR

HOMETOWN HAMBURGERS

HUTTON

PUBLIC LIBRARY

FARMINGTON AVE

E MAIN ST

SULLIVAN AVE

BUTLER AVE

20TH ST

SAN JUAN BLVD

Berg Park

Animas River Park

LA QUINTA INN FARMINGTON

E BROADWAY ST

SCOTT AVE

REGION INN

FARMINGTON AQUATIC CENTER

SPARE RIB BBQ

CASA BLANCA B&B

PANCAKE ALLEY

BUS STATION

KOKOPELLI'S CAVE

CRESTRIDGE DR

30TH ST

BROOKSIDE POOL

LA PLATA ST

N DUSTIN ST

ORCHARD AVE

THREE RIVERS EATERY & BREWERY

ANDREA KRISTINA'S

W BROADWAY ST

ANIMAS ST

ASH-KII'S NAVAJO GRILL

KB DILLON'S

PIÑON ST

MUNICIPAL DR

AIRPORT DR

PIÑON HILLS BLVD

BUTLER AVE

La Plata River

LA PLATA HWY

FOUR CORNERS REGIONAL AIRPORT

W MAIN ST

APACHE ST

LOS HERMANITOS

MURRAY DR

San Juan River

BISTI HWY

To BISTI/DE-NA-ZIN WILDERNESS

TWIN PEAKS BLVD

BLM OFFICE

SILVER RIVER ADOBE INN

MAIN ST

To Shiprock

To Salmon Ruins and Bloomfield

516

516

64

170

371

64

© AVALON TRAVEL

© ZORA O'NEILL

one tiny part of the Bolack Electromechanical Museum

are just 30 minutes' drive, so it's easy to hit the highlights in one day.

## Farmington Museum

In the same building as the convention and visitors bureau, the Farmington Museum (3041 E. Main St., 505/599-1174, www.farmingtonmuseum.org, 8 A.M.–5 P.M. Mon.–Sat., free) has some surprisingly high-quality exhibits. The centerpiece is From Dinosaurs to Drill Bits, a rather loud and overtly gee-whiz display, complete with video holograms, about the oil and gas industry—underwritten by major corporations, naturally. Once you get away from the hissing steam and chattering touchscreen games, you'll find a tasteful display on Farmington's general history, as well as an interesting replica trading post and information on just how the posts' complex, usually cashless economies functioned.

## ◖ B-Square Ranch

A 12,000-acre spread, B-Square Ranch (3901 Bloomfield Hwy./U.S. 64, www.bolackmuseums.com, 505/325-4275, tours by appointment

only, 9 A.M.–3 P.M. Mon.–Sat., free) is home to two of the weirdest museums in New Mexico. It's not exactly the contents of the museums (hunting trophies and electrical gizmos) that are odd—it's the glimpse you get into the obsessive minds of the men behind them.

At the main ranch house, the **Bolack Museum of Fish & Wildlife** is the work of Tom Bolack, oilman and erstwhile lieutenant governor of New Mexico, who until his death was an outspoken environmentalist—and a passionate hunter. One-hour tours begin with Bolack's "big five" hunting trophies from Africa and carries on through a veritable menagerie of taxidermy, with thousands of specimens from all over the globe, as well as tiger-skin rugs, elephant-foot spittoons, and specimen trays of Indonesian flying lizards. And then there's the whole display of marine life, including a shark.

On the other side of the property, Tom Bolack's son, Tommy, is steadily adding to the **Bolack Electromechanical Museum,** a jumbled but awesome array of obsolete or near-obsolete technology: electric meters, radio antennae, TV cameras, a vintage DC-3, and one of Elvis's Cadillacs. The walk through the collection takes two hours and is peppered with odd information about the family and Tommy's interests, which include pyrotechnics and country music (he plays his slightly warped 45s every Sunday on 97.9 KISS FM from 4 to 7 P.M.).

The ranch driveway is immediately west of Browning Parkway, running south, marked by a small sign. Make reservations for tours at least a day ahead, and at least four days ahead for a Saturday tour.

### Salmon Ruins & Heritage Park

Ten miles east of Farmington, these ruins (6131 U.S. 64, 505/632-2013, www.salmonruins.com, 8 A.M.–5 P.M. Mon.–Fri., 9 A.M.–5 P.M. Sat. and Sun., $3) are not exactly the best place to contemplate the mysteries of the ancients, what with the nonstop traffic drone from the highway just above and the dilapidated mobile homes that clutter the view behind the 11th-century semicircular complex.

But the site is intriguing for this very reason: Here, the layers of accumulated culture include the present day, as well as homesteaders' cabins and a gnarled apple orchard planted in the 19th century. And even though the area feels crowded now, you can see why the spot, next to the San Juan River and towering cottonwoods, must have been appealing to each wave of settlers. The buildings from the earliest period, between 1088 and 1263 (when the place was abandoned following a major fire), were probably built by colonists from Chaco, as they use the same masonry style and a similar layout. There are more than 300 rooms in a single large block.

The "heritage park" aspect of the site includes the rough timber home of George Salmon, whose family helped preserve the ruins, as well as facsimile hogans, tepees, and other examples of local architecture over the millennia. The small **museum** here is also quite good, with its emphasis on tools and daily life. In the winter (November–April), the ruins don't open till noon on Sundays.

Salmon Ruins & Heritage Park

COURTESY OF FARMINGTON CVB

The **San Juan County Archaeological Research Center and Library** (505/632-2013), based at Salmon Ruins, runs small-group tours around Chaco Canyon as well as some of the more obscure sites on Navajo land. Rates for an eight-hour outing, including a sandwich lunch, are typically $250 for groups of four or fewer.

## ENTERTAINMENT

For the most part, Farmington turns in early—if you can't find fun at the places mentioned here, there's always the mall and multiplex cinema on East Main Street, on the north side of town.

### Nightlife

Your best bet for a relaxed bar scene is **Three Rivers Brewery & Tap Room** (101 E. Main St., 505/324-2187, noon–midnight daily), where most people play pool while savoring pints of the house-made Chaco Nut Brown Ale and other brews. Also downtown, **K. B. Dillon's** (101 W. Broadway, 505/325-0222, 11 A.M.–9 P.M. Mon.–Sat.) is a bit rowdier; there's a steakhouse attached, if you need something to soak up the beer. On summer weekends, the locals (and bored long-stay oilmen) head to the track at **Sunray Park & Casino** (39 Rd. 5568, 505/566-1200, www.sunraygaming.com) for the horse races. And every Friday and Saturday afternoon in the summer, there's **live music** on the small square at the corner of Main Street and Orchard Avenue.

## Special Events
Farmington's main get-together is the **Totah Festival** (505/326-7602), a Navajo art market on Labor Day weekend. The city also hosts the **Connie Mack World Series** (www.cmws.org), in August, the final contest of the youth baseball teams that aren't in the Little League.

## SPORTS AND RECREATION
With three rivers and dramatic sandstone formations nearby, as well as quite a few in-town parks, the Farmington area is very good for getting out and about. For maps, permits, fishing licenses, and more information on these and other activities, stop in at the **BLM Farmington field office** (1235 La Plata Hwy., 505/599-8900, 8 A.M.–5 P.M. Mon.–Fri.).

## City Parks and Pools
The relatively wild-feeling **Animas River Park** is set along the riverbank on the east side of town, with trails winding through the trees. It's a pretty place for a morning run or a sunset stroll, and the paved waterside path, dotted with picnic tables, runs a full five miles. The easiest access to this walk is at **Berg Park,** on the west bank of the river, off Scott Avenue; on the east bank, the **Riverside Nature Center** (505/599-1422, 10 A.M.–6 P.M. Tues.–Sat., 1–5 P.M. Sun., free) has more trails, as well as a village of fat prairie dogs.

On the northeast edge of town, **Lions Wilderness Park** is the largest one in the city, with an outdoor amphitheatre, an 18-hole **disc golf course,** and access to hiking and biking trails into the rocky hills behind.

For swimming, **Farmington Aquatic Center** (1151 N. Sullivan St., 505/599-1167, $5) is the biggest complex, with water slides

and all the rest, but **Brookside Pool** (1901 N. Dustin St., 505/599-1188, $1.50) is nicer in the summer because it's outdoors.

## Glade Run Trail System
Local mountain bikers developed the BLM-managed Glade Run Trail System through the sandstone cliffs north of the city. It's the site of the venerable **Road Apple Rally** (505/599-1140, www.roadapplerally.com), which has run every October since 1981 (back then, competitors rode single-speed, fat-tire cruisers). You can do the rally route (30 miles, starting in the Lions Wilderness Park) on your own, or one of several other loops through the foothills.

It's easy to get lost in the network of single-track and dirt roads—download a map from www.4corners.info, but an expert at **Cottonwood Cycles** (4370 E. Main St., 505/326-0429, 10 A.M.–6 P.M. Mon.–Fri., 10 A.M.–5 P.M. Sat.) should be able to get you oriented better. The Glade Run trails are also open to **hikers,** though bicyclists get the right-of-way.

## ◖ Bisti/De-Na-Zin Wilderness
Some 45,000 acres of barren shale hills and weird rock formations, this wilderness area is about 30 miles south of Farmington, most directly accessible by Highway 371. You really have to be self-sufficient to enjoy this place—there are no marked trails, no bicycles or groups of more than eight people allowed, and no services, water, or information at the access points. But if you can commit a few hours to a hike (or better, camp on a moonlit night), you will find it one of the more fascinating terrains in the state. It's also relatively easy to navigate, as the ravines and washes form natural paths, and the larger formations and hills are good landmarks (though you should bring a compass).

The BLM-managed patch of land combines what once were two separate areas, and there are still two distinct access points. The Bisti side (36.5 miles south on Hwy. 371, then 2 miles east on gravel Road 7297) is less than stunning when you get out of your car—you probably passed more intriguing hoodoos (wind-eroded pillars of sandstone) on the drive down. The land in front of the small parking area just looks like eroded pavement, with scab-like bits of shale dotted across fine gray dust; the low hills look like mud-caked elephants. Farther off, deep red hills are a byproduct of intensely hot coal fires millions of years ago.

Walk roughly southeast about 30 minutes (two miles), and you'll be surrounded by pre-carious-looking towers of rock and undulating walls of ravines; another 1.5 hours due east from here, and you'll pass all of the best formations. Keep an eye out for fossils in the rocks and chunks of petrified wood on the ground.

The access point to De-Na-Zin is on County Road 7500, 14 miles east from Highway 371, and 10.9 miles west of U.S. 550—the pull-off on the north side of the dirt road is marked only by a small sign that's easy to miss. Here, you must hike across about half a mile of low scrub before you turn down into the washes.

## ACCOMMODATIONS

Many of Farmington's visitors are here for work, which creates a market for decent hotels in all price brackets—though none are particularly cheap. All the chain hotels are represented, most located on the east and north fringes of town.

### Under $100

In the budget category, independent **[ Region Inn** (601 E. Broadway, 505/325-1191, www.theregioninn.com, $55 s, $60 d) matches all the chain hotels in amenities but charges significantly less; there's free wireless Internet, and even an outdoor pool. Not far from downtown and the river walk along the Animas, the location is very convenient, and the on-site Mexican restaurant, Tequila's, is not bad. If it's full, your next best option is **La Quinta Inn Farmington** (675 Scott Ave., 505/327-4706, www.lq.com, $85 d), which is in very good shape. It's on the north side, behind the mall.

### $100-150

If you can find it, down a precipitous little gravel road just off U.S. 64 on the west side of town, **Silver River Adobe Inn** (3151 W. Main St., 505/325-8219, www.silveradobe.com, $105 s, $115 d) makes a wonderful, natural oasis. The breakfast room, packed floor to ceiling with plants, overlooks the river, and the whole place has a pleasant, hand-built-in-the-1970s feel, complete with solar panels, as well as exposed adobe-brick walls in the two rooms and one suite.

In a quiet residential neighborhood, **[ Casa Blanca Inn** (505 E. La Plata St., 505/327-6503, www.4cornersbandb.com, $135 d) encompasses three separate properties—all humdrum split-level ranch homes on the outside, but the interiors are completely transporting, a tasteful and uncluttered mix of heavy, hand-carved furniture, brick and wood floors, and decorative treasures like Guatemalan bedspreads and Chinese vases. The main "hacienda" has two separate garden areas and includes the Vista Grande suite, with a wraparound sun porch. Across the street are two smaller properties, with two rooms each.

### $150 and up

For sheer novelty value, you can't beat **Kokopelli's Cave** (3204 Crestridge Dr., 505/326-2461, www.bbonline.com/nm/koko-pelli, $260 d), a "luxury cave dwelling" in the cliffs on the north side of town. To get to your fully appointed, 1,650-square-foot home, you have to edge along a sandstone path down the side of a cliff face—so once you're in, you'll probably stay in for a night or two. But with a full kitchen, a barbecue grill, a hot tub, and a deck with a great view, you're pretty well set.

## FOOD

Meals in Farmington are rarely anything to write home about, but there are a few reliable options among the scores of fast-food outlets.

### Coffee and More

**[ Andrea Kristina's** (218 W. Main St., 505/327-3313, 7 A.M.–9 P.M. Mon.–Wed., 7 A.M.–9 P.M. Thurs. and Fri., 9 A.M.–9 P.M. Sat., $8) is a small bookstore and a larger coffee bar. It also has buttery pastries, sandwiches named after famous authors, and a heaping turkey, avocado, and bacon salad. Thursday is open-mic night, and Saturday usually has some kind of acoustic performance scheduled as well. For a standard American diner breakfast, **Pancake Alley** (501 E. Main St., 505/327-9312, 6 A.M.–8 P.M. Mon.–Sat., $7) is a solid option; it's a popular hangout with the Farmington police force.

## Brewpub

In a stately old downtown building that once housed a drugstore and the daily *Times-Hustler,* the sprawling ( **Three Rivers Eatery & Brewery** (101 E. Main St., 505/324-2187, 11 A.M.–9 P.M. Mon.–Sat., noon–9 P.M. Sun., $8–17) is a very popular hangout that has something on the menu for just about everyone—even homemade root beer for kids, in addition to the adult concoctions, all served at the old soda fountain at the front of the tin-ceiling room. The menu also shows a love of drink, with entrées like the super-marinated Drunken Steak. Sandwiches are fresh-tasting items like herbed chicken salad. After dinner, you can roll next door to the bar and pool tables.

## New Mexican

Venerable **Los Hermanitos** (3501 E. Main St., 505/326-5664, 6 A.M.–9 P.M. Mon.–Sat., $10) is so old-school that the "vegetarian" section of the menu includes trout and halibut. The real action is in the giant stuffed sopaipillas and anything involving *carne adovada.* There's another branch on the west side (2400 W. Main St., 505/327-1919).

A rare opportunity to eat Navajo food, made by and for Navajo, the very popular ( **Ash-Kii's Navajo Grill** (123 W. Broadway, 505/326-3804, 7 A.M.–8 P.M. Mon.–Thurs., 7 A.M.–7 P.M. Fri., 10 A.M.–7 P.M. Sat., $7) is a cheerful diner run by a family that used to sell food at flea markets—all the favorites are here, with squash stews, Navajo tacos, and mutton sandwiches. But there are a few novelties too, like the Ace pizza, topped with bits of lamb. Wash it down with Navajo tea (an herb called *cota*).

## Meat and More Meat

For a tasty sandwich and hand-cut fries, the tiny white building that is **Hometown Hamburgers** (2133 E. Main St., 505/326-5580, 10 A.M.–10 P.M. Mon.–Sat., 11 A.M.–6 P.M. Sun., $4) is the place to go. It beats McDonald's in quality *and* quantity: Really hearty eaters can order a one-pound patty.

It's a little disorienting to walk into **Spare Rib BBQ** (1700 E. Main St., 505/325-4800, 10 A.M.–8 P.M. Tues.–Sat., $8), which looks exactly like a roadside joint somewhere in the South—except the picnic tables are indoors, on carpeting. Hush puppies, sweet tea, and collard greens are all on the menu next to succulent pulled pork.

## INFORMATION AND SERVICES

The **Gateway Park Visitors Center** (3041 E. Main St., 505/326-7602, www.farmingtonnm. org, 8 A.M.–5 P.M. Mon.–Sat.), in the same building as the Farmington Museum, is the place to pick up flyers and maps (including an excellent one published by the chamber of commerce). For **Internet access,** stop by the Farmington Public Library (2101 Farmington Ave., 505/599-1270, 9 A.M.–7 P.M. Mon.–Thurs., 9 A.M.–5 P.M. Fri. and Sat., 1–5 P.M. Sun.), where you can use the computers for 30 minutes.

## GETTING THERE AND AROUND

Thanks to the oil and gas industry, **Four Corners Airport** (FMN), on the west side of town, is fairly busy. It receives flights from Denver and Phoenix (via Page, Arizona) on Great Lakes Airlines (800/554-5111, www. flygreatlakes.com). The major national car rental chains have branches at the airport.

**Greyhound** (800/231-2222, www.greyhound.com) bus service connects Farmington with Albuquerque and Durango, running once a day from the bus stop (126 E. Main St., 505/325-1009, 8:30 A.M.–7 P.M. Mon.–Sat.).

# Aztec

A half-hour drive northeast from Farmington, Aztec nearly counts as a suburb. But with its pretty restored main street lined with brick-front shops, including a giant historical museum, this town of 7,000 definitely has its own character. Like Farmington, a lot of the economy is based on the gas industry. In 1921, Aztec became the first town in the state to use natural gas to heat homes. Billboards at the edge of town boast the current number of friendly residents, "plus six old soreheads." These half-dozen cranks aren't actually all that nasty—they're six town figures elected each year based on their civic activity and general charm, and honored in a parade.

## SIGHTS

The scenery around here is a study in dusty tones, with white and beige rocks studded only with sagebrush and the occasional piñon tree—a stark backdrop for the Ancestral Puebloan ruins on the north side of town that are worth the visit for the great kiva alone.

### Aztec Ruins National Monument

The "place by flowing waters" (84 County Rd. 2900, 505/334-6174, www.nps.gov/azru, 8 A.M.–6 P.M. daily in summer, 8 A.M.–5 P.M. daily in winter, $5) was misnamed Aztec by American settlers in the 19th century, who assumed people from central Mexico had established this place. The ruins don't have the dramatic setting of Chaco Canyon or Mesa Verde, but they're the best place to see Anasazi (Ancestral Puebloan) architecture if you can't make it to those more remote spots.

The main excavated area is only a portion of a larger city—when you're up on a high point looking over the surrounding ground, you'll see that the other "hills" are really unexcavated rubble. The cleaned-up **West Ruin** contains some 400 rooms, as well as a few nice details that show off the Ancestral Puebloans' knack for building. As you walk out of the visitors center and along the side wall of the great

house, for instance, notice the band of green stone embedded in the wall, apparently an intentional bit of decoration. This is also a rather neat place to explore because you can go inside many of the rooms, some of which have their original ceilings: 800-year-old timber, insulated with mud-daubed twigs. The interior walls would have been plastered; some were painted as well.

But the really fascinating detail here is the fully reconstructed **great kiva,** a submerged room 40 feet across, the roof of which originally weighed 95 tons. Descending the stairs into the gloom, stepping onto the packed earth of the floor, you can easily imagine the whole community (or at least the men) gathered together for meetings and ceremonies.

Culturally, Aztec appears to have been first affiliated with Chaco Canyon; later, its construction style imitated that used at Mesa Verde in Colorado. It was occupied only for about two centuries and finally abandoned before 1300.

A number of burials found in the lower rooms have led archaeologists to reexamine the long-held assumption that these buildings—and similar complexes at other Ancestral Puebloan sites—functioned like apartment blocks. According to that theory, lower rooms were most often used for storage—but here at Aztec, the ritually prepared bodies suggest that the rooms had a more specialized use, and that perhaps these stone buildings were entirely dedicated to ceremonies and city administration, while people actually lived in outlying structures made of perishable materials that haven't stood the test of time.

The small **museum** addresses this issue, just one in the ever-changing field of archaeology, with a small item in one corner noting that the exhibits have yet to be updated to reflect the new ideas about the use of great houses. No matter, as the items on display are particularly interesting regardless of what theory they prop up. There's a shred of a woven reed mat, a portion of a blanket made of turkey feathers and rabbit fur, and an original ladder (rare, because they were so heavily used and usually left out in the elements), among other small comforts of life eight centuries ago.

## ⟨ Aztec Museum & Pioneer Village

The ultimate in small-town historical collections, the Aztec Museum & Pioneer Village (125 N. Main Ave., 505/334-9829, 10 A.M.–4 P.M. Tues.–Sat. June–Sept., 10 A.M.–4 P.M. Thurs.–Sat. Oct.–May, $3) has the usual array of old telephone switchboards, vintage eyeglasses, and farming implements—but it has an enormous number of them, all obsessively laid out in what seems like an endless series of rooms.

And just when you thought you were done browsing through the complete interior of an old barber shop and the large gun room, you go outside to find … an entire town. Set in orderly rows, all the usual Old West establishments are there, built at a slightly smaller scale: the sheriff's office, the one-room schoolhouse,

the general store, the village doctor, even the church, which in this case was a real building from a nearby community that was moved here and scaled down to fit with the others. And of course, each building is kitted out with period-specific knickknacks.

## SPORTS AND RECREATION

The mountain biking and hiking trail called **Alien Run** traces a route up Hart Canyon, past the site of an alleged UFO crash. It's a scenic bit of single-track, with a few patches of slick sandstone. The official length is nine miles, though locals are working on extending it. About four miles in, a plaque marks the site where in 1948 the remnants of a 100-foot-wide disc were spotted, along with dead creatures resembling small humans; according to locals, the crash was swiftly followed by heavy-breathing military reps who whisked all the evidence away—though apparently the site does register a slightly abnormal amount of radiation. To reach the trailhead, take U.S. 550 north four miles, then turn right on County Road

© ZORA O'NEILL

the great kiva at Aztec Ruins National Monument

2770. Follow this three miles to a left turn, then it's half a mile up a hill and another half mile right along the fence to a gate and parking lot. The trail is mobbed at the end of March, when Aztec hosts its annual **UFO Symposium** (505/330-4616, www.aztecufo.com).

## ACCOMMODATIONS
At the **Step Back Inn** (103 W. Aztec Blvd., 505/334-1200, www.stepbackinn.com, $98 d), the rooms nod to the past with Victorian-style armoires and reproduction wallpaper. Some elements feel a bit worn, but it's made up for with homemade cinnamon rolls at breakfast. For those on a serious budget, the motel-style **Enchantment Lodge** (1800 W. Aztec Blvd., 505/334-6143, www.enchantmentlodge.com,

$50 s, $60 d) looks a little sketchy, but the rooms are clean and basic.

## FOOD
Like Farmington, Aztec is short on good food. But **Main Street Bistro** (122 N. Main Ave., 505/334-0109, 7 A.M.–2 P.M. Mon.–Fri., 8 A.M.–noon Sat., $8), across the street from the Aztec Museum, offers good strong coffee, homemade pastries, and quiche.

## INFORMATION AND SERVICES
The **Aztec Welcome Center** (110 N. Ash St., www.aztecchamber.com, 505/334-9551, 8 A.M.–5 P.M. Mon.–Fri.), run by the chamber of commerce, can answer all pressing questions.

# Bloomfield

The town of Bloomfield (www.bloomfieldnm. info), at the intersection of U.S. 64 and U.S. 550, is about the same size as Aztec but doesn't really present any strong reason for visitors to stop. It's the gateway to the best state park in the region, though, and the **Best Western Territorial Inn & Suites** (415 S. Bloomfield Blvd., 505/632-9100, www.bestwestern.com, $105 d) is the closest you can stay to Chaco Canyon without camping.

## NAVAJO LAKE STATE PARK
Approaching Navajo Lake (1448 Hwy. 511, 505/632-2278, www.nmparks.com, $5/car), Highway 539 crosses the dam itself in an unnerving, guardrail-free swoop. The lake is the second largest in the state (after Elephant Butte), its 15,500 acres of water stretching like fingers up into Colorado. The glassy surface reflects the sky and year-round snow on the Rocky Mountains to the north. The main access point (of three) is **Pine Site,** just across the dam on Highway 511, with a visitors center and a large developed **campground** ($10, $14 with electric) that has great views over the lake, although it's somewhat removed from the

water's edge. This entrance also leads to the main **marina,** offering houseboat rentals and a snack bar. This area can get pretty packed in the summertime, but the shoulder seasons can be beautifully empty. The alternate access to the lake is at **Sims Mesa Site,** on the east side via Highway 527, which has a significantly smaller camping area and can be a little quieter in high season.

### Fishing
The park boundaries also encompass a portion of the San Juan River downstream that's renowned for its fishing—rainbow, cutthroat, and brown trout, as well as kokanee salmon and largemouth bass are among the species that thrive here. The San Juan's "quality waters," as they're called, have special regulations: The first quarter-mile after the dam is catch-and-release only, and in the next 3.5 miles, you may use only flies with a single barbless hook, and you can keep only one fish of 20 inches or more. There are pull-offs for riverbank access all along Highway 511. On the opposite bank (reached via Road 4280 off Highway 173) is pretty, tree-shaded **Cottonwood Campground,**

© ZORA O'NEILL

**houseboats on Navajo Lake**

with nearly 50 sites. You can pick up a fishing license at any of the lodges and guide shops in the community of Navajo Dam, at the junction of Highways 173 and 511.

## Simon Canyon

Technically not part of the state park but accessible by the same road as Cottonwood Campground, Simon Canyon is BLM land that has been labeled an "area of critical environmental concern," due to the presence of golden eagles, prairie falcons, and other treasured species. Use is restricted to hikers and anglers, and the trails are not frequently used. The main route, up through the canyon that runs due north where Road 4280 dead-ends, also passes a Navajo defensive fort, built in the 18th century on a pillar of rock.

# Jicarilla Apache Nation

Ninety miles east of Farmington, the village of **Dulce** is the center of the 750,000-acre Jicarilla Apache Nation (575/759-3242, www.jicarillaonline.com), which stretches east as far as Chama and south almost to the town of Cuba. The area does not represent the ancestral homelands of this band of Apache—originally, they had lived around the Platte and Arkansas Rivers in what is now central Colorado. But they were pushed south by white settlers in the 19th century, eventually scattering to live with other tribes as far south and east as Tucumcari. The current reservation wasn't designated until 1887, when the band's numbers had dwindled to just 330 and the group had split into two factions. Although the land was hard-won, it proved very fortunate when oil and gas were discovered on it in the 1930s. Profit from these resources, as well as a casino in Dulce and the luxurious Lodge at Chama, has made this a relatively prosperous reservation.

The tribe now numbers about 3,500 members, with 2,000 or so based in Dulce. The village is set in a high, grassy valley that feels hidden away from the rest of the world, with bison, cattle, and sheep grazing beneath the snow-capped Rockies.

## Sights

The name Jicarilla means "little basket"—just one of the many fine crafts this Apache band is known for. The **Jicarilla Museum of Arts & Crafts** (575/759-3242, 8 A.M.–5 P.M. Mon.–Fri.), midway through town on U.S. 64, displays some excellent examples.

## Events

On the third week in July, the **Little Beaver Roundup** is a well-attended powwow and rodeo in Dulce that's open to visitors, and photography is permitted. Similar events, plus traditional footraces, mark **Go-Jii-Ya,** the tribe's feast day on September 15; it takes place at Stone Lake.

## Recreation

Most visitors come here to hunt mule deer and elk on the reservation lands, or to fish in one of the many lakes (575/759-3255, www.jicarillahunt.com). **Stone Lake,** 18 miles south of Dulce, has pretty campsites around its three miles of shoreline ($5).

# Chaco Culture National Historical Park

State politicians make periodic threats to pave the two rutted access roads to Chaco Culture (505/786-7014, www.nps.gov/chcu, sunrise–sunset, $8/car, good for seven days), but fortunately this has not yet come to pass. Much of the appeal of Chaco is its location in a valley that has remained relatively untouched since the Ancestral Puebloans (Anasazi) departed sometime in the 13th century. The long, bumpy ride to this hidden valley gives you time to get into the right frame of mind—you're turning back the calendar 800 years as you drive.

Chaco finally appears through a small pass in the reddish rocks, with the striking Fajada Butte directly in front of you. The long valley, bordered with sheer cliff faces, was once home to more than 6,000 people, and now just you and the other visitors who made the drive are there to appreciate the ruins.

## Planning Your Time

This is one of New Mexico's greatest treasures, and even if you're not a big fan of ruins, the remote setting makes the place well worth the drive for an afternoon visit. If you're intrigued by ancient culture or wildlife, then you may want to plan several days here, pitching a tent at the campground near the entrance

to the valley. And regardless of how long you stay, don't get too caught up in following trail guides or hitting all the spots on a map. Unless you're a specialist, you won't discern too

low doorways at Chaco Culture National Historical Park

© ZORA O'NEILL

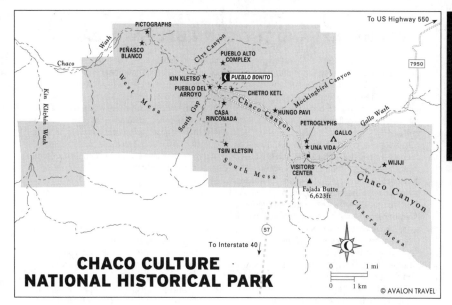

**CHACO CULTURE NATIONAL HISTORICAL PARK**

© AVALON TRAVEL

much difference in the various settlements in the valley, so don't burn yourself out trying to see every one. Better to spend time in one quiet spot, listening only to the rush of ravens' wings, the whisper of the breeze, and the other subtle sounds of this now-empty place.

Some maps and GPS devices suggest that Highway 57 provides access to Chaco Canyon on the north side. It does not. Instead, you must turn off Highway 550 onto County Road 7900, which is paved; after eight miles you turn onto the smaller County Road 7950 (well signed), and the paving gives out. The full drive is 21 miles and takes no more than 45 minutes when conditions are good. You can also approach the site from the south, via paved Highway 371 from Thoreau and Highway 9, then dirt Highway 57, but you'll want a high-clearance vehicle, and patience—the top practical speed on this bumpy road is 35 miles per hour at best. You should call ahead (505/786-7014) to check conditions before taking this route.

## History

The first people to settle in Chaco Canyon

arrived sometime between 5,000 and 10,000 years ago, but a distinctive Chacoan culture (also called Anasazi and Ancestral Puebloan) only developed around A.D. 850. In an arid valley with a harsh climate and very little water, the people of Chaco worked extremely hard to build a society that supported thousands of residents and spread its influence all over the region.

Aerial surveys done in the 1980s revealed a network of roads connecting the settlements here with some 150 outlying communities, farms, and forests where timber was gathered. The roads were perfectly straight (even going up and over cliffs and mesas, rather than around) and up to 30 feet wide—all representing a great deal of effort for a culture that did not have wheels or beasts of burden. Chaco was at the center of a sophisticated trade network, as shown by the tropical bird feathers, baby macaw skeletons, copper bells, and seashells, all from Mexico, that have been uncovered here. It is also likely that the people who lived here were from many different tribes and bands, rather than a single distinct culture—this would explain how today's Pueblo people,

# THE ANASAZI AND THE CANNIBALISM DEBATE

The Anasazi – the culture that established the elaborate cities in Chaco Canyon and the cliff dwellings at Bandelier National Monument – have long been a mystery and a topic of debate among archaeologists because their society appears to have collapsed abruptly in the 13th century.

The popular conception of the Anasazi has been of a peaceful, egalitarian society based on agriculture, an image further enhanced by the Pueblo Indians' push to rename the Anasazi (a Navajo term meaning "ancient ones" or "ancient enemies") Ancestral Puebloans. Modern Puebloans point out that the Anasazi are not some foreign, archaic people who mysteriously vanished, but the forebears of today's American Indians in the Southwest.

But a theory advanced by physical anthropologist Christy Turner suggests the Pueblo Indians might be better off disavowing their ancestors. In his 1999 book *Man Corn: Cannibalism and Violence in the Prehistoric American Southwest*, Turner proposed that the Anasazi culture was a violent one obsessed with ritual consumption of human flesh. Granted, it may not have been exactly the Anasazis' fault – the cannibalism could have been introduced by a Mexican culture, perhaps the Toltecs, and used against the Anasazi as a means of terrorizing them. In any case, his theory suggests yet another stress that could have contributed to the Anasazi collapse and answers another nagging question: What about all those piles of mangled human bones and fire-blackened skulls found at Chaco Canyon, Mesa Verde, and other Anasazi sites?

Many of Turner's colleagues were highly skeptical, and Pueblo Indians were, and still are, outraged at the accusations about their people – Turner and other archaeologists were banned from their excavations in Mesa Verde. In the years since Turner published *Man Corn*, however, the evidence to support his theory seems to have grown – for instance, he discovered a coprolite (preserved human feces) that tested positive for human proteins. Whether or not cannibalism was a regular part of Anasazi life, the evidence Turner uncovered does create a bleak and violent picture of life in what today appear to be peaceful valleys and canyons.

who all claim ancestry from here, speak a number of languages.

Far more impressive, though, is the Chacoans' knack for large-scale construction, often taking into account solar and lunar alignments as well. They developed the **"core and veneer"** style of building, in which walls consisted of an inner mass of rubble faced with thin panels of sandstone, which had been chipped from the surrounding cliffs. With this sturdy technique, they raised the ceremonial complexes we now call **great houses,** which could be up to five stories tall. That the walls are thickest on the first floors, then taper at each subsequent level, suggests that the Chacoans had planned the construction before setting out, even though the growth of the largest great houses, such as Pueblo Bonito, took place over a couple of centuries.

Chacoan ceilings were another durable innovation. They were made of layers of wood stacked at right angles: First, whole tree trunks (which were dried before use, to reduce their weight), then thinner, stripped poles, then twigs, then scraps of juniper bark, all smoothed over with a layer of plaster. Many of these roofs survive, nearly a thousand years later—even more impressive when you consider that most wood had to be carried in from the Chuska Mountains, 50 miles west.

The Chacoans' sophistication is also evident in the **"sun daggers"** discovered at the top of Fajada Butte—there, three rocks are positioned to allow light to fall in a particular pattern on a spiral drawn on a boulder behind. The sun falls on it differently according to the time of year. On the summer solstice, a dagger of light shone through the rocks directly across the center of the spiral; on the winter solstice, two daggers framed the spiral; and on the equinoxes, a smaller dagger of light marked a smaller spiral off to one side. The cycles of the moon are also reflected in shadows. Unfortunately, the rocks shifted in recent years, in part due to visitors wearing away the dirt at their base, and the daggers are no longer aligned. Visitors are no longer allowed on the butte.

The pace of construction slowed in the 12th century, and by 1300 or so, the canyon seems to have been empty, and the Chacoans dispersed—some to what is now Hopi territory in Arizona, some south to Zuni, others to the Rio Grande pueblos. No one has determined for certain whether the migration was due to environmental degradation, attacks from outside, or some other factor, and every new archaeological discovery seems to open up more possibilities, rather than confirm any one theory.

## VISITORS CENTER & CAMPING

Stop at the visitors center (8 A.M.–5 P.M. daily) first to pay, pick up a map, find out what birds and animals have been spotted recently, and get a free backcountry permit if you think you'll be hiking. During the summer, you might want to join a ranger-led tour of Pueblo Bonito (also free). If your schedule allows, time your visit with a **Chaco Night Sky Program,** a periodic event that takes advantage of Chaco's location, more than 75 miles from any population center. Visitors can peer through a number of high-powered telescopes, and the sky positively glitters at night.

Before you reach the visitors center, **Gallo Campground** offers 48 sites ($10), water, restrooms, and a dump station for RVs.

### Una Vida

These small ruins, accessible via a 1.6-mile trail from behind the visitors center, represent the earlier phase of great-house building in Chaco, begun around 850. They're worth a quick look if you have time, if only to see how an unexcavated (yet well-preserved) site differs from one where all the debris has been cleared. Blowing sand has gradually accumulated, just as the walls themselves have slowly crumbled. You

can see evidence of later occupation, probably by shepherds in the 19th century—the slabs of stone have been freshly piled up, in a different style from the original building. If you follow the trail up behind the ruins, you'll see a few petroglyphs chiseled into the rock.

## CANYON LOOP DRIVE

A nine-mile one-way loop runs up to the northwest end of the canyon and back, with parking areas near each great house.

### Hungo Pavi

Like Una Vida, this is one of the earlier complexes in the valley, built between 940 and 1040; also like the other ruins, it's largely unexcavated. If you're short on time, you can easily skip this, though the gentle curve of the back wall and the numerous tiny windows in it are rather striking.

### Chetro Ketl

The defining element of Chetro Ketl, built over a century beginning around 1010, is its huge raised plaza. The elevated platform, some 12 feet high, required tons of packed earth and stone in its construction. With more than 500 rooms, it's the second largest great house in Chaco. It also displays a long colonnaded wall—a very rare style in this region, and perhaps an idea borrowed from Paquimé, in northern Mexico, a city with which the Chacoans are known to have traded. You can also walk from Chetro Ketl to Pueblo Bonito (the next stop on the ruins road), along a flat, quarter-mile trail that passes clusters of petroglyphs on the canyon wall.

### C Pueblo Bonito

The largest complex in the canyon, Pueblo Bonito is presumed to be the ceremonial heart of the Chaco community, and it represents the pinnacle of Chacoan engineering. It began just as a sliver of an arc, a few rooms deep, in the mid-800s and by the 12th century grew into a compound with more than 600 rooms, at least 30 kivas, and walls that rise up to five stories in some sections. Roads led straight to it from every smaller settlement in the area. Due to the various styles of masonry used in the construction, you can see where the various phases begin and end, and where, for instance, an old wall and a new one converge to enlarge the arc. In some sections, the masonry is as regular as brick; in others, you can see where worn stone has been reused.

The 0.6-mile trail leads first through an alarming array of sandstone boulders that seem to have just yesterday tumbled down from the cliff above. (In fact, they fell in 1941, crushing part of the compound.) The route then continues through the Pueblo Bonito complex, including some of the enclosed rooms, but it is hard to get a true sense of the scale of the place from the ground. If you have time and energy, a hike up to the mesa top via the Pueblo Alto trail is highly recommended.

### Wetherill Cemetery

One of the few relics in this valley from a more recent era, this tiny cemetery near the end of the ruins road is easily overlooked. It is the final resting place of Richard Wetherill, a Colorado rancher who became a profiteering archaeologist. He was the first to bring Cliff Palace at Mesa Verde to national attention, and in 1896, he was hired by the American Museum of Natural History to dig up relics at Chaco Canyon. Wetherill is also credited with being the first to apply the name Anasazi to the cultures that inhabited the Four Corners area between the 9th and 12th centuries.

At that time, archaeology was only just developing as a science, and many academics in the field saw Wetherill—who worked on his own, removing pots and other valuable items as he pleased—as a threat to the accurate study of these ancient places. It was irrelevant that Wetherill was often far more knowledgeable about the area and the culture than they were. Wetherill was disparaged as a "pot-hunter," and the 1906 Antiquities Act was devised to designate national monuments and keep people like him off of them—Wetherill had actually staked a homestead claim on the land around Pueblo Bonito. He was operating a trading post

there when he was shot and killed by a Navajo man in 1910. His wife, Marietta, is also buried here, along with several unnamed Navajo.

### Pueblo del Arroyo

This is a beautiful spot in spring or summer during the rains, when the tall cottonwoods are green from the water in the wash that gives Pueblo del Arroyo its name. The large, rounded stones used in many of the rooms indicate a slightly later construction than Pueblo Bonito and Chetro Ketl. Those sites are built of thin, regular, sharp-edged slabs—the rock that was easily collected from the mesa top. This was eventually used up, forcing a switch to this more irregular stone. For the most part erected in the early 12th century, it also displays some of the "tri-wall" construction that is more common in Mesa Verde.

### Kin Kletso

If you've been noting the different styles of masonry throughout the various great houses, then you should also stop at Kin Kletso, at the far north end of the road, and a short walk from the parking lot. It displays the clearest example of what's dubbed the **McElmo style** of masonry (after the McElmo Valley in Colorado), associated with Mesa Verde. Its presence in Chaco Canyon is taken as an indication that the two communities were in regular contact (although now archaeologists debate over who influenced whom). Whereas the best Chacoan stone walls incorporate thick rubble cores and exceedingly regular facing stones, McElmo masonry is characterized by a relatively thin rubble core and the use of large, rounded pieces of sandstone on the surface, chinked with tiny, irregular bits of rock. It was first used at Chaco in the early 1100s.

### Casa Rinconada

Relatively isolated from the other great houses, Casa Rinconada is an enormous **great kiva**, meant to hold hundreds of people. Unlike other kivas, it stands alone, rather than as part of a larger complex, and it is aligned on a north–south axis with the great house of New Alto, on the opposite mesa top. It displays all the signature elements of a kiva, from the wall niches to the two raised floor vaults, which may have been topped with wood to create large drums.

If you want to visit just the kiva, bear right at the fork in the trail shortly after it begins. The trail then loops south, past a number of small villages, similar to the great houses, but on a much more limited scale. The oral histories of the contemporary Pueblo people—Zuni, Acoma, Hopi, etc.—all refer to Chaco Canyon as their ancestors' home; however, the Puebloans represent such a variety of languages and traditions that Chaco must have been home to a mix of peoples even then. Some archaeologists have proposed that these distinct villages near Casa Rinconada were inhabited by one of the different peoples.

## HIKING TRAILS

For all the longer hikes, you must have a permit, available from the visitors center, or, if you're indecisive, at the trailhead. There's no fee, and no limit on numbers—this is just a way for rangers to keep track of who's out in the wilderness.

### Pueblo Alto

This 5.1-mile loop hike, which runs off the north end of the valley from behind the Kin Kletso ruins (park at Pueblo del Arroyo), is definitely the most worthwhile of the day hikes, as long as you can handle the first clamber up the seemingly vertical cliff face to reach the canyon rim. From here, it's a level walk back along the mesa top to a point where you can peer down on Pueblo Bonito—the geometry of the buildings, and the successive layers of development all pop into focus from this perspective. You can backtrack from the Pueblo Bonito overlook, which makes for a 3.2-mile hike, or carry on to the Pueblo Alto Complex. The trail then passes by stairs and ramps the Anasazi carved in the cliffs, through a slot canyon, and back up to the mesa edge for a view over Chetro Ketl. You finish by climbing back down the same route to Kin Kletso. Allow between three and four hours for the full hike.

### Peñasco Blanco

From the Pueblo de Arroyo parking lot at the north end of the ruins road, this longer out-and-back leads to seldom-seen Chacoan and Navajo petroglyphs (rock carvings) and pictographs (paintings on the rock), and the unexcavated ruins of Peñasco Blanco, the third-largest great house in the canyon, with a unique oval layout. It's a bit of a drab hike just for this, but mostly level. The first batch of pictographs is two miles in. The whole hike, 7.2 miles round-trip, will take between four and six hours; it can be especially tiring due to the sandy ground along most of the route.

### South Mesa

Partially along some old Chacoan roads, this 3.6-mile loop takes you from near Casa Rinconada on the west side of the canyon to the unexcavated great house Tsin Kletsin, which appears to have been used as a lookout and signal post, as the view from its main kiva has sightlines to six other great houses. The trail first rises to the mesa top, about 450 feet, then descends through South Gap via one of the ancient roads. The full trip can take up to four hours, or you can just hike up to Tsin Kletsin and back in about two.

### Wijiji

A perfectly flat hike (also accessible to bicyclists), this trail leads 1.5 miles through a natural wash to a great house from A.D. 1100, a piece of wholly planned architecture, apparently built in a single phase, unlike the other great houses in the area. Though relatively small, it is exceptional for its symmetry. Allow between two and three hours.

## PUEBLO PINTADO

A separate, unexcavated great house about 20 miles southeast of Chaco and technically part of the same park, Pueblo Pintado is recommended for completists only. If you come here after an extensive visit to Chaco, you will almost certainly wonder why you made the drive; however, if you happen to be going to nearby Crownpoint for the rug auction, then you might want to stop in.

# U.S. 550 South to Bernalillo

The drive back south to the Albuquerque area is a scenic one, with a couple of possible stops in some lesser-visited wilderness areas.

## CUBA

Your best bet for a post-Chaco pick-me-up is in the town of Cuba, 48 miles south on U.S. 550, where **( El Bruno's** (6449 Main St., 575/289-9429, 11 A.M.–10 P.M. daily, $11) serves solid northern New Mexican food (distinct from the rest of the northwest, Cuba is an old Hispano town, founded in the late 18th century). There are occasional reports of bad meals, but when it's good, it's great—and you can't really argue, as it's one of the few restaurants for miles around. It's known for stuffed sopaipillas, tamales, and the Cubita sandwich (a play on the classic ham-and-Swiss cheese *cubano*), which you can enjoy on a shady patio or in a cool dining room built onto what used to be the town's ice cream stand.

## CABEZON PEAK

West of U.S. 550, the bulging "big head" butte is a wilderness study area managed by the BLM. The sides of the 2,000-foot formation are popular for rock climbing, or you can hike up to the peak for a view as far as Mount Taylor. According to Navajo legend, Mount Taylor represents a slaughtered giant whose head rolled to form Cabezon, while his blood settled into El Malpais. To reach the trailhead, turn off U.S. 550 at County Road 279, about 20 miles north of San Ysidro. Then go 12 miles southwest to BLM Road 1114, which leads to the parking area in 3 miles.

## OJITO WILDERNESS AREA

These badlands were designated wilderness in late 2005, so they are still relatively unmarked by trails—see www.ojito.org for some possible directions to take. The terrain is mostly stark, striped red hills, scored by rivulets of glittering white gypsum—not quite as dramatic as Bisti/De-Na-Zin, but also not as remote. The

© ZORA O'NEILL

the front patio at El Bruno's restaurant

partial skeleton of the herbivore *Seismosaurus* was discovered here in 1979, and you can spot fossils in the canyon walls.

From U.S. 550, turn onto Cabezon Road (County Road 26), south of San Ysidro, then bear left at the fork—the parking area for the wilderness is about 10 miles in, on the left. On the way (about 4 miles in), you reach the parking area and trailhead for **White Mesa Bike Trails,** an eerie range of gray gypsum hills traced by 15 miles of single- and double-track. The system runs in two concentric loops. About a third of it, the "Dragon's Back" section, is exceptionally challenging, while the rest is fairly accessible to all riders. Although the trails were laid out for two-wheelers (and a stretch for horses), they're also open to hikers.

Both Ojito and Cabezon are managed by the **BLM Rio Puerco field office** in Albuquerque (435 Montaño Blvd. NE, 505/761-8700).

# LAS CRUCES AND THE SOUTHWEST

Driving south from Albuquerque along I-25, your perception of New Mexico may shift dramatically: Here in the river basin, the land is green and lush. All the way to the city of Las Cruces, where New Mexico State University is known for its agriculture program, the Rio Grande nurtures alfalfa fields and pecan and pistachio orchards, as well as acres and acres of green chile. Turning out tons of the stuff every year, the town of Hatch is a pilgrimage site for the chile-addicted. To the north, the Bosque del Apache is a vast river-fed bird sanctuary that attracts giant sandhill cranes, among other migratory birds.

But the land beyond the reach of irrigation is a somewhat brutal contrast. The Chihuahuan Desert, the largest in North America, begins around Socorro and stretches south all the way to Zacatecas in Mexico. From a car window, the view can be monotonous and dreary—no wonder Spaniards along the Camino Real trade route called this waterless stretch the Jornada del Muerto (Journey of Death). Up close, though, you'll see a terrain studded with a surprising variety of yucca and cactus, as well as roadrunners, jackrabbits, and coyotes. And when the scenery does shift, as in the Florida Mountains near Deming or at the strange outcroppings called the City of Rocks, it is all the more striking amid this barren expanse.

Farther to the west rise the mountain ranges that mark the Continental Divide, where the ancient Mogollon people made their home—you can see their old living spaces at the Gila Cliff Dwellings. Elsewhere in the Gila Wilderness Area, the largest reserve in the state,

COURTESY OF LAS CRUCES CVB

# HIGHLIGHTS

**◖ The Very Large Array:** Studding the plains west of Socorro, 27 giant radio telescopes look into deep space. You can see them up close free at the operation's visitors center (page 241).

**◖ The Lightning Field:** An equally innovative, yet completely different, use of these central plains, Walter de Maria's mesmerizing sculpture requires a long drive and a 24-hour time commitment. But it's immensely worthwhile for land-art fans and anyone intrigued by the beauty of the Western landscape (page 242).

**◖ Bosque del Apache National Wildlife Refuge:** Some of the best bird-watching in the state happens on these wetlands near the Rio Grande. Time your visit with the arrival of the sandhill cranes in October if you can (page 243).

**◖ Mesilla:** This adobe village adjoining Las Cruces remains a great deal like it was when it was founded in the mid-19th century and is relatively free of touristy modern details. Don't miss the Fountain Theatre (page 254).

**◖ New Mexico Farm & Ranch Heritage Museum:** Ancient tractors, lots of livestock, and crafts demonstrations are among the attractions at this vast museum that tells the history of New Mexico in a practical yet fascinating way. Plenty of activities make it great for kids (page 257).

**◖ City of Rocks State Park:** An odd metropolis in the middle of nowhere, these cool rock formations form an interesting skyline in the flatlands between Deming and Silver City. It's a great place for a picnic or overnight camping (page 266).

**◖ Hot Springs on the Gila River:** If want solitude, hike into the Gila wilderness to soak

LOOK FOR ◖ TO FIND RECOMMENDED SIGHTS, ACTIVITIES, DINING, AND LODGING.

in natural pools; if you want an immediate restorative after a long drive, stop in at one of the man-made tubs near the Gila cliff dwellings (page 276).

**◖ Catwalk Trail:** This trail through a winding, pink-walled canyon is a remnant of the old mining industry, utilizing a maintenance bridge for a pipeline. With a stream rushing some 20 feet below the catwalk, it's an easy but thrilling trek, and a great photo opportunity (page 279).

THE SOUTHWEST

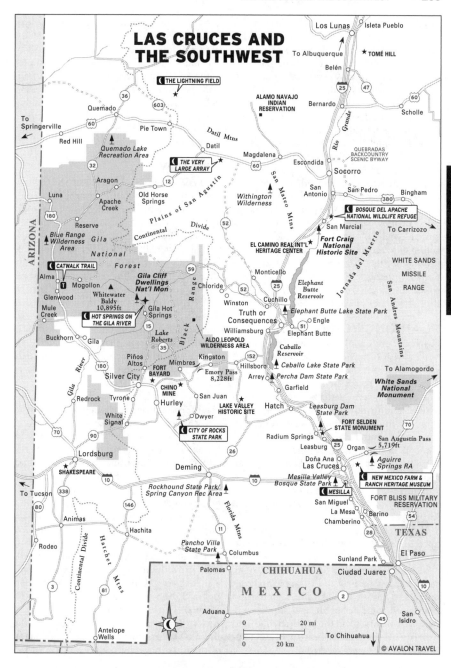

# LAS CRUCES AND THE SOUTHWEST

THE SOUTHWEST

© AVALON TRAVEL

you'll also see the remnants of the phenomenal, if short-lived, mining boom of the late 19th century. Silver City, on the southern edge of the Gila, has held up quite well and now harbors a laid-back creative community that holds "Carpe mañana" as its unofficial motto.

Along the north side of the Gila Wilderness, the mountains descend into the Plains of San Agustin, a great empty bowl where you'll see herds of pronghorn antelopes—as well as the giant white radio telescopes that make up the Very Large Array, a major space research center. This area is ranch land, with an independent ethos that seems held over from the rough-and-tumble mining days and range wars. Landowners in Catron County are required by law to carry a gun, and it's not uncommon to see folks swaggering around with full hip holsters. But even the most weather-beaten westerner will sweeten up in Pie Town, where, just as you'd expect, you can get a fresh slice of America's favorite dessert.

## PLANNING YOUR TIME

Given the driving distances involved, it's difficult to visit New Mexico's southwest if you're also interested in Santa Fe or other northern destinations. You're better off focusing on this area exclusively, perhaps even flying in to El Paso and working your way north, rather than driving down from Albuquerque. You can lounge around Truth or Consequences for a couple of days, and Las Cruces and Silver City both merit a long weekend, though you could get the spirit of each place in a day. What will interest most visitors, however, is the Gila wilderness, where hiking and relaxing in hot springs can occupy a day or a whole week.

Relatively speaking, the plains west of Socorro hold less appeal, but it's nice to at least cruise through this ranching area if you can (and it does complete a logical driving loop), as it's a sharp contrast to the hippie-holdover outlook in Silver City. Likewise, Deming and points west could be left off an arts- or hiking-focused itinerary. (And the bootheel south and west of Lordsburg holds great appeal to naturalists, as pure empty desert.)

Even if you're not planning to hike, at least make time to drive Highway 152 to Silver City, or, for hardier drivers, the Bursum Road to Mogollon and beyond. I-25 can be a bit monotonous; frontage roads, though not an option the entire way, are nearly as fast due to light traffic, and significantly more appealing, especially south of Truth or Consequences, where Highway 185 runs through the chile heartland.

## HISTORY

This corner of New Mexico saw the first extensive human habitation in the American Southwest, with the Mogollon (moh-gui-YONE) and Mimbres cultures (named for the places in which relics of their culture were first discovered) settling here around A.D. 700. With the exception of the late-era Gila Cliff Dwellings and the remnants of a few pit houses, however, these ancient people left few traces. Around 1300, about the same time that the ancestral Puebloans (Anasazi) left Chaco and Bandelier, the Mogollon abandoned their territory, for reasons that are still not clear. Presumably they moved east to the Rio Grande to meld with and expand the Pueblo culture that had just started there.

They were replaced by the Apache, a nomadic people divided into several bands spread across what's now Arizona, New Mexico, and northern Mexico. The Chiricahua and the Mimbres Apaches ranged over what's now the Gila Wilderness Area, and Geronimo, the most famous of this band, said he was born at the headwaters of the Gila River in 1829. Their aggressive raiding culture put them at odds with the Mexican government, then the American one, which was keen to protect the gold miners who'd arrived in the new territory in the 1850s.

The U.S. army was soon engaged in a small-scale war with the most tenacious Apache leaders, such as Cochise, Victorio, the woman fighter Lozen, and Mangas Coloradas (Red Sleeves). Instrumental in the fight was the African-American cavalry, better known as the Buffalo Soldiers; they also helped build many of the forts in southern New Mexico. In the meantime, Apache women and children were being forcibly resettled as far away as Florida and Alabama; the Chiricahua were the only American Indians who were not granted a reservation.

Geronimo finally surrendered in 1886, but violence continued to mar the region. The mining boomtowns (now focused on silver) that sprang up overnight were brutal, lawless places. Then the towns faded almost as quickly when silver currency was replaced with the gold standard in 1893. Meanwhile, south of the mountains, the growing cattle-ranching industry had its own share of vicious infighting, which consumed big businessmen, mercenary cattle rustlers, hit men, and every politician in the southern flatlands; assassinations were not uncommon. And the small town of Columbus, on the border with Mexico, was all but demolished by Pancho Villa in a 1916 raid.

These early battles have been replaced by struggles in the courtroom between preservationists and cattle ranchers. As the long-term damage of overgrazing has become more obvious, environmentalists have been able to successfully sue to take more wilderness acreage out of ranchers' control. Longstanding debates—over reintroduction of the Mexican gray wolf, for instance—have yet to be resolved, making the contrast all the more stark between deep-rooted families who've lived on and worked the land for generations and transplants who've moved here for the natural beauty.

**THE SOUTHWEST**

# South from Albuquerque

The desert terrain beyond Albuquerque on I-25 doesn't look immediately promising, and there's no escaping to a more scenic frontage road in this stretch. Los Lunas and Belén have their own heritage, in farming and railroads, but in recent years they have become bedroom communities for Albuquerque. By exit 152, though, you can strike out into truly remote New Mexico along the Quebradas Scenic Backcountry Byway.

## ISLETA PUEBLO

The southernmost of the pueblos, Tiwa-speaking Isleta (505/869-3111, www.isleta-pueblo.com) had a good deal of interaction with the first Spanish settlers and was the

## EL GRINGO SINGS THE BLUES

One of the state's best-loved Mexican singers is not Mexican at all. He's an American with German roots by the name of Shawn Kiehne. On stage, he goes by El Gringo. Born into a Los Lunas ranching family, he worked summers on a ranch outside of El Paso, alongside a crew of immigrants. It was there he learned Spanish and got into melodramatic *norteño* music – that distinctively twangy, accordion-filled Mexican-country stomp that's popular all along the border. He started singing under his pseudonym in 2003, and in 2005, he won second place on *El Gigante de Mañana,* an *American Idol*-style show on Univision.

He writes and sings in Spanish, with a slightly flat American accent, and his heart clearly lies right on the border. In his signature *corrida* (ballad), he declares, "To my illegal friends who live in the United States/As a gringo I want to tell you to keep dreaming and fighting/This country needs your effort and your work." El Gringo has a self-titled album and tours the United States wherever there are Mexicans to cheer him on. He occasionally plays concerts in bigger venues around Albuquerque – check the tour schedule at www.myspace.com/elgringo7.

only community that didn't participate in the Pueblo Revolt of 1680, during which many of its people fled to Hopi lands and intermarried. Notably, Isleta was home to a New Mexico civil rights hero, Miguel Trujillo, who in 1948 successfully sued the New Mexico government for American Indians' right to vote, ending 24 years of the state's disregard of federal law.

Visitors can see the whitewashed **St. Augustine Church,** a beautiful example of early mission architecture; established in 1612, it was rebuilt in 1716, and it now glows with whitewashed walls and a sky-blue back wall. Take exit 215, heading south on Highway 47, then west on Highway 147 to the village. The pueblo celebrates the **Feast of St. Augustine** August 28–September 4, with the biggest dances on the first and last days.

## LOS LUNAS AND BELÉN

These two towns are of more interest to visitors now that the Rail Runner train from Albuquerque has made them an easy outing. The Los Lunas Rail Runner station is in a residential neighborhood, and Main Street is a 15-minute walk away. You're better off disembarking in Belén, where at least the **Harvey House Museum** (104 N. 1st St., 505/861-0581, 12:30–3:30 P.M. Tues.–Sat., 1–3 P.M. Sun., donation) is across Reinken Avenue (walk over the bridge) and just south of the depot. It tells the story of Belén's past as a major rail hub. Just across the street, **Pete's Café** (105 N. 1st St., 505/864-4811, 11 A.M.–8 P.M. Mon.–Thurs. and Sun., 11 A.M.–8:30 P.M. Fri. and Sat., $9) has been open since 1949. Chile con queso—a melty, Velveeta-heavy mess—starts every meal, and everything else is similarly basic and popular, up to the homemade pies for dessert.

## Tomé Hill

Midway between the two towns, west of I-25 and the Rio Grande, Tomé Hill is an important pilgrimage site, especially on Good Friday; it is topped with three 16-foot-high crosses. A natural lookout point, the hill was a landmark on the Camino Real, and that history is commemorated with a sculpture at the base of the trail.

crosses atop Tomé Hill

© ZORA O'NEILL

A 20-minute climb gives a good view down the Rio Grande; keep an eye out for petroglyphs on the rocks near the top. Take exit 203 from I-25, head east, then south about three miles on Highway 47 and turn east. Tomé's old town church is across Highway 47 to the west.

## QUEBRADAS BACKCOUNTRY SCENIC BYWAY

This 24-mile dirt road, which runs in a jagged arc down to U.S. 380, just south of Socorro, more than makes up for the previous miles of dreary highway driving. The rounded hills here are striped with rainbow hues, and the scrub desert teems with hawks, mule deer, and foxes. Requiring two to three hours, the route makes a good slow way to the Bosque del Apache if you're planning late-afternoon bird-watching

(or you could come back up this way after a morning tour). Don't attempt the drive if it has rained recently—the route is named for the deep "breaks," or drainage channels it crosses, and the mud in the bottoms can be impossible to pass. Look out for sandy patches at all times, as well as the occasional hardy mountain biker.

Finding the start of the route is a little tricky: Leave I-25 at Escondida (exit 152), then go north for 1.3 miles on the east-side frontage road; turn east at Escondida Lake and continue for 0.8 miles, crossing the river, to Pueblito, where you turn right at a T intersection. After about a mile, you see a sign for the byway beginning on your left (west); the road ends on U.S. 380 about 10 miles east of San Antonio and the road to the bosque.

# Socorro and the Plains of San Agustin

The small town of Socorro is the gateway to the Plains of San Agustin, a dry prehistoric lake bed that's now a vast bowl of grazing land. U.S. 60 used to be a well-used cross-country route; now this part of the state, though beautiful, is seldom visited and holds few of the typical charms for visitors (and even fewer services). The tiny ranching-focused communities that mark the west edge of the plains—Datil, Pie Town, and Quemado—are, not coincidentally, spaced a day's horseback ride apart.

## SOCORRO

Once a pueblo that offered food to conquistador Don Juan de Oñate, Socorro (Succor, or Relief) now shelters people en route to the *Bosque del Apache,* as well as the students of the **New Mexico Institute of Mining & Technology** (a.k.a. New Mexico Tech), which has been training engineers since 1889 on an attractive Mission-style campus on the west edge of town. In the center, closer to the freeway, is a small time-warp historic plaza, where **Socorro Fest** (www.socorrofest.com) is held every October.

### Sports and Recreation

Socorro's student population fosters a strong bicycling culture, and the surrounding hills are crisscrossed by a number of excellent roads and trails. Visit **Spoke N' Word Cycles** (575/835-9673, 10 A.M.–6 P.M. Tues.–Sat.), on the plaza, for guidance.

### Accommodations and Food

Wet your whistle at the **Capitol Bar** (575/835-1193, noon–2 A.M. Mon.–Sat., noon–midnight Sun.) on the plaza, which doesn't seem to have changed much in its century of doing business—this is one of those dim, swinging-door saloons that you thought existed only on movie sets. **Manzanares Street Coffeehouse** (110 Manzanares St., 575/838-0809, 7 A.M.–6 P.M. daily), just off the plaza, is a popular non-alcoholic hangout.

For a full meal, try **Socorro Springs** (1012 N. California St., 575/838-0650, 10:30 A.M.–10 P.M. daily, $9), a brewpub on the north end of the main drag through town with a diverse menu, from morning coffee and omelets through late-night flame-grilled burgers and creative pizzas. Another local favorite is **Frank & Lupe's El Sombrero** (210 Mesquite St. NE, 575/835-3945, 11 A.M.–9 P.M. daily, $7), where the salsa verde is tasty, the tamales are appropriately rich with lard, and the airy interior courtyard is pretty and relaxing. It's just east of I-25 on the north side (exit 150).

As for accommodations, chain motels are the only real options here—the **Motel 6** (807 S. U.S. 85, 575/835-3500, www.motel6.com, $34 d) on the south side is basic but fine for overnight, and the **Holiday Inn Express** (1040 N. California St., 888/465-4329, www.hiexpress.com, $109 d) is positively plush. If you want something with a bit more character, head down the road to Magdalena.

## MAGDALENA

Established in 1884, Magdalena was a commercial hub for this corner of the state for about 50 years. Ranchers drove their cattle here, and miners shipped their ore, all to be loaded on the rail spur that ran to the main line at Socorro, 27 miles east. But the last cattle drive happened in 1970, and the rails were torn out in 1981. The thousand or so people here now are a mix of artists and solitary types escaping the relative bustle of Socorro. U.S. 60 becomes 1st Street in town; Main Street runs north–south in the center.

Follow signs south from U.S. 60 to the **Box Car Museum** (Main St., 575/854-2261, 11 A.M.–4 P.M. Mon., Tues. and Fri., 11 A.M.–9 P.M. Wed., 9 A.M.–2 P.M. Sat., donation), a small collection of historical artifacts, including some items from the remote Alamo Navajo reservation (29 miles north), set next to the former train depot.

### Sports and Recreation

The little-visited mountains south of town provide a great chance to hike or mountain bike in solitude. The main trail access point is **Water Canyon Campground,** reached via Forest Road 235, which runs south from U.S. 60 11 miles east of Magdalena. Southwest of Magdalena in the San Mateo Mountains, the

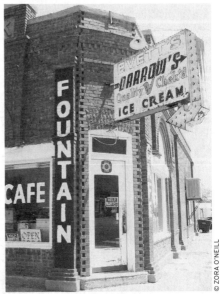

a vestige of Magdalena's boom years as a cattle station

remote **Withington Wilderness Area** is almost always devoid of people. For info on trails here and closer to town, visit the **Magdalena Ranger District office** (575/854-2281, 8 A.M.–4:30 P.M. Mon.–Fri.), on the east side.

### Accommodations and Food

About the only place to eat (aside from the gas station convenience store) is the **Magdalena Café and Steakhouse** (109 S. Main St., 575/854-2696, 7 A.M.–1:30 P.M. Mon.–Wed., 7 A.M.–1:30 P.M. and 5–7 P.M. Thurs. and Fri., 7 A.M.–12:30 P.M. Sat., $9), set in a pretty old building with shiny wood floors and cozy booths.

There are two motels in Magdalena, and both are good. The **Western Motel & RV Park** (404 1st St., 575/854-2417, www.thewesternmotel.com, $42 s, $52 d) has a rustic-country feel, with flower boxes and lace curtains in the windows, though the all-over pine paneling may be a bit overwhelming for some (there's one adobe room, the former maternity hospital). **High Country Lodge** (303

1st St., 575/854-2062, highcountry@gotsky. com, $45 d) has a standard motel layout, but the attractive decorating, with faux-parquet floors and towels coordinated with blankets, sets the place apart.

## ◖ THE VERY LARGE ARRAY

A little more than 20 miles west of Magdalena, strange structures jut out of the plains. These are the 27 radio telescopes—which look like enormous satellite dishes—that compose The Very Large Array, a research center devoted to the study of deep space. Reach the **visitors center** (8 A.M.–sunset daily, 575/835-7243, www.vla.nrao.edu/genpub/tours) by turning south onto Highway 52 and following signs to the VLA access road. The center explains, first of all, just what radio astronomy is, as well as how the telescopes are focused to see deep into the Milky Way and show images as precise as shading on Mercury's poles that may be ice. Then you can walk up close to one of the telescopes, as large as a baseball diamond and weighing 230 tons; with any luck, the array

© ZORA O'NEILL

**radio telescopes on the plains of San Agustin**

will be refocusing, and you'll get to see the massive structure slowly, grindingly turn, eerily in synch with all the others stretching up to 20 miles away.

For a long back-road drive, continue south on Highway 52, passing through a 600-acre private elk reserve and the ghost towns of Winston and Chloride, to eventually connect with I-25 just north of Truth or Consequences.

## DATIL

For visitors and Datil's 50 or so locals, life centers on the **Eagle Guest Ranch** (U.S. 60, 575/772-5612, 6 A.M.–9 P.M. Mon.–Sat.), an all-purpose gas station, saloon, diner, and taxidermy shop. Radio techies from the VLA rub shoulders with hunting parties, and the motel rooms will do in a pinch. It's a chummy, frontier-feeling place, but most people blow right through on their way to . . .

## PIE TOWN

Aside from Truth or Consequences, no other town name in New Mexico looks as intriguing on a map as Pie Town. In fact, "town" is overstating it, as it has a population of about 45, a single working pay phone, and two cafés.

The place got its name in the 1920s, when an entrepreneur began dishing out a sweet pick-me-up to famished homesteaders and, later, intrepid cross-country motorists. But after the federal interstate diverted traffic, the pie market dried up, and the place went pie-less for decades. In 1994, a disappointed visitor to Pie Town took matters into her own hands and opened the ◖ **Pie-O-Neer Café** (U.S. 60, 575/772-2711, 10 A.M.–4 P.M. Fri.–Mon.). The place features, along with more standard flavors, New Mexico Apple Pie (which works in green chile and piñon— much better than it sounds), as well as cheeseburgers and Texas-style chili con carne. There's also a small **cabin** to rent ($125), with a clawfoot tub and pie waiting in the fridge— a great way to make sure you don't miss any of the action at the annual **Pie Festival,** the second weekend in September.

THE SOUTHWEST

© ZORA O'NEILL

**Who wouldn't stop?**

And even if you come through town earlier in the week, you won't miss out on pie. **Daily Pie Café** (U.S. 60, 575/772-2700, 8 A.M.–3 P.M. Tues.–Sat.) has a great selection of New Mexican and diner standards along with the sweets; consult the "pie chart" to see what varieties are available that day. This is also the hangout for some of Catron County's crustiest ranchers; keep your cool when folks swagger in with guns strapped to their hips.

## QUEMADO

Quemado is little more than a wide spot along the highway, but it does provide some basic services for travelers. The **Largo Motel** (U.S. 60, 575/773-4686, $65 d), on the west edge of town, has very comfortable beds. Its café touts its "good pies/hot chile," and delivers on both counts.

You can also camp at **Quemado Lake Recreation Area,** about 20 miles south of U.S. 60 on Highway 32; the 131-acre lake is stocked with trout, and camping facilities range from RV hookups to pleasantly shady spots for tents. A hiking trail heads to a lookout tower in the

ponderosa forest above. Bears can be a problem here during dry summers, and the camping facilities may be closed; check with the **Quemado Ranger District office** (575/773-4678, 8 A.M.–4:30 P.M. Mon.–Fri.), just off U.S. 60 at the intersection with Highway 36.

## ☖ The Lightning Field

Quemado is also the unlikely starting point for a visit to an elaborate work of land art called *The Lightning Field* (575/898-3335, www.lightningfield.org, May–Oct.). Sculptor Walter de Maria laid out the work in 1977, setting 400 stainless-steel poles in a grid measuring one mile by one kilometer. The light glints off the poles, and summer storms create a field of crackling, brilliant electricity across their pointed tips. De Maria envisioned an immersive experience, in which the viewer, in pure isolation, watches the light shift over the course of the day. To this end, casual visitors are not allowed, and the road to the site is unmarked; you must make reservations for an overnight stay and leave your car in Quemado. At $150 per person ($250 during the prime storm months of July and August), the basic accommodations may seem a bit steep, but this ranks as one of the state's most remarkable places to spend the night, not to mention one of the great places to meditate on New Mexico's phenomenal landscape.

# Bosque del Apache

Back on I-25, continuing south from Socorro, the highway passes alongside Bosque del Apache, one of the largest nature reserves in the United States. Access is via Highway 1, south from U.S. 380. The small town of San Antonio, on U.S. 380 near the northern border of the reserve, provides basic tourist services and is a good place to get lunch before or after a visit.

## SAN ANTONIO

Just a blip on the map, this town nonetheless buzzes with birders. It's also where the world's first Hilton hotel opened—not part of Conrad Hilton's international chain, but the one opened by his father when he moved here in the 1880s. Conrad was born shortly thereafter, grew up to be his father's business partner, and went on to develop hotel properties around the world.

### Accommodations

If you want to wake up and get straight to the birds, **Casa Blanca B&B** (13 Montoya St., 575/835-3027, www.casablancabedandbreakfast.com, $80 d) can put you up for the night in one of three cozy rooms in an 1880 Victorian farmhouse; it's closed June–September. **Acosta's** (15 Pino St., 575/835-1688, www.socorro-nm.com/acostas.htm, $60 s, $80 d) has five basic rooms and is open year-round. You can camp at the **Bosque Birdwatchers RV Park** (575/835-1366, $15), just 100 yards north of the reserve border on Highway 1.

### Food

San Antonio manages to support two legendary burger joints: the **Owl Bar & Café** (U.S. 380, 575/835-9946, 8 A.M.–8:15 P.M. Mon.–Sat., $6), which has always gotten all the press, and the lesser-known **Manny's Buckhorn** (U.S. 380, 575/835-4423, 11 A.M.–8 P.M. Mon.–Fri., 11 A.M.–2:45 P.M. Sat., $6), just across the street. Both serve beer and green-chile cheeseburgers, both have chummy local staff and plenty of lore, so how to choose? Go to the Owl if you like your burgers thin, to Manny's if you like them a little fatter. Actually, the Owl gets an extra point for historic detail: The bar here is from Pop Hilton's old hotel.

If, for some reason, you're not in the mood for a burger, follow the signs for **Acosta's** (15 Pino St., 575/835-1688, 7 A.M.–7 P.M. Mon.–Sat., 7 A.M.–3 P.M. Sun., $8), one block south off U.S. 380, for homemade New Mexican food (including especially good tamales) served in a tiny dining room.

## ◖ BOSQUE DEL APACHE NATIONAL WILDLIFE REFUGE

Occupying 57,191 acres on either side of the Rio Grande, this bird sanctuary is in a sense a manufactured habitat: Controlled flooding creates the marshes that draw the birds, which find food on farm plots dedicated to tasty grains. But this is really restoring a process that happened naturally before the Rio Grande was dammed upriver. The birds certainly have no objection. Arctic geese, sandhill cranes, bald eagles, and a whole variety of ducks settle in for the winter, happily ensconced in the rich ponds. In the spring, migratory warblers and pelicans stop off on their way back to points north, while great blue herons make their spring nests here. Summer is relatively quiet, as only the year-round species are still here: hummingbirds, swallows, flycatchers, and the like.

Five miles inside the north border of the reserve, you pass the **visitors center**

Sandhill cranes spend the winter at Bosque del Apache National Wildlife Refuge.

© DICK THOMPSON

(7:30 A.M.–4 P.M. Mon.–Fri., 8 A.M.–4:30 P.M. Sat. and Sun.), where you can pick up maps and find out what birds have been spotted that day. A bit farther south on Highway 1, a 12-mile paved car loop passes through all the marsh-lands and the grain fields; at certain points along the drive, you can get out and hike set trails, such as a quarter-mile boardwalk across a lagoon or a trail to the river. Some areas are open to mountain bikers. The loop drive opens when birdlife is at its best, one hour before sun-rise; cars need to be out by an hour after dark. With all its marshlands, the bosque is also a mosquito sanctuary—slather on plenty of re-pellent before you start your drive.

The biggest event of the year is the arrival of the sandhill cranes—they were the inspi-ration for the refuge, as their population had dwindled to fewer than 20 in 1941, but now more than 15,000 of these graceful birds with six-foot wingspans winter over in the bosque. They're celebrated annually at the five-day **Festival of the Cranes** (www.friendsofthe-bosque.org) in November, when birders gather to witness the mass morning liftoffs and eve-ning fly-ins.

# El Camino Real

South of the Bosque, the Chihuahuan Desert scenery takes over, with dusty grasses occa-sionally punctuated by yucca trees. Highway 1, the interstate frontage road now designated the **Camino Real National Scenic Byway,** grants a quieter perspective and leads directly to the two major sights in this area: the re-mains of a Civil War–era fort and a monu-ment to El Camino Real de Tierra Adentro (the Royal Road of the Interior) forged be-tween central Mexico and Santa Fe during the Spanish colonial period. Just one of a network of trade routes through Spanish territory in the Americas, this north–south trail brought fur and silver into the heart of Mexico, from where it was shipped out to seaports. I-25 parallels the old route, which was so heavily traveled that wagon ruts are still visible. Unfortunately the casual tourist won't see them, as most of these hallowed spots fall within the bounds of Armendaris Ranch and Ladder Ranch, owned by Ted Turner, who promotes bison grazing and management of endangered wildlife on his million-plus acres.

## FORT CRAIG NATIONAL HISTORIC SITE

One of the largest forts in the Southwest and the staging point for the crucial Battle of Valverde during the Civil War, Fort Craig (9 A.M.–5 P.M. daily, free) is a long way to drive for precious little to see. Only true military buffs will have the imagination to bring the few building outlines and crumbling earthworks to life. As a place to stretch your legs, though, you could do worse: The site is near the Rio Grande (a bit of a walk over level ground), in view of Black Mesa to the north. In the days of the Camino Real, this striking landmass came to be known as the Mesa del Contadero, as its position right next to the river formed a natural chute for counting livestock herds. In February 1862, the north side of the mesa saw the Battle of Valverde, in which the fort's forces managed to damage a Confederate supply train, setting the stage for a more decisive Union victory in the Battle of Glorieta about a month later. Five days a week, you can also see the basic **visitors center** (9 A.M.–4:30 P.M. Thurs.–Mon., free); ask the resident volunteer to unlock it if necessary.

## EL CAMINO REAL INTERNATIONAL HERITAGE CENTER

Hidden from view about 2.5 miles east of I-25 (exit 115), the Camino Real International Heritage Center (575/854-3600, www.caminorealheritage.org, 8:30 A.M.–5 P.M. Wed.–Mon., $5) is well worth a detour. The stark modern museum stands on a windswept bluff with no sign of human population in sight—a fitting locale for this tribute to the often-difficult Spanish trade route that for centuries linked Zacatecas, Mexico, with the frontier town of Santa Fe. Inside the heritage center, the information-packed exhibits describe the major points along the royal road; outside are traditional gardens, a dramatic vista on the Chihuahuan Desert, and a six-mile trail north to Fort Craig.

## SPACE: NEW MEXICO'S FINAL FRONTIER

With all its empty land (not to mention the constant rumors of extraterrestrial visitations), southern New Mexico seems like a logical place to build a commercial spacecraft industry. At least that's what the state was betting when it established the Office of Space Commercialization and earmarked $225 million to encourage the private development of Spaceport America on a plain 25 miles south of Truth or Consequences. Critics said that money would be better spent on terrestrial needs like anti-poverty programs. Since construction began in 2009, the project now seems close to liftoff.

The biggest vote of confidence has come from far-ranging entrepreneur Richard Branson, who extended his Virgin brand to its farthest limit so far: Virgin Galactic, which has its "mission control" at the spaceport. Its ship, the VSS Enterprise, will arrive at the spaceport in 2011 and launch commercial flights sometime soon after.

Located on the bleak stretch of the historic Camino Real known as the Jornada del Muerto (Journey of Death), the spaceport is hardly typical tourist fodder, but Virgin Galactic's customers will necessarily be a tough bunch, as they'll undergo a week of training and meeting with astronauts and other space experts in preparation for their launch into the stratosphere. The trip will last only a few minutes, giving passengers just enough time to savor the view of the blue-green globe hanging in the blackness of space. They'll also be a wealthy bunch – the whole experience will cost about $200,000.

As this book went to print, the spaceport was considering guided tours of the complex on weekends. Visit www.spaceportamerica.com for news.

# Truth or Consequences

For decades, the town of Hot Springs was just a dot on the map 150 miles south of Albuquerque. Its bathhouses had once been packed with health-seekers enjoying the underground reservoir of mineral-rich water, but by the mid-20th century, the place had slumped into obscurity. Around this time, the popular radio show *Truth or Consequences* was offering national publicity to any town willing to change its name to match the show's, and the Hot Springs council took the bait. The stunt was completed in the spring of 1950, with host Ralph Edwards and a convoy of press and celebrities on hand. National notoriety faded, but T or C (as it's commonly known) has managed to hang on, acting as a diversion from the interstate for through travelers, as well as a bargain retirement spot for refugees from frigid Minnesota and Dakota winters.

Since 2000, the town has gotten a bit of a boost, as a significant number of younger artists have relocated here from the coasts, opening galleries, vintage stores, and cool motels in the small downtown area. Their influence has helped invigorate the hot-spring industry as well, and now T or C is a pleasant, if a bit ramshackle, place to spend a night or two.

## SIGHTS

Drivers will enter T or C either at its farthest north end (exit 79), where Highway 181 turns into the long commercial strip known as North Date Street, or on the south side (exit 76), where Highway 187 runs through an adjunct town called Williamsburg, then turns into Broadway in T or C. Both routes lead downtown, bounded by Main Street and Broadway, where the galleries are located (note that many are closed at least Monday and Tuesday). Most of the commercial bathhouses and hotels with springs are on or south of Main Street.

### Downtown

T or C's must-see sight is **Geronimo Springs**

**Museum** (211 Main St., 575/894-6600, 9 A.M.–5 P.M. Mon.–Sat., noon–4 P.M. Sun., $5). A fantastic small-town collection, it documents both the monumental and the mundane in T or C since its founding. Countless rooms display everything from mammoth skulls to portraits of local bankers to an authentic log cabin. Local rebel Geronimo gets a lot of attention, as does town-maker and radio and TV host Ralph Edwards.

Otherwise, you'll likely spend your time strolling the semicircle bordered by Main Street and Broadway, where a good portion of the Depression-era shopfronts have been revived with galleries and quirky shops. Of the more than 15 galleries, **RioBravoFineArt** (110 Broadway) is the oldest, representing, among others, the town's best-known painter, Delmas

a vintage door in Truth or Consequences

© ZORA O'NEILL

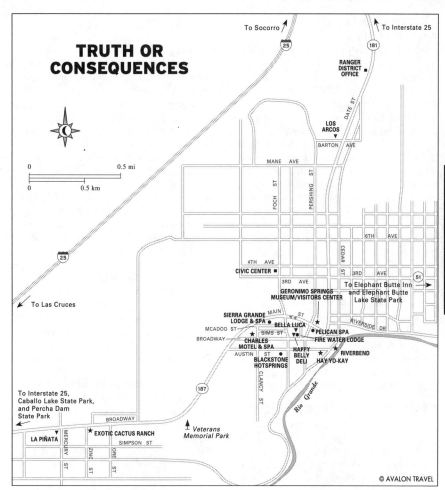

Howe, who made his name with lush murals and homoerotic cowboy portraits.

## Farther Afield

You can see some of Howe's wall art at the town's **Civic Center** (W. 4th Ave. between Grape St. and N. Foch St.), which is covered in his signature flower blooms. On the south side, stop in at the **Exotic Cactus Ranch** (1600 S. Broadway, 575/894-0790, 9 A.M.–3 P.M. Thurs.–Sun. in summer, call for winter hours), even if you don't have a desert garden. Thanks to its elaborate stock, it functions as much as a museum of obscure flora as it does a practical and beloved resource for local gardeners. Also in this area is **Veterans Memorial Park** (996 S. Broadway, 575/894-0750, www.torcveteransmemorial.com), which contains a half-scale replica of the Vietnam Memorial in Washington, D.C., as well as a museum of military history (10 A.M.–4 P.M. Tues.–Sat., free).

## ENTERTAINMENT AND EVENTS

Nightlife is scant in T or C: You'll usually find some people propping up the bar at the **Ivory Tusk Tavern** at the Elephant Butte Inn (401 Hwy. 195, 575/744-5431, 2–9 P.M. daily). A few folks might also be lounging at Riverbend's outdoor group pool, but generally lights go out across town by 10 P.M. or so. The most festive night out is the downtown **Gallery Hop** (Main St. and Broadway, www. torcart.com, 6–9 P.M.), on the second Saturday of every month. Doors stay open late, and residents toddle from spot to spot, sharing gossip and free refreshments.

Annual events also draw crowds. The biggest is the **Ralph Edwards Fiesta,** celebrated with style on the first weekend in May every year since 1950. Edwards himself attended until 1999, often with assorted TV and movie personalities in tow. Even without him (he died in 2005), the festivities are grander than you'd expect for such a small town, pulling together what feels like all of T or C's disparate population of 8,000, with the Old Time Fiddlers Association marching alongside youngsters dressed as aliens. Expect lots of goofy floats, art cars, Spam-craft contests, and more.

## SPORTS AND RECREATION

Truth or Consequences caters to both the layabout and the sportsman: The former can relax in the town's various warm baths, while the latter can enjoy a trio of man-made lakes just minutes from town. If you'll be heading west into the Gila National Forest from here, stop by the **Black Range Ranger District office** (1804 N. Date St., 575/894-6677, 8 A.M.–4:30 P.M. Mon.–Fri.), in the Lakeway Shopping Center, to pick up maps and other info, as well as necessary fishing permits. **Rio Grande Guide Service** (575/894-3454, www.riogrande-guideservice.com) is a good local outfitter; its main focus is fishing trips on and around Elephant Butte Lake, but it can also arrange hiking and camping tours.

## Hot Springs

Of the dozen or so spots to enjoy a warm dip, **Riverbend** (100 Austin St., 575/894-SOAK, www.nmhotsprings.com, 8 A.M.–10 P.M.) is easily the best. Perched at the water's edge, the cascading communal pool ($10/hour) offers four different water temperatures. With lounge chairs and the latest operating hours in town, this area can become a spontaneous party a couple of nights a week. If you're feeling less social, opt for one of three private tubs, similarly open-air and facing the river ($15/hour).

If the weather's not conducive to outdoor soaking, head for **Hay-Yo-Kay** (300 Austin St., 575/894-2228, www.hay-yo-kay.com, 11 A.M.–7 P.M. Wed.–Sun.), a restored bathhouse from the 1920s—the indoor pools for one or two people are basic, but meticulously clean; rates start at $6 for half an hour. A couple of newer, outdoor pools are shielded from the weather and can accommodate larger groups. The rooftop whirlpool tubs at the **Charles Motel and Spa** (601 Broadway, 575/894-7154, www.charlesspa.com, $5/hour) are also popular, with views across the valley, but the facilities seem no different from standard hot tubs.

## Elephant Butte Lake State Park

Named for a distinctive rock formation in the center of the water, 40-mile-long Elephant Butte Lake is the largest body of water in New Mexico and a favorite of boaters and other lovers of water sports. Although the mild weather in this area makes it a pleasant recreation spot year-round, the lake can get very busy in the summertime, with the party spilling over to the small town of Elephant Butte, immediately north of Truth or Consequences on Highway 181.

The state park itself (575/744-5923, www. nmparks.com, $5/car) contains a huge number of **campsites.** Reservations are recommended for the busy RV ($14) and developed sites ($10) on the southern half of the lake (exit 79 from I-25). Follow the frontage road along the west edge of the lake to quieter campsites such as North and South Monticello Point, or just pitch a tent at the water's edge.

During a day visit, you can paddle around in a canoe (one standard route is down the river from just south of the dam to Caballo Lake), or head to one of the sandy beaches that appear when water levels are low. Campers and day-trippers alike should stop first at the **visitors center** (575/744-5421, 7:30 A.M.–4:30 P.M. daily) near the south end, to pay fees and check on current water and wind conditions. All of the major services are around here too, at the marinas or in town. **Marina del Sur** (101 S. Hwy. 195, 575/744-5567, www.marinadelsur.info) rents pontoon boats, houseboats, and kayaks.

## Caballo Lake State Park

This smaller lake (Hwy. 187, 575/743-3942, www.nmparks.com, $5/car) 16 miles south of Truth or Consequences is quieter than Elephant Butte, frequented mainly by anglers out for white bass and walleye. The **Lakeside Recreation Area** has boat access and a few easy hiking trails. The developed sites ($8 for tents, $14 for RVs) at Stallion Campground, overlooking the lake, are preferable to those at Appaloosa, and the primitive camping area is fairly private; you can also park your car about a mile north of the park entrance and hike in to camp at **Eagle Point.**

South of Caballo Dam, the **Riverside Recreation Area** has fairly attractive developed camping spots right on the water, though the spaces are not particularly private-feeling. The best ones are at the far south end of the recreation area.

## Percha Dam State Park

Five miles farther south of Caballo Lake, this small recreational area is a birding hot spot. The annual Migration Sensation fest at the end of April draws aviophiles on the lookout for vermilion flycatchers, among other rare migratory birds. Otherwise, though, the area is not particularly lush and can feel a little dusty despite the big old cottonwood trees that line the river.

## ACCOMMODATIONS

The best options are downtown and near the river, while the true cheapies are on North Date Street; a few chain hotels are very close to the interstate.

### Under $100

A renovated old motor court, ◖ **Blackstone Hotsprings** (410 Austin St., 575/894-0894, www.blackstonehotsprings.com, $75 d) has seven rooms decorated (tastefully) in retro-TV themes, from The black-and-white Twilight Zone to the 1950s space-age Jetsons space. Some setups have patios and/or kitchenettes, and private hot springs fill every room's large soaking tub.

In a similar motor-court setting, **Fire Water Lodge** (311 Broadway, 575/740-0315, www.firewaterlodge.com) doesn't look like much from the outside, but its rooms are some of the most attractive and well priced in town— the walls are painted in glowing colors, and the furniture, hand-carved by the owner, fits perfectly in each space. One suite has just a kitchen ($70); the others also have hot spring–fed tubs built in ($80 and up).

If these places are full, try the **Pelican Spa** (306 S. Pershing St., 575/894-0055, www.pelican-spa.com, $55 s, $95 d), which has a number of comfortable, color-soaked rooms—some at the main location and others in an old-fashioned motor-court annex nearby. Only one has an in-room hot tub, though—all other guests share a large separate spa area at the South Pershing address.

### $100-150

**Elephant Butte Inn** (401 Hwy. 195, 575/744-5431, www.elephantbutteinn.com, $100 d) is ideally situated for anyone who also plans to spend time at the lake, and it's also the best choice for people who might be leery of the more unorthodox digs down in T or C. Its very standard-issue rooms reflect its chain-hotel past, but the friendly owners make the place feel more personal.

By far the ritziest choice in T or C, **Sierra**

THE SOUTHWEST

**Grande Lodge & Spa** (501 McAdoo St., 575/894-6976, www.sierragrandelodge.com, $129 d, $279 suite) has 16 wood-floor rooms decorated in a spare Southwest-meets-Mid-East style. Those on the front upstairs have balconies with a view of the mountains. The luxe spa has indoor and outdoor baths. Rates drop slightly during the week.

## FOOD
The town's favorite New Mexican joint is **La Piñata** (1990 S. Broadway, 575/894-9047, 8 A.M.–8 P.M. Mon.–Sat., $9), on Broadway south of the downtown area, a casual place where you can get all the usual chile-and-cheese-smothered offerings.

On the other end of the culinary spectrum, **BellaLuca** (303 Jones St., 575/894-9866, 11 A.M.–9 P.M. Mon., Wed., and Thurs., 11 A.M.–10 P.M. Fri. and Sat., 10 A.M.–8 P.M. Sun., $11) serves crispy-crust pizzas, inventive pastas and more, in a very sleek setting with floor-to-ceiling windows and art on the walls. Not everything hits the mark, but the food is always fresh (organic eggs and more) and appealing.

For a hearty lunch, head to **Happy Belly Deli** (313 Broadway, 575/894-3354, 7 A.M.–3 P.M. daily, $6 sandwiches), where the New Yorker proprietors pride themselves on quality bagels, meaty sandwiches, and other standards.

For morning brew, stop by ◖ **Black Cat Books and Coffee** (128 Broadway, 575/894-7070, 8 A.M.–5 P.M. Fri.–Mon.), where you can sip your java and nibble a buttery scone while you browse the stacks for secondhand reading material.

In the mood for a hefty dry-aged steak, shrimp cocktail, and deep-fried zucchini strips? Seek out the time-warp Americana of **Los Arcos** (1400 N. Date St., 575/894-6200, 5–9:30 P.M. Mon.–Thurs. and Sun., 5–10:30 P.M. Fri. and Sat., $12), which was surely T or C's finest dining experience in 1959—after which, the clock appears to have stopped.

## INFORMATION
Stop in at the helpful **visitors center** (211 Main St., 575/894-1968, 9 A.M.–noon and 1–5 P.M. Mon.–Fri., 11 A.M.–4 P.M. Sat.) for a map of the town and scads of brochures to surrounding attractions.

# Geronimo Trail

Named for the fearsome leader who held out against the Southern Apache Agency until his capture in 1886, this route (www.geronimo-trail.com) winds through the former territory of his tribe, including the Black Range, the longest and most rugged stretch of mountains in the state, where many of the battles between U.S. troops and the Apaches were waged. But you'll see little evidence of that period (except perhaps in place names like Massacre Canyon). More prevalent are the relics of the short-lived silver boom of the late 19th century. Some of the saloons, general stores, and banks from that era still stand, empty and listing dangerously or propped up and turned into museums.

The route is technically a complete loop, but

the leg that forms the west side of the circuit (Forest Road 150) is 46 miles of rudimentary dirt that can't be recommended for standard cars. Most people will drive the northern section to the ghost towns of Chloride and Winston, or traverse just the southern section on the winding mountain road to Silver City. Many of the more interesting sights are short side trips off the main trail. Before you head out, fill your tank—there are no gas stations on the route west of T or C.

## THE NORTHERN ROUTE
Head north out of T or C along the I-25 frontage road, then turn west into the Cuchillo Mountains on Highway 52.

## Winston and Chloride

After passing through **Cuchillo**, founded in the 1850s, the road winds up and over the mountains to Winston. A picturesque array of wood buildings set on a wide plain, Winston got its name from a generous shop-owner who gave credit to residents suffering through the crash of 1893, when silver was devalued and prospectors lost everything. Now it's a relatively lively community—at least compared with neighboring Chloride, a few miles up the road. Established in 1879, Chloride went bust less than 20 years later. The "hanging tree" still stands in the middle of Wall Street, and the **Pioneer Store Museum** (575/743-2736, 10 A.M.–4 P.M., donation) is crammed with 19th-century accoutrements. The museum owners can advise on nearby trails up to abandoned mines.

## Monticello

Backtrack on Highway 52 about halfway, then cut east on dirt Tortilla Flats Road to Monticello, a pretty farming community that was an early Spanish settlement. Ringed with lavender plots and grape arbors, it is still centered on the traditional plaza established in the 1850s. You can then return to T or C via Highway 142.

## THE SOUTHERN ROUTE

Twelve miles south of Truth or Consequences, Highway 152 heads west into the Black Range, passing a couple of old mining towns. The mountain scenery is striking, though the road is serpentine and slow going, and best driven in the daytime.

## Hillsboro

Seventeen miles along the road, Hillsboro is a pretty little mountain village with an Old West feel. It became the seat of Sierra County in 1884, then managed to weather the silver devaluation and a bitter murder trial in 1899, as cattlemen's feuds and other range rivalries split the whole region. But in the early 20th century, it suffered floods and the flu epidemic, and

after a long legal struggle, lost its county-seat status to Hot Springs (later T or C) in 1936, along with most of its remaining population. Just to be certain there was no going back, the courthouse was dismantled; you can still see its ruins along the "high road" through town.

On the east edge of town, the exceedingly dusty **Black Range Museum** (Hwy. 152, 575/895-5233, 11 A.M.–4 P.M. Thurs.–Sat., 1–5 P.M. Sun., $2 donation) merits a poke around if you happen to arrive during its rare open hours. Half the entertainment is in the owner, who is a bottomless well of Hillsboro lore. The haphazard collection includes fittings from "The Chinaman's Café" that occupied this building after legendary madam-made-good Sadie Orchard sold the property to Tom Ying.

Hillsboro's best-known restaurant nowadays is the 🄲 **Barbershop Café** (200 Main St., 575/895-5283, 10 A.M.–3 P.M. Thurs.–Sun., $8), a homey place in a beautiful vintage building. The barbecue brisket is tasty, and so is the grilled veggie sandwich (especially with a side of homemade potato chips), but save room for the important stuff: lavish desserts like chocolate–Grand Marnier cake and bourbon-spiked bread pudding. Call ahead in winter—the owners usually close for a stretch.

## Lake Valley Historic Site

From the main junction in Hillsboro, you can detour south on Highway 27, which winds out of the mountains and into the rolling hills that surround the Lake Valley Historic Site, an especially well-kept relic. The slumping buildings with rusted tin roofs are all the evidence that remains of the richest single silver mine ever discovered, in 1881: a glittering cavern lined with solid ore that prospectors dubbed The Bridal Chamber. The find was marred by typical tragedy for that period, as George Daly, the man who'd led the exploration, was killed by Apaches the same day the trove was unearthed. The strike prompted all the usual expansion, with saloons, stagecoach and railroad service, and plenty of gunfights. Although the silver crash and a catastrophic fire in 1895 ruined this town, Lake Valley was inhabited by a few hardy old-timers until as recently as 1994. As a result, some of the buildings are in recognizable shape, and the schoolhouse is still used for special events. Stewards should be on-site to give you a walking-tour map and answer questions; if not, you can usually find copies of the map at the entrance to the site.

Highway 27 ends at the intersection with Highway 26, and the alleged town of Nutt— all that's there is the aptly named **Middle of Nowhere Bar.** Head east to Hatch (18 miles) or southwest to Deming (28 miles).

## Kingston

Back in Hillsboro, you continue nine miles west on Highway 152 to where a DEAD END sign points to Kingston. (Signage is poor at the turn-off—if you see a sign for the Kingston Spit & Whittle Club, you've gone too far). A population of more than 7,000 made this the largest town in New Mexico in 1890, when the surrounding mountains were being stripped of their silver in mines called Ready Pay and Opportunity. Contemporary celebrities like Butch Cassidy, Mark Twain, and Billy the Kid all passed through, and Lillian Russell performed in the opera house, but the market panic in 1893 inspired a mass exodus. All that's left now is a community even smaller than Hillsboro, a clutch of buildings along a narrow road. The only one that looks just as it did during the boom years is the faithfully restored 1884 **Percha Bank** (575/895-5032, www.perchabank.com, 10 A.M.–4 P.M. Fri.–Sun. June–Aug., free), complete with all the woodwork and fittings, as well as an enormous working vault. The owners of the bank museum also do attractive letterpress printing, and a gallery space exhibits local art.

If you care to stay a while, the ◖ **Black Range Lodge** (119 Main St., 575/895-5652, www.blackrangelodge.com, $79 s, $95 d) is an atmospheric mountain outpost where you'll get a real sense of the outdoors. The main building, with its heavy stone walls and wood ceiling beams, may inspire memories of summer camp for some. The bedrooms upstairs are far better than bunks, however, with sensible, not-too-frilly antiques, old quilts, and cozy radiant heat in the floors. A separate building showcases the owners' expertise in straw-bale construction; the upstairs guesthouse ($149) has a full kitchen and a deck, while the downstairs studio ($110) has a kitchenette. A larger property across the street is ideal for groups or families. Kids will appreciate the unlimited foosball and Pac-Man in the game room. Full breakfast (with eggs from the resident chickens) is provided; for dinner, you're welcome to cook your own food in the kitchen.

### West to Silver City

After Kingston, Highway 152 snakes up to Emory Pass (elev. 8,228 feet) on a route that can be very tedious and tiring in even the best of weather. If you anticipate heavy rain, better to take the southern route to Silver City; snow often closes the pass entirely.

At the pass, however, the view is of pure blue sky and craggy peaks melting into the far distance. If you want to enjoy an even grander view, park your car at the scenic vista and start up the **Black Range Crest Trail** (no. 79), which runs 4.7 miles north to Hillsboro Peak, at 10,011 feet. The trail starts from the parking area, a short way off the main road, traversing the ridgeline and climbing to a fire tower in a broad meadow. Water is scarce, so stock up for the round-trip, which should take about four hours.

Continuing to Silver City through the Mimbres Valley, you will pass **Chino Mine** and **Fort Bayard**—both of these sites are described in the *Trail of the Mountain Spirits* section in this chapter.

# Mesilla Valley

Heading due south from T or C on I-25 (or, more scenically, on Highway 187 and Highway 185), you return to the fertile river valley and the heartland of New Mexico's distinctive cuisine. This is chile country, where the bulk of the state's crop is grown and processed. In the summer, the fields are hot and still and solidly green. By the fall harvest, the air is almost noticeably spicy (those with allergies, beware!).

## HATCH

This community has earned a much bigger name than its population of 2,000 would suggest. Every Labor Day weekend, the **Hatch Chile Festival** celebrates the town's most famous crop. As you'd imagine, food vendors are plentiful, but you can also shop for chile-theme crafts and wave at the Chile Festival Queen while you ponder that eternal question—red or green? If your visit doesn't coincide with the fiesta, head to **B&E Burritos** (303 N. Franklin St., 575/267-5191, 7 A.M.–6 P.M. Mon.–Fri., 7 A.M.–3 P.M. Sat., $6), the most esteemed place to eat the hot stuff in Hatch. It's on the right when coming in from I-25, set back a bit at the corner of West Hill Street.

## FORT SELDEN STATE MONUMENT

Fort Selden (1280 Ft. Selden Rd., 575/526-8911, 8:30 A.M.–5 P.M. Wed.–Mon., $3), 22 miles south of Hatch and 16 miles north of Las Cruces, was never the site of a dramatic battle—but that doesn't mean a visit here is dull. On the contrary, because the small museum isn't bogged down in troop maneuvers, it has space to dedicate to the

## UTOPIA ON THE RIO GRANDE

Even before the Hog Farm and other communes were established in the 1960s, New Mexico was the subject of utopian plans. In 1882, a New York City dentist named John Newbrough claimed angels had channeled his hands to type almost a thousand pages of revelation in a manuscript he called *Oahspe*. The text lays out an elaborate cosmology in which, among other things, the earth moves along with the sun through different regions of space, each of which has a spiritual effect on the human race. It also details a plan for dealing with the world's orphans, through the building of a model village called the Shalam Colony that would be dedicated to children's education.

*Oahspe's* text inspired followers, who called themselves Faithists, and it was with 20 of these people that Newbrough set about realizing Shalam Colony on the banks of the Rio Grande about a mile from the village of Doña Ana, north of Las Cruces. Set on 1,500 acres of rich farmland and funded by a wealthy Bostonian, the colony featured some 35 buildings, clever innovations such as heated chicken pens, and a grand residence for the children. But the realities of farming proved difficult to the inexperienced Faithists, and only about 50 orphans ended up being sent to the place. When Newbrough died of the flu in 1891, Shalam was already suffering, and even though his wife and the Boston investor (who married in 1893) struggled to keep the place afloat, the group finally dispersed in 1901, and the few remaining children were shipped to orphanages in Texas and Colorado.

A few Faithists carried on and settled in other parts of the West, but the only remnant of the Shalam Colony's social experiment is a historic marker on Highway 185. If this piques your interest, stop in at the **Shalam Colony & Oahspe Museum** (1145 E. Mesa Ave., 575/524-9830, by appointment only, free) in Las Cruces, which maintains a photo archive about the community and the *Oahspe* text.

humdrum details of life on the 19th-century frontier. Here you learn, for instance, that women often accompanied their husbands to forts, and that a soldier's diet consisted of not much more than flour, bacon grease, and the occasional apple. Recipes, building fixtures, and remnants of letters flesh out the portrait of the soldiers stationed here to act as escorts for trading caravans. Established in 1865, the adobe fort itself has melted to the outlines of a few walls surrounding a central parade ground; a monument to the Buffalo Soldiers, many of whom were stationed here, sits adjacent.

## Las Cruces

With the Rio Grande running through the center and scenic mountains jutting up to the east, Las Cruces resembles a miniature Albuquerque in its geography. But this city of 92,000 is distinct in several respects. As the home of New Mexico State University, which has a dedicated Chile Pepper Institute, this is a farm town and proud of it. And while Las Cruces may not literally abut Mexico (El Paso, Texas, 42 miles south, gets in the way), the neighboring country's influence is strongly felt here, in a cross-border culture that's distinct from the Hispano communities in the northern part of the state.

### SIGHTS

Although Las Cruces was founded in 1849, few relics remain. The most notable landmarks are its mural-adorned water towers—you'll see a few coming in from the north on I-25. The historic area is the adobe enclave of Mesilla on the city's east side. Strictly speaking, it's an entirely separate town from Las Cruces, but many locals just think of "Old Mesilla" as a particularly picturesque neighborhood.

### ◖ Mesilla

For the most scenic approach, drive to Mesilla via University Avenue in the south—fields line either side of the road, and you'll feel that you have indeed arrived in a separate town when you turn north on Calle de El Paso. The historic village, which has largely preserved its original adobe architecture, centers on a trim plaza that's more sedate than Albuquerque's or Santa Fe's, but also less plagued with tourist tackiness. The twin-spired **Basilica of San Albino** (575/526-9349, 1–3 P.M. Mon.–Sat.), which dates from 1905, stands on the north side of the plaza. It replaces an earlier adobe one built in 1855, when the settlement of Mesilla had finally attained, after seven years, some security from Apache raids, as well as legal surety when the Gadsden Purchase settled the dispute over the land on which Mesilla sat.

Basilica of San Albino stands at the north side of Mesilla's plaza.

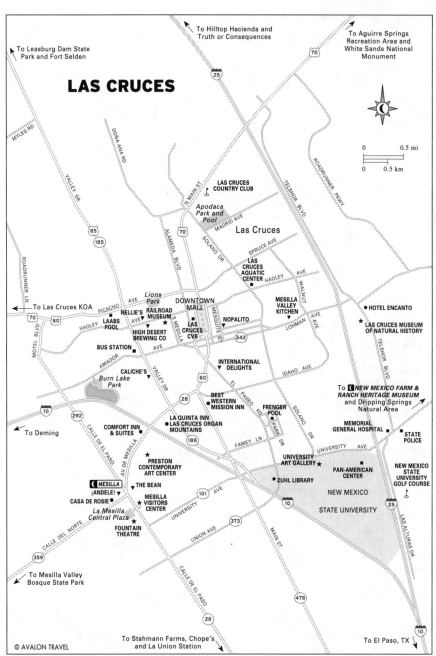

© AVALON TRAVEL

## LAS CRUCES: KEEPING THE CROSSES

In September 2005, two Las Cruces residents filed a suit in federal court alleging that the city logo was an unconstitutional use of religious symbols. The logo, three stylized crosses surrounded by a sunburst, is drawn from the literal meaning of Las Cruces, a name that is supposed to have derived from the tradition of placing crosses to mark graves along the trade route that came through the Mesilla Valley. The plaintiffs in the suit claimed that Las Cruces could just as well mean The Crossroads, referring to the city's location on the Camino Real and other historic byways; therefore, the religious symbols have no historical roots and are illegal.

The lawsuit sparked fervent debate in the city and a notable outcry in favor of the cross logo: "Keep the Crosses," read bumper stickers and window decals, and local radio stations discussed the matter endlessly. The logo's designer, a self-described "long-haired, no-religion Black Sabbath music lover" when he devised the image in 1974, was surprised at the furor and, naturally, supported keeping the image. Finally, in late 2006, a federal judge dismissed the lawsuit, ruling that the crosses were secular in this context.

This wasn't the first time New Mexico has had to take a hard look at its civic icons. In 1985, the ACLU successfully sued to have the Bernalillo County seal altered. A large gold cross used to hang in the sky over a pasture full of sheep, alongside the slogan "Con Esta Vencemos" ("With This We Conquer"), but now the sheep graze under a clear blue sky. (The ACLU declined involvement in the Las Cruces case.) On the opposite side of the fence, the zia symbol, resplendent on the state flag, has drawn criticism for decades from the Zia Pueblo Indians, who resent the use of this sacred image in a secular (and Anglo) context. In December 2005, Governor Bill Richardson established a trust fund for the pueblo's youth.

---

If you want to do a thorough tour of Mesilla's historic buildings, stop in at the **visitors center** (2231 Avenida de Mesilla, 575/524-3262 ext. 117, www.vivamesilla.org, 9:30 A.M.–4:30 P.M. Mon.–Thurs., 10 A.M.–2 P.M. Fri. and Sat.), inside the town hall, for an annotated map. It will point out such venerable spots as the **Fountain Theatre** (2469 Calle de Guadalupe, 575/524-8287, www.mesillavalleyfilm.org, $7), one block south of the plaza. Open since 1870 and operating as a cinema since 1905, it's a tiny, anonymous adobe building, the anti–movie palace, but a great place to see a film, as you settle in between walls painted with murals of the Rio Grande. It was established by Albert Jennings Fountain, the powerful political leader who lived in Mesilla with his Mexican wife; his family performed melodramas on its stage. Fountain later disappeared, along with his young son, a victim of the range wars; his presumed murder prompted a contentious 1899 trial of cattleman Oliver Lee in the town of Hillsboro.

The Fountain family's effects are on view at the **Gadsden Museum** (1875 W. Boutz Rd., 575/526-6293, by appointment only, $2), which has a replica of the old town jail from which Billy the Kid escaped in 1881, as well as many artifacts of Mesilla's Mexican and Spanish heritage.

After you've toured around the plaza, walk to the west, to the residential section, where you'll get an idea what the all-adobe village looked like 150 years back. (Be respectful when taking photos, though.) Up the road, just off Calle de El Paso road via Calle de Alvarez, **Preston Contemporary Art Center** (1755 Avenida de Mercado, 575/523-8713, www.prestoncontemporaryart.com, 1–5 P.M. Tues.–Sat.) is a large complex housing artists' studios and gallery space. Quarterly exhibits show a diverse and colorful assortment of abstract work.

### Downtown Las Cruces

A pedestrian mall built along Main Street in the 1950s proved a detriment, rather than a boon, to business, so the city decided in late 2005 to partially restore the street. (The north and south ends remain blocked to traffic.) The district is interesting to visit only as a vision of urban planning in flux, and to see the town's favorite movie palace of yore, the **Rio Grande Theatre** (213 N. Main St., 575/523-6403, www.riograndetheatre.com). Its Italianate facade was attractively restored in 2005, and it now hosts live performances. Nearby too is the old **State Theater,** home to the long-running Las Cruces Community Theatre (313 N. Main St., 575/523-1200, www.lcctnm.org). You could also stop in at the **Las Cruces Museum of Art** (491 N. Main St., 575/541-2137, 10 A.M.–4 P.M. Mon.–Fri., 9 A.M.–1 P.M. Sat., free), at the north end of the mall, to appreciate the local talent, and the truly absorbing **COAS: My Bookstore** (317 N. Main St., 575/524-8471, 9 A.M.–6 P.M. Mon.–Sat., 11 A.M.–5 P.M. Sun.) crammed with second-hand titles of every kind.

## New Mexico State University

Founded in 1888, NMSU, home of the Aggies, is set on the south side of town in the triangle formed by the intersection of I-10 and I-25, on a modern campus with a few Spanish and Southwestern touches. On the northwest corner of campus on East College Avenue, next to the visitors center (where it's easiest to park), look in at the **Zuhl Museum** (575/646-3616, www.nmsu.edu/zuhl, 8 A.M.–5 P.M. Mon.–Fri., free), a collection of geological items; particularly beautiful are the slabs of petrified wood. In Williams Hall, on University Avenue just east of Solano Drive, the **University Art Gallery** (575/646-2545, www.nmsu.edu/art-gal, 11 A.M.–4 P.M. Tues.–Fri., noon–4 P.M. Sat., free) has a beautiful collection of painted wood *retablos* (saint portraits) from the 19th century; during the summer, the gallery is open only until 4 P.M. each day. Just opposite to the west, in Kent Hall, the **University Museum** (575/646-3739, noon–4 P.M. Tues.–Fri., 9 A.M.–4 P.M. Sat., free) displays recent archaeological finds.

## ◖ New Mexico Farm & Ranch Heritage Museum

Even avowed city slickers will find something intriguing at this museum (4100 Dripping Springs Rd., 575/522-4100, www.frhm.org,

© ZORA O'NEILL

up close and personal at the New Mexico Farm & Ranch Heritage Museum

9 A.M.–5 P.M. Tues.–Sat., noon–5 P.M. Sun., $5), on the east edge of town near the Organ Mountain foothills. Indoors, trace the history of agriculture in New Mexico by peeking inside a traditional Mogollon pit house, then reading and listening to the personal histories of the various homesteaders who replaced the Spanish in the 1860s. Space is given to Blackdom, the African-American farmers' settlement begun in the Pecos Valley and relocated to Las Cruces in 1921, as well as the travails of various other immigrant groups in the state. Ag geeks can admire giant cotton pickers and learn more about the Spanish acequia system of irrigation. Outside, the museum sprawls for acres, encompassing a dairy barn and pens where visitors can inspect goats, sheep, and longhorn cattle. Look out for demonstrations of sheep shearing, blacksmithing, home canning, and the like. Throughout, the volunteer docents have the zeal and enthusiasm of missionaries—you too may have a real appreciation for vintage tractors by the time you leave.

## Other Sights

The modest **Las Cruces Museum of Natural History** (700 S. Telshor Blvd., 575/522-3120, 10 A.M.–5 P.M. Mon.–Thurs. and Sat., 10 A.M.–8 P.M. Fri., 1–5 P.M. Sun., free) is set inside a mall, but that doesn't detract from its educational mission. The small space is evenly split between terrariums showcasing native plants and reptiles and slicker temporary exhibits on topics like dinosaur eggs. It's scheduled to move to a location on Main Street in 2011.

The old Santa Fe depot houses the **Las Cruces Railroad Museum** (351 N. Mesilla St., 575/647-4480, 10 A.M.–4 P.M. Thurs.–Sat., free), with some nice period details in the furniture. But of course the real fun is in the model-train room, which recreates the AT&SF line around Las Cruces.

Just south of Las Cruces on Highway 28, the pecan trees of **Stahmann Farms** cover 4,000 acres in orderly rows, making it the largest family-owned orchard in the United States. After driving past more than a mile of trees, stop in at the **farm store** (22505 Hwy. 28, 575/525-3470, www.stahmanns.com, 10 A.M.–5 P.M. Mon.–Sat., 11 A.M.–5 P.M. Sun.) for fresh-picked nuts and butter pecan ice cream, as well as other Southwestern culinary items. Tours of the orchards start in mid-April, running every Wednesday at 2:30 P.M.

## ENTERTAINMENT

With a student body of more than 16,000, NMSU is a strong influence on local nightlife, so casual bars with free-flowing beer are the norm. Special events highlight the city's ties to Mexican culture.

### Bars and Nightlife

"None of our beers suck," boasts **High Desert Brewing Co.** (1201 W. Hadley Ave., 575/525-6752, 11 A.M.–midnight Mon.–Sat., noon–10 P.M. Sun.), but they needn't set standards so low. This brewpub's products are all quite savory, and they wash down good basic bar grub. There's live music Tuesday, Thursday, and Saturday, though you'd never guess it from the outside of the place, which looks like an office.

Populated with a crew of regulars, **El Patio Cantina** (2172 Calle de Parian, 575/526-9943, 5–11 P.M. Mon., 4–11 P.M. Tues., 2 P.M.–2 A.M. Wed.–Sat., noon–midnight Sun., $3) is a great casual hangout on the plaza in Mesilla. Wednesday night is jazz night, and weekends are usually booked with bands that get the mixed crowd—a true cross-section of Las Cruces—boogying to classic-rock covers.

### Festivals and Events

The premier annual event in Las Cruces is the **Whole Enchilada Fiesta** (575/526-1938, www.enchiladafiesta.com), over three days in late September. The festival of *lucha libre* (Mexican wrestling), motorcycle shows, and food vendors takes place in the city recreation area east of downtown and culminates in the construction of the world's largest enchilada, using 750 pounds of cornmeal, 175 pounds of grated cheese, and 75 gallons of red-chile sauce.

Other city parties have a south-of-the-border flavor, but in a more traditional way.

Mesilla's plaza is dedicated to celebrating Mexico's victory in the 1862 Battle of Puebla on **Cinco de Mayo,** with fireworks, music, piñatas, and folk-dancing performances on the weekend closest to May 5. Likewise, the **Diez y Seis de Septiembre Fiesta** commemorates Mexico's independence movement with all the usual fun on the weekend nearest September 16. At the end of October, the spooky fun of **Dia de los Muertos,** the Day of the Dead, gives kids a chance to see a different sort of Halloween.

NMSU's Pan-American Center fills with the blare of trumpets for four days in November, for the **Las Cruces International Mariachi Conference & Festival** (575/525-1735, www.lascrucesmariachi.org), which draws a long roster of musicians from northern Mexico, California, and across the Southwest. The daytime shows in Young Park are convivial.

## SPORTS AND RECREATION

The mountains' proximity makes Las Cruces a very outdoorsy town. The **Southwest Environmental Center** (275 N. Downtown Mall, 575/522-5552, www.wildmesquite.org, 9 A.M.–6 P.M. Mon.–Fri.) is a great resource for anyone interested in the wild areas around the city—ask here for trail recommendations, and learn what the latest efforts to protect the desert have yielded.

### Hiking

The most accessible day hikes are in the foothills of the Organs, directly east of Las Cruces. **Dripping Springs Natural Area** (575/522-1219, 8 A.M.–7 P.M. Apr.–Sept., 8 A.M.–5 P.M. Oct.–Mar., $3/car) is 10 miles east of the city, at the end of Dripping Springs Road. The visitors center is also the head of the 1.5-mile Dripping Springs Trail, which winds through the ruined buildings of the 19th-century resort that gives the area its name. Just before you reach the visitors center, **La Cueva Picnic Area** is high enough that it affords a fine view across the basin. A trail from here leads past a cave that was the home of an Italian hermit for a few years in the 1860s, until he was found

dead with a knife in his back; his murder was never solved.

Running six miles up and over the mountains to the east side, **Baylor Pass Trail** is a bit more challenging. It begins in the foothills east of Baylor Canyon Road—look for the turn 1.9 miles south of U.S. 70. After ascending about 1,600 feet to the pass, you have a view of both the Mesilla Valley to the west and White Sands to the east, then the trail descends over two miles to end in **Aguirre Springs Recreation Area** (575/525-4300, $3/car), a campground on the east side of the mountains. It takes about four hours to traverse; alternatively, you could make a shorter—but steeper—hike by starting on the east end and going only up to the pass and back, about 2.5 hours. From the same campground, you have access to **Pine Tree Trail,** a 4.5-mile loop that's a little shadier, without much altitude gain—it takes only about three hours to do the circuit.

### Bird-Watching

Encompassing three miles of wetlands on the west side of the Rio Grande, **Mesilla Valley Bosque State Park** (575/523-4398, 8 A.M.–5 P.M. daily Sept.–Mar., 7 A.M.–5 P.M. Mon.–Fri., 7 A.M.–7 P.M. Sat. and Sun. Apr.–Aug., $5/car) was well known as one of the best birding spots in southern New Mexico well before it was established as a state park in 2007. Entrance is via the visitors center on the northern side, where birding tours go out at 8:15 A.M. on weekends; take Calle del Norte (Hwy. 359) west from central Mesilla, then drive south 1.2 miles within the park.

### Biking

Las Cruces is flat and relatively slow-paced, making it very easy to get around on two wheels; empty roads and rugged trails nearby cater to any recreational style. **Ride On Sports** (525 S. Telshor Blvd., 575/521-1686, www.rideonsports.com, 10 A.M.–8 P.M. Mon.–Fri., 9 A.M.–8 P.M. Sat., 11 A.M.–6 P.M. Sun.) is the best local shop, offering all kinds of gear and plenty of tips on where to ride.

One of the best-loved mountain biking trails

is north of the city, just off Highway 185 in the Robledo Mountains on the west side of the Rio Grande. **Robledo Trail** (also known as SST Trail) is 6.5 miles of single-track (13 miles round-trip) with lots of technical challenges—definitely for experienced riders only. Ask Ride On Sports for precise directions to the trailhead. A more accessible circuit, **"A" Mountain Trail** (also signed as Tortugas Mountain Trails) starts just 10 minutes east of the NMSU campus and loops around a cone-shaped hill bedecked with a big red capital "A." The counterclockwise route around the low peak is the easier option, though beginning riders might still have to walk in a couple of spots.

## Rock Climbing

With the near-vertical Organ Mountains always in view, it's no wonder Las Cruces has a strong climbing scene—in fact, when considered with the great rocks closer to El Paso, it's one of the best areas for bouldering and climbing in the United States. The options are too many to detail here, so your best bet is to visit **Outdoor Adventures** (1424 Missouri Ave., 575/521-1922, www.outdooradventures-lc. com, 10 A.M.–6 P.M. Mon.–Fri., 10 A.M.–5 P.M. Sat.) for guidance and maps.

Perhaps the best-known rocks in the area are at **Hueco Tanks State Historic Site** (www. huecotanks.com for climbing details), east of El Paso; day reservations are required ($5 pp), and overnight camping is allowed. Closer to Cruces, **Peña Blanca,** in the southern section of the Organ Mountains, is less charted—no chalk marks or bolts are permitted here, so you're basically dealing with problems your way.

## Sports Facilities

Las Cruces has several public pools. **Laabs** (701 W. Picacho Ave., 575/524-3168) is a modern outdoor pool with slides, open only during the summer. Covered **Frenger** (800 Parkview Dr., 575/523-0362) is open year-round. At press time, the larger year-round Las Cruces Aquatic Center was set to open at Solano Drive and Hadley Avenue. Admission to all pools is

$2.75 for adults, $2 for teens, and $1.75 for children.

## ACCOMMODATIONS

Las Cruces is short on distinctive lodging. A couple of very nice B&Bs are set on the fringes of town, but there's nothing that's both special and centrally located. Of the chain operations, the most conveniently located ones are on Avenida de Mesilla, before you reach Mesilla proper.

## Under $100

Picacho Avenue is the zone for cheap motels, though none of those that fall into this price category can be recommended. You'll get more for your money at the **Las Cruces KOA** (814 Weinrich Rd., 575/526-6555, www.lascruces-campgrounds.com), west of the city just south of U.S. 70; here you have fantastic views of the mountains, not to mention a heated swimming pool and wireless Internet. Bring your own sleeping bags for the cabins ($55), or pitch a tent or RV at sites with water and optional electric hookups ($27–52). The shared bathrooms are kept very clean. You can also camp at **Leasburg Dam State Park** (Hwy. 157, 575/524-4068, www.nmparks.com), 15 miles north of town adjacent to Fort Selden. The park, which runs along a series of irrigation canals, is favored by kayakers and birdwatchers; it has 31 developed campsites ($8 for tents, $14 for RVs).

Of the many chain hotels in town, **La Quinta Inn & Suites Las Cruces Organ Mountains** (1500 Hickory Dr., 575/523-0100, www.lq.com, $65 d) is in excellent shape and has a small pool, as well as larger, newer rooms than the other La Quinta, just across the intersection (though that one is serviceable as well). The **Best Western Mission Inn** (1765 S. Main St., 575/524-8591, www.bwmission-inn.com, $80 d) is older but well kept, and its large rooms have nice little Southwestern details like tile mirror frames. Rates include a full breakfast, and you can often get very good online discounts.

## $100-150

Driving out to ◖ **Hilltop Hacienda** (2600 Westmoreland Ave., 877/829-7142, www. hilltophaciendalascruces.com, $125 d) on the northeast fringe of the city, you might be afraid you'll be pitching your own tent in the middle of the desert. In fact, this quiet B&B is set amid beautifully tended gardens full of honeysuckle, wildflowers, and pomegranate and cypress trees. Watch the sunset from one of several quiet patios or the hot tub, perched on the hillside. The three guest rooms share a private kitchen, and guests also have access to private trails around the hacienda's 17 acres.

The city's plushest hotel, **Hotel Encanto de Las Cruces** (705 S. Telshor Blvd., 575/522-4300, www.hotelencanto.com, $129 d) perches on a hill on the west side, affording great views across the valley. Inside, the decor is a rich palette of tan and wine, with a hint of Spanish colonial style, and the beds are particularly comfortable. Request either a west-facing top-floor room for a great sunset view or something on the pool level, where patios open onto the swimming area.

Walking distance from the Mesilla plaza, **Casa de Rosie** (2140 Calle del Norte, 575/647-1832, www.casaderosie.com, $125 d) is a cozy B&B in a rambling adobe house with a pretty central patio. Rosie is a lively hostess, and guests praise the huge breakfasts, with homemade sweet rolls, bagels, and more. Bicycles are available, and it's a reasonable ride to Mesilla Valley Bosque State Park.

## FOOD

As with sightseeing, eating is a little livelier in Mesilla, with a couple of landmark spots clustered around the plaza. But central Las Cruces has a few hot (as in spicy-hot) spots as well.

### Mesilla

Chandeliers, gleaming dark wood, gilt ceilings, and fogged mirrors give **Double Eagle** (2355 Calle de Guadalupe, 575/523-6700, www. double-eagle-mesilla.com, 11 A.M.–10 P.M.

Mon.–Sat., noon–9 P.M. Sun., $29), on the plaza, an air of bygone romance. One of the city's most venerable (and expensive) restaurants, it's the place locals go for big dates, family parties, and wedding receptions. For the price, the food is not as satisfying as it should be, but it's worth stopping in at least for a drink or an appetizer, to soak up the grand atmosphere and poke through all the ghostly rooms. The more budget-friendly option is the casual New Mexican café **Peppers** (575/523-4999, $11), which occupies two smaller front rooms and the central courtyard with a fountain; you can order off either menu at dinnertime.

Rivaling Double Eagle for historic credibility, **La Posta** (2410 Calle de San Albino, 575/524-3524, www.laposta-de-mesilla.com, 11 A.M.–9 P.M. Sun.–Thurs., 11 A.M.–9:30 P.M. Fri. and Sat., $11), just across the plaza, dishes up New Mexican standards in an old adobe that was a stop on the Butterfield Overland Mail & Stage route. The rambling compound, decked out with parrots and knickknacks, is a bit of a tourist trap, so you won't feel like you're getting off the beaten track, but the food is decent.

But you'll get better, spicier eats at Mexican diner ◖ **¡Andele!** (1950 Calle del Norte, 575/526-9631, 8 A.M.–2:30 P.M. Mon., 8 A.M.–9 P.M. Tues.–Sun., $9) nearby. The place specializes in delicious *tacos al carbon* (with meat fresh off the grill) and rich, red-chile-flecked posole. You can either sit down and eat inside, or stop by the takeout operation just across Calle del Norte.

Just across the street from ¡Andele!, ◖ **The Bean** (2011 Avenida de Mesilla, 575/523-0560, 7 A.M.–9 P.M., $3) is the most popular place to chill out with a cup of joe. Set in an old gas station, the coffeehouse hosts an array of quirky regulars, while serving up pastries, omelets, and grilled sandwiches all day long. At night, it's more of a teen hangout, with the occasional band playing.

### Downtown

As pizza purists demand, it's all about the crust

at ◀ **Zeffiro Pizzeria Napoletana** (136 N. Water St., 575/525-6757, 11 A.M.–2 P.M. and 5–8 P.M. Mon.–Sat., $7), where pies come out of the wood oven with almost comically blistered and bubbling edges. Toppings run from typical pepperoni to lemon slices and asparagus. The place gets busy early, especially if there's a concert at the nearby Rio Grande Theatre. The same team runs the student-friendly **Zeffiro New York Pizzeria** (901 University Ave., 575/525-6770, 11 A.M.–9 P.M. Mon.–Sat.), where you can get a somewhat greasier pizza by the slice.

An entirely unlikely outpost of Hawaiian cuisine, **Ono Grindz** (300 N. Downtown Mall, 575/541-7492, 10:30 A.M.–3 P.M. and 4–8 P.M. Mon.–Fri., 7:30 A.M.–2 P.M. Sat., $8) dishes up fish tacos, teriyaki beef and even sweet-sour Hawaiian-style macaroni salad. The atmosphere is festive, with brightly painted walls and steel guitar music. Look for it in the back corner of the complex at East Las Cruces Avenue.

The **farmer's market** on Main Street usually has a number of good snack vendors—tamales and more. It sets up Wednesday and Saturday (8 A.M.–noon), with more activity on the latter day.

## Elsewhere in Las Cruces

**Nellie's** (1226 W. Hadley Ave., 575/524-9982, 8 A.M.–2 P.M., Tues.–Sat., $7) promises "chile with an attitude," though the service is perfectly pleasant; equal parts meat and green fire, it's the chunky "four-alarm chile" that really gets in your face. Huevos rancheros are a slightly mellower way to start your day.

With its checked tablecloths and country-style chairs, **Mesilla Valley Kitchen** (2001 E. Lohman Ave., 575/523-9311, 6 A.M.–2:30 P.M. Mon.–Sat., 7 A.M.–1:30 P.M. Sun., $7) manages to feel homey despite its view of a parking lot in the Arroyo Plaza strip mall. The food, best at breakfast, is short-order staples, with a New Mexican twist and often better-than-average ingredients: Butter-pecan syrup tops granola pancakes, and avocado crops up in a lot of the big sandwich combos.

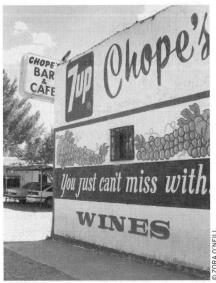
© ZORA O'NEILL

Chope's, a road-food icon south of Las Cruces

Las Cruces is short on global cuisine, but **International Delights** (1245 El Paseo Rd., 575/647-5956, 7 A.M.–midnight Mon.–Sat., 8 A.M.–midnight Sun., $7) satisfies a lot of cravings. The menu includes Middle Eastern standards like falafel along with familiar deli combos and a good selection of coffee, tea, and pastries, including baklava with local flair: date pecan, vanilla piñon, and more. Look for it in the back corner of a strip mall next to Albertson's supermarket.

On a hot summer night, there's no better place to be than **Caliche's** (590 S. Valley Dr., 575/647-5066, 11 A.M.–10 P.M. daily, $4), which serves frozen custard under pink and blue neon. A caliche (Spanish for hard clay) is the local equivalent of a St. Louis–style concrete, a shake so thick you have to eat with a spoon. Of course there are New Mexican mix-ins such as pine nuts and red chile.

## Outside of Las Cruces

Locals often make road trips to a couple of nearby destinations for dinner. **Chope's** (Hwy. 28, 575/233-3420, 11:30 A.M.–1:30 P.M. and

5:30–8:30 P.M. Tues.–Sat.), a down-at-the-heels roadhouse in the village of La Mesa, about 20 minutes' drive south of town, is famous for its heavily egg-battered chile rellenos. We prefer the red chile beans, and the rural New Mexican ambience (go early, as the crowd moves on from eating to drinking by 7 P.M. at least). Farther south, in Anthony, **La Union Station** (Hwy. 28, 575/874-2828, 11 A.M.–3 P.M. Tues.–Thurs., 11 A.M.–8 P.M. Fri., 8 A.M.–8 P.M. Sat. and Sun.) draws crowds for its massive Mexican buffet, hearty green-chile posole, and live music on weekend afternoons.

## INFORMATION AND SERVICES

**Las Cruces Convention & Visitors Bureau** (211 N. Water St., 575/541-2444, www.lascrucescvb.org, 8 A.M.–5 P.M. Mon.–Fri.) has free high-speed Internet service, along with a helpful staff and piles of brochures.

On the old plaza, **Mesilla Book Center** (2360 Calle Principal, 575/526-6220, 11 A.M.–5:30 P.M. Tues.–Sat., 1–5 P.M. Sun.) stocks area history books, guides, and other Western-theme tomes.

## GETTING THERE AND AROUND

Rather than making the drive from Albuquerque, many visitors to Las Cruces fly into El Paso (ELP), only about an hour's drive away. **Las Cruces Shuttle** (575/525-1784, www.lascrucesshuttle.com) runs an airport transport service six times daily (five on weekends). Rates are $43 one-way, or $70 round-trip. Despite its optimistic name, Las Cruces International Airport (LRU) receives only private planes.

The **Greyhound bus** (800/231-2222, www.greyhound.com) stops at the station (390 S. Valley Dr., 575/524-8518, 6 A.M.–11 P.M. daily). Two buses run daily from Albuquerque; nine run from El Paso.

**RoadRunner Transit** (575/541-2500) is the city bus system, though buses run infrequently, and only until 7 P.M. Monday through Saturday. Fare is $1 (exact change, bills accepted) or $2.25 for a day pass, and buses are equipped with front bike racks. Route no. 40 runs to Mesilla from downtown; visit www.las-cruces.org for a full schedule and map.

# West to the Bootheel

Heading west from Las Cruces, I-10 runs through the flatlands up to the Chiricahua Mountains on the Arizona border. Most of the area is unrelenting desert, known for dust storms and shimmering heat. The Florida Mountains, which jut 2,800 feet above the surrounding plain, are the only major interruption.

## DEMING

"Pure water and fast ducks" boast billboards advertising Deming's charms, and surely no other town in the United States can make such a claim to fame. The water comes from a large aquifer under the city of 15,000; as for the speedy birds, they're part of the Great American Duck Race, the city's biggest annual event. The business leaders who came up with the scheme in 1980 (to rival Ruidoso's horse-racing industry) admit the initial brainstorming session did involve liquor.

Like T or C, Deming is popular with retirees from the upper Midwest, and its greater cityscape is one of RV and trailer parks, as well as truck stops. But its old downtown, south of the intersection of Pine and Gold, shows a surprising elegance, with some arts and antiques outlets reviving a few of the old storefronts. Street addresses with directionals (SW, NE, etc.) are outside of town, not in central Deming.

### Sights

Most visitors start with the **Deming-Luna Mimbres Museum** (301 S. Silver Ave.,

THE SOUTHWEST

© ZORA O'NEILL

the drive to Spring Canyon, in Deming's Florida Mountains

9 A.M.–4 P.M. Mon.–Sat., 1:30–4 P.M. Sun., closed Sun. July–Aug., donation), one block south of Pine Street. Set in a 1917 armory, the museum is the county's vast repository of historic flotsam, lovingly curated and carefully arranged. Novelty whiskey bottles, nutcrackers, geodes, beautiful Mimbres pottery—it's all here, in incredible detail and profusion.

At the end of South Silver Street, the redbrick **Luna County Courthouse,** restored in 2006, looks like it would be more at home in Iowa. It was built in 1910, then in 1916 saw the trial of many of Pancho Villa's alleged accomplices in the rebel leader's raid on Columbus, New Mexico; four of the "Villistas" were subsequently hanged on the green lawn in front of the building.

The **St. Clair Winery** (1325 De Baca Rd. SE, 575/546-2408, 9 A.M.–6 P.M. Mon.–Sat., noon–6 P.M. Sun.), established by a French family in 1984, occupies 15 acres a few miles outside of town (head east on Pine Street)—just part of some 120 acres the group owns. You can tour the facilities and taste a wide range of wines; the better ones are under the

D.H. Lescombes label—especially the syrah, which does well in the sun here.

## Entertainment and Events

Deming's annual hoedown is the last weekend in August, when the **Great American Duck Race** (888/345-1125, www.demingduckrace. com) takes over. In addition to the headline duck sprint, festivities include a cash-prize tortilla toss, outhouse races, a parade with more fake foam beaks than you can count, and a balloon rally.

## Sports and Recreation

Beat the summer heat at **Sam Baca Aquatic Center** (815 W. Buckeye St., 575/546-7958, $2), which has several big outdoor pools, with frolicking kids segregated from the lap-swimmers. It's open summers from mid-May through the end of September; call for hours.

For a more outdoorsy experience, head southeast to the Florida (Flowering) Mountains, so named for the colorful wildflowers that blanket their steep slopes in springtime. In summer,

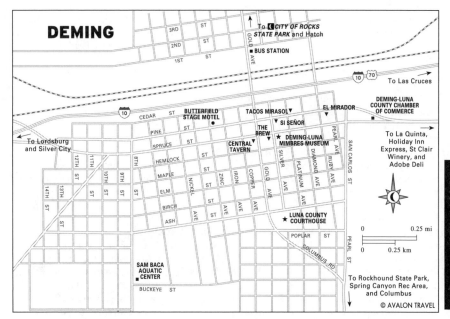

though, they can feel a bit barren and hot, and nowhere more so than at **Rockhound State Park** (Rockhound Rd., 575/546-6182, www. nmparks.com, $5/car). Its setting in the foothills is picturesque, especially around sunset, but a day poking around with a pickax (you're allowed to carry out 15 pounds of finds) is rewarding only for the truly geologically minded. Everyone else will probably be satisfied with the exhibits of geodes and other mineral miracles in the visitors center, or the nearby **Basin Range Volcanics Geolapidary Museum and Rock Shop** (6235 Stirrup Rd. SE, 575/546-4021, 9 A.M.–5 P.M. Thurs.–Tues.), at the intersection of Highways 141 and 143.

For more scenic hiking and good bird-watching, head to **Spring Canyon Recreational Area** (8 A.M.–4 P.M. Wed.–Sun.), immediately adjacent to Rockhound. While you're out, you have a slim chance of spotting an ibex, a variety of goat with large curving horns. The Department of Game and Fish imported them from Iran and released them here in 1970, as part of a now-discontinued program to create

an exotic game-hunting industry; about 400 of the animals live in the mountains now.

## Accommodations

Travelers seldom plan to spend the night in Deming, but if you're deciding between here and Lordsburg for the night, Deming is definitely the better bet, with a larger selection both at the lower end and in more upmarket chain options. Ordinarily, you should have no trouble rolling into town without a reservation, but be sure to book ahead when the duck races are on at the end of August.

On the budget end, you might be tempted by the fabulous neon sign at the **Butterfield Stage Motel** (309 W. Pine St., 866/544-0011, $35 s, $45 d), and you'll be glad to know it's not a bad choice; the rooms are a little tired but generally clean, and some have kitchenettes.

Oriented toward the highway off-ramp rather than town, **La Quinta** (4300 E. Pine St., 575/546-0600, www.lq.com, $80 d) and **Holiday Inn Express** (4600 E. Pine St., 575/546-2661, www.holidayinn.com, $70 d) are the best, most up-to-date options among the chain names.

## Food

Deming doesn't look like a promising gourmet stop, but it is a good place to sample some Mexican (as opposed to *New* Mexican) food, mostly from Mexico City and north. **Tacos Mirasol** (309 E. Pine St., 575/544-0646, 9 A.M.–9 P.M. daily, $5) is a tiny but sparkling-clean roadside hut that does tacos, of course, but also Mexican-style sandwiches (*tortas*), which consist of a choice of meat on a soft fluffy roll, usually slathered with avocado, mayonnaise, and a thin layer of refried beans. Both come with a tangy-hot tomatillo salsa; cut the heat with a banana milkshake or fresh limeade.

The same family runs ◖ **El Mirador** (510 E. Pine St., 575/544-7340, 6 A.M.–9 P.M. Mon.–Sat., $8), the kind of neighborhood diner where Border Patrol officers scoop up the soupy tortilla-and-tomato-sauce dish called *chilaquiles,* while at the next table, recent immigrants chow down on *chuletas* (pork chops). The sun shines in on three sides, and the service is fast and bilingual. Prices are more than reasonable, and everything is fresh, right down to the big glasses of carrot juice and the straight-from-the-fryer *churros* for dessert.

For New Mexican, the time-warp **Si Señor** (200 E. Pine St., 575/546-3938, 9:30 A.M.–8 P.M. Mon.–Sat., 10 A.M.–3 P.M. Sun., $6) falls into the "so bad it's good" category. The sticky vinyl tablecloths, walls tiled like a 1970s bathroom, and fluorescent lights are offset by low prices, huge portions, and an ingenious platter of chicken-fried steak slathered with green chile and cheese (the "milanesa").

If you'd like something more traditionally American, like a big rib-eye steak, make the trek out of town to the **Adobe Deli** (3970 Lewis Flats Rd. SE, 575/546-0361, 11:30 A.M.–10 P.M. Mon.–Sat., $20). The restaurant-bar is set in an old schoolhouse and gym, where the walls are bedecked with hunting trophies, and a cinema screen dominates one wall. In addition to steak, there's onion soup, which employs St. Clair wine and local cheese to deliciously goopy effect. Lunch (served till 5 P.M.) is deli sandwiches, as well as the soup. Take Pine Street east out of town, and turn right on Lewis Flats Road.

For something in the coffee-and-pastry vein, head for **@theBrew** (208½ S. Silver St., 575/546-2828, 7 A.M.–3 P.M. Mon.–Fri., $3). The entrance is around the back, by the Wells Fargo parking lot.

At press time, the **Central Tavern** (200 S. Gold St., www.demingbrew.com) was set to open as Deming's first on-premises brewpub, with a menu of pizzas and build-your-own salads.

## Information

Make your first stop in town the **Deming-Luna County Chamber of Commerce** (800 E. Pine St., 575/546-2674, www.demingchamber.com, 9 A.M.–5 P.M. Mon.–Fri., 9–11 A.M. Sat.), where you'll find a chatty staff, free coffee and Wi-Fi, and answers to all your area questions.

## Getting There

The **Greyhound bus** (800/231-2222, www.greyhound.com) comes in once a day from Las Cruces and drops you at the gas station (501 N. Gold St., 5 A.M.–10 P.M. Mon.–Sat., 6 A.M.–9 P.M. Sat.).

## ◖ CITY OF ROCKS STATE PARK

Bristling out of the flat basin north of Deming, City of Rocks (575/536-2800, www.nmparks.com, $5/car) does indeed resemble a metropolis. Hardened lava, eroded over 35 million years, forms towering pinnacles and bulbous growths, creating a skyline straight out of Dr. Seuss. With expansive views across the flatlands and all sorts of birds and other wildlife to check out up close, City of Rocks makes a great spot for a picnic and short hike, or an overnight in one of the 52 campsites (10 have water and electrical hookups). The visitors center is well equipped, with showers for overnighters. The park is 24 miles from Deming (28 miles from

© ZORA O'NEILL

the "skyline" at City of Rocks State Park

Silver City) on U.S. 180, then 4 miles northeast on Highway 61.

## COLUMBUS

Devastated in a raid by Pancho Villa in 1916, the border town of Columbus is still not exactly jumping. It's a small place, centered on a park and a WPA-built town hall, with most of its commerce and community linked with Mexico in some way. As you drive south from Deming on Highway 11, the terrain grows sandier, more dotted with cactus and yucca, and generally more like what people imagine Mexico to look like. You may see a giant white blimp in the sky—it's an aerostat, a balloon-borne radar system used by the U.S. Border Patrol.

### Pancho Villa State Park

The southeast corner of the main crossroads (Highways 9 and 11) in Columbus, formerly a U.S. Army encampment, has been transformed into a small state park (Hwy. 9, 575/531-2711, www.nmparks.com, 8 A.M.–5 P.M. daily, $5/car). It houses an excellent museum dedicated to

Villa's 1916 attack, in which 90 of Columbus's 400 residents were killed. The subsequent manhunt for the Mexican rebel leader, led by General John J. Pershing, involved some 2,000 troops traveling by car and airplane—the first mechanized military campaign in history. The museum does a great job of portraying both the personal tragedy felt in Columbus and the impressive scale of Pershing's military operation, which proved to be a crucial training ground for World War I. South of the museum and a large cactus garden are about 60 **campsites** ($8 car, $14 RV) with good facilities but in somewhat spartan surroundings.

### Columbus Historical Society Museum

Round out your cultural experience with a quick visit to the Columbus Historical Society Museum (575/531-2620, 10 A.M.–4 P.M. daily Sept.–Apr., 10 A.M.–1 P.M. Mon.–Fri., 10 A.M.–4 P.M. Sat. and Sun. May–Aug., donation), across the intersection from the state park. Housed in the old train depot, it has nifty train paraphernalia, as well as some morbidly interesting items, such as a replica death mask of Pancho Villa and a diorama showing the wreckage of the town in 1916.

## Palomas

The town of Palomas, Mexico, is not particularly remarkable, but it's somewhat illuminating to see just how different it is from its sister American town. Immediately past the border gates is a five-block strip of dentist offices, pharmacies, fruit-pop vendors, and taco shops. One mega-mart, the impossible-to-miss **Pink Store** (575/531-7243, 9 A.M.–7 P.M. daily), sells crafts from all over Mexico, plus the obligatory margaritas at the in-house restaurant. Crossing the border is usually as easy as being waved through; coming back to American soil, however, you'll need to show your passport, and your car may be subject to X-ray. It's a little easier to walk over (though you'll still need a passport); parking is available for a fee just before the border, and the Pink Store can arrange a golf-cart escort if you buy too much to carry yourself.

### Accommodations and Food

In this relative middle of nowhere, homey **Martha's Place** (204 Lima Rd., 575/531-2467, www.marthasplacebedandbreakfastcolumbusnewmexico.com, $70 d) is a great surprise—in fact, you might want to make the detour from Deming if you prefer B&Bs. Each of the five sunny rooms has a balcony. **Patio Café** (211 Broadway, 575/531-2495, 8–11 A.M. and noon–3 P.M. Mon.–Sat., $6) is about the only dining option in town, but it's a good one—the namesake outdoor area is shady and filled with flowers, a respite from the desert outside. Half-pound burgers are the centerpiece of the menu, but green-chile stew and any breakfast dish are generally winners as well.

## LORDSBURG

Aesthetically, Lordsburg is lacking—a quick cruise around town suggests this is where the chain-link-fence salesman made his first million. It's also a bit tragic economically, as the freight train industry that drove the place has all but died, leaving a desolate strip of 1st Street (now Motel Drive) running parallel to the tracks.

Nonetheless, there is a fascinating exhibit at the **Lordsburg-Hidalgo County Museum** (710 E. 2nd St., 575/542-9086, 1–5 P.M. Mon.–Fri., free), presenting the history of POW camps in New Mexico during World War II—one was located near Lordsburg, and German and Italian prisoners were put to work farming. The rest of the museum is a bit of a jumble, though there are some relics from local mines (another defunct Lordsburg industry).

### Accommodations and Food

Thanks to the U.S. Border Patrol setting up headquarters here, Lordsburg's accommodation options have improved in recent years. **Best Western Western Skies Inn** (1303 S. Main St., 575/542-8807, www.bestwestern.com, $80 d) and **Comfort Inn & Suites** (400 Wabash St., 575/542-3355, www.choicehotels.com, $90 d) are both in good shape; both have pools.

For New Mexican food, head into town to **El Charro Café** (209 Southern Pacific Blvd., 575/542-3400, 8 A.M.–10 P.M. daily, $7), a family-run diner just north of the railroad tracks, or **Ramona's** (904 E. Motel Dr., 575/542-3030, 9 A.M.–8 P.M. Tues.–Sat., 8 A.M.–2 P.M. Sun., $6), a tiny cafe with pretty curtains in the windows. Right at the freeway off-ramp, **Kranberry's** (1405 S. Main St., 575/542-9400, 6 A.M.–10 P.M. daily) is a decent diner-style restaurant.

### Shakespeare

Two and a half miles south of Lordsburg on Highway 494, this ghost town (575/542-9034, www.shakespeareghosttown.com, $4) is touted as the big attraction in the vicinity. It's open only one or two weekends a month—fine if your schedule overlaps, but not worth planning a special outing unless you or your kids have a fascination with the Old West. If you go on a reenactment day ($5), scheduled about three weekends a year, you'll get to see shootouts, hangings, and can-can girls; a special candlelit evening tour includes ghost stories.

# Silver City

Called just "Silver" by the locals, this casual mountain burg ranks high on quality-of-life lists in the national press. It has lured many of its 11,000 population from out of state with a near-utopian combination of outdoor activities, an educated populace (Western New Mexico University is here), and beautiful housing stock that dates from the city's boom in the late 19th and early 20th centuries. Unlike more slapdash towns, Silver was built to last, and its stone and cast-iron structures—many now painted fanciful colors by resident artists—have helped the town maintain its grandeur. Over the decades, it has been home to Billy the Kid, who came here in 1873 at about age 13 and got into trouble from the

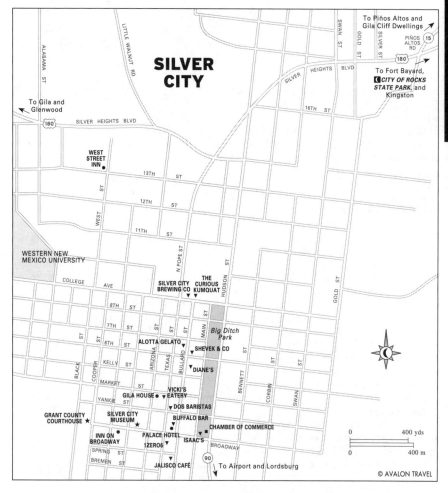

© AVALON TRAVEL

start, then many wealthy tuberculosis patients in the 1890s.

Contemporary hippies have set the mellow pace downtown and drive the local food co-op, the First Church of What's Happening, and other local institutions, while rat-race dropouts, young artists, and a small gay and lesbian community have bought up the territorial-style bungalows and downtown storefronts, repainted them in candy colors, and created a distinctive, unpretentious cultural scene. It also happens to encourage culinary creativity as well—there are more exceptional restaurants here than you'd expect in a town this size.

Navigating in Silver is not immediately intuitive because the main drag is Bullard Street, though Hudson Street, a couple of blocks east, is larger and runs directly south from U.S. 180. The original Main Street, which ran parallel to and between Bullard and Hudson, was washed away in a series of floods between 1895 and 1903, leaving what's evocatively called the Big Ditch. A greenery-filled chasm some 50 feet below the street level, it's an unorthodox park for an unorthodox populace. Most of the rest of Silver's attractions are on the west side of it.

## SIGHTS

The first stop in learning about the town, the **Silver City Museum** (312 W. Broadway, 575/538-5921, 9:00 A.M.–4:30 P.M. Tues.–Fri., 10 A.M.–4 P.M. Sat. and Sun., $3 donation) is an intriguing, polished collection in an old Victorian home. You'll see photos of Main Street before and after it became the Big Ditch, a fascinating exhibit on the culture and economy of tuberculosis treatment in New Mexico, and more than you thought you wanted to know about mining history and science. Be sure to climb up to the cupola to take in the view of the whole town.

Just up the hill at the end of Broadway, the **Grant County Courthouse** is a small but elegant building. The highlight is 1934 murals depicting the local ranching and mining industries.

a gallery door on Yankie Street

© ZORA O'NEILL

## ENTERTAINMENT AND EVENTS

Although it's a college town, Silver City isn't too rowdy at night. A few bars strung out along Bullard give a good mix of evening options within a few blocks. And many people make the drive to *Pinos Altos* for music at the saloon there.

### Bars and Nightlife

Just about everyone in town mixes at the bare-bones **Buffalo Bar** (211 N. Bullard St., 575/538-3201, 10 A.M.–2 A.M. Mon.–Sat., 10 A.M.–midnight Sun.), better known as "The Buff." It has pool tables on one side and a big dance club on the other. Across the street, sprawling **Isaac's Bar** (200 N. Bullard St., 575/388-4090, 11 A.M.–midnight Mon. and Tues., 11 A.M.–1:30 A.M. Wed.–Sat., noon–midnight Sun.) is another local hangout, with a big beer selection, a menu of bar food like duck-fat fries and nachos, and events like trivia nights, as well as live music.

© ZORA O'NEILL

the Buffalo Bar - a.k.a. the Buff - in downtown Silver City

routes through the surrounding mountains, is known as a warm-up for the Tour de France. If you're a cycling fan, this is a great time to see teams sweat up close. Plan well ahead around this time: All hotels are packed for the event, and surrounding highways are restricted on certain days.

The **Gila River Festival** (575/538-8078, www.gilaconservation.org) rallies an excellent roster of musicians and artists for an environment-friendly party in mid-September. While the center of the action is Silver City, activities such as guided hikes, bird-watching, and archaeological tours take place in the forest to the north. It's a great opportunity to explore less-visited spots in the company of experts.

## SPORTS AND RECREATION

Surrounded on almost every side by the Gila National Forest, Silver is an outdoors-oriented town. For hiking, see the *Gila Wilderness Area* section. The **Silver City Ranger District office** (3005 Camino del Bosque, 575/388-8201, 8 A.M.–4:30 P.M. Mon.–Fri.) is just north of U.S. 180 off the 32nd Street Bypass on the east side of town; this office manages only the portions of Gila National Forest that lie south of Silver.

### Biking

The staff at **Gila Hike & Bike** (103 E. College Ave., 575/388-3222, 9 A.M.–5:30 P.M. Mon.–Fri., 9 A.M.–5 P.M. Sat., 10 A.M.–4 P.M. Sun.) are veterans, with lots of tips on where to ride in the area. Ambitious road cyclists can trace some of the routes of the Tour de Gila, while mountain bikers can head to **Little Walnut Picnic Area,** north of town via Little Walnut Road from near the intersection of U.S. 180 and Highway 90. This is the starting point for a couple of short, relatively easy outings, as well as one seven-mile loop that's more challenging. You can get detailed trail guides from Gila Hike & Bike or at www.silvercity.org (search for "Southwest New Mexico Bicycling Guide"). If you're an advanced rider looking for a solid day-long route, ask about the 18-mile **Continental Divide Loop,** which

At the north end of Bullard, **Q's Southern Bistro** (101 E. College Ave., 575/534-4401, 11:30 A.M.–9 P.M. Mon.–Thurs., 11:30 A.M.–midnight Fri. and Sat.) serves beer-friendly snacks and draws a crowd to its big back patio, where there's a DJ or live band on weekends. Next door at **The Curious Kumquat** (111 E. College Ave., 575/534-0337, 5–10 P.M. Thurs.–Sat.), you can drink wine or very eclectic beers over excellent tapas.

### Special Events

The whole town turns out for Silver's biggest cultural event, the **Silver City Blues Festival** (www.mimbresarts.org), over Memorial Day weekend. Since 1995, it has gained a strong reputation, and the likes of Odetta and the Holmes Brothers have graced the stage at Gough Park, the Buffalo Bar, and the Buckhorn Saloon.

Every May, hundreds of pro cyclists descend on Silver for the **Tour de Gila** (www.tourofthegila.com), a race that, thanks to its winding

uses a portion of that through trail and ends at Little Walnut.

## ACCOMMODATIONS

Lodging in Silver City is a little pricier than you might expect, with few solid deals. Most hotels and motels are on U.S. 180 on the east side of town (also called Silver Heights Boulevard), which is not walkable to downtown. A few B&Bs are more central, but usually require booking well in advance.

### Under $100

The only hotel downtown, the ◖ **Palace Hotel** (106 W. Broadway, 575/388-1811, www.zianet.com/palacehotel, $48 s, $65 d) embodies the phrase "faded charm," but it is moderately priced and full of historic ambience—even if the beds can be a bit saggy. Noise from Bullard Street and Broadway can be a problem; the quietest of the 22 rooms are no. 61 ($48), a cozy hideaway with one double bed in the back of the building, and no. 59 ($79), a two-room suite. A basic continental breakfast is included in the rate.

**Gila House Hotel** (400 N. Arizona St., 575/313-7015, www.gilahouse.com, $90 d) is a three-room B&B adjacent to a gallery. The Southwestern-tinged rooms, all with tile floors, are a bit small, but the price is right, the hosts are friendly, and it's hard to beat the location, one block off Bullard.

### $100-150

With a broad front porch with views across town, the **Inn on Broadway** (411 W. Broadway, 575/388-5485, www.innonbroadwayweb.com) is a historic home from 1883 only a few blocks from the main drag and across from the Silver City Museum. Three sunny rooms upstairs ($125–160) are spacious, with especially nice bathrooms (although some might find the old-fashioned hand shower in the Hummingbird Room a bit of a nuisance). The cozier downstairs room ($140) has a marble fireplace. Decorating styles range from subdued Victorian to subdued Western.

About ten blocks from downtown, **West Street Inn** (1303 West St., 575/534-2302, www.weststreetinn-nm.com) rents three well-kept apartments with full kitchens, ideal if you'll be in town for a few days—there's a two-night minimum. Casa Bonita ($125) is good for groups or families, with two bedrooms and a yard; the other two apartments ($105) are one-bedrooms with king beds.

## FOOD

Silver has a handful of amazing places to eat, all in the downtown area. But most restaurants close early—and some of the best are open only a few days a week.

### Cafés

Get your java at **Javalina** (201 N. Bullard St., 575/388-1350, 6 A.M.–10 P.M. daily, $3), a rambling, old-style coffeehouse with wood floors, lots of couches, and people sitting for hours over a game of chess or the daily paper. In the evenings, you might catch a bluegrass group or other performer here.

Set in an old historic house, **Vicki's Eatery** (315 N. Texas St., 575/388-5430, 11 A.M.–3 P.M. Mon.–Sat., 8 A.M.–2 P.M. Sun., $7) is a prime spot for lunch, with big sandwiches that range from familiar and hearty (green-chile turkey melt) to the more exotic (chutney and turkey). It also has taken the Sunday brunch crown from Diane's.

### International

Two restaurants with limited hours are worth planning your visit around. Decked out with Bollywood art and Mexican crafts, ◖ **1zero6** (106 N. Texas St., 575/313-4418, www.1zero6-jake.blogspot.com, 5–8:30 P.M. Fri.–Sun., $17) is small and thoroughly personal. Each night's menu has just a few options, but they could be anything from tortellini Bolognese to Indonesian chicken in a banana leaf, all cooked from scratch, and with such a reverence for flavor you'd think there's a grandmother in the kitchen. The chef posts the menus on his website on Wednesdays; locals know to go early or call to put dibs on the dish they want, as portions are limited. A BYOB policy makes it an excellent value.

Equally globe-trotting but more wildly creative, **( The Curious Kumquat** (111 E. College Ave., 575/534-0337, $18) is the work of Chef Rob, a mad scientist in the kitchen. He draws on super-local sources (chickens from the town 4H club!) as well as the stock of the Kumquat's adjacent international grocery, so the dinner menu might feature imaginative vegetarian Indian, pork-belly blue corn tacos, and a sous-vide Filipino-style embutido. Once a month, he pulls out all the stops for a ten-course hyper-modern menu. If you're not in town for dinner (5–10 P.M. Thurs.–Sat.), do stop by for lunch (11 A.M.–2 P.M. Mon.–Sat.), which is more familiar (green-chile corn chowder) but just as delicious. And no matter what, get some sweet treat—this is the chef's not-so-secret passion.

Long-established **( Shevek & Co.** (602 N. Bullard St., 575/534-9168, 5–8:30 P.M. Sun.–Tues. and Thurs., 5–9 P.M. Fri. and Sat., $18) has a refined, personal menu that goes all over Europe for inspiration: A crepe filled with chorizo and dates complements chicken in a blood-orange sauce and chilled fruit soups. Vegetarians will find a lot to like, including a four-course meat-free tasting menu. The wine list is largely Old World, and carefully selected to match the food. The elegance of the food isn't always matched by the decor, which can run to standard plastic furniture on the back patio. But don't be deterred—Shevek knows his stuff.

## Local Favorites

Silver residents love **Diane's** (510 N. Bullard St., 575/538-8722, 11 A.M.–2 P.M. and 5:30–9 P.M. Tues.–Fri., 9 A.M.–2 P.M. and 5:30–9 P.M. Sat., 9 A.M.–2 P.M. Sun.)—it's the go-to spot for familiar flavors like meatloaf ($17) and lasagna ($15). But compared with the options above, it's not so imaginative, and the food can be inconsistent. Breakfast goes for the gut, when the house bakery cranks out green-chile toast to be topped with eggs and hollandaise sauce ($9).

Occupying a string of old storefronts on the south end of downtown, **Jalisco Café** (100 S.

THE SOUTHWEST

© ZORA O'NEILL

**just one marvelous nibble at The Curious Kumquat**

Bullard St., 575/388-2060, 11 A.M.–8:30 P.M., $10) is the most popular New Mexican joint in town. Along with a small selection of seafood dishes, you'll get all the green- and red-chile-smothered classics, though they're not nearly as hot as the menu warns, and the green chile is typical of southern New Mexico, all mellow and creamy—a relief for some diners, a travesty for others. Everyone can agree on the sopaipillas, which are huge and perfectly pillowy.

### Dessert

No meal is complete without a scoop or two from **Alotta Gelato** (619 N. Bullard St., 575/534-4995, noon–9 P.M. Sun.–Thurs., noon–10 P.M. Fri. and Sat., $2), where the devoted owners craft the richest flavors possible and preside over a sugar-buzzed clientele of addicted locals. The pistachio comes with an elaborate warning—you may never have tasted something so intensely nutty. Thoughtfully, there's a perfectly reasonable child-size scoop for those who may have previously gorged themselves at Silver's other excellent dining options.

## INFORMATION

The **Silver City-Grant County Chamber of Commerce** (201 N. Hudson St., 575/538-3785, www.silvercity.org, 9 A.M.–5 P.M. Mon.–Fri.) is just east of Big Ditch Park at Broadway. It's open on weekends only if there's a special event on, but there's info available out front all the time, and its website is very thorough.

## GETTING THERE

**Grant County Airport** (SVC), about 10 miles southeast of Silver City, receives flights twice daily (except Sunday, when there's one) from Albuquerque on Great Lakes Airlines (800/554-5111, www.greatlakes-sav.com). But most people make the drive from Albuquerque (4.5 hours) or El Paso (2.5 hours). In the latter case, **Las Cruces Shuttle** (575/525-1784, www.lascrucesshuttle.com) runs bus service once a day; rates are $80 one-way or $130 round-trip, or $60/$90 from Las Cruces. Silver City is not served by Greyhound.

# Trail of the Mountain Spirits

A romantic name for the usual driving circuit out of Silver City, the Trail of the Mountain Spirits (www.tmsbyway.com) runs north on Highway 15 through the little town of Pinos Altos, then up to Gila Cliff Dwellings National Monument and many hiking trails into the wilderness. After backtracking from the cliff dwellings, the route continues through the pine forest east on Highway 35, past Lake Roberts, over the Continental Divide to Bear Canyon Lake, and through the village of Mimbres. Highway 152 then leads back west to Silver City via the region's modern mining center around Bayard.

## PINOS ALTOS

About seven miles north on Highway 15, a sign points to the optimistically named Pinos Altos Business Loop. In fact, this tiny community offers just a couple of commercial attractions to visitors, and that's the way people like it— "P.A.," as the town is known, is the retreat for folks who think Silver is too big and busy. The all-purpose community center is **Pinos Altos Ice Cream Parlor** (30 Main St., 575/534-1997, 10 A.M.–6 P.M. Mon.–Sat., $4), which doubles as the post office; slurp down a thick shake while the locals gossip on the porch outside. You can also stop in at the obligatory **Pinos Altos Museum & Curio Shop** (33 Main St., 575/388-1882, 10 A.M.–6 P.M. Mon.–Sat., 10 A.M.–5 P.M. Sun., $2), an 1860s log cabin packed with cast-iron gewgaws; it sets the tone for the rest of the buildings in the area, which are functional if not always accurate replicas of what used to stand here in the 19th century.

In the evenings, **Buckhorn Saloon** (32 Main St., 575/538-9911, 6–10 P.M. Mon.–Sat., $26)

© ZORA O'NEILL

view from the Gila Cliff Dwellings

serves steaks in a wood-paneled, wild West setting; it's open for drinks starting at 3 P.M. and continuing past the dinner hour, with live music starting around 7 P.M. in the adjacent **Pinos Altos Opera House.** Also look for **Hearst Church** (Golden Ave., 10 A.M.–5 P.M. Fri.–Sun. May–Oct.), an odd pitched-roof adobe structure built in 1898 by William Randolph Hearst's mother, Phoebe, who had gained her family fortune from a gold mine in the area; it's now home to the Grant County Art Guild (575/538-8216, www.gcag.org). It's west of the main street—follow signs for the "Historic Route" as you come into town.

## GILA HOT SPRINGS

A small collection of services for wilderness visitors, the village of Gila Hot Springs is the last chance to stock up before heading farther north. **Doc Campbell's Post** (575/536-9551, 10 A.M.–5 P.M. daily) sells basic provisions, fishing and hunting licenses, and homemade ice cream. For overnight stays, **Wilderness Lodge** (575/536-9749, www.gilahot.com), off the road to the right as you enter town, is a rustic

but comfortable bed-and-breakfast in an old schoolhouse. Five standard rooms ($78) share a bathroom, while a two-room suite ($105) has its own facilities. Guests have access to pools fed by the nearby natural hot springs. (For more on the springs, see the *Recreation Around the Cliff Dwellings* section in this chapter.)

## GILA CLIFF DWELLINGS NATIONAL MONUMENT

The big destination on the byway is these cliff-side ruins (8:30 A.M.–5 P.M. daily June–Aug., 9 A.M.–4 P.M. daily Sept.–May, $3), just past Gila Hot Springs and 44 miles north of Silver City. Compared with the ruins at Bandelier National Monument or Chaco Canyon, these are relatively small and in a less spectacular setting, but if these are the only cliff settlements you'll be near on your trip, don't miss them. The drive up from Silver, along a narrow road often with no center stripe, takes 2.5–3 hours.

Stop in first at the **visitors center** (575/536-9461, www.nps.gov/gicl, 8 A.M.–4:30 P.M. daily), which gives a basic overview of the environment as well as the Mogollon culture that inhabited the cliff dwellings for only a generation near the end of the 13th century, through excavated relics of daily life such as reed mats and mosaic work. You can also pick up USGS maps and good books about the area.

A two-mile drive gets you to the pay station at the **trailhead** and a basic nature center, where enthusiastic rangers will let you know what kind of animals are out and about. You reach the **caves** themselves via a mile-long loop trail that takes about an hour to walk. The route is level for the first half, then increasingly steep as it winds up and through the dwellings. The trail passes three of the five caves, which once housed up to 60 people in about 40 rooms; the central one is a large, bi-level arrangement that included the central ceremonial chambers. Much of the wood you see in the rooms is original, preserved perfectly in the dry air; the Mogollon, who did not have steel, shaped it by burning it and hacking it with stone tools.

## RECREATION AROUND THE CLIFF DWELLINGS

As the most easily accessible part of the Gila wilderness, with some very scenic hiking along canyon bottoms, the trails in this area are the most used—but that doesn't mean they're crowded. You'll be sharing trails with dedicated Silver City residents and a few other visitors, and once you get out a ways, you're likely to be alone.

### Hiking

The three forks of the Gila River converge right near the cliff dwellings, and the canyons formed by the water are a nice place to walk, though you should be prepared for wet and muddy stream crossings. In summer, it's best to time hikes so you're out of canyons by mid-afternoon, to avoid flash floods caused by rainstorms. At 34 miles, the **West Fork Trail** (no. 151) is the longest in the Gila wilderness. The first 3 miles provide a pleasantly varied, fairly easy day hike. The trail begins at Scorpion

Campground, across from the Gila Cliff Dwellings. Just off the trail to the south after the first river crossing, a small ruined cabin sits next to the grave of one William Grudging, murdered in 1893—eerie evidence of the violent past of this otherwise peaceful setting. Further traces of past inhabitants can be seen at a small cliff dwelling on the west side, which marks the turnaround point for most day hikers. Others do the full length as a multi-day backpacking trek.

Given the complex network of trails in this area, it's easy to make a number of loop hikes through varied terrain. Ask for suggestions in the visitors center, where you can also pick up a topographical map.

## ◖ Hot Springs on the Gila River

A refreshing warm bath in the great outdoors is a fine motivator for a hike, and there are several natural springs in the vicinity of the visitors center. The closest ones to the visitors center are **Light Feather Hot Springs,** just half a mile up the Middle Fork Trail (which starts behind the visitors center); however, the water here is scalding hot, and you may have to reroute the river water to dilute it to a usable temperature. The deep pools of **Jordan Hot Springs** are worth the longer hike (about eight miles) up the same trail; you can shorten the trip by starting at the trail behind TJ Corral, farther up the road to the cliff dwellings, but get precise directions from the visitors center.

If you'd rather not hike, you can still enjoy the warm waters at developed hot springs. Look for signs to **Gila Hot Springs Campground** (575/536-9551, www.gila-hotspringsranch.com, $3) about a mile after you cross the Gila River. The pools, kept at different temperatures, are attractively designed and blend in nicely with the natural surroundings, and the price is a bargain. You can also camp here for just $1 more. Down the same access road (helpfully labeled "Access Road"), **Wildwood Retreat & Hotsprings** (575/536-3600, www.silver-city.com/wildwood, $5) has a similar setup but with more modern facilities; you can camp here ($10)—and even rent camping equipment—but it's closed during the winter months.

## LAKE ROBERTS

Returning to the intersection with Highway 35 and heading east, you reach Lake Roberts, a pristine 69 acres stocked with trout. Shaded heavily by tall pine trees, it's a popular getaway during the summer months; you can **camp** at the lake, in developed sites ($7) or undeveloped ones (free), which have no water. There are also several lodges in the area. The first you reach, at the intersection with Highway 15, is **Breathe Inn Lodge** (575/536-3206, www.breatheinnlodge.com, $50 s, $60 d, $90 suite). The rooms, which are in several attached mobile homes, have all the charm of a barebones summer camp, but they're functional, clean, and well priced. Plus, there's no better place to wake up if you love birds, as the main lodge building, which houses a **café** (8 A.M.–4:30 P.M. Sun.–Tues., 8 A.M.–9 P.M. Wed.–Sat., $6), is surrounded by feeders and draws just about every species in the Gila to the floor-to-ceiling windows. During the Hummingbird Festival in early June, the lodge is packed; be sure to book ahead.

Farther down the road to the east, **Lake Roberts Cabins & Store** (869 Hwy. 35, 575/536-9929, www.lakeroberts.com) is a complex of cozy rooms, along with a few RV parking spots and room for camping ($5) near a creek that runs through the property. The cabins are single and duplex arrangements, often with wood floors and walls, as well as kitchenettes—perhaps the most atmospheric is Cedar ($99), with its heavy roof beams. Families or bigger groups can book one of the mobile homes; secluded Pine sleeps 5, while Juniper ($125) has room for up to 10.

Past the lake, the least rustic option is **Spirit Canyon Lodge** (684 Hwy. 35, 575/536-9459, www.spiritcanyon.com), which rents small rooms in its main pine-paneled building ($73) and a separate back cottage ($175) that's ideal for families. The **café** (5–7 P.M. Fri., 8 A.M.–6 P.M. Sat. and Sun., $7) serves breakfast all day, burgers and steaks for lunch and dinner, and German food on Saturdays.

## MIMBRES VALLEY

The wide, green valley surrounding the village of Mimbres is the epicenter of the ancient culture of the same name, best known for its elegant black-on-white pottery designs. Now, though, you're most likely to think of it as a place to fill up your tank, as it has a number of gas stations and convenience stores. The **Gila Wilderness Ranger District office** (Hwy. 35, 575/536-2250, 8 A.M.–4:30 P.M. Mon.–Fri.) is here.

Just after the turnoff to the old Spanish settlement of **San Lorenzo,** Highway 35 dead-ends at Highway 152, which runs west to Silver City.

## CHINO MINE

Off the east side of Highway 152, you can't help but notice the monumentally altered landscape around the Chino Mine, the pit of which measures more than a mile across. The oldest continuously mined claim in the United States, it was first known by Apaches, who took copper from the area. In 1799, the Spanish, with the help of convict labor, began extracting copper and sending it to Mexico. Production was so great that the majority of the early 19th-century copper coins from Mexico and Spain can be traced back to Santa Rita del Cobre, as the mine was known then. Open-pit mining began in 1910, eventually swallowing up the town of Santa Rita that had grown adjacent to the mine. The hole now reaches 1,600 feet into the ground, dwarfing the trucks and shovels that toil on its terraces, and the majority of Grant County's population is employed here in some capacity. You can't miss Chino from the road, but if you want an up-close look, stop at the observation point maintained by Phelps Dodge, just south of mile marker 6. If you're able to ignore the obvious environmental ravages, it's an impressive piece of land art.

## FORT BAYARD

Just after the junction of Highway 152 with U.S. 180, Fort Bayard (www.fortbayard.org)

was built in 1866 by the Ninth Cavalry, some of the Buffalo Soldiers who earned renown fighting the Apaches. During the 1920s, it was a center of tuberculosis treatment for the military, and the tidy rows of white barracks are a product of that period; it's a veterans' hospital today. There are no formal sights for visitors, except for the adjacent national cemetery, and the **Fort Bayard Days** reenactments in mid-September. The Silver City chamber of commerce runs a free walking tour on the second Saturday of every month.

# Gila National Forest

The larger region surrounding the more tightly controlled Gila Wilderness Area, the Gila National Forest encompasses some 3.3 million acres, stretching west to Arizona and north as far as Quemado. From Silver City, U.S. 180 runs north about 45 miles to the junction with Highway 12 and the town of Reserve. For much of the drive, the road is surrounded by public lands, and where it is not, the national forest is not far off. Passing

## EXPLORING THE GILA WILDERNESS

Covering 558,000 acres, the Gila Wilderness Area is the largest such protected area in any state but Alaska, and it's also the first. With the adjacent 200,000 acres of the Aldo Leopold Wilderness Area (part of the original designation in 1924, now named for the man who was instrumental in establishing the protection), plus the Gila National Forest to the south and north, it's an almost overwhelming place to explore. The terrain ranges from piñon forests dotted with spring wildflowers and the peaks of the Mogollon Mountains to dramatic canyons and the flat beds of the three forks of the Gila River – especially nice during the fall, when the more than 20 species of deciduous trees turn color. As an added perk, the violent volcanic activity of millennia past created an abundance of natural hot springs, which can provide great motivation for a challenging slog up a stream.

The most common access point is on the south side, via Highway 15 north of Silver City. This serpentine road winds up through pine trees to the Gila Cliff Dwellings National Monument and several well-used trailheads. Another solid hike is to Mogollon Baldy (elev. 10,770 feet) via a forest road and trail on the east side of the wilderness.

While you're driving or hiking around, keep your eyes open for the area's rich wildlife. At lower elevations, javelinas (small wild pigs) are plentiful, as are packs of coatimundis. Nimble, raccoon-like animals with long snouts, coatis usually live in more tropical climates; southern New Mexico is the only area they're found in the United States. You might see one scampering across the road, or napping in a tree. Less exotic, skunks are plentiful (four different species, in fact), and you'll surely encounter at least the traces of one at some point on your trip. In the higher mountains, you may see herds of mule deer and elk. The eponymous Gila monster, a venomous lizard that can grow up to two feet in length, makes its home here, as do lots of rattlesnakes. Be alert in the springtime, when the snakes have just come out of hibernation and are on the prowl for mates. Wear boots that come above your ankles, and don't place your feet between rocks or in crevices when hiking.

Whatever you're planning in the wilderness area, always check first with one of the Gila National Forest district offices in Mimbres, Truth or Consequences, Glenwood, Reserve, Silver City, and Quemado for current conditions and fire regulations, as well as high-quality maps. You can also check current advisories online at www.fs.fed.us/r3/gila.

through rolling grassy plains and between mountain peaks, it's a beautiful—and often empty—drive.

## GILA

Not to be confused with Gila Hot Springs, the village of Gila is often a jumping-off point for trips into the wilderness area or down the Gila River to the southwest; it's also close enough to Silver City that it counts as a sort of suburb.

Set on 90 acres with a stream running through, **(** **Casitas de Gila** (50 Casita Flats, 575/535-4455, www.casitasdegila.com) is a great way to enjoy the area in comfort. Nightly rates go down the longer you stay—and once you get a glimpse of the night sky from the hot tub, you'll probably want to settle in. The five apartments, furnished with custom Mexican woodwork, have kiva fireplaces, kitchens stocked with breakfast food, and private patios. Foldout couches in the living rooms make the standard casitas ($160) family-friendly, while a larger two-bedroom option ($210) can sleep seven.

## GLENWOOD

The road north from Gila skirts the mountains and races through grasslands, reaching the small town of Glenwood after about 30 miles. Stop in at the **Glenwood Ranger District office** (575/539-2481, 8 A.M.–4:30 P.M. Mon.–Fri.) for information on local hikes and the status of the Bursum Road to Mogollon. Leah Jones of **Gila Wilderness Ventures** (575/539-2800, www.gilawildernessventures.com) runs day trips as well as multi-day pack outings in the Gila.

## **(** Catwalk Trail

A Civilian Conservation Corps project in the 1930s, the Catwalk Trail ($3/car) is a hanging walkway over a stream for the first half of its 1.1 miles. With the metal grating more than 20 feet above the water in some stretches and the pink canyon walls pressing in on either side, it's a very scenic hike that's also easy going. The catwalk follows the route of a water pipeline built in the 1890s as part of a mining

Careen through a canyon – easily – on the Catwalk Trail.

operation. The first half mile of the trail is fully wheelchair-accessible, and the second half, after the end of the catwalk, is also a very easy stroll. The turn-off for the trail is in the middle of Glenwood, well marked as Highway 174 (Catwalk Road).

### Accommodations

For an overnight stay, the **(** **White Water Motel** (U.S. 180, 575/539-2581), next to the post office near the south entrance to the town, is a gem—the kind of simple place where the owners clearly care about details. The 10 rooms are tidy, comfortable, and trimmed with lace curtains, with back porches overlooking a shady garden and stream. Configurations range from one double bed ($49) to three twin beds and a double ($67), great for families or groups; some have small refrigerators. You can also camp in the area at **Bighorn Campground,** which is adjacent to the Catwalk trailhead; it has just five tent spots (and no room for RVs), however, and no water.

## Food

**Blue Front Café** (U.S. 180, 575/539-2561, 5–8:45 P.M. Wed., 11 A.M.–8:45 P.M. Thurs.–Sun., $8) is short on decor, with peeling wallpaper and faded posters, but it's strong on hearty food, serving barbecue brisket all day every Saturday and Sunday. The rest of the week, the menu is typical New Mexican, with a tasty selection of homemade desserts.

## MOGOLLON

Unlike many old mining towns, Mogollon bursts with color and cheer. Its old buildings, including the **Silver Creek Inn** (866/276-4882, www.silvercreekinn.com, $100 d or $350–400 weekend package with meals), the **Purple Onion Café** (575/539-2710, 9 A.M.–5 P.M. Fri.–Sun.), and the village **archives,** are painted in vibrant shades. But don't make the place a destination unless it's a weekend between May and October—everything's shut otherwise. The village is nine miles up Highway 159, which locals call the **Bursum Road.** From a turn east about three miles north of Glenwood, it starts off easily enough, crossing rolling scrub, but then it ascends steeply into the mountains. About halfway into the climb, the road reduces to a harrowing single lane with steep switchbacks and no guardrails. Even those who've cut their teeth on other New Mexico back roads will find this one anxiety-inducing.

But the view across the rolling grasslands below is stunning, and you can make this a daylong scenic drive by carrying on past Mogollon, where the road grows increasingly rough and enters aspen glades that glow gold in the fall. After **Ben Lilly Campground** (with seven tent sites), it is ordinarily possible to drive north (signed as Forest Road 28) to come out at Highway 12 midway between Reserve and Datil. It's also possible (but only for very sturdy cars) to continue east on Forest Road 142, then south on Forest Road 150 to Silver City. From after the first snowfall until early June, Bursum Road is usually locked above Mogollon, and if it has rained recently, you're better off winding your way very, very carefully back down the way you came in. Avoid

doing this at sundown, however, as the glare just adds to the risk.

### Crest Trail to Mogollon Baldy

One of the many trails off the Bursum Road, the Crest Trail (no. 182) begins eight miles east of Mogollon, on the south side of the road at Sandy Point. You can bag two peaks on the six-mile trail, hitting Whitewater Baldy (elev. 10,895 feet) after a steep ascent and a walk along a scenic ridge, then up and down a bit till you reach Mogollon Baldy, just a few feet lower in elevation. Plan at least six hours for the full out-and-back hike.

## ALMA

Once a hideout for Butch Cassidy, this wide spot in the road is the turn-off for a good hiking trail into the Gila.

### Mineral Creek Trail

This trek between the towering walls of a narrow canyon is scenic, varied, and rewarding. The canyon walls are striped in vibrant colors, and you'll pass small waterfalls, the ruins of the mining town of Cooney, and an apple orchard. You'll also have the opportunity to take a dip when the water is high. The first 1.5 miles, which include small waterfalls, pools, and the Cooney ruins, make a nice alternative to the Catwalk as an easy family hike. Be prepared to get your feet wet, as you'll be crossing the stream frequently. Allow six to eight hours for a full exploration of the canyon (the trail actually ends up at Highway 159 after 14 miles).

To reach the trail (no. 201), turn east in Alma onto Mineral Creek Road, a dirt track; this turns into Forest Road 701 and dead-ends at the trailhead after 5.5 miles. Just before mile 5, look for "Cooney's tomb," a giant boulder made into the gravesite for miner James Cooney and a few of his men, who were killed here by Apaches in 1880.

## BLUE RANGE WILDERNESS AREA

North of Alma, about two miles past Saliz Pass between mile markers 25 and 26, County

Road CO13 leads west to this 29,000-acre patch of wooded mountains. Connected to a much larger wilderness area across the border in Arizona, it is seldom visited but best known as the place where the first family of Mexican gray wolves was released into the wild in the United States in 1998—much to the dismay of local ranchers, who maintain a vocal anti-wolf campaign. Now the area supports between 50 and 60 of the endangered predators, and the few people who do visit the place have come in hopes of hearing them howl at night. The standard backpacking route is along the **WS Mountain Trail** (no. 43), which runs 8.8 miles roughly north–south through the middle of the wilderness. Much of it is a relaxing hike, as it follows canyon bottoms and streambeds (usually dry). You can camp around WS Mountain (elev. 8,430 feet), just over the border in Arizona. The trail starts at **Pueblo Park Campground,** 5.6 miles up County Road CO13 from U.S. 180. At the campground you'll also find a 1.5-mile interpretive trail that shows some of the traces of Mogollon culture in the area.

## RESERVE

Hunting is a big business in the Catron County seat, with expeditions leaving from here and plenty of taxidermy shops in town. Reserve, first settled by Mexican homesteaders in the early 1800s, is notorious for an 1884 shootout between 80-odd Texan cowboys and the local deputy sheriff, Elfego Baca, who held off the gang for 36 hours, until they ran out of ammunition. In what many saw as a blatantly racist move, Baca was later brought to trial for murdering one of the cowboys; he was finally acquitted when he displayed the bullet-riddled door he'd hidden behind. Look for a memorial to Baca at the main crossroads.

If you're not hunting, there's precious little to do in Reserve, though there is a gas station. If you have to stay the night, the basic motel **Rode Inn** (200 Main St., 575/533-6661, www.rodeinnmotels.com, $68 d) will do, but it's priced higher than what you'll find farther north in Quemado. The **Reserve Ranger District office** (575/523-6331, 8 A.M.–4:30 P.M. Mon.–Fri.), on Highway 12 just west of town, has information on the Gila National Forest, as well as the wilderness area.

For food, **◖ Adobe Café and Bakery** (U.S. 180., 575/533-6146, 7 A.M.–3 P.M. Mon. and Wed.–Sat., 7 A.M.–8 P.M. Sun., $8), just south of Reserve, on U.S. 180 about a quarter-mile from the junction with Highway 12, is a real treat, with a fresh, varied menu of breakfast goodies, salads, and creative sandwiches like the "Gyr-Faux," a tasty lamb wrap. Service can be a bit slow, though. For dinner, **Ella's** (96 Main St., 575/533-6111, 7 A.M.–8 P.M. Tues.–Sat., 7 A.M.–2 P.M. Sun. and Mon., $7), in Reserve proper, will do just fine—locals in Carhartts and hats dig in to chicken-fried steak and enchiladas.

# CARLSBAD CAVERNS AND THE SOUTHEAST

Long barren lands stretch between the few major tourist sights in southeastern New Mexico, and those sights are often far from typical: the giant bat-filled rooms of Carlsbad Caverns National Park, the ghostly gypsum dunes at White Sands National Monument, the cryptic carvings dotting the rocks at Three Rivers Petroglyph Site, a museum dedicated to UFOs in Roswell. In short, the area is not the state's most immediately appealing, but you'll find surprising things here if you make the drive.

And what a long drive it is. The blank expanse the Spanish dubbed the Llano Estacado starts in Fort Sumner (where Wild West sharpshooter Billy the Kid finally met his end in 1881) and stretches east and south into Texas. The roads are straight, the horizon often shimmers with heat, and soon you can't tell if you've been driving for 20 minutes or two hours. The occasional oil derrick or herd of cattle breaks up the monotony, and tiny towns loom up suddenly and disappear in the rearview mirror just as fast. Portales, center of the "peanut basin of the Southwest," is a rare green spot, thanks to its access to a deep aquifer, and Roswell is the area's largest settlement, and perhaps its strangest, as many people are still obsessed with an alleged crash-landing of an alien spacecraft here in 1947.

The Sacramento Mountains mark the western end of the plains. Here, the small resorts of Cloudcroft and Ruidoso cater to Texans who've fled the maddening flatlands, and the steep trails at Ski Apache, with a base elevation of 9,600 feet, provide excellent winter

© ZORA O'NEILL

# HIGHLIGHTS

◖ **The Blue Hole:** Santa Rosa's surprising claim to fame is this freshwater pool, both impressively deep and beautifully clear. Stop here for a refreshing dip, or, if you're certified, even a dive – the last activity anyone expects on a trip to New Mexico (page 286).

◖ **Bosque Redondo Memorial:** The Long Walk of 1864, a formative cataclysm in the modern history of the Navajo, is commemorated on the grounds of Fort Sumner. It's the same place Billy the Kid was shot and killed 17 years later (page 289).

◖ **International UFO Museum & Research Center:** Mysteries of deep space revealed! Government conspiracies uncovered! Plush alien dolls for sale! Roswell's most popular museum may seem campy, but it takes its mission very seriously (page 299).

◖ **Anderson Museum of Contemporary Art:** Roswell is also home to this excellent collection of artwork in every media, which rivals the galleries in Santa Fe in quality and wins for sheer gutsy enthusiasm (page 300).

◖ **The Big Room:** Some 600,000 visitors a year tour the main cave at Carlsbad Caverns National Park – for good reason. It's amazing in both its vast scale and its smallest details, such as clusters of tiny stalactites as delicate as lace. Silence is requested on the tour – not hard, as you'll be too awed to speak (page 309).

◖ **Heart of the Sands:** Visiting the eerie landscape at the center of White Sands National Monument is sort of like going to the beach and the North Pole all at once. It's certainly unlike any place you've ever seen (page 320).

◖ **Lincoln State Monument:** The late 19th century's "most dangerous town in

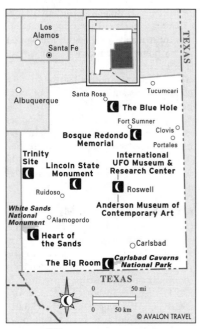

LOOK FOR ◖ TO FIND RECOMMENDED SIGHTS, ACTIVITIES, DINING, AND LODGING.

America" is now a quiet place, half of its main-street buildings preserved as museums that conjure life in Billy the Kid's era, without all the usual Wild West kitsch (page 326).

◖ **Trinity Site:** You can visit the site of the first atomic bomb blast (fittingly set in a stretch of the stark Jornada del Muerto desert) only two days a year, but it's an essential stop if your schedule allows (page 329).

THE SOUTHEAST

entertainment. At the foot of the mountains, orderly Alamogordo is home to the International Space Hall of Fame. It's the closest town to White Sands, a 275-square-mile lunar landscape that's fascinating as a natural attraction, but also inextricably linked with the world's first atomic bomb test, which took place in this desert in 1945.

Carlsbad Caverns, another natural wonder, fortunately has no such legacy. Getting there requires the longest drive of all, nearly to the Texas border in the south. But when you see the so-called Big Room, the vast main cave that drips with stalactites and takes more than an hour to explore, you'll know there's nothing else like it in New Mexico, nor in the whole country.

## PLANNING YOUR TIME

Even more so than southwestern New Mexico, this southeastern section requires long drives in between the sights. If you're focusing on Carlsbad, White Sands, and either Cloudcroft or Ruidoso, it can make sense to fly in to El Paso (ELP), then stay in either Las Cruces (one hour's drive) or Alamogordo (about two hours); the town of Carlsbad also receives commuter flights from Albuquerque.

Driving from Albuquerque, you could take the leisurely route via the Salinas Pueblo missions and Carrizozo, reaching Ruidoso or Alamogordo by dinnertime, then carrying on to White Sands the next day—or you could cruise down the interstate and get straight to White Sands by the afternoon. In any case, allow about three hours for a basic visit to the park, or more if you plan to do any hiking or photography. Carlsbad Caverns calls for the better part of a day to see just the basics, though the more adventurous small-group

tours are well worth allotting a second afternoon for. Both these places get busy in the summer, but the sands absorb crowds better. The caverns are substantially better in the off-season, though.

## HISTORY

Hundreds of millions of years ago, the groundwork for southeastern New Mexico's modern history was already effectively written in stone: The dinosaurs that roamed the swampy banks of the sea would eventually be transformed into the fossil fuel that many a contemporary Lovingtonian or Artesian makes a living extracting today.

In between these bookends, New Mexico's southern plains and mountain ranges saw much the same patterns as the rest of the state. The U.S. army clashed with the resident Indian tribes: General James Carleton ordered Kit Carson, "All Indian men of that [Mescalero] tribe are to be killed whenever and wherever you can find them." Billy the Kid got up to no good, including meeting his end, at the age of 21. And railroad lines and highways (especially the legendary Route 66) brought modern thrills to previously untouched patches of plain.

But a single cataclysmic event makes this area unique, for better or worse. Just before sunrise one summer morning in 1945, White Sands was lit brighter than high noon by a towering mushroom cloud—the successful test of the first atomic bomb, which was then deployed over Japan to win WWII. During the Cold War, White Sands was the proving ground for some essential technology in the space race. In these respects, the region is an odd juxtaposition of humankind's most current obsessions against timeless landscape.

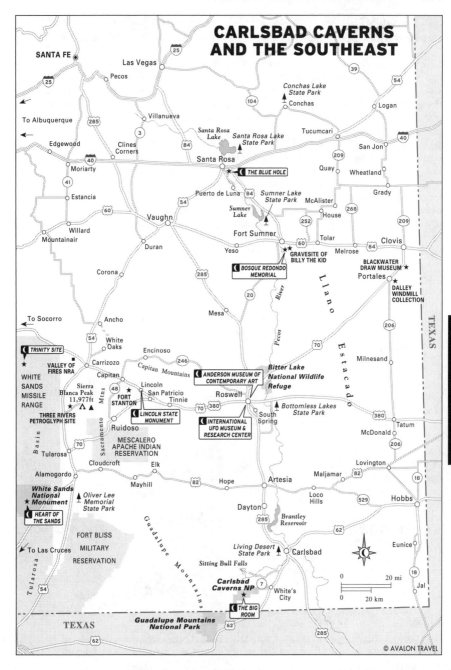

# CARLSBAD CAVERNS AND THE SOUTHEAST

© AVALON TRAVEL

# East on the Interstate

After crossing the pass between the Sandia and Manzano Mountains east of Albuquerque, I-40 heads into the high plains. Get used to the scenery, because it won't change until well into Texas. The wind blows constantly across gold tufts of grass, and the barbed-wire fences are clotted with tumbleweeds. The most excitement along this stretch is counting down the billboards to truck stops like the Flyin' C, where you can stock up on everything from moccasins to fireworks. It's not quite the glamour of Route 66 of old, but the combination of tacky signage, big sky, and a whole lot of nothing says "American road trip" like nothing else.

## EDGEWOOD

Off exit 187 in Edgewood, **Wildlife West** (505/281-7655, www.wildlifewest.org, 10 A.M.–6 P.M. daily mid-Mar.–Nov., noon–4 P.M. daily Dec.–mid-Mar., $7) is a better-than-average roadside attraction. This "enhanced zoo" is a 122-acre wildlife sanctuary for wolves, cougars, elk, and other native animals.

Just north of Walmart, **Katrinah's East Mountain Grill** (150 Hwy. 344, 505/281-9111, 7 A.M.–8 P.M. Tues.–Sat., 8 A.M.–2 P.M. Sun., $8) is a great road-food find, with a menu of standard diner goodies, from enchiladas to veggie wraps, all made from exceptionally fresh ingredients—definitely worth a stop if you're feeling hunger pangs in this stretch of highway.

## SANTA ROSA

This town of 2,500 is easy to cruise past on I-40, but if you think a refreshing swim sounds nice, take time out for the "City of Natural Lakes," where cool springs well up alongside the Pecos River. Starting in 1901, Santa Rosa was a stop on the Chicago, Rock Island & Pacific freight line, and in the 1930s, the place began to grow as Route 66 travelers passed through (John Steinbeck set a scene of *The Grapes of Wrath* here, which was then re-created for film in the town in 1940). Its stretch of the historic highway, which runs parallel to I-40 to the south, is lined with stately old warehouses on one side and lurid neon on the other.

## ◖ The Blue Hole

But most people come to Santa Rosa for a more natural attraction, and a thoroughly unexpected one: the Blue Hole (dawn–dusk daily), an 81-foot-deep pool of water that's a constant 64°F year-round. Only about 80 feet across, it doesn't look like much from the surface, but it's more impressive when you consider that water is gushing from the spring at the bottom at 3,000 gallons per minute (check the overflow channel on the south side to get an idea just what that number means). The steady temperature and perfect clarity of the water makes it a popular place for scuba divers—who create an incongruous image with the tumbleweeds

diver down in Santa Rosa's Blue Hole

blowing by in the background. And the place is popular with local kids, who can spend a whole summer day doing cannonballs off the high rocks on one side. (There are less adventurous ways of getting into the water, including cement stairs.) Admission is free, but to dive you'll need a permit ($8), available from the visitors center in town or the adjacent **Blue Hole Dive Training Center.** To reach the Blue Hole, get off at exit 278 or 275 and follow signs to Blue Hole Road (also a section of Historic Route 66).

If you want more room to play, backtrack on Blue Hole Road to **Park Lake,** an adjacent natural spring that's the town's biggest recreation spot. Zip down the free water slide, rent a pedal boat, or just jump into the cool, refreshing water. (By comparison, **Santa Rosa Lake State Park,** the product of a dam on the Pecos River north of town, is quite dull next to these natural springs.)

### Route 66 Auto Museum

For car buffs, the Route 66 Auto Museum (2866 Historic Rte. 66, 575/472-1966, 7:30 A.M.–6 P.M. Mon.–Sat., 10 A.M.–5 P.M. Sun. Apr.–Oct., 8 A.M.–5 P.M. Mon.–Sat., 10 A.M.–5 P.M. Sun. Nov.–Mar., $5), on the east side of town, is a big gleaming showroom of curvaceous machines from the heyday of American road-tripping.

### Accommodations

Santa Rosa has the normal chain places, with a couple, such as **La Quinta** (2277 Historic Rte. 66, 575/472-4800, www.lq.com, $78 d), in better condition than their counterparts in Tucumcari. If you want a vintage Route 66 motel, though, the only recommendable places are down the highway in Tucumcari.

### Food

If you're wondering whether to eat here or hold out till Tucumcari, eat here—Santa Rosa boasts of its PDL chile, a special strain grown around the village of Puerto de Luna, just to the south; it's usually eaten in its green form. Hit the **C Comet II** (217 Historic Rte. 66, 575/472-

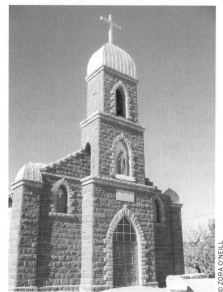

Nuestra Señora del Refugio Church in Puerto de Luna

FOOD, 6 A.M.–10 P.M. daily, $8), which is bathed in neon and does steaks and homemade pie along with the usual New Mexican menu. The Comet is substantially better than the inescapable landmark, **Joseph's Bar & Grill** (865 Historic Rte. 66, 575/472-3361, 6 A.M.–10 P.M. daily, $7), which rests more on its iconic "Fat Man" logo (salvaged from a Depression-era restaurant) than its food—though the décor is impressively kitschy.

### Information

On the main drag in the historic district, the **Santa Rosa Visitor Center** (244 S. 4th St., 575/472-3763, www.santarosanm.org, 8 A.M.–5 P.M. Mon.–Fri.) sells dive permits for the Blue Hole, in addition to stocking all the usual brochures.

## PUERTO DE LUNA

Santa Rosa's historic roots are in this tidy collection of tin-roofed adobe buildings in a protected valley 10 miles south of I-40 on Highway 91. Founded in 1842, it was the county seat in the 1880s and was later the childhood home of writer Rudolfo Anaya, who described the place in detail in his seminal novel *Bless Me, Ultima*. It's also alleged to be the place Billy the Kid enjoyed his last Christmas dinner, en route to jail in Lincoln while in the custody of Pat Garrett. The village's annual celebration, the **Fiestas de Nuestra Señora del Refugio** (575/472-3763), takes place over Fourth of July weekend.

The pretty drive down from Santa Rosa winds through red-striped rocky hills and chile fields. You can backtrack up Highway 91 or carry on south to where the highway meets Questa Road, which then runs into U.S. 84 about 10 miles south of Santa Rosa. This is just one small leg of the larger **Mesalands Scenic Byway,** which zigzags across I-40 between Santa Rosa and Tucumcari—the next leg is Highway 156 from Santa Rosa, then Highway 209 north to Tucumcari.

## SUMNER LAKE STATE PARK

A welcome bit of lushness amid the dry grasses, Sumner Lake (Hwy. 203, 575/355-2541, www.nmparks.com, $5/car) is an excellent birding spot, as it's on a major migration route (check the canyon below the dam in summer). The **camping** spots ($8–14), spread out in four areas and set amid cottonwoods and junipers, are very pretty. The state park is midway between Santa Rosa and Fort Sumner, six miles west of U.S. 84 via Highway 203.

## FORT SUMNER

A small town bedecked in Old West–style detailing, Fort Sumner is 42 miles south of I-40 and Santa Rosa via U.S. 84. It's best known as the final resting place of Henry McCarty, a.k.a. Henry Antrim, a.k.a. William H. Bonney, a.k.a. Billy the Kid. It was here in 1881 that Lincoln County Sheriff Pat Garrett finally tracked down the gunfighter and shot him (in ambush, in the dark, the Kid's fans will point out), to mete out justice for the 21 men Billy had allegedly killed in his short life—he was only 21, in fact, when he died in a farmhouse kitchen.

But for more than a century, the lurid story of the town's Wild West antihero had all but obliterated the memory of what Fort Sumner had first been: a failed reservation-turned-concentration-camp for about 9,000 Navajo and 500 Mescalero Apache for five years during the Civil War. In 2005, a state monument finally gave more public recognition to this tragic period in the settling of the American West.

### Sights

In town proper, there's little to see but the **Billy the Kid Museum** (1435 E. Sumner Ave., 575/355-2380, 8:30 A.M.–5 P.M. daily mid-May–Sept., 8:30 A.M.–5 P.M. Mon.–Sat. Oct.–mid-May, $4), a tourist outpost of the highest order, the sort of place where the rooms full of collections just keep coming: antique cars, blacksmithing tools, a replica of Billy the Kid's grave, and of course a gift shop. You could also seek out the **WPA murals** in the De Baca County Courthouse (514 Ave. C, 575/355-2601, 8 A.M.–4:30 P.M. Mon.–Fri.), just north of Sumner Avenue at the intersection with 7th Street.

The real action is all down the road: Head 3 miles east of town on U.S. 84, then 3.5 miles south on Billy the Kid Road, and you reach the so-so **Old Fort Sumner Museum** (575/355-2942, 9 A.M.–5 P.M. daily, $3.50) and, behind it in a rather desolate little cemetery, the *Real* **Gravesite of Billy the Kid** (to distinguish it from the model displayed up in town). Would-be outlaws should first pay their respects to William Bonney, who, perhaps due to his repeated jailbreaks in life, is now penned in by a wrought-iron fence as well as cemented over, along with a couple of his "pals." Also buried nearby: Lucien B. Maxwell, owner of the enormous Maxwell Land Grant in northern New Mexico, as well as this property, after the fort was decommissioned. It was in Maxwell's son's home, less than a mile toward the river, that Billy the Kid was fatally shot. The museum offers yet another collection of Old West relics and plenty more detail about the 21-year-old star of the Lincoln County War.

## Bosque Redondo Memorial

Immediately south on the road from here, the Bosque Redondo Memorial (3647 Billy the Kid Rd., 575/355-2573, www.nmmonuments.org, 8:30 A.M.–5 P.M. daily, $5) is a long-overdue museum and monument to the exceptional misery endured by most of the Navajo and a handful of Mescalero Apache, beginning in 1863. Force-marched in from the northwest and northeast corners of the state to this newly designated reservation, the people endured what the Navajo came to call the Long Walk, a midwinter trek of hundreds of miles, during which the weakest were shot for holding up the group and many women and children were sold into slavery. The two bands, which had little in common culturally and shared only a history of raiding each other, were penned in here and told to make a life together. But the allotted stretch of river basin was not enough land to support so many, so crops failed and disease tore through the overcrowded communities. The Mescalero Apache defied the U.S. military and left as a group two years into the terrible experiment. Nearly 3,000 Navajo—almost a third of the tribe—died in what they named H'weeldi (Place of Suffering) before they were allowed to return to their homelands in 1868.

The museum is a conceptual modern building—Navajo hogan meets Apache tepee—with a detailed exhibit on the camp, plus extra room for rotating displays on other low points in human rights history. Out back, a path leads past the site where the Navajo leaders finally signed the treaty that released them (and established the Navajo Nation) in 1868, and into the greenery alongside the river, where the fort itself used to stand. It's a deceptively pretty scene, considering what happened here.

### Accommodations and Food

The **Billy the Kid Country Inn** (1540 Sumner Ave., 575/355-7414, $36 d), across from the Billy the Kid Museum on the east end, is a good local hotel—all rooms have mini fridges and microwaves.

A big cinder-block building on the west end

of town, **Sadie's** (257 Sumner Ave., 575/355-1461, Wed.–Mon., $7) is busy serving huge burgers and New Mexican food to locals at its plastic-tablecloth-covered diner tables. Or at least it does when it's open, which happens according to an inscrutable system. If it's closed, head to **Fred's** (1408 Sumner Ave., 575/355-7500, 11 A.M.–8 P.M. Tues.–Sat., $7), which draws raves for the quality of its chile, guacamole, and chicken-fried steak; check out the neat old wood bar in the back.

### Information

Visit the **Fort Sumner Chamber of Commerce** (707 N. 4th St., 575/355-7705, www.ftsumnerchamber.com, 9 A.M.–4 P.M. Mon.–Fri.) for all the basic tourist details.

## TUCUMCARI

For the California-bound on Route 66, Tucumcari was the first real stop on New Mexico's 465 miles of the Mother Road. "Tucumcari Tonight!" urged the billboards leading up to the town's neon-lined strip, where thousands of hotel beds waited. The neon glow has turned to a flicker, and the number of beds is down to about 1,200 (and the number of desirable ones quite a lot fewer). But Americana buffs should definitely get off the highway here, to see the Tepee Curios shop and the glow of the Odeon Theater marquee, and even to bunk down in one of the well-preserved old motor courts. And dinosaur freaks will find a great museum.

Tucumcari's legacy goes back farther than Route 66. Back in the railroad-building days it was dubbed Six-Shooter Siding. The gunplay quieted down a little once regular trade got going along the newly laid rails (Tucumcari's Main Street is oriented with the old depot, not with Route 66), and the place took the name of nearby Tucumcari Mountain. The railroad provided steady employment even when I-40 led motorists away, but in 1999, the railroad closed its operations here. Now the sturdy, low bungalows that line the wide side streets seem to be the only thing keeping the town from being blown away in the winds—but the residents are stubborn and dedicated to keeping the place alive.

## Sights

After you've cruised all the neon signs on Historic Route 66 (a.k.a. Tucumcari Boulevard), check out Tucumcari's *other* main drag: Turn north on 1st Street and drive about eight blocks up to **Main Street** and the train depot. Nice murals adorn some buildings, and the 1936 Odeon Theater is still in business on 2nd Street.

The surprisingly spiffy **Mesalands Dinosaur Museum** (222 E. Laughlin St., 575/461-3466, 10 A.M.–6 P.M. Tues.–Sat., $6) is in this area too, one block east of 1st Street and two blocks north of Tucumcari Boulevard. The exhibit hall contains a huge number of beautiful bronze casts of dinosaur skeletons (neat, because you're allowed to touch them), as well as some dinosaur eggs and lots of other fossils. It also owns a full 30-foot-long *Torvosaurus* skeleton—the only known evidence of this giant carnivore.

Two blocks farther north (look for the windmill), the **Tucumcari Historical Museum** (416 S. Adams St., 575/461-4201, 8 A.M.–5 P.M. Mon.–Sat., $5) takes up an entire two-story redbrick house with old saddles, slot machines, and Indian relics, then spills over into a yard full of vintage boxcars, Route 66 paraphernalia, and more.

## Sports and Recreation

In the summer, locals decamp to one of New Mexico's bigger reservoirs, **Conchas Lake State Park** (575/868-2270, www.nmparks. com, $5/car), northwest of town 34 miles on Highway 104. It stretches for about 25 miles, its coastline weaving along many inlets, sandy beaches, and canyons. The setting is rather austere, however, and there's very little shade—it's nicer to visit in the cooler spring or fall, when crowds are lighter as well.

## Accommodations

Tucumcari has a handful of excellent-value retro motels—worth a stop just to enjoy a taste of the past. A relic of the Route 66 days,

© ZORA O'NEILL

vintage Route 66 architecture in Tucumcari

the pink-and-turquoise **Blue Swallow Motel** (815 E. Route 66 Blvd., 575/461-9849, www. blueswallowmotel.com, $50 s, $65 d), on the east side of town, dates from 1939, with 12 cozy, plaster-wall rooms with tiled showers and patches of wood floor. Many of the carports adjacent to the rooms are used for storage, but otherwise the place has been kept up quite well by the proud owners.

The Blue Swallow is open only March–October, however. **Motel Safari** (722 E. Route 66 Blvd., 575/461-1048, www.smalltown-america.com, $49 d) is open year-round and has been renovated with great care—firm beds, borderline chic furniture, and flat-panel TVs are offset with retro touches like old-fashioned black phones in the rooms.

If you want to go even cheaper, check out the **Historic Route 66 Motel** (1620 E. Route 66 Blvd., 575/461-1212, www.rte66motel.com, $30 s, $36 d). It might not have a fabulous neon sign, but its architecture will make mid-century modernists swoon. The owners, who renovated the place in 2007, have kept some groovy touches in its rooms, such as the turquoise vinyl chairs that may be from the original 1967 design.

## Food

Although it's bigger than Santa Rosa, Tucumcari doesn't have as many restaurants. A couple, though, will do in a pinch. Sombrero-topped **La Cita** (812 S. 1st St.) is better for a photo op than for a meal; instead, try **Pow Wow Restaurant & Lizard Lounge** (801 W. Route 66 Blvd., 575/461-2587, 6 A.M.–10 P.M. Sun.–Thurs., 6 A.M.–midnight Fri. and Sat., $8). It's a town hangout, thanks to its pool table and bar; the restaurant serves sandwiches and New Mexican dishes in a pastel Southwest-style dining room—it's a perfectly serviceable place to have lunch or dinner.

For lunch, **Cornerstone Deli** (711 E. Route 66 Blvd., 575/461-3326, 11 A.M.–7 P.M. Mon.–Sat., $6) serves sandwiches with ingredients from the local small-scale Tucumcari Mountain Cheese Factory (foodies: check it out at 823 E. Main St.), as well as homemade potato chips and super-creamy frozen custard.

## Information

The **Tucumcari-Quay County Chamber of Commerce** (404 W. Route 66 Blvd., 575/461-1694, 9 A.M.–5 P.M. Mon.–Fri.) has the usual assortment of information.

## Getting There

Running along I-40, **Greyhound** (800/231-2222, www.greyhound.com) stops in Tucumcari three times a day. The bus stops at the McDonald's (2608 S. 1st St., 575/461-1350, 5 A.M.–midnight daily).

# The Llano

Texans refer to these barren plains as the Llano, and it makes sense to use the term because so much of this area could be mistaken for the neighboring state, from the fields of cattle to the oil derricks that dot the horizon. The dairy industry also flourishes here—adding a distinctive tang to the air, mixing with the smell of petroleum.

"West West Texas" rarely sees tourists, but some of this land is exceptionally pretty: South on Highway 209 from Tucumcari, for instance, takes you closer to the mesas and leaves the visual clutter of billboards and semi trucks behind. Scored by deep channels, the red earth is studded with cholla cactus and a delicate-looking variety of yucca, as well as black, brushy mesquite. The occasional farmhouse—often built only feet away from a ruined homestead from 50 years ago—shows the incredible optimism required to live in this windy, harshly beautiful landscape. (If you jog west toward Fort Sumner, you'll see the state actually profiting from the rough climate here, through a field of wind turbines that feed into the electricity grid.)

## CLOVIS

Like so many other chronically windy spots on the plains, Clovis has an ongoing problem keeping its sign boards straight, so WELCOMET OCLOVIS will have to do. Busy as it is with rail freight, cattle auctions, and training at the adjacent air force base, Clovis doesn't really court tourists anyway. It had its last moment in the national spotlight in 1957, when Buddy Holly and his pals recorded "That'll Be the Day" in a music studio here. And even though its population is 33,000 and growing, it feels like a fairly small town, especially along its wide brick Main Street that dead-ends against the rail yard. This downtown area has not been "revived" in the typical sense—many of the art deco buildings have been occupied by the same businesses for decades. Only the glamorous Hotel Clovis, once the tallest building west of Dallas, is boarded up, now overshadowed by grain silos.

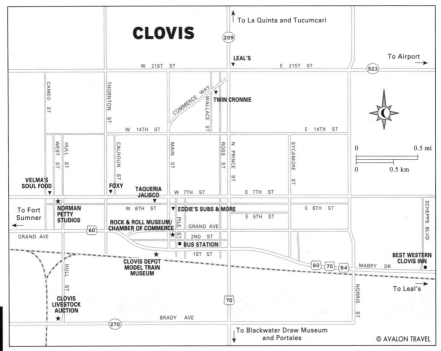

# THE *LLANO ESTACADO*

The early explorers on Francisco Vásquez de Coronado's first excursion through the west, in 1541, referred to the stretch east from the Sacramento Mountains as the *llano estacado*, describing the place as an endless sea of green, with grass as high as their horses' bellies – an evocative image, but it doesn't explain exactly what the conquistadors may have meant by the word *estacado*.

The common translation is "stockaded" or "staked" plains – which hardly clarifies the issue. Some academics have reasoned that the great green expanse was as disorienting as being at sea, so the Spanish horsemen pounded stakes in the ground to mark their way. The "stockaded" camp reasons that the Spanish thought the mesas that punctuated the flatlands – particularly the 300-foot-high Caprock Escarpment near Tucumcari – stood up, straight-walled, like defensive forts. A third, far less common interpretation proposes that in 16th-century Spanish, *estacado* also had the meaning of "covered in spikes." That is, these were the "stickered plains," due to the spiny yucca plants and thorn-covered mesquite bushes that flourish here. Whatever the case, although the "sea of grass" that Coronado traversed is not so green today, the mesas remain as stark and straight.

## Sights

It's open only by appointment, but **Norman Petty Studios** (1313 W. 7th St., norman-pettystudios@superoldies.com) is so influential that it deserves mention regardless. Petty was a young professional musician who'd scored with the hit version of the song "Mood Indigo" in 1956, but found himself disillusioned with the industry. Intending to record his own music, he came back home and set up a production studio in the building adjacent to his parents' filling station. He instead got a big break when Buddy Holly, a foundering country singer, came up from Lubbock to record a couple of tracks. Petty quickly took Holly from western crooner to pop sensation, then launched the careers of Roy Orbison and Waylon Jennings. No one talks much about "the Clovis Sound" these days, but in the late 1950s, it was unmistakable. The Beatles, who saw Holly in concert in 1958, were indelibly marked by it, and the young Rolling Stones covered "Rave On." Petty continued to produce into the 1970s and died in 1984.

Some of the ephemera from these golden days is collected at the **Norman & Vi Petty Rock & Roll Museum** (105 E. Grand Ave., 575/763-3435, 8 A.M.–noon and 1–5 P.M. Mon.–Fri., $5). One exhibit details the roots of a Petty-inspired annual jam, now revived as the **Clovis Music Festival** (575/763-3435, www.clovismusicfestival.net), every September. The studios are also open during that weekend.

Otherwise, Clovis's attractions are just the regular business activities: You can watch the action every Wednesday morning at **Clovis Livestock Auction** (504 S. Hull St., 575/762-4422) at the corner of Hull and Brady, south of the tracks. Or follow the freight trains' comings and goings from the bridge over Hull Street or at the **Clovis Depot Model Train Museum** (221 W. 1st St., 575/762-0066, www.clovis-depot.com, noon–5 P.M. Wed.–Sun. Mar.–Sept., call for hours Oct.–Feb., $5 per person or $15 per family). The restored 1950s depot contains a number of operating scale models, and rail fans can even listen in to the real-time

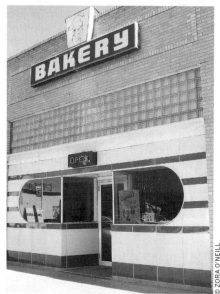

Art Deco style in downtown Clovis

communications in the yard, as they're piped in over speakers in the depot.

## Accommodations

Most of the hotels and motels in Clovis are on Mabry Drive, parallel to the railroad tracks through town—which makes for a bad night's sleep if you're sensitive to noise. If you can afford it, go for the town's branch of **La Quinta** (4521 N. Prince St., 575/763-8777, www.lq.com, $93 d), one of a very few options on the north side of town, with a nice indoor pool and well-kept, suite-layout rooms. If not, **Best Western Clovis Inn** (2912 Mabry Dr., 575/762-5600, www.bestwestern.com, $80 d) is probably the best of the Mabry Drive choices, a perfectly functional chain motel, and you can barely hear the trains when the air-conditioning is on.

## Food

Local favorite ◖ **Leal's** (3100 E. Mabry Dr., 575/763-4075, 10:30 A.M.–9 P.M. Mon.–Sat.,

10:30 A.M.–3 P.M. Sun., $8) is more Tex-Mex than New Mex, serving dishes like a Topped Sopaipilla (rather than the stuffed variety) and red and green chile sauces that are flavorful but not terribly hot, along with *carne guisada* (long-stewed beef in a tomato-and-chile sauce) and a Texas-style bowl of chili. There's a second location on the north side of town, but regulars swear by the original.

For *Mexican* Mexican, head to **( Taqueria Jalisco** (217 W. 7th St., 575/763-1865, 7 A.M.–9 P.M. daily, $7), where you can get a huge slab of steak and homemade flour tortillas, as well as deep-fried *gorditas,* stuffed *tortas,* and creamy, cinnamon-spiked *horchata* to drink—far more food than you can eat, served with style (the trompe l'oeil mural takes you right to Mexico's Pacific coast), at astonishingly low prices.

A popular spot for the noon meal is **Eddie's Subs & More** (517 N. Main St., 575/762-6911, 10:30 A.M.–5 P.M. Mon.–Fri., $6), good for hamburgers, enchiladas, and green-chile stew—in addition to the aforementioned heroes, served on fresh-baked bread. **Velma's Soul Food** (1420 W. 7th St., 575/769-0707, 11 A.M.–2 P.M. Mon.–Sat., $6) dishes up pit barbecue and all the sides. It may not be the greatest ever, but the dining room, with its gold vinyl tablecloths, and Velma herself are American relics. Beware the tooth-achingly sweet cobblers.

Then there's the category of 1950s-style drive-in restaurants, the likes of which are seldom seen these days—especially not of this caliber. **( Foxy** (720 W. 7th St., 575/763-7995, 7:30 A.M.–10 P.M. Sun.–Thurs., 7:30 A.M.–11 P.M. Fri. and Sat., $5) excels at crispy taquitos and steak fingers, while **Twin Cronnie** (709 Commerce Way, 575/763-5463, 8 A.M.–10 P.M. daily, $5) is the home of a tasty combination involving two hot dogs, chile, and a round bun, among a million other menu items.

## Information

The Clovis **chamber of commerce** (105 E. Grand Ave., 575/763-3435, www.clovisnm.org, 8 A.M.–noon and 1–5 P.M. Mon.–Fri.) has

its offices downtown, but the staff is not really geared to walk-in queries. Its website is very thorough.

## Getting There

Clovis Municipal Airport (CVN), six miles east of town, receives two flights a day (except Sunday, when there's one) from Albuquerque on Great Lakes Airlines (800/554-5111, www.greatlakesav.com). **Greyhound** (800/231-2222, www.greyhound.com) stops at the station (121 E. 2nd St., 575/762-4584, 11 A.M.–5 P.M. Mon.–Fri., 12:30–2:30 P.M. Sat.); buses come from Las Cruces once a day.

## BLACKWATER DRAW MUSEUM

Midway between Clovis and Portales, this archaeology museum (42987 U.S. 70, 575/562-2202, 10 A.M.–5 P.M. Mon.–Sat., noon–5 P.M. Sun. June–Aug., closed Mon. Sept.–May, $3) shows relics from the "type site" for the ancient culture dubbed Clovis Man, the oldest known culture in the New World—or at least the oldest one that researchers can agree on. Excavations in the late 1940s and early 1950s revealed distinctive fluted spearheads embedded in a mammoth carcass, effectively proving the existence of humans in North America at the end of the last ice age, in roughly 11,300 B.C. The site, nearby on Highway 467, is also important because it shows so many layers of occupation: Remnants of the later Folsom Man culture are stacked atop the Clovis points, and early agricultural efforts on top of that. (Your museum admission also gives you access to the site—ask for directions.)

This is all well illustrated in the museum, which explains the logic of archaeology in addition to the ancient history itself. You'll find a reproduction mammoth head—just to get an idea of the scale those early hunters were up against—as well as a number of other glass cases illustrating the development of hunting technology and culture in the region across the ages. In winter, the museum is officially shut on Mondays, but you'll often find the door open and the staff inside, allegedly tending to their own work but still just as ready to chat about the exhibits.

## PORTALES

Home of Eastern New Mexico University, some prairie chickens, and a whole lot of peanut farmers, Portales is a pretty but not terribly exciting. The farmland surrounding Portales may produce a mere 30 million pounds of legumes a year—only 1 percent of the nation's peanut crop—but that accounts for 90 percent of the exceptionally tasty red-skinned Valencia variety. Its downtown, fanning out from a deco-goes-West courthouse (look for the cowboy friezes above the windows), hasn't quite gotten in on the revitalization movement, and the most attractive area of town is the campus of dark brick buildings and green lawns in the southwest corner of town. On the 21-mile drive down from Clovis, you might see the biggest tumbleweeds of your trip—just slow down and let 'em roll on by.

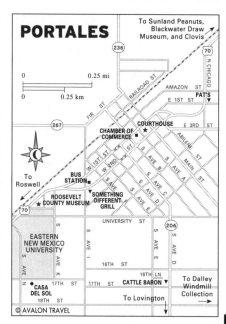

### Sights

On the ENMU campus, the **Roosevelt County Museum** (575/562-2592, 8 A.M.–5 P.M. Mon.–Fri., 10 A.M.–4 P.M. Sat., 1–4 P.M. Sun., free) is a very manageable size, with some great paintings (see the cowboy's ode to the mountain lion in the main hall) and cool dioramas, along with items from Japan and Peru, donated by well-traveled locals. The museum is at West 2nd Street and University Place. Weekend hours in summer may vary—call ahead.

About two miles northeast of town, **Sunland Peanuts** (42593 U.S. 70, 575/356-6638, 8 A.M.–5 P.M. Mon.–Fri.) is the area's biggest processing plant for the tasty little legumes—it makes peanut butter and other tasty treats, all available in the gift shop. Visitors are welcome for free tours of the plant (samples included) on Mondays, Wednesdays, and Fridays at 2 P.M.; call ahead to let them know you're interested.

Perhaps Portales's most obscure attraction, the **Dalley Windmill Collection** (S. Kilgore Ave. at 18th St.) is the largest private collection in the country, with about 85 of the things clustered in the owner's front yard. Fans of old

farm equipment should turn south on Kilgore Avenue from Highway 467 and drive about a mile; the house is on your right. You're welcome to walk up and sign the guestbook under the tree.

### Events

ENMU sponsors the annual **Peanut Valley Festival** (575/562-2242) near the end of October—sadly, it's not *completely* peanut-obsessed, what with distractions like a big craft fair, funnel-cake booths, and the like, but it is a lively time to be in town. Birders descend on the area in April for the **High Plains Prairie Chicken Festival** (575/762-6997), a get-together of grouse fans to marvel at the birds' mating rituals—it all takes place in nearby Milnesand, which claims to be the Lesser Prairie Chicken Capital of New Mexico.

### Accommodations

Along with the chain hotels, there's **Casa del Sol** (1401 W. 17th St., 575/356-5966, www. casadelsolportales.com, $75 d), an attractive cottonwood-shaded adobe built in the 1940s by architect John Gaw Meem—a surprising outpost of Pueblo Revival style. It has two rooms, one in the main house and another in a more private outbuilding.

## Food

Sample Portales's produce in a deliciously creamy peanut-butter shake at **( Pat's** drive-in (100 N. Chicago Ave., 575/356-5841, 11 A.M.–9 P.M. Sun.–Thurs., 11 A.M.–10 P.M. Fri. and Sat., $5), where you can also fill up on taquitos, burgers, and chili dogs.

An old drive-in, redone with a faux-Italian interior, **Something Different Grill** (805 W. 2nd St., 575/356-1205, 11 A.M.–9:30 P.M. daily, $7) serves passable pasta, stuffed baked potatoes, and teriyaki bowls to locals of all ages. The staff is exceptionally nice. It doesn't serve alcohol, though.

If you're feeling "fancy," locals recommend the **Cattle Baron** (1660 S. Ave. D, 575/356-5587, 11 A.M.–9 P.M. Sun.–Thurs., 11 A.M.–10 P.M. Fri. and Sat., $20). You see these steakhouses all over this part of New Mexico—it's a respectable mini-chain where you can't really go wrong with a big slab of beef, a baked potato, and a trip to the salad bar.

## Information

The **Roosevelt County Chamber of Commerce** (100 S. Ave. A, 575/356-8541, www.portales.com, 8 A.M.–5 P.M. Mon.–Fri.) can help you out with maps, brochures, and, most importantly, free peanuts.

## Getting There

**Greyhound** (800/231-2222, www.greyhound.com) drops passengers at the station (820 W. 2nd St.); buses come from Las Cruces once a day.

## TATUM

When you're driving through Tatum, keep an eye on the street signs—the cut-metal silhouettes are the work of **Westcraft Metal Art,** which specializes in this decoration that's essential to any well-turned-out ranch gate. You

**Westcraft Metal Art in Tatum**

© ZORA O'NEILL

can visit the operation a few blocks west of the main intersection (500 W. Broadway, 575/398-5295), where the company also sells smaller gift items.

## LOVINGTON

The seat of Lea County, Lovington has a handsome art deco courthouse and tidy streets. The town-operated **Lea County Museum** (103 S. Love St., 575/396-4805, www.leacountymuseum.org, 1–5 P.M. Tues.–Fri., 10 A.M.–5 P.M. Sat., free), across from the courthouse, contains all the usual pioneer-era items. In addition, one room is dedicated to Western writer Max Evans, who lived until the age of 12 in nearby Humble City, now all but vanished (Evans rechristened the place Starvation, Texas, in one of his novels).

If you're hungry in Lovington, hit the **Lazy 6** (102 S. 1st St., 575/396-5066, 10 A.M.–2 P.M. Mon.–Thurs., 10 A.M.–8 P.M. Fri., $6), where the knickknack-to-customer ratio is 10 to 1, even when the place is packed for lunch. Don't let it distract you from the good home cooking, though. It's one block west of Main Street. **Main Street Café** (201 N. Main St., 575/396-1800, 5 A.M.–8:30 P.M. Mon.–Sat., $7) is also good, serving three meals a day and particularly strong on breakfast.

## HOBBS

Yet another oil town with a Texan sensibility and the smell of, shall we say, "money" in the air, Hobbs is just five miles from the border and the largest settlement in Lea County, with nearly 30,000 residents. It's a destination only for people working in the industry, students at New Mexico Preparatory College and the College of the Southwest, and fans of gliding—the flat land and empty skies are made for delicate sailplanes.

### Sights

Wild West fanatics will want to pay their respects at the **Western Heritage Museum and Lea County Cowboy Hall of Fame** (5317 Lovington Hwy., 575/392-6730, www.museumshobbsnm.org, 10 A.M.–5 P.M. Tues.–Sat., $3), a sleek bit of architecture that renders an oil derrick in green glass. The 29,000-square-foot complex on the north edge of town honors local ranching and rodeo stars (more like saints, really, to judge from the way their personal effects are enshrined) and gives an overview of the region's history, from dinosaur stomping ground to wild territory to modern source of black gold (first tapped in 1927).

More obscure is the **New Mexico Wing, Confederate Air Force Museum** (U.S. 62/180, 575/397-3202, 8 A.M.–sunset daily, free), a dusty hangar at the Hobbs airport filled with WWII planes and other items.

## ARTESIA

Never mind the cliché image of, say, a Navajo man on a cell phone in front of a centuries-old adobe house. Instead, one of the most discordant views of New Mexico can be had at the junction of U.S. 285 and U.S. 82 in Artesia: This presents one of the most discordant views in New Mexico. Look west and you'll see an attractive, modernized Main Street that boasts a beautiful movie palace, lots of shops, and sturdy old buildings. Look east and you see the state's largest oil refinery, all concrete towers, blinking lights, and plumes of steam and smoke. If you keep your back to the refinery, you can spend a pleasant hour or two (or more, if you go to a movie), checking out the **Artesia Historical Museum & Art Center** (505 W. Richardson Ave., 575/748-2390, www.artesiamuseum.com, 9 A.M.–noon and 1–5 P.M. Tues.–Fri., 1–5 P.M. Sat., free), in a pretty area two blocks south of Main Street. Larger-than-life bronze statues dot the main drag, including a very cool series of life-size figures in the midst of a cattle-rustling operation, arranged across three intersections. It's a very orderly town, thanks to the presence of a major federal law-enforcement training center.

### Practicalities

For food, head to **The Wellhead** brewpub (332 W. Main St., 575/746-0640, 11 A.M.–9 P.M. Mon.–Thurs., 11 A.M.–10 P.M. Fri. and Sat., $10), where you can get burgers, steaks, or enchiladas with red chile from The Shed in Santa Fe.

If you care to spend the night, **Heritage Inn** (209 W. Main St., 575/748-2552, www.artesiaheritageinn.com, $98 d) is a historic hotel that has been smartly renovated on the points that matter (modern bathrooms and comfy beds). Opened in 2009, the glitzier **Hotel Artesia** (203 N. 2nd St., 888/746-2066, www.hotelartesia.com, $115 d) looks like it has been beamed in from Miami. The 52 spacious rooms are done in a somewhat generic sleek modern style, with every convenience for business travelers. Incongruous with the surrounding streets, the lobby lounge is popular after work.

Stop in at the **Artesia Chamber of Commerce** (107 N. 1st St., 575/746-2744, www.artesiachamber.com, 9 A.M.–5 P.M. Mon.–Fri.), in the old train depot for additional info. The **Artesia MainStreet** program (510 W. Main St., 575/746-1117, www.artesiamainstreet.com, 9 A.M.–5 P.M. Mon.–Fri.) offers a walking and driving tour around this surprisingly large town (pop. 13,200).

# Roswell

Launched into national notoriety in 1947 by an alleged UFO crash (and subsequent government cover-up) on a nearby ranch, Roswell has been marked indelibly by the odd events. Ever since popular fascination was renewed with a lot of "truth-seeking" exposés in the 1980s, the town has become a sort of pilgrimage site for true believers as well as seekers of American kitsch. The city takes its mission seriously: The streetlights look like little green alien heads, the city seal sports a glowing disc, and the McDonald's resembles a space ship about to lift off.

But there's a lot more to this city of 50,000, the largest metro area in this region. Founded in 1870, it has its roots in ranching, then agriculture, after an artesian well was discovered in 1890; Chaves County is now the largest dairy producer in the state. The town is anchored by a 1910 courthouse with a tall, green-tiled dome (built by Isaac Hamilton Rapp, who was also instrumental in designing Santa Fe's zoning codes to create a homogenous downtown).

Over the longer term, Roswell has probably been more influenced by the presence of the New Mexico Military Institute, established 1891. There's a strong conservative streak in this city, to the point it's hard to even find a bar at night. As if to balance the scales, Roswell has hosted a small clan of contemporary artists every year since the mid-1960s, which has fostered a strong appreciation for the arts and two excellent museums. In short, there are enough disparate elements here to keep a visitor entertained for a day or two.

## SIGHTS

The central intersection is at North Main Street (U.S. 285) and West 2nd Street (U.S. 70/380), also the location of the UFO museum. Like debris around a crash site, space-theme shops and other attractions (many relying heavily on

The beaux-arts Chaves County courthouse was built in 1911.

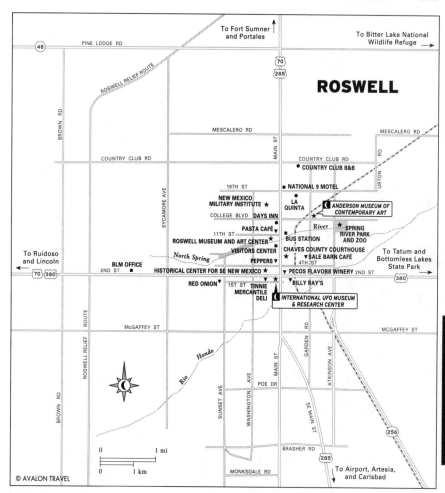

fluorescent paint and black lights) dot the surrounding blocks.

## **⟨ International UFO Museum & Research Center**

Most visitors to Roswell make a beeline to this converted movie theater (114 N. Main St., 575/625-9495, www.iufomrc.org, 9 A.M.–5 P.M. daily, $2), where the events of July 1947 are dissected with obsessive care. As kitschy as everything surrounding the museum

is, its core is very serious. The dense mass of data—newspaper clippings, affidavits, faded photos—is a little overwhelming and presented with a minimum of gloss; an audio tour only heaps on more detail. Related issues such as ancient alien cults, Area 51, abductions, and crop circles get the same thorough documentary treatment. The mood lightens a bit with a section about Roswell in the movies, and a photo studio where you can have your picture taken being "beamed up." The museum was

Roswell's main attraction: the International UFO Museum & Research Center

founded by two men who were peripherally involved in the incident, and they're occasionally at the front desk, ready to talk shop with anyone who asks.

Plans are afoot to move the museum to a cool new building at Main and 8th, but it likely won't happen within the lifespan of this book.

## Roswell Museum and Art Center

The wide-ranging city museum (100 W. 11th St., 575/624-6744, www.roswellmuseum.org, 9 A.M.–5 P.M. Mon.–Sat., 1–5 P.M. Sun., free) is a real treasure. The original gallery space, built in 1937 as a WPA project, is an attraction in itself, with high viga ceilings and tin chandeliers; it contains work by local luminaries like Peter Hurd and Henriette Wyeth, as well as a beautiful collection of Western paraphernalia, such as finely wrought spurs and elaborate beaded deerskin tunics.

The place celebrates science too, with an exhibit on space-flight visionary Robert Goddard, who moved from Massachusetts to Roswell in

the 1930s to continue his work on liquid-fueled rockets—his workshop has been re-created, piece by piece, in one room. Adjacent to the main museum, the **Robert H. Goddard Planetarium** (912 N. Main St.), the second-largest in the state, has public shows one week a month; call the museum for the schedule.

## ◖ Anderson Museum of Contemporary Art

As good as the Roswell Museum is, it's no match for this 17,000-square-foot space (409 E. College Blvd., 575/623-5600, www.roswellmoca.org, 9 A.M.–noon and 1–4 P.M. Mon.–Fri., 1–5 P.M. Sat. and Sun., free), an invigorating collection from the past four decades, in media ranging from oil paintings to wood inlay. The works on view are representative samples from an artist-in-residence program established in 1967 by oilman Donald Anderson. Since then it has hosted luminaries like abstract expressionist Milton Resnick and sculptor Luís Jiménez (best known for his *Blue Mustang* outside the Denver airport), along with scores of others still working and developing their reputations.

In the museum, many of the products of the "gift of time" (as the foundation calls the residency) are set alongside photos of the artists themselves, posing as a group or relaxing with their families in the compound they're granted on the fringes of town—a sort of yearbook photo accompanying the art, which also pegs it to a certain period. It's an unorthodox approach (as is the way pieces are hung, packed in close and covering nearly every surface), and it lends an exuberance to the place that's hard to resist, even if you're not generally a fan of contemporary artwork.

## General Douglas L. McBride Military Museum

A visit to this array of military paraphernalia (575/624-8220, 8 A.M.–4 P.M. Mon.–Fri., free) is more an excuse to get inside the giant fortress that is the New Mexico Military Institute, on North Main Street at College Boulevard. Like the courthouse, the main building was designed

## NEW MEXICO'S ALIEN OBSESSION

In 1947, America's skies seemed to fill with UFOs, with strange encounters reported in Washington State, then in early July in Idaho and, more notoriously, in Roswell. This latter event, in which a "flying disc," complete with alien crew, was said to have crashed on a ranch outside of town, quickly led to revisions of the stories, the military's involvement, and a haze of confusion over what actually happened.

The Roswell incident was followed in the next several years by scores of sightings, putting the United States in the grip of a UFO frenzy. A 1950 book titled *Behind the Flying Saucers*, by a reporter for *Variety* named Frank Scully, only fanned the flames of wild speculation. That book described yet another strange encounter in New Mexico: In March 1948, just nine months after the Roswell incident, the residents of Aztec, near Farmington, apparently had a similar occurrence in their own backyard – although no one actually saw the disc in the sky or at the crash site, as all but a scrap had been whisked away by the military. In fact, Scully was the first to investigate

the crash, when he was in the area investigating the "Farmington Armada" spotted earlier in the year.

Two years later, it was revealed that the spaceship wreckage Scully had seen was actually the work of Silas Newton and Leo Gebauer, who had been seeking investors in their device for finding oil – the crash had been their back story for the alien technology that allegedly drove their gadget, and they hoped to secure investors in their scheme. The two con men were convicted of fraud in 1953.

That didn't stop UFO enthusiasts from reviving the Aztec story in the 1980s, along with the Roswell incident, which became the subject of fresh fascination. Now both towns have a respectable alien-inspired tourism industry. The general perception in New Mexico toward these and other events (such as the creepy cattle mutilations in the 1970s, and ongoing reports of alien abductions) is not one of feverish conviction, nor of outright dismissal. It's more an attitude of resigned acceptance – as if the UFOs are just one more weird happening in a very weird state.

by I. H. and W. M. Rapp, who also laid out a master plan for its expansion. The institution trains about a thousand high school and college prep students from all over the country, and alumni have included newscaster Sam Donaldson, hotelier Conrad Hilton, historian Paul Horgan, painter Peter Hurd, actor Owen Wilson, and even Miss New Mexico 2001. The entrance to the museum is in the back of the main building; head west on College, then turn right on Kentucky, then through the gates at Duty Street.

### Historical Center for Southeast New Mexico

The trials of pioneer living are detailed at the town's historical museum (200 N. Lea Ave., 575/622-8333, 1–4 P.M. daily, free), a 1912 Prairie-style brick bungalow filled with period furniture and mannequins. You can pick up a

brochure for a walking tour around Roswell's other historic houses, in a variety of styles.

## ENTERTAINMENT

You're lucky to find even a restaurant open past 8 P.M. in Roswell, much less a bar. The city lets loose for a couple of annual parties, though.

### Nightlife

It's slim pickings on the drinking front, but **Billy Ray's** (118 E. 3rd St., 575/627-0997, 11 A.M.–midnight Mon.–Sat.) has a decent scene, with good bar food, homemade soups, and full meals (lunch only on Monday) if you want them—but most people are there for drinks, and maybe karaoke.

You can sample wine from many of the state's best producers at **Pecos Flavors Winery** (305 N. Main St., 575/627-6265, 10 A.M.–7 P.M. Mon.–Thurs., 10 A.M.–8 P.M.

Sat. and Sun.), though the tasting bar shuts at 5 P.M. Thanks to a handsome antique wood bar and a convivial atmosphere, this feels more like a town hangout than a formal tasting room, and it's a nice place to put your feet up after walking around downtown. It also stocks other local bounty, such as salsas and pistachios, and occasionally hosts live music in the evenings.

## Special Events

The town dedicates Fourth of July weekend to visitors from space, as well as around the world, for the **Amazing Roswell UFO Festival** (888/ROS-FEST, www.roswellufofestival. com), which melds serious science with all the geekiness of a *Star Trek* convention. More than 50,000 space fans gather for an alien costume contest, screenings of vintage sci-fi films, a nighttime disc-golf tourney, and lectures by scientists and assorted actors. By contrast, the **Eastern New Mexico State Fair & Parade** (575/623-9411, www.enmsf.com), in early October, seems pretty mundane.

## SPORTS AND RECREATION

A big park in town caters to kids, while a state park to the east offers a few opportunities for swimming and mountain biking. Overall, though, the flat terrain around Roswell doesn't lend itself to exciting outdoors activities. The **BLM Roswell field office** (2909 W. 2nd St., 575/627-0272, 8 A.M.–4:30 P.M. Mon.–Fri.), on the far west edge of town, is the contact point for questions about nearby public lands.

## Spring River Park and Zoo

Like many small-town zoos, the animal component of Spring River Park and Zoo (1306 E. College Blvd., 575/624-6760, 10 A.M.–8 P.M. daily in summer, 10 A.M.–5:30 P.M. daily in winter, free) is a little distressing—although the massive prairie dog village (allegedly the largest in the state) is always a crowd-pleaser, and there's a fishing hole just for kids. Do go to see the 1926 carousel—a ride on its hand-carved wooden horses costs just a

quarter; a miniature train also loops around the grounds. The park is the head of the **Spring River Trail,** a five-mile paved route to the town golf course.

## Bottomless Lakes State Park

The water at Bottomless Lakes (575/624-6058, www.nmparks.com, $5/car) does not actually descend to the center of the earth. But the pools at this state park just east of Roswell are a rare phenomenon in New Mexico. Like the Blue Hole in Santa Rosa, they began as water-filled caverns, then the ceilings collapsed. Lea Lake, the deepest and largest of the pools here, plunges 90 feet. It's also the only lake open for swimming and diving, but it's a pretty small patch of water for the crowds that descend on it in the summertime.

There's tent camping at Cottonwood Lake, adjacent to the park office. (If you're interested in archaeology, ask here for directions to **Garnsey Arroyo,** a barely excavated bison "kill site" from about 500 years ago.) You'll find RV camping farther down the access road at Lea Lake.

**Skidmarks Trail,** good for biking or hiking, runs for a little more than three miles over some of the limestone bluffs on the north edge of the park area. Wildflowers bloom here in the spring, and you'll see lots of water birds. Look for the trailhead just as you turn onto the loop road around the park (if you get to Lazy Lagoon, you've gone too far).

To reach the park, head east of Roswell 12 miles on U.S. 380, then drive south on Bottomless Lakes Road for 3 miles—the turn for the park access road is on the right (west) side of the highway.

## Bitter Lake National Wildlife Refuge

Established in 1937, the Bitter Lake refuge (4067 Bitter Lakes Rd., 575/622-6755) encompasses nearly 25,000 acres of grasslands, dunes, and wetlands around the Pecos River. As at Bottomless Lakes, there are a number of freshwater sinkholes, which teem with distinctive wildlife. The area is great for birding, as well as for spotting more than 90 species of colorful dragonflies and damselflies, best viewed in late summer. There's even a **Dragonfly Festival** in early September. To reach the refuge headquarters, from North Main Street (U.S. 70/285), turn onto East Pine Lodge Road east and follow it until it turns into Bitter Lakes Road and runs into the park.

## ACCOMMODATIONS

All of the hotels and motels are along the northern section of Main Street (U.S. 70/285) or at the far west end of 2nd Street (U.S. 70/380), and there's not much available beyond the usual chains.

### Under $100

Of the cheaper places on North Main, the one-story **National 9** motel (2001 N. Main St., 575/622-0110, www.national9roswell. com, $45 s, $50 d) is clean and tidy, and its 60 rooms are all furnished with a fridge and a microwave—most were in the middle of a renovation in 2010.

Among the chains, **Days Inn** (1310 N. Main St., 575/623-4021, www.daysinn.com, $60 s, $64 d) offers very good value. It's well kept and even has a small pool for hot summer days. It's a two-story motel-style layout—walls and ceilings are a bit thin, so a second-floor room is preferable. A full breakfast is included in the rate, but it's pretty institutional.

### $100-150

The one B&B in town, **Country Club Bed & Breakfast** (400 E. Country Club Rd., 575/624-1794, www.countryclubbnb.com, $100 d) occupies a beautiful Victorian house on the far north side of town. There are just two rooms, but they're furnished nicely, without too much lace; bathrooms are on the small side, though.

Opened in mid-2006, **La Quinta** (200 E. 19th St., 575/622-8000, www.lq.com, $129 d) meets the generally good standards of this chain. Just east of Main Street, on the north side of town, it's a little out of the way, but preferable because it's set back a little from the heaviest traffic. It also has an indoor pool.

## FOOD

Just a few blocks from Main Street, **Tinnie Mercantile Deli** (412 W. 2nd St., 575/622-2031, 10 A.M.–5 P.M. Tues.–Sat.) is a good lunch spot, with the usual sandwiches (all named after surrounding towns), soups, and salads. Perhaps more important for many people, though, is its full selection of espresso drinks.

With pink-and-red decor and a mostly Spanish-speaking waitstaff, the **Red Onion** (1400 W. 2nd St., 575/622-3232, 7 A.M.–4 P.M. daily, $7) transports you to Mexico for breakfast or lunch, with big platters of migas (scrambled eggs with tortilla bits mixed in) and other standards, complete with tropical-flavor Jarritos sodas to wash it down. It also has a surprisingly appetizing lunch buffet 11 A.M.–2 P.M. Look for it in a half-empty strip mall a bit out of the center on the west side.

Both a meal and a sightseeing opportunity, the **Sale Barn Café** (900 N. Garden St., 575/622-1279, 7 A.M.–2 P.M. Mon.–Thurs., 9 A.M.–2 P.M. Fri., $7) sits alongside the Roswell Livestock Auction. If you go on a Monday morning, you can watch cattle get sold off, which will either improve or kill your appetite, depending on your outlook. The menu is straight-up diner-style New Mexican, plus a tasty pecan crumble, and an excellent cross-section of characters walking through. On Mondays, closing time is really whenever the auctions end.

For dinner, **Peppers** (500 N. Main St., 575/623-1700, 11 A.M.–10 P.M. Mon.–Sat., $10) is one of the most popular restaurants in town. It feels a bit like a family-owned Chili's, with an all-over-the-place menu. It's strongest on meat, from fajitas to baby-back ribs, but there's also a good vegetarian burrito and some other solid New Mexican dishes. Wash it all down with a microbrew and get a seat on the patio if you can.

THE SOUTHEAST

For solid red-sauce Italian, **Pasta Café** (109 W. 12th St., 575/624-2319, 11 A.M.–9:30 P.M. Sun.–Thurs., 11 A.M.–10:30 P.M. Fri. and Sat., $11) does the job. Despite the name, the place is a bit more formal than a café, and the menu's not just pasta—it also has well-executed favorites like a delectably light eggplant Parmesan. It's also one of the only good places in town open for dinner on a Sunday night.

## INFORMATION AND SERVICES

The **Roswell Convention & Visitors Bureau** (912 N. Main St., 575/624-7704, 8:30 A.M.–5 P.M. Mon.–Fri., 8:30 A.M.–4 P.M. Sat., 9 A.M.–3 P.M. Sun.) has info on all parts of the state and offers free wireless Internet access.

## GETTING THERE AND AROUND

**American Airlines** (800/443-7300, www. aa.com) operates one flight daily from Los Angeles to Roswell (ROW). The airport is five miles south of town.

**Greyhound** (800/231-2222, www.grey-hound.com) runs one bus a day from Las Cruces to the station (1100 N. Virginia Ave., 575/622-2510, 8 A.M.–4 P.M. Mon.–Fri., 11:30 A.M.–3:30 P.M. Sat.); from Albuquerque, you must go as far as Amarillo to transfer.

Roswell has a surprisingly good bus system, **Pecos Trails Transit** (575/624-6766, www. roswell-nm.gov/pecostrails.htm). The most useful bus for visitors is no. 1, which runs up and down Main Street roughly every half hour; the no. 2 bus runs east–west along 2nd Street. Fare is $0.75.

# Carlsbad

Tourists rarely hear the word Carlsbad without "caverns" tacked on the end, which means that few people come to see the town itself (the national park is 30 miles farther down U.S. 62/180). But the place is pleasant, thanks to an orderly plan laid out in 1888 and the Pecos River rolling through the middle in a broad blue ribbon. Shaded with big old trees, the river makes a great place to swim in the summer. You'll be excused if you make a beeline for the caves, though.

## SIGHTS

Canal Street may be the big north–south route now, but the historic main drag was Canyon Street, which still has a few cute shops, galleries, and antiques stores, as well as a pueblo revival courthouse, its front door bordered with cattle brands. The main landmark in town is the Pecos River, which glides along the east side, wide and deep. On the north edge, the **Pecos River Flume** is a serious bit of engineering to bring irrigation water to farm plots, erected in wood in 1890 then rebuilt more

permanently in 1903, making it the largest concrete structure in the world at the time.

## Carlsbad Museum & Art Center

The town's surprisingly good museum (418 W. Fox St., 575/887-0276, 10 A.M.–5 P.M. Mon.–Sat., free) holds a small trove of excellent Southwestern art, including some beautiful pieces by Ernest Blumenschein and other early Taos painters. There's also a few early photographs of the caverns, a real stagecoach, and lots of pottery.

## Living Desert State Park

Immediately north of Carlsbad on U.S. 285, this zoo and gardens (575/887-5516, www. nmparks.com, 8 A.M.–5 P.M. daily June–Aug., 9 A.M.–5 P.M. daily Sept.–May, $5) is a great place to familiarize yourself with the habitat in this area. Planted with all manner of endemic cactus, grasses, and yucca, the place also keeps quite a few native animals in cages, so you can get an up-close look at elk, peccary, and even bobcats and a black bear with a penchant for

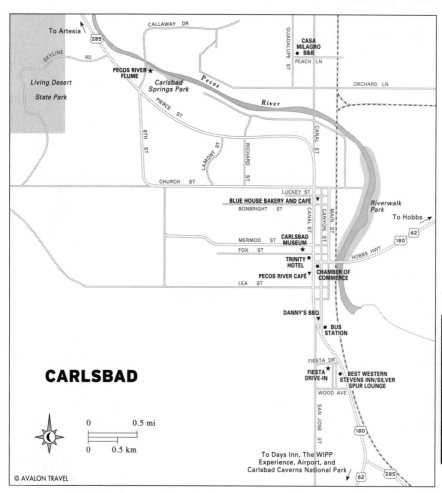

painting. They're all rescue animals, which is generally a positive thing, but they can still look a little forlorn, as they're usually alone in their pens. Note that the last entrance is an hour and a half before closing time.

## ENTERTAINMENT
In the summer, hit the drive-in; in the winter, cruise the Pecos.

### Nightlife
The three-screen **Fiesta Drive-In** (401 W. Fiesta Dr., 575/885-4126, www.fiestadrivein. com) still draws crowds to first-run movies year-round. Fully renovated in 2004, it's fairly high-tech for an outdoor cinema, and the concessions stand includes burgers and fries, in addition to the usual popcorn and candy.

As for bars, **Trinity Hotel** (201 S. Canal St., 575/234-9891, 5–10 P.M. Mon.–Sat.) is a popular gathering place, with a long wood bar in a high-ceiling room. Only beer, wine (most from around New Mexico), and faux cocktails are served, but there's a good selection

## HOT ROCKS IN CARLSBAD

When many New Mexicans think of Carlsbad, they think of an entirely different sort of cave from the ones preserved in the national park here. More than 2,000 feet below ground is a vast, deep salt bed into which massive halls have been carved. This is the Waste Isolation Pilot Plant, a nuclear waste dump that opened in 1999.

Bitterly fought from the day it was proposed in 1979, the site became a symbol of a strange sort of New Mexican fatalism: Judging from decades of prior oafishness, corner-cutting, and corruption, most people believed New Mexican leaders were just too incompetent to pull off such a tricky, potentially dangerous operation. Fortunately, over more than a decade in operation, WIPP hasn't seen any major glitches.

It helps that the salt caves are meant to contain low-level waste, such as contaminated lab suits and rubber gloves from Los Alamos National Labs. But now, because the site has been deemed a success, one state senator is proposing it also receive higher-level radioactive waste, such as that destined for the now-shuttered Yucca Mountain site in Nevada. The idea has geologists and state residents worried that this "hot" material will cause the salt to erode and lead to leaks.

While this debate rages, the state still runs a chipper little exhibit about the current operation, **The WIPP Experience** (4021 National Parks Hwy., 800/336-WIPP, 8:30 A.M.-3:30 P.M. Mon.-Thurs., free), which involves a video and (yippee) free salt samples.

of snacks to go alongside. For a rowdier night out, the **Silver Spur Lounge** (1829 S. Canal St., 575/887-2851), in the Best Western Stevens Inn, is the place to go for live country music, free snacks during happy hour (4–7 P.M.), and big-screen TV.

### Special Events

If you're in Carlsbad in the winter, don't miss **Christmas on the Pecos** (575/887-6516, www.christmasonthepecos.com, $12.50 Sun.–Thurs., $17.50 Fri. and Sat.), an extravaganza of twinkling lights, leaping reindeer, and even glowing margarita glasses all strung across more than a hundred homes on either side of the river. You view the spectacle from a pontoon boat gliding along the water; the whole ride takes about an hour. The city has obligingly extended the "Christmas" season from Thanksgiving to New Year's Eve, and you should book tickets in advance, especially for weekend tours.

## SPORTS AND RECREATION

Essential when the temperature climbs above 90°F in the summer, Carlsbad offers a number of ways to cool off in the water.

### Pecos River

As soon as winter's light chill lifts, all of Carlsbad turns its attention to the Pecos River. The great **Beach Recreation Area,** at the end of Church Street, is essentially the city's public pool, with protected swimming areas, a little island for diving, and even a few palm trees and seagulls (migrants from the Gulf of Mexico), to lend an authentic beachfront feel. With **Carlsbad Cruise Lines** (575/302-7997), you can rent pedal boats and kayaks ($12/hour) or take a cruise on an old-fashioned paddle-wheel riverboat ($5). A **river walk** runs 4.5 miles along the water on both banks.

### Sitting Bull Falls

West of town, this 130-foot cascade (8 A.M.–5:30 P.M. daily April–Sept., 8:30 A.M.–4:30 P.M. Oct.–Mar., $5/car) is a nice spot for an easy hike on a paved path, a picnic, and a dip in the small, icy pool. Sixteen miles of dirt trails also wind through the area. There are two access points: 7 miles south of Carlsbad, turn on County Road 409, or 12 miles north of town, turn on Highway 137. Either way, the drive takes about 45 minutes from the highway.

© ZORA O'NEILL

Sitting Bull Falls

## ACCOMMODATIONS

Because they have a captive clientele in the half-million visitors to the caverns every year, the hotel scene in Carlsbad is bleak. Rooms are high-priced for what you get, and unfortunately, none of the independents are good (with the exception of the high-end historic hotel). Just about all hotels are on the southern end of Canal Street and its continuation, National Parks Highway (U.S. 62/180), for an easy start on the drive to the caverns. You might want to consider staying in Artesia—although you'll have to allot an extra hour's driving time.

### Under $100

**Days Inn** (3910 National Parks Hwy., 575/887-7800, $56 s, $72 d) has everything you need, including cushy beds and an indoor pool. Bathrooms are small but clean, and everything's very well kept up. Rates include a basic continental breakfast.

### $100-150

The **Best Western Stevens Inn Carlsbad** (1829 S. Canal St., 575/887-2851, www.bestwestern.com, $110 d) is a warren of 220 rooms in a range of classes, and maintenance isn't airtight, but overall it's reliable. With their newer furniture, the junior suites are worth the extra $10 or so; there's a small pool on the premises.

Out on the fringes of town, where the lots are larger and horses graze, **Casa Milagro** (1612 N. Guadalupe St., 575/887-2188, www.casa-milagro-nm.com, $105 d) is set in a big old whitewashed farmhouse surrounded by tall shade trees. The rooms are a bit creaky and snug and not entirely new-looking (and only one has a private bath), but the rural surroundings are relaxing—a good option if you can't face another chain hotel. Full breakfast is included, and there's an option of dinner too.

Opened in late 2009, **Trinity Hotel & Suites** (201 S. Canal St., 575/234-9891, www.thetrinityhotel.com, $129 s) is the revival of a stately old bank building downtown, and a welcome addition to Carlsbad's otherwise dreary hotel scene. Despite the historic vibe, rooms are thoroughly modern, with sleek black furniture and all the tech trimmings, offset by the occasional exposed brick wall. One of the suites ($199) even has a whirlpool tub on an outside porch. Prices seem steep, but they're barely a notch above the top-end chain hotels; room layouts (most with just one bed) are best for couples.

## FOOD

As with hotels, Carlsbad isn't bursting with choice—the best options are open only for lunch. Most places are on or very near Canal Street.

Even if you intend just to pop in for a quick coffee and morning pastry, you might find yourself spending hours at the ◖ **Blue House Bakery & Café** (609 N. Canyon St., 575/628-0555, 6 A.M.–1 P.M. Tues.–Fri., 6 A.M.–noon Sat. and Mon., $6). The atmosphere in the sunny, brightly painted place (which really is a house on a quiet block) is relaxing and familiar. The menu ranges from homemade granola to daily soups and sandwiches.

**Pecos River Café** (409 S. Canal St., 575/887-8882, 6:30 A.M.–2 P.M. Mon.–Fri., $8) is better than its architecture (a former Pizza Hut) might suggest. Thanks to its spicy green-chile enchiladas and other New Mexican platters, it's packed at lunch—go early or late to skip the rush.

The eponymous owner of ◖ **Danny's Place BBQ** (902 S. Canal St., 575/885-8739, 11 A.M.–9 P.M. Wed.–Mon., $10) is obsessive, in a good way. He earned himself a reputation for quality 'cue while operating a pit off the side of the Dairy Queen he managed. Now he has his own spot, with nothing on the menu but smoked meat in a sweet-hot sauce (though the meat's so succulent, it's fine plain). There are the usual sides, including some great bacony pinto beans.

For a slightly dressed-up dinner scene, the **Trinity Hotel Restaurant** (201 S. Canal St., 575/234-9891, 7 A.M.–2 P.M. and 5–9 P.M. Mon.–Sat., 8 A.M.–2 P.M. Sun., $14) has a familiar menu of pastas and steaks at dinner, and a mix of sandwiches for lunch. It doesn't break any new ground, but it's better than a chain restaurant, and the split-level, wood-floor dining room is elegant and buzzing with conversation. Breakfast is also good, with fresh pastries and sun shining in through the big front windows.

## INFORMATION AND SERVICES

Stop in at the **Carlsbad Chamber of Commerce** (302 S. Canal St., 575/887-6516, www.carlsbadchamber.com, 9 A.M.–5 P.M. Mon., 8 A.M.–5 P.M. Tues.–Fri.) for a visitors guide and a detailed map.

## GETTING THERE

**Greyhound** (800/231-2222, www.greyhound.com) buses come through from El Paso, Texas, once a day, stopping at Food Jet (3102 National Parks Hwy., 575/628-0768, 5 A.M.–midnight daily).

**New Mexico Airlines** (888/564-6119, www.flynma.com) flies in to Carlsbad airport (CNM) from Albuquerque, on three flights daily. The airport is south of town on U.S. 62/180.

# Carlsbad Caverns National Park

One of the country's most awesome natural wonders, Carlsbad Caverns (575/785-3137, www.nps.gov/cave, $6) is mesmerizing even in the basic two-hour stroll around the biggest cavern. But you could easily spend days here (your entrance ticket is good for three), visiting ever more obscure underground worlds.

The park is 23 miles south of the town of Carlsbad and seven miles in on a winding access road. In prime conditions, it takes about 45 minutes to get to the **visitors center** (727 Carlsbad Caverns Hwy., 8 A.M.–7 P.M. daily June–Aug., 8 A.M.–5 P.M. daily Sept.–May). But as of 2010, the parking lots and roads were being repaved, which required the use of a shuttle bus for the last portion, from the intersection at the highway (a tourist-trap "town" called White's City). The project will likely be completed in 2011—check the website for notices of possible delays.

If you're visiting in the peak summer months, allow an extra hour's waiting time at the vistors center. Probably the best time to go is in December, before the holidays, or in January and February, because you'll have the whole place to yourself, and the caverns take on a perfectly ghostly silence. In summer, though, you get to see hundreds of thousands of bats fly out every evening, and the 56°F temperature underground is a treat.

Always pack a sweater, no matter how hot it is outside, and wear sturdy shoes, even if you're only going on the main self-guided tours. You might want to pack a lunch too, as the cafeteria at the caverns is pretty institutional. Fill your gas tank in Carlsbad, as once you head

© NEW MEXICO TOURISM DEPARTMENT/DAN MONAGHAN

**the hiking entrance to Carlsbad Caverns**

south you're at the mercy of one pricey station in White's City.

## ◖ THE BIG ROOM

The basic entrance ticket gives you access to two major parts of the cave: the **Natural Entrance Trail** (last entrance 3:30 P.M. daily June–Aug., 2 P.M. daily Sept.–May), which descends about 800 feet in the course of a mile, on a paved trail dense with switchbacks, and The Big Room (last entrance 5 P.M. daily June–Aug., 3:30 P.M. daily Sept.–May), the largest cave in the Carlsbad complex. If you don't feel up to hiking down (or don't have the time), an elevator will whisk you straight to the cavern floor, in a 754-foot trip that will make your ears pop. Instead of floors, the elevator display shows 50-foot increments. The walk down is recommended, though, as it gives you a better sense of what it must have been like for cowboy Jim White to first explore this place in the early 20th century. It also gives an idea of the scale you'll be dealing with once you get underground—at one point, you have to hike around Iceberg Rock, a 200,000-ton boulder

that fell a few hundred thousand years ago, and that accounts for about a third of the 1.5-hour-long trek. (Note that you're only permitted to hike down the Natural Entrance Trail, and not up.)

Don't expect the lurid colored lights you see in many "show caves"—since the late 1970s, The Big Room has been lit in tasteful white lights. (But it's not all natural—there's still a snack bar down on the cave floor, as well as restrooms, discreetly hidden behind rock formations.) It's no less impressive for the make-under: "Big" doesn't even begin to describe the scope of the place, which soars above you like a cathedral and off into the distance for more than 1.25 miles. If you think of caves as claustrophobia-inducing, this one will change your mind.

Scientists theorize that The Big Room—and many of the other caverns in this network—began to form more than 20 million years ago, as the petroleum deposits under the Guadalupe Mountains reacted with groundwater to create sulfuric acid, which ate through the stone to form vast hollow spots under the ground.

THE SOUTHEAST

# GUIDED TOURS IN CARLSBAD CAVERNS

Double-check schedules at www.nps.gov/cave.

| Tour | Cost | Duration | Length | Age Limit | Schedule |
|---|---|---|---|---|---|
| King's Palace | $8 | 1.5 hours | 1 mile | 4 and up | Summer: 10 A.M., 11 A.M., noon, 2 P.M., 3 P.M. Winter: 10 A.M. and 2 P.M. |
| Left Hand Tunnel | $7 | 2 hours | .5 mile | 6 and up | 9 A.M. daily |
| Lower Cave | $20 | 3 hours | – | 12 and up | 1 P.M. Mon.–Fri. |
| Slaughter Canyon Cave | $15 | 2 hours, plus driving time | 1.25 miles, plus 0.5 mile steep hike to entrance | 8 and up | Summer: 10 A.M. daily Winter: 10 A.M. Sat. and Sun. |
| Hall of the White Giant | $20 | 4 hours | – | 12 and up | 1 P.M. Sat. |
| Spider Cave | $20 | 4 hours | – | 12 and up | 1 P.M. Sun. |

These spaces began to fill with stalagmites and stalactites about 500,000 years ago, and now the delicate formations—still growing in some parts of the caverns—are a wonderland of shapes, from hulking towers that ripple like clay to delicate needles that look more like icicles than stone.

For both routes, you can rent an **audio tour** for $3—it includes some interesting information, but don't get too caught up in listening to every entry. It's much more rewarding just to look and let your imagination roam.

## RANGER-LED TOURS

Especially in the summertime, you may want to join one of the side tours, for which the number of visitors is capped. They cost extra, but they're a chance to enjoy a little more quiet and, of course, see a lot more of the caverns. You should try to decide before you arrive whether you want to take any of these tours. Reservations (877/444-6777, www.recreation.gov) are recommended at peak times, and even

on crowd-free days, if you'd like to see more once you're down in the Big Room, then you have to come back up to the surface to buy the extra ticket.

The easiest addition to your itinerary, **King's Palace** is the deepest part of the caves open to the public. Limited to 75 participants, the tour passes giant formations as well as tiny details such as a bat's skeleton grown into a stalagmite. Best of all, it includes a few minutes with the lights turned off, when you get to stand in the cool, smothering black. Like the Big Room walk (but unlike all the other ranger-led tours), the trail is paved and not particularly steep except at the entrance.

For sheer sense of discovery, **Left Hand Tunnel** is a must. On the trek, limited to 15 people, you carry just a flickering lantern through fantastic rock formations—made all the more bizarre as they loom up out of the darkness in front of you. **Lower Cave** requires a bit more exertion, starting with a clamber down 50 feet of rope and very sketchy-feeling ladders—great fun for some, but a deal-breaker for others. The formations here include toothpick-like stalactites and the perfectly round and white formations called "cave pearls."

**Slaughter Canyon Cave** is the only cave that's not accessible through the visitors center. Instead, you have to drive five miles south of White's City, then turn west onto a well-signed county road; allow 45 minutes' drive time from the visitors center. Once in the cave, though, the walk isn't too difficult and it goes past formations like the glittering, crystal-covered column dubbed the Christmas Tree.

Finally, for people who aren't afraid of tight spaces, **Hall of the White Giant** and **Spider Cave** are strenuous but rewarding trips. Each one takes about four hours, and you have to bring batteries and gloves (the rangers provide headlamps and helmets). Expect to wiggle through some very narrow tunnels and get muddy in the process.

### BAT FLIGHTS

From late May through mid-October, twilight at Carlsbad is marked by an exodus of bats rushing out from the depths of the caverns and into the bug-filled night. At their peak in July and August, about 400,000 of the critters fly out each evening. Half an hour before sunset at an amphitheater at the top of the Natural Entrance Trail, rangers give a short talk about the bats (ask at the visitors center or call 575/785-3012 for times). When the bats pour out, you hear the soft flapping of their wings and feel the rush of air as they pass overhead. If you're an early riser, you can also come at dawn (well before the visitors center is open) to see the bats return to the cave.

Most are of the Brazilian free-tail variety, which migrate to Mexico in the winter. Another group of larger cave *Myotis* live in the Lake of the Clouds, the deepest point in the cave system; they too come out every night, and if you're at the underground cafeteria near closing time, you might feel them whir through. Whether you're underground or at the amphitheater, keep your camera stowed—the flash and auto-focus devices disorient the animals.

### ABOVE GROUND

Although the park's main attraction is underground, the regular scenery isn't bad either—especially when you look up at night. Throughout the summer, the park hosts **Star Party** events, with rangers on hand with telescopes—check the park website (www.nps.gov/cave) for schedules.

You can also explore the desert landscape along hiking trails or the 9.5-mile gravel **Walnut Canyon Desert Drive,** starting at the visitors center parking lot. Get free backcountry permits and topo maps at the visitors center.

### WHITE'S CITY

This so-called town at the junction of U.S. 62/180 and Highway 7 is just an unreconstructed tourist trap—there's a bad restaurant, two dumpy hotels, a wildly overpriced gas station, and a junk-filled gift shop. You might want to blindfold or at least distract your kids as you drive past the giant water slide (for hotel guests only), or you'll never hear the end of it. The **Greyhound** bus can be prevailed upon to pull up here, though it's not a regularly scheduled stop.

### GUADALUPE MOUNTAINS NATIONAL PARK

Adjacent to the caverns land and just over the border in Texas, Guadalupe Mountains National Park (915/828-3251, www.nps.gov/gumo, $5) is mentioned here because it's where people usually camp ($8) when visiting Carlsbad Caverns. The largest area, with both tent and RV sites (but no hookups), is **Pine Springs Campground,** near the visitors center, about 35 miles south of White's City on U.S. 62/180.

You can also **hike** the exceptionally scenic **McKittrick Canyon,** where a 6.8-mile out-and-back trail leads through a narrow limestone canyon thick with deciduous trees—truly stunning in late October, when the leaves turn, though often crowded. If it's too mobbed, try the 4.2-mile **Devil's Hall Trail,** which starts at Pine Springs Campground, for a similar canyon-bottom route.

# Cloudcroft

The closest bit of high altitude to the Texas flatlands, the Sacramento Mountains draw vacationers with a drawl, and have been doing so since 1899, when a local railroad man built a resort at Cloudcroft, now accessible by U.S. 82 due west of Artesia. The village of Cloudcroft is still barely more than a cluster of rustic cabins with a few gift shops in between—but the view from up here, looking down as far as White Sands, is incredible, especially when the clouds are gathering below you. The view straight up is great too—hence the location of a major solar observatory nearby.

## SIGHTS

The main street in town is Burro Avenue, just north of U.S. 82—here's where you'll find a row of Old West–style false-front buildings along a wooden boardwalk. The whole town is so small you can easily walk everywhere.

Cloudcroft's creaky wooden boardwalk runs along Chipmunk Avenue.

## Sacramento Mountains Historical Museum

Across the street from the chamber of commerce, the local museum (U.S. 82, 575/682-2932, 10 A.M.–4 P.M. Mon., Tues., Fri., and Sat., 1–4 P.M. Sun. in summer, 10 A.M.–4 P.M. Fri. and Sat. in winter, $5) is the usual assortment of memorabilia from the past, plus a "pioneer village" made up several old log cabins, furnished with antique tools and furniture.

## Sunspot

Sixteen miles south of Cloudcroft on Highway 6563 (geekily named for the wavelength of the orange-red light we associate with images of the sun; most people call it Sunspot Highway), Sunspot National Solar Observatory and privately owned Apache Point Observatory take advantage of the high altitude and clear skies to spy on the solar system. Visitors can wander around on their own or, on Saturdays and Sundays in summer, join the guided tour at 2 P.M. at the Sunspot visitors center (575/434-7190, 9 A.M.–5 P.M. daily Mar.–Jan.). On your way up here, you'll pass **Karr Canyon,** another nice place for a picnic.

## SPORTS AND RECREATION

Cloudcroft has a lot to do year-round. As long as you're adjusted to the altitude, the hiking trails are not too strenuous. Check current conditions with the **Sacramento Ranger District office** (4 Lost Lodge Rd., 575/682-2551, 7:30 A.M.–4:30 P.M. Mon.–Fri.).

## Winter Sports

Two miles east of town on U.S. 82, **Ski Cloudcroft,** sometimes called Snow Canyon (575/682-2333, www.skicloudcroft.net, $35 full-day lift ticket), is a ski area with a separate tubing area; it's a modest, not-too-challenging hill. There's more reliable fun in town, with **ice skating** (575/682-4585) on a rink at the west end of Zenith Park, and tubing all over the hills. For a little more room to frolic, head up Highway 6563 to **Triple M Snowplay Area** (575/682-2205, www.triplemsnowplay.com), which even has a small lift to drag tubers back up the hill—it's $20 for a full-day pass with tube rental. Many of the town's rail trails are good for **cross-country skiing.**

## Hiking

The old railroad that used to zigzag up the mountain is gone, but the railbed makes for excellent hiking on the well-maintained **Cloud-Climbing Rail Trail.** The **Mexican Canyon Loop** is probably the best introduction—it's just 2.5 miles and leads to the picturesque (and vertigo-inducing) Mexican Canyon Trestle, built in 1899. The trail starts on the west edge of town, off the south side of the road, where a replica of the original train depot stands. For a map on the rest of the rails-to-trails network, stop in at the chamber of commerce.

Another popular route is **Osha Trail** (no. 10), maintained by the National Forest Service. It runs three miles through relatively level, shaded forest that's especially pretty when the leaves change in the fall. The trailhead is west of town, on the opposite side of the road from the Mexican Canyon trestle.

## Mountain Biking

The 28-mile **Rim Trail** is legendary for its amazing views as it winds along the spine of the mountains, roughly parallel to Sunspot Highway (Hwy. 6563). It's intermediate difficulty, climbing about a thousand feet over the course of the whole ride, though it has some zippy downhill sections, as well as some jarring rocky terrain. Only the first 13 or so miles are official Forest Service trail (no. 105), but it runs all the way to Sunspot, then down to Forest Road 90 to the southeast; you can cut in at the observatory and take the paved road back downhill. The trailhead is just off Highway 6563—look for parking on the right side almost immediately after you make the turn from Highway 130.

A handful of other loop trails start in town and nearby. Stop in at the chamber of commerce or the exceptionally helpful **High Altitude** (310 Burro Ave., 575/682-1229, 10 A.M.–5:30 P.M. Mon.–Thurs., 10 A.M.–6 P.M. Fri. and Sat.), a shop that also organizes a race every April, for maps and other guidance.

## ACCOMMODATIONS

The main type of accommodation in town is the guest cabin, though you don't have quite the same choice as in Ruidoso. Location isn't too essential, considering how small the town is.

### Under $100

Halfway down the mountain on the way to Tularosa, the excellent **❖ Cloudcroft Mountain Park Hostel** (1049 U.S. 82, 575/682-0555, www.cloudcrofthostel.com) has three rooms with eight bunks each ($17 pp), as well as two basic private rooms ($30) and one big family room ($50), all with access to shared baths and a big common area and kitchen. Everything's clean and colorfully painted, with a casual but orderly atmosphere.

**Summit Inn** (Chipmunk Ave. at Curlew Pl., 575/682-2814, www.summitinn-nm.com, $55 s, $72 d) has clean and airy rooms, with tiny kitchenettes, vintage TVs, and showers (no tubs). Don't bother with the cabins, though—they're relatively expensive and short on charm.

At the east end of town, **Spruce Cabins** (100 Lynx Ave., 575/682-2381, www.sprucecabins. com, $75 d) are pleasant enough standalone apartments with a faintly rustic feel—some elements of the decor veer toward 1970s mobile home, but that's offset by attractive quilts on the beds and cozy wood-burning fireplaces.

Smack in the center of town, **Cloudcroft Hotel** (306 Burro Ave., 575/682-3414, www. cloudcrofthotel.com, $80 s, $95 d) is affordable and very well kept. Each of the eight rooms is carefully decorated and fastidiously clean; all have claw-foot tubs and lots of pine paneling. There are a couple of odd rooms that don't have interior windows—potentially dreary, but a bargain if you're going to be spending the days outside, and a bit quieter than those on the front of the building (though room no. 1, with access to the front balcony, is a gem).

**Burro Street Boardinghouse** (608 Burro Ave., 575/682-3601, $89) has just three rooms, but each one is very nicely done, with choice antiques and details like vanity sinks. The building is a big, airy pine-paneled A-frame, and the owner is an old Cloudcroft hand. She also operates **The Crofting B&B** (300 Swallow Pl., 575/682-3604, www.cloudcroft.com/crafting, $89 d), a larger house that's usually un-hosted—nice if you want to have a place more to yourself. Some of the upstairs rooms here have little balconies.

## $100-150

At the top of the hill—and the top of the price range—**The Lodge** (601 Corona Pl., 800/395-6343, www.thelodgeresort.com, $115 s, $145 d) is a fairly well-restored relic from the early railroad era. The current structure, with its vaguely Tyrolean look, was built in 1911 by the Alamogordo & Sacramento Railway, to re-place a 1901 lodge that burned down. The 58 rooms range from fairly small standard queens to more lavish suites—each furnished with custom drapes and other details. With lots of chintz, brocade, and dark wood, the over-all effect may be historically accurate, but the rooms can feel cramped. Rooms in the Retreat wing ($315 d) are newer construction and have fireplaces and whirlpool tubs. Down the hill, the Pavilion is the oldest section, a large wood cabin with a wraparound porch—the rooms

here are a bit more rustic, and rates (from $135) include breakfast at Rebecca's, the resort's main restaurant.

## FOOD

Cloudcroft's unofficial social center, the **Western Bar & Café** (304 Burro Ave., 575/682-9910, 6 a.m.–9 p.m. daily, $7) sat-isfies just about every social need, whether you want a breakfast omelette, a cold beer, or a crazy night of karaoke (the bar is open till 11 p.m. during the week and 1 a.m. on Friday and Saturday). The vibe is friendly and the crowd is eclectic.

There are a couple of other places on Burro Avenue for sandwiches, and **Rebecca's** (575/682-2566, 7–10:30 a.m., 11:30 a.m.–2:30 p.m., and 5:30–9 p.m. Mon.–Sat., 7 a.m.–2 p.m. Sun.), at The Lodge, is good for historic ambience, though the prices for fancy sandwiches and steaks are a little high (about $12 at lunch, $24 and up at dinner). You can stop in at the lounge, open throughout the af-ternoon, and have just a drink and a snack.

## INFORMATION

Cloudcroft's **chamber of commerce** (U.S. 82, 866/874-4447, www.cloudcroft.net, 10 a.m.–5 p.m. Mon.–Sat.) occupies a tiny cabin on the east side of town. Despite the cramped quarters, it has just about any info on the town you could need.

# Alamogordo

For most visitors, Alamogordo functions as the gateway to the stunning White Sands National Monument, the largest field of pure gypsum in the world. It also has a couple of interesting sights of its own, though people seldom plan a trip around them. Founded in 1899 as a railroad stop, the town has been shaped more by the early space industry and Holloman Air Force Base, which also trains German pilots. It fits between the railroad tracks and the foothills of the Sacramento Mountains, with some 35,000 residents in a low-rise sprawl—though it feels much smaller than this.

## SIGHTS

Navigating Alamogordo is straightforward: Almost everything is located on or very near White Sands Boulevard (U.S. 54/70), which runs roughly north–south through town. New York Avenue, one block east, is Alamogordo's historic downtown, though there's very little of it left—it runs for just a couple of blocks south

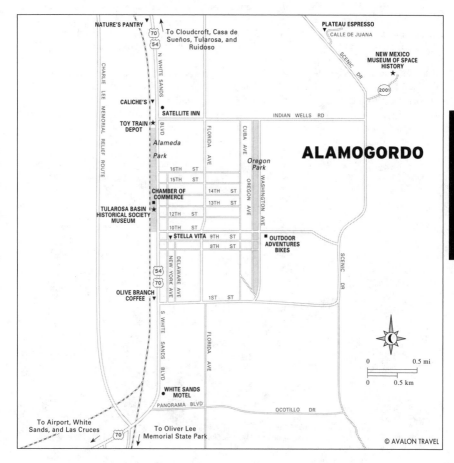

© AVALON TRAVEL

of 10th Street. The space museum is far up in the foothills, but it's easy to find your way, as it's visible from a long way off.

## New Mexico Museum of Space History

This state-run museum (1100 Oregon Ave., 575/437-2840, www.spacefame.org, 9 A.M.–5 P.M. daily, $6) began in 1976 as a hall of fame for astronauts, including the first chimpanzee in space, who's buried here. Then it morphed into this comprehensive look at space exploration—which in many ways got its start through rocket tests in the Tularosa Basin below. Working your way down through four floors, you pass assorted relics from the space race, a chunk of moon rock, and more. But perhaps the most interesting items are those that hint at what everyday life in zero gravity is like, such as the space station interior model and a space-flight hygiene kit. Overall, it's a surprisingly un-high-tech museum, both in the way things are displayed and in the items themselves. The cobbled-together rockets and

patched-up spacesuits serve as a reminder just how mechanical and hardware-driven space exploration has been—not a sleek, digital process at all.

The current state of space exploration looks a little slicker: The bottom floor of the museum is devoted to the X Prize, which encourages commercial space flight, and a hangar outside contains a model of the first winner: glossy, bulbous SpaceShipOne, covered in corporate-sponsor logos. Next to it, a 1940s accelerator for testing G-forces looks brutally primitive.

## Toy Train Depot

You can't miss Alamogordo's nifty miniature train: It runs straight through town, parallel to White Sands Boulevard. The northern endpoint is the Toy Train Depot (1991 N. White Sands Blvd., 575/437-2855, noon–4:30 P.M. Wed.–Sun., $4, plus $4 for train ride), the model-train collection of a retired rocket scientist; one of the layouts shows the old route up to Cloudcroft. But the real fun is outside on the larger-scale tracks. The museum has two

THE SOUTHEAST

rockets at the New Mexico Museum of Space History

© ZORA O'NEILL

trains that run kids down to Alameda Park and back, plus a smaller-gauge one that runs loops around the yard—kids might get to drive it themselves, if they're well behaved.

## Tularosa Basin Historical Society Museum

This is a very grand name for the usual assortment of pioneer gear and old furniture (1301 N. White Sands Blvd., 575/434-4438, 10 A.M.–4 P.M. Mon.–Fri., 10 A.M.–3 P.M. Sat., 1–3 P.M. Sun., free). The highlight of the collection is an American flag with 47 stars; there's also some information about Trinity Site, as well as the older Hispano community of La Luz, just north of Alamogordo.

## Alameda Park and Zoo

Just behind the museum and to the south, the oldest zoo (1321 N. White Sands Blvd., 575/439-4290, 9 A.M.–5 P.M. daily, $2.50) in the Southwest has about 90 species on view, including some frisky otters and even some kangaroos, which don't look too out of place in this desert. There's also a nice shaded picnic area inside.

## SPORTS AND RECREATION

Most of the good hiking and mountain-biking trails are farther up the mountains near Cloudcroft. For general info on trails and other recreation on the desert floor, stop in at the **Lincoln National Forest supervisor's office** (3463 Las Palomas Rd., 575/434-7200, 7:30 A.M.–4:30 P.M.) or **Outdoor Adventures Bikes & Sports** (1516 10th St., 575/434-1920, 10 A.M.–6 P.M. Mon.–Fri., 10 A.M.–5 P.M. Sat.), where you can also rent gear.

### Hiking

The one big rec area nearby is **Oliver Lee Memorial State Park** (409 Dog Canyon Rd., 575/437-8284, www.nmparks.com, $5/car), 12 miles south of Alamogordo. After you've been to White Sands, it's hard to muster the energy to hike in the regular old desert, but lush Dog Canyon has water all year-round, making it a pretty green oasis where you'll see everything from moss to orchids growing, if you look closely. The 5.5-mile **Dog Canyon Recreational Trail** begins at the visitors center and heads up to a ridge with great views of the desert basin—a very strenuous climb, with an elevation gain of 3,100 feet. Many hikers just go about 2.5 miles in to a stone cowboy cabin, then turn around. There are also more than 40 developed **campsites** here ($8–14)—the closest car-camping option to White Sands National Monument.

## ACCOMMODATIONS

A rare case in which an eye-catching sign actually points to quality lodging, **White Sands Motel** (1101 S. White Sands Blvd., 575/437-2922, $45 s, $50 d) is a tidy, old-fashioned little place—the rooms are snug, but they're kept clean, and many of them are set well back from the main road, so the traffic noise is slightly diminished. Rooms all have mini-fridges, microwaves, and wireless Internet. In the same price range, **Satellite Inn** (2224 N. White Sands Blvd., 575/437-8454, www.satelliteinn.com, $40 s, $50 d) is a bit more modern-feeling, if a little bland; amenities include Internet access and laundry facilities, and there's a small pool in the parking lot.

Your only other options are chain motels, and those are not entirely reliable—though at least the Holiday Inn Express is new.

## FOOD

It's slim pickings for distinctive dining in Alamogordo—and no surprise most people wind up eating at the chain restaurants on White Sands Boulevard.

### Coffee and Lunch

For your morning brew, head to **Olive Branch Coffee & Deli** (123 N. White Sands Blvd., 575/443-8151, 6 A.M.–6 P.M. Mon.–Sat., 7 A.M.–4 P.M. Sun.), which roasts its own beans and also dishes up basic breakfasts. If you need a pick-me-up after the Space Museum, **Plateau Espresso** (2724 N. Scenic Dr., 575/434-4466, 6 A.M.–10 P.M. Sun.–Thurs., 6 A.M.–11 P.M. Fri. and Sat.) will do the trick, while providing awesome views over the city from its patio.

For a healthy lunch, the deli counter at the back of **Nature's Pantry** (2909 N. White Sands Blvd., 575/437-3037, 8 A.M.–7 P.M. Mon.–Sat., $7) makes vegetarian-friendly wraps and sprout-stuffed sandwiches, which you can wash down with a shot of wheatgrass juice or a smoothie—a great antidote to standard roadside fare.

All matte gray and faux stone, **Stella Vita** (902 New York Ave., 575/434-4444, 11 A.M.–2 P.M. Mon.–Thurs., 11 A.M.–2 P.M. and 5–9 P.M. Fri., 5–9 P.M. Sat., $9) is by far the most stylish place in Alamogordo. The menu is slightly fancified Americana—think Applebee's, but nicer. At lunch, the menu is heavy on salads. At dinner (only two nights a week), you can get steaks and pork chops (about $20 per entrée). Service is very attentive.

## Dinner

It requires a 20-minute drive to the south edge of Tularosa, but for its *carne adovada* ribs alone, **€ Casa de Sueños** (35 St. Francis Dr., 575/585-3494, 10:30 A.M.–8 P.M. Mon.–Fri., 11 A.M.–8:30 P.M. Sat., 10:30 A.M.–8 P.M. Sun., $11) is worth the trek. This ingenious fusion of traditional New Mexican chile with barbecue savor is just one of several tasty (and very meaty) dishes on the menu. You can also get the usual enchiladas and rellenos, as well as burritos to go. And although it's just off the

west side of the highway, the ambience inside is warmly lit, with a pretty patio out back.

**Caliche's** (2251 N. White Sands Blvd., 575/439-1000, 11 A.M.–10 P.M. daily, $4) is an outpost of the frozen-custard specialist in Las Cruces. It's no balanced meal, but given the options in Alamogordo, you're excused if you have a thick shake for dinner.

## INFORMATION

The **Alamogordo Chamber of Commerce** (1301 N. White Sands Blvd., 575/437-6120, www.alamogordo.com, 8 A.M.–5 P.M. Mon.–Fri.) dispenses a very detailed free map, though its information on local businesses isn't always current.

## GETTING THERE AND AROUND

**Greyhound** (800/231-2222, www.greyhound. com) connects Alamogordo to Las Cruces once a day, stopping at the station (3500 N. White Sands Blvd., 575/437-3050, 7–11 A.M. and 4–8 P.M. Mon.–Fri., 7–9 A.M. and 5–8 P.M. Sat. and Sun.).

**New Mexico Airlines** (888/564-6119, www.flynma.com) runs two flights daily between Alamogordo Municipal Airport (ALM; 575/439-4110) and Albuquerque. El Paso (ELP) is 90 miles away.

**Enterprise** (400 N. White Sands Blvd., 575/434-9010, 8 A.M.–6 P.M. Mon.–Fri.) rents cars in this area.

# White Sands National Monument

White Sands (575/479-6124, www.nps.gov/whsa, $3), 275 square miles of blinding, shimmery gypsum, is a surreal and magnificent place. At every turn, you have to remind yourself what you're really looking at. In the summer, temperatures exceed 100°F, but the sand looks like no desert you've ever seen. On a cool winter day, especially after rainwater has pooled along the road, your brain can't stop thinking snow and ice. For the best photography, as well as a break from the heat, you'll probably want to visit either early or late in the day—but there is also something appropriately overwhelming about this featureless landscape at high noon.

Although the barren dunes at the core of the park are the most popular image of the place, there's a surprising amount of life here, from tiny kangaroo mice to the beleaguered tufts of skunkbush sumac that are the last holdouts as the sand shifts around them. A number of nature trails lead off the eight-mile-long **Dunes Drive,** and if you have time, you should definitely join one of the ranger-led walks—usually near sunset.

## VISITORS CENTER

Stop in at the pleasantly old-fashioned visitors center (8 A.M.–7 P.M. daily mid-Apr.–Aug., 8 A.M.–6 P.M. Mar.–mid-Apr. and Sept.–Oct., 9 A.M.–5 P.M. Nov.–Feb.) at the main gate to check the schedule of ranger tours and maybe pick up a plastic sled from the gift shop, for sliding down the dunes. Among the ranger outings is a car trip to **Lake Lucero** ($3 pp, reserve ahead), the crystal-filled lake bed that's the source of the sands, as well as the occasional full-moon **bicycle tour.** If you plan to do any backcountry hiking, you'll need to get a permit here ($3)—there's only one designated hike-in camping area, about a mile from the road, so check there's a vacancy.

© ZORA O'NEILL

White Sands National Monument

## DUNES DRIVE

Open 7 A.M. to sunset, the road leads from the shaggy, brush-covered hills at the edge of the white desert into the pure dunes at the center. In between is the transition area, where hills are being carved away by wind and yuccas teeter on lone sand pedestals. As long as you park in one of the designated pullouts, you're welcome to walk wherever you like, but make careful note of landmarks before you set out; even in the areas with lots of vegetation, it's easy to wind up walking in circles.

The first stop on the drive, **Playa Trail** runs 500 yards along the border where the gypsum meets the regular desert terrain, ending up at a playa, the term for a depression that forms a temporary lake after rainfall. These playas are all over White Sands (Lake Lucero is the largest), as well as in the desert areas of the rest of New Mexico. Of all the trails, this is probably the least remarkable—skip it if you're not planning to spend all day here.

The one-mile-long **Dune Life Nature Trail** does a quick loop up to the top of a dune and past the most typical types of vegetation. At least stop to pick up one of the trail guides, which can help you identify the animal tracks you'll see all over the dunes. The **Interdune Boardwalk** is another quick trail—a very easy way to check out some of the more common plants, without trudging through sand.

## ◖ HEART OF THE SANDS

This is the main destination inside the park. You can set up camp in one of the mod metal picnic shelters (which include grills), then go out to clamber, slip, and slide up and down the pristine white hills. (There are also restrooms out here, but no water.) The **Alkali Flat Trail** leads out from the end of the parking area—it's a 4.6-mile loop into the most austere part of the dunes, without a scrap of vegetation visible. This can be extremely disorienting once you're out of view of the parking lot—heed the stern warnings to turn back if you can't see the orange trail markers, which periodically get covered with sand. Allow about three hours for the whole hike, and be sure to register at the trailhead before you proceed.

# Ruidoso

North of Alamogordo and east on U.S. 70, Ruidoso (Noisy) is named for the audible stream that flows through a canyon in the center. Like Cloudcroft, it's a little spot of Texas in the high mountains and very much a resort town, dedicated to golf (there are five courses in the immediate area), horse racing in the summer, skiing on southern New Mexico's highest mountain in the winter, and shopping year-round. On the drive up on U.S. 70, you pass through the Mescalero Apache reservation, which was established in 1883 and occupies some 463,000 acres.

One of the more prosperous in the state, the tribe (which got its name from the Spanish, who remarked on its ritual use of peyote, or mescal) operates the ski area as well as a rather luxurious resort and casino, about 20 minutes' drive south of town.

## SIGHTS

The main drag of Ruidoso is Highway 48, which runs in an L along the two main streets, Sudderth and Mechem Drives. The town is divided into districts roughly between the major intersections. Midtown refers to the stretch of Sudderth Drive between Mechem Drive and Carrizo Canyon Road, and the highest concentration of gift shops and galleries housed in rustic pine cabins and gaily painted Victorians. Uptown is to the west, encompassing the businesses on Mechem Drive north of its intersection with Sudderth. Upper Canyon refers to Main Road—essentially, the western extension of Sudderth Drive where it winds up the river. At the west end of town, "The Y" is the junction of Highway 48 and U.S. 70, also referred to as downtown, with most of the

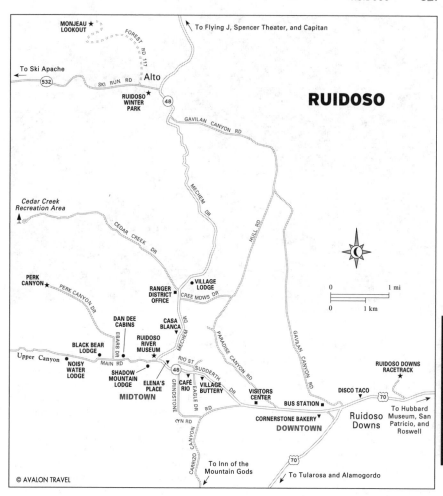

chain businesses. Farther east along U.S. 70, Ruidoso Downs is technically a separate town, but there is no physical gap between it and its neighbor.

## Hubbard Museum of the American West

Horse-lovers should head straight to this rambling museum (841 U.S. 70 W, 575/378-4142, www.hubbardmuseum.org, 9 A.M.–5 P.M. daily, $6), built around one woman's enormous collection of all things equine, from stirrups to saddles to stagecoaches. To round out the romance of the cowboy era, there's also a tribute to the famous quarter horses that have raced at Ruidoso Downs.

## Ruidoso River Museum

The only other official sight in town is this museum (101 Mechem Dr., 575/257-0296, www.ruidosorivermuseum.com, 10 A.M.–5 P.M. Thurs.–Mon., $5) that mixes the expected

© ZORA O'NEILL

**festive winter lights in midtown Ruidoso**

Lincoln County lore with odder items: a narwhal tusk, silverware from the *Titanic,* a glittery jacket once owned by Liberace, and one of Mother Theresa's rosaries, to name just a few. See it to believe it.

## ENTERTAINMENT

Midtown is the place to be at night, but the track is where the action is on weekend afternoons.

### Nightlife

For margaritas, **Casa Blanca** (501 Mechem Dr., 575/257-2495, 11 A.M.–10 P.M. daily) is the top spot, enhanced by a great patio surrounded by tall pines. After the first round of drinks and dinner, action usually moves to the two dueling mega-bars in Midtown: **The Quarters** (2535 Sudderth Dr., 575/257-9535) and **Win, Place and Show** (2516 Sudderth Dr., 575/257-9982), which play both kinds of music (that'd be country *and* western) to inspire some speedy two-stepping around the big dance floors. The Quarters also has pool tables.

### Gambling

Memorial Day through Labor Day, **Ruidoso Downs** (U.S. 70, 575/378-4431, www.ruidownsracing.com) hosts races Thursday–Sunday, starting at 1 P.M. There are a few thoroughbred meets, but historically Ruidoso has been a quarter-horse track. The All-American Futurity, which draws nearly 20,000 people to town over Labor Day weekend, has been dubbed the world's richest quarter-horse race, thanks to its purse of more than $1 million—not bad money for 21 seconds worth of racing. (As in any futurity, owners have to start the gambling early—they buy into the race as soon as a horse is born, with incremental payments over the next two years.)

Next to the racetrack, the 15,000-square-foot **Billy the Kid Casino** is a bonanza of slot machines and off-track betting. But the spacious **Inn of the Mountain Gods Casino** (287 Carrizo Canyon Rd., 800/545-9011, 8 A.M.–4 A.M. Sun.–Thurs., 24 hours Fri. and Sat.) is a more pleasant setting than Ruidoso Downs. Here you can play a few table games, including poker, along with all the usual dinging machines.

## Spencer Theater for the Performing Arts

Just up the road from Ruidoso in the satellite community of Alto, Spencer Theater for the Performing Arts (108 Spencer Rd., 575/336-4800, www.spencertheater.com) juts up like a white wedge from the plain. With seats for 515, it hosts touring musical productions as well as local performers. The building alone is an attraction—the architect is New Mexican Antoine Predock, and the interior features a large number of Dale Chihuly glass sculptures. There are guided tours on Tuesdays and Thursdays at 10 A.M. (call to reserve).

## Fun for Kids

Up the road in Alto, **Flying J Ranch** (575/336-4330, www.flyingjranch.com, June–Aug.) is unapologetically cheesy, but it may be just the thing if you have kids to delight. Expect pony rides, staged gunfights, and gold panning, followed by a whole lotta grub and a wholesome, Opry-style stage show. The price is actually relatively old-timey, too: $24 for adults, $14 for kids.

Sure, there are *real* golf courses in the area, but **Funtrackers** (101 Carrizo Canyon Rd., 575/257-3275, 10 A.M.–9 P.M. daily in summer, Sat. and Sun. in winter) has 18 miniature holes, as well as go-carts, an arcade, and more. Even Ruidoso's **public swimming pool** (515 Sudderth Dr., 575/257-2795, noon–4:45 P.M., $3) is pretty fun, with a giant loop-de-loop slide.

## SPORTS AND RECREATION

For details on national forest areas, contact the **Smokey Bear Ranger District office** (901 Mechem Dr., 575/257-4095, 7:30 A.M.–4:30 P.M. Mon.–Fri.). Birders should keep an eye out for hummingbirds, which summer here in great numbers.

## Winter Sports

Head 18 miles north to **Ski Apache** (575/464-3600, www.skiapache.com, $55 full-day lift ticket), which gets more than 15 feet of snow every year. Of the 55 trails, 45 percent are advanced, with a vertical drop of 1,900 feet across the mountain. Snowboarders have the run of the trails, as well as the Boneyard, a special park with all kinds of rails and jumps. Don't go driving up here just on a lark, though—Ski Run Road is dangerously narrow, so uphill traffic is banned 3–6 P.M. during ski season.

Nonskiers can head to **Ruidoso Winter Park** (575/336-7079, $20) for tubing and sledding, just a quarter mile up Ski Run Road; it has a nifty conveyor to take you back up the slope, and it's open late some nights, with bonfires and marshmallows.

## Hiking

In the summer, the same mountain offers some great hiking. The starting point for one good hike—or just a pretty spot for a picnic—is **Monjeau Fire Lookout Tower,** which affords a panoramic view from 10,356 feet. From there, the Crest Trail (no. 25) runs to the ski area. To reach the tower, a nifty rock construction from 1940 by the Civilian Conservation Corps, take Highway 48 to Ski Run Road (Hwy. 532), then turn right after one mile onto Forest Road 117—it's a bumpy, bumpier, bumpiest five miles to the lookout point.

Back in town, check out **Two Rivers Park,** located right behind the visitors center (720 Sudderth Dr.)—a little walking trail follows the river all the way into Upper Canyon, sometimes so far below the main road level that you forget you're in the middle of town.

## Mountain Biking

Handy **Perk Canyon Trail** begins basically in people's backyards and runs about three miles up to some open meadows. To get to the trailhead, take Main Road to Ebarb Drive in the Upper Canyon section; turn right, go two blocks to Perk Canyon Road, and turn left. The paved road dead-ends at the trail. To head farther into the mountains, your best bet is along **Bonito Lake Road** (Forest Road 107, off Hwy. 37), where a number of old mining roads head up canyons and narrow into challenging single-track. But any biker who comes to this area is usually headed for the more dramatic trails around Cloudcroft.

## ACCOMMODATIONS

The signature lodging of Ruidoso is the cozy wood cabin, complete with kitchen and fireplace, and most of these are in what's called Upper Canyon, on Main Road, which follows the river up a narrowing route. If country-cute is not to your taste, you might prefer the guesthouses at the Hurd La Rinconada Gallery in San Patricio, 20 miles east of town. The majority of the chain hotels are at the east end of town, around The Y, but it's hard to find anything decent for less than $80.

### Under $100

The cheapest lodging in Ruidoso is of course camping, but this is only feasible in summer. **Eagle Lake Campground** (575/336-4668, May–mid-Sept., $15), about four miles up Ski Run Road, is on Mescalero Apache land, with nice amenities such as a bathhouse; there's also fishing in the lake. **Monjeau Lookout** has just four campsites, but they're prime ones, with great views; you'll have to carry in water, though. If there's no room here, head farther up Ski Run Road to **Oak Grove,** with 30 sites, including a few walk-in spots that are wonderfully secluded under oak trees; again, you'll have to bring your own water.

At **Shadow Mountain Lodge** (107 Main Rd., 575/257-4886, www.smlruidoso.com, $89–95) in the "historic" Upper Canyon, where many cabins have been around for decades, you have a choice of rooms in the central lodge or in standalone cabins. All are geared to couples, with king beds in the pine-paneled lodge and queens in the cabins, which are more modern but still rustic enough. There are fireplaces and kitchenettes in all the rooms.

### $100-150

The oldest place in Upper Canyon, and still one of the most pleasantly old-fashioned, is **Dan Dee Cabins** (310 Main Rd., 575/257-

2165, www.dandeecabins.com, $109 d), where some buildings date from 1938. They've been well maintained, and the oldest ones, such as Starlight and Miss Chief, are preferable for their wood-paneled walls, stacked-stone fireplaces, and few pieces of antique furniture. (The more modern ones feel a bit too much like mobile homes.)

At the uppermost end of Upper Canyon, **Noisy Water Lodge** (1013 Main Rd., 575/257-3881, www.noisywaterlodge.com, $109 d) is isolated enough that you can hear the river bubbling along outside. Its cabins are all very nicely appointed, with carpeting and extras like whirlpool tubs and fireplaces, depending on which you choose. One-, two-, or three-bedroom arrangements accommodate anyone from honeymooners to big families.

For a less rustic vibe, **Black Bear Lodge** (428 Main Rd., 575/257-1459, www.blackbearruidoso.com, $119 d) is a bed-and-breakfast in a single large log cabin. The place has four spacious rooms, each with a king-size bed, whirlpool tub, and gas fireplace. They're done with tasteful Mission-style furniture and solid colors—incongruous with the common living room, where teddy bears and quilts abound. There's a large shared kitchen too.

In town on the north side, the **Village Lodge** (1000 Mechem Dr., 575/258-5442, www.villagelodge.com, $109 d) is a sprawling condo complex with spacious, well-maintained one-bedroom suites, all outfitted with full kitchens and wood-burning fireplaces. With pull-out sofas, they can sleep up to six people.

### $150-250

**Inn of the Mountain Gods** (287 Carrizo Canyon Rd., 800/545-9011, www.innofthemountaingods.com, $189 d) is a lovely small-scale resort run by the Mescalero Apache. The large rooms are done in a subdued Southwestern style, and all but a few have balconies overlooking the lake that the building arcs around. (It's definitely worth the $20 to upgrade to these lakeview rooms; the ones with mountain views are usually smaller as well.) Compared with what you'd pay for similar amenities and service closer to Santa Fe, as well as with far more rustic cabins up in Ruidoso proper, the place is a relative bargain—though the assumption is that you'll also spend money at the casino, golf course, and overpriced restaurant on the premises.

## FOOD

Ruidoso's best dining is at the casual end. Many places cater to blander Texan palates—if you're looking for spice, you won't find it here.

### Breakfast and Lunch

**Cornerstone Bakery & Café** (359 Sudderth Dr., 575/257-1842, 7:30 A.M.–2 P.M. Mon.–Sat., 7:30 A.M.–1 P.M. Sun., $8) helps you start the day right—with French toast, for instance, or a BEST sandwich (bacon, eggs, spinach, and tomatoes), or a super-sticky sweet roll. This is many residents' and regular visitors' morning favorite, so the atmosphere is very homey and chummy, and you see a good slice of the town come through.

Good thing **The Village Buttery** (2107 Sudderth Dr., 575/257-9251, 10:30 A.M.–2:30 P.M. Mon.–Sat., $8) doesn't open too early, or you might be tempted to start your day with pie. For lunch, you can get hearty soups, quiches, and sandwiches with a Texan twist (pimento cheese, say) before you embark on a tour of the pie case. Despite the café's name, the crusts aren't bursting with butter—the pies with crumb crusts are preferable.

### Pizza

For pizza, head to super-casual ◖ **Café Rio** (2547 Sudderth Dr., 575/257-7746, 11:20 A.M.–7:50 P.M. daily, $8), which earns the local vote for best pie. All the usual toppings are on offer, along with rarer treats like artichoke hearts and capers, and the rest of the menu reflects the owners' quirky outlook, with items like shrimp jambalaya and Portuguese kale soup. You can wash it all down with a good selection of microbrews, or a big milkshake.

### Mexican and New Mexican

In a big converted old house overlooking the river, pretty **Casa Blanca** (501 Mechem Dr., 575/257-2495, 7 A.M.–9 P.M. Mon.–Thurs., 7 A.M.–10 P.M. Fri. and Sat., 9 A.M.–9 P.M. Sun., $12) is a town institution, and about as formal as Ruidoso gets—which isn't very. Its signature appetizer is crispy strips of green chile—because how else to improve on New Mexico's signature vegetable than by sticking it in the deep-fryer? The rest of the menu is typical Tex-Mex, well executed, especially with a margarita to wash it down.

More casual and homey with a welcoming, family-run feeling, **Elena's Place** (2800 Sudderth Dr., 575/630-8022, 11 A.M.–9 A.M. Tues.–Sat., 11 A.M.–3 P.M. Sun., $9) has all the usual New Mexican dishes, with especially light and delicious chiles rellenos. But one of the owners is straight from Mexico, so there are also goodies like fish tacos and really meaty burritos to choose from. It's set in a funky round building, with patio seating out back. Also check out the cool bar on the lower level.

The irresistibly named **Disco Taco** (141 U.S. 70 E, 575/378-4224, 7:30 A.M.–8 P.M. daily, $7) serves up authentic *norteño*-style food. Just east of Ruidoso Downs, the low-atmosphere, diner-style restaurant specializes in all manner of grilled meats (and we do mean *all* manner) and hangover-curing menudo.

## INFORMATION

The Ruidoso chamber of commerce operates a very cheery **visitors center** (720 Sudderth Dr., 575/257-7395, www.ruidosonow.com), positively bursting with information and helpful staff—the lobby section is even open 24 hours.

Ruidoso's local bookshop, **Books Etcetera** (2340 Sudderth Dr., 575/257-1594, 10 A.M.–5 P.M. Mon., Tues., and Thurs.–Sat., noon–4 P.M. Sun. in summer) is well-stocked with local tomes as well as games and other diversions for kids.

## GETTING THERE

**Greyhound** (800/231-2222, www.greyhound.com) stops at the station (138 Service Rd., 575/257-2660, 9 A.M.–5 P.M. Mon.–Fri., 9 A.M.–noon Sat.) once a day from Las Cruces.

**THE SOUTHEAST**

# Billy the Kid Trail

This scenic driving route forms a triangle with Ruidoso, Tinnie, and Capitan at the points. The loop is an easy day's drive, meandering through orchards, horse farms, and deep forest. If you're feeling thorough, you can stop first at the **Billy the Kid Interpretive Center** (U.S. 70, 575/378-5318, 10 A.M.–5 P.M. Thurs.–Tues.) in Ruidoso Downs, next to the Hubbard Museum.

## SAN PATRICIO

This bucolic village in a valley 20 miles east of Ruidoso glows with the sort of light painters praise—no surprise, then, that it was the home of artists Peter Hurd and Henriette Wyeth, daughter of N. C. Wyeth. One of their children owns the family ranch and operates **⟨ Hurd La Rinconada Gallery and Sentinel Ranch** (100 Rinconada Ln., 800/658-6912, www.wyethartists.com), which displays the family's work. It also rents some beautiful **guest homes,** scattered over the Wyeth ranch land. These are an excellent alternative to staying in Ruidoso—the smallest ones ($140) cost little more than you'd pay at the high end in town, and they're much larger and more attractive overall, furnished with original art and antiques. **Benson Fine Art** (575/653-4081, 10 A.M.–5 P.M. daily) is another highly respected gallery in the village, showing not just contemporary painting and sculpture (almost all with a Southwestern bent) but also jewelry, pottery, and even a few pieces of antique furniture.

## TINNIE

Just east of the junction of U.S. 70 and U.S. 380, Tinnie is a dot on the map with one attraction. Folks from Ruidoso drive up here for a fancy night out or big brunch at **Tinnie Silver Dollar Steakhouse and Saloon** (575/653-4425, 5–9 P.M. Mon.–Thurs., 5–10 P.M. Sat., $28), the old town general store that has been converted to a luxe steakhouse (run by the Cattle Baron mini-chain). The real appeal is

the building's interior, which was restored in the 1950s with German stained glass and a gorgeous hardwood bar from Chicago. During the day, you can stop in at the **deli** and have a sandwich on the wraparound porch.

## ⟨ LINCOLN STATE MONUMENT

More of an open-air museum than a town, Lincoln is an artfully preserved Old West village where many of the buildings on the main street have been turned into public monuments. A stroll up and down the road is a rare chance to meditate on history without the distraction of souvenir vendors.

During the Lincoln County War (1878–1881), when the area was wracked by endless retaliatory killings triggered by a struggle to control the town dry-goods business, the national press dubbed this "the most dangerous town in America." The local feud also put Billy the Kid, who'd been causing low-grade trouble around New Mexico for years, in the spotlight. He burnished his outlaw reputation when he took sides with the upstart Tunstall faction and the band of "Regulators" who later sought vengeance for Tunstall's murder. Near the end of the war, Billy made a daring escape from the town jail, killing two guards in the process.

### The Museums

You can learn all about the Kid's exploits—as well as the Mexican families who first settled the town in 1846, and the Buffalo Soldiers who bunked at nearby Fort Sumner—at the **Anderson-Freeman Visitors Center & Museum** (U.S. 380, 8:30 A.M.–4:30 P.M. daily, $5). Then tour the other buildings in town, which have been filled with period furnishings and a few smaller historical displays. (A couple of them are open only April–October.) The Montaño Store, for instance, is kitted out with 19th-century stock, and you can see the holes in the courthouse wall where Billy the Kid fired bullets as he made his getaway.

© ZORA O'NEILL

**Many of the buildings in Lincoln have been preserved as museums.**

## Accommodations and Food

"No guests gunned down in over 100 years," boasts the 🄲 **Wortley Hotel** (U.S. 380, 575/653-4300, www.wortleyhotel.com, $85 s, $95 d), which was formerly owned by Sheriff Pat Garrett. The historic building is smack in the middle of town, so after visiting the museums, you can toddle over here and settle into a rocking chair on the porch to watch the sun go down. Rooms are simply furnished and whitewashed—no faux-rustic paneling here. The restaurant serves great breakfast (included in the room rate) and lunch. Officially it's open only Wednesday through Sunday (8 A.M.–3 P.M.), but it might accommodate you if it happens to have guests that need feeding too. And as of late 2010, there were plans to start serving dinner on the weekends—call to check. The other option is the **Ellis Store** (U.S. 380, 800/653-6460, www.ellisstore.com), an atmospheric tumbledown stone complex where you can stay in the main house with private baths ($99–109) or share a bathroom for less in the rambling mill house ($89).

For dinner, you'll have to reserve ahead for a gourmet meal at the Ellis Store ($15). You can also get a homey breakfast or lunch, or dinner on request, at the beautiful **Dolan House** (826 Calle la Placita, 575/653-4670, 9 A.M.–3:30 P.M. Fri.–Tues., $9), a restored adobe home, complete with a giant fireplace, wood floors, and big, heavy furniture.

## FORT STANTON-SNOWY RIVER NATIONAL CONSERVATION AREA

A well-signed detour off U.S. 380, Fort Stanton itself doesn't merit a drive—it's a somewhat creepy place that was last used as a drug-rehab center for convicts. Past the fort, though, is a wilderness reserve most remarkable for being set over the third largest cave system in the state. If you're an experienced caver, you can explore on your own (you must get a permit from the BLM field office in Roswell), and camp by the cavern entrance. Otherwise, **Fort Stanton Cave Tours** (1204 Mechem Dr., Ruidoso, 575/937-1074, www.fortstantoncavetours.com) runs expeditions into the caverns, complete with miner's lamps and lots of wriggling your way into massive stalactite-heavy halls. The basic two-hour tour is $30, and it's open to anyone age eight and above; longer tours are more expensive and strenuous. You must call ahead at least a couple of days in advance to reserve; the guides need at least four people to run a tour.

## CAPITAN

Capitan might have a pioneer history, but you'd never know it. This town is all about Smokey Bear—the tiny cub discovered clinging to a tree after a fire raged across 17,000 acres in the Capitan Mountains in 1950. Badly burned, the cub was nursed back to health, dubbed "Smokey," and eventually shipped off to the National Zoo in Washington, D.C., where a generation of school kids got to visit the living symbol of fire prevention. (The image of Smokey Bear was invented in 1944—but the campaign didn't catch on until the real, adorable bear took over the mantle.) Smokey died in 1976, but, like Elvis, his spirit lives on, especially here in Capitan, where he's buried, and where nearly every business name is some ursine pun. The place really goes crazy for **Smokey Bear Days,** on the first weekend in May.

### Sights

The state forestry office operates **Smokey Bear Historical Park** (118 W. Smokey Bear Blvd., 575/354-2748, www.smokeybearpark. com, 9 A.M.–5 P.M. daily, $2). It's a bit dry, in a 1970s-education way, though kids will probably be impressed by the displays of forest-fighting gear, and adults might be interested to see how the fire-prevention ads have changed over the years. There's also a short walking trail to Smokey's grave.

### Accommodations and Food

**Smokey Bear Motel** (316 Smokey Bear Blvd., 575/354-2253, www.smokeybearmotel.com, $55 s, $70 d) is a string of little rooms with handmade wood furniture, including rocking chairs—not bursting with character, but they'll do in a pinch. They're not as well kept as similar places in Ruidoso, but they're also much less expensive.

For meals, **Café Z** (103 Lincoln St., 575/354-0977, 11 A.M.–8 P.M. Thurs.–Sat., 10 A.M.–2 P.M. Sun., $7) hits the spot with smoky (no pun intended) meatball sandwiches and brisket tacos, as well as creative, Mexican-ish salads and other veggie-friendly dishes.

# Northern Tularosa Basin

Both U.S. 70 and U.S. 380 descend to meet U.S. 54, which runs north through a broad, dry valley between the Sacramento and San Andres Mountains. Much of it is part of the White Sands Missile Range, which does extensive testing for the military and private industries.

## THREE RIVERS PETROGLYPH SITE

Five miles off U.S. 54, in an unremarkable stretch between Tularosa and Carrizozo, this BLM-managed land (8 A.M.–7 P.M. daily Apr.–Oct., 8 A.M.–5 P.M. Nov.–Mar., $2/car) is easy enough to drive right past. Even when you get up close, it's hard to see what all the fuss is about. A trail leads up to a series of low hills, marked by volcanic rock that appears to cover the ridgeline like scabs. Look carefully, though, and you'll soon see why these 50 acres are now protected: The dark rocks are scored with thousands of intricate designs, alive with lizards, mountain goats, snakes, and other figures or flecked with checkerboards and spirals. Because it's so far from any modern settlement, the area has barely been marred by more recent carving (as the West Mesa in Albuquerque has).

Archaeologists estimate that the inscriptions here date from between 900 and 1400, when the Mogollon people had a settlement nearby (a separate short trail leads to its remnants), and the farther off the trail you go, the more pure carvings you'll see.

Farther down County Road B-30 about eight miles, just at the base of massive Sierra Blanca, **Three Rivers Campground** ($6/car) is a very pretty place with 14 tent or RV sites, a creek running nearby, and trails running up into the hills. Unlike campgrounds at higher elevations, this one is open year-round, and it's rarely crowded.

## CARRIZOZO

A booming railroad town until the early 1950s, Carrizozo is the seat of Lincoln County, but you wouldn't guess it from the general quiet of the place. It now holds a handful of galleries, some beautiful old shop fronts, and the dispenser of the best ice cream sodas in the state: **Roy's Gift Gallery** (1200 Ave. E, 575/648-2921, 9:30 A.M.–6 P.M. Mon.–Fri., noon–5 P.M. Sat.). The eponymous Roy, a Carrizozo native who has been at his craft since 1978, works at an old marble counter, with fountain fixtures

THE SOUTHEAST

© ZORA O'NEILL

one of thousands of rock carvings at Three Rivers Petroglyph Site

from the 1930s. Once the town drugstore, the 1909 building is still outfitted with all its original display cabinets. If you wanted something more nutritious (but why?), you could go to the **Outpost Bar & Grill** (415 Central Ave., 575/648-9994, 11 A.M.–8 P.M. Mon.– Sat., noon–8 P.M. Sun.), where the green-chile cheeseburger ranks with the Owl Café in San Antonio in terms of devoted fans—though this writer finds it too skimpy on the green stuff. And if you see apple cider on the menu, order it—it's from a nearby orchard.

If you haven't given yourself a stomachache yet, you could also stop in at the **Carrizozo Heritage Museum** (103 12th St.), which has a small collection devoted to local history.

At the corner of Central Avenue and Airport Road, one block south of the intersection of U.S. 54 and U.S. 380, the **chamber of commerce** (575/648-2732, www.carrizozochamber.org) has its office in a vintage caboose, though it's open very seldom. You can always grab a few basic brochures from the display outside.

## VALLEY OF FIRES NATIONAL RECREATION AREA

Four miles west of Carrizozo on U.S. 380, these little-visited badlands (575/648-2241, $3 pp or $5/car) are far smaller but more striking than El Malpais National Monument, west of Albuquerque. The product of an explosion just 1,500 years ago, the lava here is newer, which means the rocks are shinier, craggier, and generally just a more dramatic black, unlike the duller, almost purple hue of older volcanic stone. Up close, you'll be surprised at how much scrubby greenery has managed to grow up around the flow—a short **nature trail** leads around part of the site.

The **campground** ($7–18) has 25 sites, more than half with electricity hookups, as well as showers and restrooms. The nicest spots are in campground no. 3, down in a little gully.

## ◖ TRINITY SITE

This portion of White Sands Missile Range, where the first atomic bomb was detonated on July 16, 1945, is open to the public only on the first Saturday in April and October, 8 A.M.–2 P.M. If this happens to coincide with your schedule, do try to go. At first, it doesn't seem like there's much to see beyond the ranch house where the bomb was assembled and the small depression left in the sand by the explosion, but then small details, such as shards of the green glassy substance created on the desert floor by the heat of the bomb, pop out the more you look around. Perhaps the most disturbing thing about the place is just how normal it looks.

Access is via the Stallion Gate to the missile range, off U.S. 380, at a turn south 53 miles west of Carrizozo or 12 miles east of San Antonio. Call the missile range public affairs office (575/678-1134) to confirm dates and directions. If you're in the Alamogordo area around this time, you can join a car convoy for the 72-mile drive, starting in the Tularosa High School parking lot; contact the chamber of commerce (575/437-6120) for details.

THE SOUTHEAST

## WHITE OAKS AND ANCHO

The heart of White Oaks is the **No Scum Allowed Saloon** (575/648-5583, noon–late Fri. and Sat., noon–6 P.M. Sun.), which is cheerier than its name suggests—you might stumble on amazing fiddle playing or a biker bash. The bar is open year-round, but the rest of this former mining settlement is near-silent in the off-season. Near the end of April, it opens up with its annual **artist studio tour** (575/648-2732, www.whiteoaksnewmexico.com). Even then, the most intriguing buildings—such as spooky, fenced-off Hoyle's Castle to the south, and the equally looming Gumm House, on a hill on the north side—are closed to visitors. The brick schoolhouse and a little miner's home both contain small museums that are open weekends in the summer. The turn for White Oaks is three miles north of Carrizozo on U.S. 54; head east on Highway 349.

Neighboring Ancho, up U.S. 54 another 15 miles, then east on Highway 462, is even more desolate, though it thrived until the early 1920s, thanks to a brick-making industry. But it does have a bizarre museum that goes by the honest name of **My House of Old Things** (575/648-2456, May–Oct., $3). Set in the old train depot, it has been open since 1963 and is

© ZORA O'NEILL

the most hospitable bar in White Oaks

a sprawling collection of everything from cigar bands to a telegraph machine, maintained by a man who has been ranching in the valley for more than 60 years.

# BACKGROUND

## The Land

Sharp peaks, windswept cliffs, deep gorges, harsh desert, sweeping plains—everything about New Mexico's landscape is dramatic. The light glints off surfaces at surprising angles, and the scenery can change at any bend in the road. The altitude ranges from around 2,800 feet down by the Texas border to more than 13,000 at Wheeler Peak (the state's highest, north of Taos), but the average altitude is about 5,700 feet—so if you're not gasping for breath from the scenery alone, you almost certainly will be from the thin air.

### GEOGRAPHY AND GEOLOGY

Much of New Mexico's landscape is the product of volcanic activity, beginning hundreds of millions of years back and ceasing (at least for now) only about 1,500 years ago. The main mountain ranges, which form part of the Continental Divide, are relatively young, pushed up in the Eocene era between 55 million and 34 million years ago, when shock waves from the collision of the North American plate and the Farallon plate caused the continent to heave. Just a few million years later, the **Rio Grande Rift**—one of the biggest rift valleys in the world—formed, as eras' and eras' worth of accumulated rock was pulled apart by shifting faults, leaving the perfect path for the river when it began to flow about 3 million years ago. The water carved deep canyons, perfect slices of

© ZORA O'NEILL

© CHRIS DAHL-BREDINE

**The Rio Grande Gorge was formed by seismic activity.**

geologic time, where you can see layers of limestone, sandstone, clay, and lava stacked up. The best example is the 800-foot-deep Rio Grande Gorge, cut through the lava plateau that stretches west from Taos. Just 1.2 million years back, a volcano's violent eruption and subsequent collapse created the huge **Valles Caldera,** and even as recently as A.D. 500, molten lava hardened into black badlands in the Tularosa Basin.

Below all this is evidence of a more stable time. For some 4 billion years, the land was completely underwater, then spent hundreds of millions of years supporting prehistoric sealife—hence the marine fossils found at the top of the Sandia Mountains, 10,000 feet above the current sea level. Dinosaurs, too, flourished for a time—one of the first, *Coelophysis,* a nimble meat-eater, lived during the Triassic period around Abiquiu, and heftier herbivores left their tracks all along the northeast part of the state.

## CLIMATE

Much more than simple latitude, the relative altitude determines the climate in New Mexico,

where river-bottom central Albuquerque can be crisp and cloudless while Sandia Peak, 20 miles away and almost 5,000 feet up, is socked in by a blinding snowstorm. Nowhere, though, is it a particularly gentle or mild climate—expect sudden changes in weather and temperature extremes.

At all but the very lowest elevations, winter is cold—days usually between 40°F and 55°F—but rarely cloudy, with a few snowstorms that never add up to quite as much moisture as people hope for. Come spring, which starts in late April or May, the number of wildflowers that dot the hills is a direct reflection of the previous winter's precipitation. Little rain falls in May and June, typically the hottest months of the year, with temperatures climbing into the 90s—though temperatures can still drop 40 degrees at night.

By early July, the "monsoon" season (as locals call it) brings heavy, refreshing downpours and thunderstorms every afternoon for a couple of months. It's remarkable—if a bit dismaying—to see how quickly all the water vanishes after each torrential rain. (If you're out hiking in this season, steer clear of narrow canyons and arroyos during and after rains, as they can fill with powerful, deadly flash floods in a matter of minutes.) September, October, and November are again dry, with the temperature dipping lower each month.

The higher the elevation, the later the spring: At 8,500 feet, snow could still be on the ground in May. Summer nights are rarely warm, and winter chill sets in sooner too, with fresh snow often falling in late October or November, although it takes well into December for a good base layer to build up at the ski areas.

## ENVIRONMENTAL ISSUES

The state's unforgiving climate and geography have made it a perpetual challenge for human inhabitants. For thousands of years, New Mexicans have been facing the same dilemma: never enough water. In prehistoric times, farming in the river valley was relatively easy, if subject to erratic flooding. But

Wind farms are cropping up across the state's flatlands.

at higher elevations, mountain streams had to be channeled into irrigation ditches. This system was perfected by the Spanish settlers, who called their ditches acequias, a word they'd learned from the Arabs *(al-saqiya)*, who used the system to cultivate the Iberian Peninsula.

But now, as an ever-growing population demands more amenities, the traditional ways of managing water have given way to more complex legal wrangling. And there's no relief in sight: Some 49 billion gallons of water are pumped out of the middle Rio Grande aquifer every year, and only a portion of that is replenished through mountain runoff. Albuquerque started using filtered river water in late 2008. Santa Fe already has the lowest per-capita water use in the country and doesn't have any more resources to tap. "Smart growth" gets lip service in city council meetings, although construction continues apace on Albuquerque's arid West Mesa. Neo-homesteaders on the fringes are installing cisterns to catch rain and systems to reuse gray water, but these features are still far from standard.

Another result of New Mexico's dry climate is that years of relative drought have made tinderboxes of the forests. In 2000, the National Forest Service started a "controlled burn" (a hotly debated strategy for thinning invasive undergrowth in choked woodlands) that got very out of control and nearly destroyed the town of Los Alamos, along with 45,000 acres of trees. It was the largest wildfire ever in New Mexico, and the smoke and flames could be seen in Albuquerque. Pecos Wilderness Area, too, suffered from fire in 2000 and is still recovering. Each summer is a waiting game, as residents brace for fires in wilderness or near homes.

Visitors to New Mexico can help the picture by following local environmental policies—complying with campfire bans in the wilderness, for instance, and keeping showers short. Golfers may want to consider curtailing their play here. New courses are springing up in every new casino resort and high-end residential development, despite the fact that they're intense draws on the water table.

## LEAVE NO TRACE

So as not to upset the rather precarious environmental balance in much of New Mexico, you should internalize the ethic of "leave no trace," whether you're out for a day hike or a weeklong backpacking trek. Let the phrase first guide your trip in the planning stages, when you equip yourself with good maps and GPS tools or a compass, to avoid relying on rock cairns or blazes, as well as repackage food and other items to minimize the waste you'll have to pack out. Also try to keep your group size under six people, and don't take pets with you.

On the trail, resist the urge to cut across switchbacks, and slog through the center of the trail, even if it has been widened by others trying to avoid mud. Be quiet and courteous, to avoid disturbing wildlife and other hikers. Leave what you find, whether plants, rocks, or potsherds or other relics of the past.

Camp only where others have, in durable areas, at least 200 feet from water sources; dig cat holes 200 feet away, too. Pack out your toilet paper and other personal waste, and scatter dishwater and toothpaste. Safeguard food in "bear bags" hung at least 15 feet off the ground. Campfires are typically banned in New Mexico – please honor this policy, and keep a close eye on camp stoves. Pack out all cigarette butts.

While most leave-no-trace ethics apply to backpackers, day hikers should also maintain a strict policy regarding litter. Tossing an orange peel, apple core, or other biodegradable item along the trail may not cause an environmental disaster, but it reminds other hikers that humans have been there and intrudes on the natural solitude of New Mexico's wilderness.

# Flora and Fauna

Just as humans have managed to eke a life out of New Mexico, so have plants and animals—and a rather large variety of them, considering the harsh circumstances. The state supports the fourth most diverse array of wildlife in the country.

## FLORA

Although much of the plant growth in New Mexico is nominally evergreen, the overall aspect of the landscape can skew toward brown, until you get up into the wetter alpine elevations.

### Vegetation Zones

Below 4,500 feet, New Mexico's **Lower Sonoran** zone, largely in the river valleys in the southern part of the state, is dotted with cactus, yucca, and scrubby creosote bushes. The **Upper Sonoran** zone, covering the areas between 4,500 and 7,000 feet, is the largest vegetation zone in the state and includes the high plains in the northeast and most of Albuquerque and Santa Fe, where the Sandia and Sangre de Cristo foothills are covered with juniper and piñon trees. The **Transition** zone, from 7,000 feet to 8,500 feet, sees a few more stately trees, such as ponderosa pine, and a lot of the state's colorful wildflowers: orange Indian paintbrush, bright red penstemon, purple lupine. Above 8,500 feet, the **Mixed Conifer** zone harbors just that sort of tree—along with clusters of aspens. The **Subalpine** zone, starting at 9,500 feet, is home to Engelmann spruce and bristlecone pine, while 11,500 feet marks the tree line in most places and the beginning of the **Alpine** zone, where almost no greenery survives. At 11,973 feet, the top of Sierra Blanca, near Ruidoso, is the southernmost example of this zone in the United States.

### Trees and Grasses

Trees are the clearest marker of elevation. In very low areas—such as the Chihuahuan

© ZORA O'NEILL

just one of the scores of varieties of yucca, the state flower

Desert outside of Las Cruces—you'll see almost no trees, only some of the more desertlike plants: assorted cactuses, such as **yucca,** the state flower that comes in many spiky varieties and usually produces towering stalks of blooms in May; the common **cane cholla;** and the humble **tumbleweed.** Along the Rio Grande and the Pecos Rivers, thirsty **cottonwoods** provide dense shade; many of the biggest trees, with their gnarled, branching trunks, have been growing for centuries. In the spring, their cotton fills the air—hell for the allergic, but the source of a distinctive fragrance—and in the fall, their leaves turn pure yellow. Willow and olive are also common.

In the foothills, **piñon** (also spelled pinyon), the official state tree, is everywhere, a slow-growing, drought-resistant scrub tailor-evolved for the New Mexican landscape. When burned, its wood produces the scent of a New Mexico winter night, and its pinecones yield tasty nuts. Alongside piñon is **shaggy-bark juniper,** identifiable by its loose strips of bark, sprays of soft needles, and branches that look

twisted by the wind. In season, it's studded with purple-gray berries—another treat for foraging humans and animals alike. On the ground in the foothills, also look for clumps of sagebrush and bear grass, which blooms in huge creamy tufts at the ends of stalks up to six feet tall.

Up in the mountains, the trees are a bit taller—here you'll find the towering **ponderosa** pine, the bark of which smells distinctly of vanilla. Look for tall trees with thick, almost crusty chunks of reddish-black bark. At slightly higher elevations, dense stands of **aspen** trees provide a rare spot of fall color in the evergreen forests. The combination of their golden leaves and white bark creates a particularly magical glow, especially in the mountains near Santa Fe. The highest mountain areas are home to a number of dense-needled hardy pines, such as blue-green **Engelmann spruce, corkbark fir, bristlecone pines,** and **subalpine fir,** with its sleek, rounded pinecones. Hike your way up to stands of these, which are tall but with sparse branches, and you'll know you're close to the peak.

## FAUNA

As with plants, what you see depends on whether you're down in the desert or up on the mountain slopes. And you'll have to look very carefully, because a lot of the animals that have survived this long in dry, harsh New Mexico are the sort that have blended in with their surroundings—which means there are a lot of brown critters.

### Mammals

In the open, low-elevation areas on city fringes (and sometimes in the occasional vacant urban lot), look for **prairie dogs,** which live in huge communities of underground warrens. If you're camping, the first little creatures you'll meet are squirrels and chipmunks—at higher elevations, look out for **Aber's squirrel,** with its tufted ears and particularly fluffy tail. Long-haunched, clever, and highly adaptable, **coyotes** roam the lower elevations and are not shy about nosing around backyards; they make a barking yelp at night. On the plains, you may see **pronghorns** (often called pronghorn antelopes, though it is not a true antelope) springing through the grasses, while hefty **mule deer** flourish in mountain forests, such as the Pecos Wilderness. Herds of even larger **elk** live in the high valleys; Rocky Mountain elk are common, thanks to an aggressive re-introduction effort in the early 20th century to make up for overhunting. A group of the largest variety, Roosevelt elk, whose fanlike antlers are the stuff of dreams for trophy hunters, roams in Valles Caldera. **Bighorn sheep** live in the mountains around Taos and in the Gila wilderness.

**Black bears** crash around the forests, though their name is misleading—at any given time, they can be brown, cinnamon-red, or even nearly blond. Smokey Bear, the mascot of the National Forest Service, was from New Mexico, a cub rescued from a forest fire in Capitan. Drought has on many occasions driven the omnivorous beasts into suburban trash cans to forage, with tragic results for both people and the animals. If you're camping, take thorough measures to keep your food away from your camp and out of reach of animals.

And then there's the elusive **jackalope**, a jackrabbit hare sporting elaborate antlers. Alas, it seems now to appear only on postcards, although you may occasionally see a taxidermied head in a curio shop.

## Birds

New Mexico's state bird is the **roadrunner,** which can grow up to two feet long. It nests in the ground and feeds on insects and even rattlesnakes, and its feet are specially adapted to racing on the sands of the lower desert elevations in which it lives. Blue-and-black **Steller's jays** and raucous all-blue **piñon jays** are some of the most common birds in the foothills and farther up in the mountains, where you can also see bluebirds, black-masked mountain chickadees, and Clark's nutcrackers, which hoard great stashes of piñon nuts for winter. Also look around for varieties of **woodpeckers,** including the three-toed variety, which lives at

higher elevations. On the very highest peaks are **white-tailed ptarmigans,** which blend in with their snowy environment. But you can't miss the bright-yellow-and-red **Western tanager,** a shot of tropical-looking delight in the Transition zone forests.

In the late summer, keep an eye out for tiny, red-throated **Rufous hummingbirds** on their way to Mexico for the winter, along with hundreds of other birds that use the center of the state as a migratory corridor. The Sandia Mountains and the Las Vegas National Wildlife Refuge, among other spots, are on the flight path for **red-tailed hawks, eagles,** and other raptors—they're especially numerous in the springtime.

With more than 450 species spotted in New Mexico, this list is only scraping the surface. If you're a dedicated birder, first contact the **Randall Davey Audubon Center** in Santa Fe, which leads bird walks, or the **Rio Grande Nature Center** in Albuquerque. **Bosque del Apache National Wildlife Refuge,** south of Albuquerque, is a must-visit, especially in the winter when thousands of **sandhill cranes**—and even the occasional rare **whooping crane**—rest in the wetlands. You may want to take a trip with Jim West of **WingsWest Birding** (800/583-6928, www.wingswestnm.com), who has been leading groups around New Mexico, from the Pecos to Las Vegas, since 1996. He offers four-hour, eight-hour, and full dusk-till-dawn outings to some of the best spots all over the state, and he's also willing to take people out for several days at a stretch.

## Fish

**Trout** is the major endemic fish, found in the cold waters of the Rio Grande as well as the San Juan, Chama, and Pecos Rivers. The cutthroat is particularly beloved in New Mexico—the only variety of trout originally found on the eastern side of the Continental Divide, whereas the more aggressive rainbow and brown trout are interlopers. The Rio Grande cutthroat, the official state fish, is now quite uncommon. Another local fish in jeopardy is the **Rio**

**Grande silvery minnow,** listed as endangered since 2004. The last of the Rio Grande's five native fish, it's in such a dire state that biologists are scooping them out of the water individually during bad dry spells and taking them to the Albuquerque aquarium for safekeeping. The hope is that they will breed and be able to be returned to their original habitat during wetter conditions.

## Reptiles

One can't step foot in the desert without thinking of **rattlesnakes,** and New Mexico has plenty of them, usually hidden away under rocks and brush, but very occasionally sunning themselves in full view, much to hikers' alarm. The New Mexico ridgenose variety is an endangered species, while the predominant species in the Rio Grande Valley, the **Western diamondback,** can grow to be seven feet long. Although its venom is relatively weak, it has an impressive striking distance of almost three feet. Around Taos and Santa Fe, the main species is the prairie rattlesnake, which is only about four feet long at most.

More benign cold-blooded critters include all manner of **lizards,** such as the **short-horned lizard** (a.k.a. horny toad), a miniature dinosaur, in effect, about as big as your palm. You'll see it primarily in desert and the scrubby foothills.

## Insects and Arachnids

Because it's so dry, New Mexico isn't too infested with bugs. The ones that are there, however, can be a bit off-putting to a visitor, particularly if you chance upon the springtime **tarantula migration,** usually in May—it's not a true seasonal relocation, just the time when all of the male tarantulas come out of their dens to go on the prowl for mates. The fist-size spiders move in waves, hundreds at a time, and occasionally back roads are closed to let them pass; if you'll be camping in the desert in the spring, ask the ranger's office about the status. Though they're big and hairy, they're not poisonous.

**Scorpions,** though, can be somewhat toxic, if very rarely deadly. In the southern desert areas, the most common variety is the

© ZORA O'NEILL

Watch out for rattlesnakes whenever you hike.

bark scorpion, which nestles in rock crevices and woodpiles and can find its way into your shoes or the bottom of your sleeping bag. Its sting can cause anything from severe pain to difficulty breathing and should be treated with antivenin as soon as possible. Hard-shelled, segmented **desert centipedes** are another creepy-crawly you might see; they're often out at night and can grow up to nine inches long.

# History

The historical and cultural continuity in New Mexico is remarkable. Although the state has been transformed from ice-age hunting ground to home of the atom bomb, many people claim roots that stretch back hundreds, even thousands, of years.

## ANCIENT AND ARCHAIC CIVILIZATION

New Mexico was one of the first places to harbor humans after the end of the last ice age. Archaeological findings indicate that some 12,000 years ago, people were hunting mastodons and other big game across the state. Mammoth bones, arrowheads, and the remains of campfires have been found in the Sandia Mountains east of Albuquerque; Folsom, in northeastern New Mexico; and Clovis, in the south. Sometime between 8000 and 5000 B.C., these bands of hunters formed a small temporary settlement just north of Albuquerque, but it was not enough to stave off the decline of that ancient culture, as climatic shifts caused the big game to die off. Nomadic hunter-gatherers, seeking out smaller animals as well as seeds and nuts, did better in the new land, and by 1000 B.C., they had established communities built around clusters of pit houses—sunken, log-covered rooms dug into the earth.

Along with this new form of shelter came an equally important advance in food: Mexican people gave corn kernels (maize) and lessons in agriculture to their neighbors, the **Mogollon,** who occupied southern New Mexico and Arizona; by A.D. 400, the Mogollon had begun growing squash and beans as well and had established concentrated communities all around the southern Rio Grande basin. This culture, dubbed the Basketmakers by archaeologists, also developed its own pottery, another skill learned from the indigenous people of Mexico. So when the Mogollon made contact with the Ancestral Puebloans (also known as the Anasazi) in the northern part of the state, they had plenty to share.

## THE PUEBLOS FORM

The year 700 marks the beginning of the **Pueblo I** phase—the time when disparate groups began to form larger communities in the upland areas on either side of the northern Rio Grande. Pit houses were still in use, but aboveground buildings of clay and sticks were erected alongside them. Increasingly, the pit houses were sacred spaces, chambers in which religious ceremonies were carried out; these are now known as kivas and are still an integral part of pueblo life. The **Pueblo II** era dates from 850 and is distinguished by the rise of Pueblo Bonito in Chaco Canyon, northwest of Santa Fe, into a full-scale city and perhaps capital of a small state. It was home to an estimated 1,500 people ruled by a religious elite. But Chaco abruptly began to crumble around 1150 (perhaps due to drought, famine, or warfare), marking the beginning of the **Pueblo III** period, when the people who were to become today's Puebloans began building their easily defended cliff dwellings—most famously in the Four Corners area, at Mesa Verde, but also farther south, on the Pajarito Plateau in what's now called Bandelier National Monument, and in Puyé, on Santa Clara Pueblo land. A drought at the end of the 13th century cleared out the Four Corners, marking the start of the **Pueblo IV** era and provoking the population to consolidate along the Rio Grande in clusters of sometimes more than a thousand interconnected rooms. These communities dotted the riverbank, drawing their sustenance both from the river water and from the mountains behind them.

## THE SPANISH ARRIVE

These settlements were what the Spanish explorer **Francisco Vásquez de Coronado** and his crew saw when they first ventured into the area in 1540. Their Spanish word for the villages, *pueblos,* stuck and is still the name for both the places and the people who live in them. Coronado wasn't all that impressed, however, because the pueblos were made out of mud, not gold as the Spanish had been hoping. So after two years and a couple of skirmishes with the natives, the team turned around and headed back to Mexico City. It took another half a century for the Spanish to muster more interest in the area. This time, in 1598, Juan de Oñate led a small group of Spanish families to settle on the banks of the Rio Grande, at a place they called San Gabriel, near Ohkay Owingeh (which they called San Juan Pueblo). About a decade later, the settlers moved away from their Indian neighbors, to the new village of Santa Fe. The territory's third governor, Don Pedro de Peralta, made it the official capital of the territory of Nuevo México, which in those days stretched far into what is now Colorado and Arizona.

This time the colonists, mostly farmers, were motivated not so much by hopes of striking it rich but simply of making a living. Moreover, they were inspired by Catholic zeal, and Franciscan missionaries accompanied them to promote the faith among the Puebloans.

It was partly these missionaries and their ruthless oppression of the native religion that drove the Indians to organize the **Pueblo Revolt** of 1680. The Franciscans' "conversion" strategy involved public executions of the pueblos' medicine men, among other violent assaults on local traditions. But the Spanish colonists were no help either. In their desperation to squeeze some wealth out of the hard land, they exploited the only resource they had, the slave labor of the Indians, who were either conscripted for projects or stolen from their families. (The Indians did their share of poaching from Spanish families too, creating a sort of violent cultural exchange program.)

The leader of the Pueblo Revolt was a man named **Popé** (also spelled Po'pay), from San Juan Pueblo. Using Taos Pueblo as his base, he traveled among the other communities, secretly meeting with leaders to plan a united insurrection. Historians theorize he may have used Spanish to communicate with other Puebloans who did not speak his native Tewa, and then he distributed among the conspirators lengths of knotted rope with which to count down the days to the insurrection. Although the Spanish captured a few of the rope-bearing messengers (Isleta Pueblo may never have gotten the message, which could explain its being the only pueblo not to participate), they could not avert the bloodshed. The Puebloan warriors killed families and missionaries, burned crops, and toppled churches. Santa Fe was besieged, and its population of more than 1,000 finally evacuated in a pitiful retreat.

The Spanish stayed away for 12 years, but finally a new governor, Diego de Vargas, took it upon himself to reclaim the land the Spanish had settled. He managed to talk many pueblos into peaceful surrender, meeting resistance only in Taos and Santa Fe, where a two-day fight was required to oust the Indians from the Palace of the Governors. The Spanish strategy in the post-revolt era was softer, with more compromise between the Franciscans and their intended flock, and a fair amount of cultural and economic exchange. The threat of raiding Comanche, Apache, and Navajo also forced the Spanish and Indians to cooperate. Banding together for defense, they were finally able to drive the Comanche away, culminating in a 1778 battle with Chief Cuerno Verde (Green Horn). The decisive victory is celebrated in the ritual dance called Los Comanches that's still performed in small villages by Spanish and Indians alike.

© ZORA O'NEILL

1643 — DE VARGAS — 1704

Diego de Vargas reclaimed the city of
Santa Fe following the Pueblo Revolt.

The other bonding force was trade. The
Spanish maintained the **Camino Real
de Tierra Adentro** (Royal Road of the
Interior), which linked Santa Fe with central Mexico—the route follows roughly
the line carved by I-25 today. Caravans
came through only every year or two, but
the profit from furs, pottery, textiles, and
other local goods was enough to keep both
cultures afloat, if utterly dependent on the
Spanish government.

## MEXICAN INDEPENDENCE AND THE FIRST ANGLOS

Spain carefully guarded all of its trade routes
in the New World, even in a relatively un-
profitable territory like Nuevo México. The
only outside trade permitted was through
the Comancheros, a ragtag band of men
who traded with Comanche and other Plains
Indians, working well into what would later be
Oklahoma, and even up to North Dakota. The
Spanish governor encouraged them because
their tight relationship with the Comanche

helped protect New Mexico and Texas against
intruders.

Interlopers were certainly not welcome—
only a few enterprising fur trappers, lone mountain men in search of beaver pelts, slipped in.
Spy-explorer **Zebulon Pike** and his crew were
captured (perhaps intentionally, so Pike could
get more inside information) and detained
in Santa Fe for a spell in 1807. But in 1821,
Mexico declared its independence from Spain,
liberating the territory of Nuevo México along
with it. One of the first acts of the new government was to open the borders to trade. Initially
just a trickle of curious traders came down the
rough track between St. Louis and Santa Fe,
but soon a flood of commerce flowed along the
increasingly rutted and broad **Santa Fe Trail,**
making the territory's capital city a meeting
place between Mexicans and Americans swap-
ping furs, gold, cloth, and more.

## THE MEXICAN-AMERICAN WAR AND AFTER

Pike's expedition, conducted just as Lewis and
Clark were returning from their march across
the Louisiana Purchase, not only gave the U.S.
government new information on the locations
of Spanish forts and other details, it also helped
fuel the country's general expansionist fervor.
By the 1840s, **"manifest destiny"** was the
phrase on every American's lips, and the government was eyeing the Southwest. It annexed
Texas in 1845, but New Mexico, with its small
population and few resources, didn't figure
heavily in the short-lived war that resulted—
the Mexican governor surrendered peacefully
to General Stephen Kearny when he arrived in
Santa Fe in 1846. In Taos, though, the transition was not accepted so readily, as a brief but
violent uprising instigated by Hispano business
leaders with help from Taos Pueblo Indians resulted in the beheading of the first American
governor, Charles Bent.

During the **Civil War,** New Mexico was
in the way of a Texan Confederate strategy
to secure the Southwest, but the rebels were
thwarted in 1862 at the Battle of Glorieta Pass.
The territory stayed in the hands of the Union

until the end of the war, and people were more concerned with the local, increasingly brutal skirmishes with the Apache and the Navajo, in which the U.S. army tried to subdue the tribes and protect the homesteaders and profitable gold, silver, and coal mining claims that were being developed. This latter industry indirectly bred further violence in the 1870s in the form of the Lincoln County War and the Colfax County War, two extended brawls in which some of the era's most notorious outlaws were involved.

Even more significant to New Mexico's development was the arrival of the **railroad** in 1880, as it was laid through Raton Pass, near Santa Fe, and very close to Albuquerque. Virtually overnight strange goods and even stranger people came pouring into one of the more remote frontier outposts of the United States. Anglo influence was suddenly everywhere, in the form of new architecture (redbrick was an Eastern affectation) and new business. Albuquerque, almost directly on the new railway tracks, boomed, while Santa Fe's fortunes slumped and Taos all but withered away (its peak had been back in the late days of the Camino Real).

But while wheeler-dealers were setting up shop in central New Mexico, some more intrepid souls were poking around in the less-connected areas farther north. These tourists were artists who valued New Mexico not for its commercial potential but for its dramatic landscapes and exotic populace who seemed untouched by American ways. From the early 20th century on, Santa Fe and Taos were cultivated as art colonies, a function they still fulfill today.

## FROM STATEHOOD TO WORLD WAR II

Based on its burgeoning economy, New Mexico became the 47th state in the union in 1912, effectively marking the end of the frontier period, a phase of violence, uncertainty, and isolation that lasted about 300 years, longer here than anywhere else in the United States. In addition to the painters and writers flocking to the new state, another group of migrants arrived: tuberculosis patients. Soon the state was known as a health retreat, and countless people did stints in its dry air to treat their ailing lungs. One of these people was J. Robert Oppenheimer, whose mild case of TB got him packed off to a camp near Pecos for a year after high school. He loved northern New Mexico and became familiar with some of its more hidden pockets, so when the U.S. Army asked him if he had any idea where it should establish a secret base for the **Manhattan Project,** he knew just the place: a little camp high on a plateau above Santa Fe—its name was Los Alamos. This was the birthplace of the atomic bomb, a weird, close-knit community of the country's greatest scientific minds (and biggest egos), all working in utter secrecy. Only after the bomb was tested at White Sands and Fat Man and Little Boy were dropped over Japan was the mysterious camp's mission revealed.

## RECENT HISTORY

With the invention of the A-bomb, New Mexico was ushered into the modern era—not just because it produced world-changing technology, but also because the high-paying jobs at Los Alamos and Kirtland Air Force Base in Albuquerque helped pull some of the population out of subsistence farming and into a life that involved cars and electricity. Even with these modern trappings, though, the character of the state remained very conservative and closed, so when the 1960s rolled around and New Mexico looked like the promised land to hippies, the culture clash was fierce. Staunch Catholic farmers even took potshots at their naked, hallucinogen-ingesting neighbors who fantasized about getting back to the land but had no clue how to do it. After a decade or so, though, only the hardiest of the commune-dwellers were left, and they'd mellowed a bit, while the locals had come to appreciate at least their enthusiasm. Even if the communes didn't last, hippie culture has proven remarkably persistent—even today, distinctly straight Hispanos can be heard saying things like, "I was tripping out on that band, man," and the state still welcomes Rainbow Gatherings, would-be Buddhists, and alternative healers.

The end of the 20th century saw unprecedented growth in New Mexico's bigger cities. As usual, Albuquerque got the practical-minded development, such as the Intel plant and the financial headquarters for Gap Inc., while Santa Fe was almost felled by its own artsiness, turned inside-out during a few frenzied years when movie stars and other moneyed types bought up prime real estate. In just a matter of months in the early 1990s, rents went up tenfold and houses were selling for more than $1 million. The city has yet to work out the imbalance between its creative forces, which did save the city from utter decline, and the weird economic ones through which the richest people live in faux-adobe homes on real dirt roads, and the poorest put a fresh coat of mud on their houses every year, but at least the paving runs up to their doors.

Meanwhile, Taos and Las Cruces have grown slowly but steadily, as have the pueblos, thanks to the legalization of gambling on their lands, but all of these communities have a touch of old New Mexico about them, where the frontier flavor and solitude can still be felt.

# Government and Economy

Up until very recently, New Mexico hasn't looked so good on paper, what with high statistics for corruption, nepotism, and poverty. But that has also inspired a good deal of activist sentiment, and politics are lively as the economy has begun to slip out of some of its old restrictive patterns.

## GOVERNMENT

New Mexico's political scene is as diverse as its population, a fractious mix of Democrats, Republicans, Greens, Libertarians, anarchists, independents, and irredeemable cranks. The presidential contests of 2000 and 2004 were too close to call, requiring recounts to determine the winners by a hair (Gore in 2000, Bush in 2004). But in 2008, the election went squarely to Obama, after he rallied Hispanics with the slogan "Obamanos!" New Mexico got more attention when Obama tapped Governor Bill Richardson, a Democrat who previously served as the U.S ambassador to the United Nations and ran for president, as a potential cabinet member—but Richardson stepped down after some checks into his business dealings. Nonetheless, Richardson carried out his term as governor, ending on the same popular note he was elected on. (Don't be fooled by his Anglo last name: Richardson is Mexican American, and a fluent Spanish-speaker. So far, he has been the only Hispanic governor in the United States.) In 2010, New Mexico got its first woman governor, Republican Susana Martinez. The election would've been historic either way: Her opponent was Democrat Diane Denish, lieutenant governor under Richardson.

New Mexico is also notable for its high Hispanic representation in every level of government. The state Hispanic population is about 45 percent, the highest of any state, and the congress is 44 percent Hispanic. This proportional representation has helped keep the immigration debate at a polite pitch—unlike neighboring Arizona, where the Hispanic population is 30 percent, but only 16 percent in the legislature.

On a local level, corruption charges and entrenched cronyism are still rampant. When any scandal breaks (nepotistic assignment of highway repair contracts, for instance, or politicians repeatedly arrested for DUIs, and then cleared), pundits can't help but comment that the old Spanish *patrón* system, in which small-town bosses dole out benefits to their loyal supporters, seems to still be at work. "New Mexico is a third-world country" is another common quip.

The system is even more muddled by the Indian reservations, each of which acts as a sovereign nation, with its own laws, tax regulations, police forces, and government. Indians vote in U.S. and state elections, but in the pueblos, most domestic issues are decided by each pueblo's tribal governor, war chief, and a few other officials elected by a consensus of men in the kiva. The Navajo Nation, perhaps due to the fact that it has more than 250,000 people to manage, as well as a substantial amount of natural resources, does practice direct democracy. In its system, the reservation, which reaches into Arizona and Utah, is divided into "chapters," and their representatives, voted on by men and women alike in a popular election, participate in the Navajo Council, which convenes in the capital at Window Rock, Arizona. Since a reform in 1991, the Navajo system has had three branches, like the American one. In 2006, Lynda Lovejoy was the first woman to run for president; she made a strong showing against incumbent Joe Shirley. In 2010, she lost by a small margin to former vice president Ben Shelly.

state government buildings in Santa Fe

© ZORA O'NEILL

## ECONOMY

New Mexico has always lagged at the bottom of the country's economic ratings: In 2008, 17.1 percent of the population was living below the poverty level—not great, but at least a few rungs up from the bottom, compared with states like Mississippi. It's also 46th out of 50 in the number of high school graduates and the number of college graduates per capita. Statistics in the pueblos and reservations are even grimmer, with up to 50 percent unemployment in some areas—though this is changing due to casino-fueled development. The Navajo Nation, in particular, has extensive landholdings and a population hungry to spend money on the reservation, but due to an infrastructure that's more 19th than 21st century, no businesses are interested in investing here. The same could in fact be said for many of the rural sections of the state, on Indian land or no.

As of 2010, the state was still battling the effects of the recession, which knocked its unemployment rate from an all-time low of 3.8 percent up to the 8 percent range. Nonetheless, Albuquerque continues to be a **manufacturing** center for all manner of things, from computer chips to mattresses to specialty running shoes. And the city where Microsoft was founded (then Bill Gates and Paul Allen moved back to Seattle to be close to their families) is doing better at fostering **technology** development these days, as home to a range of tech specialists catering to Sandia National Labs and an **aerospace** manufacturing park growing on the west side. On the horizon is a solar farm that would produce electricity for 300,000 homes and, under the direction of the New Mexico Space Commission, the development of spacecraft by private companies at Spaceport America near Truth or Consequences.

Significant profits from coal, copper, oil, and natural-gas extraction—most in the southern part of the state, as well as in the northwest—keep the economy afloat. That's the big money, but the **agricultural** sector, from dairy cows in the south to apple orchards along the Rio Grande to beef jerky from the numerous cattle ranches, contributes a decent amount to the pot. And Santa Fe's **arts** sector shouldn't be overlooked—galleries post sales of $200 million every year, though they're criticized for sending much of that money right back out of the state to artists who live and work elsewhere. Finally, governor Richardson actively courted the **film industry,** nicknamed "Tamalewood," leading to a boom in movies shot against the dramatic backdrops of the state.

Even if the economic situation isn't ideal, it's nothing New Mexicans aren't used to—low income has been the norm for so long that a large segment of the population is, if not content with, at least adapted to eking out a living from very little (the median family income is only around $43,000). In this respect, the state hasn't lost its frontier spirit at all.

# The People

New Mexico's 1.8 million people have typically been described as a tricultural mix of Indians, Spanish, and whites. That self-image has slowly begun to expand as residents have delved deeper into history and seen that the story is a bit more complex.

## DEMOGRAPHY

The typical labels of Indians, Spanish, and Anglo are used uniquely in New Mexico. First, **Indians:** New Mexicans generally don't use the term "Native American." So you'll see "American Indian" in formal situations, but even the "American" part is a bit laughable, considering "America" wasn't so named until Christopher Columbus made his voyage west. In any case, "Indian" refers to a number of different peoples who do not share a common culture or language: Navajo on the west side of the state, Jicarilla and Mescalero Apache, and the Puebloans of the Rio Grande and west as far as Acoma and Zuni. (The latter term, Pueblo, is another problematic one, as it refers not to a particular tribe, but to a larger group of people who speak four distinct languages but are banded together by a common way of living.) With about 10 percent of the population claiming American Indian ancestry (which is 10 times the national average), traditions are still strong. Though of course they've changed, as neon-dyed feathers trim kids' ceremonial headdresses, and wealth from casinos funds elaborate museums as well as new housing projects.

**Spanish** really means that: the people,

primarily in northern New Mexico, whose ancestors were pure-blood Spaniards, rather than the mestizos of Mexico. For many families, it's a point of pride similar to that of Mayflower descendants. Over the years, particularly during the 20th century, a steady influx of Mexican immigrants has blurred racial distinctions a bit, but it has also helped preserve the local Spanish culture, in that it has reinforced the use of Spanish as a daily language and spurred pride in the culture's music and other folkways. Increasingly, the word **Hispano** is being used to label New Mexico's distinct culture with centuries-old Spanish roots, though this still doesn't accurately cover the **Basques,** who came here both during the conquest (Juan de Oñate, the first Spanish governor, was Basque) and in the early 20th century as sheepherders. And the recent discovery of families of **crypto-Jews** (Spanish Jews who nominally converted to Catholicism but fled here to avoid the Inquisition) has added another fascinating layer to the Spanish story.

**Anglo** is the most imprecise term of all, as it means anyone who's not Spanish or Indian. Originally used to talk about the white traders who came to hunt and sell furs and trade on the Santa Fe Trail, it still refers to people who can't trace their roots back to the conquistadors or farther. If you're a Vietnamese immigrant in Albuquerque, you're an Anglo. If you're a Tibetan refugee in Santa Fe, you're an Anglo. And even if you're an African-American farmer who settled here after the Civil War,

# LUMINARIAS OR *FAROLITOS?*

The cultural differences between Santa Fe and Albuquerque don't apply just to the number of art galleries per square block and whether you eat posole or rice on the side with your enchiladas. Every Christmas, an ugly debate rears its head: What do you call a paper bag with a bit of sand in the bottom and a votive candle inside? These traditional holiday decorations, which line the driveways and flat adobe rooftops in both cities in the last weeks of December, are known as luminarias in Albuquerque and most towns to the south, and as *farolitos* in Santa Fe and all the villages to the north.

To complicate matters, another common holiday tradition in Santa Fe and other northern towns is to light small bonfires of piñon logs in front of houses. And Santa Feans call these little stacks of wood...luminarias. *Faroli-*

*tos*, they argue, are literally "little lanterns," which certainly describes the glowing paper bags quite well – and under this logic, the use of *farolito* has spread a bit in Albuquerque, at least among people who weren't raised saying luminaria from birth.

But Albuquerqueans have Webster's on their side; the dictionary concurs that luminarias are paper-bag lanterns and notes the tradition comes from Mexico, where the bags are often colored and pricked with holes. (Perhaps Albuquerque's relative proximity to the border – and its larger proportion of Mexican immigrants – has shaped the language over the years?) In any case, because this author's own loyalties are to Albuquerque, the argument is settled, at least in these pages: Luminaria it is.

© NEW MEXICO TOURISM DEPARTMENT/DAN MONAGHAN

luminarias on Albuquerque's Old Town plaza

in some circles you're an Anglo. (According to 2008 estimates, about 42 percent of the population is non-Hispanic white; Asians are only 1.4 percent, and African Americans make up 3 percent.) But all Anglo culture is shot through with Spanish and Indian influence, whether among the organic garlic farmers from California who rely on their acequias for water or the New Age seekers who do sweatlodge rituals.

Even with this liberal application of "Anglo," the tricultural arrangement is a bit limiting, as it doesn't assign a place to contemporary immigrants from Mexico and other Latin American countries, and their numbers are growing steadily. It also doesn't acknowledge the strong Mexican-American **Chicano** culture that's shared across the Southwest, from Los Angeles through Texas. The U.S. census form lumps both newer arrivals and old Spanish under "Hispanic"—a category (distinct from race) that made up about 45 percent of the population in 2008.

## LANGUAGE

**English** is the predominant language, but once you get off the beaten track, you'll hear **Spanish** used more and more—about 29 percent of the population speaks it. Spanish-speakers in northern New Mexico were for centuries only the old Hispano families, communicating in a variant of Castilian with a distinct vocabulary that developed in isolation. This "Quixotic" dialect changed little until the 20th century, when immigrants began to arrive from Mexico and elsewhere in Latin America. For much of the 20th century, English was the only permissible classroom language, although many school districts required Spanish as a foreign language. Since the 1990s, education policy has shifted to include bilingual classrooms.

Additionally, you'll occasionally hear Indians speaking their respective languages. Of the four main Pueblo tongues, **Tiwa, Tewa,** and **Towa** are part of the Tanoan family of languages (Kiowa, spoken by Plains Indians, is the fourth member). They are all somewhat related but mutually unintelligible, roughly equivalent to, say, French,

Spanish, and Italian. Tewa is the most widely spoken, used in all of the pueblos just north of Santa Fe: Ohkay Owingeh, San Ildefonso, Santa Clara, Pojoaque, Tesuque, and Nambé. Four pueblos speak Tiwa—Taos and Picurís share one dialect, while Isleta and Sandia, in an odd pocket near Albuquerque, speak a different dialect. Towa is now spoken only at Jemez Pueblo. Part of the greater Athabaskan family, the **Navajo** and **Apache** languages are related to each but distinct from one another.

**Keresan** (spoken in Laguna, Acoma, Cochiti, Kewa, San Felipe, Santa Ana, and Zia) and **Shiwi** (spoken only at Zuni Pueblo) are what linguists call "isolates." Like Basque, they are unconnected not only to neighboring languages, but also to any other language. Additionally, each Keresan-speaking pueblo has developed its own dialect, such that immediately adjacent communities can understand each other, but those farthest apart cannot.

One interesting phenomenon of the Pueblo languages is that their speakers have managed to keep them relatively pure. Despite centuries of Spanish and English influence, Tewa vocabulary is still less than 5 percent loan words—probably due to the way speakers have long been forced to compartmentalize it, using it for conversation at home and switching to English or Spanish for business and trade. For centuries, the Franciscan priests, then the U.S. government attempted to stamp out Native American languages. Following the Civil War, Puebloan children were moved forcibly to boarding schools, where they were given Anglo names and permitted to speak only English, a policy that continued for decades.

Only in 1990, with the passage of the **Native American Languages Act,** were American Indian languages officially permitted in government-funded schools—indeed, they are now recognized as a unique element of this country's culture and encouraged. This has created an interesting practice in Taos, where the Tiwa language is a ritual secret that outsiders are not permitted to learn. But one Taos public school has Tiwa classes for younger students, open only to tribe members and taught by approved

# THE SECRET BROTHERHOOD: NEW MEXICO'S PENITENTES

In almost every small Hispano village in northern New Mexico is a modest one-story building called a *morada* – the meeting place of Los Hermanos Penitentes (The Penitent Brothers), a lay Catholic fraternity with deep roots in medieval Spain and a long and varied history that has often put it at odds with the church itself.

The Penitentes developed in New Mexico in the early colonial era and were at the height of their influence during the so-called Secular Period (1790–1850), when the Franciscans had been pushed out by church leaders in Mexico but no new priests were sent to the territory. The brotherhood, likely modeled after penitential fraternities in the Old World, cared for the ill and conducted funerals as well as settled petty disputes and even elections. They generally maintained the spiritual and political welfare of their villages when there were no priests or central government to do so.

What the Penitentes are best known for, however, is their intense religious ritual, which includes self-flagellation, blood-letting, and mock crucifixion – activities that took place in public processions for centuries but were driven underground following official church condemnation in the late 19th century. The secrecy, along with sensational journalism by visitors from the East Coast, fueled gruesome rumors about the brotherhood. Penitentes used real nails in their crucifixion reenactments, people said, and the man drawn by lot to be the *Cristo* had a good chance of dying (no eyewitness recorded the practice on paper, though). One well-documented ritual involves pulling *la carretera del muerte*, an oxcart filled with rocks and a wooden figure of Doña Sebastiana, the Angel of Death. Morbid imagery bred morbid curiosity: Photos in a *Harper's* magazine story from the early 20th century show Anglos looking on agog as Penitentes clad in white pants and black hoods whip themselves.

In 1947, after years of concerted lobbying (but not an official renunciation of its bloody rituals), the Penitentes were again accepted into the fold of the Catholic church. The *hermanos mayores* (head brothers) from all of the *moradas* (meeting houses) convene annually in Santa Fe, and the group, which has an estimated 3,000 members, has the outward appearance of a political and public-service club.

The rituals, though, do continue, most visibly during Holy Week. This is when the group's devotion to the physical suffering of the human Jesus is at its keenest. The Penitentes reenact the stations of the cross and the crucifixion, and although ketchup is more prevalent than real blood now and statues often stand in for the major players, the scenes are solemn and affectingly tragic. On some days during Holy Week, the *morada* is open to non-Penitentes for various rituals – a rare chance for outsiders to see the meeting place of this secretive group.

---

teachers; as an added measure against the language being recorded, the classroom has no chalkboard. Less formal instruction within the pueblos as well as on the Navajo Nation has also helped the Indian languages enjoy a renaissance lately.

## RELIGION

Four hundred years after the arrival of the Franciscan missionaries, New Mexico is still a heavily **Catholic** state—even KFC offers a Friday-night fish fry during Lent. But the relative isolation of the territory produced some variances that would no doubt disturb the Vatican. In both Indian and Spanish churches, the pageantry of medieval Christianity is preserved. Las Posadas, the reenactment of Mary and Joseph's search for lodging in Bethlehem, is a festive torch-lit tradition every December, and during the annual Holy Week pilgrimage to Chimayó, devoted groups stage the stations of the cross, complete with hundred-pound wood beams and lots of fake blood.

The Pueblo Indians play on church-as-theater too: During Christmas Eve Mass, for instance, it's not uncommon for the service to come to an abrupt end as the priest is hustled off the pulpit by face-painted clown figures who make way for the parade of ceremonial dancers down the aisle. In both cultures, the Mexican Virgin of Guadalupe is highly revered, and a number of saints are honored as intercessors for all manner of dilemmas, from failing crops to false imprisonment.

Eastern religions have a noticeable presence as well, and even a bit of political clout—a community of primarily American-born converts to **Sikhism** in Española, for example, is a major donor to both big political parties. Santa Fe is home to a substantial number of **Buddhists,** both American converts and native Tibetan refugees who have relocated to this different mountainous land. Stupas can be found up and down the Rio Grande.

# Food

New Mexicans love their food so much, they have been known to enshrine it on lottery tickets, with scratch cards named Chile Cash, Chips and Salsa, and Sopaipilla Dough (promising "lots of honey and plenty of money"). The state cuisine is a distinctive culinary tradition that shouldn't be confused with Tex-Mex or south-of-the-border Mexican—even though most locals will say they're going out for "Mexican" when they mean they want a bowl of purely *New* Mexican green-chile stew. (But if you're eating *mole* or *ceviche,* that's "Mexican-Mexican," and you can get more of it the farther south you drive.)

## ALL CHILE, ALL THE TIME

The cuisine's distinguishing element is the **New Mexico chile pepper,** also called the Hatch chile, for the name of the southern New Mexican town that's the center of the industry.

## RED CHILE SAUCE

Use only freshly ground New Mexico red chile for this sauce – not the "chile powder" sold in most grocery stores. The sauce will keep in the refrigerator for a month, and you can use it to top eggs or steaks, or devote the whole batch to a tray of enchiladas. (If you're doing the latter, you'll want to keep the sauce relatively runny, so you can easily coat the tortillas with sauce before filling them.) The flavor is best if it is prepared ahead and left to sit overnight.

*Yield: 2 cups*
½ c. New Mexico red chile powder
1 tsp. ground cumin
1 tsp. ground coriander
2 Tbsp. all-purpose flour
2 Tbsp. vegetable oil (or lard)
2 or 3 cloves garlic, crushed or minced
2 c. water or chicken stock
1 tsp. dried oregano (optional)

Measure the chile, cumin, coriander, and flour into a heavy-bottomed saucepan and place over medium-high heat. Stirring frequently, toast the spices until they are just fragrant and the flour has darkened slightly. Turn the heat down to low and push the chile mix to the sides of the pan so it is not directly over the flame. Pour in the oil, then add the garlic and stir until fragrant. Then stir the spices into the oil-garlic mixture – you will have a very coarse paste. Stirring constantly, slowly add half of the water or stock. The mixture should thicken and become velvety. Add the remaining water or stock and the oregano, mix well, turn heat to low, and let sauce simmer for about 20 minutes, until it is somewhat reduced and thickened to your liking. If the mixture becomes too thick, simply add more water.

In the north, Chimayó is another big chile-producing town. When the chile is picked green, it is roasted and frozen, to be used whole to make chiles rellenos (stuffed with cheese and fried in batter) or cut into chunks and used as the base of a meaty green-chile stew or blended into a sauce. In northern New Mexico, that sauce is pure chile, maybe thinned with chicken broth; in the southern part of the state, it's more like a green-chile gravy, with a creamy base.

Other chiles are left to ripen, then dried in the sun, where they turn dark red and leathery. The dry red chiles are then ground into powder or strung up whole in long chains called *ristras,* for use later in sauces or marinades. While some dishes, such as *carne adovada* (pork shoulder marinated with red chile), are only ever made with one type, most other items—enchiladas, burritos, and eggs (huevos rancheros), to name a few—can be ordered with either variety, so a standard question in restaurants is "Red or green?"

The chile is coupled with the traditional Native American triad of **corn, squash,** and **beans.** The beans are typically brown, meaty pintos, served whole in a stew or mashed up and "refried" (not actually fried twice—the term is a mistranslation of Spanish *refrito,* which means "really fried"). Corn makes its way into tortillas as well as into hulled kernels of hominy, called posole here and often cooked into a hearty stew with lamb or beef, chile, and oregano. Ground corn paste (masa) is whipped with lard (or Crisco, if you're "healthy") and wrapped around a meaty filling, then tied in a corn husk and steamed to make a **tamale** (a local corruption of the Spanish *tamal*). Squash comes in a common side dish called *calabacitas,* sautéed with onions and a touch of green chile. Spanish settlers brought lamb, which finds its way into tacos and stews.

Traditional Indian cuisine isn't so distinct from what everyone else eats—its one major element is **frybread,** a round of deep-fried dough served with honey or filled with ground meat, cheese, and lettuce to make an "Indian taco"; a "Navajo taco" often uses shredded lamb or mutton in place of ground beef. Bread baked in a traditional domed adobe *horno* oven is also popular, and the Zuni make a distinctive sourdough this way. On the reservations, you'll see these mud ovens in the yards of even modern houses. Game meat, such as deer, is also a major component of Indian cooking, though you'll rarely see it in restaurants.

Green chile makes its way into standard American fare as well. It's a popular pizza topping (great with pepperoni or ham), and the **green-chile cheeseburger** is a top choice at fast-food restaurants. Try the statewide Blake's Lotaburger mini-chain for excellent fresh burgers, as well as hand-cut fries and cherry Coke with extra syrup. Also look out for **breakfast burritos,** big flour tortillas filled with scrambled eggs, hash browns, and some kind of meat—bacon, crumbled sausage, or sometimes Mexican chorizo, a spicy pork sausage. Some places sell them as on-the-run food, in which case, green chile is added to the mix, and the whole thing is wrapped in foil. At sit-down places, you can opt to get the thing smothered in either red or green chile sauce and topped with cheese.

**Sopaipillas** are another New Mexican invention—they're little square bits of dough that puff up like pillows when deep-fried. They're used to mop up chile and beans during the main meal, then slathered with honey for dessert. (In a disturbing trend, some restaurants are switching to a honey-flavored corn syrup, because it's cheaper and doesn't crystallize—if you encounter this, complain at top volume.) **Bizcochitos,** little anise-laced butter cookies, are the state's official sweet treat. Wash it all down with a **margarita,** which purists insist should involve only lime, tequila, and triple sec and be served on the rocks in a salt-rimmed glass. You can get a slushy frozen margarita, but it's usually the mark of a restaurant that's pandering to tourists.

## HOW TO TAKE THE HEAT
When your server plunks down a heavy white ceramic plate covered in melted cheese and oozing chile sauce, the words "this plate is very hot" cover only half of the story. Every year the

*Hornos*, or outdoor adobe ovens, are a common sight in New Mexico.

harvest varies a bit, and the chile can be mild or so spicy as to blister lips and produce a dizzying (and addictive) endorphin rush. Locals look back on particularly incendiary seasons with that mixture of awe, fear, and longing that junkies reserve for their best scores. In general, green chile tends to be hotter than red, but it's a good idea to ask your server what to expect.

You can protect yourself against chile-induced burns by ordering a side of sour cream with your enchiladas or burrito—although be warned that this is seen as a "Texan" affectation and may be derided by your fellow diners. Locals usually just reach for a sopaipilla, the starch from which can absorb some of the chile oils. But don't gulp down water, which only spreads the searing oils around your mouth. Beer is a marginal improvement. If all else fails, there's the distracting power of margaritas.

## FINE DINING AND WINE

While there are plenty of time-warp diners and mom-and-pop hole-in-the-wall joints in New Mexico, dining can also be very sophisticated, keeping pace with the national trend toward local and organic produce. This movement hasn't been such a huge leap here; many small family farms didn't have to "go organic" because they were never industrialized in the first place. At white-tablecloth places, Southwestern fusion is the byword, with chile working its way into foie gras appetizers and even high-concept desserts. The fine dining scene is enhanced by a burgeoning wine industry, the product of Spanish settlers in the 17th century but enjoying a resurgence since the 1980s. Gruet Winery in Albuquerque is the best-known New Mexico producer, especially for its excellent sparkling wine. This is a boon to dining out, because you can get inexpensive fizzy wine by the glass almost everywhere. *Local Flavor*, a monthly tabloid magazine, and the glossy quarterly *Edible Santa Fe* cover artisanal food and high-end dining, which is centered in Santa Fe but has its proponents elsewhere in the state as well.

## VEGETARIAN FOOD

New Mexican food isn't a meat-centric cuisine, but vegetarians will have to be vigilant, as many chile dishes are traditionally made with beef or chicken stock as well as lard for flavoring. The closer you get to Texas, the more likely it is that red chile sauce will have bits of meat in it. Decades of hippie influence, though, have resulted in many menus stating clearly whether the chile is meatless. And quite a lot of restaurants have an unreconstructed 1970s worldview, with alfalfa sprouts and squash casseroles galore.

# Arts and Crafts

New Mexico is a hotbed of creativity, from Santa Fe's edgy contemporary art scene to traditional Spanish folk artists working in remote villages, using the same tools their great-grandfathers did, to whole Indian villages, such as Zuni, devoted to the production of fine silverwork. Here's what to look out for in the more traditional crafts.

## POTTERY

New Mexico's pottery tradition is perhaps the state's most thriving one, drawing on millennia of craftsmanship. About 2,000 years ago, the **Mogollon** people in the southern part of the state began making simple pots of brown coiled clay. A thousand years later, the craft had developed into the beautiful black-on-white symmetry of the **Mimbres** people. Later, each of the pueblos developed its own style; by the 20th century, some traditions had died out, but almost all felt some kind of renaissance following the work of San Ildefonso potter **María Martinez** in the first half of the 20th century. Along with her husband, Julian, Martinez revived a long-lost style of lustrous black pottery painted with geometric designs to make a subtle matte-on-shiny finish. The elegant pieces, at once innovative and traditional, inspired Anglo collectors (who saw the couple's work at the 1934 Chicago World's Fair, among other places) as well as local potters. Today, many artists make their livings from pottery, sold both in galleries and out of people's homes in the pueblos.

The various tribal styles are distinguished by their base clay, the "slip" (the clay-and-water finish), and particular shapes. Taos and Picurís pueblos, for instance, are surrounded by beds of micaceous clay; the mica helps the pots withstand heat well (they're renowned for cooking beans) and lends the pottery a subtle glitter. Acoma Pueblo specializes in intricate black-and-white painted designs. Pottery from Ohkay Owingeh (formerly called San Juan) is typically reddish-brown with incised symbols. And Santa Clara Pueblo developed the "wedding jar," a double-neck design with a handle. Traditional Navajo pottery is distinguished by "pitch" glaze (a coating of pine resin over the clay, giving it a shiny, waterproof finish) and "fire clouds," the grayish smudges left when burning wood has pressed against the clay during firing.

A whole other field of contemporary design is thriving too, with artists working in glass, for instance, or applying traditional decorative motifs to large-scale sculpture. If you're interested in buying, you can start by looking around Santa Fe and Albuquerque galleries—if there's a particular style that catches your eye, then visit the specific pueblo, where you may be able to buy directly from the artisan and perhaps see where the piece was made.

## TEXTILES

After pottery, **weaving** is probably the state's largest craft industry. Historically, Indian and Spanish weaving styles were separate, but they have merged over the centuries to create some patterns and styles unique to the Rio Grande Valley. Prior to the arrival of the Spanish, American Indians had already developed a weaving tradition—the Spanish explorers marveled especially at the Navajo cotton blankets, woven in whole panels on wide looms (Spaniards had been working with narrow looms and stitching two panels together) and featuring patterns of stepped diamonds. Spanish weavers introduced the hardy Churro sheep, with its rough wool that was good for hand-spinning, as well as new dyes, such as indigo (although the blue-tinted rugs are often called **Moki** rugs, using a Navajo word).

In the early 1800s, in an attempt to make a better product for trade, the Spanish government sent Mexican artists north to work with local weavers. Out of this meeting came the distinctive **Saltillo** styles (named for the region the Mexican teachers came from), such as the running-leaf pattern, which Rio Grande weavers alternated with solid-color stripes. In the 1880s, New Mexican artisans first saw quilts from the eastern United States, and they adapted the eight-pointed star to their wool rugs; another popular motif from the 19th century is a zigzag pattern that resembles lightning. One item that shows up in antique shops is the **Chimayó blanket,** an invention of the tourist age in the early 20th century, when Anglo traders encouraged local Hispano weavers to make an affordable souvenir to sell to visitors looking for "Indian" blankets. They're handsome, single-width rugs with a strong central motif, perhaps the iconic Southwestern-look rug. Also look for **colcha** work, a Spanish style in which a loose-weave rug is decorated with wool embroidery. It was revived in the 1930s by Mormons, and you will occasionally see beautiful examples from this period in collectors' shops. Contemporary weaving can draw on any and all of these innovations and is practiced just as often by a young Anglo as a Hispano grandmother. A strong small-batch wool industry in New Mexico helps the scene tremendously—expect to see vivid color-block contemporary pieces alongside the most traditional patterns.

## JEWELRY

The Indians of New Mexico have been making jewelry for thousands of years, though the familiar forms seen today date only from the mid-19th century, when the Navajo of western New Mexico pioneered silversmithing (it's thought they learned it during their internment at Fort Sumner) and taught it to the Pueblo Indians. The most iconic piece of Southwestern jewelry, a signature Navajo design, is the turquoise-and-silver **squash-blossom necklace,** a large crescent pendant decorated with flower-like silver beads. Actually derived from Spanish pomegranate decorations, rather than native plant imagery, it's readily seen in every Southwest jewelry store. Look also for shell-shape **concho belts** (also spelled concha), silver "shells" linked together or strung on a leather belt, and the San Felipe specialty, **heishi,** tiny disks made of shell and threaded to make a rope-like strand. The Zuni carve small animal **fetishes**—bears, birds, and more—often strung on necklaces with heishi. In addition to turquoise, opals are a popular decorative stone, along with brick-red coral, lapis lazuli, and black jet and marble. Whatever you buy, the gallery or artisan should supply you with a written receipt of its components—which stones, the grade of silver (sterling, ideally), and so forth.

## Shopping for Turquoise

Although New Mexico's turquoise is all mined out, the stone is still an essential part of local jewelry-making; most of it is imported from mines in China. It is available in shades from lime-green to pure sky-blue, and much of it has been subjected to various processes to make it more stable and versatile, which affects the price.

Rare gem-grade turquoise is the top of the line—a piece from now-empty mines like Lander or Lone Mountain can cost $40 per carat. "Gem-grade" applies only to **natural stones**—those that have not been chemically treated in any way—and is based on the piece's matrix (the spiderweb of dark veins running through it, which you should be able to feel in any natural turquoise, regardless of grade), luster, and hardness. Gem-grade turquoise pieces from still-functioning mines in China or Tibet will cost significantly less ($10–20 per carat) but will be of the same quality as some premium American stones.

© MICHAEL HAYES

Each pueblo has a distinct style of turquoise jewelry.

Slightly less splendid natural stones are graded jewelry-quality, high-quality, or investment-quality—but they are not quite hard enough to guarantee they will not change color over decades. They cost $2–5 per carat. For any natural stone, the seller must provide you with a written certificate of its status.

Turquoise that has been **stabilized,** or submerged in epoxy resin to prevent color change, makes up the bulk of the market. Because good natural turquoise is increasingly difficult to come by and turquoise is such an unreliable stone, stabilization is a perfectly acceptable way of making a great deal of the stuff usable. Because it's less expensive, it allows for a little waste in the carving process, and good-quality stabilized turquoise is often found in expensive jewelry with elaborate inlay. Average-quality stabilized stone, the next grade down, is used by perhaps 70 percent of American Indian artisans—it can stand up to being carved and is very well priced. Though it ranks relatively low in the range of turquoise available, it produces an

attractive piece of jewelry—perhaps not with the elaborate spiderwebbing of a rare piece, but with an overall good color and luster.

Below this are low-quality stabilized stones that have been artificially colored (often called "color shot," or, more confusing, "color stabilized"). **"Synthetic"** stones are actually real turquoise—small chunks mixed with a binding powder of ground turquoise or pyrite, then pressed into shapes and cut. The result is surprisingly attractive, with natural spiderwebbing, but it should be clearly labeled as synthetic. **Treated** turquoise has been submerged in water or oil to make it heavier and shinier, a scam with only temporary results—best avoided, but by its nature, it's seldom honestly labeled.

Aside from the treated stuff, don't worry too much about getting "bad" or "cheap" turquoise—because each stone is different, the more important thing is to find a piece that's attractive to you and is priced to reflect its quality. Just remember that the words "genuine," "authentic," or "pure" have no real meaning—only "natural" commands a premium. Shopping in New Mexico provides many opportunities to buy direct from the artisan—under the portal at the Palace of the Governors in Santa Fe, for instance. Otherwise, just avoid shopping in too-good-to-be-true stores that are perpetually "going out of business" or "in liquidation."

## WOOD AND TINWORK

When Spanish colonists arrived in New Mexico, they had few resources, little money, and only the most basic tools. The first group of settlers included one carpenter, whose skills helped the group both fill their houses with heavy wood **furniture** (still made today) and worship—for chief among the wood-carvers was (and is) the *santero* or *santera,* who carves images of saints out of wood. These images, called **santos,** can be either flat *(retablos)* or three-dimensional *(bultos)* and are typically painted in lively colors, though some outstanding work has been produced in plain, unpainted wood. Santo styles have shown remarkable continuity over the centuries—the most notable break from tradition was *santero* Patrocinio Barela, whose work, sponsored by the WPA in the 1930s, employed fluid, modernist shapes that utilize the natural curves and grains of the wood. His sons and grandsons practice the art today. For centuries, the piousness of the *santero* was valued at least as much as his skill in carving, though many contemporary carvers do their work for a large market of avid collectors. One popular figure is

decorative tin mirror with painted glass

© ZORA O'NEILL

San Isidro, patron saint of farmers, from 12th-century Spain.

Look also for **straw marquetry,** another product of hard times in the colonial period, in which tiny fibers of "poor man's gold" replaced precious metals as inlay to make elaborate geometric designs on dark wood. Tinwork is another ubiquitous craft, found in inexpensive votive-candle holders as well as elaborately punched and engraved mirror frames and chandeliers.

# ESSENTIALS

## Getting There

### BY AIRPLANE

**Albuquerque International Sunport** (ABQ; 505/244-7700, www.cabq.gov/airport) is the main access point to the region. It's served by all major U.S. air carriers, though only Southwest Airlines runs occasional direct flights from the East and West Coasts. Fares fluctuate on the same schedule as the rest of the country, with higher rates in summer and over holidays; in the winter, it's wise to choose a connection through a more temperate hub, such as Dallas (American) or Salt Lake City (Delta).

Small **Santa Fe Municipal Airport** (SAF; 505/955-2900), west of the city, receives

direct flights from Dallas and Los Angeles with American Eagle. For visiting the southern half of the state, you might find it easier to fly into **El Paso International Airport** (ELP; 915/780-4749, www.elpasointernationalairport.com), Texas, just an hour's drive from Las Cruces.

### BY BUS

**Greyhound** (800/231-2222, www.greyhound.com) connects New Mexico with adjacent states and Mexico. Routes run roughly along I-40 and I-25, with little service to outlying areas. If you're coming from elsewhere in the Southwest, you may want to investigate

© ZORA O'NEILL

**El Paso-Los Angeles Limousine Express** (915/532-4061 in El Paso, 626/442-1945 in Los Angeles, 505/247-8036 in Albuquerque, www.elpalimo.com), the biggest operator of bargain bus service for the Mexican immigrant population—its route runs east–west from El Paso to Los Angeles, stopping in Las Cruces, Deming, and Albuquerque. It also connects Denver and Albuquerque. It's both less expensive and more comfortable than Greyhound. It helps to have some basic Spanish when calling.

## BY TRAIN

**Amtrak** (800/USA-RAIL, www.amtrak.com) runs the Southwest Chief daily between Chicago and Los Angeles, stopping in **Raton, Las Vegas, Lamy** (18 miles from Santa Fe, connected with a shuttle), **Albuquerque,** and **Gallup.** Traveling by train, if you have the time to do it, is a rewarding experience, as you'll get a great sense of New Mexico's isolation—as well as what a dramatic change the railroad made when it arrived in 1880.

Arriving in Albuquerque, you're in the middle of downtown with full services available, but other stops are usually nothing more than an unstaffed depot. From Chicago, Amtrak pads its schedule heavily between Lamy and Albuquerque—so if the train is running behind, you'll be late arriving in Lamy, but generally will still get to Albuquerque on schedule.

Amtrak's Sunset Limited train, from Florida to Los Angeles via the southern edge of the state, is significantly less useful—it requires a bus transfer from El Paso to **Las Cruces,** and then makes stops in **Deming** and **Lordsburg.**

# Getting Around

Practically speaking, you will need a car. Traveling between towns by bus or train is feasible, but it certainly limits what you can see; buses rarely run more than once a day between any two points, and they travel only on the main highways. To cover the longer distances, flying is a possibility—**New Mexico Airlines** (888/564-6119, www.flynma.com) and **Great Lakes Aviation** (800/554-5111, www.flygreatlakes.com) are the two companies with flights between Albuquerque and Alamogordo, Carlsbad, Clovis, Farmington, and Silver City.

Within Albuquerque and Santa Fe, you can often get around by walking, biking, or public transport, but getting to or around anywhere smaller requires your own wheels.

## BY CAR

Driving New Mexico's scenic byways is one of the pleasures of traveling here. All of the major car-rental chains are at Albuquerque's airport, in a single convenient center; see the respective city chapters for other rental companies and offices. In Santa Fe, parking can be limited, and it's easy enough to get around on foot, so you may prefer not to rent a car for the days you're in the city.

All but a few roads described in this book are passable year-round and don't require four-wheel drive or any other special equipment, though be prepared in winter for ice and snow anywhere other than central Albuquerque and the southernmost section of the state. Also check your car rental agreement for restrictions on driving on dirt roads—a rare clause in the United States, but occasionally employed by smaller companies. Needless to say, this is a liability, as it's almost impossible to go anywhere interesting in New Mexico without winding up on a dirt road at some point.

## BY BUS

**Greyhound** (800/231-2222, www.greyhound.com) connects Albuquerque with Santa Fe, Taos, and Las Cruces, as well as most other midsize towns. The most useful route is along I-25 from Las Cruces to Albuquerque and Santa Fe, and the east–west run along I-40. After this, you're getting into trickier territory,

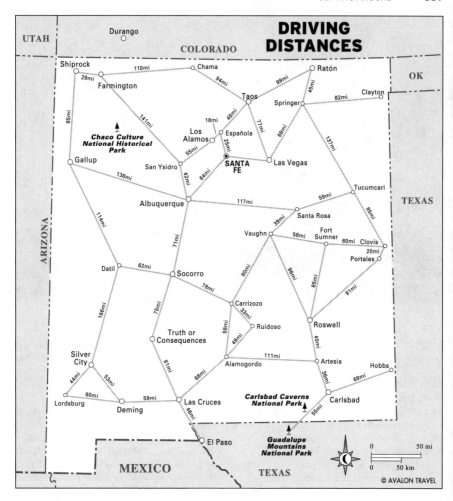

# DRIVING DISTANCES

UTAH

COLORADO

OK

TEXAS

ARIZONA

MEXICO

TEXAS

Durango

Shiprock

Farmington

110mi

Chama

94mi

Taos

Ratón

Springer

99mi

45mi

Clayton

82mi

29mi

85mi

141mi

18mi

46mi

Los
Alamos

Española

77mi

68mi

137mi

**Chaco Culture
National Historical
Park**

55mi

25mi

**SANTA
FE**

Las Vegas

Gallup

San Ysidro

42mi

64mi

138mi

Albuquerque

117mi

Santa Rosa

Tucumcari

59mi

85mi

71mi

39mi

Vaughn

Fort
Sumner

58mi

60mi

Clovis

20mi

Portales

114mi

Datil

62mi

Socorro

78mi

80mi

96mi

85mi

91mi

166mi

75mi

Carrizozo

33mi

Ruidoso

Roswell

Truth or
Consequences

58mi

49mi

Silver
City

81mi

68mi

111mi

Alamogordo

Artesia

40mi

Hobbs

44mi

53mi

36mi

69mi

60mi

59mi

Las Cruces

**Carlsbad Caverns
National Park**

Carlsbad

Lordsburg

Deming

46mi

55mi

El Paso

**Guadalupe
Mountains
National Park**

0          50 mi

0      50 km

© AVALON TRAVEL

with transfers in Las Cruces for any part of the southeast, and no service at all in the southwest mountains (Deming and other towns on I-10 are served, though).

## BY TRAIN

**Amtrak** (800/USA-RAIL, www.amtrak.com) doesn't cover enough territory in New Mexico to be a practical option, but the trip between Albuquerque and Gallup or Albuquerque and Las Vegas is short enough to be a pleasant

outing, and in both towns, you can see a reasonable amount on foot once you've arrived. Given the schedules, you could visit each place on an overnight trip without involving a car.

The **Rail Runner** (866/795-RAIL, www.nmrailrunner.com) commuter train connects Albuquerque and Santa Fe, with convenient downtown stations in both cities, making a car-free visit quite feasible—you can even pop up to Santa Fe just for the day. The train passes through odd pockets of Albuquerque and

© ZORA O'NEILL

The Rail Runner arrives near Santa Fe's plaza.

stunning, untouched pueblo lands. The 90-minute train ride costs $7, or $8 for a day pass.

## BY BIKE

With beautiful vistas, often deserted roads, and a strong community of both road cyclists and mountain bikers, New Mexico can be a great place to get around on two wheels, as long as it's not your main form of transport. Whether you'll be riding your own bike or renting one here, always pack a patch kit—goathead thorns and broken glass are particular scourges of the highway shoulder. You may want to install tire liners.

Within cities, central Albuquerque is particularly bike-friendly and evolving all the time, while Santa Fe has some bike lanes. Las Cruces is moderately accommodating.

## TOURS

If you have a particular interest, such as art or archaeology, or just a limited amount of time to see the area, you may want to arrange a custom tour. **Destination 505** (505/424-9500, www.destination505.com), a Santa Fe–based company, has a roster of area-savvy experts in archaeology, Pueblo Indian culture, and history to act as guides. Daylong tours or walking tours are recommended in destination chapters.

# Accommodations

Whether you want to lay your head in a refurbished Airstream trailer or a cave carved in a cliff face, you can do it in New Mexico. Throughout the book, these distinctive choices (along with many exceptionally comfortable bed-and-breakfasts, lodges, and small hotels) are emphasized over chain options as much as possible. But just because the chains are not listed doesn't mean they're not available—and in many small towns, they're the only option. As of last pass in 2010, generally the newest franchises were from Holiday Inn Express.

The prices listed are the official high-season rack rates—that is, what you'd pay if you just walked in off the street, with no discounts; tax is not included. Most often, the numbers are the least expensive room for one person in one bed (a single, abbreviated *s*) and two people in two beds (a double, abbreviated *d*)—suites and other premium rooms can of course run a lot higher. High season is usually June–August and, in the mountains, the ski season is January–March. Expect slightly higher rates in the week following Christmas and during special events, such as Indian Market in Santa Fe, but overall you will probably be able to secure lower rates than those listed simply by looking online or calling the hotel directly.

Note that while many hotels tout their swimming pools, they are often forced to leave them empty due to water restrictions imposed during severe droughts (which, these days, is nearly all the time). If you've booked at a hotel specifically for the pool, you might want to check the status before your trip, so you don't wind up paying a premium for a service you can't use. Santa Fe is usually the strictest area in the state, and it also limits hotels to changing towels and bed linens only every four days.

## RANCHES AND RETREATS

With all its wide-open spaces, New Mexico has lot of lodging particularly suited to big groups or families, or to people just looking to pass some quiet time alone. In the *Santa Fe* chapter, look

## ONLINE HOTEL BOOKING

Albuquerque and Santa Fe have more hotels than can possibly be reviewed here, with many options that are more than adequate, if not particularly special – unless they can be booked cheaply. In Albuquerque, online booking often shows major discounts for:

- Best Western Rio Grande (www.riograndeinn.com)
- Sheraton Albuquerque Uptown (www.sheratonabq.com)
- La Quinta (www.lq.com) on the west side (but not the east)

In Santa Fe, the following are reliable and often less than $100:

- King's Rest Court (505/983-8879)
- Santa Fe Suites (www.thesantafesuites.com)
- America's Best Value Inn Lamplighter (www.abvilamplighter.com)
- Fort Marcy Suites (www.allseasonsresortlodging.com)

For deals on high-end properties in Santa Fe, "blind" booking sites Hotwire and Priceline are your friends. Hotwire divides Santa Fe neighborhoods in such a way that you can often narrow down the hotels on offer. In the "Santa Fe Mountain" neighborhood, for instance, the only five-star property is Encantado (www.encantadoresort.com); Bishop's Lodge is also up this way, rated as a four-star property. Around Santa Fe Plaza, the only four-and-a-half-star property with a pool is La Posada de Santa Fe (laposada.rockresorts.com) – grossly overpriced normally, but fine if you can get it for less than $150 per night. A four-star property with a spa is either Hotel Santa Fe (www.hotelsantafe.com) or the Inn and Spa at Loretto (www.innatloretto.com). Happy deal-hunting!

for **Rancho Jacona,** which has family-friendly houses with kitchens, a swimming pool, and lots of farm animals and sprawling gardens, and **Ghost Ranch,** which has basic sleeping and meeting facilities in a gorgeous natural setting. A step up in price takes you to **Bishop's Lodge,** which in addition to the usual hotel perks has hiking trails and a stable of horses. In the *Taos* chapter, see **Mabel Dodge Luhan House,** which has a huge communal kitchen and dining area. In Ruidoso (see *Carlsbad Caverns and the Southeast*), **Noisy Water Lodge** has a big old lodge building with a fireplace that's perfect as a group get-together spot.

In addition to these places, **Cimarroncita** (U.S. 64, 575/376-2376, www.cimarroncita. com) is a beautiful spot midway between Eagle Nest and Cimarron, high in the Sangre de Cristos. It doesn't take in regular overnight guests, but it can be rented to groups. A former girls camp, it has been converted to more grownup tastes, with all-white linens and clawfoot tubs in the shared bathrooms. The staff can organize fishing, horseback riding, and other activities.

© ZORA O'NEILL

**New Mexico offers hotels for every taste.**

## Conduct and Customs

New Mexico may be a part of the United States, but it can sometimes feel quite foreign, particularly in the high mountain Spanish villages and in the Indian pueblos. But basic courtesy still rules, starting with limiting your cell-phone use in public—this is still considered a bit tacky in both the cities and the small towns. Also, women should dress somewhat modestly for visiting the older Catholic churches—at least put a layer over a tank top.

New Mexico is not a wealthy state, and the gap between rich and poor can be wide; in general, people don't appreciate conspicuous displays of wealth, and it's doubly rude to flash cash, fancy gadgets, and jewelry in tiny subsistence-living villages and pueblos. Be

thoughtful when taking photos, particularly of people's homes—always ask permission, and consider that some of the more "scenic" elements of New Mexico are also the products of poverty, which some people may not be proud to have captured on film.

You can help the local economy by favoring New Mexican–owned businesses, rather than chain operations. Also try to buy directly from artisans wherever possible. In these situations, don't get too bent on bargaining—the item you're purchasing represents not just raw materials and hours of work, but a person's particular talent, skill, and heritage; insisting on an extra-low price belittles not just the item, but the artisan as well.

## PUEBLO AND RESERVATION ETIQUETTE

Visiting pueblos and reservations calls for particular behavior. Remember that you are not at a tourist attraction—you are walking around someone's neighborhood, so peeking in windows and wandering off the suggested route (most visitors centers will give you a basic map to follow) isn't polite. If you want to take photos, you'll usually need a camera permit, for an additional fee; always ask permission before taking photos of people, and ask parents, rather than children, for their consent. Most pueblos ban alcohol as well—if not all the time, then certainly on feast days.

Some pueblos are more welcoming than others—San Ildefonso, for instance, is open year-round, whereas Jemez is completely closed, except for some feast days. It's flawed logic, then, to seek out the less-visited places or go in the off times in order to have a less "touristy" experience because the private pueblos will not be at all welcoming to strangers poking around among their homes. The most rewarding time to visit *is* on a big feast day—although you won't be the only tourist there, you have a better chance of being invited into a local's home. In general, many Pueblo Indians, as well as Navajo, find loud voices, direct eye contact, and firm handshakes off-putting and, by the same token, may not express themselves in the forthright way a lot of other Americans are used to. Similarly, a subdued reaction doesn't necessarily mean a lack of enthusiasm.

# Tips for Travelers

## STUDY AND VOLUNTEERING

From afternoon cooking classes to a semester-long intensive on adobe building techniques, the opportunities to learn in New Mexico are broad. Santa Fe and Albuquerque are both home to renowned alternative healing, herbal medicine, and massage schools, more than can be listed here; if you're interested, visit www.naturalhealers.com for a list.

### General Education

Look first into the art, music, and outdoors programs at **Ghost Ranch** (877/804-4678, www.ghostranch.org), both at the beautiful property in Abiquiu and at the Santa Fe campus; of particular interest is **Zoukfest** (www.zoukfest.com), a world folk-music workshop, in November. The El Rito campus of **Northern New Mexico College** (575/581-4115, www.nnmc.edu), north of Abiquiu, runs the **Heritage Retreat Center,** offering Spanish immersion classes and short-term workshops in traditional crafts.

### Cooking Classes

**Santa Fe School of Cooking** (116 W. San Francisco St., 505/983-4511, www.santafeschoolofcooking.com) offers day classes not only in contemporary Southwestern cuisine, but also in traditional Native American cooking (author Lois Ellen Frank instructs) and New Mexican standards; nice farmers market trips and restaurant walking tours are offered too.

An experienced chef and former restaurant owner runs **Cooking Studio Taos** (575/776-2665, www.cookingstudiotaos.com); class topics cover the globe, with one New Mexican class a month. In Dixon, **Comida de Campos** (505/852-0017, www.comidadecampos.com) offers classes on cooking in a traditional outdoor *horno,* and occasionally in clay-pot cooking, all in a beautiful farm setting.

### Permaculture and Alternative Construction

At Santa Fe's **Ecoversity** (2639 Agua Fria St., 505/424-9797, www.ecoversity.org), you can dip in with daylong sessions on topics like making your own biodiesel, beekeeping, or setting up edible gardens. **Seeds of Change** (888/762-7333, www.seedsofchange.com), dedicated to preserving biodiversity in agricultural products, occasionally runs tours of its six-acre research farm in El Guique, just outside of Santa Fe.

If you're interested specifically in northern New Mexico's solar architecture movement, you can take a three-day **Earthship Seminar** (575/751-0462, www.earthship.org), a crash course in building the off-the-grid rammed-earth houses that are springing up around Taos. The Earthship Biotecture organization also accepts volunteers. For more on local building styles, look into the intensive semester-long classes in adobe construction at **Northern New Mexico College** (575/581-4115, www.nnmc.edu).

## FOREIGN TRAVELERS

As for any destination in the United States, check before departure whether you'll need a **visa** to enter; most European and Latin American nationals do not need one, however.

New Mexico uses the **United States dollar,** and currency exchange is available at most banks as well as in better hotels, though the rates in the latter case will not be as good. For the best rates and convenience, withdraw cash from your home account through **automatic teller machines** (ATMs), located in bank lobbies and, increasingly, in shops and restaurants; check first, though, what fee your home bank and the ATM's bank will charge you for the transaction. Otherwise, **travelers' checks** from known brands are accepted—American Express is well known, Visa and Thomas Cook less so. It's best if you can buy them in U.S. dollar amounts, though, rather than British pounds, to avoid an additional transaction while traveling.

**Tipping** etiquette is similar to elsewhere in the country: 15–20 percent on restaurant bills (though often restaurants will add 15 percent or so to the bill for groups of six or more); $1 or so per drink when ordered at the bar; 15 percent to cab drivers; $1 or $2 to staff who

Don't worry – you can get cash from an ATM almost anywhere.

handle your luggage in hotels; and $1 or $2 per day to housekeeping in hotels—envelopes are often left in rooms for this purpose, though if you don't see one, don't assume a tip won't be appreciated. **Bargaining** is usually accepted only if you're dealing directly with an artisan, and sometimes not even then—it doesn't hurt to ask, but don't press the issue if the seller won't budge.

**Electricity** is 120 volts, with a two-prong, flat-head plug, the same as Canada and Mexico.

## TRAVELERS WITH DISABILITIES

Wheelchair access can be a little frustrating in some historic properties and on the narrower sidewalks of Santa Fe and Taos, but in most other respects, travelers with disabilities should find no more problems in New Mexico than elsewhere in the United States. Public buses are wheelchair-accessible, for instance, and you can even get out in nature a bit on paved trails such as the Santa Fe Canyon Preserve loop or the Paseo del Bosque in Albuquerque. If you'll be visiting a lot of wilderness areas, you should get the National Park Service's **Access Pass** (888/467-2757, www.nps.gov), a free lifetime pass that grants admission for the pass-holder and three adults to all national parks, national forests, and the like, as well as discounts on interpretive services, camping fees, fishing licenses, and more. Apply in person at any federally managed park or wilderness area; you must show medical documentation of blindness or permanent disability.

The **Governor's Committee on Concerns for the Handicapped** (491 Old Santa Fe Tr., 505/827-6465 voice, 505/827-6329 TDD, www.gcd.state.nm.us) occasionally publishes a print guide outlining accessibility features of major sights, restaurants, and more, but you may still want to call places ahead to make sure they can accommodate you.

## SENIORS

Senior discounts are available at most museums and other attractions. If you'll be visiting a number of wilderness areas, look into a **Senior Pass,** a lifetime pass for people 62 and older that grants free admission for the pass-holder and three additional adults to national parks, National Forest Service lands, and many other areas, as well as a 50 percent discount on activities such as camping and boat-launching. The pass can be purchased only in person at a federally managed wilderness area for just $10; for more information, contact the **National Parks Service** (888/467-2757, www.nps.gov).

**Road Scholar,** formerly known as Elderhostel (877/426-8056, www.roadscholar. org), runs more than 40 group trips in northern New Mexico, from a five-day general introduction to Santa Fe history to slightly longer tours focusing on the legacy of Georgia O'Keeffe, for instance, or strategies in Native American museum curation and conservation. Prices are very reasonable.

## TRAVELING WITH CHILDREN

Hispanic and American Indian cultures are typically very child-friendly, so your little ones will be welcome in most environments, including restaurants and hotels. The only exception would be some of the more formal restaurants in Santa Fe and Albuquerque. Kids are sure to be fascinated by ceremonial dances at the pueblos, but be prepared with distracting games, as long waits are the norm. Prep children with information about American Indian culture beforehand, and brief them on the basic etiquette at dances, which applies to them as well. Kids will also enjoy river rafting (relaxing, less risky "floats" along placid sections of the Rio Grande and Rio Chama are best) as well as skiing; Taos Ski Valley in particular has a very strong program of classes for youngsters. Though the specific prices are not listed in this guide, admission prices at major attractions are almost always lower for children than for adults.

## GAY AND LESBIAN TRAVELERS

Santa Fe is one of the major gay capitals in the United States, second only to San Francisco in the per-capita rates of same-sex coupledom, and particularly popular with lesbians. There are no designated "gay-borhoods" (unless you count RainbowVision Santa Fe, a retirement community) or even particular bar scenes—instead, gay men and lesbian women are well integrated throughout town, running businesses and serving on the city council. Two weeks in June are dedicated to Pride on the Plaza, a festive time of gay-pride arts events and parades. Albuquerque also has a decent gay scene, especially if you want to go clubbing, which is not an option in quieter Santa Fe. As for smaller towns and pueblos, they're still significantly more conservative.

Gay culture in the state isn't all about cute shops and cool bars. One big event is the annual **Zia Regional Rodeo,** sponsored by the **New Mexico Gay Rodeo Association** (505/720-3749, www.nmgra.com). It takes place every June in Albuquerque, with all the standard rodeo events, plus goat dressing and a wild drag race.

# Health and Safety

Visitors to New Mexico face several unique health concerns. First and foremost are the simple environmental hazards of **dehydration, sunburn,** and **altitude sickness.** The desert climate, glaring sun, and thin ozone layer conspire to fry your skin to a crisp and drain you of all moisture. (On the plus side, sweat evaporates immediately.) Apply SPF 30 sunscreen daily, even in winter, and try to drink at least a couple of liters of water a day, whether you feel thirsty or not; remember to ask for water in restaurants—it's usually brought only on demand, to cut down on waste. After you start feeling thirsty, you're already seriously dehydrated, and at risk of further bad effects: headaches, nausea, and dizziness, all of which can become full-blown, life-threatening **heatstroke** if left untreated. It doesn't even take serious exertion—just lack of water and very hot sun—to develop heatstroke, so if you're feeling at all woozy or cranky (another common symptom), head for shade and sip a cold drink. Gatorade or a similar electrolyte-replacement drink is a good choice.

Staying hydrated will also help stave off the effects of the high elevation, which most visitors will not be used to. The mildest reaction to being 7,000 feet or more above sea level is simple lethargy or lightheadedness—you will probably sleep long and soundly on your first night in New Mexico. Some people do have more severe reactions, such as a piercing headache or intense nausea, especially if they engage in strenuous physical activity. Unfortunately, there's no good way to judge how your body will react, so give yourself a few days to acclimate, with a light schedule and plenty of time to sleep.

More obscure hazards include **West Nile virus** (wear a DEET-based insect repellent if you're down along the river in the summer); **Hanta virus,** an extremely rare pulmonary ailment transmitted by rodents; and the even rarer **bubonic plague** (a.k.a. The Black Death), the very same disease that killed millions of Europeans in the Middle Ages. Luckily, only a case or two of the plague crops up every year, and it's easily treated if diagnosed early. **Lyme disease** is so far nonexistent, as deer ticks do not flourish in the mountains.

If you'll be spending a lot of time hiking or camping, take precautions against **giardiasis** and other waterborne ailments by boiling your water or treating it with iodine or a SteriPen (www.steripen.com)—even the clearest mountain waterways may have been tainted by cows upstream. **Snake bites** are also a small hazard in the wild, so wear boots that cover your ankles, stay on trails, and keep your hands and feet out of odd holes and cracks between rocks. Only the Western

*Descansos* mark a dangerous spot on the low road to Taos.

diamondback is aggressive when disturbed; other snakes will bolt and will not bite if you simply back away quietly.

And the general **outdoor safety rules** apply: Don't hike by yourself, always register with the ranger station when heading out overnight, and let friends know where you're going and when you'll be back. Pack a good topographical map and a compass or GPS device; people manage to get lost even when hiking in the foothills, and if you're at all dehydrated or dizzy from the altitude, any disorientation can be magnified to a disastrous degree. Also pack layers of clothing, and be prepared for cold snaps and snow at higher elevations, even in the summer.

## CRIME AND DRUGS

Maybe it's partially the influence of American Indian culture, with its strong tradition of hallucinogen-induced shamanism, but recreational drug use is not uncommon in New

Mexico—generally in a relatively benign form, with marijuana fairly widespread (former governor Gary Johnson, though not a user himself, has been a strenuous advocate for its legalization).

But as in much of the rural United States, crystal methamphetamine is an epidemic, and some villages in northern New Mexico have also been devastated by heroin use, with overdose deaths at a rate several hundred times higher than the national average. A side effect has been a lot of petty theft, especially in isolated areas such as trailheads; always lock your car doors, and secure any valuables in the trunk. Don't leave anything enticing in view.

Drinking and driving is unfortunately still common, especially in rural areas; be particularly alert when driving at night. A distressing number of crosses along the roadside (*descansos*) mark the sites of fatal car accidents, many of which had alcohol involved.

# Information and Services

## MAPS AND TOURIST INFORMATION

Before your trip, you may want to contact the **New Mexico Tourism Board** (800/733-6396, ext. 0643, www.newmexico.org) for a free visitors guide; the board's website is packed with background information and listings of special events. The organization also publishes the monthly *New Mexico* magazine (www.nmmagazine.com), which covers both mainstream attractions and more obscure corners of the state. If you plan to do a lot of hiking, you can order detailed topographical maps from the **National Forest Service** office in New Mexico (505/842-3292) or from the Bureau of Land Management's **Public Lands Information Center** (www.publiclands.org). Santa Fe and Albuquerque also have active convention and visitors bureaus, and many smaller towns' chambers of commerce can be

extremely helpful; look for their contact details under the *Information and Services* heading associated with each town.

## TELEPHONE AND INTERNET

Mobile phones on the GSM network (Cingular, T-Mobile) get very poor or no reception in rural areas. The corridor between Albuquerque and Santa Fe is fine, but if you'll be spending a lot of time outside of these two cities, you might consider a CDMA phone (Verizon is reliable), particularly if you're counting on it for emergency use.

Internet access is widespread, though DSL and other high-speed service has not yet arrived everywhere. There are not many Internet cafés catering to travelers, but you should be able to find one or two places with hourly rates in each city; when in doubt, head to the public library. Wireless hot spots are prevalent, and the city of

Albuquerque even maintains a few completely free ones—most notably in the airport. Thick adobe walls can be a hindrance to consistent reception, however.

## TIME ZONE

New Mexico is in the mountain time zone, one hour ahead of the West Coast of the United States and two hours behind the East Coast. It's –7 GMT during the winter and –6 GMT in summer, when daylight saving time is followed statewide.

In New Mexico, *"Hasta la vista"* is more than a quote from a movie.

# RESOURCES

## Glossary

*abierto* Spanish for "open"

*acequia* an irrigation ditch, specifically one regulated by the traditional Spanish method, maintained by a *mayordomo,* or "ditch boss," who oversees how much water each shareholder receives

*adobe* a building material of sun-dried bricks made of a mix of mud, sand, clay, and straw

*arroyo* a stream or dry gully where mountain runoff occasionally flows

*asado* pork stew with plenty of red chile

*atrio* the churchyard between the boundary wall and the church entrance, usually used as a cemetery

*bizcochito* anise-laced hard cookie, traditionally made with lard but now more commonly baked with butter

*bosque* Spanish for "forest," referring specifically to the cottonwoods and other wetlands growth along a river

*bulto* a three-dimensional wood carving, typically of a saint

*caldera* a basin or crater formed by a collapsed volcano

*canal* a water drain from a flat roof; pl. *canales*

*carne adovada* pork chunks marinated in red chile, then braised; the result is meatier and dryer than *asado.*

*cerrado* Spanish for "closed"

*chicharrón* fried pork skin, usually with a layer of meat still attached, incorporated into burritos and bowls of chile

*chile* not to be confused with Texas-style meat-and-beans chili; refers to the fruit of the chile plant itself, eaten green (picked unripe then roasted) or red (ripened and dried)

*chimichanga* a deep-fried burrito; allegedly invented in Arizona

*colcha* a style of blanket, in which loom-woven wool is embellished with long strands of wool embroidery

*enchilada* a corn tortilla dipped in chile sauce then filled with cheese or meat, then topped with more chile; can be served either rolled or flat (stacked in layers)

*farolito* in Santa Fe and Taos, a luminaria

*genízaro* during Spanish colonial times, a detribalized Indian who lived with Spaniards and followed Catholic tradition, usually due to having been taken as a slave

*gordita* a variation on the taco, with a thicker tortilla-like shell, often deep-fried; these are a more traditionally Mexican dish (though in that case rarely fried) and are available only in the southern part of the state

*heishi* fine disk-shaped beads carved from shells

*horno* a traditional dome-shaped adobe oven

*jerga* a Spanish-style wool blanket or rug, usually loosely woven and barely decorated, meant for daily use

*kachina* an ancestral spirit of the Pueblo people as well as the carved figurine representing the spirit; also spelled katsina

*kiva* the sacred ceremonial space in a pueblo, at least partially underground and entered by a hole in the ceiling. Only men are allowed in the kiva, and outsiders are never permitted to enter.

*latillas* thin saplings cut and laid across vigas to make a solid ceiling

**lowrider** an elaborately painted and customized car with hydraulic lifts

**luminaria** in Albuquerque, a lantern made of a sand-filled paper bag with a votive candle set inside; in Santa Fe and Taos, refers to small bonfires lit during the Christmas season

*menudo* tripe soup, said to be good for curing a hangover

*morada* the meeting space of the Penitente brotherhood

*nicho* a small niche in an adobe wall, usually meant to hold a santo

**Penitente** a member of a strict Catholic brotherhood

**petroglyph** a rock carving

**pictograph** a painting on a rock surface

*portal* the covered sidewalk area in front of a traditional adobe structure; pl. *portales*

**posole** stew of hominy (soaked, hulled corn), pork, and a little chile, either green or red

**pueblo** literally Spanish for "village," the word for the various communities of American Indians settled along the Rio Grande Valley; also identifies the people themselves, though they are not of the same tribe and speak several different languages

*rajas* rough-hewn slats laid over vigas to form a ceiling; also, strips of roasted chile

**ramada** a simple structure built of four sapling posts and topped with additional saplings laid flat, to form a shade structure and a place to hang things to dry

**reredos** an altar screen, usually elaborately painted or carved with various portraits of Christ and the saints

*retablo* a flat portrait of a saint, painted or carved in low relief, usually on wood

*ristra* a string of dried red chiles

**santo** a portrait of a saint, either flat (a *retablo*) or three-dimensional (a *bulto*)

*sipapu* the hole in the floor of a kiva, signifying the passage to the spirit world

**sopaipilla** square of puffed fried dough, served with honey for dessert, as well as with the main meal, for wiping up sauces

**tamale** a corn husk filled with masa (hominy paste) and a dab of meat, vegetables, or cheese, then steamed; usually made in large quantities for holidays

*terrón* a building material of bricks cut out of sod and dried in the sun – similar to adobe, but much more rare in New Mexico

**Tewa** the language spoken by the majority of Pueblo Indians; others in the Rio Grande Valley speak Tiwa, Towa, and Keresan

*torreón* a round defensive tower built in Spanish colonial times

*vato* a cool Chicano, usually driving a lowrider

*viga* a ceiling beam, usually made of a single tree trunk and cut to extend outside the building walls on either side

*zaguán* a long central hallway

# Suggested Reading

## HISTORY

Deutsch, Sarah. *No Separate Refuge.* New York: Oxford University Press USA, 1989. Not a light read due to its scholarly tone, but the definitive history on the transition from Hispano to Anglo dominance in New Mexico and the power struggles involved, beginning with the railroad's arrival in 1880.

Egan, Timothy. *The Worst Hard Time: The Untold Story of Those Who Survived the Great American Dust Bowl.* New York: Mariner Books, 2006. The town of Clayton features a bit in the pages of this highly readable history that really conveys the misery and environmental folly of the period.

Hordes, Stanley. *To the Ends of the Earth: The History of New Mexico's Crypto-Jews.* New York: Columbia University Press, 2005. A rather exhaustive, but nonetheless intriguing, account of the Jewish families who fled the Inquisition and lived in the Southwest as Catholic converts. The communities, some still practicing distinctly Jewish rituals, came to light only a few decades ago.

Horgan, Paul. *Great River.* Middletown, CT: Wesleyan University Press, 1991. Two enormous tomes (*Vol. 1: The Indians and Spain* and *Vol. 2: Mexico and the United States*) that won the Pulitzer Prize for history, and deservedly so: They're packed with drama and intrigue, all on a base of meticulous analysis of primary sources. Horgan's *Lamy of Santa Fe* (Wesleyan, 2003) is also highly recommended, as a balanced examination of the contentious archbishop's life in New Mexico.

Martinez, Esther. *My Life in San Juan Pueblo.* Champaign: University of Illinois Press, 2004. Born in 1912, Martinez has a lot of stories to tell. This free-flowing book incorporates her memories with larger pueblo folklore, and a CD with recordings of some of her stories is included.

Poling-Kempes, Leslie. *Valley of Shining Stone: The Story of Abiquiu.* Tucson: University of Arizona Press, 1997. Georgia O'Keeffe fans will like the personal stories of those in her circle in the 1930s, while historians will appreciate the detailed, linear second half of the book, which gives a more objective overview of the transformation of this remote valley into an artists' haven.

Reisner, Marc. *Cadillac Desert: The American West and Its Disappearing Water.* New York: Penguin, 1993. Not specifically about New Mexico, but an excellent analysis of the Southwest's water shortage and how the U.S. government's dam-building projects exacerbated it. Apocalyptic, sarcastic, and totally compelling.

Salaz-Marquez, Ruben. *New Mexico: A Brief Multi-History.* Albuquerque: Cosmic House, 1999. A good introduction with an easy-to-follow timeline format; very thorough, though not much analysis.

Sides, Hampton. *Blood and Thunder: An Epic of the American West.* New York: Doubleday, 2006. Working from the story of Kit Carson and the campaign against the Navajo, including the Long Walk, Sides tells the gripping story of the entire American West. He's an excellent storyteller, and the 480 pages flow by in a rush of land grabs, battles on horseback, and brutality on both sides.

Simmons, Marc. *New Mexico: An Interpretive History.* Albuquerque: University of New Mexico Press, 1988. The state's historian laureate presents an easy, concise overview of the major historical events. Also look into his more specialized titles, such as *The Last Conquistador: Juan de Oñate and the Settling of the Far Southwest* (Norman: University of Oklahoma Press, 1993).

Smith, Mike. *Towns of the Sandia Mountains.* Charleston, SC: Arcadia, 2006. This slim volume of vintage photographs and juicy stories in extended captions is about a very specific region, but could tell the story of much of New Mexico in its shift to modernity.

Usner, Donald J. *Sabino's Map: Life in Chimayó's Old Plaza.* Santa Fe: Museum of New Mexico Press, 1995. A balanced and gracefully written history of the author's hometown, illustrated with fond photos of all the craggy-faced characters involved. Usner's follow-up, *Benigna's Chimayo: Cuentos from the Old Plaza* (Santa Fe: Museum of New Mexico Press, 2001), is equally good, relating his grandmother's story of the village and her trove of folktales.

## LITERATURE AND MEMOIRS

Anaya, Rudolfo. *Bless Me, Ultima.* New York: Warner, 1994. Anaya's story of a young boy coming of age in New Mexico in the 1940s is beautifully told, and an interesting depiction of life in that era. The book, first published in 1973, launched Anaya into his role as Chicano literary hero; his later books, such as *Alburquerque* (1992) are not quite so touching, but they always have a lot of historical and ethnic detail.

Evans, Max. *Hi-Lo to Hollywood: A Max Evans Reader.* Lubbock, TX: Texas Tech University Press, 1998. Prolific Western author Evans coined the term "Hi-Lo Country" for New Mexico's eastern plains (the novel of the same name was made into a film, as was another novel, *Rounders*), and all of his works, whether essay or fiction, somehow reflect the rolling expanse and the particular dilemmas of the modern cowboys who work on them. A ranch kid himself, he has an eye for detail and a direct and

affectionate tone; this reader includes many of his own favorite pieces.

Hillerman, Tony. *Skinwalkers.* New York: HarperTorch, 1990. Hillerman's breakout detective novel, set on the Navajo Nation, weaves a fascinating amount of lore into the plot—which all comes in handy when Tribal Affairs police Joe Leaphorn and Jim Chee investigate three homicides. Hillerman spun Leaphorn and Chee into a successful franchise, and all of the books show the same cultural depth.

Mallery, Barbara Vogt. *Bailing Wire and Gamuza: The True Story of a Family Ranch near Ramah, New Mexico.* Albuquerque: University of New Mexico, 2004. Arranged like a family scrapbook, this memoir recounts the author's homesteading life between 1905 and 1986.

Nichols, John. *The Milagro Beanfield War.* New York: Henry Holt, 2000. The first title in Nichols's "New Mexico Trilogy" is also the best, a ripping tale of comic intrigue in a small Hispano village, all started by a little dispute over acequia access. It was made into a film by Robert Redford in 1988.

Pillsbury, Dorothy. *Roots in Adobe.* Santa Fe: Lightning Tree Press, 1983. Pillsbury's charming stories (which occupy three other *Adobe*-based titles) capture the strangeness and warmth of Santa Fe culture in the 1940s. The author tells hilarious stories of settling into her little adobe home and all the characters she meets.

Silko, Leslie Marmon. *Ceremony.* New York: Penguin, 1988. Silko's classic novel about the impact of the atomic bomb on Native Americans' worldview (and that of all Americans) is brutal, beautiful, and bleak.

Waters, Frank. *The Woman at Otowi Crossing.* Athens, OH: Swallow Press, 1987. Longtime Taos resident Waters fictionalizes the story of a woman whose isolated café catered to Los Alamos scientists during the bomb-building years. Waters is particularly fascinated with the often mystical relationship between the land of the Southwest and the people who live on it—his *The Man Who Killed the Deer* (Athens: Ohio University Press, 1970), about a crime in the Taos Pueblo community, does the same.

## ART AND CULTURE

Clark, Willard. *Remembering Santa Fe*. Layton, UT: Gibbs Smith, 2004. A small hardback edition of selections from the Boston artist who stopped off in Santa Fe in 1928 and stayed to learn printmaking and produce a series of charming etchings depicting Santa Fe life.

Eaton, Robert. *The Lightning Field*. Boulder, CO: Johnson Books, 1995. Eaton served as a forest ranger in Chaco Canyon for five years, so his eye is for the empty and the starkly beautiful destinations around the state, including the art installation of the title (in Quemado, in western New Mexico). His essays, each focusing on a different destination, combine history and strong description. Seek this title out if you want to get well off the usual track.

Gandert, Miguel. *Nuevo México Profundo: Rituals of an Indo-Hispanic Homeland*. Santa Fe: Museum of New Mexico Press, 2000. Like Enrique Lamadrid's work, but with a slightly broader scope. There's an attempt at scholarly analysis in the text, but it's really about the 130 beautiful photographs.

Hammett, Kingsley. *Santa Fe: A Walk Through Time*. Layton, UT: Gibbs Smith, 2004. A light, largely visual tour of the capital's history and rich trove of weird legends, as told through its buildings.

Lamadrid, Enrique. *Hermanitos Comanchitos: Indo-Hispano Rituals of Captivity and Redemption*. Albuquerque: University of New Mexico Press, 2003. Fascinating documentation, in descriptive prose and rich black-and-white photos, of the traditional Spanish dances of northern New Mexico, such as Los Comanches and Los Matachines.

Lummis, Charles F. *A Tramp Across the Continent*. Lincoln: University of Nebraska, 1982. In 1884, fledgling journalist and Cincinnati resident Lummis decided to walk to his new job in Los Angeles; this book is the product of his journey. The sections on New Mexico really shine, and Lummis was so entranced that he later moved to the territory. He wrote a number of other books about American Indian culture, and he was the first to write stories about the Penitente brotherhood in the national press.

Myers, Joan. *Pie Town Woman: The Hard Life and Good Times of a New Mexico Homesteader*. Albuquerque: University of New Mexico, 2001. The biography of a woman captured in famous Farm Security Administration photos from 1940, this book also muses on the power of memory and photography.

Padilla, Carmella, and Juan Estevan Arellano. *Low 'n Slow: Lowriding in New Mexico*. Santa Fe: Museum of New Mexico Press, 1999. Lovingly lurid color photographs by Jack Parsons are the centerpiece of this book, which pays tribute to New Mexico's Latino car culture—an art form that has even landed a lowrider from Chimayó in the Smithsonian. In the interviews with the car owners, the painstakingly transcribed *vato* slang is a little distracting at times, but it certainly conveys their enthusiasm.

Parhad, Elisa. *New Mexico: A Guide for the Eyes*. Los Angeles, CA: EyeMuse Books, 2009. Informative short essays on all the distinctive things you see in New Mexico and wonder what the backstory is: concha belts, beat-up pickup trucks, blue sky. The richly illustrated book makes good pre-trip reading, or a souvenir when you return.

Price, V.B. *The City at the End of the World*. Albuquerque: University of New Mexico Press, 1992. Journalist and poet Price writes a travel guide to New Mexico's biggest metropolis but disguises it as a discourse on urban theory, recommending his favorite spots in the context of the city's unique position and growth processes—sometimes a little dense as well as overblown, but interesting nonetheless. Black-and-white photographs by Kirk Gittings highlight the stark landscape.

Robinson, Roxana. *Georgia O'Keeffe: A Life*. Lebanon, NH: University Press of New England, 1998. A strong and intimate biography, focusing on the celebrated painter's role as a proto-feminist and her difficult relationships

## NATURE AND THE ENVIRONMENT

Coltrin, Mike. *Sandia Mountain Hiking Guide*. Albuquerque: University of New Mexico Press, 2005. Basically a print version of Coltrin's meticulously maintained website (www.sandiahiking.com), with thorough trail descriptions, GPS coordinates, and a foldout map of the east and west slopes of the mountain.

Crawford, Stanley. *Mayordomo: Chronicle of an Acequia in Northern New Mexico*. Albuquerque: University of New Mexico Press, 1993. A short, fascinating diary of a year in Crawford's life as a garlic farmer, detailing water wranglings and the subtle shift in seasons. *A Garlic Testament* is a later book that goes into more detail about farming.

Julyan, Robert, and Mary Stuever, eds. *Field Guide to the Sandia Mountains*. Albuquerque: University of New Mexico Press, 2005.

A thorough guide illustrated with color photographs, detailing birds, animals, plants, even insects of the Sandias—worth picking up even if you'll be in the Santa Fe area, as much of the wildlife is the same.

Kricher, John. *A Field Guide to Rocky Mountain and Southwest Forests*. New York: Houghton Mifflin, 2003. A comprehensive book covering both flora and fauna: trees, birds, mammals, you name it. It's illustrated with both color photos and drawings. It's not encyclopedic, but it's a great basic reference. Peterson guides are also available for narrower categories—reptiles and amphibians, for instance, and butterflies.

McFarland, Casey and S. David Scott. *Bird Feathers: A Guide to North American Species*. Mechanicsburg, PA: Stackpole Books, 2010. While not New Mexico–specific, it is the only guide of its kind, and its authors grew up in the state and know the birdlife well. Great for serious birders and curious hikers, with beautiful detailed photographs.

Sibley, David Allen. *The Sibley Field Guide to Birds of Western North America*. New York: Knopf, 2003. The New Mexican birder's book of choice, with 810 species listed, some 4,600 color illustrations, and a handy compact format. Generally beats out Peterson's otherwise respectable series.

Tekiela, Stan. *Birds of New Mexico: Field Guide*. Cambridge, MN: Adventure Publications, 2003. A great book for beginning birders or curious visitors, with 140 of the state's most common species listed, many illustrated with photographs.

# FOOD

Frank, Lois Ellen. *Foods of the Southwest Indian Nations.* Berkeley, CA: Ten Speed Press, 2002. Beautiful photographs are a highlight of this thorough documentation of a little-covered cuisine—they help make an ancient culinary tradition accessible and modern, without subjecting it to a heavy-handed fusion treatment. For good reason it earned a James Beard Award.

Kagel, Katharine. *Café Pasqual's Cookbook: Spirited Recipes from Santa Fe.* San Francisco: Chronicle, 1993. Re-create your best meals from the legendary restaurant that set the standard for Santa Fe fusion cooking. Chef Kagel is a charming contrarian, too, which makes for great reading.

# Internet Resources

## TRAVEL INFORMATION

Use official sites produced by chambers of commerce and convention bureaus to look up specific businesses, or to find out what special events will be going on during your trip. If you want more opinionated information, look to privately run sites.

### Official Tourism Sites
### Albuquerque Convention and Visitors Bureau
### www.itsatrip.org

The basic official intro to the city and surrounding areas, with events listings as well as hotel-booking services. A good starting point for research.

### Indian Country New Mexico
### www.indiancountrynm.org

A coalition of tourism groups in the Four Corners region maintain this basic overview website.

### New Mexico Board of Tourism
### www.newmexico.org

The best of the official sites, this one has very thorough maps, suggested itineraries, and background info like weather. You can even do a live online chat with the New Mexico Visitors Center in Santa Fe.

### Northeast New Mexico
### www.nenewmexico.org

Good descriptions of various towns, with a bit more history and lore than you usually get from similar sites. The site covers a larger area than the same chapter in this book—there's also information about Santa Rosa, Tucumcari, and the Enchanted Circle.

### Santa Fe Convention and Visitors Bureau
### www.santafe.org

Near-exhaustive listings of tourist attractions

and services on this slickly produced site. Primarily, though, you'll just want to order the CVB's visitors guide.

### Other Travel Information
### Hiking in the Sandia Mountains
### www.sandiahiking.com

Mike Coltrin hiked every trail in the Sandias over the course of a year, covering about 250 miles. He detailed each hike, complete with GPS references, here.

### Public Lands Information Center
### www.publiclands.org

Buy USGS, Forest Service, and other topographical maps online from the Bureau of Land Management's well-organized website. Good stock of nature guides and other travel books too.

### Sangres.com
### www.sangres.com

Scores of articles and travel details about the mountain communities, culture, and history of northern New Mexico, as well as southern Colorado.

### Southern New Mexico Travel & Tourism
### www.southernnewmexico.com

This site offers heaps of information about even the most obscure towns in the southern half of the state, but many of the articles are undated, so it's hard to tell whether facts are current.

## NEWS AND CULTURE
### Albuquerque Journal
### www.abqjournal.com

The state's largest newspaper is available free online only for the day of publication—you must pay an annual subscription fee to read the archives. But skimming the headlines can give you a good idea what the big local issues are.

### Alibi
### www.alibi.com

Albuquerque's free weekly has been cracking wise since 1992, taking a critical look at politics as well as restaurants. Sometimes the staff is too hungover to list all the movie times, but otherwise they're right on target. Its annual "Best of Burque" guide is a good listing of local recommendations.

### Duke City Fix
### www.dukecityfix.com

This Albuquerque-centric blog covers everything from politics to gossip about the restaurant scene.

### Free New Mexican
### www.freenewmexican.com

The free online version of the *Santa Fe New Mexican* requires registration, but its archives contain good restaurant reviews, trail descriptions, and weekend outings, as well as all the news about the city.

### Las Cruces Sun-News
### www.lcsun-news.com

The paper of record in Las Cruces, covering issues all across the southern half of the state, especially border debates.

### New Mexico Independent
### www.newmexicoindependent.com

Excellent, serious online news publication, watching the state capitol as well as the border. OK—maybe it's not all serious: editor Gwyneth Doland is also known for her hilarious takes on politics.

### New Mexico Politics with Joe Monahan
### www.joemonahan.com

Analyst Monohan's obsessive, snarky blog charts the circus that is state politics, with plenty of examples why New Mexico still can't shake its "third-world country" rep.

### Santa Fe Reporter
### www.sfreporter.com

Santa Fe's weekly, like Albuquerque's, is politically sharp and often funny. Get opinionated reviews and news analysis here, along with appropriately snarky blogs.

### Steppin' Out
### www.steppinoutnewmexico.com

The online version of a handy monthly, published in Socorro, that covers the arts scene all over southern New Mexico. The cultural listings are as exhaustive as you'll find.

### Taos Horse Fly
### www.taosdaily.com

Rumor-mongering, way-left-of-center political commentary, and listings of activist meetings—check the pulse of Taos here.

# Index

# List of Maps

# Acknowledgments

Thanks to my mother, Beverly McFarland, who once again lent her car and her curiosity—I think we minimized the U-turns a bit this time. And thanks to my father, Patrick O'Neill, who finally got to see up close what it is I do (and don't do); you were an enthusiastic travel companion and great at pointing out photo opportunities. And thanks of course to both my parents for raising me in such a fine place. Thanks also to the usual New Mexico crew: Susan Loubet, Gwyneth Doland, Sandra Stengel, Tony Geller, Barbara Sundberg, Melu Uriarte, Kent Caldes, Jesse Wood, Jenna Hansche, and Casey McFarland. I'm especially grateful to the warm welcome I got in Silver City: thanks, Mitch Hellman and Nick Seibel for the inside scoop!

I certainly couldn't have done this without the assistance of the staff at Avalon, which has tightened up my words and added the graphics and maps that really bring the whole project to life.

I'm most grateful to the readers who take time to write with comments, compliments, reviews, queries, and corrections (of course it's a cantilever truss--what was I thinking?). I value this feedback more than anything, and I'm always happy to hear that the book has wound up in good hands!

# www.moon.com

DESTINATIONS | ACTIVITIES | BLOGS | MAPS | BOOKS

**MOON.COM** is ready to help plan your next trip! Filled with fresh trip ideas and strategies, author interviews, informative travel blogs, a detailed map library, and descriptions of all the Moon guidebooks, Moon.com is all you need to get out and explore the world—or even places in your own backyard. While at Moon.com, sign up for our monthly e-newsletter for updates on new releases, travel tips, and expert advice from our on-the-go Moon authors. As always, when you travel with Moon, expect an experience that is uncommon and truly unique.

**MOON IS ON FACEBOOK—BECOME A FAN!**
**JOIN THE MOON PHOTO GROUP ON FLICKR**

# MAP SYMBOLS

| | | | | | | | | |
|---|---|---|---|---|---|---|---|---|
| ▦ | Expressway | 【 | Highlight | ✕ | Airfield | ⚓ | Golf Course |
| ▦ | Primary Road | ○ | City/Town | ✈ | Airport | Ⓟ | Parking Area |
| ▦ | Secondary Road | ◉ | State Capital | ▲ | Mountain | ▱ | Archaeological Site |
| ====== | Unpaved Road | ⊛ | National Capital | ✚ | Unique Natural Feature | ⌂ | Church |
| ------ | Trail | ★ | Point of Interest | | | ⌷ | Gas Station |
| ·········· | Ferry | • | Accommodation | 🦌 | Waterfall | ◌ | Glacier |
| ⊶⊶⊶ | Railroad | ▼ | Restaurant/Bar | ⚑ | Park | ▨ | Mangrove |
| ▨ | Pedestrian Walkway | ▪ | Other Location | 🚩 | Trailhead | ▨ | Reef |
| ▥ | Stairs | ∆ | Campground | ⛷ | Skiing Area | ▨ | Swamp |

# CONVERSION TABLES

$°C = (°F - 32) / 1.8$
$°F = (°C \times 1.8) + 32$
1 inch = 2.54 centimeters (cm)
1 foot = 0.304 meters (m)
1 yard = 0.914 meters
1 mile = 1.6093 kilometers (km)
1 km = 0.6214 miles
1 fathom = 1.8288 m
1 chain = 20.1168 m
1 furlong = 201.168 m
1 acre = 0.4047 hectares
1 sq km = 100 hectares
1 sq mile = 2.59 square km
1 ounce = 28.35 grams
1 pound = 0.4536 kilograms
1 short ton = 0.90718 metric ton
1 short ton = 2,000 pounds
1 long ton = 1.016 metric tons
1 long ton = 2,240 pounds
1 metric ton = 1,000 kilograms
1 quart = 0.94635 liters
1 US gallon = 3.7854 liters
1 Imperial gallon = 4.5459 liters
1 nautical mile = 1.852 km

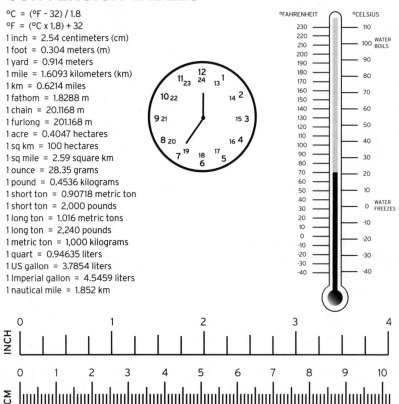

**MOON NEW MEXICO**
Avalon Travel
a member of the Perseus Books Group
1700 Fourth Street
Berkeley, CA 94710, USA
www.moon.com

Editors: Elizabeth Hansen, Leah Gordon
Series Manager: Kathryn Ettinger
Copy Editor: Annie Blakley
Graphics and Production Coordinator:
    Lucie Ericksen
Cover Designer: Lucie Ericksen
Map Editor: Albert Angulo
Cartographers: Kat Bennett, Chris Hendrick
Indexer: Judy Hunt

ISBN-13: 978-1-59880-733-2
ISSN: 1543-6187

Printing History
1st Edition – 1989
8th Edition – April 2011
5 4 3 2 1

Title page photo: Hot Air Balloons © Paul Schneider/ 123RF
Other front matter photos: pages 5, 6 bottom, 7, 10, 11, 13–15 top, 16, 19–23 left, 24: © Zora O'Neill; page 4: © New Mexico Tourism Department/ James Orr; page 6: © www.itsatrip.org; page 8: © newmexicostock.com; page 12: © Gak Stonn; page 15 bottom: © Jay Blackwood; page 18: courtesy Farmington CVB; page 23 right: © MarbleStreetStudio.com

Printed in Canada by Friesens

## KEEPING CURRENT

If you have a favorite gem you'd like to see included in the next edition, or see anything that needs updating, clarification, or correction, please drop us a line. Send your comments via email to feedback@moon.com, or use the address above.